HOLLYWOOD LEFT AND RIGHT

HOLLYWOOD LEFT AND RIGHT

HOW MOVIE STARS SHAPED AMERICAN POLITICS

STEVEN J. ROSS

OXFORD
UNIVERSITY PRESS

OXFORD
UNIVERSITY PRESS

Oxford University Press, Inc., publishes works that further
Oxford University's objective of excellence
in research, scholarship, and education.

Oxford   New York
Auckland   Cape Town   Dar es Salaam   Hong Kong   Karachi
Kuala Lumpur   Madrid   Melbourne   Mexico City   Nairobi
New Delhi   Shanghai   Taipei   Toronto

With offices in
Argentina   Austria   Brazil   Chile   Czech Republic   France   Greece
Guatemala   Hungary   Italy   Japan   Poland   Portugal   Singapore
South Korea   Switzerland   Thailand   Turkey   Ukraine   Vietnam

Published by Oxford University Press, Inc.
198 Madison Avenue, New York, NY 10016

www.oup.com

Oxford is a registered trademark of Oxford University Press

Library of Congress Cataloging-in-Publication Data
Ross, Steven Joseph.
Hollywood left and right : how movie stars shaped American politics / Steven J. Ross.
   p.   cm.
Includes bibliographical references and index.
ISBN 978-0-19-518172-2
1. United States—Politics and government—20th century. 2. Motion picture industry—United States—Influence.
3. Motion picture producers and directors—Political activity—United States—History—20th century.
4. Motion picture actors and actresses—Political activity—United States—History—20th century. I. Title.
E743.R675   2011
791.4302'8092273—dc22   2011006037

9 8 7 6 5 4 3 2 1

Printed in the United States of America
on acid-free paper

For
Linda, Lydia, and Gaby

CONTENTS

★

ACKNOWLEDGMENTS

★

After ten years of working on this project, I find myself indebted to many friends and institutions. I am grateful to the University of Southern California for its unstinting research support and to the Academy of Motion Picture Arts and Sciences for granting me its Film Scholars Award. This book never could have been completed without the cooperation of librarians and archivists around the country. The following institutions and people were especially helpful in guiding me to important sources: the Cinema/Television Library (Ned Comstock) and Special Collections (Dace Taube and Claude Zachary) at the University of Southern California; the Margaret Herrick Library (Barbara Hall, Faye Thompson, and Linda Mehr); the Robert F. Wagner Labor Archives, Tamiment Library (Kevyne Baar) at New York University; the Huntington Library (Peter Blodgett); the Herbert Hoover Presidential Library (Matt Schaefer); Special Collections, UCLA Library; the Special Collections Department and the Theater Arts Collection, New York Public Library; the Schomburg Center for Research in Black Culture, New York Public Library; Oral History Collection and Special Collections, Columbia University Library; the Wisconsin Historical Society; and the Film Studies Center, Museum of Modern Art. A special thanks to Marc Wanamaker at Bison Archives and Brent Earle at Photofest for gathering photographs for the book.

Over the years, my arguments were sharpened by exchanges with participants in the Columbia University American History Seminar, the Shelby Cullom Davis Center Seminar at Princeton University, the Center for the United States and the Cold War Seminar at New York University, and the Los Angeles Institute for the Humanities at USC. Thanks to my research assistants Dina Bartolini, Caroline Garrity, and Andreas Petasis. Thanks, too, to the many people who allowed me to interview them and offered perspectives I could never have obtained from just looking at written material. My appreciation also goes out to Peter Hirsch and Jessica Lehman who loaned me their mountain cabin to finish writing this book.

I owe an enormous debt of gratitude to friends who have read and commented on the manuscript. For nearly thirty years, the Los Angeles Social History Study Group has served as a model of friendship and nourishment, intellectual and culinary. I am indebted to the helpful advice offered by Thomas Andrews, Hal Barron, Carla Bittel, Karen Brodkin, Nancy Fitch, Tobie Higbe, John Laslett, Craig Loftin, Jennifer Luff, Becky Nicolaides, Jan Reiff, Seth Rockman, Troy Rondinone, Diana Selig, Frank Stricker, Allison Verzally, Jessica Wang, and Leila Zenderland; and especially Bob Slayton, who read through chapters more than once and always did so with good cheer and helpful guidance. I am also lucky to have many friends who took time from their own busy work to comment on the entire manuscript. They helped make this a far better book than I could have done on my own: Elinor Accampo, Joyce Appleby, Lois Banner, Marjorie Becker, Leo Braudy, Richard Fox, Michael Kazin, Gary Kornblith, James Lafferty, Richard Miller, Ed Perkins, Richard Schickel, Dan Schnur, and Vanessa Schwartz.

I was also fortunate to get perceptive critiques and suggestions from David McBride, my wonderful editor at Oxford University Press. Sandy Dijkstra, my agent, believed in this project from the beginning and offered advice and encouragement that was always appreciated. I want to extend a very special thanks to two friends who read through the manuscript several times. Jon Boorstin helped make this a far more readable book by urging me to be a writer, not just an academic. Phil Ethington has been a close friend, colleague, and intellectual guide for many years. He has read through the book more times than anyone else and never flagged in his very smart advice and support. He also has excellent taste in movies and beer.

My final acknowledgments go out to my family. I want to thank my children, Lydia and Gaby, for bearing with me for many years as I alternated between working on the book and serving as department chair. Lydia proved a marvelous reader, going through every chapter with a perceptive eye. Gaby pushed my knowledge and pleasure in new directions by exposing me to some fabulous music. My greatest debt of gratitude goes to my wife and best friend, Linda Kent. Her many years in the television movie business gave me an insider's view of how the entertainment industry really worked. More importantly, she spent the last decade listening to me talking about the book over and over again during our morning walks and then reading endless drafts of chapters. She has made my life richer in more ways than I could ever describe. This book is dedicated to the loves of my life, Linda, Lydia, and Gaby.

HOLLYWOOD LEFT AND RIGHT

INTRODUCTION: MOVIE STARS AND POLITICS

Political Hollywood started much earlier than most people realize. In 1918, FBI leaders William J. Burns and J. Edgar Hoover were so worried about the power of movie stars to affect the political consciousness of a nation that they ordered secret agents to maintain close surveillance over suspected Hollywood radicals. Four years later, Bureau agents confirmed their worst fears. "Numerous movie stars," they reported, were taking "an active part in the Red movement in this country" and were hatching a plan to circulate "Communist propaganda . . . via the movies."[1] The Cold War politicians who launched the Red Scare's infamous House Un-American Activities Committee in the late 1940s also feared the power of movie stars to alter the way people thought and acted. They understood that movie audiences were also voters, and they asked themselves: Who would people be more likely to listen to: drab politicians or glamorous stars? What if left-leaning celebrities such as Charlie Chaplin, Humphrey Bogart, Katharine Hepburn, and Edward G. Robinson used their star appeal to promote radical causes, especially Communist causes?

Such fears about radicalism in the movie industry reflect long-standing conventional wisdom that Hollywood has always been a bastion of the political left. Conventional wisdom, however, is wrong on two counts. First, Hollywood has a longer history of conservatism than liberalism. It was the Republican Party, not the Democratic Party, that established the first political beachhead in Hollywood. Second, and far more surprising, although the Hollywood left has been more numerous and visible, the Hollywood right—led by Louis B. Mayer, George Murphy, Ronald Reagan, Charlton Heston, and Arnold Schwarzenegger—has had a greater impact on American political life. The Hollywood left has been more effective in publicizing and raising funds for various causes. But if we ask who has done more to change the American government, the answer is the Hollywood right. The Hollywood left has the political glitz, but the Hollywood right sought, won, and exercised electoral power.

Can such a counterintuitive argument really be true? What did the Hollywood right achieve to merit such a claim? There have been two foundational changes in twentieth-century U.S. politics. The first was the creation of a welfare state under Franklin D. Roosevelt, a development that established a new relationship between government and the governed and crystallized differences among conservatives, liberals, and radicals. The second was the gradual dismantling of the welfare state that began under a movie star, Ronald Reagan. The conservative revolution of the 1980s could not have happened without the groundwork laid by Louis B. Mayer, his protégé George Murphy, and his protégé Ronald Reagan.

Although movie industry conservatives began wielding power in the 1920s, the Hollywood right did not emerge as a major force in American politics until after the postwar era. Once they did, their impact was tremendous. During the 1950s and early 1960s, Murphy and Reagan used their fame, charm, and communication skills to help build an insurgent grassroots constituency by speaking to conservative groups throughout the nation. The two stars articulated an ideological agenda that called for dismantling the New Deal, returning power to the state and local levels, reducing taxes, and waging war against all foes of American security—Communists in particular. During the mid-1960s, the two former stars designed innovative campaign strategies that drew on their experiences as actors to accomplish what more established politicians like the prickly Barry Goldwater could not do: sell conservatism to a wide range of previously skeptical voters. By making conservatism palatable, Murphy and Reagan helped make the conservative revolution possible.

As Murphy and Reagan demonstrated, movie stars do more than just show us how to dress, look, or love. They teach us how to think and act politically. "If an actor can be influential selling deodorants," Marlon Brando explained just before the 1963 March on Washington, "he can be just as useful selling ideas." Speaking more recently about the relative importance of Washington and Hollywood in the public mind, former-Republican-turned-Democratic Senator Arlen Specter remarked, "Quite candidly, when Hollywood speaks the world listens. Sometimes when Washington speaks, the world snoozes."[2]

Americans have long maintained a love–hate relationship with movie stars. Audiences connect with movie stars at an emotional level and with a sense of intimacy they rarely feel about politicians. We love stars when they remain faithful to our fantasy images of them, but we condemn them when they reveal their flaws or disagree with our politics. The public "choose the stars and then make Gods of them," director William deMille observed in 1935. "They feel a peculiar sense of ownership in these romantic figures they have created—and, of course, an equal sense of outrage in those cases where their idols turn out to have feet of clay."[3]

While there is a long tradition of political activity in Hollywood, there is an equally long-held fear that being too political can destroy a career. When former child star Jackie Cooper returned from World War II, he "was frightened of everything that was tainted with any kind of politics. My mother always said, 'The actor has to stay out of politics—think what you want, vote—but you want Catholics, Jews, Arabs, everyone to go to the box-office, and any way you campaign, you'll lose some box-office.' I think it's true." Jump ahead in time to 1999 and the living room of Arianna Huffington, where actor Billy Baldwin, then president of the Creative Coalition—a group of liberal star activists—was trying to recruit new members. When asked about possible reprisals against outspoken actors, he confessed, "I can't tell you how many famous stars came up to me and said, 'Billy, I'm happy to write you a check, but my agent or my lawyer says I can't appear on stage representing your organization. It might endanger my career.'"[4]

Hollywood Left and Right tells an important story that has escaped public attention: the emergence of Hollywood as a vital center of political life and the important role that movie stars played in shaping the course of American politics. My cast of characters features ten activists: five on the left and five on the right. Their stories, told in rough chronological order, reveal how

Hollywood's engagement in politics has been longer, deeper, and more varied than most people would imagine. Each person was either the first or most important practitioner of his or her particular form of activism and each left an important legacy. Alternating between stars on the left and the right, the following nine chapters take us from the early twentieth century to the present. They examine the lives and beliefs of their central characters at the height of their political activism and end when that activism stopped or when they got elected to office, for then they became politicians rather than movie stars.

Whatever their ideological differences, all ten people believed that movie stars had a right and an obligation as citizens to participate in the nation's political life. Yet the ways in which they did so was influenced by the changing structure of the movie industry and by the changing nature of local and national politics. As both evolved over the course of the century, so too did the forms of movie star politics.

The movie industry began as a small-scale business with hundreds of producers, distributors, and exhibitors scattered throughout the country. There was little political engagement by actors and actresses during the early silent era because the star system was still emerging and performers did not want to risk losing their audience by engaging in partisan activities. Charlie Chaplin was the first major star to use movies as an ideological weapon, and he did so in a way that both amused and politicized audiences. A socialist sympathizer who hated joining groups, his films mocked the power and legitimacy of authority figures from the local cop to Adolf Hitler. Because he had complete control over his films (as producer, director, writer, star, and later distributor), Chaplin could make anything he wanted. There was no studio head to tell him what he could or could not do. This left the world's most popular movie star free to put his politics directly on the screen where they could be seen, and perhaps acted upon, by millions of Americans.

The 1920s signaled the rise of a new type of film industry, an oligarchic studio system centered in Los Angeles and financed by some of the largest industrial and financial institutions in the nation. As the studio system known as "Hollywood" matured, so too did the focus of political engagement. With a business-oriented Republican Party dominating the national scene throughout the decade, powerful studio figures such as Metro-Goldwyn-Mayer's Louis B. Mayer turned to electoral politics both to meet the needs of his industry and to advance the fortunes of his favored party. More than any other figure, Mayer was responsible for bringing the Republican Party to Hollywood and Hollywood to the Republican Party. Mayer was not a movie star, but he created stars and pioneered the uses of stardom and media for partisan ends. During his tenure as studio chief and head of the California GOP, he injected showmanship into the party's nominating conventions, showed Republicans how to employ radio more effectively, and inaugurated the first "dirty tricks" campaign by employing fake newsreels in 1934 to defeat Democratic gubernatorial candidate Upton Sinclair. Hollywood Democrats had no one to rival the power of the man who helped swing the 1928 Republican presidential nomination to his good friend Herbert Hoover.

Studio moguls such as Mayer ruled Hollywood politics during the 1920s, but the devastating effects of the Great Depression and the election of the charismatic Franklin D. Roosevelt in 1932 prompted many actors and actresses to become politically active, often for the first time. Movie stars such as Edward G. Robinson used their celebrity to draw attention to a wide variety of causes. At a time when the vast majority of the American public preferred to turn a blind eye to the growing dangers of Nazism and fascism, Robinson and dozens of other left stars marched in the streets, organized radio shows, and issued declarations condemning Hitler that attracted international attention. Movie star participation in issue-oriented politics also generated a new era of Hollywood fundraising and giving as Robinson, Gene Kelly, Melvyn Douglas, and others helped bankroll numerous progressive causes.

Concerned about potential audience backlash at the box office, studio heads moved to limit the unprecedented activism of their famous employees. The financial success of the studio system made it possible for actors and actresses to make unprecedented amounts of money, but at the cost of restricting their freedom by tying them to lengthy contracts that gave studio heads the ability to shape a star's image and control his or her offscreen activities. Studios were willing to tolerate some partisan activism, but stars who strayed too far from the political mainstream had their careers cut short, blacklisted or graylisted by fearful industry executives.

The end of the studio system in the late 1940s and early 1950s freed actors and actresses to speak out on a wide range of issues. Just as the Depression and New Deal sparked the rise of the Hollywood left, the Cold War and the Red Scare gave powerful new life to the Hollywood right. The publicity generated by the House Un-American Activities Committee hastened the rise of the Cold War and Hollywood's Cold Warriors. Led by George Murphy and then by Ronald Reagan, a small number of ideologically driven stars engaged in conservative movement politics. Unlike issue-oriented politics, which focused on a discrete set of problems, movement politics demanded a long-term commitment aimed at restructuring the very foundations of American government.

From the late 1940s to the mid-1960s, Murphy and Reagan joined with conservative groups around the nation in an effort to overturn the most important liberal achievement of the twentieth century, the New Deal state. By reshaping the partisan uses of television and skillfully employing it to sell conservative messages, the two men reshaped American politics for the next five decades. During their political careers, Murphy, who was elected California's senator in 1964, and Reagan, elected governor in 1966, preached the politics of fear and reassurance, of dire foreign threats coupled with reassuring promises to preserve domestic tranquility. Their rivals on the left preached the politics of hope and guilt, of what America could be but how prejudice and selfishness prevented us from realizing those dreams. In the skillful hands of Murphy and especially Reagan, fear and reassurance proved a far greater motivator of voters than hope and guilt.

As the worst excesses of the Red Scare died down, Hollywood leftists became increasingly involved in radical movement politics. Harry Belafonte and Jane Fonda worked hard to challenge what they viewed as dominant systems of power that led to inequality at home and imperialism and war abroad. Beginning in the early 1950s and continuing through the 1980s, the two stars, though acting independently of one another, helped build coalitions that attacked racism, promoted civil rights, opposed the war in Vietnam, and struggled for women's rights and greater social and economic justice. Belafonte served as the most important Hollywood figure in the civil rights movement and as one of Dr. Martin Luther King Jr.'s two closest friends. Likewise, Jane Fonda, perhaps the most reviled star in Hollywood history, worked to change the course of American politics first through the antiwar movement and then as cofounder of the Campaig for Economic Democracy, a progressive organization that called for radical changes in government policies. Fighting on multiple fronts, they both opened production companies and made films that promoted their political agendas.

Charlton Heston, who began his political life on the left and gravitated to the right, was the first prominent practitioner of image politics. His monumental performance as Moses in *The Ten Commandments* (1956), and subsequent roles in which he played three saints, three presidents, and two geniuses, allowed him to forge a cinematic persona of such gravitas that he repeatedly used it to lend authority to his offscreen role as political spokesman. In the 1960s, he championed civil rights. However, following the fracturing of the Democratic Party in 1968 and the decline of its long-standing New Deal coalition, Heston moved to the right. Working tirelessly on behalf of conservative causes and candidates, "Moses," as many thought of him, used his involvement with the National Rifle Association to help swing several key states to George Bush in 2000 and thereby enable him to win the presidency.

The democratization of Democratic Party leadership that pushed Heston to the right opened new opportunities for left stars such as Warren Beatty to play a prominent role in national politics. Drawing on his skills as an actor, director, writer, and producer, Beatty served as part of the inner circle of three presidential campaigns, helping to shape the messages and media strategies of George McGovern's run in 1972 and Gary Hart's two unsuccessful bids in 1984 and 1988. Like Charlie Chaplin, Harry Belafonte, and Jane Fonda, Beatty also opened his own production company and used the screen to convey his political ideas to millions of potential voters. At a time when American politics were shifting increasingly rightward, he made two left films—*Reds* (1981) and *Bulworth* (1998)—that few other major actors would have touched.

The explosion of 24/7 news and entertainment media in the late twentieth century opened opportunities for yet another form of political engagement. Arnold Schwarzenegger merged Mayer's, Murphy's, and Reagan's creative use of media with Heston's use of image politics to fashion a new era of celebrity politics. Often ridiculed in the press as a political lightweight, the Austrian-born star understood what many establishment figures did not: entertainment venues such as *Entertainment Tonight* and *Access Hollywood* were not a debasement of politics but an expansion of the arenas in which political dialogue could occur, especially among Americans who tended not to vote. During his run for governor in California's 2003 recall election, the popular action hero relied on these outlets rather than on mainstream newspapers or television news shows to spread his message to voters.

With few allies in the state's conservative-dominated GOP, Schwarzenegger's victory demonstrated that candidates no longer needed to have deep roots in one of the parties. Image and celebrity were now powerful enough to win an election without traditional party support.

These ten activists do not represent a complete history of Hollywood politics. Dozens of other politically engaged stars are worthy of study, and many of them make brief appearances in this book. Likewise, some of the most important figures in Hollywood rarely make it into the narrative—power figures such as Lew Wasserman, legendary head of the Music Corporation of America. With the exception of Mayer, the most influential Hollywood conservative during the first three decades of the twentieth century, my focus is on the movie stars who formed Creative Hollywood rather than the behind-the-scenes wheelers and dealers who comprised Corporate Hollywood.[5]

The goal of this book is not to demonize one side of the political spectrum and praise the other. Rather, it seeks to understand how each of these ten people saw the world, why they became political, what they hoped to accomplish, how they affected political life, and, in several cases, the steep personal costs of their activism. Their political lives were characterized by many of the same qualities that led to their cinematic success. All ten were charismatic and all ten were willing to put in the long hours and hard work needed to be successful in their craft and, later, in their political endeavors.

In a town where narcissism is only slightly less widespread than oxygen, each of these Hollywood activists gave their time and risked their careers for their beliefs. How many of us would be willing to throw away the chance to earn millions of dollars to defend causes we cared about? This is the story of Hollywood politics as seen through the prism of ten people willing to do just that.

THE FIRST POLITICAL MOVIE STAR:
CHARLIE CHAPLIN

When is a dinner party something more than just good food and conversation? When it is given by Charlie Chaplin, or so thought FBI deputy head J. Edgar Hoover. In August 1922, America's favorite Tramp hosted a soirée to introduce Hollywood liberals and leftists to Communist labor leader William Z. Foster. Several days later, director William deMille was visited by two of Hoover's secret agents who grilled him about the party (which deMille did not attend) and demanded to know whether his friend Chaplin was a Communist. When the unnerved director admitted that Chaplin had once confessed he was a socialist, "a look of satisfaction passed between the two men; they had probably known all the time; it would have gone ill with me had I lied." The agents sent Hoover a memo reporting that Chaplin was part of a Communist plot to use movies to make a "propagandist appeal for the cause of the labor movement and the revolution."[1]

Four years earlier the federal government had used Chaplin to sell war bonds to an adoring public. Now they feared the effect his films would have "upon the minds of the people of this country" if the world's most famous comedian became an outspoken advocate for radical causes. They had good reason to be concerned.[2]

American culture was becoming increasingly visual during the early twentieth century. The rise of the movies marked a significant shift not only in terms of entertainment but also in the delivery of information and ideas. Chaplin was at the vanguard of a new form of political communication that bypassed traditional authority figures and spoke directly to millions of immigrants and working-class people who felt as though no one cared about them or understood the problems they faced. But Chaplin did. His silent films did not promote Communist causes as the FBI feared, but they did mock the power and legitimacy of those who gave ordinary Americans a hard time: employers, foremen, police, judges, the idle rich, and even world leaders. Whatever their partisan loyalties, workers and immigrants shared Chaplin's distrust of those in powerful positions. His films gave life to those sentiments in a way that amused and inspired millions. As one newspaper observed in 1915, "Charlie Chaplin could become President if he were to have political ambitions."[3] No wonder Hoover had Chaplin tailed for the next forty years.

Chaplin's story illuminates the evolving intersection of movie stars, politics, and celebrity culture. No silent star brought political messages to a mass public more effectively than the man millions of moviegoers affectionately called "Charlie." Yet Chaplin was also a surprisingly shy and insecure man; he was insecure about money, women, and his own intellectual abilities. During his early years in Hollywood, he was afraid that being too political would cause him to lose his audience and plunge back into poverty. Chaplin had ideas, but the unschooled star was too insecure to articulate any explicit political agenda. His first films reflected his instinctual anti-authoritarian politics but never offered any solutions to the problems caused by those in power.

Chaplin's interactions with admiring intellectuals in the 1920s and 1930s changed him from a naive radical to a more self-conscious political filmmaker. Reporters in the United States and Europe solicited his opinions on world affairs not because he was an expert but because he was a celebrity with a professed interest in politics. His celebrity, in turn, affected his politics. By the mid-1930s, he was wealthy and self-confident enough to confront the most urgent issues of the day. As fascism spread across Europe, Chaplin joined with Orson Welles, Edward G. Robinson, Melvyn Douglas, and other Hollywood stars in speaking out against Nazism in Germany and economic injustice at home. *The Great Dictator*, a 1940 film that mocked

Adolf Hitler and Benito Mussolini, contained a final scene in which Charlie delivered a highly polemical speech calling for world peace and understanding, one of the first times he talked on the screen.

Ironically, Chaplin was most effective politically when his movies were silent. When he began speaking out in the early 1940s, on and off the screen, he lost a good part of his audience. "Once he opened his mouth," observed Robinson, "he ceased to be universal and became an actor." As Chaplin grew increasingly outspoken, outraged conservatives tried to stop him from ever making another film.[4]

More than any other star of the silent era, Chaplin helped legitimize the idea that politically engaged actors could be taken seriously, though often at considerable cost to their careers.

FROM LONDON TO LOS ANGELES

Why does anyone become political? More intriguing, why would an actor risk his or her livelihood, especially a lucrative one, to take a political stand? In Chaplin's case, his politics were borne out of childhood experiences that left him with a dread of poverty and hostility toward religion, the police, and charitable institutions. Had Charlie's early life been the subject of a Charles Dickens novel, it would have been called *Declining Expectations*. Growing up poor might have been easier for him than adjusting to what he experienced: the slow but steady descent from middle-class comfort into abject poverty. Few other stars would be so genuinely empathetic with the plight of the poor. Charlie Chaplin did not simply act the Tramp; he was the Tramp.

Charles Spencer Chaplin was born in London on April 16, 1889, to music hall performers Charles and Hannah Chaplin. Charles was Hannah's second husband and Charlie her second child. Following the birth of her son Sydney and subsequent divorce, Hannah married her former sweetheart, Charles Chaplin. Three years later, she gave birth to Charlie.

The Chaplins were reasonably successful entertainers, and Charlie remembered his early years as being "modestly comfortable; we lived in three tastefully furnished rooms."[5] But theirs was not a happy home. Charles Senior was an alcoholic who spent most of his earnings on booze. Tiring of her husband's drunken stupors, Hannah left him and took her sons with her.

Hannah's descent from modest theatrical success came soon after she contracted a bad case of laryngitis. Unable to perform or collect money from her ex-husband, she pawned her jewelry and depleted her savings. With no financial resources left, Hannah moved her boys from their comfortable three-room flat to a one-room flat and then into accommodations that grew "progressively drabber."[6] The Chaplins plunged into the harsh underbelly of Victorian London, with its stark contrasts between wealth and poverty. For Charlie, being poor and not having much to eat was not so bad. It was the humiliation he suffered because of poverty, such as accepting handouts from condescending reformers and church officials, that he found so hard to accept.

Hannah grew so ill and the family so poor that they were forced to enter the Lambeth Workhouse in June 1896. Three weeks later, six-year-old Charlie and ten-year-old Sydney were transferred to the Hanwell School for Orphans and Destitute Children, a drab institution situated twelve miles outside London. It was at Hanwell that Charlie learned how authority could be misused. Every Friday morning 200 to 300 boys were marched into a large gym and lined up military style to watch alleged miscreants await their trial and punishment. The guilty had their wrists strapped to the sides of a desk and were beaten across the buttocks with a thick birch cane. The spectacle was so terrifying that "invariably a boy would fall out of rank in a faint."[7] Many years later, Chaplin recollected how he had been falsely charged with setting fires in the bathroom and given three strokes with the dreaded cane. The experience taught him a lifelong lesson about the dignity of quiet suffering, a quality that would distinguish his cinematic Tramp.

The next several years proved equally difficult. His mentally ill mother was sent to the Cane Hill Lunatic Asylum, and Charlie was transferred to a workhouse. Hannah was soon released and moved her two boys into a cheap flat near a pickle factory. But the family was so wretchedly poor that they could not afford a traditional home-cooked Sunday dinner. With his mother perpetually strapped for cash, nine-year-old Charlie dropped out of school and went on tour with a troop of clog dancers known as the Eight Lancashire Lads. He followed that by taking a series of odd jobs around London.

Hunger, humiliation, and death marked the next few years of his youth. When Charles Chaplin died of alcoholism in May 1901, the family could not afford to bury him. Worse yet, malnourished Hannah grew so ill that authorities sent her back to Cane Hill Lunatic Asylum and twelve-year-old Charlie was forced to fend for himself.

The Chaplin family fortunes began to change in 1903 when Fred Karno's vaudeville company hired older brother Sydney and Charlie secured a job with a traveling theatrical company. Charlie used the opportunity to perfect his comic stagecraft; shortly afterward he joined his brother in the successful Karno Troupe. In September 1910, the young comedian embarked on an extended American tour with Karno's traveling company. Having dropped out of school as a young boy, Charlie used his long periods on the road to educate himself. He began reading Emerson, Whitman, Twain, Poe, Hawthorne, and Irving. His hostility toward organized religion, borne of the church's mistreatment of his family, was given greater intellectual focus after reading Robert Ingersoll's *Essays and Lectures*. "This was an exciting discovery," he recounted. Ingersoll's "atheism confirmed my own belief that the horrific cruelty of the Old Testament was degrading to the human spirit."[8] The diminutive comic also perfected his musical skills, learning how to play violin and cello with considerable aplomb, talents he would draw upon in his later films.

Karno's troupe received mixed reviews, but Charlie attracted the attention of Mack Sennett, head of the Keystone Comedy Company. The Los Angeles–based producer offered the comedian a one-year contract that paid him the considerable sum of $150 a month for the first three months and $175 a month for the remaining nine months ($3,320 and $3,870, respectively, in 2009 dollars). Chaplin accepted and arrived at Keystone's studio in December 1913 ready to begin his film career.[9]

THE TRAMP ARRIVES

When his train pulled into Los Angeles' Union Station, politics was the last thing on Chaplin's mind. Like so many immigrants, he was focused on financial success. Hired to replace departing star Ford Sterling, Chaplin made his cinematic debut in February 1914 playing an urban dandy in *Making a Living*. Keystone's production schedule was almost as frantic as the action in its films; in three months, Chaplin appeared in eleven films. Performing a variety of roles during these hectic weeks, he developed what soon became his signature character, the Tramp.

There are many stories of how the Tramp came to be. Chaplin's own version is that while filming *Mabel's Strange Predicament* (1914) the cameraman asked him to dress in comical attire. Drawing on his British music hall experiences, he decided to "make everything in a contradiction—baggy trousers, tight coat, large head, small hat, a cane, raggedy, and at the same time, a gentleman, and I didn't know how I was going to do those."[10] He borrowed Fatty Arbuckle's oversized trousers; Charles Avery's diminutive jacket; Ford Sterling's size fourteen shoes, which Chaplin (a size five) wore on the wrong feet to keep them from falling off; a small derby that belonged to Arbuckle's father-in-law; and Mack Sennett's false moustache, which he trimmed to caterpillar size.

The Tramp proved immensely popular, so much so that Sennett allowed Chaplin to write and direct nineteen of the next twenty-five films in which he appeared. Chaplin's transition from British émigré to American movie star took slightly more than one year. In January 1915, movie fans voted him the nation's number one film comedian. Charlie soon left Sennett for Essanay Studios and then for the Mutual Film Corporation, which gave him a signing bonus of $150,000 and a weekly salary of $10,000 ($3.3 million and $221,000 in 2009 dollars), a salary exceeded only by the president of U.S. Steel.[11]

By October 12, 1917, when he completed *The Adventurer*, Charlie reigned as the world's most famous comic star. Nevertheless, Chaplin and his Tramp were not universally loved. As a Detroit newspaper headline declared, "Low Grade Persons Only Like Charlie Chaplin and Mary Pickford, Says Pastor." Men and women of the genteel class, explained stage actress Minnie Maddern Fiske, found Chaplin to be a vulgar buffoon. "Chaplin is vulgar," Fiske agreed, but so too, she added, were Aristophanes, Rabelais, Fielding, and Swift.[12]

POLITICS AND THE DANGEROUS NEW MEDIUM

To understand Chaplin's meteoric rise, we need to understand why his films touched audiences so deeply. Early movie theaters were places of magic where fantasies appeared every day and the impossible always seemed possible. By 1910, five years after the opening of the first nickelodeon (a name that combined the cost of admission with the Greek word for theater), nearly 30 percent of the nation's population flocked to the movies each week. Ten years later, almost half the country attended one of the nation's 15,000 movie theaters on a weekly basis; by 1930, admission figures approached 100 percent of the population. The new medium proved especially popular with immigrants and working people, the "dangerous classes," as elites frequently called them. Movies were one of the few amusements that financially strapped families could afford. Contemporary writers referred to the movies as the "academy of the working man," the "poor man's amusement," and a medium built upon the "nickels of the working class."[13]

Chaplin entered the cinematic world at a moment when American politics were extraordinarily diverse and when groups on both the left and the right were using film as a medium of entertainment and propaganda. From the late nineteenth century until the end of World War I in 1918, political parties included conservative Prohibitionists and Republicans, more moderate Democrats and Progressives, and Populists and Socialists who openly challenged capitalism. Radicalism seemed far more viable during the Progressive era than today. In 1912, Socialist Party presidential candidate Eugene V. Debs shocked the political establishment by capturing nearly one million votes (6 percent of the total). Voters around the country elected socialists to over a thousand offices, from city council to Congress. Likewise, an insurgent labor movement expanded its ranks from 440,000 in 1897 to three million by 1917.[14]

The ideological diversity of early silent films mirrored the ideological diversity of American politics. Indeed, movies were political long before movie stars. During the early years of the new industry, the minimal demands of technical expertise and the low cost of production ($400 to $1,000 a reel in many instances) allowed groups we would not usually associate with Hollywood—from socialists and militant trade unionists on the left to the National Association of Manufacturers and the American Bankers Association on the right—to produce films aimed at swaying public opinion. For millions of Americans, many of whom could neither read nor understand English, movies provided an important visual language that allowed them to see what was happening in the nation. Radical filmmakers used the screen to show that their cries of injustice were real—that class oppression did exist within our borders. Conservative business organizations parried these visual claims by making movies showing the extraordinary efforts they had undertaken on behalf of employees. By 1915, these polemical productions had grown so numerous that drama critic Walter Eaton warned of the day when movies would foster bitter cleavages between "the proletariat . . . and capitalist class."[15]

None of these productions, however, rivaled the popularity of Chaplin's films. Although his thinking would evolve in later decades, his early politics were simple, humanitarian, and naive. His visual politics were not Democratic, Republican, or Socialist, but deeply anti-authoritarian. All "authority is a simple target for comedy or ridicule," he explained, whether "it's a General, Admiral, or whoever it is—policeman—anybody that's pompous and with an exaggerated ego."[16] Beneath the humor he depicted the harsh daily realities of an urban industrial world whose leaders and institutions seemed unsympathetic to the plight of ordinary working people. He used ridicule as a powerful weapon for taking down one's seemingly invincible betters. The comedian understood that hopeful humor was food for the soul.

Chaplin was the Charles Dickens of his century, exposing the hardships and injustices of a world he knew all too well. A childhood of poverty and humiliation turned the young filmmaker into an instinctual radical, favoring the poor over the rich, labor over capital, and humane socialism over harsh capitalism. No one in power was spared from the Tramp's sharp cinematic barbs. He attacked authority figures up and down the class scale: from the follies of the extremely wealthy to the pretensions of the new middle classes to the foibles of the working class. Given his own background and the fact that a majority of early urban audiences were workers and immigrants, it is hardly surprising that his films mocked the local authority figures who gave working people the hardest time. Far from being escapist, his films offered viewers a vision of a more hopeful future.

Chaplin's early movies were a modern version of the Brer Rabbit tales told by American slaves in the nineteenth century, tales in which the weak but wily rabbit continually bested animals that were bigger, stronger, and determined to eat him. Writing, directing, producing, and starring in his films enabled Chaplin to put his politics directly on the screen. However, his lack of self-confidence as a political thinker and fear of losing his fortune limited the scope of his ideological attacks. Unlike radical filmmakers of the time, Chaplin rarely challenged capitalism or urged rebellion; nor did he offer solutions to contemporary ills. Instead he portrayed familiar dilemmas and individual responses to them. The Tramp never resorted to collective action, as socialists urged, because he always knew how to outwit employers, police, and other authority figures.

Chaplin's anti-authoritarian films gave life to the fantasies of his audience. In *The Count* (1916) and *The Rink* (1916), he delighted in lambasting the affectations of elite "society" and their fawning obsession with European aristocracy. In *Work* (1915) and *The Floorwalker* (1916), he skewered the upwardly mobile middle-class who liked to pass themselves off as richer and smarter than they really were. *The Immigrant* (1917) depicted the difficulties endured by men and women who crossed the ocean in steerage and their degrading encounters with immigration officials (who get a swift kick in the rear from the Tramp) upon arriving at Ellis Island. Chaplin put these experiences on the big screen for everyone to see, especially native-born Americans who had little sense of the difficulties faced by the newly arrived.[17]

Such anti-authoritarian politics might seem strange for a man who found himself suddenly wealthy and courted by Los Angeles elites. But Chaplin never thought of himself as a rich man. Indeed, he had a lifelong reputation for profound cheapness. As his friend, radical writer Max Eastman observed, Charlie lived "in dread of poverty" and was "afraid all the time that he will be taken to that orphan asylum again." The poor boy from London's East End could never get comfortable in the luxurious world of Hollywood, "a misfortune," Eastman noted, "that keeps him in touch, at least, with the common man!"[18]

THE POLITICAL USES OF STARDOM

Like most actors of the time, Chaplin initially refrained from participating in political causes. Although organizations and individual filmmakers made movies to promote their ideological agendas, movie stars maintained a low political profile during these early years, largely because they were trying to carve out careers in this relatively new industry. There were some exceptions. Actors Viola Barry and Francis X. Conlan and directors Augustus Thomas and Hall Caine openly proclaimed their socialist loyalties. Comedienne Mabel Normand did more than just talk. In the spring of 1913, she visited scores of nickelodeons in Los Angeles campaigning for the Socialist Party ticket and speaking out on behalf of women's suffrage. "I really think when women's suffrage invades California," she wrote that August, "I shall run for mayor of Los Angeles on the suffrage ticket."[19] Yet, these exceptions aside, few actors said much about the political issues of the day.

The United States government was the first to use movie stars for explicitly political purposes. Shortly after the United States entered World War I in

April 1917, Secretary of the Treasury William McAdoo persuaded the nation's leading screen idols—Charlie Chaplin, Mary Pickford, Douglas Fairbanks, and William S. Hart—to tour the country in April and May of 1918 hawking war bonds to movie-mad citizens. Prior to the war, explained Chaplin's one-time assistant Harry Crocker, "Hollywood stars had maintained a strict silence on the subject of religion, politics or civic subjects." They feared "that if an actor took sides in any matter, he was bound to alienate a portion of his public. And that was bad, as [theatre magnate] Sid Grauman would have said, 'for the old box officeroo.'" But patriotism knew no party and selling Liberty Bonds, actors decided, was an exception. McAdoo's expectations of celebrity-driven sales proved correct. Throngs of nearly 100,000 people repeatedly mobbed the stars, who sold as much as $2 million in war bonds in a single afternoon.[20]

The war bond tour gave Chaplin his first insight into the political uses of stardom. He discovered that people were more interested in hearing what he or Mary or Doug had to say than any congressman, senator, or even president. As he traveled around the country, the normally tongue-tied comedian had to deliver speeches to frenzied crowds. In April 1918, he stepped onto a

FIGURE 1.1 Charlie Chaplin selling war bonds to an enthusiastic crowd on Wall Street in April 1918. SOURCE: ACADEMY OF MOTION PICTURE ARTS AND SCIENCES

podium in Washington, D.C., and declared, "The Germans are at your door! We've got to stop them! And we will stop them, if you buy Liberty Bonds! Remember, each bond you buy will save a soldier's life—a mother's son!—will bring this war to an early victory!" Afterward, the three celebrities went to the White House and met President Woodrow Wilson (see fig. 1.1).[21]

Despite his war work, Chaplin privately insisted he was a pacifist, a position that generated hostility on both sides of the Atlantic. By 1915, a year after the war began in Europe, the actor was widely criticized in England for not returning to fight for his native land. After the United States entered the fray in April 1917, Chaplin received thousands of letters and white feathers (symbols of cowardice) from angry citizens demanding that he enlist. Public pressure finally led the diminutive comedian to register for the selective service draft in Los Angeles on June 5, 1917. But the government agency rejected the twenty-eight-year-old for being undersized (between 5'4" and 5'5") and underweight. The tight-fisted star tried to curry public favor by donating $1,000 to the war relief fund and producing a ten-minute film, *The Bond*, for the government in 1918.[22]

Willing to sell bonds that might help bring the war to a rapid end, Chaplin was appalled at the militarist fervor that swept the nation. His loathing of war led him to make his first self-consciously polemical film, the antiwar comedy *Shoulder Arms* (1918). Friends tried to dissuade him from producing what many would consider an antipatriotic film. However, a lucrative deal with the First National Exhibitors' Circuit gave the movie star enough money to build his own studio and make whatever he wanted.

In *Shoulder Arms*, Chaplin depicts the so-called glories of war as anything but glorious. Spoofing the militarism he hated so much, Charlie abandons the Tramp to play the most awkward member of the "Awkward Squad," a group of soldiers totally incapable of doing the most basic military maneuvers. While filled with hilarious scenes of battles gone awry (most notably, Charlie trying to cross no man's land disguised as a tree trunk), the film also evokes the pathos of frightened young men finding themselves an ocean away from family, living and dying in trenches, and fighting a war that seemed even more chaotic than Charlie's comic antics.

Despite the initial fears of his friends, the three-reel film opened to rave reviews in October 1918 and became a smash hit with troops and civilians alike. It "took a gentle genius like his," Grace Kingsley wrote in the *Los Angeles Times*, "to transmute into golden laughter the flickering high-lights of comedy which capriciously illumine the grim background of war." When peace was finally declared on November 11, 1918, Chaplin was filled with joy and melancholy. Civilization as "we had known it," he lamented, "would never be the same—that era had gone. Gone, too, were its so-called basic decencies—but, then, decency had never been prodigious in any era."[23]

Chaplin would never be the same either. Two issues haunted the world's most famous man over the next thirty years: his suspect patriotism and his troubled love life. The political uses of movie stars during World War I established an important precedent: using celebrities to promote official government policy. During future wars, the alliance of Hollywood and Washington, D.C., would again draw on movie stars to raise funds and entertain the troops abroad. However, the Treasury Department's initial success also sparked government fears: If stars could sell war bonds with such effectiveness why not political ideas that challenged official policy? Patriotism, from the administration's point of view, meant unquestioning support of government positions. Despite his participation in the war bond drive, Chaplin's failure to fight led many to question his political loyalties. This questioning grew especially ugly during World War II and the subsequent Red Scare.

Chaplin's star persona was further tarnished by what many viewed as his scandalous love life. Over the next several decades, he entered into four marriages, three divorces, and numerous affairs. Chaplin liked young women, very young women. During his years in Hollywood, he had relationships with Edna Purviance (19), Mildred Harris (16), Lita Grey (16), May Collins (14), Louise Brooks (18), Merna Kennedy (17), and Oona O'Neill (16).[24] Once his affairs became public, Charlie discovered that audiences did not like their fantasies punctured by stars whose politics or romances became too public or too scandalous. The downside of stardom, as he sadly learned, was a loss of private life. The press, restrained in its handling of the first divorce, proved less inhibited in criticizing his subsequent affairs. The intensely private comedian found his love life making front-page news throughout the 1920s, 1930s, and 1940s.

The Political Evolution of Charlie Chaplin

The period between 1918 and 1931 marked a turning point in Chaplin's life and politics. His celebrity brought him into contact with intellectuals and radicals on both sides of the Atlantic who helped transform the unschooled star into a more confident political thinker. Imbued with a new self-assurance, Chaplin began voicing his opinions on a range of controversial issues. He also produced a series of films that challenged the dominant class politics of the era.

Chaplin's political evolution began at the end of the war when he became acquainted with two of the nation's most prominent radical intellectuals: Upton Sinclair and Max Eastman. Considered by many to be America's greatest socialist writer, Sinclair put into words the oppression and abuse of authority that Chaplin tried to convey on the screen. His most celebrated novel, *The Jungle* (1906), was a scathing critique of the meatpacking industry that eventually led to the passage of the Pure Food and Drug Act (1906).

Chaplin first became interested in socialism after meeting Sinclair. His initial contact with the "professorial looking man, with iron grey hair, pince-nez glasses and a perpetual sweetness of the mouth" came in August 1918 when the two had lunch at Sinclair's home in Pasadena. The soft-spoken socialist bluntly asked the wealthy actor, then the richest man in Hollywood with a fortune estimated at $5 million in 1922 ($64 million in 2009 dollars), if he believed in the profit system. "It was a disarming question," Chaplin admitted, "but instinctively I felt it went to the very root of the matter, and from that moment I became interested and saw politics not as history but as an economic problem."[25]

The two quickly became friends, spending time at each other's homes and at Chaplin's studios where they discussed politics and movies. Sinclair's goal, he told Charlie, was to turn him "into a Socialist." It is not surprising that Chaplin was attracted to Sinclair; in addition to being an interesting thinker, he was one of the first radicals to use the screen to communicate ideas to a mass audience. He turned *The Jungle* into a film in 1914 and maintained close ties with leftist filmmakers well into the 1930s.[26]

While Sinclair piqued Chaplin's interest in radical politics, Max Eastman introduced him to New York artists and intellectuals who believed that modernist art in all its various forms (including film) could be used to transform the world in revolutionary ways. The son of two Protestant ministers, Eastman pursued radical politics through periodicals such as *The Masses*, which he edited until its suppression by the government in August 1917, and *The Liberator*, which he founded in March 1918 with his sister

Crystal Eastman. His writers constituted a who's who of the American left: Floyd Dell, John Reed, Sherwood Anderson, Randolph Bourne, and Carl Sandburg. The ruggedly handsome Eastman was one of the few prominent socialists who managed to publicly oppose the war, support the Russian Revolution, and still stay out of jail.

Chaplin and Eastman crossed paths at a time when radical activists were the subjects of national debate and repression. The rapid spread of radicalism across Europe after the Russian Revolution in October 1917 and the emergence of two American-based Communist parties raised fears among government leaders that the "Red Terror," as the press dubbed it, had crossed the Atlantic Ocean. The dynamiting of Attorney General A. Mitchell Palmer's home and reports of mail bombs being sent to government officials led federal and state authorities to initiate policies aimed at suppressing radicalism. Constitutional rights were violated and personal liberties trampled as thousands of Communists, socialists, and radicals who committed no crimes were arrested, jailed, or deported because of their political beliefs. The Red Scare reached its peak in January 1920 when, on a single evening, Attorney General Palmer ordered the arrest of 4,000 alleged Communists in thirty-three cities.[27]

Chaplin met Eastman for the first time in November 1919, when the latter gave a speech in Los Angeles denouncing the repeated abuses of civil liberties by government authorities. Dining together that evening, they began a friendship that lasted until Eastman's rightward turn in the early 1940s. The writer found the movie star to be an intellectually curious, if not a fully accomplished, thinker; "he has intellect as well as imagination." Eastman was impressed that the "most famous man in the world" was reading Oswald Spengler's *Decline of the West* and James Joyce's short stories.[28]

Eastman quickly learned that rumors about the comedian's cheapness were true. When Chaplin said he wanted to help fund *The Liberator*, the editor's eyes lit up, until the millionaire handed him a gift of $25. "Charlie likes radical ideas; he likes to talk about transforming the world," Eastman recounted, "but he doesn't like to pay for the talk, much less the transformation." Chaplin also refused to publicly support his new friend. He feared the possible effects that radical pronouncements might have on his box office, especially in the midst of the Red Scare. When asked by a reporter in November 1919 whether he had contributed to Eastman's radical periodical, a not entirely honest Charlie responded, "I am absolutely cold on the

Bolshevism theme; neither am I interested in Socialism. . . . If *The Liberator* is seditious, it certainly should be suppressed."[29]

Chaplin never lost his anxiety about money or his reputation for being cheap. "He could break his arm pulling away from the check," one of his tennis partners remarked. However, his willingness to speak out on controversial issues took a major leap forward in the fall of 1921. Depressed by his recent divorce and worn out by making seventy-one films in seven years, Charlie traveled to England to attend the premiere of *The Kid*. In the course of his journey, he found himself the focal point of a newly emerging cult of celebrity, one in which fame trumped expertise. As he crossed the United States by train, the comedian was surprised that people continually solicited his opinions about contemporary political events. When he arrived in New York, reporters queried him about a range of controversial issues. "My radical views have been much misunderstood," he told the assembled gathering. "I am not a Socialist, nor am I looking for a new order of things. But I do believe that conditions can be much improved and that the lives of the working classes can be made far more pleasant than they are now." Growing more comfortable, Charlie also called for the government to establish trade relations with the Soviet Union.[30]

During his time in New York, Max Eastman exposed Chaplin to an intellectual world unknown to him in Los Angeles. The movie star met bohemians and radicals who cared deeply about the world of ideas and about the links between art and politics. He loved Greenwich Village and its intense intellectual life. He loved talking with African American truck drivers who waxed eloquently about the beauties of *Roget's Thesaurus*, and waiters who quoted Karl Marx and William Blake with every course they served. He also met luminaries such as novelist Waldo Frank; poet Hart Crane; and the controller of the Port of New York, Dudley Field Malone, and his wife, Margaret Foster, a suffragist activist.

Chaplin's political/intellectual evolution continued during his nearly two-month trip to Europe. Charlie set sail on the *Olympic* luxury liner on September 3, 1921, and arrived at Southampton six days later. Within three days of his return, England's native son received 73,000 letters, 28,000 of which asked for money. The crowds and letters were expected; the broad reach of his celebrity was not. The self-educated lad received invitations to dine with Europe's leading intellectuals. During the next few weeks, he met with socialist and playwright George Bernard Shaw, E. V. Lucas (editor of

Punch), and writers H. G. Wells, J. M. Barrie, and Thomas Burke. Despite his exhilarating visit to Greenwich Village, Charlie was still insecure about his intellect. According to his Yale-educated assistant and confidant Harry Crocker, he felt flummoxed during his meeting with Shaw, made foolish comments to Wells, and proved a reticent dinner guest at many parties in England. "So tongue-tied and confused did he become when in the presence of his idols that his experiences with them were not felicitous."[31]

Tongue-tied or not, Charlie was flattered that people whom he so admired took him seriously. During dinner with Wells, the two men discussed socialism, Russia, and a range of world problems. The socialist writer complimented Chaplin by telling him he was a man who noticed things, who observed and analyzed. "That alone," Chaplin wrote, was "worth the entire trip from Los Angeles to Europe." The movie star found himself equally celebrated in France, where he was awarded the Order of Public Instruction. Reporters constantly queried him about his views on world affairs. "He is being taken so seriously," reported the *New York Times*, "that several editorials have been written condemning or approving his judgment."[32]

The joy of meeting so many of his literary idols was tempered by the scenes of destitution and despair he saw throughout Europe. As he drove through Brixton, he passed "a lot of painted ladies" who were looking for young men. "Some of the young fellows are minus arms and many of them carry various ribbons of military honor. They are living and eloquent evidence of the war and its effects." Chaplin found Berlin equally ravaged by war. "It still had an atmosphere of defeat, with its tragic aftermath of armless and legless soldiers begging on almost every street corner."[33]

Charlie left Europe on October 18 with mixed feelings. He was pleased at being welcomed into the world of intellectual elites but unnerved by what he saw. "If I could only do something," he wrote in his memoir. "Solve the unemployment problem or make some grand gesture, in answer to all this." But he was only an actor. What could he do?

Chaplin returned home more willing to endorse radical ideas and organizations. During a visit to Socialist Party headquarters in New York that October, he told his admirers, "It is a pity that the Socialist forces of the world were not united, because if they were not split up and quarreling with each other they could accomplish big things." Four months later, in an interview in the *Literary Digest*, he attacked the British class system, something highly unusual for movie stars during the 1920s.[34]

Although the star's political awareness continued to evolve over the decade, he still preferred private conversations to public pronouncements, for such venues never put him at financial risk. Those who listened to his views discovered that Chaplin, though inclined toward radicalism, was an eclectic political thinker who subscribed to no specific ideological school of thought. Harry Crocker, who worked as his assistant from October 1925 through October 1929, was the frequent recipient of Chaplin's political discourses. In his unpublished memoir, Crocker explained how many of the actor's "views could not help but offend persons who believed in the capitalistic system, as I do, in the American way of life. In arguing the cause of labor, Charlie frequently gave expression to ideas that could be considered socialistic in a capitalistic nation. It was these expressions of opinion which led some people to regard him, even in 1921, as a Bolshevik, and, in the 1940s, a Communist; yet these ideas were mild enough in themselves."[35]

Crocker proved correct in assessing how others viewed his employer's politics. Chaplin's friendship with Upton Sinclair and Max Eastman, and his occasional willingness to speak out on controversial issues, attracted the attention of the FBI. Following Chaplin's August 1922 dinner party for Communist leader William Z. Foster, Bureau deputy head Hoover added the actor to the FBI watch list, eventually collecting 1,900 pages of reports on the star. Hoover also turned his files over to R. M. Whitney, director of the ultraconservative American Defense League. In 1924, Whitney published *Reds in America* and singled out Chaplin as someone especially "interested in radical movements and a heavy contributor to radical funds, much of which found its way into Communist channels."[36] Whitney was half right: Charlie was interested in radical politics, but he was far too cheap to be a heavy contributor to any cause.

Chaplin arrived back in Los Angeles on October 31, 1921, determined to be a more serious filmmaker. His postwar films displayed a determination to combine entertainment with critiques of class inequalities, all done in humorous fashion. This new resolve came at a time when government officials pressured movie industry leaders to join their Americanism Campaign and produce films aimed at halting the spread of "Bolshevism and radicalism." The Hollywood–Washington alliance worked. Studios hesitated producing any film during the 1920s that was overtly favorable to labor or radical causes. A strong left perspective virtually disappeared from the screen as industry officials succeeded in driving independent radical film companies out of business. Leftists also suffered bitter defeats off the screen. Accused by business and government groups of aiding Communism, labor union and Socialist Party membership steadily declined during the 1920s.[37]

Chaplin refused to join the anti-Red crusade. He could be more politically independent than most filmmakers because he was more economically independent. In January 1919, a year after organizing his own studio, he joined with Douglas Fairbanks, Mary Pickford, and director D. W. Griffith to launch their own distribution company. United Artists, the partners insisted, would "protect the independent producer and the independent exhibitor" against the abuses of the rapidly expanding Hollywood studio system. Now in full control of production and distribution—as well as writing, directing, and starring in his films—Chaplin could do as he pleased.[38]

During the 1920s, Chaplin produced a series of works that challenged the dominant conservative politics of the era. Postwar audiences, argued Hollywood insiders, wanted to forget about death and instead celebrate the good life. They wanted movies about money, sex, beauty, and luxury. No one did this better than Cecil B. DeMille. He was the master of cross-class fantasies, "society films" as they were often termed, that explored romantic interactions between upper-class and working-class protagonists. "Your poor person," the conservative Republican declared in 1925, "wants to see wealth, colorful, interesting, exotic." And that is what he gave them: lavish hotels, magnificent mansions, fashionable clothing boutiques, and exotic nightclubs where the moneyed set amused themselves. Audiences watching films such as *Male and Female* (1919) and *Saturday Night* (1922) were treated to voyeuristic glimpses of the lifestyles of the extremely rich, while at the same time receiving conservative messages that suggested they were ultimately better off remaining within their own class. "Be satisfied and content with your life" was the dominant ideology of these films.[39]

Chaplin's cinematic critiques of the class system so venerated by DeMille proved especially important because they appeared at a time when the rise of luxurious movie palaces turned moviegoing into a regular part of middle-class and even upper-class life. Chaplin understood that movies helped shaped the way vast numbers of Americans understood their world. In the 1920s, few middle-class people knew what a millionaire's life—or a poor person's life—was like. But Chaplin changed that. His films offered a "keyhole into the way the other half of the world lives," he explained in 1925, "people one hasn't seen, ways, conventions, wastes and savings, graces and disgraces, hearts one does not know."[40] Still reluctant to make explicitly radical films, his goal was to heighten political awareness rather than provide specific solutions.

Chaplin's postwar films offered moviegoers a sharp political contrast to those of DeMille's. The two admired each other's skills but remained ideological opposites. "I detest his political views," the political conservative wrote of the comedian.[41] While DeMille looked at American life from the top down, Chaplin depicted the same world but from the bottom up and did so with an empathy for working-class life that was absent in DeMille's productions. Like the conservative director, Chaplin's movies are filled with scenes of luxurious summer resorts and stately mansions teeming with men in tuxedos and women in elegant gowns. But he also exposed audiences to charity hospitals that cared for unwed mothers, flophouses populated by rootless transients, and cold attic rooms inhabited by the poor. In *The Kid* (1921) and *The Idle Class* (1921), the rich are not people to be admired, but hypocrites who denounce how the poor care for their children but do nothing to help. Likewise, the authorities who run charity hospitals and orphanages are more concerned about their institutions than the people they are supposed to serve.

While these films were filled with humor and biting social commentary, Chaplin wanted to show that he was something more than just a comedian. "I have always been ambitious to do serious things," he told reporters in October 1923. "That is why I have written and produced 'A Woman of Paris.'" Premiering that September, the movie marked a sharp departure for the man most people associated with slapstick comedy: a psychological drama that rebelled against the sentimentality and breezy shallowness of postwar American cinema. This was the first time that the actor did not star in one of his films. Insisting that he was "no Valentino," Chaplin cast Adolphe Menjou (a well-known conservative) as the wealthy Parisian bachelor Pierre Revel, a notorious womanizer who, like Chaplin, preferred mistresses to marriage.[42]

Drawing on his recent experiences in Europe, Chaplin presented a glimpse of a world few would ever see: the world of the Parisian wealthy. But class relations are far more nuanced in *A Woman of Paris* than in DeMille's spectacles. Rejecting DeMille's stock caricatures, he offered viewers more fully realized portraits of the class divide. In order to change the world, his film implies, people need to know whom they are going up against. Unlike the rich in DeMille's films, who are always silly if not downright stupid, Chaplin suggests that men of wealth must be taken seriously. Pierre Revel is no fool; he is smart, sophisticated, and usually gets what he wants. Likewise, the poor are not simply good-hearted, salt-of-the earth types. They are intelligent and calculating.

Critics and directors such as Ernst Lubitsch and Sergei Eisenstein hailed *A Woman of Paris* as a masterpiece, but it proved less successful with audiences. In fact, it barely earned back its costs. Audiences wanted Chaplin to be funny.

Fearful of losing his fame and fortune, Chaplin resumed the role of the Tramp in his next film, *The Gold Rush* (1925). Yet this was a different kind of comedy than in the past, a more fully realized comedic drama filled with character development rather than just slapstick. The basic plot line has Charlie prospecting for gold in the brutal Alaskan wilderness. Amid the well-known scenes of the Tramp eating his own shoe, conducting a dance with two potatoes, and turning into a human-sized chicken, Chaplin depicts a tough world in which the pursuit of wealth is filled with hunger, betrayal, violence, and death. Yet *The Gold Rush* is ultimately a film about the triumph of the little man. Unlike DeMille's working-class characters who are cautioned to remain content with their lot, the Tramp strikes it rich and gets the girl. While DeMille was the master of class fantasy deferred, Chaplin offered audiences a more satisfying vision of class fantasy realized. The film was a major hit and squelched any concern that Charlie had lost his touch.

Chaplin's subsequent productions were slowed down by his marriage, the birth of two children, a messy divorce from Lita Grey, and the death of his mother, Hannah. In 1928, he returned to the screen with the mildly anti-authoritarian comedy *The Circus*, and then three years later with the moving *City Lights*. Released in January 1931, in the midst of the Great Depression—when millions of men and women lost their jobs, their savings, their homes, and their dignity—the film is a poignant romantic comedy that contrasted the insincerity of the rich with the selflessness of a poor Tramp. Chaplin once again skewers the hollowness of the extravagant elite lifestyle venerated by so many in the 1920s and seemingly so out of place in the harsh years of the early 1930s.

City Lights is filled with humorous scenes of the Tramp and his millionaire friend driving in a Rolls-Royce, drinking at ritzy nightclubs, and attending wild parties. But the Tramp, like his creator, is never fooled by the trappings of wealth. "The saddest thing I can imagine," Charlie wrote in his autobiography, "is to get used to luxury."[43] The film offers no solutions, but it reminds audiences not to trust men of wealth and power. While such messages were not revolutionary, let alone radical, Chaplin nevertheless remained one of the few major filmmakers of the time to place such left-leaning ideas at the heart of his productions.

City Lights was a successful anomaly: a silent film made in the new era of sound. Although Chaplin wrote a musical score and added sound effects, he was reluctant to abandon the iconic silent Tramp. To do so, he feared, would diminish the character's universality. "To the French," observed his friend William deMille, the Tramp "is a Frenchman, as he is Russian in the Soviet Union. If he ever spoke he would lose his personality and become much more finite, less universal."[44]

The film earned kudos from the public and critics alike. *City Lights* became Chaplin's biggest financial hit, grossing over $5 million by 1935.[45]

CHAPLIN SPEAKS

The 1930s and 1940s marked yet another stage in Charlie Chaplin's political evolution. Spurred on by the combined effects of the Great Depression, a world tour in 1931–1932, the election of Franklin D. Roosevelt, and the rise of fascism in Europe, the increasingly self-confident star now believed he had something to say. So he did.

In February 1931, the actor traveled to London for the British premiere of *City Lights* and then continued on a sixteen-month trip that took him to Europe, Africa, and the Far East. During the tour, Europe's leading intellectuals and politicians, many of whom cared less about his ideas than meeting the world's most famous celebrity, again sought Chaplin out. In England, he talked politics with George Bernard Shaw, H. G. Wells, Winston Churchill, Aldous Huxley, Lady Astor, John Maynard Keynes, and Mahatma Gandhi; in Germany he met with members of the Reichstag who opposed the rising Nazi party; in Italy he had a brief audience with Benito Mussolini. Along the way, he witnessed the suffering wrought by an economic depression that gripped the entire world. "I am reputedly a comedian," he quipped during the tour, "but after seeing financial conditions of the world I have decided I am as much an economist as financiers are comedians."[46]

Chaplin arrived back in Los Angeles on June 10, 1932, convinced he was a world citizen and needed to address matters that concerned all humanity.

"Patriotism is the greatest insanity the world has ever suffered," he told a re-porter. "Patriotism [in Europe] is rampant everywhere, and the result is going to be another war." Having established an international audience for his films, Charlie hoped to do the same for his politics. While in the Far East, he began working on an essay, "The Economic Solution," that he hoped to present to the League of Nations. Upon his return to Hollywood, he wrote an account of his travels that was serialized in *Woman's Home Companion*—and later published as *A Comedian Sees the World* (1933)—in which he chronicled his political thoughts and conversations with world leaders. Unafraid to be explicitly political, Chaplin used this opportunity to lay out his political agenda: the need for a single international currency, a more humane capitalism, shorter working hours, and greater rights for labor.[47]

Franklin Roosevelt's election in November 1932 sparked Chaplin's first involvement in electoral politics. Like other actors, he was inspired by the charismatic president's ambitious New Deal program. Breaking his long-standing reluctance to give public speeches, Chaplin delivered a talk over national radio in October 1933 endorsing FDR's National Recovery Admin-istration and its "Buy Now Campaign." This is especially significant in light of his decision to turn down a $650,000 offer to do radio commercials two years earlier, which he did in order to preserve the "mystery" and "illusion" of the silent character he had created on the screen.[48]

Chaplin also lent his star power to help Upton Sinclair during his 1934 campaign to win the governorship of California on his End Poverty in Cali-fornia (EPIC) platform. When the Socialist-turned-Democratic candidate first approached his friend for an endorsement in December 1933, Chaplin refused, telling him, "I realize it would be a mistake for me to identify myself in politics. As in the past, my principle is to maintain a non-partisan atti-tude." But the actor changed his mind and agreed to participate in a satiric skit Sinclair wrote, "Depression Island," which the two men performed at a campaign rally. Casting aside his aversion to organized political activity, Chaplin joined with Hollywood Communists such as Lillian Hellman and Donald Ogden Stewart, and progressives such as Groucho Marx, in lending his name to the Authors' League for Sinclair. The candidate, in turn, prom-ised the star a position in his cabinet if elected.[49]

More willing to speak out publicly, he nevertheless saved his sharpest pronouncements for the medium he knew best. The actor-director-writer shifted his cinematic attacks from the local scene to the national and, finally, to the international. During the 1920s, he disparaged the excessive materialism of the age. In the mid-1930s and early 1940s, he critiqued the cruel nature of industrial capitalism and Nazism. His villains evolved from local authority figures to fascist leaders who were bringing the world to the brink of war.

Modern Times, originally titled *Commonwealth* and *The Masses*, opened in New York on February 5, 1936, to rumors that it was filled with Communist themes. Begun in the depths of the Great Depression, *Modern Times* is another reworking of Chaplin's childhood traumas updated and set in the factories, alleyways, and crumbling shantytown Hoovervilles of 1934 America. This would be the last film in which the Tramp appeared. *Modern Times* is a story of human perseverance set amid a harsh world dominated by heartless industrialists, abusive police, indifferent politicians, insensitive clergy, and allusions to dreaded orphanages and mental institutions.

Like *City Lights, Modern Times* is not entirely silent. It has sound effects and a musical score written by Chaplin but virtually no dialogue. The film opens with a shot of hundreds of sheep being herded and then cuts to hundreds of sheep-like workers emerging from a subway on their way to the Electro Steel Corporation, where huge machines dwarf human beings. Anticipating the Big Brother world of George Orwell's *1984*, Chaplin reveals a factory where cameras are everywhere (including bathrooms) and employees are constantly monitored by the company president who watches them on a closed-circuit television in his office.

During the next fifteen minutes, Chaplin cleverly mocks the dehumanizing assembly line and scientific management methods so despised by American workers. The factory boss hopes to eliminate wasted lunchtime by feeding employees with a machine, thereby allowing them to continue working during meals. The Tramp is the guinea pig and of course the machine goes haywire throwing food all over the place. A frazzled Chaplin returns to the assembly line but soon gets caught in the conveyor belt and passes through the wheels and gears of the surreal machinery. The work of modern times drives him crazy and he winds up in a hospital suffering from a nervous breakdown.

The inspiration for the early part of the film, and especially the scene in figure 1.2, dated back to 1918, when Chaplin visited Henry Ford's automobile factory in Detroit as part of his Liberty Bond tour. Chaplin was appalled by the inhumane workings of an assembly line that required men to perform one task over and over again until they figuratively became part of the

FIGURE 1.2 Chaplin mocked the inhumanity and insanity of industrial life and the Great Depression in *Modern Times* (1936). SOURCE: PHOTOFEST

machinery. Once again, Chaplin uses humor to deliver his political message. He turns his critique of industrial capitalism and the enslavement of man by machine into an opportunity for comic antics. We see the small but smiling Tramp best the assembly line by passing unharmed through the gigantic cogs of industry. This is Chaplin's version of "Man Bites Dog."[50]

The Tramp eventually leaves the hospital cured but without a job. In a scene of self-parody, Chaplin, who was constantly accused of being a Communist, bends down to pick up a red flag that fell from a passing construction truck. Just as he starts waving it, hoping to catch the driver's attention, demonstrators carrying protest signs in English and Spanish ("Liberty or Death," "Unidad," "Libertad") come around the corner and fall in behind him. Chaplin suddenly finds himself leading the group and is immediately arrested as a Communist agitator and sent to jail. In a sad commentary on American life, we see that the Tramp lives far better in prison than on the streets: he gets three meals, a warm room, a clean bed, and spends the day reading newspapers and listening to the radio. He enjoys it so much that when released, he tries to get himself arrested and sent back to the one place a poor man can survive without fear.

Soon after leaving jail, the Tramp meets and falls in love with the Gamin, played by Paulette Goddard, whom Chaplin would marry after the film's opening. She lives in a shack down by the docks and steals food in order to feed her unemployed father and two younger sisters. When her father is killed by police during a protest, pitiless state authorities come to take her and her sisters to an orphanage, just as they once did for Charlie and Syd. But the Gamin escapes and joins up with the Tramp.

The remainder of the film is filled with more arrests, more strikes, more unemployment, more homelessness, and more heartbreak—all portrayed for laughs. The final scene finds the Tramp and the Gamin walking down an open road, with the latter crying, "What's the use of trying?" But the always optimistic Tramp tells her to "Buck Up," and the film ends with the couple walking away—hopefully to a better life—with smiles on their faces.

Reactions to *Modern Times* varied widely. Some praised it for its biting satire of modern life, while others condemned it as propaganda. Leftists generally applauded the film, but a number of radicals criticized the star for not offering any political solutions. Despite Chaplin's growing offscreen activism, his movies still sought to expose problems rather than solve them. For all its satire of American life, *Modern Times* never confronted real politicians or contemporary foreign policy, something Chaplin would do in his next film, *The Great Dictator*.

Now wealthy beyond his dreams, the forty-seven-year-old Chaplin was free to do whatever he wished. What he wished, he told Max Eastman, was to do something that would "give him more spiritual satisfaction." That led him to deal with an evil he considered far greater than mass production: Adolf Hitler. The more he read about Hitler's "attacking of minority people, or people that didn't agree with him," the more he felt compelled to confront the situation on the screen. "If he had won," Charlie explained, "the world would have been Nazi for the next thousand years. Those things you can't bear to think of." Coincidentally, Hitler and Chaplin were born four days apart, in April 1889, and came from equally harsh childhoods marked by difficult fathers, sick mothers, and the need to leave their native land to achieve success. The authoritarian dictator hated the anti-authoritarian filmmaker. The Nazi government circulated propaganda claiming Chaplin was Jewish and, in 1936, banned *Modern Times* on the ground that it "inclines toward bolshevism." Officials also prohibited a planned revival of *The Gold Rush* because its "spirit" did not conform to the new German ideology.[51]

Chaplin's familiarity with Nazism was heightened by his friendship with European émigrés who fled to Los Angeles in the 1930s, many of whom were Jews. His friends included prominent figures such as Albert Einstein, Aldous Huxley, Sergei Eisenstein, Lion Feuchtwanger, Thomas Mann, Bertolt Brecht, and the many left-wing salonists who flocked to Salka Viertel's Santa Monica home.[52]

The rapid politicization of the Hollywood community during the 1930s deeply affected Chaplin and dozens of other stars. The fear of Nazism in Germany and the outbreak of civil war in Spain in 1936 led Hollywood liberals, radicals, and a small number of conservatives to fight on two fronts: some battled fascism off the screen, while others preferred to wage their battles directly on the screen. Those pursuing the former course organized a wide range of progressive "Popular Front" groups, most notably the Hollywood Anti-Nazi League, dedicated to fighting fascism abroad and at home. "No other cause so gripped Hollywood during the 1930s," observed one newspaper reporter. Caught up in the heady politics of the moment, the normally reticent Chaplin attended meetings of the Hollywood Anti-Nazi League and, following the outbreak of war in September 1939, the Committee to Defend America.[53]

Believing his movies more effective than his offscreen activities, Chaplin focused on making a film that mocked Hitler and his fascist allies. An incomparable mimic, Charlie spent hours watching newsreel footage of the Führer, observing his mannerisms and listening to the inflection of his voice as he addressed the crowds. After hearing the star's imitation of the Nazi leader in August 1939, a reporter remarked, "If you were in the next room and heard Chaplin doing it, you would think you were listening to Hitler, although not one word Chaplin utters is really a German word."[54]

Making a film attacking Hitler proved far more controversial than Chaplin anticipated. Producers who wished to turn out starkly anti-Nazi movies—such as Walter Wanger and Harry and Jack Warner—were repeatedly constrained by Hollywood's self-censorship board, the Production Code Administration (PCA), and its antisemitic head, Joseph Breen. Created in 1934 to forestall federal censorship of motion pictures, PCA rules prohibited filmmakers from attacking or mocking foreign governments and their leaders. When Hitler and Mussolini promised to ban the films of any studio that offended them, and all Hollywood films if necessary, Breen stepped up his efforts to stop producers from endangering the industry's highly profitable foreign revenues. Indeed, not everyone thought Hitler was so evil. As late as January 1939, PCA censors attempted to halt production of Warner Bros.' *Confessions of a Nazi Spy*, the nation's first explicitly anti-Nazi film, explaining that to "represent Hitler only as a screaming madman and a bloodthirsty persecutor, and nothing else, is manifestly unfair, considering his phenomenal public career, his unchallenged political and social achievements, and his position as head of the most important continental European power."[55]

Rumors about Chaplin's proposed film *The Dictator* (its original title) were followed by pressure from Nazi sympathizers to halt production. In October 1938, Dr. George Gyssling, the German consul general in Los Angeles, wrote Breen objecting to the proposed film about "a defenseless little Jew, who is mistaken for a powerful dictator." If these rumors "should prove true," he added, it "will naturally lead to serious troubles and complications." Several Los Angeles–based Nazi groups sent Chaplin letters threatening "to create riots" and "throw stink bombs into the theaters and shoot up the screen wherever it would be shown." The actor contacted San Francisco Longshoremen's Union head Harry Bridges, a Communist and militant antifascist, and asked him to send twenty or thirty of his toughest men to the film's opening. This way, "if any of these pro-Nazi fellows started a rumpus, your folks might gently stamp on their toes before anything got seriously going."[56]

Opposition from so many quarters delayed production but did not stop it. Outside pressure made Chaplin even more determined to put his message on the screen. "I did this picture for the Jews of the world," he told a reporter. "I did it because I wanted to see a return to decency and kindness and humanity." In a moment of uncharacteristic generosity, Chaplin ordered United Artists to turn over a share of the film's European rental income to the Vienna Jewish Kulturgemeinde to facilitate the emigration of Jews from Central Europe.[57]

Chaplin and other political filmmakers were slowed down by the outbreak of war on September 1, 1939. Fearing the disastrous financial impact antifascist films might have on European markets, motion picture industry czar Will Hays forbade American studios that wished to receive a PCA seal (a necessity for most theaters) from developing films with an obvious anti-Nazi bias. The ban remained in effect from September 15, 1939, until January 1940.[58] On September 9, 1939, as Nazi troops marched across Europe, Chaplin began shooting *The Great Dictator*, hopeful that the ban would be lifted before he was done. The film was completed a year later and premiered in New York on October 15, 1940.

The Great Dictator is a tale of mistaken identity set in two interconnected worlds: the pseudo-Nazi epicenter of power ruled by Adenoid Hynkel, dictator of Tomania, and the Jewish ghetto inhabited by his double, the Jewish barber. Both roles are played by Chaplin. More than just a mocking of Hitler and Mussolini, the film is an impassioned defense of the plight of European Jewry at a time when antisemitism was rife in America. The movie opens in 1918 and we see the hapless barber, now a German soldier, save the life of a German fighter pilot. The film then cuts to scenes of Hynkel's rise to power and we hear Chaplin do a wonderful imitation of Hitler, spouting gibberish German. Instead of a swastika, Tomania's national symbol is the "double cross." Chaplin's humor disappears as we move inside the Jewish ghetto and see storm troopers harassing Jews. The barber, who has been an amnesiac since the end of the war, escapes from the hospital and returns to his barbershop to see the word "JEW" painted on his boarded-up front window. He has no idea who the Nazis are and cannot understand why his people are being persecuted. He soon meets Hannah (Paulette Goddard), who explains what transpired during his convalescence.

The Great Dictator served as a visual wakeup call for the many Americans who cared little about Hitler's persecution of the Jews. Coming some thirty-five minutes into the film, the scene of Chaplin resisting the Nazi-like thugs who surround him (see fig. 1.3) marked the first time that images of Jewish ghettos and subsequent warnings about concentration camps appeared in a major Hollywood production. Although set in World War II, the scene of the seemingly vulnerable barber confronting a crowd of bullies reflected an updated version of the Tramp confronting—and ultimately besting—a wide range of bullies.

The film soon cuts back to Hynkel's palace where the dictator proclaims his megalomaniac desire to be "Emperor of the World." When his chief aide Commander Schultz, the pilot whom the barber saved during World War I, objects to his needless persecution of Jews, an angry Hynkel sends him to a "concentration camp." This is probably the first time that term was heard on American screens. Storm troopers come into the ghetto, beat up residents,

FIGURE 1.3 *The Great Dictator* (1940) was one of the first Hollywood films to show Jewish ghettos and Nazi persecution of Jews. SOURCE: CINEMA/TV LIBRARY, USC

and eventually burn down the entire Jewish district. Some of the towns-people escape to nearby Osterlich (read Austria), but the barber is arrested and sent to a concentration camp.

In the meantime, Hynkel meets with Benzini Napaloni (Chaplin's stand-in for Benito Mussolini) to plot a strategy for invading peaceful Osterlich. Napaloni is a ridiculous leader who can barely get out of his private train car let alone invade a nation. As played by Jack Oakie, he is closer to Chico Marx than a ruthless totalitarian dictator. While the two world leaders confer, the barber and Schultz escape the camp dressed in Tomanian uniforms. Hynkel, who has gone hunting, is mistaken for the barber and arrested by his own troops. The barber in turn is mistaken for Hynkel, but proves unable to stop the invasion of Osterlich. The film cuts to Osterlich's ghetto, where we see young Jews who resist the invaders shot to death, and the survivors rounded up for deportation to concentration camps.

In the final scene, modeled on Hitler's infamous Nuremberg rallies, massive crowds await a victory speech by Hynkel. The barber slowly walks up to the platform and, in a hesitating voice that gets stronger as he goes on, addresses the gathering. The six-minute speech is an amalgam of Chaplin's political views. Everything he has learned, thought, or felt makes it into the speech. Chaplin rails against nationalism, militarism, and an industrial world that has turned men into machines. He tells the gathered minions:

> I'm sorry, but I don't want to be an emperor. . . . I don't want to rule or conquer anyone. I should like to help everyone—if possible—Jew, Gentile, black man, white. The way of life can be free and beautiful, but we have lost the way. Greed has poisoned men's souls—has barricaded the world with hate—has goose-stepped us into misery and bloodshed.

After urging soldiers not "to give yourselves to brutes" who "enslave you," the increasingly passionate barber concludes his speech with a humanist, antinationalist plea that Chaplin's critics would later label as Communist:

> Let us fight for a new world—a decent world that will give men a chance to work—that will give youth a future and old age a security. . . . Let us fight to free the world—to do away with national barriers—to do away with greed, with hate, and intolerance. Let us fight for a world of reason—a world where science and progress will lead to all men's happiness. Soldiers, in the name of democracy, let us unite!

The film ends with the soldiers cheering and with Hannah and the Jews of Osterlich looking optimistically toward the horizon.

Chaplin's explicitly political film and decision to speak on the screen generated more controversy than any previous production. Sympathetic reviewers applauded *The Great Dictator* as a "frank, hard-hitting attack on Fascism" and praised his "defense of democracy at the end of the picture" as "the most impressive and important thing in the film."[59] But many critics and fans did not like the comedian turning so blatantly political. The *Motion Picture Herald* condemned the film as "stark propaganda," while the *Hollywood Reporter* called it "his poorest picture" and insisted that the star's decision to address the audience "brings a letdown to the production." *New York Times* critic Bosley Crowther, who enjoyed the film, called the spoken ending "confusing, banal, and embarrassing." His fans wanted him to be funny, not political. As one critic complained, "there are none of the belly laughs. There's none of the heart pull nor the rooting for the little fellow through his tragedies."[60]

Charlie quickly learned what happened when movie stars took stands on controversial foreign policy issues that were far in advance of public opinion and government policy. The British-born filmmaker was an internationalist in what was then a hyper-isolationist nation. As late as July 1941, 79 percent of those surveyed in a Gallup poll opposed the United States entering war against Germany and Italy. Just the rumor of Chaplin making an explicitly anti-Nazi film generated angry responses from displeased moviegoers. In February 1939, Walter W. McKenna of Ventnor City, New Jersey, wrote to influential Foreign Relations Committee member Senator Robert R. Reynolds, objecting to Chaplin "stirring up further strife and recrimination between Germany and the U.S. Government." McKenna urged authorities to deport Chaplin "for the abuse of this Nation's hospitality." Other disgruntled fans accused Charlie of being a Communist because his film attacked Hitler and Mussolini without also criticizing Soviet leader Joseph Stalin. "To the citizens of the United States," Harry Crocker explained, "the words of Chaplin sounded like rank propaganda. But then, the citizens of the United States had not seen their countries overrun and occupied, their men folk shot, their kinfolk carted off into slavery."[61]

What Chaplin viewed as actions in defense of democracy, others saw as part of a media conspiracy led by Jews to force the United States into war (Chaplin was often accused in the media and in FBI reports of being Jewish, or at least half-Jewish). Angry that Chaplin and others were using the screen to sway public opinion toward American intervention, isolationist senators Gerald Nye of North Dakota and Bennett Clark of Missouri launched the U.S. Senate Subcommittee Hearings on Motion Picture and Radio Propaganda in September 1941. Clark questioned the star's suspect loyalties, charging he had made "a great fortune" in the United States yet had refused to become a citizen. The contentious hearings were only canceled following the United States' entry into war on December 8, 1941.[62]

The antifascist star responded to the rebukes by becoming an even more public political figure. In January 1941, he accepted an invitation to perform at Roosevelt's inauguration and to deliver the final speech from *The Great Dictator* over national radio. When the Nazis invaded the Soviet Union in June 1941, he joined several groups that promoted Soviet-American friendship and sent aid to the wartorn nation. Moved by what he saw as Russia's epic resistance to Hitler's brutal onslaught throughout 1941 and 1942, Chaplin endorsed the growing call to deflect Hitler's attacks on Russia by launching a second Allied front in Western Europe.

Had Chaplin shied away from praising the Soviets he might have survived the attacks of his critics. However, the movie star got into deep trouble after making what his enemies judged as a series of pro-Communist speeches in 1942. On May 17, 1942, as Russians troops battled Nazi forces, Chaplin received a phone call from the head of the American Committee for Russian War Relief in San Francisco asking him to speak in place of former U.S. Ambassador to the Soviet Union Joseph E. Davis, who had suffered a sudden attack of laryngitis. Chaplin agreed despite his profound fear of public speaking. "I die before I go on and make a speech for anything at all," he told one interviewer. "Die and vomit."[63]

The next evening, in a hall packed with 10,000 people, including generals, admirals, and San Francisco Mayor Rossi, the keynote speaker grew increasingly agitated as he sat through a series of talks that "were restrained and equivocating." He was upset that speakers downplayed Soviet contributions to the war effort. Chaplin only intended to talk for four minutes, but "after listening to such weak palaver my indignation was aroused." He stepped up to the podium and proclaimed, "'Comrades!' And I mean comrades. I assume there are many Russians here tonight, and the way your countrymen are fighting and dying at this very moment, it is an honor and a privilege to call you comrades." Adapting Shylock's speech from *The Merchant of Venice* to the current situation, he explained, "The Communists are no different from anyone else; whether they lose an arm or a leg, they suffer as all of us do, and die as all of us die. And the Communist mother is the same as any other mother. When she receives the tragic news that her sons will not return, she weeps as other mothers weep. I don't have to be a Communist to know that. I have only to be a human being to know that." The impassioned actor spoke for forty minutes and ended by calling for a second front and urging the audience to telegram the president to that effect.[64]

Chaplin had caught speech fever. Five days later, he was the featured speaker at a Russian war relief rally in Los Angeles. In the coming months, he spoke at pro-Russian gatherings in several cities. That July, he gave a fourteen-minute speech calling for a second front that was broadcast via radio to a mass meeting of 60,000 trade unionists and their allies at Madison Square Garden. In October he addressed the Artists' Front to Win the War rally in

Carnegie Hall, a rally which Jack Warner urged him to avoid because of the organization's radical orientation. Ignoring Warner, Chaplin again called for a second front, praised Roosevelt for releasing American Communist Party leader Earl Browder from prison, and urged FDR not to deport labor leader Harry Bridges. In a November speech in Chicago, the actor-activist insisted that domestic wartime sacrifices demanded greater postwar economic justice for the poor. "I want change. I don't want the old rugged individualism—rugged for a few and ragged for the many." In December, he returned to New York and stepped up his defense of Russia. "Thank God this war is sweeping away all the hypocrisy and nonsense about communism. People are no longer shocked by it. They understand that it is a good thing. . . . I am not a Communist but I am proud to say that I feel pretty pro-Communist."[65]

Chaplin's speeches inflamed conservative critics who equated any defense of Russia with a defense of Communism. "Chaplin lately has said that he was pro-Communist," syndicated conservative columnist Westbrook Pegler told readers in December 1942, "which means anti-American." Hedda Hopper joined Pegler's Red-baiting campaign to deport the star and asked her readers why Chaplin had been allowed to make "his home, fortune and reputation in America, without ever making any attempt to become a citizen of our country."[66]

Despite mounting public accusations, Charlie never embraced Communism, though he was sympathetic to its more idealistic goals. As "an ardent champion of the under-dog and as an avowed pacifist," explained Harry Crocker, Chaplin "was a push-over for the raw trend of Communist thought." But the actor never supported state-sponsored Communism. "Certainly I have said that I believe that Communism has accomplished benefits for the Russians," he told Crocker. "But I certainly don't want Communism. I'm a Capitalist, but just because I am a Capitalist, must I blind myself to the defects of Capitalism?"[67] Any illusions he harbored about the Soviet Union were dispelled when he met composer Dmitri Shostakovich and learned how he was forced to compose his music along party lines and receive party approval before making public statements.

Chaplin's defense of Russian troops and call for a second front were fully consistent with his cinematic politics. For nearly three decades, he put his steadfast defense of the "little guy" and image of the Tramp resisting powerful bullies on the screen for millions to see. In his mind, he envisioned Russian troops playing the role of the Tramp and Hitler's Nazis the bullies.

Yet his visual politics always proved more ambiguous than his spoken words. When Chaplin moved from the screen to the speaker's podium, he wound up in bigger trouble than the Tramp had ever faced. What is often forgotten today is that many Americans found the "godless" Stalin far more dangerous than the seemingly "god-fearing" Hitler; some even suggested the United States had chosen the wrong side in the war.

Chaplin's public image was further damaged by the sensationalist publicity surrounding the Joan Barry affair and his marriage to Oona O'Neill. Barry, an actress with a history of mental illness, had a brief affair with the actor in the summer of 1941. When Chaplin tried to end it, she responded with a series of bizarre acts that included breaking into his home with a gun and threatening to kill herself. Barry was eventually arrested and ordered to leave town. In the meantime, Charlie met and fell in love with sixteen-year-old Oona, daughter of playwright Eugene O'Neill. The actor's controversial love life hit the front pages of the nation's newspapers when Barry returned to Los Angeles in May 1943 and, aided by Hedda Hopper, filed a paternity suit claiming she was pregnant with his child. The actor faced further humiliation when a federal grand jury indicted him in February 1944 for violating the Mann Act, which made it a crime to transport a woman across state lines for immoral purposes. The case was orchestrated in part by J. Edgar Hoover, who had his agents gather as much negative material on the star as possible. Chaplin was eventually cleared of the federal charges. However, a jury in a subsequent paternity suit disregarded blood tests that proved he was not the baby's father and ordered him to pay child support to Barry's baby. Chaplin's public image as a sexual predator was further inflamed when the fifty-four-year-old married Oona, his fourth wife, who had just turned eighteen in June 1943.[68]

Chaplin's controversial sex life and politics cost him the support of many former fans. "In the years gone by I've much enjoyed Charlie Chaplin's many pictures," a mother of three wrote FBI director Hoover, "but since learning so much about him and especially the sickening side of his personal life— and the fact he is not an American citizen—I'm wondering why" the government just doesn't send him "back to his 'Island' home." Hedda Hopper, who continually blasted the star in her columns, received similar letters from her readers. "Ye Gods cannot that Chaplin beast be thwarted," wrote one New Yorker, while another fan congratulated her for being "the only columnist who isn't afraid of him because the others either avoid it altogether or handle it with gloves."[69]

Chaplin's friends understood that much of public animus surrounding the scandals was caused by the actor's political activity. They believed what happened in the bedroom was no one's business, but what happened on a speaker's podium became fodder for vituperative critics. "You are the one artist of the theatre," novelist Lion Feuchtwanger told the besieged star, "who will go down in American history as having aroused the political antagonism of a whole nation."[70] Kind words, but Chaplin's days as the idol of millions were over. Moviegoers resented his turn from comic to propagandist. The Tramp was dead and Charlie would never make another film that achieved the popularity of his earlier productions.

FADE OUT

The war against Hitler and Germany ended on May 8, 1945, the war against Tojo and Japan on August 15, 1945, but the war against Charlie Chaplin continued for several decades. The onset of the Cold War and the House Un-American Activities Committee (HUAC) hearings to investigate Communist infiltration of Hollywood only added to his miseries. The horrors of war and the dropping of two atomic bombs on Japan led Chaplin to continue speaking out on and off the screen, but at the cost of losing his once adoring audience. By declaring himself "an internationalist" and warning that "if the sense of horror at the atomic bomb is to be conquered, everyone else is going to have to become an internationalist, too," he convinced his enemies that he had indeed moved into the Communist camp.[71]

Chaplin made four films over the next twenty years, but he was now seen as an ideologue and his critics refused to forgive what they viewed as his anti-American politics. His postwar movies, especially *Monsieur Verdoux* (1947) and *A King in New York* (1957), offered explicit and often heavy-handed critiques of the dehumanizing effects of capitalism and war and of the political repression exercised by HUAC. Begun in November 1942, *Monsieur Verdoux* opened in New York on April 11, 1947. Chaplin's Henri Verdoux is a modern-day Bluebeard who, after losing his job during the Great Depression, marries and murders wealthy spinsters in order to support his real family. This black comedy portrays a crazed capitalist world in which murder is simply another way of doing business. But the subtlety Chaplin achieved in earlier films rarely appears here. Caught and put on trial for his crimes, Verdoux explains to the jury that he spent over thirty years working as an honest bank clerk until unemployment forced him to earn a living by whatever means possible. "As for being a mass killer," he asks, "does not the world encourage it? Is it not building weapons of destruction for the sole purpose of mass killing? Has it not blown unsuspecting women and little children to pieces, and done it very scientifically? Ha! As a mass killer I am an amateur by comparison." When a reporter suggests that honest people do not use murder as business, Henri replies, "That's the history of many a big business. Wars, conflict, it's all business. One murder makes a villain, millions a hero."

Chaplin's outspokenness led him to forget one of his early principles of comedy. The "underlying motif of a story should be bright, not depressing," he told a reporter in 1925. Audiences "don't want the great truths brought home to them and strongly resent having pessimism of any sort thrust in their faces." Two decades later, Chaplin thought audiences were ready for a black comedy about contemporary politics. He was wrong. The opening night crowd booed the film so much that Chaplin got drunk. Most moviegoers never got a chance to see the film. Picketing of theaters by members of the American Legion and Catholic War Veterans who accused Chaplin of being a Red led to the film's cancellation in theaters across the nation. Boycott fever grew so intense that United Artists withdrew the film from American circulation in December 1948.[72] The same thing happened again in October 1952, when boycotts limited the distribution of Chaplin's film *Limelight*. Animosity toward the star grew so intense that a New York television station canceled *The Chaplin Theater* in December 1950 (a weekly series that ran his films from 1916–1917) after receiving protests from groups who insisted that "a man of very definite Communist leanings" should not be held up "as an idol to the American public."[73]

The anti-Red hysteria generated by the HUAC hearings in September 1947 hastened Chaplin's declining popularity. "I'd run every one of those rats out of the country and start with Charlie Chaplin," Hopper wrote her friend J. Edgar Hoover in April 1947. "In no other country in the world would he have been allowed to do what he's done." The columnist's loathing of the outspoken star was shared by HUAC member John Rankin, who called for his deportation and demanded that his "filthy pictures" should not be shown in American theaters. After telling Chaplin that they wanted him to testify that fall, HUAC postponed his appearance three times, a tactic the committee often used when it lacked hard evidence. A nervous Chaplin sent the committee a telegram explaining, "I am not a Communist, neither have I ever joined any political party or organization in my life. I am what you call a 'peacemonger.'"[74]

Chaplin's descent reached its nadir in September 1952 when, after setting sail to attend the London premiere of *Limelight*, he received word that U.S. Attorney General James McGranery, acting on information obtained from Hoover, had withdrawn permission for him to reenter the United States. "He has been publicly charged with being a member of the Communist Party," McGranery explained, "and with grave moral charges, and with making statements that would indicate a leering, sneering attitude towards a country whose hospitality has enriched him."[75] Chaplin would not return to the United States until April 1972. Settling in Switzerland with his family, the world's once greatest star made two more films, *A King in New York* (1957), an explicit attack on Cold War hysteria, and *A Countess from Hong Kong* (1967). Neither approached the popularity of his prewar films.

Chaplin's rise to stardom took less than two years and lasted for decades. His fall from adulation was equally quick and almost as long. In his determination to make explicitly political films, he abandoned the subtle artistic qualities that made his earlier productions so great: his ability to wrap his politics in an appealing mix of pathos and humor. Moreover, he came to believe his own celebrity and thought he could say whatever he wanted without any consequences. The Tramp might have survived by making fun of his attackers, but Chaplin the man could not.

Chaplin discovered that audiences did not want their fantasies punctured by screen idols who took controversial political stands. The star, many believed, had betrayed his public, and once betrayed, they proved unforgiving. As critic Bosley Crowther explained in April 1947, "Everyone loves Charles Chaplin—or rather, everyone loved him once, when he still answered to the name of Charlie and stuck faithfully to his little Tramp." But when he began "expressing something more than the pathos of life, a great many former admirers are cooling conspicuously toward him. What right has he, a comedian, to go solemn, they rancorously inquire. Climb back into that tramp costume, they thunder, and take those kicks in the pants as of yore! Stop making us feel uncomfortable by provoking us to think!"[76]

Chaplin's decline cannot be ascribed solely to the efforts of his enemies. His failures were as much artistic as they were political. Stars, directors, and writers often reach a creative peak and then their abilities decline. Chaplin's postwar films were simply not as good as his earlier works. It was not just a matter of a comedian no longer being funny. Chaplin never mastered sound filmmaking at the same high level as his silent films. He lost touch with his craft and his audience, and no one dared point this out to the aging star. He was old and portly and no longer displayed the sprightliness of his youth. And like many other silent stars who failed to make the transition to sound, he had a prissy high-pitched voice that did not work well in the new cinematic age.

Charles Spencer Chaplin died on Christmas Day 1977, but he left a legacy that survived long after his fall from grace. He was arguably the greatest star in the history of Hollywood and the first star whose political views were listened to by a wide swath of Americans. He made comedy an important vehicle of social and political commentary. In subsequent decades politically engaged stars such as Harry Belafonte, Jane Fonda, and Warren Beatty would follow a similar path by opening their own production companies and putting their politics directly on the screen.

Yet the comedian's career also revealed that a star's fame and box office could be undermined by political pronouncements deemed too radical by audiences and government officials. Chaplin had been in the forefront of those criticizing Nazis and praising anyone who fought against them, even if they were Communists. He had once been the most beloved man in the world, but he opened his mouth and lost his fans. Chaplin's experience sent a warning to subsequent generations of activist stars: celebrities who endorse the government's wartime policies are widely praised as patriots. However, those taking positions too far in advance of public opinion, especially during wartime—be it World War I or wars in Iraq and Afghanistan— are often attacked by disillusioned fans and angry government officials who accuse them of being unpatriotic, accusations that can damage if not destroy a career.

Hollywood conservatives found themselves able to act with greater impunity than their left counterparts. By aligning themselves with the Republican Party and embracing what the public perceived as "true Americanism," conservatives such as studio boss Louis B. Mayer succeeded in pushing forward their ideological agendas.

Political climates change and the anger of the past often fades in the nostalgic yearnings of the present. Ignorant of Chaplin's radical past, audiences today remember the best of the Tramp. To millions of people throughout the world, he remains, as Harry Crocker poignantly observed, "a symbol of the little man's fight to live, to live freely, and as richly as he may."[77] Charlie would have liked that.

2

THE MAN WHO BROUGHT HOLLYWOOD INTO THE REPUBLICAN PARTY: LOUIS B. MAYER

Louis B. Mayer would have cried like a baby at his own funeral. The emotional "mogul of moguls" would have dissolved into tears as Jeanette MacDonald sang "Ah! Sweet Mystery of Life" and Spencer Tracy delivered a moving eulogy to the overflow crowd of 2,200 people who spilled onto the streets in front of the Wilshire Boulevard Temple on the morning of October 31, 1957. The man who ruled over Metro-Goldwyn-Mayer Studios for twenty-seven years would have loved to hear the laudatory tributes of admiring Republican friends such as Vice President Richard M. Nixon and former President Herbert Hoover. Louis would have nodded his head in agreement as the city's most famous Jewish leader, Rabbi Edgar Magnin, praised him "as an ardent enemy of pseudo-liberals, Reds, and pinks." On the other hand, he would have been deeply hurt to hear Samuel Goldwyn tell reporters that the "reason so many people showed up at his funeral was because they wanted to make sure he was dead."[1]

From the middle of the 1920s until the United States entered World War II, no Hollywood figure wielded more power on or off the screen than Metro-Goldwyn-Mayer's (MGM) forceful executive vice president. "More than any other man," the *New York Tribune* remarked, Mayer "set the tone of a generation of American motion pictures." Mayer was also more responsible for bringing Hollywood into the world of electoral politics than any other figure, left or right. The man "who made [Clark] Gable, [Wallace] Beery, [Jean] Harlow, and [Spencer] Tracy household words in a million homes" was also the man who brought the Republican Party to Hollywood and Hollywood to the Republican Party.[2]

Media rants about "liberal" Hollywood and histories of alleged Communist infiltration of the movie industry during the 1930s and 1940s have left the impression that Hollywood has been exclusively involved in left politics. But Louis B. Mayer's life reveals a different story. From the start of the new industry, conservative studio leaders were more involved in electoral politics and wielded far greater influence than left-oriented stars. And "L. B.," as he was known to friends and associates, was the first to fashion a permanent connection between the increasingly business-oriented Republican Party (GOP) and the increasingly corporate-oriented movie industry. Hollywood's best rumba dancer glided between the worlds of studio politics and party politics more deftly than anyone else. He campaigned for Calvin Coolidge in 1924, served as a power broker at the Republican National Convention in 1928 where he helped secure Herbert Hoover's nomination, and then rose to become head of the California GOP from 1932 to 1934. Mayer's influence was so pronounced that a grateful President Hoover made him the first Hollywood figure to spend a night at the White House.

More importantly, Mayer redefined the relationship between the American people and American politics through his innovative uses of media and celebrity. Ruling over Hollywood's most powerful studio from 1924 until 1951, he taught Republicans how to use radio, film, and movie stars to sell candidates and ideas to a mass public. At no time was the political power of Hollywood clearer than in 1934, when he inaugurated the first "dirty tricks" campaign by producing a series of staged newsreels aimed at defeating California gubernatorial hopeful Upton Sinclair.

Mayer also affected the long-term fortunes of the GOP by turning MGM into a training ground for Republican activists and the home of a cinematic ideology that formed a core message of conservatism for decades to come.

Through his involvement in party politics and his careful mentoring of conservative stars, Mayer laid the groundwork that made it possible for actors such as George Murphy, Ronald Reagan, and Arnold Schwarzenegger to become successful politicians.

THE RISE OF LOUIS B. MAYER

Louis Burt Mayer was a big sentimental lug and the meanest son of a bitch in Hollywood. "The devil incarnate," actress Helen Hayes spat out. "Not just evil, but the most evil man I have ever dealt with in my life." He was "a Jewish Hitler, a fascist," added actor Ralph Bellamy. "He had no feeling for any minority, including his own." On the other hand, screenwriter Anita Loos thought her boss was "a wonderful old boy," the "one you went to whenever you were in trouble and needed help." Like others who knew him well, Loos felt Mayer may have been the best actor on the MGM lot. He was "very emotional and excitable. . . . He cried, and once I was with him when he was begging me to put something into a film, and he was talking about a little kiddy praying for its mama's something or other, and he got down on his knees, and tears streamed down his face."[3]

Hollywood histories are filled with stories of studio heads who began life as poor immigrants. Yet Mayer experienced perhaps the hardest childhood of any of them. No one knows exactly where or when he was born or what his original family name might have been. Lazar Burt Mayer ("Louis" came later and "Mayer" could have been Meir or some other variant) was apparently born in the town of Dumier, in an area in the Ukraine twenty-five miles north of Kiev. Although he later claimed July 4, 1885, as his birthdate and Minsk as his birthplace, his father, Jacob, insisted his son was born on July 12, 1884. Barely five feet tall, Jacob was a mean-spirited man who eked out a living as a peddler. Sarah Mayer, whom her son adored, was a gentle woman who came from peasant stock. Looking for safer settings the family migrated to England in 1886, and around 1888 settled in Saint John, New Brunswick (Canada), a town with few Jewish families.[4]

The eldest son in a family of five children, Louis was expected to contribute to the Mayers' meager income by collecting rags and scraps when not in school and to protect his two younger brothers from Jew-baiting gangs of Irish and German thugs. Young Louis, whose formal education ended when he was thirteen, proved more clever and industrious than his religiously orthodox father, whom he feared and disliked, not surprising given the elder Mayer's tendency to beat his son. Jacob spent most of his days in synagogue studying the Talmud and leaving the task of earning a living to others. By the time Louis turned fifteen, he had taken control of his father's unsuccessful scrap iron business and turned it into a profitable venture.

On January 3, 1904, the nineteen-year-old Mayer set off for Boston, carrying little money but large ambitions. He took a job with a local scrap metal merchant and within five months met and married Margaret Shenberg, the daughter of a local kosher butcher. In August 1905, Louis moved his family, which now included daughter Edith, to Brooklyn, where he opened a junk business. After encountering failure for the first time in his life, in the summer of 1907 a broke and discouraged Mayer returned to Boston with his wife and now two daughters.

The birth of the movie industry offered opportunities for ambitious entrepreneurs. With the help of family and friends, the erstwhile junk dealer leased a rundown burlesque house in the nearby town of Haverhill, Massachusetts, in August 1907 and turned it into a respectable movie theater that offered clean, family-oriented shows. As box-office receipts grew, the determined exhibitor launched five more theaters. Reluctant to share profits with distributors and producers, he started the Louis B. Mayer Company in 1913 with the idea of producing and distributing his own films. Mayer's crucial moment came in 1915, when he secured the exclusive New England distribution rights for D. W. Griffith's *The Birth of a Nation* and wound up making $250,000 ($5.5 million in 2009 dollars). His triumph was dampened only by the death of his beloved mother in October 1913. Insisting that "only God was more important to me than her," Mayer kept a portrait of Sarah over his bed for the rest of his life.[5]

Over the next decade, Mayer focused on becoming a successful producer and involved himself in a number of companies. As film production shifted from the East Coast to the West Coast, so too did Mayer, who moved his family to Los Angeles in 1918. The ambitious immigrant arrived at a critical moment in the evolution of the new industry. In 1910, Hollywood was a sleepy little town with fewer than 4,000 residents and no movie studios. Nine years later, with war-ravaged European film studios in shambles, the region's seventy-plus production companies turned out over 80 percent of the world's movies.[6]

Seizing on the opportunity to be a major player in the rapidly expanding industry, Mayer initiated a plan for success that he followed throughout his career: give audiences wholesome films, major stars, and directors who could elevate movies from mere entertainment to wishful fantasy. To that end, he signed famed actresses Anita Stewart and Norma Shearer; recruited several talented directors; and, in 1923, hired the brilliant twenty-three-year-old Irving Thalberg to be his production chief. Mayer's own turn at stardom came in April 1924, when Loew's Inc. announced that thirty-nine-year-old Louis would head up the newly organized Metro-Goldwyn-Mayer studios (a merger of the Metro, Goldwyn, and Mayer companies). The company's financial headquarters remained in New York, but production shifted entirely to Los Angeles. On April 26, Mayer presided over a lavish dedication ceremony that featured movie stars, military officers, local politicians, and congratulatory telegrams from President Calvin Coolidge and Secretary of Commerce Herbert Hoover.

Having achieved financial success, the Canadian-raised mogul slowly turned his eye toward playing a starring role in the world of American politics.

POLITICIANS AND THE MOVIE INDUSTRY

Louis B. Mayer was the first major Hollywood figure to play an important role in partisan politics, but he was not the first industry figure to ally with politicians. Long before MGM's new head set foot in California, movie producers saw the advantages of enlisting politicians in their ongoing battles against censorship. Industry needs, not partisan ideology, is what initially drove their collective politics. As early as August 1907, civic and religious leaders throughout the nation denounced the "vicious and demoralizing" effects of film and fought hard to pass laws censoring movies and establishing federal control over the industry. The Protestant elite who led these attacks were highly suspicious of a new industry run largely by Jews who bought films from Catholic France and showed them to impressionable American (and largely Protestant) children. Reluctant to let anyone tell them how to run their business, the heads of twenty-five companies organized the Motion Picture Producers' Association (MPPA) in 1916 and pledged to support any politician, regardless of party, who supported their interests.[7]

California politicians were equally interested in allying with producers, for they saw Hollywood as a place where they could go for money. In 1916, California Democratic hopefuls such as George S. Patton Sr., who was running for Senate, and Rufus Bowden, who was running for Congress, received industry funding after promising to oppose a congressional bill calling for the establishment of a federal censorship board. The normally conservative producers endorsed "near socialist" city councilwoman Estelle Lindsey when she pledged to look after their interests. By 1919, the MPPA was collecting mandatory campaign contributions from its members and asking studio employees to serve as precinct walkers for favored candidates. Of course, the MPPA expected, and received, a quid pro quo for their financial largesse. As campaign committee head Frank Garbutt told producer Hal Roach, "This is the cheapest insurance we can secure against censorship, Sunday-closing and other burdensome laws taxing and restricting the picture industry."[8]

Movie industry participation in party politics was confined largely to local and state levels until World War I, when Washington came to Hollywood for help in the war effort. While stars such as Charlie Chaplin sold war bonds, industry leaders helped the Committee on Public Information, the government's official propaganda agency, by making short films publicizing the nation's war-related activities. The Hollywood–Washington connection took a new turn in 1921, when, following a series of highly publicized Hollywood scandals, studio bigwigs moved to quell public cries for federal censorship by hiring Will Hays to lead the newly organized Motion Picture Producers and Distributors Association (MPPDA). A former Republican National Committee chairman, Hays engineered Warren Harding's presidential victory in 1920 and then served as his postmaster general. After taking over the MPPDA, the political heavyweight used his influence to kill a pending congressional censorship bill. Equally important, the teetotaling Presbyterian elder, who staffed his New York office entirely with Protestants and Catholics, gave the Jewish-dominated industry a patina of political and religious respectability.[9]

THE FIRST POLITICAL MOGUL

Although the MPPDA allied itself with individual politicians on both sides of the aisle, Louis B. Mayer went a step further by forging a direct and lasting relationship between Hollywood and the Republican Party. Mayer's rise to partisan prominence occurred during a major transition in national politics. The election of Republican Warren Harding as president in 1920 signaled an end to Democratic President Woodrow Wilson's Progressive-era activism and a return to more conservative laissez-faire government. Calling for "normalcy" after two years of war, Harding shifted power back to the business sector. When he died of a heart attack on August 2, 1923, Calvin Coolidge, who was even more probusiness than his predecessor, replaced him. "The chief business of the American people is business," the new president proclaimed. And business, he believed, should be unhindered by federal regulation or oversight because when government became too involved in the economy, it "closes the door of opportunity and results in monopoly."[10]

Mayer became a Republican for ideological and self-serving reasons. This was an era of Republican ascendancy in Los Angeles and California. As the state's onetime Attorney General Robert Kenny observed, "There were no Democratic politics to speak of in California throughout the 20's." Registered Republicans outnumbered Democrats by a 3:1 margin during the 1920s, and in 1930 the figure stood at 1,638,575 to 456,096.[11] Mayer's early struggles and triumphs led him to embrace the GOP and its entrepreneurial ideology. Being Jewish and coming from poverty, he also felt a desperate need to be recognized as a success. What better proof could there be than being accepted by the party of the wealthy WASP establishment and then moving up in its ranks?

Mayer was also drawn to politics because he believed the Republican Party could further the interests of his studio. "There certainly was an element of opportunism in my grandfather," recounted grandson Daniel Selznick. The party's increasingly corporate orientation paralleled the increasingly corporate character of the movie industry. By the early 1920s, Wall Street firms and industrial corporations were represented in the boardrooms of virtually every major film company. The eight major studios that came to dominate Hollywood—MGM, Paramount, Warner Bros., Fox, Columbia, Universal, United Artists, and RKO—expanded by selling stocks to private investors through Wall Street investment banks and borrowing from commercial banks to cover short-term production costs. Hollywood was now big business, with nearly $1 billion in capital investments by 1921. Large studios were closer in their business practices to General Motors, U.S. Steel, and DuPont than they were to the modestly sized movie companies of a decade earlier.[12]

Convinced he needed to curry powerful allies to secure his business success, the ambitious studio head plunged into local politics. Within a few months of MGM's opening ceremonies in April 1924, Mayer joined a number of community leaders in supporting a police bond issue (the only studio head to do so) and in opposing a 700 percent telephone rate increase that would have diminished studio profits. The fledgling politico proved so successful in the latter endeavor that Los Angeles Mayor George Cryer appointed him chairman of the General Citizens Telephone Committee. That fall, Mayer joined the Sixty-third Assembly District Republican Club and worked for the Coolidge-Dawes Re-Election Committee. Mayer was the only industry leader in either party to play a prominent role in the 1924 presidential campaign.[13]

The MGM chieftain had all the right instincts and persuasive abilities to be successful at politics. As director Josef von Sternberg quipped, Mayer could "convince an elephant that it was a kangaroo." Even those who disliked him, such as screenwriter Budd Schulberg, conceded, "Louis was a politician, a manipulator, and an opportunist who could have given chapter and verse to Machiavelli if only he had known how to write." What L. B. lacked in 1924 was knowledge of the insider's game. He obtained that knowledge, as well as entry into the highest levels of Republican politics, from the remarkable woman who came to be known as "Mrs. Hollywood," Ida B. Koverman.[14]

Born in Cincinnati in 1876, Koverman moved to Los Angeles sometime after World War I. She quickly established herself as one of the most important behind-the-scenes power figures in Republican circles. "She projected quick intelligence and had a contagious endearing smile," recollected Daniel Selznick. Once an aspiring concert pianist, Koverman became interested in politics while working as Herbert Hoover's secretary at the New York offices of the Consolidated Gold Fields of South Africa. Between 1924 and 1952, she served as executive secretary of the Southern California presidential campaign committees for both Calvin Coolidge and Herbert Hoover, and as a delegate to three national Republican conventions.[15]

By 1920, Koverman was living in Los Angeles and working with Republicans who wanted to shift control of the state party from progressives such as Hiram Johnson to probusiness leaders like Hoover. Ida held a number of key party positions during the decade, and she remained Hoover's most trusted California adviser, providing him with valuable information about state and local politics. The Midwesterner was a rare political commodity in her age: a woman whom political insiders trusted. She was "one woman with whom men like to work shoulder to shoulder," a reporter noted, "for they knew she would 'play the game straight, knows the finesse of politics, [and] keeps her eye on the main issue.'"[16]

The self-effacing widow met Mayer during the Coolidge presidential campaign. Impressed with her political savvy, Mayer hired her as his executive assistant and political mentor. Koverman quickly schooled her new boss in the intricacies of power politics played at the highest state and national levels, the only levels where Mayer wanted to play. Over the next three decades, observed her friend Hedda Hopper, Ida served as the "queen mother who stood behind King Louis' throne" (see fig. 2.1). When Secretary of Commerce Herbert Hoover came to Los Angeles to campaign for Coolidge in August 1924, Koverman arranged for him to tour the MGM studio and meet her new boss. The "Chief" (as Hoover liked to be called) and the mogul hit it off and began a lifelong friendship. As his daughter Irene remarked, Mayer "took great pride, great pleasure" that "Hoover listened to him on certain things."[17]

FIGURE 2.1 Ida Koverman, the guiding political force behind Louis B. Mayer; with photo of Mayer on the wall behind her.
SOURCE: BISON ARCHIVES

It is easy to see why Hoover and Mayer admired one another. Both were poor boys who had made good—in Hoover's case, rising from a hard-scrabble Iowa farm to become a wealthy mining engineer and successful politician. Both were also ambitious men never fully trusted by those at the center of power. Mayer had a contentious relationship with his corporate bosses in New York, while Hoover was considered too probusiness by the GOP's anticorporate insurgents and too internationalist by the party's Old Guard. Each man saw the other as someone who could help achieve his ambitions. The publicity-conscious Hoover believed Mayer could keep his name in the public limelight, while the studio chief thought the secretary of commerce could be useful in furthering MGM's fortunes (see fig. 2.2).[18]

While L. B. was a faithful Republican, his first loyalty was to his studio and he never hesitated to use his political connections to further his business interests. Within a few weeks of their meeting, he dashed off a letter to Hoover asking him to assist the studio with some foreign production problems. "Glad to see you anytime on twenty-four hours' notice," the Iowan

FIGURE 2.2   Louis B. Mayer and Herbert Hoover. SOURCE: BISON ARCHIVES

quickly wrote back.[19] Mayer arrived in Washington, D.C., in September 1924 and Hoover arranged for him to meet the head of the Interstate Commerce Commission. Hoover had the secretary of state send formal letters to the U.S. ambassadors in London, Paris, and Rome asking them to help his "very special friend" with any problems he incurred while shooting *Ben-Hur* in Italy. Hoover also sent Mayer an advance copy of the Federal Trade Commission's report concerning potential legal action against the movie industry.[20]

Koverman taught her boss that politics was not just about the next election. It was about developing a long-term strategy and positioning oneself to carry it out. That meant building political bases at the local and state levels and making new friends who could be helpful down the road. Mayer followed his mentor's advice and joined numerous civic, business, religious, and political groups. He gave speeches to virtually any organization that asked, usually ghostwritten by a member of the studio's publicity department or by one of its screenwriters. Ida also got Louis deeply engaged in local politics. He endorsed candidates, raised money, and worked on behalf of cutting property taxes. By the late 1920s, Mayer had become an important civic leader in Los Angeles.

LOUIS'S ROAD TO THE WHITE HOUSE

Mayer's breakthrough as a power player in Republican circles came during the 1928 presidential election. He joined Hoover's campaign in 1927 and, along with Koverman, who served as executive secretary of the Southern California Presidential Campaign Committee, traveled back and forth to Washington to meet with the presidential hopeful. Mayer was not the entertainment industry's first partisan activist. During the 1920s, movie stars who also worked in New York's theatrical world participated in presidential campaigns. Al Jolson organized Broadway stars to work for Warren Harding in 1920 and Calvin Coolidge in 1924. In 1928, Claudette Colbert, Walter Huston, and Frank Morgan headed up the Hoover-Curtis Theatrical League and campaigned for the Republican hopefuls. That same year, Fannie Brice, Eddie Cantor, Helen Hayes, George Jessel, and Ed Wynn promoted the Democratic cause by organizing "Stars for [Al] Smith."[21]

While many actors endorsed their favorite candidates, none worked inside the political trenches as effectively as Mayer. There "was very little political consciousness in the twenties," reflected Conrad Nagel, a Broadway actor who came to Hollywood in 1920, "because I myself was very active in what few political organizations did exist at that time. . . . very few of my contemporaries [were] interested in the work of either the Republican or Democratic Party."[22] Mayer soon changed that by bringing Hollywood into the world of electoral politics.

Until 1928, the studio leader had been an emerging player but not a major force within party circles. That changed after he helped secure the presidential nomination for his friend Herbert Hoover. Appointed treasurer of the Republican National Committee for California, Mayer turned Hollywood into an important new center for Republican money. He spent most the spring campaigning and raising funds for Hoover, including a $10,000 donation from director Cecil B. DeMille and $7,000 each from himself and United Artists president Joseph Schenck (approximately $125,000 and $87,700, respectively, in 2009 dollars).[23] In June, Mayer and Koverman boarded a train and set off for the Republican convention in Kansas City. He went as a delegate from California and she was one of six women invited to plan strategy with Hoover.

The Kansas City convention marked Mayer's debut on the national political stage, and many of his friends and enemies wondered how this portly Jewish immigrant who often mangled the English language would do in a native-born, Protestant-dominated political world that only grudgingly allowed in Catholics. They did not have to wait long for an answer. Delegates who expected a bumbling junk-dealer-turned-movie-huckster were surprised by Mayer's magnetism. Soon after his arrival in Kansas City, he gave a well-received speech to convention delegates in which he promised to deliver the motion picture industry to the Republican Party—a promise that infuriated Loew's president (MGM's parent company) Nicholas Schenck, a lifelong Democrat who had donated $25,000 to Al Smith.[24] While it is unclear whether Mayer ultimately fulfilled his promise, he delivered something equally significant: the support of powerful media tycoon William Randolph Hearst.

Mayer and Hearst had been friends since 1924, when Hearst moved his Cosmopolitan Pictures company along with his mistress, actress Marion Davies, to the MGM lot. To the surprise of many, the two self-serving power figures grew genuinely fond of one another. Hearst became a regular visitor to the Mayers' Santa Monica beachfront home and called Louis "son." Mayer in turn called Hearst "Chief," the publisher's preferred sobriquet (and one shared by Hoover). "Uncle William," recounted Louis's daughter Irene, "seemed to consult my father on all kinds of matters—politics, finance, and even the Hearst Corporation." The newspaper magnate was even more politically ambitious than the movie mogul, and he had long fancied himself a potential presidential candidate. After being elected to Congress in New York in 1902, he ran several unsuccessful campaigns for mayor, lieutenant governor, and governor. As late as 1924, Hearst considered himself a Democrat, but in 1928 when the party nominated corporate lawyer John Davis, whom he felt was a Wall Street puppet, he left his longtime political home.[25]

Hoover was considered the Republican frontrunner in 1928, but his nomination was anything but certain. Party conservatives considered Hoover too liberal and preferred Andrew Mellon, the millionaire banker who served as secretary of the treasury under Coolidge, and who had the backing of Hearst and his powerful newspaper chain.

Once Hearst defected from the Democrats, Mayer and Koverman immediately set about wooing him into the Hoover camp. In the weeks prior to the convention, they arranged a meeting between the candidate and the power broker at Mayer's Santa Monica home. Hoover assured Hearst he would support reforms and public works programs aimed at saving the nation from economic stagnation. Hearst left the meeting still committed to Mellon, but when it became clear that he could not win the nomination, the media giant instructed delegates loyal to the Hearst empire to support Hoover. This was enough to get Hoover nominated on the first ballot and to bolster Mayer's reputation as a man who could deliver the goods.[26]

Mayer left the convention having cemented his role as a key member of Hoover's inner circle of allies. During the next several months he proved a tireless campaigner, traveling to Washington to discuss strategy, delivering speeches to Republican groups and business organizations, making radio addresses, and raising money throughout California. The last role proved especially vital because the 1928 campaign became the costliest in history to that point, largely because of the increased use of radio advertising to reach voters. The percentage of American homes with radios rose from 24 percent in 1927 to 46 percent in 1930. With Republicans investing ever-greater amounts of money in radio broadcasts, the cost of campaigns skyrocketed from $3.7 million in 1924 to $9.4 million in 1928. As treasurer of the Republican National Committee for California, Mayer helped make the GOP's ambitious radio campaign possible.[27]

No studio head had ever risen this high in either party or played such a major role in a presidential campaign. Addressing the influential Los Angeles Women's Breakfast Club, Mayer spoke passionately about the current European situation and measures that might be taken to promote peace. The MGM chief became such a prominent part of the campaign that New York Mayor Jimmy Walker accused him and United Artists studio head Joseph Schenck of attempting to turn the entire movie industry over to the Republican Party.[28]

On November 6, 1928, Americans elected Herbert C. Hoover as president. He carried California by a margin of 1,162,323 to 614,365. Mayer and Koverman were ebullient. Rumors began circulating that the president-elect would name Mayer ambassador to Turkey, the only country willing to accept a Jew to such a high position. "I am not a candidate for any public office of any kind," Mayer told reporters in February 1929, "and even were I a candidate Mr. Hoover is not yet president, and to discuss such a thing at this time would be decidedly premature." Years later, Hoover told Mayer's biographer, *New York Times* film critic Bosley Crowther, that "Mr. Mayer decided he could not leave his responsibilities and declined to have his name submitted to the Turkish government." The president did, however, invite his friend to attend the inauguration and spend a night at the White House with his family. The latter honor was the behind-the-scenes product of the shrewd Mrs. Koverman. "This is another small boy—new at the game and used to a great deal of attention," she wrote Hoover's chief aide Lawrence Richey in January 1929. "I know he would strut around like a proud pigeon."[29]

On March 12, 1929, the once impoverished Jewish boy, his wife, and two daughters became the first guests the Hoovers entertained after moving into the White House. "He was so at home there," Louis's daughter Edith remembered, that he even complained the gravy was too thick. That night, lying in bed inside the White House, Mayer found himself unable to sleep. "I kept thinking back," he later told his friend Samuel Marx, "here I was—an immigrant boy, born in Russia, and I was a guest of the President of the United States. I didn't sleep a wink."[30]

"BOSS" MAYER

Mayer's work in the 1928 campaign inspired him to play a more prominent role in local, state, and national politics. His key contribution was not as a policy innovator, for his political beliefs—lower taxes, less government, and more freedom for private enterprise—were standard conservative fare. Mayer's signal achievement over the next decade was as architect of a new relationship between Hollywood and the Republican Party and creator of an infrastructure that promoted their mutual interests.

Like urban bosses of the late nineteenth and early twentieth centuries, Mayer enjoyed wielding political influence. The traditional form of rewarding the winning political faithful was to allow them to make patronage appointments. Mayer solidified his power and accumulated IOUs by getting people appointed to positions such as Collector of the Internal Revenue in Los Angeles, minister to Czechoslovakia, U.S. assistant attorney general, federal judge for the Southern District of California, and members of the Federal Home Loan Bank Board. He even helped the president's son Herbert Hoover Jr. get a job heading the radio department of Western Air Express.[31]

Although it was not unusual for leaders of major corporations to use their influence in Washington to secure favors, the MGM head was the first Hollywood figure to obtain direct access to the president and his cabinet. In addition to meting out patronage appointments, "Boss" Mayer persuaded the attorney general to quash his indictment in a pending stock fraud case and to prevent the consolidation of William Fox's studio with Loew's, a move that would have removed L. B. as studio head. He also cemented GOP ties to Hollywood by arranging meetings between Hoover and prominent Republicans Joseph Schenck, Cecil B. DeMille, and his new ally William Randolph Hearst. The friendship between Hoover and Mayer was so well known to the general public that a number of individuals sent the president screenplays and asked him to forward them to the MGM head.[32]

Over the next decade, Mayer also changed the Hollywood–Washington connection by infusing the Republican Party with a new element of glamour. By the late 1920s, studios were like empires and Mayer proved the most powerful emperor of all. He used his studio and its stars to draw national attention to the GOP. Just as political and world leaders paid visits to Disneyland in the 1950s and 1960s, their predecessors toured the MGM lot—the "Versailles of the movies"—during the 1920s and 1930s (see fig. 2.3). Studio guests included Calvin Coolidge, Herbert Hoover, Winston Churchill, Hugh Walpole, Speaker of the House Nicholas Longworth, and California Governor James Rolph. Mayer found the connection to political power an aphrodisiac. He loved taking visiting presidents, senators,

FIGURE 2.3 Touring the MGM studios are motion picture industry czar Will Hays, President Calvin Coolidge, Mrs. Coolidge, Mary Pickford, and Louis B. Mayer. SOURCE: BISON ARCHIVES

governors, congressmen, foreign ambassadors, and British MPs around his studio, and hosting luncheons in their honor.[33]

Glamour, celebrity, and publicity were core elements of the film industry, and Mayer used all three on behalf of visiting Republican dignitaries. Knowing that politicians could be as starstruck as the average fan, the studio chief indulged their fantasies by seating guests next to their favorite movie stars. He also made sure that prominent Republicans were photographed with MGM's most popular stars. With almost 400 journalists covering the movie capital, these pictures often appeared in newspapers throughout the country and lent GOP politicians an aura of celebrity-by-association that Democrats lacked. Such publicity proved especially useful during campaign season as star/politician photographs often bumped stories about their rivals to the back pages of local newspapers. Of course, ulterior motives also lay behind his hospitality. As one business reporter observed, "Mr. Mayer's courtesies to U.S. senators and vice admirals make it easier for MGM to borrow a battleship for *Armored Cruiser* or a fleet of Navy planes for *Hell Divers*."[34]

With Hoover's election secured and the Hollywood–Republican connection firmly in place, Mayer turned his attention back to his studio and the task of overseeing its transition to sound. On October 6, 1927, Warner Bros. shocked the world with the release of the first talking picture, *The Jazz Singer*. Metro-Goldwyn-Mayer was the Cadillac of the studio system and Mayer intended to keep it that way. Fortunately, he could rely on his highly capable head of production Irving Thalberg to oversee the conversion to sound. After a youthful flirtation with socialism, the brilliant but sickly young executive known around town as the "Boy Wonder" lost his passion for politics and focused all his energies on producing the best movies in Hollywood. Bristling under the accolades that Mayer received for MGM's success and was loath to share, Thalberg was only too happy to run the studio while his boss was off for weeks at a time pursuing his political interests in California and Washington, D.C. By the end of 1929, Mayer returned to oversee the installation of state-of-the-art Western Electric sound facilities and construction of the industry's largest sound stage. Despite Mayer's frequent political activities, the Mayer-Thalberg partnership proved highly successful. Metro-Goldwyn-Mayer never failed to make a profit during the Depression, even in the leanest years.[35]

With a sound system in place, Mayer resumed his political ascent. Once again, he turned to party insiders to help him, in this instance to Mendel Silberberg and Mabel Walker Willebrandt. In September 1930, attorney Silberberg and Willebrandt, a former U.S. assistant attorney general and close friend of Ida Koverman, orchestrated Mayer's appointment as vice-chairman of the California GOP. As the number-two man in California's dominant party, L. B. was now a political player in his own right.[36]

Life for Republicans, however, proved increasingly difficult as Hoover attempted to extricate the nation from the worst depression in its history. The stock market crash of October 1929 marked the onset of a devastating economic crisis, the Great Depression, which lasted for over a decade. With business after business shutting its doors, unemployment soared from 3.5 million people in March 1930 to over 12 million in March 1933 (25 percent of the workforce). Unable to pay their rent or mortgages, families moved out of their homes and into crudely built shelters made of packing crates and salvaged metals that were erected in city parks and abandoned lots—areas derisively known as "Hoovervilles." The number of births and weddings declined, loan sharks charged 42 percent annual interest, and even Babe Ruth was forced to take a pay cut of $10,000 in 1932.[37]

It took a tough salesman to hold onto Republican voters during such desperate times, but Mayer proved an energetic party leader and surprisingly talented public speaker. To overcome his educational limitations, he took speech lessons from MGM star Conrad Nagel. Mayer's role as the state party's vice-chairman meant even more trips to Washington conferring with Hoover and occasionally spending the night at the White House. By the beginning of 1932, L. B. was eagerly gearing up for the Chief's reelection campaign. He gladly accepted the task of coordinating campaign efforts in Los Angeles. Several of Mayer's biographers suggest he was little more than a face man, but they could not be more mistaken. Koverman may have been the behind-the-scenes political choreographer, but Mayer also knew how to exercise power. On January 28, 1932, he summoned Republican leaders from Southern California to plot strategy and build unity among the party faithful. The Republican editors of the *Los Angeles Times* were so impressed by his efforts that they commended the movie magnate "for taking the initiative in getting the campaign under way under such happy auspices."[38]

From March 1932, when the presidential campaign went into high gear, until the November elections, the Jewish mogul became the public face and radio voice of the Republican presidential campaign in California. Mayer always knew how to put a positive spin on the worst of situations. At a rally in San Bernardino, he pointed out that Theodore Roosevelt was pilloried while president but people were now building monuments in his honor. He promised that citizens would soon feel the same about Hoover. Mayer also offered his own solutions for relieving Depression-era problems: government guarantees of national bank deposits, loosening bank credit to businesses, lowering income and profits taxes, tariff reform, and increased public works projects.[39]

After meeting with Hoover in June 1932, Mayer traveled to Chicago where he served as a delegate to the Republican convention. Although he could not prevent William Randolph Hearst from returning to the Democratic Party to support Franklin D. Roosevelt, Mayer worked behind the scenes to prevent his friend Vice President Charles Curtis from being replaced on the ticket by General Edward Martin.[40]

Mayer's greatest contribution to the 1932 election was to inject show-manship and celebrity into the GOP convention and the presidential campaign. It was not evident to party leaders that elections could be a form of entertainment. But it was to Mayer, and he worked hard to make them so. Understanding that voters, like moviegoers, wanted a good show, he taught Republicans how to produce and sell a more effective drama for a mass audience. He staged the convention, now being broadcast on national radio, just as thoughtfully as he would one of his film productions. In sharp contrast to the 1928 convention, a veritable "desert of dullness" as one scholar called it, Mayer introduced a festive element by providing live music during delegate demonstrations, screening a talking film of Hoover, and arranging for balloons to flutter down onto the convention floor following the Chief's nomination. The MGM chieftain brought such flair and attention to the proceedings that *Variety* proclaimed him a national leader "of politics and the show business, the only American holding that dual honor."[41] Equally pleased party leaders rewarded him by selecting the Russian-born immigrant as one of four delegates sent to inform Hoover of his nomination.

Following the convention, Mayer mobilized scores of conservative movie stars to help Hoover. He sent Ethel and Lionel Barrymore, Lewis Stone, Conrad Nagel, Wallace Beery, Al Jolson, Colleen Moore, Jackie Cooper, and other MGM luminaries to political rallies in hopes of attracting larger crowds. The GOP leader understood that many people turned out to see their favorite stars. Yet, he hoped that after listening to a candidate's speech they would be convinced to vote Republican.

The 1932 elections also marked the first time Hollywood studios used their considerable powers on behalf of both presidential candidates. Industry rivals MGM and Warner Bros. competed politically as well as cinematically. Longtime Republicans Harry and Jack Warner bolted to FDR, with Jack agreeing to become chairman of the motion picture division of "Roosevelt for President." Like Mayer, Jack and Harry called on their stars to attend party rallies. The rival studio heads also produced "newsreels" that slanted the news toward their favored candidate.[42]

Impressed with his work, Republican leaders appointed Mayer chairman of the California GOP in September. His selection signified that Hollywood celebrity and money had dramatically changed American politics. In 1928, the studio head succeeded in persuading wealthy individuals to contribute to Hoover's campaign. In 1932, he went a step further and turned Hollywood into a vital source of campaign funds for the party and its candidates. Seeing radio as a medium of partisan propaganda as well as entertainment, the media-savvy GOP leader used much of the newly raised money to fund radio broadcasts that reached voters who did not like to attend political rallies. Mayer regularly went on air during the last two months of the campaign, usually introduced by an MGM star, and praised the embattled president as the man who "has preserved us from economic prostration at home and has maintained unimpaired our friendly diplomatic and trade relations abroad."[43]

Understanding the powerful lure of celebrities, Mayer called on his retinue of stars to add pizzazz to the presidential campaign. No group or gathering was too small for the vote-conscious Republican. When a consortium of women's clubs gathered at the Ambassador Hotel in Los Angeles prior to the election, L. B. made sure their meeting was attended by nearly two dozen stars, including Mae Murray, Theda Bara, Anita Page, and child actor Jackie Cooper, who told the group he would vote for Hoover if he were old enough to do so. A Saturday night rally at Hollywood High School drew a large crowd when word spread that Conrad Nagel and Mae Murray would address the gathering. Another rally that night featuring Jackie Cooper, Johnny Weissmuller, and Jean Hersholt attracted 3,000 people to Roosevelt High School.[44]

Mayer's sense of showmanship was never greater than at the grand rally he staged at the cavernous Shrine Auditorium six days before the election. The evening began with a torchlight procession led by movie stars who marched the faithful into the Shrine. Sparing no expense, Mayer mounted an elaborate series of entertainments that featured two complete stage shows, a band, and a twenty-five-piece orchestra. He packed the stage with an array of MGM stars, including Lionel Barrymore, Buster Keaton, Conrad Nagel, Wallace Beery, Mae Murray, Jimmy Durante, and Colleen Moore. The evening opened in dramatic style as the theater filled with the sound of Herbert Hoover addressing the audience via radio from Washington, D.C. The overflow crowd then heard speeches by Mayer, attorney Joe Scott, congresswoman Florence Kahn, and senatorial candidate Tallant Tubbs. Such celebrity-studded events soon became commonplace at rallies and conventions, but Mayer was their modern pioneer.[45]

On election eve, November 7, Louis took to the radio one last time. "History discloses that, shortly before Abraham Lincoln was re-elected, it looked as if he would go down to defeat," he told listeners. Now that the American people "had the opportunity to learn of the accomplishments of President

Hoover," he predicted the Chief would be reelected. He was wrong. After twelve years of Republican presidents, voters elected Franklin D. Roosevelt by a margin of 22.8 million to 15.8 million votes. In the once solidly Republican state of California, FDR beat Hoover 1,324,157 to 847,902. Democrats also won eleven of twenty congressional races and increased their presence in the state assembly from three to twenty-four. Though disappointed with the results, Mayer asked Hoover for a last favor: permission to photograph interior areas of the White House so that the studio could accurately recreate them for an upcoming MGM film. The president agreed. It seemed the least he could do for his loyal friend.[46]

The Dirty Tricks Campaign

Mayer's role in the Republican Party would never be quite the same after Hoover left office. Nor would the California Republican Party. By 1934, the parties were dead even in terms of registered voters. Worse yet, Republicans faced the prospect of losing the governor's office that they had controlled for the past thirty-five years. Hoover was gone, but Mayer, aided by production head Irving Thalberg, continued to reshape the course of American politics by producing a series of carefully staged newsreels in the fall of 1934 that helped undermine Upton Sinclair's bid to become California's twenty-eighth governor.

Following the GOP's disastrous results at the polls in 1932, Mayer put his energies into his studio and his love life. He proved more successful in the former than the latter. The Mayer-Thalberg team was by far the most powerful pair in the industry. In December 1931, when most studios were facing bankruptcy, MGM was praised by twelve New York bankers who rated Thalberg and Mayer as the only two executives who had "made the grade during the past year." By 1934, ten years after taking control, Mayer's 117-acre studio included 23 sound stages, the world's largest film laboratory, 61 movie stars, 17 directors, 51 writers, and a total of 4,000 employees. That year, MGM boasted the greatest number of hits—among them, *The Barretts of Wimpole Street*, *Treasure Island*, and *David Copperfield*—and the industry's highest net earnings.[47]

During the mid-1930s, the financial health of the MGM studio was never better. The same could not be said of Mayer's relations with his family. His conduct as a father and husband fell far short of the family ideal he produced for the screen. He was an extremely stern and authoritarian parent to daughters Edith and Irene. "When people say my grandpa behaved like an Emperor," Daniel Selznick recounted, "it's not far from the truth." Although a loving father, L. B. also proved tyrannical and expected absolute obedience. When Edith wanted to marry Billy Goetz, an assistant supervisor at Fox, in a modest wedding ceremony, her outraged father told her, "I'm not going to have people say I couldn't give my daughter a big wedding." Ignoring the couple's wishes, he threw a lavish reception at the Biltmore Hotel. Father and daughter eventually reconciled, but Edith learned that when "Louis the Republican" clashed with "Louis the Family Man," politics trumped family. When Goetz openly backed Democratic presidential candidate Adlai Stevenson in 1948, his father-in-law stopped speaking to him—forever. When the family patriarch died in 1957, he left $500,000 to Irene and similar amounts to her sons, but he cut Edith, Billy, and their children completely out of his will.[48]

Mayer's role as a hands-on party activist began to decline as his attention turned to reviving his love life. Married to Margaret Shenberg at the age of nineteen, he remained faithful for years and their marriage seemed a happy one. But Margaret never liked the limelight of studio life, preferring the life of a mother. Their marriage grew troubled when illness and menopausal symptoms caused Margaret to have frequent bouts of depression. She lost all interest in sex and the couple stopped sharing the same bed. Mayer's friends urged him to find a hobby. "Trocadero Louis" (named after the nightclub he frequented) soon took up ballroom dancing and golf, becoming quite accomplished at both. In July 1932, he also started seeing Adeline "Ad" Schulberg, the lively and estranged wife of his former close friend B. P. Schulberg. As Margaret's depression grew worse and Mayer's roving eye more pronounced, he started attending wild stag parties thrown by his friend Frank Orsatti, a shady character who gave up bootlegging and smuggling to become a Hollywood agent. Although not an inveterate womanizer, Mayer possessed a high sex drive. Feeling guilty about his affairs, he justified his actions by explaining that "the Talmud says a man is not responsible for a sin committed by any part of his body below the waist."[49]

In July 1934, Louis and Margaret sailed for Paris, intending to spend several months in Europe. On board at his request was the fifty-one-year-old mogul's latest crush, a twenty-four-year-old aspiring actress from Texas, Jean Howard. The hoped-for cruise romance was cut short by two unexpected events: Margaret's sudden illness and disturbing news from Ida Koverman that Upton Sinclair's bid for governor was going far better than anyone had anticipated.

In October 1933, Upton Sinclair, having changed his registration from Socialist to Democrat, published *I, Governor of California*, a book that laid out his campaign plan to End Poverty in California (EPIC). The longtime critic of capitalism promised to eliminate unemployment, provide $50 monthly pensions to widows and the needy, abolish sales taxes, drop all taxes on homes valued under $3,000, and institute a graduated income tax starting at $5,000 and increasing to a point where all incomes over $50,000 would be taxed 50 percent. In a move that infuriated Mayer and his colleagues, Sinclair also called for a special tax on the state's highly profitable movie industry.[50]

Much to the radical's delight, voters were drawn to his EPIC plan. On August 28, 1934, after months of vigorous campaigning throughout the state, Sinclair shocked the political establishment—including President Roosevelt—by capturing the Democratic nomination with more than 436,000 votes, the largest ever received in a California primary election. His chief opponent in the November contest was Frank Merriam, Hoover's California campaign manager in 1928 and a man whom one observer described as "a dull Republican wheelhorse." Raymond Haight, a maverick Republican attorney who supported the New Deal and voted for Socialist Norman Thomas in the 1932 presidential election, was the dark horse in the race.[51]

Mayer and his colleagues grew increasingly worried, for Sinclair's tax plans threatened their personal and business fortunes. During the mid-1930s, movie industry leaders earned nineteen of the twenty-five highest salaries in America. Mayer reigned as the nation's highest-salaried executive in 1937, $1.3 million—more than the heads of General Motors and U.S. Steel. Loew's executives did equally well, with J. Robert Rubin and Nicholas Schenck often occupying the second and fourth earning slots. Their financial success, however, depended on the continued profits of their studios. When polls announced that Sinclair's chances of winning rose to even money, 20th Century Pictures president Joseph Schenck flew to Miami to investigate relocating the film industry. Upon his return, the prominent Democrat promised reporters, "I'll move the studios to Florida, sure as fate, if Sinclair is elected." Sinclair's popularity grew so strong that Herbert Hoover traveled down from Palo Alto that fall to meet with Ida Koverman, while Hearst returned early from Germany to supervise the anti-Sinclair press campaign. "Unless a lot of people wake up," warned Billy Wilkerson, conservative editor of the *Hollywood Reporter*, "Sinclair is going to be the next Governor of the state."[52]

On Sunday, October 7, Mayer returned from his European trip bent on destroying Sinclair and electing Merriam. The Republican candidate, he told the press, was the only one who offered citizens "a chance to retain an able, energetic, and sincere public servant whose election will represent the rejection of radical and unsound theories and doctrines." Ironically, in 1932, Irving Thalberg had bought the movie rights to Sinclair's *The Wet Parade*. Even though the film made money, Mayer told Thalberg that he did not want to see that Bolshevik "bum" around his studio. Two years later, that "bum" threatened to undermine the health of the entire film industry.[53]

Putting his romantic woes behind him, the state GOP leader set out to mount public rallies and raise $500,000 to fund radio and newspaper advertisements. Once again, he proved an innovative if somewhat controversial fundraiser. In 1928 and 1932, the Republican mogul had succeeded in tapping his wealthy Hollywood friends. This time he required all MGM employees earning more than $100 a week, including its stars, to "donate" a day's pay to the Merriam campaign. According to MGM writer Albert Hackett, studio personnel received unsigned checks made out to Louis B. Mayer and a note that said, "'Here is the amount we think you should give. This is for the Republican candidate for governor of California. Date it and write your name and the name of your bank; sign it and send it back.'" Anyone who did not respond in three or four days received a telephone call or personal visit from one of Mayer's minions saying, "'We have not got your check yet for Governor Merriam.'... They would keep calling you harassing you about giving money." If you still hesitated to donate, "you got the word—people would say, 'I understand that if you didn't give to the Merriam campaign, they make a note of it, and when your option time comes up, they fix you.'"[54]

Mayer's policy of forced contributions proved exceedingly unpopular with actors but very popular with his peers. Partisan divisions among studio heads disappeared as Jack Warner and five other studio leaders joined MGM in "requesting" a day's salary from employees for the Merriam campaign fund. Not all Hollywood folks caved in to studio pressure. James Cagney, a left-liberal tough guy from New York's Hell's Kitchen, led a revolt of actors at

Warners against the Merriam tax. He told one friend that if the studio tried to force him to donate one day's salary he would give a week's pay to Sinclair. Cagney was joined by Edward G. Robinson, Jean Harlow, and Katharine Hepburn. Writers Gene Fowler, Jim Tully, Frank Scully, and Morrie Ryskind fought back by organizing an Upton Sinclair committee. But most actors, directors, writers, and producers simply paid the money into the Republican war chest.[55]

The studio head's next move proved even more controversial. With newspapers throughout the state warning that one-half of the nation's unemployed would rush to California if Sinclair was elected, Mayer and Thalberg intensified those fears by producing a series of staged "newsreels" designed to discredit Sinclair and heighten respect for Merriam. In the days before television and the Internet, newsreels were an especially popular way for Americans to see what was happening in the world around them. Most citizens believed these productions were factual reportage, not partisan propaganda. What made MGM's three *California Election News* productions so powerful was that they did contain an element of truth.

Thalberg sent director Felix Feist, writer Carey Wilson, and a camera crew throughout the state to interview voters about the upcoming elections. On October 19, the state's moviegoers got to watch the first of three MGM-produced newsreels. The five-minute *California Election News No. 1* opened with a series of intertitles explaining that viewers would see men and women "selected at random" expressing their opinions on the upcoming elections. The voice of the "Inquiring Cameraman" reminded the audience, "Remember, they're not actors. I don't rehearse them, I'm impartial." Although some interviews were conducted with actual voters, MGM hired a series of minor actors to play the part of ordinary voters. Thalberg and Mayer understood that casting, costuming, accents, and makeup could all be used to shape the ideological impact of the sham newsreels. Interviewees supporting Merriam were well-dressed, attractive, American-looking citizens who had jobs and property and spoke in a clear and cogent manner. Sinclair's supporters were disgruntled, dirty riffraff who occasionally stammered or spoke with foreign accents and lauded communism and socialism. "Respectable folks who liked Sinclair," MGM writer Samuel Marx observed years later, "landed on the cutting room floor along with shots of tramps who spoke for Merriam."[56] Several Haight supporters were thrown in to give the newsreels an appearance of political balance.

So what exactly did voters see and hear? In *California Election News No. 1* a blue-collar Mexican man tells the Inquiring Cameraman that he is voting for Sinclair because we "need a complete rejuvenation of our governmental system," while a prosperous Anglo male in white shirt and tie announces he will support Merriam because he opposed "Mr. Sinclair's socialistic ideas." The same visual and oral messages—especially the subtle Red-baiting and racism that suggested radicals would vote Democratic and true Americans Republican—were also delivered in the seven-minute *California Election News No. 2*. An older shirtsleeved man praises Sinclair as "the author of the Russian government and it worked out very well there and I think it should do here." In contrast, a handsome auto mechanic who curiously has no dirt on his hands or uniform peers out from under a car and explains, "First of all, I am an American and I believe Mr. Merriam will support all the principles America has stood for in the past 150 years. I have a job now and I want to keep it." *California Election News No. 3* heightened popular fears with shots of scores of bums getting off of freight trains in California and promising "to remain there permanently if the EPIC plan went into effect." Prints of all three newsreels were distributed to theaters throughout the state free of charge.[57]

Other studios followed MGM's lead and produced short films intended to sway citizens to vote Republican. A newsreel aimed at African Americans featured popular boxer-turned-preacher Oscar Rankin declaring support for Merriam and suggesting that Sinclair might outlaw churches. The cinematic assault against Sinclair was so great that even the conservative *Hollywood Reporter* remarked, "Never before in the history of the picture business has the screen been used in the direct support of a candidate. Maybe an isolated exhibitor here or there has run a slide or two, favoring a friend, but never has there been concerted action on the part of all the theaters in a community to defeat a nominee."[58]

These carefully staged visual assaults were replicated in many of the state's newspapers. When Hearst's *Los Angeles Examiner* ran a half-page picture on October 25 that showed a group of hoboes streaming into California, a number of readers quickly spotted movie stars Dorothy Wilson and Frankie Darrow among the rootless "bums." The purported "news" photograph was really a still from Warner Bros.' 1933 film *Wild Boys of the Road*.[59]

Not all viewers believed or approved of what they saw on the screen or read in the newspapers. A number of Sinclair supporters were so infuriated that they stormed box offices demanding refunds and insisting that managers pull the offending partisan material from the screen. *Variety* reported that "near riots" broke out in dozens of movie theaters screening *California Election News No. 3*. Protests grew so intense that on November 4, the chief of Fox's West Coast chain of theaters ordered exhibitors to stop showing *No. 3*, while Warners pulled the newsreels from all their theaters.[60]

The outraged, however, were greatly outnumbered by the fearful. In early September it looked like Sinclair would be the Golden State's next governor. However, on November 6, after weeks of being exposed to scare tactics in newspapers, radios, and movie theaters, California voters went to the polls and elected Frank Merriam. The victorious Republican received 1,138,620 votes, Sinclair 879,537 and Raymond Haight 302,519. "There is little doubt," observed MGM insider Samuel Marx, "that the doctored newsreels provided the knockout blow against Sinclair's gubernatorial aspirations." When actor and Democratic activist Fredric March blasted MGM's scurrilous newsreels as "a dirty trick" and "the damndest unfairest thing I've ever heard of," Irving Thalberg shot back, "Nothing is unfair in politics. We could sit down here and figure dirty things out all night and every one of them would be all right in a political campaign."[61]

Soon after the election, Governor-elect Merriam sent a letter of appreciation to his many supporters in Hollywood and included a special thanks to that "splendid hard worker, Louis. B. Mayer."[62] Ironically, once in office Merriam imposed a series of new taxes on the movie industry. He was voted out of office four years later.

TRAINING MOVIE STARS FOR POLITICS

The dirty tricks campaign of 1934 was the last time Mayer played a decisive role in state or national elections. Within two years of Sinclair's defeat, Hollywood turned increasingly Democratic. A poll taken on the eve of the 1936 presidential election found movie industry personnel favoring FDR over Republican Alf Landon by a 6:1 margin. Even Mayer, a delegate to the Republican convention that year, was loath to support the unimpressive Landon. Although serving as vice-chair of the California GOP, he privately assured FDR's comptroller of the currency that he would not openly oppose Roosevelt. L. B. remained true to his word and was rewarded with an invitation to the White House the next year. According to one story, Mayer entered the Oval Office, put his watch on FDR's desk, and said,

"Mr. President, I'm told that when anyone spends eighteen minutes with you, you have them in your pocket." Exactly seventeen minutes later, the studio head got up, thanked the President, and walked out.[63]

The Hoover-Mayer alliance allowed the mogul to reach the pinnacle of political power. No other studio head, not even the Warner brothers (who soon returned to the Republican fold), were in and out of the Oval Office as frequently as the MGM boss. However, with Hoover deposed and Republican prospects dim, Mayer was not interested in being a minority leader. Nevertheless, he remained a power to be reckoned with. As a *New Yorker* profile observed in April 1936, "In politics and public affairs, particularly as they related to California and the film industry, Mayer has no potential rivals at all."[64]

Retreating from day-to-day partisan politics, Mayer played a crucial role in aiding the party's long-term prospects. At the same time that he focused on bringing Republicans to Hollywood, he also brought Hollywood into the Republican Party. He did this by turning MGM into a training ground for GOP activists. During the 1920s and 1930s, Mayer used studio visits by prominent political leaders both to court them and to educate actors interested in learning more about politics, especially Republican politics. At the elaborate luncheons that accompanied these visits—with surroundings carefully designed by MGM art director Cedric Gibbons—stars such as Robert Montgomery, Robert Taylor, Adolphe Menjou, Conrad Nagel, Lionel Barrymore, Marie Dressler, James Stewart, Jeanette MacDonald, and George Murphy were seated next to guests and encouraged to engage in conversation.

Mayer also invited prominent speakers to talk with actors, directors, producers, and writers about a wide range of contemporary issues. The studio head hoped to "educate" any star willing to listen, making them conservatives if he could. In December 1933, political historian Mark Sullivan spoke to Mayer's protégés about the problematic nature of Roosevelt's monetary policies. Months later, Maryland Governor Harry Nice treated the MGM faithful to a similar critique of FDR's "irrational expenditure of public money." Other gatherings featured talks by local politicians or Mayer himself, who by the mid-1930s repeatedly denounced FDR's "wholesale spending" and the "appalling taxes, Communism, foreign imports and the theoretical fancies of young professors" advising the administration. These meetings, observed one historian, were "the Hollywood equivalent of the political salons of the east, where power brokers rubbed shoulders."[65]

The studio chief also called on Ida Koverman to help his politicizing efforts. Dubbed by one reporter as the "guiding angel of all the kids on the lot," she made sure that young stars had "teachers for everything, speech, music, dancing, and sports." She also taught them the basic elements of political life. Koverman invited her favorite stars to her home to mingle with people she thought they should meet—politicians, lawyers, conservative movers and shakers, and Herbert Hoover himself. A keen judge of communication skills, she mentored George Murphy, Robert Montgomery, and Robert Taylor, "a special protégé and pet," on the importance of presenting ideas in a way that would reach audiences. She gave them the same advice as she gave her beloved Chief: always speak to voters in a clear, simple way. Koverman understood the concept of pithy sound bites long before the term was invented. Hoover's radio speeches, she explained, "are always very meaty and constructive," but "at times I have noticed that they were over the head of the ordinary person."[66]

Although luncheons and private gatherings were important occasional events, the studio commissary served as the daily forum for the political education of MGM personnel, right and left. The MGM commissary was known for its excellent, inexpensive food and its unrivaled chicken soup. For Mayer, offering good cheap food was less a matter of largesse than practicality; having studio personnel remain on the lot for lunch meant more efficient moviemaking. The soup, however, was personal. As a poor boy, Louis thought the ultimate extravagance in life was chicken soup with lots of chicken in it. He swore that if he ever became a rich man he would have chicken soup every day of his life. Although Mayer did not keep this vow, he ordered the MGM commissary to have a daily chicken soup special: 30 cents for the biggest chicken-filled bowl of soup in the city. "It was so good that you couldn't bear it," raved journalist Adela Rogers St. Johns, "and one bowl would be enough for a meal."[67] The first thing any visitor venturing into the kitchen saw was a plaque engraved in gold with Mayer's beloved mother's recipe for the soup.

The commissary was more than just a place to eat lunch. It was where Republican and Democratic activists talked and debated politics. Left-leaning actor Edward G. Robinson, who made The Last Gangster at MGM in 1937, found that it "was politically the most schizophrenic of lots." Studio executives "almost to a man, were antiliberal," the writers were leftists, and the actors a mix of both. "The writers' table was a hotbed of progressive thought; those writers who didn't agree ate with the directors, whose table was a hotbed of people who longed for the reincarnation of Calvin Coolidge." Political discussions were so intense that waitresses had a hard time taking orders over the din. Actors invited to dine at the commissary with Mayer were encouraged to order the chicken soup and then listen to his "acid comments on Eleanor Roosevelt, Harold Ickes, and Mrs. [Frances] Perkins." Loyal Republicans readily concurred, while ardent New Dealers like Robinson remained silent.[68]

Mayer's vision of using his studio to build a Republican base in Hollywood paid off not only in terms of soliciting stars to participate in political campaigns but also in creating a leadership cadre that would influence the political direction of the industry and the nation in coming years. Two early Screen Actors Guild presidents, Robert Montgomery (who served from 1935 to 1938 and again from 1946 to 1947) and George Murphy (who served from 1944 to 1946) were Mayer protégés. The two also headed up the Hollywood Republican Committee in the late 1940s. Murphy, who entered MGM in 1936 as a "dormant Democrat" and became "an active Republican" in 1939, learned a great deal from Koverman, but he also credited Mayer with getting him into "the civic thing." L. B. was especially fond of the former song-and-dance man. When Koverman retired in 1954, he asked him to take over her job of keeping "in touch with the political scene."[69] Murphy, in turn, mentored his SAG successor, another Democrat-turned-Republican by the name of Ronald Reagan. All three men would become active at the highest level of American politics, instructing presidents on how to sell ideas via the media and, in Reagan's case, becoming president.

CINEMATIC CONSERVATISM

Mayer left yet another legacy. He was the producer of political visions that laid out the kind of optimistic "American" values that future conservative leaders used to reassure an often-anxious nation. Mayer understood that politics extended beyond the electoral arena. Movies reached people of all political persuasions and the ideas they contained could change the ways in which people thought about themselves, their values, and their leaders. For her father, Irene explained, movies served as "a potent force and an important weapon. He believed they would have a profound influence on the public, his country, and eventually the world." In terms of sheer numbers, movies commanded the attention of far more Americans than did politicians. In 1936, 88 million Americans flocked to the movies each week, a figure that greatly exceeded the 45.6 million votes cast in the presidential election that year.[70]

Make no mistake, the man whom producer Joe Mankiewicz insisted "could have run General Motors as successfully as MGM" could be just as ruthless and cynical as any corporate head. Whether it was politics or religion, Mayer's actions were always guided by his bottom-line mentality. Jewish moguls may have created "an Empire of their own," as cultural historian Neal Gabler argues, but the author overestimates Mayer's commitment to Judaism. When business interests clashed with Jewish interests, the MGM head consistently chose the former. Unlike staunch antifascists Jack and Harry Warner, Mayer did not want to risk studio profits by engaging in any political controversy that threatened highly lucrative foreign markets. When the Warner brothers responded to Adolf Hitler's institution of antisemitic laws by shutting down their German offices in 1934, not only did Mayer continue trading with Germany but he curried the government's favor by inviting ten leading Nazi newspaper editors onto his lot in June 1939, less than three months before the outbreak of World War II.[71]

Film allowed Mayer to create his own ideal world, and he had a clear vision of what he wanted to see on the screen: clean, wholesome films that celebrated the best of American values, films that an entire family could enjoy without embarrassment. The sudden death of Irving Thalberg in September 1936 was both a tragedy and an opportunity for the studio head. Both men believed they were responsible for MGM's success and resented the accolades the other received. Mayer was thought of as the "business brains of the studio" while Thalberg was hailed as its creative genius. Now L.B. had a chance to prove he could be both. His primary goal was always to produce films that would attract audiences and make money. To that end, he still entrusted daily operations and creative direction to his underlings. Yet, from time to time, he let them know about his passion for particular kinds of films. He must have done something right, for as successful as he was with Thalberg, it was only after Irving's death—and a subsequent string of major hits—that Mayer became what biographer Bosley Crowther called the "Hollywood Rajah."[72]

Thalberg had always objected to Mayer's sentimentality and taste for popular but mediocre fare. Yet the studio chief felt he understood the desires of mainstream America; audiences wanted to be entertained, but they also wanted something in which to believe. And that is precisely what he gave them. Mayer's cinematic ideology was a stark contrast to the progressive social-issue movies coming out of the Warner Bros. studio. While Warner Bros.' films repeatedly exposed what was wrong in American life—poverty, corruption, lack of opportunity—Mayer offered Depression-era audiences an antidote to hopelessness and despair. His favorite films were brimming with optimism and heralded everything that was right with America. He created an updated Victorian world where anything was possible, so long as one subscribed to what he viewed as the Holy Trinity of American life: Family, God, and Country. "Louis truly thought of his company not just as an entertainment factory," explained writer Budd Schulberg, "but as a mighty pillar of society holding up the House of Rectitude that was America. In his Byzantine mind, God, Country, the GOP, and MGM had become a holy quaternary."[73]

For Mayer, success was a matter of individual effort and not collective action. The family, not the state, was the only institution one needed to turn to for help in hard times. These may now seem like old-fashioned values, but at the time MGM went against the tide of the New Deal's more collectivist vision of increased reliance on government. Unlike Samuel Goldwyn, who famously quipped, "If you want to send a message, send it Western Union," Mayer wanted to shape a discourse of American life that would influence audiences long after the movie ended. He wanted the messages of his films to seep into public consciousness in a way political speeches rarely did. Like many successful immigrants, Mayer loved his adopted nation and made films that emphasized the best of American life. He loved America so much that he closed his studio on July 4 every year for a dual celebration of his and the nation's birthday.[74]

Mayer's vision of America was most explicitly articulated in his favorite MGM productions, the Hardy Family series. The machinations of the Hardy Family proved so popular that the studio released fourteen films between 1937 and 1943. "The best pictures [I] ever made—the only pictures I really ever took an active hand in," he told a reporter years later, "were the Andy Hardy series." He delighted in watching daily rushes and added his input whenever he felt it was necessary. Director Billy Wilder recounts being on the set one day when Mayer grabbed an unruly Mickey Rooney (who played Andy Hardy) by the lapels and screamed, "You're Andy Hardy! You're the United States! You're the stars and stripes. Behave yourself, you are a symbol!"[75]

The Hardys represented the ideal family that Mayer never had: the perfect family where father and mother loved one another and raised children in an atmosphere of affection, respect, and obedience. The first four films in the series—*A Family Affair* (1937), *You're Only Young Once* (1938), *Love Finds Andy Hardy* (1938), and *Judge Hardy's Children* (1938)—established a basic paradigm that was followed in subsequent productions.[76] The films are set in Carvel, an idyllic small town located along the banks of a gently curving river in an unspecified region of America. The Hardys are neither wealthy nor poor, but the quintessential middle-class American family: mom, dad, two daughters, and a son. Judge James Hardy is a wise and thoughtful man, and Mayer's ideal leader. In *A Family Affair*, Judge Hardy (played by Mayer's favorite, Lionel Barrymore, and later by Lewis Stone) risks being defeated in his reelection campaign by halting construction on a popular aqueduct project that would bring jobs to the financially strapped community. Standing firm as the town turns against him, Hardy explains that he has been doing what is right for the past twenty years and is not about to change his ways, even if it costs him reelection. But of course in the end the wily judge saves the day when he discovers that the aqueduct is a developer's scam that would have ruined the town's businesses. Doing the conservative thing, the MGM film tells us, is always the right thing.

A Family Affair delivers messages about family and patriarchy with scenes showing the Hardys gathered near the hearth, the younger members respectfully standing, the older ones sitting, daughter Marion's boyfriend courting in suit and tie, and everyone focused on the head of the household, Judge James K. Hardy. Messages about class mobility are also subtly woven into the film. The scene in figure 2.4 also provides an image of the kind of simple but elegant middle-class home that hardworking Americans could aspire to own.

The Hardy Family films laid the visual foundation of a conservative ideology that heralded the attributes of local governance and condemned the corruption of an overly active federal government. Indeed, political corruption and New Deal socialism were the focal points of *Judge Hardy's Children*. When the judge is asked to travel to the nation's capital to head a special commission hearing a case involving utility company monopolies (something similar to the government-sponsored Tennessee Valley Authority, controversial to Republicans like Mayer), he brings the entire family with him. Daughter Marian falls under the sway of political lobbyists who get her

FIGURE 2.4 Mayer's perfect American family gathers in *A Family Affair* (1937). The Hardy Family films were Mayer's favorite series. SOURCE: CINEMA/TV LIBRARY, USC

to reveal inside information about the case. When they attempt to blackmail the judge, he returns to Carvel ready to resign. However, Andy saves the day by reminding his father of the lessons he taught him: patriotism meant fighting even when the odds seemed impossible. The judge heeds his son and goes on radio to expose the lobbyists and their duplicitous efforts on behalf of the quasi-socialist monopolies. In following with Mayer's own political inclinations, the judge's commission ruled against the "illegal" TVA-like monopoly.

Babes in Arms (1939), though not part of the Hardy Family series, features MGM's two most famous stars—Mickey Rooney and Judy Garland—and offers Mayer's most explicit tribute to American life and values. In this film, hard work and determination lead to success, even in the midst of the Great Depression. Mickey and Judy save their vaudevillian parents and friends from ruin by staging a successful musical. The nearly eight-minute-long closing number, "In God's Country," repeatedly proclaims that everything is better in America where "smiles are broader and freedom's greater."

As the song reaches its climactic end, a backdrop of the Capitol Building appears and out comes a car with Rooney dressed as FDR and Garland as Eleanor. After Mickey gives a "fireside" talk, a mélange of Americans ask the president what he plans to do about pensions, wages, the budget, and foreign relations. His optimistic response is that everything can be solved by working together. Mayer's only regret was that it was Roosevelt and not Hoover sending out the message.

Audiences loved the Hardy Family films. Each episode grossed three or four times its cost and MGM made a total of $25 million on its most financially successful series ever, leading *Variety* to call it "the biggest money-maker in relation to investment in the planet's history." In 1939, theater owners named Rooney the industry's top box-office star, the first of three consecutive years he would hold that honor. When told that the Hardy Family films were not up to the artistic standards of some of the Thalberg-era productions, Mayer snapped back, "Any good Hardy picture made $500,000 more than *Ninotchka* made." Likewise, *Babes in Arms*, which cost $745,341, grossed $3,335,000. *Wizard of Oz*, also released in 1939, cost $2.8 million and grossed only $3,017,000.[77]

If these films and their messages seem like well-worn clichés, it is because men like Louis B. Mayer helped make them so. The studio chief took traditional values and updated them to please audiences. A "successful picture, at any time," director William deMille observed in 1935, "represents what a majority of the 70 million want at that time. For, believe me, if they don't want it they say so in no uncertain terms." Mayer's critics thought him overly sentimental and the Hardy Family films lightweight treacle. But the unbridled success of *Babes in Arms* and the Hardy Family series suggests that he did indeed have his finger on the pulse of audience fantasies and desires. The power of these movies lay in their ability to offer viewers comfort, hope, and, faith. Moreover, as the first studio to make films aimed at the teenage and youth markets, MGM's products exposed millions of adolescents to Mayer's worldview and perhaps even inspired a new generation to envision and embrace the conservative family values so dear to Republicans.[78]

At the very least, these films helped shrink the cultural divide between Hollywood and its conservative critics, many of whom felt the movie industry was out of touch with mainstream values. Mayer offered these people a vision of the America they wanted to see: not necessarily the "real" America, but the America they fantasized about. This was the same perceptive quality that made the political right so successful in subsequent decades.

Members of the Academy of Motion Picture Arts and Sciences were equally impressed with the films and awarded the Hardy Family series a special Oscar in 1942 for "furthering the American way of life." More importantly, Mayer's message continued to be articulated by his protégés. When asked to explain George Murphy's surprise election to the Senate in 1964, actor Robert Ryan responded, "Murphy's got an M-G-M philosophy. You know, the way Louis B. Mayer was in the dream business—pretty people, nice kids, lovely homes, that kind of stuff."[79] A similar message was sounded in 1984, when a calm, reassuring Judge Hardy–like Ronald Reagan ran for reelection promising a militarily and economically depressed nation, "It's Morning in America." Mayer may have removed himself from the center of partisan politics, but his impact on American political life endured for decades to come.

THE DECLINE OF LOUIS B. MAYER

Once he set the infrastructure of the Hollywood–Republican relationship into motion, Mayer had nothing new to add, especially after Herbert Hoover disappeared from public life. As the MGM head faded from the political scene to occupy himself with movies and his latest passion, racehorses, Hollywood entered a new era in its political history. The unprecedented activity of large numbers of actors, directors, writers, and producers in the mid-1930s shifted industry politics and ideology decidedly to the left. A new generation of left activists such as Edward G. Robinson, Melvyn Douglas, Fredric March, Katharine Hepburn, and Humphrey Bogart supplanted conservatives like Mayer, Cecil B. DeMille, and Robert Montgomery. Yet, after World War II, they in turn would be overshadowed by a resurgent Hollywood right led by MGM stalwarts who took up the mantle of Cold War anti-Communist conservatism.

Unlike her boss, Ida Koverman remained a powerful behind-the-scenes party activist for several more decades. She served as a delegate and committee member to GOP conventions in 1944 and 1948, and she worked hard but futilely to get conservative Robert Taft nominated in 1952. Always a party loyalist, she joined with Hedda Hopper in organizing the Women's Brigade for Eisenhower and Nixon. When she died of a heart attack on

November 24, 1954, the headline of the *Los Angeles Herald Express* proclaimed, "Mrs. Hollywood Passes." Her funeral was a star-studded event attended by Mayer, Jimmy Stewart, Barbara Stanwyck, Edward G. Robinson, George Murphy (who delivered the eulogy), and dozens of other celebrities. Telegrams of condolence were sent by Herbert Hoover, Chief Justice Earl Warren, and FBI head J. Edgar Hoover.[80]

Mayer's reign as the Hollywood Rajah came to an end in August 1951 when the sixty-five-year-old mogul was forced out of what he thought of as his studio. Worse yet, from his point of view, liberal Democrat Dore Schary replaced him. Believing that Mayer's Depression-era nostalgia and sentimentality no longer appealed to postwar audiences, MGM's corporate heads in New York replaced him with a man who could usher the studio into the modern age, both cinematically and politically. Schary, as Hedda Hopper disparagingly remarked, "thought pictures should carry a social message, not exist exclusively on their merits as entertainment."[81]

On his final day at MGM, studio executives and secretaries gathered on the steps of the Thalberg building and applauded Mayer as he walked down a red carpet laid out for the occasion. Yet, the parting was an unhappy one. Although he became chairman of the board of Cinerama, life after MGM proved a disappointment. When Republicans nominated General Dwight D. Eisenhower as their standard-bearer instead of the more conservative Robert Taft, the disenchanted former mogul moved further to the right, so far to the right that he joined the Hollywood committee for the reelection of Red Scare leader Senator Joseph McCarthy. "The more McCarthy yells," the former mogul proclaimed in April 1954, "the better I like him. He's doing a job to get rid of the termites eating away at our democracy. I don't care how many toes he steps on, including mine, as long as he gets the job done."[82]

Despite a bitter last decade, the "czar of Hollywood movie producers," as the *New York Times* called him in 1957, had ruled MGM for nearly thirty years. Mayer remained convinced to the very end that he, not Schary or Thalberg, knew best how to infuse films, and his disciples, with the politics of true Americanism. "I know what the audience wants," he told a reporter just prior to his resignation. "Andy Hardy. Sentimentality! What's wrong with it? Love! Good old-fashioned romance. Is it bad? It entertains. It brings the audience to the box-office."[83] Who could say that he was wrong? Certainly not George Murphy or Ronald Reagan. They believed in the same kind of America as Mayer and tried to integrate his political vision into the very fabric of American life.

But before they could do so, other Hollywood stars and producers would articulate a very different vision of America—a vision that ultimately got many of them into more trouble than they had ever known.

LITTLE CAESAR AND THE HUAC MOB: EDWARD G. ROBINSON

December 9, 1938, marked the beginning of payback time for the man millions of Americans knew as "Little Caesar." Caesar's payback did not involve machine guns mowing down rival mobsters but instead came in the form of political action against the greatest villain of the day: Adolf Hitler. Two months after European leaders signed the infamous Munich Pact allowing Hitler to annex part of Czechoslovakia, Edward G. Robinson joined with fifty-five film industry leaders in calling upon Congress to boycott all German products until the Nazis stopped persecuting Jews and other minorities. "The world," Robinson told reporters, "is faced with the menace of gangsters who are much more dangerous than any we have ever known." It would be heartening to think that Americans embraced the daring pronouncements of their favorite stars, but that was not the case. While some applauded Robinson's actions and spoke glowingly of his power "to mold public opinion of today as well as that of the future," others denounced him as a Communist "pseudo-statesman" and threatened box-office reprisals once "every Christian in the country" recognized "[you] for what you really are. A cheap, big-mouthed ignorant Jew lacking in a sense of public decency and decorum."[1]

Americans today like to talk nostalgically about World War II as the "Good War," a war where "good" and "evil" were easy to identify. During the 1930s, however, the vast majority of Americans preferred to turn a blind eye to events in Europe. Indeed, 95 percent of those polled in November 1936 opposed U.S. participation in any European conflict; even as late as July 1941, 79 percent still opposed America entering the war.[2]

There was one place where Hitler and his allies met with marked resistance: Hollywood. Film scholars refer to the 1930s as the "Golden Age of Hollywood," a time when movies were at their lavish best. The 1930s were also the "Golden Age of Hollywood Politics," the decade when Hollywood and its stars emerged as a major force in the nation's political life. While Charlie Chaplin concentrated on visual politics and Louis B. Mayer on electoral politics, Edward G. Robinson engaged in what soon became the dominant form of Hollywood activism: issue-oriented politics. Robinson showed how a mobilized community of movie stars could use their celebrity to draw national attention to the most controversial issues of the day and help sway public opinion. At a time when most Americans ignored the expansionist policies of fascist leaders Adolf Hitler, Benito Mussolini, and Francisco Franco, Robinson and dozens of left celebrities marched in the streets, went on the radio, and issued political declarations that attracted widespread attention.

Movie stars who had previously shied away from politics found themselves politicized in the 1930s by the disastrous effects of the Great Depression and the spread of Nazism and Communism both abroad and at home. While some were active on the left and others the right, most stars staked out the liberal center. And few exhibited greater commitment to democratic equality than Edward G. Robinson. From the mid-1930s to the late 1940s, Eddie, as his friends called him, participated in a wide range of progressive causes. Yet, despite a distinguished wartime record, Robinson's career as a major star ended when he was accused of being a Communist in 1950. Although America's favorite cinematic gangster eventually cleared his name, it came at the cost of a ruined career, over $100,000 in legal expenses, and the need to humiliate himself by writing an article, "How the Reds Made a Sucker of Me," for *The American Legion Magazine* in 1952.[3]

Studies of political activism in the movie industry during the 1940s and 1950s usually focus on the House Un-American Activities Committee

(HUAC) and its attack on the ten writers, directors, and producers who refused to testify, commonly known as the Hollywood Ten. Yet, in many ways, this familiar history is far less significant than the story of Edward G. Robinson and the rise and fall of left-oriented politics. Everyone in the movie industry knew that most of the Hollywood Ten— especially John Howard Lawson, Lester Cole, Ring Lardner Jr., and Dalton Trumbo—were or had been Communist Party members. Therefore, it was upsetting but not surprising when HUAC went after them. However, Hollywood activists were truly frightened when Red-hunters targeted those who were decidedly not Communists, particularly Eddie Robinson. In late 1947, the longtime star was completing Arthur Miller's *All My Sons* and getting ready to shoot *Key Largo* with Humphrey Bogart and Lauren Bacall. Three years later, he was persona non grata in the industry he so loved.[4]

In an era dominated by studios and powerful moguls such as Louis B. Mayer, Robinson's story reveals the collective power that could be wielded by movie stars. During the 1930s and 1940s, actors and actresses used their celebrity to alert citizens to dangers they believed threatened the very core of democracy. Yet Robinson's story also reveals how a diverse array of conservatives brought a temporary halt to the emergence of Hollywood as a powerful progressive force in American politics. The successful efforts of Cold Warriors to bring down the militant left-liberal sent a warning to other stars that speaking out on controversial issues could endanger their box office and possibly ruin their careers, a warning that remains true to this day.

THE RISE OF EDDIE ROBINSON

Few Hollywood stars reacted more angrily to charges of being un-American than Edward G. Robinson. Born on December 12, 1893, Emanuel Goldenberg was ten when his family escaped the brutal antisemitism in Bucharest, Romania, by traveling steerage to the United States and settling in the tenements of New York's Lower East Side. His mother, Sarah, and father, Morris, an Orthodox Jew and builder, decided to leave their homeland shortly after their son Jack had his skull crushed by a Jew-baiting mob. Lacking the money to migrate as a family, Morris sent his eldest son Zach to New York, where he earned enough money to bring over his two brothers; they, in turn, sent for their father and eventually for the rest of the household. Eddie landed in New York on February 14, 1903, ready to begin a new life.[5]

Like Charlie Chaplin, Robinson's childhood encounters with persecution and injustice shaped a political worldview that lasted a lifetime. In the years after his arrival at the Castle Garden immigration center, Robinson devoted himself to three great passions: social justice, acting, and modern art. The young boy never forgot the brutal antisemitism he suffered in his homeland. Attending Public School 20 near the family's cramped Broome Street tenement flat, he soon added English to the Romanian, German, Hebrew, and Yiddish he already spoke. Eddie enjoyed making impassioned speeches to family and friends. "When I was twelve," he reflected years later, "I wanted to be a rabbi, to instill the right sort of ideas into people and make them great influences in the world." Eventually realizing that he would "have to be either a moron or a charlatan . . . to pass as a sacrosanct gent day after day," he sought justice in the world of electoral politics. His first partisan activity came in 1909, when the fifteen-year-old high school student campaigned for William Randolph Hearst, who was running for mayor of New York as an independent reform candidate. Young Mr. Goldenberg proved so effective that Hearst's campaign committee drove him to Manhattan's theater district—his first ride in a car—where he implored crowds to reject corruption and vote for Hearst.[6]

Discouraged by Hearst's subsequent defeat, he decided to pursue other paths of justice. While studying at Townsend Harris High School, he was drawn to criminal law. "I had, I found, a deep and abiding sympathy and compassion for the underdogs of the world." He was determined to "defend and champion the dregs of mankind, the human beings who were abused and exploited, knocked down, as it seemed by a bully civilization." In 1910, the precocious seventeen-year-old entered City College of New York and, as classmate and future actor Sam Jaffe recounted, remained "active in causes, always wanting to help people." Eddie also discovered a passion for theater, and when the American Academy of Dramatic Arts awarded him a scholarship, he gave up college and thoughts of law in favor of the stage. He entered the academy at nineteen and changed his name from Goldenberg to Robinson, "a name I had heard while sitting in the balcony of the Criterion Theater."[7]

Robinson made his first professional appearance in Binghamton, New York, in April 1913 in the play *Paid in Full*. For the next several years, he went wherever there were parts: vaudeville, stock, and legitimate theater. His career was interrupted by a brief stint in the Navy during World War I. Initially a conscientious objector, he changed his mind about the war after a German U-boat sank the *Lusitania* in 1915. He applied to work in naval intelligence but wound up peeling potatoes at a naval base in the Bronx. When he saw the mutilated bodies of soldiers coming back from Europe after the Armistice, it confirmed his initial instinct that "war is not right." This led him to vote for Socialist Party candidate Eugene V. Debs in the 1920 presidential election because of Debs's outspoken opposition to the war.[8]

By the early 1920s, the Romanian émigré had established himself as a popular actor on the Broadway and Yiddish stages. In 1923, he made his screen debut playing an old man in *The Bright Shawl*. His next film came six years later, in the early talkie *The Hole in the Wall* (1929) with Claudette Colbert. Acting did not lessen his interest in social justice. A captivating orator, Robinson frequently spoke to New York unionists about a range of contemporary issues. "I'd drive to a Union Hall—longshoremen, meat packers, bakers, whatever," he recounted. "I seldom knew the topic before I arrived. As I'd head for the speaker's platform, the chairman would throw me a topic. And I'd go on for 45 minutes. It kept me on my toes."[9]

Confident as an orator and actor, Robinson proved less secure in love. In 1923, the thirty-one-year-old was still living at home with his parents and rarely dated. It was not until he moved to Manhattan in 1925 that he met Gladys Lloyd. An aspiring stage actress, Lloyd was a Philadelphia Quaker, divorcée, and mother of a young daughter. When the couple married in a civil ceremony in 1927, Eddie still had not told his Orthodox parents about his non-Jewish fiancée. Despite his romantic inexperience, he realized there was something wrong with his wife. "There was always a thin curtain between us," he painfully recounted, and even after twenty-five years of marriage "the wall never came down." Only later did he realize that Gladys was a manic-depressive, "one moment loving and the next cool." Robinson compensated by finding a less troubled passion: art. During a trip to Europe in 1923–1924, he fell in love with the Impressionists and began buying their work. Over the next dozen years, he purchased paintings by Degas, Renoir, Monet, Van Gogh, and Cézanne and built what soon became one of the greatest privately held Impressionist and Post-Impressionist collections in the country. The chief curator of the

Louvre "was nearly in tears at the wonder of the collection" when he visited the actor's home in September 1935.[10]

Robinson never believed he had the looks to be a movie star. "My physical handicaps were great, I knew. I was short and in my own mind I believed that all actors should be tall, fair, and handsome. My mirror told me that I was none of these things." Irving Thalberg disagreed and offered him $1 million in 1930 to make six pictures over three years, an offer Robinson turned down when the MGM executive refused to allow him to do an occasional Broadway play. Instead, he signed a more flexible deal with Warner Bros.[11]

The 5' 7," 165-pound, stocky actor with black hair, brown eyes, and thick lips did not look like a traditional leading man, but he was perfect for the part of Rico Bandello, the gangster hero of *Little Caesar*, in the 1931 production that made him a star and an American icon. Robinson helped redefine the image of the tough male star, and especially the image of the American gangster (Jack Warner originally wanted to cast Clark Gable). His Rico was no dirty thug but, as we can see in figure 3.1, an elegantly

FIGURE 3.1 Robinson in his iconic role as *Little Caesar* (1931). SOURCE: PHOTOFEST

dressed criminal who proves tougher than most men. After being shot by rival mobsters, he grabs his arm and standing his ground calmly stares at the failed assassins.

Little Caesar made Robinson the hottest actor on the Warner Bros. lot. In August 1932, he was the fifth-highest-paid performer in Hollywood. Seven years later, a string of hits—*The Whole Town's Talking* (1935), *Bullets or Ballots* (1936), and *Confessions of a Nazi Spy* (1939)—propelled him to the number three spot; his $255,000-a-year salary was exceeded only by Gary Cooper ($482,820) and James Cagney ($368,333). Robinson's fame also rivaled that of the nation's greatest politicians. When he arrived at a New York train station in 1932, he was mobbed by adoring fans who ignored fellow passenger President Herbert Hoover.[12]

THE POLITICIZATION OF HOLLYWOOD

Throughout the early 1930s, Robinson focused his energies on his skyrocketing career, his new family (Eddie Jr. was born on March 19, 1933), and his growing art collection. Yet, like many other stars, he soon found himself swept up in an unprecedented wave of political activism. During the 1920s, only a small number of producers and stars, mainly Republicans, participated in party politics. But after 1932, the entire town, left and right, was caught up in the same political passions that gripped the nation.

The politicization of Robinson and the Hollywood community was sparked by several factors. The devastating effects of the Great Depression, the rapid spread of fascism in Europe, and the election of a charismatic president who brought a dramatic flair to politics inspired previously complacent movie industry personnel. Before Roosevelt, Robinson explained, his life revolved around "acting, painting, music, [and] all of the arts." But FDR made politics "no longer merely a politician's 'job'—he made it the concern of every human being . . . and in doing so he left the artist with no excuse to remain aloof from it." This proved especially true for many Broadway actors who migrated to Hollywood after the coming of sound. Lured by weekly salaries two to ten times greater than they made on the stage, these men and women tended to be more educated, cultured, and politically engaged than those who had spent their entire career in what Robinson and others condescendingly referred to as "the low-brow world of motion pictures." Broadway stars, explained Republican actor Conrad Nagel, were "interested in more things than just Hollywood, the motion pictures, and his particular job. Many of them did have very definite and profound and clear-cut political convictions, on all sides."[13]

The influx of stage stars pushed Hollywood to the left and helped turn the movie capital into a new political force in American life. The overwhelmingly liberal orientation of actors, then and now, can be partially understood as a byproduct of the demands of their craft. Playing a variety of characters, many of whom they did not necessarily like, fostered a sense of empathy and ability to understand issues and people outside their personal experience. When asked if he would ever play Hitler in a film, Robinson said no, explaining "that a capable actor could make of Hitler a sympathetic, human character." Many stars also experienced years of economic hardship before succeeding and felt a sense of kinship with the poor and oppressed. Hollywood's increasingly cosmopolitan composition also contributed to its liberal inclinations. Leo Rosten, who spent 1937 to 1940 conducting a sociological study of the movie industry, found the town filled with "actors from Tasmania, Brooklyn, Stockholm; directors from Pasadena, Tiflis, Sicily; writers from Budapest to Wapakoneta, Ohio; cameramen from China to New York; producers from Minsk to Wahoo, Nebraska." Living and working together created a sense of tolerance, if not genuine acceptance, among movie personnel.[14]

The rise of liberal Hollywood was also fueled by what many actors and writers viewed as the unfair policies of conservative studio heads. When Louis B. Mayer ordered a 50 percent across-the-board paycut for all employees in March 1933 (a move followed by other producers), he "created more communists than Karl Marx," recounted screenwriter Albert Hackett, and "made more Democrats than anybody in the world." Outraged writers responded by forming the Screen Writers Guild in April 1933; two months later, eighteen actors organized the Screen Actors Guild. Although studios soon scaled back their cuts, forced contributions to Frank Merriam's gubernatorial campaign in 1934 led many previously quiescent stars to become Democratic activists.[15]

Studio and domestic issues were certainly important, but events in Europe ignited the greatest political passions in Hollywood. As conditions abroad worsened, movie stars began questioning their responsibilities as citizens to speak out against forces they felt threatened democracy. "Depression was withering away at America," Robinson recounted, "and there seemed no solution; Hitler was gathering his brown forces in Germany; Spain was splitting at the seams; Mussolini was making the trains run on time just as certainly as he was abridging human freedom; the Soviet Union sat on the land between Europe and Asia licking its chops, waiting to pounce." The Robinsons' home on Beverly Hills' Rexford Drive served as a cultural and political center, and the couple spent countless evenings discussing European problems with their closest friends, Fredric March and Florence Eldridge and Melvyn and Helen Gahagan Douglas. As fellow Jews, Robinson and Douglas—born Melvyn Hesselberg—were especially concerned about the spread of antisemitism at home and the indifference of so many Americans. Something, they agreed, had to be done.[16]

Robinson, Douglas, and hundreds of actors, writers, directors, and producers soon joined the struggle to stop the spread of Nazism in Europe and to lend support to the Loyalist forces fighting fascists in Franco's Spain in 1936. Given the large numbers of Jewish movie industry personnel and European émigrés who populated Hollywood in the 1930s, it is not surprising that antifascism emerged as the focal point of political action. Of the 1,500 film professionals who fled Germany after 1933 and Austria after 1938, over one-half settled in Hollywood. Robinson joined with others in bringing émigrés such as Thomas Mann, Lion Feuchtwanger, and Arnold Schoenberg to Los Angeles. By 1936, the movie community knew that fascist forces in Europe were on the move: Germany was reoccupying the Rhineland, Italy was annexing Ethiopia, Spanish fascists were battling Republican forces in a bloody civil war, and Hitler and Mussolini had formalized their Axis alliance.[17]

Hollywood's new activists were at the forefront of internationalist politics at a time when most Americans were still isolationists, a situation that led many Americans to see the movie capital as a bastion of liberalism and, worse yet, liberalism on behalf of Jews and foreign interests. Antisemitism was a fact of life in America and few citizens were willing to risk war to aid European Jews. According to polls taken in 1938 and 1940, nearly two-thirds of Americans believed that Jews as a group had "objectionable traits" and over 50 percent thought that Nazi Germany's antisemitism stemmed partially or wholly from the actions of German Jews.[18]

Not everyone in the world's movie capital was frightened by the growing power of Hitler, Mussolini, and Franco. "There were people in Hollywood who supported their views," explained a worried Robinson.

"'Oh,' the thoughts went, 'Hitler will forget the anti-Semitism; it's only a passing phase. And he *will* stop the spread of Communism.'" A deeply concerned Paulette Goddard, Charlie Chaplin's costar in *Modern Times* and a Jew by birth, told one reporter in October 1936 that many industry figures were "falling easy victims to fascism," which was "fast outdistancing Communism in the film colony." One of the most outspoken conservative stars was "America's Sweetheart," Mary Pickford. A longtime admirer of Il Duce, Pickford cheerily noted in March 1934, "Italy has always produced great men and when she needed one most Mussolini was there. Viva Fascismo! Viva Il Duce!" Three years later, she lavished equal praise on Adolf Hitler, remarking to one reporter that he "seems to be a very great fellow, too, for the German people. Things look much better over there."[19]

In addition to combating isolationist sentiments, Hollywood activists found themselves battling fascists in their own backyard. "The Silver Shirts and the Bundists and all the rest of these hoods are marching in Los Angeles right now," Jack Warner warned in 1938. "There are high school kids with swastikas on their sleeves a few crummy blocks from our studio." Pro-Nazi groups such as the German-American Bund and the American Nationalist Party (ANP) joined with other local fascist organizations in stirring up antisemitic hatred and accusing Hollywood activists of being Communists. Calling on loyal "Christian Vigilantes" to boycott movie industry filth, one ANP poster proclaimed, "Hollywood is the Sodom and Gomorrha [*sic*] where International Jewry controls Vice-Dope-Gambling—where young Gentile girls are raped by Jewish producers, directors, casting directors who go unpunished."[20]

By the mid-1930s, Hollywood's liberal community had emerged as a hotbed of political activism and focus of national attention. The intensity of so many issues, observed Leo Rosten, led scores of stars to abandon the long-standing idea perpetuated by "managers, press agents and producers, that the actor or actress must remain a kind of a romantic, glamour idol or symbol, who never gets into the kinds of things which would lose him or her the esteem of the fans" or "alienate the Democrats or the Republicans" who went to the movies. Stars spoke out and what they said, Rosten observed, was "reported to the world in greater detail than any other single group in the world, with the possible exception of Washingtonists. . . . People would know Clark Gable or Greta Garbo in parts of the world where they didn't know the name of their own prime minister or the mayor of their own little town."[21]

Hollywood's political engagement took several forms during these years: some became involved with mainstream parties; others allied with third parties like the Communist Party (mostly writers and directors); others still participated in issue-oriented politics by promoting one or more specific causes. Like most stars, Eddie Robinson fell into the last category. His politics might be best described as "left-liberal." He was not a radical trying to replace capitalism with socialism, nor did he think in terms of larger systems that led to inequality, war, and imperialism. Rather, he was militantly devoted to the Bill of Rights and the cause of equal justice for all people. The habitual cigar smoker who liked to wear old clothes and refrain from physical exercise gave his time, money, and support to virtually every progressive group that spoke out on behalf of democracy and against religious, ethnic, and racial intolerance. Known as the softest touch in town, Robinson donated more than $250,000—$3.1 million in 2009 dollars—between 1939 and 1949 to 850 political and charitable groups.[22]

Political categories and alliances were far more fluid during the 1930s than in the postwar years. This was not a time when sharp distinctions were drawn between left and center, liberal and Communist, and, in some instances, radical and conservative. Hatred of Nazism led Robinson and other Hollywood liberals, Communists, and some Republicans to join a wide range of "Popular Front" groups, most notably the Hollywood Anti-Nazi League, the Motion Picture Artists Committee to Aid Republican Spain (which had 15,000 members at its peak), and the Joint Anti-Fascist Refugee Committee. Forged by the Communist International in 1935, the Popular Front represented a broad coalition of groups and individuals on the left, center, and right who put aside sectarian differences and united in a common effort to fight the spread of fascism. Whether Popular Front groups contained Communists or not seemed irrelevant at the time; political causes were more important than political labels. It was only during the late 1940s and 1950s, explained screenwriter Philip Dunne, that "witch-hunters . . . succeeded in twisting this meaning into something far more sinister: a front in the sense of a false front of compliant liberals behind which Communists could hatch their nefarious plots." Communists were infiltrating the movie industry in the

1930s, but this small group seemed far less threatening than Hitler and his minions.[23]

Robinson's desire to stop Hitler led him to join dozens of organizations, but none proved as important as the Hollywood Anti-Nazi League (HANL). Founded in April 1936, the HANL was the city's best known and most diverse Popular Front organization. Far from being a dilettante celebrity group, the HANL marked the beginning of a new kind of issue-oriented politics. In a Hollywood ruled by studios that controlled what messages went on the screen, movie stars found an alternative way to reach a broad public. They used their celebrity to raise public awareness about the dangers Nazism posed in Europe and the United States. The organization—whose 4,000 to 5,000 members included liberals and leftists such as Robinson, Melvyn Douglas, and Fredric March and conservatives such as Bruce Cabot, Joan Bennett, John Ford, and Dick Powell—mounted frequent demonstrations and rallies, held talks on topics such as "Hitlerism in America," sponsored two weekly radio shows that publicized fascist activities, published its own biweekly newspaper *Hollywood Now*, called for boycotts of German products, and blockaded meetings of the Los Angeles German-American Bund. Heated protests by the HANL also succeeded in cutting short Hollywood visits by Benito Mussolini's son Vittorio in September 1937 and by Leni Riefenstahl, Hitler's favorite filmmaker, a year later.[24]

By January 1938, Hollywood was thoroughly politicized. "There is hardly a tea party today," Ella Winter wrote in the *New Republic*, "or a cocktail gathering, a studio lunch table or dinner even at a producer's house at which you do not hear agitated discussion, talk of 'freedom' and 'suppression,' talk of tyranny and the Constitution, of war, of world economy and political theory." The *Los Angeles Times* reported that studio moguls were so worried about the increased activism of their stars that they considered inaugurating "a squelch campaign against anything savoring of political activities, even incorporating a clause in contracts covering this, like the famous morals clause." Unlike their stars, Jewish studio executives refused to venture too far in front of public opinion. Upon returning from Germany in 1934, Irving Thalberg told Louis B. Mayer that "a lot of Jews will lose their lives" but "Hitler and Hitlerism will pass; the Jews will still be there."[25]

Industry leaders had good reason to be concerned. The internationalist pronouncements of Robinson and other Hollywood activists soon came to haunt them as the House Un-American Activities Committee (HUAC) began portraying antifascists as the allies of Communists bent on destroying America. Ironically, the impetus behind HUAC came from New York Jewish Congressman Samuel Dickstein. In 1934, he called for a House investigation of pro-Nazi propaganda and subversion in the United States. When Congress approved the plan in 1938, they made Texas Representative Martin Dies the chair and excluded the Jewish politician from HUAC. The publicity-hungry Texan immediately launched an investigation of Hollywood, which he called a "hotbed of Communism," but paid little attention to fascist groups that many considered far more dangerous. In August 1938, HUAC investigator Edward Sullivan turned the nation's attention to the movie capital when he accused the HANL of being a Communist front. While the HANL certainly did have Communist members, most shared Robinson's attitude that he would join with anyone, "Stalinists, Quakers, Holy Rollers . . . anarchists, or Republicans" willing "to fight against the black horror that was beginning to sweep Europe."[26]

Not everyone shared Robinson's Popular Front attitude. Anti-Communist right-wing organizations such as the Patriotic Sons of America denounced actors who lent their name to the antifascist cause. Worse yet, as Hollywood politics shifted increasingly leftward, public opinion moved to the right. When asked by pollsters in August 1938 whether they would like the Roosevelt administration to become more liberal or more conservative over the next two years, 72 percent of respondents hoped for a conservative turn.[27]

STAR POLITICS, AUDIENCE RESPONSE

Undaunted by efforts to intimidate him, Robinson entered the national political stage on December 9, 1938, when fifty-six prominent stars, writers, directors, and studio heads—including James Cagney, Joan Crawford, Henry Fonda, Groucho Marx, Rosalind Russell, Bette Davis, Paul Muni, Melvyn Douglas, Harry Warner, and Jack Warner—gathered at his home to discuss the worsening situation in Germany and western Europe. They constituted the "Committee of 56," named after the number of signatories to the Declaration of Independence, and they signed a "Declaration of Democratic Independence" that they sent to Congress and the president. The Declaration called for a boycott of all German products until the nation ended its aggression toward other nations and stopped persecuting Jews and all minorities. Conscious of their star power, the Committee staged a second signing for the press. Photographs and stories of the star-studded group and their cause appeared in newspapers throughout the world.[28]

Robinson was a big movie star, but did audiences really care what celebrities had to say about American foreign policy? He certainly hoped so. The main point of issue-oriented politics was to use movie stars' celebrity to draw attention to causes that might otherwise be ignored. Perhaps the industry's "standard wisdom" was wrong; perhaps citizens would not be offended by stars who spoke out on controversial issues.

In the weeks following the release of the Declaration, people deluged Robinson with letters that praised or condemned his actions. Henry Bortin Jr. of Laguna Beach, California, congratulated him for using his "high position to take this kind of stand" and exerting "a great deal of influence with the American public." He and his wife promised to repay the actor by attending "all pictures in which you have a part" and hoped that his "strong stand will pay you financial dividends at the box office as well as spiritual dividends of happiness in your own conscience." Others pledged to sign copies of the boycott petition being circulated around the country.[29]

Robinson's call to boycott Germany also elicited numerous antisemitic letters denouncing the signatories and threatening future retributions. The National Association of Southerners warned Robinson that his outspoken political activity was "far afield from your profession and can only cause your popularity to wane with millions of Americans who are unsympathetic to Jewish activities." A self-proclaimed "Bible Christian" from Minneapolis chastised the actor for "entering upon a new field of endeavor—that of advising the President and Congress. What arrogance! Who do you think you are anyway? Because a lot of silly men and women worship you does not prove that you [actors] are gods who may tell our government what or what not it is to do." The "movie colony may root for the Jews all they wish," she added, "but don't think that the people of the United States are going to fall in with your plans. . . . Those of us who know World History and the Bible know that the Jews have always been in trouble up to their ears. . . . They are trouble makers."[30]

Many angry writers conflated anti-Nazism with pro-Communism, an association that would haunt left activists for decades to come. "You and your bunch are making it your business to boycott Germany," wrote one Cleveland resident. "But! Nary a word or statement against Russia and its

persecution of Christians—oh, me!" An even greater number of corre-
spondents were upset that Robinson and his group denounced Christian
Germany rather than what they perceived as the far more dangerous athe-
istic Soviet Union; after all, Hitler, they mistakenly believed, was a God-
fearing Christian while Stalin sought to destroy religion. Harwood
Motley, an avid Robinson fan, urged him to attack Communism as well as
Nazism, and included an article from a religious periodical, *Our Sunday
Visitor*, that threatened "a boycott of the pictures" made by politically
offensive stars.[31]

Motley's letter raised studio executives' worst fears: that movie star
activism would alienate audiences and adversely affect box-office receipts.
Moguls believed that fans wanted stars to remain emotional fantasy figures, not political guides. "When a Joan Crawford denounced the invasion
of Ethiopia," observed Leo Rosten, "when a Fredric March pleaded for
ambulances for Spain, it was like harsh voices destroying a cherished
dream." Judging by the letters Robinson received, industry leaders were
not mistaken. Outraged by the star's attack on Hitler and Germany, National Gentile League founder D. Shea announced that his organization,
which he claimed represented 12 million "True Blue Americans," was declaring "a Nonattendance strike" against Robinson and others who had the
"same attitude against Gentiles."[32]

Antisemitic diatribes and threats of box-office reprisals did not dissuade
Robinson from doing what he considered to be his political and moral duty.
The activities of the Hollywood Anti-Nazi League reached tens of thousands
of citizens, but committed antifascists like Robinson knew they had to reach
millions if they wanted to alter isolationist attitudes. To that end, the actor
supplemented his offscreen activism by making movies that enabled him "to
combine entertainment and larger implications that 'point up' social aspects
and encourage social awareness." Film and radio, he insisted, "are the most
immediate and powerful forces in the world for informing men and shaping
public opinion."[33]

Fortunately for Little Caesar, Harry and Jack Warner felt the same way.
The brothers, whose father fled pogroms in Poland and immigrated to Balti-
more in 1883, were determined to help European Jews being persecuted by
Nazi thugs. When Hitler declared an official boycott of Jewish businesses in
April 1933 and demanded that Hollywood studios fire all German Jews, the
Warners responded by closing their German offices in July 1934 and refusing

to conduct any business with the Nazi regime (MGM, Paramount, and Fox continued operating there until 1939). Their studio, Jack told a reporter in 1936, would always "strive for pictures that provide something more than a mere idle hour or two of entertainment." The Warners alerted a complacent public to the dangers of Nazism at home and abroad by producing a series of antifascist films: *Black Legion* (1937), *Confessions of a Nazi Spy* (1939), *Juarez* (1939), *Espionage Agent* (1939), *British Intelligence* (1940), *The Sea Wolf* (1941), and *Underground* (1941).[34]

Like the Warners, Robinson wanted to make movies that would help "my people." When he heard rumors in 1938 that the studio wanted to turn FBI agent Leon Turrou's account of foiling a domestic Nazi-spy ring into a film, he begged Jack for a role. As the star told one reporter, he would "gladly work as first assistant to the prop boy if it would help him get a crack at Adolf Hitler." The Warners responded by casting him as the crusading Turrou, who tracked down the spies and brought them to trial. By participating in *Confessions of a Nazi Spy*, the first film to portray Nazis as a threat to America, Robinson felt "that I am serving my country just as effectively as if I shouldered a gun and marched away to war."[35]

In order to circumvent Production Code Administration prohibitions against attacking or mocking foreign governments, Warners had to ensure that *Confessions* was based entirely on fact. Consequently, the film's final scene (see fig. 3.2) shows Robinson's crusading FBI agent character and New York City's district attorney receiving a facsimile of a special edition newspaper announcing "NAZI SPIES SENTENCED." Four real-life Nazi spies were convicted of violating U.S. espionage laws in November 1938 and sentenced in a New York federal court the next month.

Robinson's work in *Confessions* steeled his resolve to star in movies that advanced his political ideas. Convinced that "exposing even surface conditions is all to the good," he accepted roles in several other Warner Bros. Jewish bio-pictures and antifascist films: *Dr. Ehrlich's Magic Bullet* (1940), which FDR screened at the White House that March; *A Dispatch from Reuters* (1940); and *The Sea Wolf*, in which he played the tyrannical Captain Wolf Larsen, "a Nazi in everything but name." Robinson's political activism also extended to radio, which he saw as another way to influence public opinion. In *Big Town*, a series that ran from 1937 to 1942, he played crusading newspaper editor Steve Wilson, who each week battled one of the many problems plaguing American life. *Big Town*'s sponsor, he

FIGURE 3.2 Robinson plays a crusading FBI agent who foils a Nazi spy plot in *Confessions of a Nazi Spy* (1939). SOURCE: PHOTOFEST

explained in December 1938, wanted him "to entertain the public and create good will for the product. Yet, within reasonable limits they permit my program to devote itself to vital social and economic issues." The weekly shows he helped write were "constructed primarily to create awareness and then to establish a mood favorable" to reaching solutions. *Big Town* proved enormously popular and ranked second only to *The Jack Benny Show*.[36]

Robinson's efforts to persuade citizens that anti-Nazism was distinct from Communism suffered a fatal blow when Hitler and Stalin signed a nonaggression treaty on August 24, 1939. Liberals had been willing to unite with Communists so long as they stood in opposition to Hitler. But the day after the pact was signed, disillusioned members resigned en masse from the Hollywood Anti-Nazi League, which quickly changed its name to the Hollywood League for Democratic Action. Like many others, Robinson rejected arguments made by Stalin's American defenders that the Soviet Union was simply stalling for time while it geared up for an inevitable fight against Hitler. The pact also led to a new round of anti-Communist investigations of Hollywood. During a Grand Jury hearing in August 1940, John Leech, a former organizer for the Communist Party (CP), insisted that the HANL was conceived by the CP for the purpose of playing upon the fears of Hollywood Jews and their sympathizers. We were "making suckers out of 95 percent of those who joined the organization," Leech boasted. These charges sparked yet another set of HUAC hearings later that month, and a year later by California's own Un-American Activities Committee.[37]

Hot War, Cold War

When war broke out in Europe on September 1, 1939, Robinson began delivering speeches denouncing Nazism and right-wing isolationist groups such as America First. Over the next three years, he participated in an ever-wider array of organizations: the National Bureau for the Right of Asylum and Aid to Political Refugees, the American Committee for the Protection of the Foreign Born, the Committee to Defend America, and, after Hitler's invasion of the Soviet Union on June 22, 1941, the Russian War Relief Association of California and the National Council of American-Soviet Friendship. He also used his radio show as a platform to call for military preparedness. The actor proved so successful in this regard that the American Legion gave him an award in 1941, the same one they gave Louis B. Mayer in 1940, for his "outstanding contribution to Americanism through his stirring patriotic appeals on his nation-wide broadcast of *Big Town*." The popular radio show ran until July 1942, when Robinson quit after his sponsor refused to let him raise issues related to the war.[38]

Once the United States entered the conflict, Robinson interrupted his film career to serve his country. In October 1942, four months after he volunteered for military service, the Office of War Information appointed the forty-nine-year-old "as a Special Representative of the Overseas Operation Branch of this Agency at London, England." Once in London, Robinson used his dramatic and linguistic skills to deliver radio addresses in half a dozen languages to countries under Nazi domination. Placing patriotism over personal safety, he returned to Europe in 1944 and was the first movie star to travel to Normandy to entertain the troops some twenty-seven days after D-Day. During his time back home, Robinson sold war bonds, donated $100,000 to the USO, talked to workers at shipyards and defense plants, and appeared in numerous government-sponsored rallies (see fig. 3.3). He also stepped up his involvement in the Hollywood Democratic Committee. He served on its executive board and in 1944 campaigned with great enthusiasm for FDR and congressional candidate and friend Helen Gahagan Douglas.[39]

After the Soviet Union rejoined the Allied forces in June 1941, an array of Soviet-American groups approached the well-known activist to speak on behalf of our new war allies. Addressing a September 1942 rally organized by the Jewish Anti-Fascist Committee of the USSR, he praised the crowd for joining "together in their hatred of Hitlerism" and urged them to "remain together in love of humanity." No fan of Communism, Robinson supported anyone who fought the Nazis. Unable to attend a February 1943 dinner honoring the Red Army, he sent the following tribute: "Only the historians of tomorrow will be able to appraise the courage, valor, and achievements of

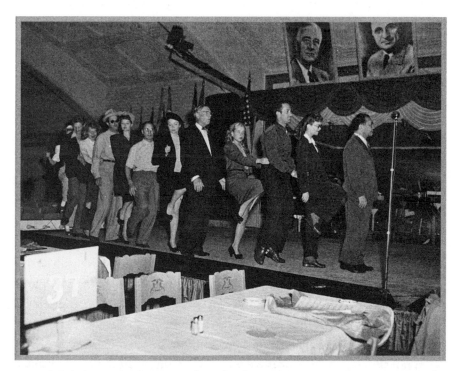

FIGURE 3.3 Robinson leads a conga line of Hollywood Democratic Committee stars who campaigned for FDR and Truman in 1944. SOURCE: CINEMA/TV LIBRARY, USC

the Red Army of today." The National Council of American-Soviet Friendship honored his war work by electing him to its board of directors in August 1944, and he continued supporting the organization after the war.[40]

Robinson's pride in his war work was diminished by difficulties at home. Gladys was "miserable and bored" living in Hollywood and resented the attention her husband received. The couple bickered all the time. After Pearl Harbor she suffered a mental breakdown and was sent to a Pasadena hospital for shock treatments. Gladys sued Eddie for divorce and then withdrew her suit after her hospitalization. She repeated this pattern several times over the next decade as she went in and out of mental clinics. Her treatments proved so costly that the actor had to curtail his volunteer activities in order to accept several lucrative film roles. Young Eddie Jr. (known as Manny) proved to be equally troubled. He was thrown out of several schools and had acquired a drinking problem by the age of twelve. Robinson took comfort by retreating into the art gallery he built in his Beverly Hills home to house his growing collection.[41]

The conclusion of the war in Europe and Japan marked the beginning of a Cold War against the Soviet Union and an equally chilling war against Hollywood activists. Although the second Red Scare (the first came in 1919) is usually associated with HUAC and Senator Joseph McCarthy, the postwar climate of fear had its roots in wartime Hollywood's anti-Communist movements. Long before HUAC resumed its hearings in the spring of 1947, the Hollywood right accused movie industry activists of associating with Communists and insisted that their political ideas posed a threat to national security. Leftists and liberals initially scoffed at these claims but soon found themselves under assault from a number of quarters.

Opposition to the Hollywood left was institutionalized in February 1944, when industry conservatives organized the Motion Picture Alliance for the Preservation of American Ideals (MPA). Pledging to "combat the rising tide of Communism, Fascism and kindred beliefs that seek by subversive methods to undermine and change the American way of life," the MPA grew from seventy-five to several hundred and included die-hard conservatives such as Walt Disney, Barbara Stanwyck, Robert Taylor, Adolphe Menjou, Ward Bond, Hedda Hopper, and John Wayne. The members of the MPA were not the only ones concerned with Communism in the movie capital. The FBI received reports that Reds were taking over movie industry unions and inserting dangerous propaganda into American films. Around 1933, explained one Bureau report, the Communist International "realized the value of the motion picture as a propaganda medium, and in 1935 a directive was issued by the Communist Party to make an intensive drive in the cultural groups, writers, artists, actors, actresses and others to enlist their assistance toward the Communist cause." Beginning in August 1942, FBI head J. Edgar Hoover ordered Los Angeles agents to investigate Communist infiltration of Hollywood, an investigation that lasted several decades and was aided by MPA members who served as FBI informants.[42]

In August 1945, however, Hollywood progressives still outnumbered MPA activists. For Robinson, issue-oriented politics did not die with the end of war. Defeating Nazism and fascism steeled his determination to forge a more democratic and less prejudiced postwar world. "[W]e were prepared for Utopia," he reflected years later, "a world safe for democracy, no more war, no more bestiality." He joined with Myrna Loy, Danny Kaye, and dozens of other stars in drumming up public support for the United Nations and working with the Hollywood Democratic Committee's oddly named successor, the Hollywood Independent Citizens Committee of the Arts, Sciences and Professions (HICCASP), to lobby for a congressional bill that would have provided national health care for all Americans.[43]

The actor's hopes for international peace were soon punctured by what he perceived as dangerous anti-Soviet policies advocated by western leaders. In March 1946, Winston Churchill gave his famous "Iron Curtain" Speech at a meeting with President Harry Truman and proposed that Great Britain and the United States form a military alliance against Stalin and the Soviet Union. Robinson responded by sending Truman a telegram: "Hope his [Churchill's] outmoded viewpoint never becomes the policy or procedure of our country as it is a threat to the solidarity of UNO and to peace."[44]

The cinematic tough guy remained equally committed to protecting democratic rights for all Americans. Hailed by black leaders in October 1944 as "one of the great friends of the Negro and a great advocator of Democracy," Robinson was especially outspoken in demanding equality for African Americans after the war.[45] Endorsing the call of the Fair Employment Practices Commission to end workplace discrimination in May 1945, he reminded citizens that the nation did "not make race, creed or color a requirement for our fighting forces, and we should not make any accident of birth an obstacle to anyone wishing to participate in production after the war." When Truman agreed to Southern senators' demand to set restrictive poll taxes, Robinson sent a telegram in April 1946 urging him to "re-evaluate your statement that poll taxes be determined on the basis of States' Rights inasmuch as many voters both black and white are deprived of free votes which is fundamental to democracy." He also endorsed the creation of a Jewish state in Palestine and the erection of memorials for the six million Jews killed during the war.[46]

Growing increasingly aggressive in his quest for justice, Robinson also entered the bitter battles within his own industry. He incurred the lasting enmity of powerful anti-Communist labor leader Roy Brewer by supporting the left-wing Conference of Studio Unions in its battle to replace Brewer's corrupt International Alliance of Theatrical Stage Employees Union as the movie industry's main labor organization. He also alienated the growing number of Hollywood anti-Communists by opposing the Screen Actors Guild requirement that members sign loyalty oaths. Any "attempt to curb freedom of expression and set arbitrary standards of Americans," he argued, was "in itself disloyal to both the spirit and the letter of the Constitution."[47]

With the nation at "war," albeit a Cold War, political statements made by movie stars were scrutinized with new vigor. By 1946, the optimistic mood embraced by so many citizens at the war's end gave way to a new climate of fear as Americans worried that the Soviet Union, which put its first nuclear reactor on line on Christmas Day, might use atomic weapons against the United States. Conservative Republicans regained control of Congress that year and anti-Communist groups extended their campaigns to include attacks against liberals, unions, civil rights groups, and even religious bodies.

Political differences hardened as the Cold War created good-versus-evil melodramas that left no room for shades of gray. Before the Red Scare, explained Gene Kelly, "there just seemed to be two sides—all those who were Democratic, no matter how far left they were . . . and all those who hated Roosevelt and were against him." Political labels grew murkier after the war as Hollywood liberals such as Melvyn Douglas and Philip Dunne, believing the Soviet Union posed a threat to democracy, joined the Americans for Democratic Action (ADA) and united with conservatives in supporting anti-Communism while opposing conservatives on domestic issues. Conservative Red-hunters, however, often overlooked such distinctions. By 1947, outspoken activists like Myrna Loy discovered that "people in the middle—the so-called liberals—were painted with the same brush as the 'left.'" Popular Front alliances split apart as formerly united progressives divided into two factions: liberal anti-Communists who attempted to prove their "true" Americanism by expelling radicals from their organizations; and militant liberals and leftists who resisted any effort to abrogate free speech rights protected by the Constitution.[48]

Refusing to join the ADA's liberal anti-Communist crusade, Robinson grew more aggressive in opposing reactionaries, especially those who would abridge basic freedoms guaranteed in the Bill of Rights. "Today it is not enough just being liberal," he insisted in September 1946. "One must be militantly anti-Fascist." However, his refusal to denounce Communists led many movie fans to see him as a dangerous radical. Saying that he preferred Robinson's movie characters to his offscreen political persona, F. B. Putnam of El Monte, California, blasted the actor in March 1946 for associating with "large numbers of commies" and "stirring up racial and religious hatred." Dick Mooney, an old friend from New York, was concerned to see the star's name listed in the newspaper "with several alleged Un-Americans." Robinson assured him that the accusations were false. "I suppose in these critical times, we will have to become accustomed to being called names by those who are influenced by those who want to confuse the issues." Robinson promised that he would not stop speaking out. "I am fighting for those American things which I hold dear. . . . [T]he sanity of the American people will win out against any offensive of reaction."[49]

Robinson overestimated the "sanity" of the American people. Little Caesar was about to battle a tougher group of thugs than he ever faced on the screen: the HUAC mob. Although HUAC found little hard evidence of Communist infiltration of Hollywood before the war, it resumed closed hearings in Los Angeles on May 7, 1947, much to the chagrin of local FBI agents who resented the shoddy work done by Committee investigators. The Committee was "more concerned with having 'big-named' people appear," complained one Los Angeles agent, "than with developing some real information of value."[50] Whether their information was accurate was beside the point: HUAC wanted publicity. The bigger the star, the greater the publicity and the more funding the Committee was likely to get from Congress. It is interesting to speculate whether HUAC, which was not popular with most congressmen in 1945–1946, would have become a strong national presence without its Hollywood crusade. Despite widespread fears about Communist infiltration of American institutions, HUAC did not initially go after atomic spies or radicals working in defense plants, people who might legitimately be seen as threatening national security. They went after movie stars.

Neither fairness nor justice could be expected from a committee chaired by headline-hungry J. Parnell Thomas (R-NJ), a "pompous" man whom even the FBI did not trust. Committee members also included antisemites such as John Rankin of Mississippi, who blasted Jews as "long nosed reprobates" responsible for Communism and Red efforts "to undermine and destroy America." The Committee was emboldened by a December 1947 poll in which 59 percent of those surveyed believed American Communists owed their primary loyalty to Russia and 62 percent favored outlawing the Communist Party.[51]

The Committee began its hearings by calling a parade of "friendly" witnesses that included Screen Actors Guild officers (Ronald Reagan, Robert Montgomery, George Murphy) and members of the Motion Picture Alliance (James McGuiness, Ayn Rand, Adolphe Menjou). Sounding a theme echoed by the others, Menjou insisted that Hollywood was filled with "what I call the lunatic fringe, the political idiots, the morons, the dangerous Communists, and those who have yet to be convinced." Studio heads called to testify, such as Jack Warner and Louis B. Mayer, were polite but uncooperative. They did not want the federal government meddling in their business. Despite his vocal anti-Communism, Mayer initially resisted firing anyone who could make money for his studio. Screenwriter Lester Cole, an active Communist, recalled how shortly after he came under suspicion, Mayer called him into his office and told him, "I don't give a shit about the law. It's them goddam commies that you're tied up with. Break with them. . . . I believe you're great. Dough means nothing. We'll tear up the contract, double your salary. You name it, you can have it. Just make the break." Cole refused.[52]

In September 1947, HUAC subpoenaed forty-three prominent Hollywood figures and demanded that they testify before the Committee. The ten writers and directors who refused to answer questions regarding possible Communist affiliations were voted in contempt by Congress in November, tried in federal court the following year, and sentenced to twelve months in jail. Hollywood liberals and leftists responded to HUAC's subpoenas by organizing the Committee for the First Amendment (CFA). Like actress

Marsha Hunt, many were "angry that headline-hunting Congressmen would use Hollywood and the motion pictures as a step to their own self-glorification." The group—which included Hunt, Robinson, Humphrey Bogart, Lauren Bacall, Katharine Hepburn, Danny Kaye, Judy Garland, Frank Sinatra, and Gene Kelly—denounced HUAC's actions, arguing that "any investigation into the political beliefs of the individual is contrary to the basic principles of our democracy." It was the Constitution, the group declared, and not the Hollywood Ten that they were defending.[53]

Using their celebrity to attract national attention, forty of the CFA's most prominent members chartered an airplane and flew to Washington, D.C., on October 26. Robinson could not make the trip because he was shooting Arthur Miller's *All My Sons*, but he joined CFA members that evening in a special ABC national radio broadcast that condemned HUAC and upheld the right to free speech. Hoping to prevent government interference in their industry, the producer-based Motion Picture Association of America (MPAA) initially backed the CFA, taking out ads in the *New York Times* and *Washington Post* criticizing HUAC and supporting the Hollywood Ten. "Tell the boys not to worry," MPAA president Eric Johnston reassured them a week earlier. "There'll never be a blacklist."[54]

A disastrous opening-day testimony by writer and militant Communist John Howard Lawson quickly turned public sympathy against the subpoenaed men. That afternoon, CFA members were shocked when MPAA president Johnston, sensing which way the political winds were blowing, appeared before HUAC and, while criticizing Congress for its unproven attacks on the industry, signaled a new spirit of cooperation (or capitulation, as CFA members thought) by welcoming any investigation that might expose Communist infiltration of Hollywood. Concerned about box-office retribution, Jack Warner pressured Bogart, the group's most visible member, to return to Hollywood the next day. Fearing his career was on the line, he did. Several days later, tough guy Bogie issued a public apology confessing that his trip to Washington "was ill-advised, even foolish," and declared, "I am not a Communist."[55]

The highly publicized hearings threatened the financial health of the movie industry by turning audiences against alleged Hollywood Reds. "For the first time in the history of the Committee," the FBI reported in November 1947, "they had enough big names to win over public opinion and the newspapers to the Committee's side." Gossip columnist and MPA leader Hedda

Hopper told the FBI that month of being flooded with letters from people who claimed they would not attend movies featuring actors cited for contempt of Congress. Several days later, an FBI informant in Chapel Hill, North Carolina, recounted how when a movie trailer of Katharine Hepburn's forthcoming film, *Song of Love*, was run at a local theater the audience booed and some shouted, "She is a Communist; that's one I won't see."[56]

Hepburn was not the only one to suffer. In December 1947, the FBI reported that box-office receipts had fallen off 20 percent as a result of the Washington hearings. Agents told Bureau chief Hoover that fear of box-office reprisals, not "any change of heart," led Hepburn, Bogart, and others to back off of their attacks on HUAC and involvement with the CFA.[57]

As public sentiment shifted so too did the attitudes of studio moguls. Had the studios maintained their initial resistance to the Committee, it is doubtful that HUAC would have achieved as much success. However, on December 3, 1947, nervous industry leaders, responding to pressure from New York financiers, issued the "Waldorf Statement" (named after the New York hotel that hosted their meeting). They condemned the actions of the Hollywood Ten and pledged they would not "knowingly employ a Communist or a member of any party or group which advocates the overthrow of the government of the United States by force or by illegal or unconstitutional methods." The blacklist was now official. When director George Stevens asked Mayer, "Are you taking this action for economic reasons or for patriotism," the studio head candidly replied, "the action was taken for economic reasons." Several exhibitors had already refused to book MGM films that featured his politically besmirched stars.[58]

Robinson appeared on the initial list of actors to be investigated by HUAC. Had he been called to testify in the first round of questioning, he told writer Victor Lasky, he probably would have been considered an "unfriendly witness" and included among the Hollywood Ten. He thought they had all been set up. Little did he realize that the FBI had closely monitored his activities for several years. Bureau reports listed all the dinners Robinson hosted for political causes between 1941 and 1945, the dates of every speech and rally in which he was involved, and even suggested that he and Gladys were "involved in Russian espionage activities." In May 1945, the FBI sent the White House a confidential memo naming Robinson as one of fifty movie stars accused of being a Communist or having Communist leanings. By the summer of 1947, secret informants told the FBI that Robinson was a member of the Communist Party and that Red leaders found his political views "to be very sound and mature." Their accusations led FBI agents to place his home under surveillance and record the license plate numbers of everyone who visited him.[59]

American Federation of Labor leader Matthew Woll was the first to openly accuse Robinson of having Communist ties. In a September 1946 magazine article, he insisted, "Hollywood today is the third largest Communist center in the United States" and listed Robinson as one of the most prominent fellow travelers, a charge that was reprinted in the rabidly anti-Communist *Hollywood Reporter*. An outraged Robinson sent letters to both

> ⁘ and unfounded" and charged Woll
> ⁙n him "by innuendo, weasel words
> ⁙, he wrote, was "trying to bludgeon
> ⁙merican citizens like me, away from
> ⁙nterests and activities."[60]
> ⁙t publicity generated by the HUAC
> ⁙n and box-office prospects. "How is
> ⁙terina wrote him in October 1947,
> ⁙s a Communist fellow traveler . . . in
> ⁙same month an Illinois brick manu-
> ⁙n one of the few actors he genuinely
> ⁙d his children and grandchildren "to
> ⁙ editors of the Catholic weekly *Ave*
> ⁙Robinson's films because attending

In spite of receiving venomous antisemitic letters that referred to him as "stinking Yiddish riff raff—from stinking European ghettoes" and promised not to rest "until you scum are driven out of the entertainment field," Robinson refused to curb his political activities. Instead, he grew more assertive in supporting controversial groups such as the Progressive Citizens of America and the Conference of Studio Unions. Accusations of Red affiliations increased when he campaigned in 1948 for Communist-backed Progressive Party presidential candidate Henry Wallace, whose platform called for ending the Cold War, ending segregation, and instituting universal health care for all Americans. An actor "is not a person apart from life," Robinson declared in 1949, "but a citizen who should participate actively in his government." Being a celebrity, he insisted, "shouldn't deprive a person of his democratic rights. He should have the same opportunities as anyone to state his views and defend them." His statements were admirable but naive.[62]

The Fall of Little Caesar

Robinson soon learned that speaking out for what he believed had a price. As Cold War hysteria grew more rampant in the late 1940s, so too did accusations of Communist infiltration in all areas of American life. Fear and paranoia reached new heights in 1949–1950 as the Soviet Union exploded its first atomic bomb, China fell to Mao Zedong, and Senator Joseph McCarthy announced that he had a long list of Communists working in the State Department. In the spring of 1949, much of the nation was fixated on the perjury trial of alleged Soviet spy Alger Hiss. Press attention shifted momentarily to the espionage trial of former Justice Department analyst Judith Coplon when FBI documents were read aloud accusing Robinson and Fredric March of being Communists. Robinson dismissed the charges as "character assassinations" that emanated from the "sick, diseased minds of people who rush to the press with indictments of good American citizens." Influential *Hollywood Reporter* publisher W. R. Wilkerson wondered whether there was any truth to the charges. Unless the actor was willing to testify under oath, Wilkerson told his readers, "his half-baked denial" meant "nothing in the eyes of the public that made him a big star." Robinson also came under attack that June from right-wing Christian Nationalist Crusade leader Gerald L. K. Smith. The notorious antisemite, whom Robinson had denounced as a bigot in 1945, told a gathering of 750 people that Robinson was "one of Stalin's main agents in Hollywood" and that he "should be put in a Federal penitentiary."[63]

Robinson's frequent clashes with Red-baiters and antisemites did not initially derail his career. In 1946, the actor appeared in two major features, *Scarlet Street* and *The Stranger*; in 1947 he starred in *The Red House*, and began shooting *All My Sons*, *Key Largo*, and *Night Has a Thousand Eyes* (the latter three films premiered, respectively, in March, July, and October 1948). Producers and studio heads were willing to sacrifice a handful of radical screenwriters in order to protect well-known stars. After all, people rarely attended a film because of the writer; they went to see Humphrey Bogart,

Katharine Hepburn, Edward Robinson, or Gene Kelly. Despite his distaste for Kelly's left politics, Louis B. Mayer refused to fire the outspoken MGM star because, as an FBI informant reported, doing so "would ruin the two pictures he has in the can starring Gene Kelly and his five million dollars would go down the drain."[64]

Robinson's fortunes were about to change. As angry fan letters poured into studio offices, industry leaders moved to placate audiences by pressuring stars to refrain from taking controversial political positions. Robinson never considered himself a radical so he never felt the need to stop speaking out. But repeated accusations associating the star with Communist groups made him a box-office risk. Offers for good parts, for any parts, began to dry up. The proverbial straw that broke the back of his career came in June 1950, when the three former FBI agents who authored *Red Channels: The Report of Communist Influence in Radio and Television* charged him, along with 150 other people, with belonging to a number of Communist fronts. Although no Red affiliation was ever proven, Robinson's reign as a major star was over. By December 1950, secret Informant T-17 told the FBI that Robinson "was unable to obtain parts in movies at this time because of his past Communist activity."[65]

Outraged by the smear campaign directed against him, Robinson spent the next three years of his life, and over $100,000 of his own money, trying to clear his name and resume his career. When a three-hour visit to the editors of *Red Channels* failed to change their minds, the feisty actor wrote to HUAC requesting an opportunity to testify about his participation in alleged Communist groups. His request was granted with one caveat: because Congress was in recess and Committee members were out of town campaigning for reelection, Robinson would be questioned by HUAC's investigative staff rather than by the full Committee.

On October 27, 1950, the actor appeared before the group in Washington, D.C., with a statement that listed all the organizations in which he participated, explained the rationale behind his political activities, and accounted for every donation he made from December 16, 1938, to December 15, 1949. During several hours of questioning by senior investigator Louis J. Russell, Robinson insisted that he had "at all times subscribed to and believed in the principles of democracy." As for his participation in U. S.-Russian groups, Robinson reminded Russell that at the time Russia was our ally and the gatherings at which he spoke included the likes of

Secretary of State Cordell Hull, Assistant Secretary of State Dean Acheson, Secretary of Treasury Henry Morgenthau, and numerous U.S. senators. When Russell asked "whether or not you have ever been a member of the Communist Party of the United States or of any other country," the actor immediately shot back, "I am not now, nor have I ever been a fellow traveler or a member of the Communist Party." He had "at all times opposed every form of totalitarianism" and had employed his talents as an actor "to stimulate, among the millions of people I have reached, greater devotion to the democratic way of life." Robinson concluded by pledging to "assist and defend the United States of America in any way within my power against any enemy, including Russia, her supporters and satellites."[66]

Hoping to leave no doubts about his loyalties, Robinson wrote J. Edgar Hoover several days later asking to present his case to the FBI. Hoover, who considered himself "a Robinson fan," had met the star on the MGM lot during the filming of *The Last Gangster* in 1937. Robinson told the FBI head he "would be more than pleased to confront any such accuser at any time and place you may designate." Hoover wrote back thanking him for bringing "your observations to my attention," but explained that he could do nothing to help. A similar request by Robinson to appear before the executive board of the Motion Picture Alliance "to clear his name of the Communist stigma" was also denied.[67]

When new allegations surfaced several weeks later, the embattled star returned to Washington to testify before a HUAC subcommittee. On December 21, 1950, Robinson once again swore that he had "never been a Communist sympathizer" nor was he "active in anything that smacked of communism." Asked if it was true he had once said that he did not care whether the Soviet Union took over the United States so long as he was allowed to keep his art collection, the flabbergasted actor replied, "That is a vicious lie." In a highly emotional closing statement, Robinson explained how "my good name and my Americanism" had been "hurt by a lot of these vicious charges, and the repetition of them in a lot of irresponsible publications." He voluntarily traveled to Washington because HUAC was the "only tribunal we have in the United States where an American citizen can come and ask for this kind of relief. . . . if you find me innocent, I would like to ask that you give these facts to the American people."[68]

Choking with emotion, Robinson ended with a Patrick Henry–like appeal: "Either snap my neck or set me free. If you snap my neck I will still say I believe in America." When the Committee hesitated to choose, lead investigator Russell came to Robinson's defense, explaining that he had conducted a thorough investigation of Communists in Hollywood in 1945 and the actor's name did not appear on any document linking him to the Party.[69]

News of Little Caesar's testimony and his denial of any Communist affiliation were widely reported in the national press. "Now that Eddie Robinson has been completely cleared of those Communist charges by Uncle Sam, himself," gossip columnist Louella Parsons wrote on December 26, "it's time that all the whispering stopped." Rumors of his Red affiliation were so widespread, she added, that they were "beginning to affect his career." On January 10, 1951, HUAC released a report clearing Robinson "of ever having engaged in pro-Communist activities or any other activities against the interests of the United States." Anxious to get back to work, the actor sent copies of his testimony to Samuel Goldwyn, Louis B. Mayer, Harry and Jack Warner, Darryl Zanuck, Joseph Schenck, and Howard Hughes. Insisting he never believed Robinson was "even one-thousandth percent Communistic," the conservative Zanuck congratulated him for testifying and suggested that the actor had made a "very stupid series of mistakes" by joining organizations that contained many "fellow travelers."[70]

Chances for a quick resumption of Robinson's career were crushed when HUAC member Donald Jackson (R-CA), who hoped to tarnish all of Hollywood's Democratic activists, denied that the Committee had cleared his constituent. After receiving complaints by American Legion investigators who were "disturbed over the apparent 'whitewash' given" to Robinson, Jackson told the press that the actor had been allowed to make self-serving statements without the Committee calling witnesses "who claimed to have evidence of his alleged Red affiliations." Ready for further battle, Robinson wrote back to HUAC chairman John Wood asking for a quick hearing "because every day that it is postponed only adds further damage to my name and reputation."[71]

Not only was Robinson denied a speedy hearing, but the national furor over his case sparked a new round of HUAC investigations. Relishing the publicity and prospects for greater funding, the Committee subpoenaed John Garfield, Anne Revere, José Ferrer, and comedian Abe Burrows in March 1951. But Robinson would not be called for another thirteen months. In the meantime, his career ground to a halt. No studio was willing to take the chance of offering the politically tainted actor a starring role. "Eddie's hotter than a two-buck pistol," one producer told a friend. "It costs at least a million to make a picture. I'm not interested in having my pictures boycotted." Except for "a single week's work in a Ben Hecht production in '51," one magazine observed in December 1952, "Robinson hasn't made a picture since he starred in *House of Strangers* in '49." Actually, he did make one film, *My Daughter Joy*, which was shot in England and released as a Columbia B-list film in 1950. This was quite a comedown for a man who just a few years before had been one of the industry's most highly paid stars. A distraught Robinson appealed to Screen Actors Guild president Ronald Reagan for assistance, but the SAG officer and FBI informant, whom Robinson had alienated during Hollywood's contentious postwar labor battles, refused to help him.[72]

Eddie's problems were compounded by family difficulties during the late 1940s and early 1950s. Gladys suffered yet another series of breakdowns and was taken to a sanitarium under restraint and given electroshock treatments. After her release, she continued to be plagued by paranoid episodes and, in early 1952, demanded a divorce from Robinson, whom she accused in widely reported press accounts of plotting against her. Worse yet, Gladys was traveling to Europe and spending extravagant amounts of money on hotels and clothing despite the fact that her husband was no longer working—this on top of the mounting medicals bills to pay for her treatments. Eddie's troubles also extended to his son Manny, who was constantly in trouble with police and in the courts, where he appeared on charges of disturbing the peace, passing bad checks, drunk driving, theft, and armed robbery.

Robinson was not entirely blameless for the decline of his family life. He simply did not know how to cope with his troubled wife or son. He had never been in a close relationship with a woman, let alone one who suffered from mental problems, until he met Gladys at the age of thirty-one. He now responded to their constant fighting by moving into a separate bedroom. Despite sending Manny to psychiatrists and private schools, Robinson proved equally incapable of helping his son. Unable to cope, the actor spent his days at home reading, painting, or showing guests his art collection.[73]

Years of battling family problems and unnamed accusers in the Kafkaesque world created by HUAC finally took its toll as Robinson sank into a severe depression. "Please Eddie get hold of yourself," William Morris agent

Bert Allenberg wrote in March 1952. "I know you are human and entitled to moments of weakness and depression and God knows you have been strong and courageous beyond belief during this terrible period and you do have dear good friends who are loyal . . . and you will be on top again higher than ever before so have faith and confidence in yourself just as I have for you." Several weeks later, Allenberg again implored his client not "to go to pieces." This was a difficult request for Robinson to honor. The public questioning of his loyalty was so intense that the State Department refused to renew his passport in 1952 until conservative Los Angeles Congressman Sam Yorty intervened on his behalf.[74]

As the doomed mobster Cesare "Rico" Bandello asked, "Mother of Mercy, is this the end of Rico?" Almost but not quite. By spring 1952, Robinson observed, "McCarthyism was burgeoning; the cold war was in every headline; anti-communism was in high fashion. . . . All I had to do to clear myself of all these charges, new and old, was to admit publicly and in print that I was a dupe." But he refused to make any statement that portrayed him as "a fool who out of brainlessness and an overzealous consideration for mankind had been blindly led into organizations that wished to destroy America." With producers afraid to hire him, Robinson sought to clear his name by returning to the theater in September 1951 to star in Sidney Kingsley's anti-Communist play *Darkness at Noon*. The actor took the part of Rubashov, the diehard Bolshevik who comes to realize the evil nature of the Revolution. He toured with the production until it closed in Cincinnati on April 26, 1952.[75]

Despite his highly praised work in the anti-Bolshevik play, Robinson was still unable to sign on to any significant film project. Four days after *Darkness* closed, the desperate and despondent star traveled to Washington, D.C., to testify before HUAC for a third time. In a hoarse voice, the actor widely regarded as one of the brightest minds in Hollywood finally told Committee members what they wanted to hear: "I was duped and used." Insisting that he had "always been a liberal Democrat" who fought to "help underprivileged or oppressed people," a repentant Robinson confessed he had slowly come "to realize that persons I thought were sincere were Communists" and that "some organizations which I permitted to use my name were, in fact, Communist fronts." He had been consistently lied to. "Not one of the Communists who sought my help or requested permission to use my name ever told me that he or she was a member of the Communist Party." He had been a fool. "I am glad for the sake of myself and the Nation, that they have been exposed by your committee."[76]

During the course of several grueling hours of questioning, Robinson named no names but he did repudiate the progressive organizations to which he had belonged in the 1930s and 1940s. When asked if he was now "a little gun shy" about joining political organizations, he replied in a sadly defeated manner, "Oh, yes. There ain't no room for both of us [him and HUAC] in this town—one of us has got to go, and it was me." As the questioning came to a close, Robinson rallied his spirits one last time to ask his chief nemesis, Representative Donald Jackson, whether he thought the actor had ever been disloyal to his country. "I personally do not believe you were a member of the Communist Party," Jackson replied, but the "activities in which you have engaged have, to some extent and in some degree in the past lent aid and comfort to the international Communist conspiracy." The Committee's chair Francis E. Walter claimed it was beyond HUAC's purview to exonerate anyone, but he told an anxious Robinson that they "never had any evidence presented to indicate that you were anything more than a very choice sucker. I think you are No. 1 on every sucker list in the country."[77]

Walter's characterization of Robinson as the nation's "No. 1 sucker" made newspaper headlines throughout the country. "ROBINSON SAYS HE WAS DUPED BY REDS," blared one daily; "EGR CALLED 'SUCKER' FOR RED FRONTS" screamed another headline. Desperate to salvage his career, the actor continued his ritual of rehabilitation through humiliation by publishing an article in the October 1952 issue of the *American Legion Magazine* entitled "How the Reds Made a Sucker Out of Me." Robinson told readers that while he had "never paid much attention to communism in the past," he now knew how they went about duping loyal Americans. "They do not reveal themselves as communists," but pose "as fine American citizens who are for 'Peace,' or 'decent working conditions,' or 'against intolerance.'" These were lies; their real aim was "world domination, oppression and slavery for the working people and the minorities they profess to love." The contrite actor ended by swearing, "I am not a communist, I have never been, I never will be—*I am an American*."[78]

Neither his article nor his HUAC testimony succeeded in clearing his name or restoring his career. "Nobody would dare touch the sucker," he lamented. The former star was forced to enter what he called "the 'B' picture phase of my career as a movie star—or a former movie star . . . or has been." During the next several years, the only offers he received were minor roles, at greatly reduced pay, in minor films such as *Actors & Sin* (1952), *Vice Squad* (1953), *The Big Leaguer* (1953), *The Glass Web* (1953), *Black Tuesday* (1954), and *The Violent Men* (1955). Movies he would have immediately turned down in the past, he now did "for the money and something to do, my own self-esteem decreasing by the hour."[79]

Robinson was forced into one last humiliating round of testifying before HUAC when it was revealed in January 1954 that he had loaned $300 to Louis Russell, the Committee's chief investigator. On July 11, 1953, Russell wrote the embattled star explaining there had been complications after the recent birth of his child that "required specialists and expensive care." Knowing "of your desire to assist persons in emergency cases," the HUAC investigator begged Robinson to lend him $600. Ever the soft touch, Eddie sent $300. "I wish I could loan you the full amount you need," he wrote, "but my financial condition does not permit. I hope this will be of help to you." News of the loan leaked out and on January 25, 1954, Robinson once again testified before HUAC. Although he acquitted himself of any wrongdoing, another appearance before HUAC did little to restore public or studio confidence in the actor.[80]

Ironically, Robinson was restored to semi-respectability in 1956 when Cecil B. DeMille, one of Hollywood's most prominent anti-Communists, offered him a plum role in *The Ten Commandments* as the Hebrew informer Dathan. When told that Robinson was "unacceptable" for any major film, DeMille, as Robinson tells it, "wanted to know why, coldly reviewed the matter, felt that I had been done an injustice, and told his people to offer me the part." DeMille, he insisted, "restored my self-respect."[81]

DeMille may have revived the actor's self-respect but not his former career. Given his tainted political past and the fact that HUAC never officially cleared him, industry leaders still considered him a box-office risk. Yet like Charlie Chaplin, there were also a variety of nonpolitical reasons that hastened Robinson's demise. Age proved especially important in the new postwar Hollywood. Frightened by declining box-office receipts in the face of television's rise, studios turned to new genres and younger stars such as Kirk Douglas, Burt Lancaster, and Marlon Brando. Not surprisingly, sixty-year-old actors such as Robinson found it difficult to get leading roles.

Parts may disappear but not an actor's ego. Like Robinson, many aging performers believed they were still stars, if only the right role would come their way. Yet, even if such a role were to come along, it is unlikely producers would have given it to a politically suspect actor who might damage a movie's potential box office.

After making *The Ten Commandments*, Robinson waited almost three years before being offered another significant part, this time in Frank Capra's *A Hole in the Head* (1959). With movie offers scarce, he accepted "Special Guest Star" roles on television shows, an honorific billing he noted without illusion that "means you get a small salary but large billing, and nobody pays the slightest attention to it. It's what we used to call baloney."[82] Robinson continued making movies until his death in 1973, and even experienced a mild resurgence in the 1960s. Ironically, his best role of the era was as Lancey Howard, the seemingly washed-up gambler, in *The Cincinnati Kid* (1965), a film cowritten by blacklisted writer Ring Lardner Jr. Appearing in nineteen movies between 1960 and 1973, Robinson was under no illusion about his box-office prominence. Tellingly, his autobiography, published after his death in 1973, ends with his getting a part in *The Ten Commandments*. By 1956, it was clear to him that his life as a major star was over. He was now just another actor, and a minor one at that.

IF YOU LIVE LONG ENOUGH

By the mid-1960s, the HUAC hearings and Hollywood Red Scare were forgotten by most Americans, but not by Robinson. He "still fussed and fumed over those terrible days," wrote co-biographer and friend Leonard Spigelgass. Others proved less concerned with his political past and Robinson began receiving the kind of public adulation he had not experienced since the early 1940s. In March 1969, California State Senator Ralph Dills introduced a resolution honoring his career and life. That same month, Republican Governor Ronald Reagan and Senator George Murphy joined the Masquer's Club tribute to their former colleague. In November, Screen Actors Guild president Charlton Heston presented Robinson with its annual award in recognition of his pioneering work in organizing the union, his service during World War II, and his "outstanding achievement in fostering the finest ideals of the acting profession."[83]

On January 11, 1973, the ailing actor received word of what he considered to be his greatest honor. In recognition of his fiftieth year in the movies, the Board of Governors of the Academy of Motion Picture Arts and Sciences voted to give him an honorary Oscar at the upcoming awards ceremony. The inscription read, "To Edward G. Robinson, who achieved greatness as a player, a patron of the arts, and a dedicated citizen. . . . In sum, a Renaissance Man. From his friends in the industry he loves." Tragically, he never lived to receive his award. On January 26, the former Emanuel Goldenberg died of cancer at Cedar Sinai Hospital in Los Angeles. Over 1,500 friends attended his funeral ceremony at Temple Israel, and another 500 people crowded outside to pay their last respects. In October 2000, Little Caesar received his final tribute when the United States Post Office unveiled its Edward G. Robinson postage stamp, the sixth in its Legends of Hollywood series.[84]

POLITICAL LEGACIES

If Eddie Robinson's story were made into a movie, it would be filled with pathos. The actor who prided himself on being a true American, above all else, was indelibly scarred by the events of the late 1940s and 1950s. "I may have taken money under false pretenses in my own business, and I may not have been as good a husband or father or friend as I should have been," he confessed at his December 21, 1950, HUAC hearing, "but I know my Americanism is unblemished and fine and wonderful." But it was deeply blemished by the anti-Red campaign. Worse yet, Robinson was so burned by his experiences with HUAC that he retreated from virtually all political activity. Toward the end of 1950, he asked groups he had long been associated with "to immediately discontinue the usage of my name in connection with your organization or any of its actions." He did not even want to be on their mailing list.[85]

The worst loss Robinson suffered was that of his self-respect. He had done nothing wrong—nothing more than anyone committed to democracy would have done. Nevertheless, in order to earn a living he demeaned himself by kowtowing to HUAC. Looking back on his testimony two decades later, Robinson wrote with evident anguish that he knew in 1950 the Committee wanted him to confess that he had been "a dupe, a sucker, a fool, an idiot . . . an unsuspecting agent of the Communist conspiracy. I didn't say it because I didn't believe it." But by 1952, "[my] defenses were down and

I said it. My judgment was warped and I said it. My heart was sick and I said it." The pain of these confessions never subsided. Leonard Spigelgass, co-author of Robinson's 1973 autobiography, tells how in recounting these events the actor talked "*so* rapidly, *so* passionately, that I had extreme difficulty putting it down. The tears were streaming down his cheeks; but his voice was steady, and I have no doubt that the period in which he was accused of disloyalty was still weighing heavily on him and that he was seeking to make it meaningful."[86]

Robinson saw himself as a man trapped with few choices. But he did have more options than most other blacklisted or graylisted stars. Ego, as well as political conviction, got in his way. He could have returned to Broadway where the effects of Red-baiting were far less pronounced than in Hollywood; but that would mean admitting his days as a movie star were over. He could have sold his art, but that would have been like selling a child. He could have moved out of Beverly Hills, but that too would be admitting that his enemies had defeated him. He naively believed that his faith in the Bill of Rights would save him. It did not. As his family life and career fell apart, he caved in.

Edward G. Robinson's story is more than just the sad tale of a decent man caught in a web of events beyond his control. In many ways, his persecution and political retreat had a far more devastating effect on the film community than that of the Hollywood Ten. Politically aware actors knew that most of the Ten were Communist Party members. But Robinson was no radical, let alone a Red. When queried about his political activity during the 1930s and 1940s, Betty Warner Sheinbaum (Harry Warner's daughter and friend of young Communists Maurice Rapf and Budd Schulberg) exclaimed, "Eddie Robinson? He wasn't political!" She explained that he "was not a spokesman or party member," characteristics radicals of the time associated with being political. "He was a very sweet man, very kind and gentle and gentlemanly. He was off beat in that he was primarily interested in painting, literature and artists."[87]

Robinson's downfall sent an even greater chill throughout the industry than the incarceration of the Hollywood Ten. Actors, directors, writers, and producers did not condone HUAC's actions, but they understood why the Committee pursued such well-known radicals. Robinson was quite another case. If the government could drive a left-liberal like Eddie out of the business, a man whom even anti-Communists like Ronald Reagan called "one of the warmest-hearted, truly kind people in the world," then they could go after anyone. And if a star of Robinson's magnitude could not survive such attacks, was anyone safe? A whole generation of Hollywood activists took note of his fate and, as Lauren Bacall noted, "relinquished their political opinions or at least stopped voicing them" in order to protect their families, their jobs, and their lives. They were not being overly cautious. As late as July 1961, federal judge Edward Tamm refused to order Hollywood studios to lift their ban against hiring actors and writers suspected of being Communists. Two months later, Jack Warner told delegates to the American Legion's national convention that there were no jobs for Communists, fellow travelers, or Fifth Amendment–takers at Warners.[88]

The cost of the era's right-wing activism needs to be measured not just in terms of the damage it did to individuals, but in the way it reshaped American politics by halting the emergence of Hollywood as a progressive force in national life. From Roosevelt's victory in 1932 until the presidential elections of 1948, left activists such as Robinson, Melvyn Douglas, Myrna Loy, Olivia de Havilland, and Lena Horne played an important role in publicizing progressive causes and electing Democratic candidates. As George Pepper, executive director of the Hollywood Democratic Committee, wrote White House aide David Niles in July 1945, "We in Hollywood have a tremendous reservoir of talent which, in my opinion, has never been utilized to its full capacity. That the opposition realizes the potential of this talent is proven by their constant attempts to smash the democratic forces in Hollywood." After the war, movie stars used their celebrity to heighten support for the United Nations, civil rights legislation, and the emerging nuclear freeze movement. But by 1953, Hollywood was no longer the progressive force it had been over the past two decades.[89]

Robinson's story also helps illuminate the long-standing myth of "liberal" Hollywood. Like any myth, this one contains elements of truth. Individual actors, writers, directors, and producers were in the vanguard of liberal and radical activities in the 1930s and early 1940s. However, the studios that constituted the core of the movie industry had (with the exception of Warner Bros.) repeatedly proven themselves politically conservative and unwilling to risk profits to promote liberal causes. Nevertheless, it was the stars' politics, not that of their employers, that made "Hollywood" synonymous with "liberalism," an association that was fixed in the popular imagination by years of highly publicized anti-Communist investigations. Activists who attacked Hitler without simultaneously attacking Stalin were vilified by conservative critics as either Communists, Communist dupes, or, at best, naive liberal dupes. By the early 1950s, "liberal Hollywood" was seen by many citizens as a danger to American security, a sin many liberals paid for by being blacklisted.

At the same time that Hollywood liberals and leftists went underground, conservative movie stars George Murphy and Ronald Reagan were busily laying the groundwork for their emergence as political stars in the 1960s. Both men built their political careers by portraying themselves as staunch Cold Warriors who battled threats posed by the Soviet Union and its loyal— or duped—fellow travelers. By 1947, Murphy was denouncing the left and calling for a new kind of movie industry politics. "For too long a time," he told the Hollywood Republican Committee (which he chaired), "a vociferous minority has misled the public at large to believe the majority of Hollywood actors and actresses are radicals, crackpots, or at least New Deal Democrats. We know this is not the case. We believe it is time for Republicans in the entertainment world to take a militant stand."[90]

During the next two decades, he and Reagan did just that by speaking to Republican groups throughout the country, taking leadership positions in state party politics, and, in the 1960s, successfully running, respectively, for U.S. senator and governor of California. Never forgetting the experiences of the late 1940s and early 1950s, the two anti-Communists continually played the Red card and attacked liberals for underestimating the dangers posed by Soviet enemies. As late as 1979, Murphy was still telling the press that he "would be surprised if the Communists weren't infiltrating it [Hollywood] today."[91]

A chill political wind swept over Hollywood in the wake of HUAC and McCarthyism, and it did not subside until after John F. Kennedy's election in 1960. Yet even then, the scars and fears of the 1950s remained imprinted on the memories of many stars. As late as 2002, actress Lee Grant froze and went into a near trance when asked about her experiences with HUAC. When large numbers of liberal and left movie activists once again took public positions on contemporary political events during the early 1960s, they generally focused on domestic concerns such as civil rights and not on foreign affairs. Why? Because domestic issues were the only ones they could speak out on without immediately being labeled as Communists.[92]

When Eddie Robinson first read the script for *Little Caesar*, he realized it was more than just a gangster story; it was like reading a Greek tragedy.

Cesare "Rico" Bandello, Robinson reflected years later, was a "man who defies society, and in the end is mowed down by the gods and society, and doesn't even know what happened. . . . In his own mind, he thought he was doing the right thing, and that's the way you color him."[93] Robinson could have been talking about his own life.

HOLLYWOOD AND THE CONSERVATIVE REVOLUTION: GEORGE MURPHY AND RONALD REAGAN

When Hollywood actors George Murphy and Ronald Reagan announced their intentions to run, respectively, for California senator in 1964 and governor in 1966, political pundits greeted their candidacies with derision. Las Vegas bookies were so certain of Murphy's defeat that they made him a twenty-to-one long shot. Subsequent upset victories did little to quell contempt inside and outside the movie industry for these seemingly rank political amateurs. Asked in 1968 what he thought of the idea of Ronald Reagan as president, studio head Jack Warner quipped, "No. Jimmy Stewart for President, Ronald Reagan for his best friend."[1]

As history shows, their detractors were wrong. Murphy and Reagan proved far more politically savvy than they were given credit for. Each combined his experience as an actor with twenty years of work with Republican groups to design innovative campaign strategies that propelled them into office in the mid-1960s and laid the groundwork for the conservative revolution of the

1980s. While neither man could claim to be the ideological brains behind the conservative movement, they accomplished what more experienced politicians such as Barry Goldwater could not: they figured out how to sell conservatism to a wide range of skeptical voters. By making conservatism palatable, Murphy and Reagan made the conservative revolution possible.

Murphy and Reagan opened the doors for yet another kind of Hollywood politics, movement politics. Practiced by those on the right as well as on the left, movement politics are less a top-down phenomenon than a bottom-up grassroots mass movement embraced by diverse coalitions of groups and individuals who share a common ideology and determination to bring radical changes to the nation's political, social, and economic systems. Movement politics demanded a more intense commitment than any other form of political engagement. The most dedicated movement activists were willing to work for ten, twenty, or even thirty years to turn their ideas into national policy. For Murphy, Reagan, and the millions of Californians who voted for them, the goal was not simply to win an election but to alter the very foundations of American government by overturning the most important liberal achievement of the twentieth century, the New Deal state.

During the early 1960s, the most powerful impetus for conservatism did not come from Washington, D.C., or Arizona, but from Hollywood and Southern California, and it was led by a pair of relative political unknowns. George Murphy and Ronald Reagan provided the conservative movement with a new kind of leadership, one better equipped for the new age of television in which a candidate's image was as important as his or her ideas. Conservatives admired Goldwater, but his prickly personality and image as a man who might start a nuclear war frightened millions of potential voters. Politics was becoming a world of performance, and politicians who knew how to sell themselves in an appealing fashion gained an important edge over their opponents. Murphy and Reagan were among the first Hollywood figures to realize how television had changed electoral life. Relying on the medium to an unprecedented extent, they designed campaigns that drew upon their cinematic image as "good guys" and used their skills as actors to sell conservative ideas to a mass public. By reshaping the political uses of media, the two men reshaped American politics for the next five decades.

Ronald Reagan is generally considered the man who brought Hollywood, politics, and sound bites into the television age. But the lesser-known

Murphy was the true pioneer. During the 1920s and 1930s, Louis B. Mayer taught Republicans how to use radio and movie stars to their advantage. Murphy, who served as a delegate to three Republican conventions and as chairman of the California GOP in 1953–1954, took the Hollywood–Washington nexus a step further by instructing presidential candidates Thomas Dewey and Dwight Eisenhower on how to use television to great effect. He then employed that knowledge to develop what would later be known as the "Reagan strategy"—winning over independents and blue-collar Democrats—to effect the upset election of 1964: defeating Pierre Salinger for a seat in the U.S. Senate. Murphy was the trailblazer, but Reagan proved a far more skilled politician. A consummate communicator, he showed how a few simple ideas could achieve powerful force when said in a sincere and trustworthy manner. Those skills proved powerful enough to get him elected as governor of California and then as president of the United States.

The election of these two men also signaled a new American attitude toward celebrity. The public was beginning to concede that actors had the right to take themselves seriously as politicians. Reagan demonstrated how a candidate's image and ability to communicate proved of far greater importance to voters than his or her sheer brilliance. In July 2010, the *New York Times* reported that only 5 percent of those polled believed that intelligence was the most important quality in a presidential candidate.[2]

The focal point of this chapter is not their political careers, but how Murphy and Reagan came to have those careers. Both entered Hollywood in the 1930s as liberal Democrats and then shifted to the right as they came to see the New Deal and its postwar legacy of big government as threatening fundamental American values. During the 1940s and 1950s, they used their fame, charm, and communication skills to help build a grassroots conservative constituency by articulating an ideological agenda that called for returning power to local and state governments, reducing taxes, and waging war against all foes of American security.

Once Murphy and Reagan were elected they ceased being movie stars and became politicians. Yet, what made them want to move from the screen to the statehouse? How did two former Democrats come to envision a very different kind of America than Roosevelt had created? By helping pave the way for a conservative revolution that challenged the New Deal state, the Hollywood right, led by Murphy and Reagan, had a far greater impact in shaping the course of postwar politics than the more numerous and visible Hollywood left.

The Road to Hollywood

Like Charlie Chaplin and Louis B. Mayer, George Lloyd Murphy and Ronald Wilson Reagan traveled a rough road to Hollywood. Murphy, or "Murph" to his friends, initially grew up in a more privileged household than Reagan, "Ronnie" to his friends and "Dutch" to his intimates. Born on July 4, 1902 in New Haven, Connecticut, to Michael and Nora Murphy, George's father was a famous track coach at Yale who went on to train the U.S. Olympic track team in 1912. Like many Irish Catholics, the Murphys were devoted Democrats, the party young George favored until 1939. His maternal grandfather had been a Democratic member of the Michigan State Assembly, and during the summers powerful Boston politicos such as John "Honey Fitz" Fitzgerald (grandfather to the Kennedy clan) visited Michael Murphy at his home in Westboro, Massachusetts. After moving to Philadelphia in 1904, the famed trainer remained equally popular with local Democrats who often sought his endorsement.[3]

The Murphy fortunes took a downward turn when Michael died in 1913. Nora moved the family back to New Haven and then two years later to Detroit, where they lived with her parents in the heavily Irish Corktown neighborhood. Murphy eventually received an athletic scholarship to attend the Peddie Institute in New Jersey and then the Pawling School in New York, where he became good friends with future actor Robert Montgomery. George's talents soon took him to Yale, where he studied engineering for two years before dropping out. With money scarce, he spent summers working a number of tough but well-paying jobs: on an automobile assembly line in Detroit, as a coal miner in Pennsylvania, checking liquor deliveries for bootleggers, as a bouncer in a sleazy Newark nightclub, and, after dropping out of Yale, as a real estate salesman, auto mechanic, and runner for a New York brokerage house.

Murphy's prospects changed when he ran into his old Detroit girlfriend Julie Henkel, who had moved to New York to pursue her dream of becoming a professional dancer. Declining an offer to join his friend's brokerage house, the 5' 11," 175-pound Murphy started dancing professionally with Julie. The couple was talented enough to get bookings on the nightclub circuit and sufficiently in love to get married on December 28, 1926. Their big break came in 1929, when they replaced the leads in the long-running Broadway musical hit *Hold Everything*. Over the next few years, they appeared in three more Broadway shows and numerous nightclubs.

George's career changed in 1934, when Samuel Goldwyn signed him to play the second male lead to Eddie Cantor in *Kid Millions*. When Columbia Pictures offered him a one-year contract at a staggering $750-a-week salary, Julie retired from dancing and the couple moved to Los Angeles. Over the next two years, he made four films but never got a chance to show off his dancing skills. That would soon change. Louis B. Mayer met Murphy at a luncheon for California Lieutenant Governor George Hatfield and was so impressed that he signed the amiable actor to an MGM contract, the beginning of a twenty-two-year-long association. Shortly afterward, the mogul lent him to Universal to appear in his musical breakout role in *Top of the Town* (1937). Over the next five years, Murphy made fourteen films, including *Little Miss Broadway* (1938) with Shirley Temple and *Little Nellie Kelly* (1940) with Judy Garland. But he never had a role that turned him into box-office gold. For the rest of his career he was usually cast as the amiable best friend. Although not a star, Murphy's "good guy" persona, on and off the screen, proved a great advantage in his future political career.

Like Murphy, Ronald Reagan's path to Hollywood was both exciting and frustrating. On February 6, 1911, John and Nelle Reagan welcomed the arrival of their second son, Ronald Wilson Reagan. John, a first-generation Irishman and staunch liberal Democrat, was a ne'er-do-well shoe salesman. A serious drinking problem prevented him from holding any job too long, a fact young Ronnie learned when he discovered his father passed out dead-drunk on the porch. "Our family didn't exactly come from the wrong side of the tracks," he reminisced years later, "but we were certainly always within sound of the train whistles."[4] By the time Reagan was nine and his brother John Neil "Moon" Reagan was eleven, the family had moved from Tampico, Illinois, to several small Midwestern towns before settling in Dixon, Illinois, which remained his hometown until he was twenty-one. Nelle Wilson Reagan was responsible for bringing stability and culture into the family's life. A frustrated actress who loved organizing dramatic readings, she got her younger son interested in drama.

In the fall of 1928, Reagan received a scholarship to nearby Eureka College, a small Christian institution with 250 students. Over the next four years, he plunged into the life of the school, playing football and acting in several productions. He also proved an effective political leader. When a budget crisis led the college's new president to order drastic cutbacks in courses and faculty, students went on strike and the freshman class elected Reagan as its representative. The experience helped shape his attitude toward organized protest. After several months, the striking students succeeded in reversing the cuts and forcing the president to resign. Neither threats nor violence were needed. "Our policy of polite resistance," he recollected, "brought victory."[5]

By his senior year, Reagan knew he wanted to be in show business but with New York and Hollywood so far away, he decided to start in radio. As a young man, he listened to Franklin Roosevelt's "fireside chats" and was impressed by the way the president spoke in a calm, reassuring fashion. He used that knowledge when he went to work as a sportscaster in Iowa. Since the local station could not afford to send him to football and baseball games, Reagan used telegraph reports to create vivid play-by-play narratives. His big break came when a friend arranged for a screen test at Warner Bros. while Reagan was in Los Angeles covering the Chicago Cubs' spring training camp. When he returned to Des Moines, the sportscaster was greeted by a telegram: Warners offered him a seven-year contract starting at $200 a week.

Packing his Lafayette convertible coupe, Reagan set off for Los Angeles and began work at the studio on June 1, 1937. He debuted several weeks later in *Love Is in the Air* (1937). By the end of 1939, columnist Louella Parsons heralded the handsome 6' 1," 175-pound actor as "a great personality" who "is being rapidly groomed by Warners for stardom." His first big role came in 1940 when he played George Gipp in *Knute Rockne, All-American.* Reagan also made society-page headlines when he married actress Jane Wyman in January 1940; a year later, he was making $2,000 a week ($29,100 in 2009 dollars) and living in the Hollywood Hills. After receiving rave reviews in *King's Row* in 1942, the young actor was poised to become a major star.[6]

Reagan's career was put on hold when the army reserve officer was called to active duty in April 1942. Poor eyesight prevented him from being shipped abroad, so he was sent to "Fort Roach" (the Hal Roach studios) in Culver City to work with the Army Air Force's new Motion Picture Unit. In September 1945, Reagan was discharged from the army and ready to resume his career. However, he soon discovered that the Hollywood he returned to was not the same place he had left. Much to his chagrin, he heard rumors that Communists were trying to infiltrate industry unions and liberal organizations. Captain Reagan readied himself to fight a new enemy.[7]

To understand how and why Reagan's and Murphy's politics changed, we need to backtrack and examine how events of the 1930s and 1940s led both men to convert from New Deal Democrats to conservative Republicans.

CONVERSION EXPERIENCES AND THE RISE OF THE HOLLYWOOD RIGHT

In early 1939, as Adolf Hitler prepared for war, Murphy and Reagan prepared for their respective roles in *Risky Business* and *Hell's Kitchen*. Although the two actors did not know each other well, their lives grew increasingly intertwined over the next decade as a series of events led both liberal Democrats to become conservative Republicans. By the early 1950s, as their film careers faded, they became part of an emerging conservative movement that sought to preserve American security by fighting Communism and what they perceived as the overreaching activities of the federal government. Their repeated battles with alleged Reds during this era laid the foundation for what Murphy would later refer to as the "evil conspiracy" and Reagan as the "Evil Empire."[8]

A number of factors explain Murphy's political transformation. When he arrived in 1936, MGM was the bastion of Hollywood Republicanism and the charming Irishman caught the eye of Louis Mayer and Ida Koverman, political tutor to the studio's young stars. Mayer and Koverman shared an antipathy to Communism, taxes, and the New Deal with their new protégé. At the time, observed writer Leo Rosten, MGM was filled with "right-wing actors, writers, [and] directors" who hated Roosevelt and identified "themselves with an anti–New Deal or conservative position." Liberal Democrat Murphy found himself talking politics over lunch with conservatives such as Robert Taylor, Conrad Nagel, Jeanette MacDonald, and Robert Montgomery, his old high-school friend from Pawling. He also enjoyed long conversations with his golf partner Adolphe Menjou, a man so reactionary, quipped Edward G. Robinson, that he "never forgave King John for signing the Magna Carta." Murphy's rightward drift was further hastened by his friendship with FBI head J. Edgar Hoover (who told him that Communists were penetrating Hollywood) and by listening to the many speakers Mayer brought to MGM, most of whom accused the New Deal of creating socialism through tax policies and federal programs that competed with private industry.[9]

As Murphy grew closer to Koverman, who "nurtured, cajoled and . . . taught him all she knew," he became increasingly disenchanted with the "excesses of the New Deal." Roosevelt's attempt to subvert constitutional checks and balances by "packing" the Supreme Court proved especially troubling. Although the president failed, Murphy wondered if his MGM colleagues were right. Perhaps FDR's New Deal liberalism had gone too far. In late 1939, George Murphy switched his registration from Democrat to Republican. A conversation with Supreme Court Justice and FDR confidant Frank Murphy the following year convinced him that he had made the right decision. Justice Murphy, an old family friend from Detroit who served as FDR's attorney general before joining the court, confirmed his fears that powerful forces were "seeking to promote Socialism or some other form of centralized government."[10]

Murphy was not alone in believing the New Deal had gone too far. As most of Hollywood was shifting leftward in the late 1930s, the nation's citizens were moving in a more conservative direction. When asked in an October 1939 Gallup poll whether they would like to see the Roosevelt administration be more liberal or conservative over the next two years, 72 percent responded "more conservative." Hollywood activists, it seemed, were far to the left of public opinion, a perception that began in the 1930s and remained implanted in the public's mind to the present.[11]

With his film career stuck in second-lead roles, Murphy accepted a position as an officer in the Screen Actors Guild (SAG). He did so at a difficult moment in the organization's history. An accomplished boxer as well as dancer, Murphy proved his toughness in September 1937, when he fought off efforts by the mob-controlled Hollywood branch of the International Alliance of Theatrical Stage Employees Union (IATSE) to muscle in on SAG's jurisdiction over actors. Murphy was warned that his children would have acid thrown in their faces if he did not back off. Refusing to be intimidated, he beat back Chicago mobster Frank Nitti's henchmen. The guild's members rewarded the tough guy by electing him to their executive board in 1939, electing him as first vice-president between 1940 and 1944, and electing him president from 1944 to 1946.[12]

Murphy's greatest assets were his charm and ability to confront any crisis with a calm "can-do" attitude. Once he switched political allegiances, he used those qualities to become an important player in the Republican Party and in movie industry politics. Murphy's greatest contributions were organizational rather than ideological. Concerned that Hollywood was turning into a Democratic stronghold, he launched the Hollywood Republican Committee (HRC) in 1940. The HRC, Murphy explained, aimed to "combat the general belief that all Hollywood actors and writers belonged to the left wing. . . . I thought we ought to have a two-party system in our town as well as in the rest of the nation." When Republicans selected Wendell Willkie (another Democrat-turned-Republican) in 1940, Murphy joined the campaign serving as master of ceremonies at numerous rallies, speaking on the radio, and recruiting prominent Republican stars to help draw audiences to events: Mary Pickford, Harold Lloyd, Adolphe Menjou, Ginger Rogers, and the popular "Judge Hardy," Lewis Stone (see fig. 4.1).[13]

Recognizing Murphy's potential as a Republican leader, Mayer and Koverman helped him develop his public speaking skills. "It all started," he recounted, "when Mayer discovered I 'had a way with people,' as he put it, and that I could handle audiences of all kinds." Impressed with Murphy, the MGM studio head appointed him "troubleshooter for the motion picture industry." Throughout the 1940s, Mayer sent the actor to speak to myriad groups around the nation defending Hollywood from charges of immorality and Communist infiltration. Murphy grew into an accomplished public speaker and quickly emerged as the Republican Party's local "'take-over' guy, the M.C. at thousands of functions, always willing to do what I could to come to the aid of a party whose basic philosophy I believed in so strongly."[14]

Too old to join the military when the United States entered the war on December 7, 1941, the thirty-nine-year-old father of two headed up the Hollywood Victory Committee and arranged for movie stars to make appearances at military bases around the world. As many younger actors fought overseas, Murphy battled an enemy he considered equally dangerous: Communists who hoped to take control of the film industry.

Although the Hollywood left's participation in the prewar Popular Front is well documented, much less is known about the emergence of the Hollywood right and its impact on American politics. In the 1930s, the

FIGURE 4.1 Robert Montgomery and George Murphy were part of the Hollywood Republican Committee campaigning for Wendell Willkie in 1940. SOURCE: SPECIAL COLLECTIONS, USC

Hollywood left alerted a complacent citizenry to the dangers of Nazism and fascism. In the 1940s, the Hollywood right played an equally critical role in publicizing the dangers of Communism and laying the groundwork for the postwar anti-Communist movement. Before the war, conservatives such as Robert Montgomery joined with liberal and radical colleagues in opposing Hitler. Yet, many conservatives suspected that Communist-led Popular Front alliances were a self-serving strategy aimed at furthering the interests of the Soviet Union. Their fears were confirmed in August 1939, when Joseph Stalin entered into a nonaggression pact with Adolf Hitler and American Communist Party members immediately called for the United States to remain neutral in any possible European conflict.

Conservatives such as George Murphy found the "naiveté of some liberals toward Communism" appalling and alerted fellow citizens to the dangers Stalin posed to worldwide democracy. During the next several years, the SAG leader studied "communist tactics," read the *Daily Worker* (sent to him anonymously after his election to the SAG board in 1939), and was deeply influenced by Eugene Lyons's *The Red Decade* (1941), which saw little difference between repressive totalitarian regimes in Germany and the Soviet Union, and attacked liberals for their "irrational and indefensible" support of the latter. Murphy was especially disturbed by Lyons's report that "Communists were able to lure celebrities into their nefarious 'front' groups."[15]

Beginning in the mid-1940s and blossoming in the 1950s, the Hollywood right formed a version of the Popular Front that we might call the Conservative Front. This loose confederation of actors, producers, directors, and screenwriters was united by three factors: their hatred of FDR and an activist federal government that restricted free enterprise; their loathing of a progressive income tax that taxed corporations and wealthy individuals up to 90 percent of their earnings; and their fear that Communists were penetrating the industry's labor unions and inserting Red propaganda into American films. This informal amalgam included far right members of the John Birch Society (Walter Brennan and later John Wayne), those sympathetic to fascists (Mary Pickford), ardent Cold Warriors (Adolphe Menjou, Cecil B. DeMille, Ward Bond, Hedda Hopper, and Murphy), moderate conservatives (Gary Cooper), and, in the postwar era, concerned liberals (Ronald Reagan) who saw Communists as posing as great a danger to America in the 1940s as Nazis had posed in the 1930s.

The most zealous anti-Communists formalized their opposition in February 1944, when they met at the Beverly Wilshire Hotel and organized the Motion Picture Alliance for the Preservation of American Ideals (MPA). Louis Mayer's efforts to build a Republican constituency in Hollywood now paid off. The brainchild of MGM's most right-wing conservatives—directors Sam Wood and Clarence Brown, writer James McGuinness, and set designer Cedric Gibbons—the group declared its frustration with the "growing impression that this industry is made up of, and dominated by, Communists, radicals and crack-pots" and pledged to "fight Fascist or Communist control or any other non-American control of our unions, our guilds, our personnel, [and] our product." The initial group of seventy-five mushroomed to several hundred and included Clark Gable, Barbara Stanwyck, and Gary Cooper. According to the FBI, 200 of the organization's initial 225 members worked at MGM. When the war ended, the MPA urged the House Un-American Activities Committee

(HUAC) to return to Los Angeles and resume the investigation of Communist infiltration that had abruptly ended in August 1942.[16]

The MPA's warnings attracted the attention of a number of Hollywood Democrats who were equally concerned about Communist infiltration of their industry, people such as Ronald Reagan. When the aspiring star reported to the Warner Bros. lot in June 1937, few imagined he would become a leader of the conservative revolution. After all, he began his career as a devoted New Deal Democrat who campaigned for FDR in 1940 and worked in Hollywood's most liberal, pro-Roosevelt studio. Many years later, actress Sheila MacRae, who worked with Reagan during the 1940s, referred to him as the "Warren Beatty of his day," an actor passionately devoted to liberal causes.[17]

Over the years, writers have created many myths about Ronald Reagan. One of the most popular is that he was a charming but easily manipulated political naïf whose greatest skill lay in reading the lines given him by more experienced operatives. Those who knew Reagan in the 1940s suggest he was far savvier about politics than most people realized; his easygoing nature deceived supporters and critics alike. Leftist writer-director Bernard Vorhaus, who served with Reagan at "Fort Roach," was startled to discover that the young captain "had more knowledge of political history than any other actor I'd ever met."[18]

Throughout the war, according to Vorhaus, Reagan attended numerous "left-wing functions." It is unclear whether he went out of political sympathy or political suspicion. In September 1941, J. Edgar Hoover told his agents to include Reagan on their list of industry people who might assist them in their investigations. Yet, as late as March 1946, FBI agents raised questions about the liberal star's political loyalties. Insisting he was not a Communist, secret agent T-10 (Reagan) provided local G-Men with information in 1947 about alleged Red activity in Hollywood.[19]

Whatever the nature of his dealings with the FBI, Reagan remained a committed liberal during the war years and when he left the military in September 1945. "Like most of the soldiers who came back, I expected a world suddenly reformed," he wrote in his autobiography. To that end, he joined with Hollywood internationalists such as Edward G. Robinson in advocating a ban on the atomic bomb and signed a petition protesting U.S. support for corrupt nationalist leader Chiang Kai-shek against Communist Mao Zedong. His outspoken support of so many causes, noted one contemporary observer, made him "a favorite of the Hollywood Communists."[20]

Reagan's political conversion was gradual and occurred in several stages: from liberal to liberal anti-Communist and then to conservative anti-Communist. Until the postwar era, Reagan remained alert to but not overly concerned by alleged Red threats to national security. Patriotism led him to cooperate with the FBI, but he did not consider himself an anti-Communist nor did he believe Communists threatened the movie industry to the extent agents suggested. His initial rightward shift resulted from battling Reds on two fronts: in the Hollywood Independent Citizens Committee of the Arts, Sciences and Professions (HICCASP); and in postwar movie industry unions.

Created in June 1945, HICCASP united liberals, radicals, and Communists in an effort to counter Truman's Cold War policies with an internationalist vision that called for universal disarmament, support of the United Nations, and a foreign policy based on cooperation rather than conflict with the Soviet Union. By July 1946, HICCASP's membership had grown to 3,200 and Reagan "felt honored" to be named to its executive council along with Edward G. Robinson, Humphrey Bogart, and John Garfield. His leadership position lasted less than one month. When his brother Neil, who was spying for the FBI, warned him that the group was a left-wing front, Ronnie thought it was just "Republican propaganda."[21]

What Reagan did not know at the time was that by the middle of 1946, as tensions between the United States and the USSR heightened, Soviet leaders secretly ordered the Communist Party of the United States of America to break their long-standing alliance with liberal groups and pursue a more militant pro-Soviet line. Moscow crushed any semblance of local autonomy by clamping down on the flexibility of party leaders. The first casualty of this new policy was HICCASP.[22]

Hollywood's left community split apart in July 1946, when *Life* magazine published an excerpt of famed liberal academic Arthur Schlesinger Jr.'s *The Vital Center* in which he attacked HICCASP as a Communist front and warned that Reds were trying to turn the movie industry into the cultural servant of the USSR. The executive director of HICCASP, George Pepper, who was a Communist Party member, asked the executive council to respond to the charges. When FDR's son James Roosevelt and producer Dore Schary suggested that the organization issue a statement repudiating Communism, a motion Reagan endorsed, tempers flared and ugly words were exchanged. Roosevelt, Schary, and Reagan were denounced with epithets such as "Fascist," "capitalist scum," and "Red-baiter."[23] The shouting ended when director John Cromwell, who chaired the session, appointed a committee that included Reagan to draft a resolution favorable to both sides.

Reagan left the meeting in shock. "You can imagine what this did to my naïveté," he wrote years later. A "simple statement" he thought "any American would be proud to subscribe to" unleashed "a Kilkenny brawl." As he walked out of the contentious gathering, Schary invited Reagan to Olivia de Havilland's apartment where several liberal board members were meeting to draft an anti-Communist resolution. Many Hollywood activists believed Reagan was a hardcore leftist, so much so that when he entered the apartment and told Olivia that he thought she was a Communist, she immediately shot back, "I thought you were one. Until tonight, that is." The group drew up a resolution insisting that Communist nations could "live together in peace and good will" with "capitalist democratic nations," but they rejected Communism "as desirable for the United States."[24]

The HICCASP executive council reconvened on July 5, and when de Havilland presented their resolution another free-for-all broke out. According to Reagan, screenwriter John Howard Lawson, the secret leader of the Hollywood Communist Party, pounded on a table and angrily declared, "This committee will never adopt a statement of policy which repudiates Communism or endorses private enterprise as an economic system." When Reagan suggested the resolution should be voted on by the full membership rather than by the council, Lawson responded that the members "would not be politically intelligent enough or educated enough to make such a decision." The resolution never made it to the membership. Lawson presented it to a smaller executive committee that killed it. Reagan and scores of other liberals soon resigned.[25]

Reagan's experience with HICCASP proved to be the first in a "series of hard-nosed happenings" that began to change his view of the Communist threat. The antidemocratic instincts of Lawson and his radical allies, as well as their bullying and exceedingly bad manners, offended Reagan's sensibilities. He found Lawson's assertion that HICCASP members could not be trusted to discuss issues in a democratic manner simply intolerable. In 1947, Reagan followed other like-minded liberal anti-Communists and joined the recently organized Americans for Democratic Action.[26]

Reagan's involvement with SAG and the labor wars that plagued Hollywood from 1945 to 1947 proved even more crucial to his political conversion. Throughout his life, the actor spoke of the importance of unions, even when he broke up the air traffic controllers union in 1981. His initial commitment to unions as vehicles for protecting workers from misuses of power by employers came from his experience. Warner Bros. issued him a standard long-term contract in 1937 that bound the actor to the studio, but the studio only had to pay him twenty weeks' salary during every twenty-six-week period. Worse yet, during the twelve weeks he was laid off, he was expected to do publicity for the studio for free and prohibited from taking any job without the express permission of the Warner Bros. studio, which they usually refused to grant. When Warners asked him to travel to South Bend on his own dime to publicize *Knute Rockne*, the Midwesterner stood firm and refused to go until the studio paid all his expenses. By the time he joined SAG's executive board in 1938, he considered himself "a rabid union man."[27]

When Reagan returned to the SAG board in February 1946, he found himself working alongside a cadre of anti-Communist conservatives that included, among others, George Murphy. The two men became friends while arguing politics during production of *This Is the Army* in 1943, a film in which he portrayed Murphy's son. Socializing together after the war, usually with other Hollywood Republicans, they amused their wives and friends with their continual efforts to convert each other. "Ronnie used to sit around with Adolphe Menjou and George Murphy and talk about Communism—at parties," remarked writer Leonora Hornblow. "People would say, 'There go Adolphe and George and Ronnie talking the Red Menace.'"[28]

Reagan's opinion of the Communist threat changed as he worked with Murphy to resolve one of the most divisive disputes in Hollywood's history. Responding to years of corruption by IATSE, the Conference of Studio Unions (CSU) launched a series of strikes in 1944 and 1945 aimed at displacing the rival organization. Led by former Oakland boxer Herb Sorrell, the more radical members of the CSU demanded greater workplace democracy and supported a broad array of social and economic goals. In March 1945, IATSE's national leadership sent longtime Democrat and militant anti-Communist Roy Brewer to break the strike and reassert its lucrative control of studio labor. The conflict ended when the American Federation of Labor (AFL) awarded the CSU control over most studio set work.[29]

Brewer took the defeat hard and set out to prove that the Communist Party was supporting the CSU. Vilified by the left and hailed by the right, the IATSE leader was a complex man who was both an ardent New Dealer and a rabid anti-Communist. Cooperating with FBI agents who assured him that Reds were using the rival organization to gain "control [of] all workers in the Hollywood film industry," Brewer spread the word that Sorrell was a Communist and the CSU the Communist Party's tool. He found ready support among MPA members who welcomed him into their ranks and joined his anti-CSU crusade.[30]

Reagan knew from personal experience that studios would exploit their employees whenever possible. Consequently, like most Hollywood liberals, he supported the CSU's demand for more democratic unionism and scoffed at opponents' claims of secret Red plots. When the two men first met, Brewer recounted how Reagan "looked at me like I was the devil himself."[31] Yet, the IATSE leader changed the course of Reagan's political life by convincing him that the Communist threat was real. They began working together when another industry strike broke out in September 1946, shortly after a SAG election in which Robert Montgomery was chosen president and Reagan third vice-president.

Unbeknownst to SAG, Brewer had made a secret deal with industry executives to force the CSU out of the studios. When the studios transferred jurisdiction over set work to IATSE on September 23, CSU locals went out on strike and called upon SAG to support them. Over the next several weeks, the strike grew increasingly violent as pickets were stabbed, cars overturned, and dozens of men hospitalized. Reagan experienced the anger firsthand when rocks were thrown at the bus he rode through picket lines while shooting *Night unto Night*. This "was the first time," Neil Reagan explained, that his brother "ever saw any bunch of pickets swinging three-foot lengths of log chain at people's heads who were just trying to go in and go to work."[32]

A series of personal threats proved crucial in pushing Reagan into the anti-CSU camp. In early October, three FBI agents came to his home to explain how Reds had infiltrated the CSU and to warn that Communists had targeted him. "Now look, I don't go in for Red-baiting," he told them. The agents responded that Communists hated him so much that at a meeting the previous evening someone asked, "What are we going to do about that sonofabitching bastard Reagan?" Any suspicions the actor harbored that the

FBI was exaggerating evaporated when he received an anonymous phone call several days later threatening to throw acid in his face if he opposed the CSU. When he arrived at Warners the next day and reported what happened, the studio security chief quickly obtained a gun permit and fitted the star with a shoulder holster and a loaded .32 Smith and Wesson. Realizing that he could be killed for his political beliefs, Reagan "mounted the holstered gun religiously every morning and took it off the last thing at night," and continued the practice for several months.[33]

Political conversions are personal decisions often influenced by seemingly minor affronts. Reagan never liked confrontation. He did not favor it during the student strike at Eureka College. He hated it even more when his anti-Communist position prompted scathing personal attacks from Lawson and other radicals. By the time SAG held a second mass meeting on December 19, Reagan firmly believed Brewer's contention that Sorrell was a Communist and that Reds had infiltrated the CSU. Reagan felt there could be no other reason for Sorrell's unwillingness to settle the dispute.

The strike dragged on into 1947, and when Montgomery resigned on March 10 SAG members elected Reagan president. Reagan was now a true believer, but being a true believer can also blind one to the full spectrum of the truth. One evening during the strike, Reagan, his wife Jane Wyman, and Murphy paid a visit to Father George Dunne, a Loyola University political scientist who investigated the strike for the Catholic periodical *Commonweal*. After listening to Reagan claim "that Herb Sorrell and the CSU and all these people were Communists," Dunne explained that Sorrell was "a man of honesty and integrity" and that Brewer and the producers were using the "Red Menace" to "cloud the issue and to deceive the public." Reagan refused to listen and left the priest's home three hours later. Dunne found the SAG leader "very articulate" but felt that "this is a dangerous man, because he is so articulate, and because he's sharp. But he can also be very ignorant, as he clearly was, in my judgment, interpreting everything in terms of the Communist threat."[34]

The strike ended in October 1947, with the producer-IATSE alliance destroying the CSU. Reagan emerged from the conflict a highly respected labor leader, at least among anti-Communists. Brewer lauded him as a "fearless foe" of Communism in the labor movement, while anti-Communist studio head Jack Warner marveled that Reagan "turned out to be a tower of strength, not only for the actors but for the whole industry." On the other hand, the man many had considered one of the most affable liberals in town was now a pariah to the left. The majority of SAG actors sided with Reagan. They reelected him president in November 1947, and then to four more terms over the next four years.[35]

The strike experience led Reagan to follow other Hollywood liberals into the Americans for Democratic Action (ADA), an organization that pledged to fight totalitarianism while also pursuing a progressive domestic agenda. By 1947, he was listed on the Southern California branch's masthead along with Melvyn Douglas, Philip Dunne, and Will Rogers Jr. The ADA's brand of liberal anti-Communism differed sharply from that of conservative anti-Communists. Many of the latter were strongly influenced by Friedrich Hayek's popular bestseller *The Road to Serfdom* (1945). The Austrian-born economist argued that Nazism and Communism were the same when it came to economic and state planning, and that misguided liberals paved the way for Communism by supporting a highly active central government. Years later, Reagan would draw on Hayek's work when he spoke of "state socialism" and "benevolent monarchy."[36]

Despite his anti-Communist turn, the SAG president still considered himself a liberal. He laid out his political philosophy in a lengthy March 1947 interview with his new admirer, Hedda Hopper. "Reagan always struck me as being quiet, unassuming, and not the two-fisted fighter we needed for the [SAG] position," the conservative columnist confessed. "I was never more wrong." Explaining his recent awakening to the dangers of Communism, Reagan told her, "Our highest aim should be the cultivation of freedom of the individual, for therein lies the highest dignity of man. Tyranny is tyranny and whether it comes from right, left or center, it's evil." Yet unlike Hopper and her conservative allies, the SAG president defended liberals accused of being "fellow travelers." As he explained, "You can't blame a man for aligning himself with an institution he thinks is humanitarian but you can blame him if he deliberately remains with it after he knows it's fallen into the hands of the Reds."[37]

Reagan took a similar stance when he testified before the House Un-American Activities Committee on October 23, 1947. Appearing along with "friendly" witnesses that included former SAG presidents Montgomery and Murphy, and conservative stars Robert Taylor, Gary Cooper, Ginger Rogers, and Adolphe Menjou, Reagan agreed that a "small clique" within the guild followed "tactics that we associate with the Communist Party." However, when asked what steps should be taken to rid the movie industry of any Communist influence, he proved far more liberal than his colleagues. Unlike Taylor, who favored outlawing the Communist Party, Reagan opposed banning any party "on the basis of its political ideology. We have spent a hundred and seventy years in this country on the basis that democracy is strong enough to stand up and fight against the inroads of any ideology."[38]

Parrying statements made by stars such as Cooper, who told the committee he had turned down scripts he thought were "tinged with communist propaganda," Reagan insisted that Communists had never "been able to use the motion picture screen as a sounding board for their philosophy or ideology." He closed his testimony by reasserting his abhorrence of Communist ideology but also warned HUAC, "I hope we never are prompted by either fear or resentment of Communism into compromising any of our democratic principles in order to fight it." Hollywood could police itself; let democracy work without government interference.[39]

A key question remains unanswered: Was the liberal Democrat being properly vigilant or did he and men like Roy Brewer exaggerate the Communist threat to Hollywood? Was Father Dunne right? Did Reagan support the wrong side in the studio labor wars? The answer is complicated. Archival sources made available since the end of the Cold War reveal that the Communist Party (CP) was not just another American party but took orders from a foreign government. The CP was a secretive and undemocratic organization that enforced a "party line" set down in Moscow and run directly from its New York headquarters. The Hollywood CP, under the control of John Howard Lawson, attempted to recruit writers and movie industry unionists to the cause. Loyal party members had to follow Moscow's orders no matter what their personal feelings.[40]

Communist presence in Hollywood was real, but the CP did not impose a Soviet agenda on all progressive organizations. Most Americans who joined the CP in the 1930s did so because they wanted to stop the spread of fascism and the CP was the only party to take a public stand against Hitler. Many also joined because they believed the CP could make the United States a better place for workers, minorities, women, immigrants, and the underprivileged. Despite conservative accusations, Hollywood Communists, 300 at the party's height, did not succeed in inserting Soviet propaganda into American films. "Nobody would have dared go very far to the left in Hollywood of that day," explained onetime CP member and Hollywood Ten writer Edward

Dmytryk, "because they knew that they would be unsuccessful, couldn't get it through [the studios and Production Code Administration], and the public wouldn't accept it." To the extent that they could, CP members tried to insert "liberal propaganda, not Communist propaganda" in their films.[41]

Communists were certainly active in the CSU, but most rank-and-file members joined the union because they were disgusted with corrupt IATSE leaders who maintained a cozy relationship with studio heads. Indeed, the final report of a congressional subcommittee (the Kearns Committee) that investigated jurisdictional disputes in the movie industry concluded in March 1948 that the dispute between the CSU and IATSE was not precipitated by Communist agitators but was "probably the result of collusion between the producers and the I.A.T.S.E."[42]

While the truth is difficult for historians to detect, it was even more difficult for contemporaries living through the heat of battle. Reagan was convinced that Reds were trying to take over his industry. Even if that were not true, one cannot underestimate the role that fear played in hastening his conservative drift. The threats against the actor's life, reflected Roy Brewer, "frightened him, and he then began to realize what kind of people he was dealing with."[43]

Reagan's political activism and anti-Communist fervor took a toll on his personal life by wrecking his eight-year marriage to Jane Wyman. As he moved slowly to the right, she remained a staunch civil libertarian. In October 1947, Wyman flew to Washington with the Committee for the First Amendment to defend the Hollywood Ten. After a brief separation in February 1948, the couple divorced in July 1949. During court proceedings, she explained that her husband spent "too much time in film colony politics" and "we just didn't have enough in common to sustain our marriage."[44]

Despite his personal unhappiness, Reagan finished the decade as a Democratic activist, campaigning for Harry Truman in 1948 (see fig. 4.2). Two years later, he supported Helen Douglas's senatorial bid against rising Republican conservative star Richard M. Nixon, who dubbed her the "Pink Lady." As his marriage fell apart, the actor became increasingly active in anti-Communist organizations such as the Motion Picture Council—which included a mix of Democrats and Republicans—and the Labor League of Hollywood Voters, a Democratic group he cofounded with Roy Brewer aimed at blocking Communist penetration of the movie industry.[45] Over the next decade, as he took his anti-Communist message on the road, a

FIGURE 4.2 Reagan and Lauren Bacall support Harry Truman in 1948. SOURCE: SPECIAL COLLECTIONS, USC

series of events led him to believe that a greatly expanded federal government posed an equally dangerous threat to American security. The longtime liberal soon joined his friend George Murphy as the two became the most popular spokesmen for the rapidly growing conservative movement.

LAYING THE GROUNDWORK

During the early 1950s and 1960s, the political path the two actor-activists traveled differed considerably. Murphy went into the movement, while the movement came to Reagan. As Reagan gained public recognition as one of Hollywood's leading labor leaders, Murphy cemented his role as a key behind-the-scenes player in the Republican Party. Building on the Hollywood–Washington connection forged by Louis B. Mayer, Murphy helped change the style of American politics by preparing Republican politicians for the new media age. He also went out on the road building political networks and honing his own conservative message. Reagan, though far less

involved in party politics than Murphy, began crafting his conservative ideology in the mid-1950s while traveling the country as a national spokesman
for General Electric. By the early 1960s, both men were preaching similar
messages of fear and reassurance: fear of Communism and creeping federal
socialism, and reassurance that conservatives could save the nation by
defeating the Soviet Union and reversing the New Deal.

After turning over the reins of SAG's presidency to fellow conservative
Robert Montgomery in 1946, Murphy resumed his modest film career
making nine features for MGM between 1947 and 1952. Fittingly, in his
tenth and perhaps best film, *Walk East on Beacon!* (Columbia, 1952), he
played an FBI agent who foils a Communist spy ring. Murphy's hoped-for
cinematic career lagged in part because he proved a far more talented political organizer than actor. Under the guidance of Ida Koverman, he succeeded Mayer as the Republican Party's most important Hollywood
figure. Possessing an ego far more modest than his studio boss, Murphy
worked behind the scenes heading the Hollywood Republican Committee's presidential campaign efforts in 1947 and 1948. In June 1948, he
entered the national political stage when he, Koverman, and comedian
Harold Lloyd traveled to Philadelphia as delegates to the Republican National Convention. When the party chose New York Governor Thomas
Dewey as its candidate and California Governor Earl Warren as his running mate, Murphy arranged for celebrities to travel around the country
promoting the GOP ticket. He proved so successful that two weeks before
the election Dewey invited him to join his eighteen-man inner circle for a
series of meetings in Washington.[46]

Murphy emerged from the Washington, D.C., gathering as Dewey's
media man and helped shape a new era of image politics. The former song-
and-dance man understood in 1948 what has now become commonplace:
selling the candidate was as vital, if not more so, than selling their message.
People wanted to identify with politicians in the same way they identified
with movie stars. Voters, he believed, were attracted more by the sizzle than
the steak, and if there was ever a candidate in need of sizzle, it was the uptight
Dewey. The people Murphy met at rallies around the country found the candidate too stiff. "Why don't you spill some gravy on your vest and brush it
off?" Murphy advised Dewey. "It will make you look a little more human."
He urged the Republican governor to be more vulnerable and not always
answer questions so quickly. "Take your time," he suggested. "The audience

will appreciate a fluff once in a while." Murphy did not succeed in getting Dewey elected, but impressed party leaders named him chairman of the stage, screen, and radio division of the Republican National Committee. Two years later, Dewey made extensive use of television during his successful gubernatorial campaign.[47]

The "Irish Fred Astaire," as Adolphe Menjou called him, returned to the national political arena in 1952, stage-managing the Republican national convention, serving as a delegate, and, most importantly, helping drag party politics out of smoke-filled rooms and into the new television age. Television networks covered both parties' 1948 Philadelphia conventions, but only 172,000 households were equipped with television sets and most people watching the proceedings lived in the Northeast. Four years later, convention coverage went national as networks broadcast both Chicago-based conventions to 15.3 million homes across the country. "Television," New York Times broadcast critic Jack Gould predicted that June, "is going to wield a major and perhaps determining influence this year over both the conventions and the campaign to follow."[48]

Murphy was charged with making politics entertaining not just for delegates but also for the 50 to 60 million people who tuned in to the proceedings, and who might be swayed to vote Republican if they were sufficiently impressed. He succeeded in turning the convention into a lively show. The carefully orchestrated proceedings, Time reported that July, "made political, moral and dramatic sense." Television had changed politics by "bringing the country much closer to the words and actions of its politicians."[49]

Murphy's most important contribution came during the course of the campaign. Republicans were desperate to end the Democrats' twenty-year-long stranglehold on the presidency. Grasping the potential uses of television more quickly than Democrats, the GOP outspent their rivals by a ten-to-one margin. In addition to raising funds for TV time, Murphy coached "perspiring Republicans who suddenly found that they needed to 'project' on TV screens." Murphy also sent movie stars to rallies throughout the country to drum up support for Ike. Pleased with the actor's work, Ike asked him to run the final campaign rallies. Although Murphy preferred the more conservative Senator Robert Taft to the moderate Eisenhower, he accepted the general's offer.[50]

Organizing rallies and raising money was old-style politics. Murphy's greatest challenge in 1952 was turning Eisenhower into a more TV-friendly presence. The Republican National Committee had hired the advertising firm Batten, Barton, Durstine, and Osborne to design the scripts for Eisenhower's campaign. But the popular war hero appeared wooden on television. "His voice was flat," *Time* observed, "he looked like an old man on TV because his light hair and eyebrows did not show up, giving an impression of blankness; his rimless glasses registered as two blobs of light on the TV screen."

When Ike brought Murphy into his advisory group that October, the actor wrested control away from the public relations men, telling one, "You don't know anything about" television and "you won't handle it." Murphy asked his MGM friend Robert Montgomery to help coach Eisenhower. The pair taught the general how to sell himself on the screen. Murphy understood that messages would not matter unless voters found the messenger appealing. Under their tutelage, Ike became a more relaxed and confident speaker. People who saw him on TV and voted Republican told pollsters the general appeared "good-natured, sincere, honest, cheerful, and clearheaded," qualities one might also attribute to Murphy.[51]

Eisenhower and Murphy became friends. Following the election, which Ike won by the largest popular vote in history, the actor was one of the few Hollywood people he invited to the White House. Taken with Murphy's savvy, the president told friends he would "be delighted if we could find a way to integrate him more closely into the staff family." Murphy preferred to remain in Hollywood, so Eisenhower appointed him to several national commissions and invited him to several White House conferences. Murphy and Montgomery continued serving as Ike's media advisers throughout his presidency.[52]

Murphy left the 1952 campaign still a song-and-dance man in the eyes of the public but an increasingly important player in Republican power circles. When California GOP head A. Ronald Button was elevated to the party's national committee in October 1953, Republican Governor Goodwin Knight asked Mayer's protégé to take over as state chairman. When Murphy hesitated, knowing full well that the party was bitterly divided between liberals in the North and conservatives in the South, Knight pleaded, "George, you've got to take it. You're the only guy in the state that nobody's mad at." His appointment, which lasted until August 1954, was widely hailed in the local press. One newspaper called Murphy "long a leader of Hollywood's conservative faction," while another praised him as "an early spotter of communistic infiltration in film ranks" who "never became a witch-hunter."[53]

Murphy proved far more important to the GOP than just his role as a party chairman or media adviser. Mass movements require an ideology that attracts people, messengers who can articulate it, and grassroots networks that spread it to communities across the nation. Murphy emerged as a messenger because Louis B. Mayer gave him the opportunity to do so. While serving as MGM's "ambassador of good will," he addressed hundreds of organizations, many of which proved vital to the burgeoning conservative movement: the American Legion, chambers of commerce, Kiwanis clubs, Rotary clubs, and Young Republicans.[54]

As frightened Democratic stars withdrew from political activism in the wake of the HUAC hearings, Murphy grew increasingly outspoken in his denunciation of Communism and the New Deal legacy. The actor-activist laid out his ideas in a guest column written for influential conservative radio commentator and newspaperman Fulton Lewis Jr. in August 1951. Sounding themes that became the leitmotiv of the conservative revolution, he insisted that "Government spending should be curtailed, except for the military; that secret Socialism and Government interference with private enterprise should be stopped and done away with; that our leaders should consider, for a change, how to tax us less rather than how to spend more . . . that our national strength and ability to produce must be conserved rather than wasted." Not surprisingly, MGM's representative to America often closed his public talks with a Louis B. Mayer/Hardy Family vision of a better future. "I would like my children to have a chance to grow up in the same kind of America I did," he told one reporter, where "individual rights are respected—where opportunity exists for all. Where honesty and integrity are virtues and where a person can worship God in a way of his own choosing."[55]

The seemingly indefatigable father of two (Dennis then age fifteen and Melissa age ten) was laid low in February 1954, when doctors removed several cancerous nodes from his trachea. At the same time, his wife, Julie, suffered from a severe case of arthritis that would eventually cripple her. When Ida Koverman retired in December, Dore Schary, who replaced Mayer at MGM, appointed Murphy to fill her position as the studio's political guru. Murphy spent his time tracking upcoming legislation that affected the motion picture industry and went on the road speaking to various groups on behalf of MGM and Hollywood. When the studio launched its first television show in 1955, *M-G-M Parade*, Schary chose Ike's congenial TV man to serve as its host, a position that brought Murphy into the homes of millions of viewers.[56]

In March 1958, following a failed effort to reinstate Mayer as head of MGM, Murphy left the studio he had been with since 1936 and went to work as vice president in charge of public affairs at Desilu Productions, the company owned by Lucille Ball and her husband, Desi Arnaz. Murphy and Arnaz found common political ground in their shared loathing of Communism. Desi's father had been mayor of Santiago, Cuba, and had vigorously opposed Fidel Castro when he came to power in 1959. Murphy continued his grassroots speaking engagements, picking up dozens of awards over the next few years for his public service.[57]

In 1960 Murphy once again stage-managed the Republican National Convention. The ensuing campaign energized Republican and Democratic stars in a way not seen since 1932. Eisenhower never fired up Hollywood conservatives in quite the way Richard Nixon did; Nixon was one of California's own and on friendly terms with a number of stars. Murphy headed up the Celebrities Committee for Nixon-Lodge and recruited numerous stars to speak on the vice president's behalf, including Ronald Reagan, who served as vice-chairman of Southern California Democrats for Nixon.[58] Although disappointed with the eventual outcome of the election, Murphy and Reagan joined together the following year in the largest series of anti-Communist rallies in the region's history, rallies that helped launch their political careers. In order to understand what led Reagan to turn his back on his earlier views, we need to go back in time and trace the second stage of his political journey from liberal anti-Communist to conservative.

By the early 1950s, Reagan had participated in a number of anti-Communist groups, but he was not a hardcore conservative. In a column written for *Fortnight* in February 1951, SAG's leader defended rooting out Communists who "sought to infiltrate and control certain key industries" but also warned against the excesses of Red-baiting and ultra-patriotism in Congress. "If we get so frightened that we suspend our traditional democratic freedoms in order to fight" Communists, then the Reds will have shown "that Democracy won't work when the going gets tough." Criticizing demagogues such as Senator Joe McCarthy, Reagan urged Congress to trust the democratic process. "No new laws are needed, the present government agencies are equipped to deal with treason and we sacrifice none of our traditional democratic freedoms." A year later, he criticized HUAC for asking studios "to fire people because of their political beliefs," an action, he pointed out, that "happens to be against the law." Reagan also condemned the unfair treatment of liberals who, like himself, had "unwittingly endorsed organizations that later were identified as Communist fronts."[59]

Reagan's middle-ground anti-Communism shifted decidedly to the right after his marriage to actress Nancy Davis in 1952. When the twenty-nine-year-old Smith College graduate found herself unable to get work because she was confused with another Nancy Davis who appeared on the roster of several Communist front organizations, director Mervyn Le Roy sent her to Reagan, who along with Roy Brewer was clearing Hollywood personnel suspected of Red activity. The two met for dinner in December 1950 and immediately hit it off. The SAG leader discovered that the "slender young lady with dark hair and a wide-spaced pair of hazel eyes" was "violently opposed" to "Leftist causes." Her father, Dr. Loyal Davis, who adopted six-year-old Nancy after marrying her mother, was a diehard conservative who had little love for leftists, blacks, Jews, or Catholics. Davis, who was friends with Barry Goldwater, influenced Reagan's subsequent views on abortion and the dangers of what he referred to as "socialized medicine." Nancy and Ronnie married in March 1952 and had their first child, Patricia, seven and a half months later.[60]

Reagan's rightward shift was also hastened by years of socializing and talking politics with a small circle of conservative stars and wealthy business leaders such as tire heir Leonard Firestone, drugstore magnate Justin Dart, and car dealer Holmes Tuttle, all of whom later became members of his "Kitchen Cabinet." Reagan still remained friends with many liberals, but Nancy preferred mingling with conservatives such as Dick Powell, William Holden, and Robert Taylor. Actress June Allyson remembered how during dinner parties her husband, Dick Powell, tried "to shift Ronnie Reagan into the Republican party." By 1952, he partially succeeded as Reagan cast his first Republican vote for Dwight Eisenhower. Several years later, he struck up a friendship with conservative intellectual William F. Buckley Jr. and became a charter subscriber to the *National Review* when it debuted in 1955.[61]

Reagan was prosperous enough to own a home in Pacific Palisades and a 360-acre ranch near Malibu Lake, where he loved to ride horses on weekends. However, like Edward G. Robinson, his career stalled in the postwar years as studios cast younger actors in roles that once would have gone his way. Reagan also attributed his difficulties to his earlier typecast roles as a nice guy. "I'm weary of being dreary, of being the good, the sweet, the colorless charmboy," he confessed in 1950. "I'd make a good louse and I hope they're not out of style before I get a chance to find out." That "nice guy" image, however, would serve him well in the future.[62]

After making seventeen films between 1947 and 1953, the entertainer spent the next several years doing considerably more work in television than film and even mounted a nightclub act at the Last Frontier Hotel in Las Vegas. Financially strapped, the star soon developed a core conservative value: animosity toward federal tax policies. Like many conservatives, Reagan railed against what he and others referred to as FDR's "soak-the-rich" policies. The "handsome money" he made earlier in his career, Reagan explained, "lost a lot of its beauty and substance going through the 91 percent bracket of income tax." Once the government took your money, he lamented, "it is well-nigh impossible to earn your way out."[63]

As Reagan's cinematic star waned, his political activism rose. In February 1952, Democrats urged him to enter the congressional race for the newly formed Twenty-second District. A year and a half later, after heading Los Angeles Mayor Fletcher Bowron's Democratic reelection committee, Reagan was asked to run for the U.S. Senate, an invitation he again turned down. Over the next decade, he shunned public office in favor of participating in movement politics. Reagan was not yet a central figure in conservative circles but like Murphy he increased his appeal by speaking to numerous groups about the dangers of Communism and the threat of "collective dictatorship" that had emerged in the Soviet Union after Joseph Stalin's death in 1953.[64]

A key moment in his ideological evolution came in 1954 when General Electric (GE) advertising executive Earl Dunckel noticed the popular speaker. "Reagan's conversion began one day in 1954 when he signed his GE contract," explained Edward Langley, the public relations man assigned to work with him. "He was joining a company so obsessed with conservatism that it was not unlike the John Birch Society." General Electric was looking for a charismatic star who could host its show, General Electric Theater, and speak to company workers as part of its employee and community relations program. Dunckel, a conservative and member of the company's management team, thought Reagan would be perfect and offered him the job and a salary of $125,000 (nearly $1 million in 2009 dollars), which was four times what he made on his last feature film. Between September 1954 and March 1962, he hosted all the weekly half-hour shows and acted in thirty-six episodes. Appearing on Sunday nights after the enormously popular *Ed Sullivan Show*, *General Electric Theater* reigned as one of the top-rated television shows. "I am seen by more people in one week [on television]," Reagan marveled, "than I am in a full year in movie theaters."[65]

During the course of his eight-year tenure with the company, Reagan traveled to 135 plants and met with 250,000 workers. The company never told him what to say, so he talked to workers about the "attempted takeover of the [movie] industry by the Communists." Discovering "how completely uninformed the average audience was concerning internal Communism and how it operated," he awakened "many people to the threat in their own backyards." After delivering hundreds of speeches to GE employees, he perfected a twenty-minute pitch that he could turn "on and off like a record" and which he delivered without notes. Reagan became so good that by 1957 GE sent him to speak to chambers of commerce, civic clubs, business conventions, and groups "recognized as important political sounding boards."[66]

Working with Dunkel and GE vice president Lemuel Boulware provided the star with what he called his "postgraduate course in political science." Reagan absorbed his mentors' belief in limited government and reduced taxes; in later years, he filled his speeches with Boulware-like examples of government programs that went wrong by competing with private industry. Boulware also urged him to bypass troublesome union leaders and speak directly to rank-and-file workers' aspirations and concerns.[67]

Presenting so many talks gave Reagan the opportunity to forge a more fully developed conservative critique. At the core of the conservative/liberal divide in the 1950s was a debate that went back to the founding of the republic: Should the government promote the welfare of citizens through a strong central structure that acted on behalf of all Americans, or should government involvement be reduced to a minimum in order to allow citizens and private industry the opportunity to fashion their own destiny? New Dealers and their successors believed in the former, while conservatives were equally passionate about the latter, with one critical caveat: they favored large defense budgets with generous grants to military contractors in order to fight Communism. In 1945, Reagan cast his lot with FDR's legacy; ten years later, he was articulating a strong antifederal government message.[68]

Reagan's most significant contribution during his GE years was presenting conservative ideas in a compelling way. He did not tell audiences anything new, but when the dynamic star spoke people listened and heard the message as though it was for the first time. When the press labeled Reagan "The Great Communicator" in the 1980s, they were simply repeating what those who heard him speak thirty years earlier already knew. He offered people a reassuring vision of patriotic Americanism in the midst of a frightening Cold War. He explained how Americans could realize a better future by returning to the time-honored values of the past: small government, individual initiative, and opposition to all enemies of democracy. Reagan's message was so inspiring that one GE executive told him he was in greater demand as a public speaker than anyone save President Eisenhower.[69]

By the late 1950s, Reagan emerged as a full-fledged conservative, delivering the same messages of fear and reassurance as George Murphy. The former liberal warned Americans of the "quickening tempo in our government's race toward the controlled society." Federal agencies undermined individual initiative and prosperity by operating "thousands of businesses . . . in direct competition with private citizens who not only survive in the face of this unjust monopoly, but must pay taxes to cover the losses incurred by these government-owned competitors."[70]

The increasingly strident tone of Reagan's speeches and denunciations of government-funded programs such as the Tennessee Valley Authority (TVA) got him into trouble with his employers. Despite Boulware's denunciations of government interference, GE was the beneficiary of federal largesse, serving as one of the nation's leading defense contractors in the 1950s and 1960s. The TVA had purchased $50 million worth of equipment from GE and the company could not afford to lose such a profitable customer. When GE asked him to confine his speeches to selling products, Reagan refused. "There's no way that I could go out now to an audience that is expecting the type of thing I've been doing for the last eight years and suddenly stand up and start selling them electric toasters," he told his employers. Either he continued with his speeches, or "you get somebody else."[71] General Electric canceled the show at the end of the 1961–1962 season.

Reagan's television popularity during his GE years and image as "Mr. Norm" made him a valuable asset to conservatives. Insisting that actors were "citizens and should exert those rights by speaking their minds," the TV host assumed the role of Republican activist for the first time in 1960. That September, he headed up Democrats for Republican Congressman Alphonzo Bell; a month later, he assumed the post of vice-chairman of Southern California Democrats for Nixon (see fig. 4.3). Under Kennedy's "tousled boyish haircut," he wrote Nixon in July, "is still old Karl Marx" and his New Frontier program was "nothing new in the idea of a government being Big Brother to us all."[72]

The vice president lost the election to his charismatic Democratic opponent, but party insiders noticed Reagan's talent. When Reagan officially registered as a Republican in late January 1961, California GOP leader John Krehbiel floated his name as a possible candidate for governor in 1962. He was flattered but declined, noting that it "would represent too much of a change in my way of living and what I'm trying to do." Reagan was also smart enough to know he could not defeat Nixon, who would likely enter the race. He remained content to spread the message rather than run for office.[73]

FIGURE 4.3 Ronald Reagan, George Murphy, and Richard Nixon in the early 1960s.
SOURCE: PHOTOFEST

Reagan had reason to be optimistic about the future. His work in film and especially television placed him at the forefront of a new age of media politics in which image often overpowered substance. Murphy's work with Eisenhower helped lay the groundwork, but the televised presidential debates of 1960 revealed the medium's extraordinary power with voters. During the first debate, which reached 75 million Americans, a handsomely bronzed John F. Kennedy looked presidential, while a pale and sweating Nixon, observed CBS president Frank Stanton, "looked like death." Polls taken afterward revealed that those who watched the debates on television thought Kennedy won, while those who listened on radio gave Nixon the edge. "That night," reporter Russell Baker remarked, "television replaced newspapers as the most important communications medium in American politics."[74]

Few commentators understood television's impact on politics better than historian Daniel Boorstin. His popular book, *The Image: A Guide to Pseudo-Events in America*, published a year after the debates, described how the "language of images" had "displaced the language of ideals." Audiences preferred to focus on a candidate's visible public personality rather than his or her true private character. "More important than what we think of the Presidential candidate," Boorstin argued, "is what we think of his 'public image.' We vote for him because his is the kind of public image we want to see in the White House." Ray Price, Nixon's chief speechwriter, certainly agreed. "Get the voters to like the guy and the battle's two-thirds won." Yet Price made it clear that it was not "the guy" the public needed to like, but his image.[75]

Television also altered politics by marginalizing third parties that could not afford expensive airtime. As Socialist Party leader William Price told a 1959 congressional hearing on "Political Broadcasts," voters who relied on radio and television for their information "would never have known that such alternatives as ours were within their reach in the voting booth." Broadcasters gave liberal amounts of free time to major party candidates, but minority candidates, complained another Socialist official, "do not receive free time, comparable or otherwise."[76]

Television may have hurt minority parties, but it helped the rapidly growing conservative movement. The 1960s are often thought of as a return to liberalism, but the era also experienced the rise of a grassroots conservative movement heavily financed and promoted by large corporations (especially those receiving Defense Department funding). Southern California was a center of anti-Communist groups, and Reagan and Murphy proved eager players in the embryonic conservative revolution, especially as the religious right entered the political scene.

In August 1961, the two prominent Republicans used the medium to spread the movement's message by participating in a series of televised events organized by Christian leader Dr. Fred Schwarz as part of his Southern California School of Anti-Communism. The weeklong rallies featured celebrities such as Roy Rogers, Dale Evans, Pat Boone, and John Wayne. The opening night event attracted 16,000 to the Los Angeles Sports Arena and focused on teaching teenagers, the voters of the future, "methods of combating Red infiltration." The evening's most popular speaker was Ronald Reagan, who brought the crowd to its feet when he proclaimed, "You're a target. Communists will appeal to your rebellious nature . . . they will make you feel your patriotism is hollow. Then they will fill up the vacuum with their philosophy." The rallies proved so successful that Schwarz organized a three-hour television special at the Hollywood Bowl in October billed as "Hollywood's Answer to Communism." Broadcast live on thirty-five stations in six western states, the program was shown again two weeks later throughout the New York metropolitan area.[77]

Over the next few years, Murphy and Reagan spoke to an expanding array of grassroots groups. Reagan supplemented the pair's familiar anti-Communist warnings with denunciations of proposed programs such as Medicare, which he labeled as an effort to impose socialism on the American people. By the beginning of 1962, Reagan had purged himself of all former taints of liberalism. He knew what audiences wanted to hear and gave it to them. In a January speech to the Young Republicans, he warned that liberals had one thing in common with "Socialists and Communists—they all want to settle their problems by government action." Sounding themes he perfected on his GE tours, he denounced federal aid programs, current foreign policies, and a progressive income tax "spawned by Karl Marx as a means of eliminating the middle class."[78]

As Murphy and Reagan grew increasingly popular among conservative organizations, calls for them to run for political office grew stronger.

RUNNING FOR OFFICE

For actors and politicians timing is everything. Murphy and Reagan turned to electoral politics at the perfect moment. Richard Nixon's loss in 1960 left the Republican Party deeply split between eastern-based moderates (led by Nelson Rockefeller and Jacob Javits), western conservatives (led by Barry Goldwater), and an insurgent wing of Christian conservatives with strongholds in fundamentalist regions of the deep South, Midwest, and parts of Southern California. Holding similar views on foreign and fiscal policy, GOP moderates differed from conservatives in their more liberal attitudes toward government promotion of domestic social programs. Looking ahead to the 1964 presidential elections, California conservatives launched "Operation Take-Over," a multipronged movement to spread their ideology, build independent organizations outside of electoral politics, and seize control of the state's party from moderates.[79]

As many scholars have pointed out, there was no single conservative movement or ideology but rather a number of grassroots groups that, while disagreeing on specific policies, united around four basic ideas: militant anti-Communism, limited government, lower taxes, and social conservatism. Movement activists included a wide range of libertarians, auxiliary groups attached to the Republican Party, far-right organizations such as the John Birch Society and Ku Klux Klan, Christian fundamentalists, and powerful conservative associations such as the American Legion and National Association of Manufacturers. Periodicals such as *Human Events* and *The National Review* helped spread conservative ideas to activists throughout the nation.[80]

Murphy and Reagan's electoral success was directly tied to Southern California's emergence as the center of a plethora of socially and religiously conservative groups that preached, as one historian notes, an ideology of "staunch individualism, Protestant piety, and resentment against Washington 'collectivists.'" Ironically, this hotbed of antifederal activism owed much of its wealth and growth to Washington's largesse. In 1957, defense-related jobs accounted for 70 percent and 59 percent, respectively, of all employment in San Diego and Los Angeles counties. By the early 1960s, defense was the nation's largest business, accounting for 62 percent of the federal budget, and Southern California received the majority of those funds. As defense-related industries poured into Orange County, its population rose by 385 percent between 1940 and 1960. Overwhelmingly white (90 percent) and dominated by conservative evangelical and fundamentalist religious sects that were anti-Communist, anti-union, and suspicious of Jews, Catholics, and minorities, Orange Country served as a breeding ground for organizations that formed the core of Murphy's (and later Reagan's) support.[81]

Fueled by their success at the community level, California conservatives set out to seize control of the state's formerly moderate California Young Republicans (CYR) and California Republican Assembly (CRA). In April 1963, conservatives organized the United Republicans of California (UROC) to push their ideological agenda; a year later, the group's 10,000 members were operating 290 units in the state's fifty-eight counties.[82]

As the California right rose to power, the state's Republican Party remained bitterly divided between conservatives in the south and moderates in the north. Worse yet, registered Democrats outnumbered Republicans by a three-to-two margin. What seemed like a disastrous scenario to most experienced GOP politicians proved the opportunity of a lifetime for Hollywood's two electoral neophytes.

By early 1964 California conservatives had won numerous skirmishes but to win the upcoming senatorial elections they needed a candidate who could remain loyal to their ideology while also uniting the party's warring factions. George Murphy seemed the perfect choice. Not only did he have a longer conservative track record than Reagan, but he now worked for Patrick Frawley, one of the movement's most zealous financial backers. After leaving Desilu, Murphy accepted the self-made millionaire's offer to become vice president of Technicolor Corporation. Frawley encouraged Murphy to carry on his political work.[83]

On December 23, 1963, the sixty-year-old party activist announced his intention to run for the U.S. Senate, knowing full well that relying on his celebrity was not sufficient to get him elected. He also needed to operate as a traditional politician, building coalitions and convincing voters that he could do the job. After setting up his campaign headquarters in a small Beverly Hills storefront, the candidate hit the road with his son Dennis and drove their station wagon around the state hoping to lock up the Republican nomination.

Fortunately for Murphy, he faced little serious competition in the primaries. His chief conservative rival, San Francisco financier Leland Kaiser, had few roots in Republican politics, while former Kansas Governor Fred Hall was considered too moderate by party conservatives. That June, Murphy defeated his opponents in the primaries by a wide margin. Conservatives were overjoyed when Barry Goldwater—who boldly proclaimed that "extremism in the defense of liberty is no vice" and "moderation in the defense of liberty is no virtue"—squeaked by Nelson Rockefeller in the California presidential primary, 1,120,403 to 1,052,053.[84] Despite his momentary pleasure, Murphy knew he faced a far more difficult battle against his Democratic rival, Pierre Salinger, the former press secretary to presidents Kennedy and Johnson.

Ironically, the native-born California Democrat had lived outside the state so long he failed to meet the residency requirement needed to vote in the election. But the Kennedy-Johnson connection proved strong enough to give Salinger a close primary victory against state controller Alan Cranston. The former presidential press secretary remained confident he could defeat his far less experienced Republican opponent, a sentiment that pollsters confirmed. In April, Murphy trailed Salinger 48 to 32 percent; by mid-September, the Democrat maintained a comfortable 50 to 38 percent margin, with 12 percent of the voters undecided. Little wonder that the *Los Angeles Times* labeled the party's prospects in the upcoming senatorial election as "bleak."[85]

Murphy remained undaunted. He may have been a novice at running for office, but he had years of experience advising presidents and knew how to present a candidate's image in a way that would appeal to voters. He used that knowledge to create what would later become known as the "Reagan strategy." To win in November, he needed to unite conservative Goldwaterites and moderate Rockefeller supporters while also attracting 20 percent of the Democratic vote. He did this by bringing moderates into his inner circle, luring blue-collar Democrats with a conservative stance on social issues, denouncing Salinger as a carpetbagger, and, perhaps most important, using his celebrity to attract starstruck swing voters.

Murphy began building a new coalition by soliciting funds from conservatives, leadership from moderates, and campaign ideas from both. His financial backing came from a small cadre of wealthy conservatives, many of whom also supported Goldwater's campaign. In a masterful political juggling act, Murphy pleased the right by endorsing Barry Goldwater, but he maintained his moderate supporters by refraining from campaigning with the candidate and pointing out their differences: Murphy supported the civil rights bill (which Goldwater opposed), opposed any right-to-work law that prevented closed union shops, and supported a 25 percent cut in foreign aid rather than its complete elimination, as Goldwater wanted.[86]

Unstinting in his call to overturn the New Deal state, Murphy delivered his messages in a far less strident manner than Goldwater. The present Washington bureaucracy, he warned, threatened to turn our government into a "welfare state, or socialism, or some kind of dictatorship" that would be ruled by a "small group of the self-appointed elite, the Fabian socialists." On the foreign front, he insisted that the Red menace was "greater now than at any time in our history" and opposed American recognition of China, trade with Cuba, and the sale of surplus wheat to Russia. Murphy also added an element of reassurance to familiar messages of fear: "I want to put this country back on track, back in the wonderful condition it was in when I began to enjoy its benefits fifty years ago. If we can do this, we will have saved the future of civilization." Murphy's optimism, confessed one previously skeptical reporter, "makes you feel good . . . he has no doubts, and your own doubts can be resolved."[87]

Pierre Salinger hoped to thwart Murphy's crossover efforts by linking his opponent to Goldwater and characterizing the two as "reckless" and "heartless conservatives" who offered nothing "but doom and gloom and a dreary recital of all that they find wrong in this country and this world." Pushing his own liberal agenda, Salinger ignored his advisers and came out against the most controversial issue of the campaign, Proposition 14. Placed on the ballot by the California Real Estate Association, the measure proposed to repeal the antidiscrimination provisions of the recently passed Rumford Act (1963), which prohibited homeowners from refusing to rent or sell property to blacks, Jews, Asians, or any minority. Murphy did not like the Rumford Act, but he felt that Proposition 14 "went too far in the opposite direction."[88] With passions running high on both sides of the issue, he decided to remain neutral.

Hollywood's impact on politics was most evident in Murphy's ability to use his positive screen persona to attract voters. The eastern press delighted in derisively referring to him as "former hoofer," "former tap dancer and motion picture star," and "Shirley Temple's leading man of the 1930s." The October 16 cover of *Time* magazine showed a professional-looking Pierre Salinger dressed in a suit in the foreground while a smiling, leprechaun-like Murphy danced on top of a piano in the background. Yet, what the press saw as a liability, the candidate saw as an asset. "I had never played a bad guy. I had always been a good guy—that was my so-called 'image.'"[89]

Murphy's appearance on late-night television proved a distinct advantage. According to one reporter, several TV stations screened his old films to hurt him, but "the whole scheme backfired. Murphy emerged as a nice, clean-cut guy on screen, and I'm sure many people voted for him with this image in mind." Murphy agreed. "Those old pictures showing me dancing with Shirley Temple that keep turning up on the late night TV movies are getting me votes." As we can see in the scene from *Little Miss Broadway* (1938) in figure 4.4, Murphy comes off as the graceful and gracious "good guy" cheerfully willing to cede the spotlight to a far more talented child—an image that served him well in the campaign. These late-night films were especially popular with "the Lawrence Welk kind of people," the blue-collar voters he needed to win. Having people watch his films in bed at night, Murphy joked with one reporter, gave him "a more intimate association with my constituents than any other candidate." He also integrated TV into his campaign by filming two half-hour campaign rallies that featured Jimmy Stewart, Ricardo Montalban, and Cesar Romero.[90]

FIGURE 4.4 Murphy and Shirley Temple in *Little Miss Broadway* (1938). Such good-guy images helped Murphy's campaign.
SOURCE: SPECIAL COLLECTIONS, USC

While Salinger focused on winning the battle of ideas, Murphy focused on winning the hearts of voters. He enjoyed mingling with crowds in shopping centers, factories, union meetings, and any place where "some Democrats might be converted," shaking hands, kissing babies, and always slipping in some anecdote about his Hollywood days. The simplicity of his ideas appealed to many voters, especially women over thirty-five who flocked to work on his campaign. Murphy recalled how an elderly woman told him after one meeting, "It's wonderful the way you say things. You make important problems sound so simple that even I can understand them."[91]

The triumph of image over substance was never clearer than during the televised debate between the two candidates. When Senator Clair Engle died on July 31, Governor Pat Brown appointed Salinger to fill the position. Whatever advantage the Democrat gained was lost in early October when, despite the pleadings of his advisers, Salinger agreed to debate his rival on television. Murphy knew that television cameras cared little about political experience. Looking like a senator was more important than proving he could be a senator. Wanting to appear rested and confident, Murphy canceled all his appearances and spent the weekend rehearsing with advisers.

On Monday, October 7, Murphy entered the CBS studios feeling "relaxed and prepared," while Salinger showed up "nervous" and "uptight." As the two men stood by their podium, Murphy scored points without even saying a word: at one end of the stage stood a tall, immaculately groomed candidate who looked as though he had come right out of central casting, while at the other stood his shorter, stockier, and agitated opponent. Murphy fended off Salinger's accusations that he was a carbon copy of Goldwater by pointing to the issues on which they disagreed. He then turned the tables by calling the Democrat a carpetbagger who knew little about the state's problems and was riding on JFK's legend. "Why vote for a man who can't vote for himself?" he asked. As the debate drew to a close, viewers watched a calm Murphy make his final statement while Salinger, realizing he made a mistake by referring to his close association with Kennedy rather than discussing the state's needs, froze and broke out in a cold sweat. The Democrat left the studio in a huff and lost his temper when questioned by waiting reporters.[92]

The television debate proved crucial in swaying the minds of undecided voters. Image had trumped substance. "As a debater," observed columnists Rowland Evans and Robert Novak, "Salinger demolished Murphy, whose logic and syntax both tend to be elusive. But politicians of both parties agree that Salinger emerged as the brash, almost arrogant young man while Murphy was the comfortable old shoe." Local voters agreed. A poll released one week after the debate showed Murphy closing the gap. Salinger's 12 percent lead of early September had shrunk to a razor-thin 4 percent margin. What looked like a runaway race was now too close to call.[93]

Murphy's fortunes rose in the closing days of the campaign when he received the endorsement of the influential *Los Angeles Times*. On November 2, a Field poll showed the candidates dead-even at 43 percent each, with 14 percent of the voters still undecided. A final push by hardcore Southern California conservatives who, the *Washington Post* noted, were "doing the kind of tough precinct work that is needed to win elections," gave Murphy renewed hope of capturing the undecided.[94]

On November 3, American voters went to the polls and chose President Lyndon Johnson over Barry Goldwater by an overwhelming margin of 43.1 million to 27.2 million. Only one Republican won a Democratically held Senate seat, George Murphy. In the upset election of the year, Murphy polled 3,628,555 votes to Salinger's 3,411,912.

Postelection analysts attributed Murphy's triumph to three factors: Salinger's poor image, Murphy's ability to stick the carpetbagger label on him, and the Democrat's outspoken opposition to Proposition 14, which passed by a two-to-one margin. What pundits overlooked was his ability to lure Democratic and independent voters: 25 percent of the Democrats casting ballots voted for the former actor, while only 14 percent of Republicans voted for Salinger. The key votes came in the heartland of conservatism. Murphy lost Northern California by 150,000 votes, but he carried the southern part of the state by over 350,000 votes. Sounding a theme Reagan adopted two years later, the ebullient senator-elect told reporters, "It seems to me most Republicans don't go after Democratic votes as hard as they should. I went after Democrats and independents as actively as I went after Republicans and the results show this met with some success." Murphy was convinced that television had swung the election. "The impression you make on people is very important. . . . Salinger made a bad tactical error by agreeing to debate me on TV. I was anxious to let the public see us side by side. I was amazed at how short Mr. Salinger looked beside me and I knew then I had the advantage."[95]

Murphy's election inspired a new generation of political hopefuls in Hollywood, many of whom had built their careers around television: Democrats Steve Allen, Gary Merrill, Robert Vaughn, Dan Blocker, and Eddie Albert; and Republicans Chuck Connors and Shirley Temple-Black. While most of these stars were interested in winning elections, Ronald Reagan was interested in changing a nation. Local activists had long preferred Reagan to Murphy and urged him to run for office as early as December 1961. Reagan was solidly entrenched in conservative circles by 1962 and served as cochair of Goldwater's California campaign, but he did not burst onto the national scene until he galvanized audiences with a speech he gave on national television a few days before the November election. Known among Reagan intimates as "The Speech," Reagan had been delivering his "A Time for Choosing" address since his days at General Electric. The power of The Speech came from the clarity of his argument and his ability to speak into the television camera with maximum effect, just as FDR had done on radio. As his brother Neil explained, Ronnie had the ability to "convince people of his sincerity and genuineness, to distill complicated issues and explain them to the voting public."[96]

At the heart of the October 27 speech is a simple but powerful theme: the excesses of government and evils of Communism threatened the freedom of every American. Speaking to millions of viewers as though he was sitting in their living room, Reagan told them that in America there was "no such thing as a left or right," there was "only an up or down—up to a man's age-old dream, the ultimate in individual freedom consistent with law and order—or down to the ant heap of totalitarianism." We had come to a time for choosing "whether we believe in our capacity for self-government or whether we abandon the American Revolution and confess that a little intellectual elite in a far-distant capital can plan our lives for us better than we can plan them ourselves." Calling for vigilance against Communism, he warned, "We are at war with the most dangerous enemy that has ever faced mankind in his long climb from the swamp to the stars, and it has been said if we lose that war, and in doing so lose this way of freedom of ours, history will record with the greatest astonishment that those who had the most to lose did the least to prevent its happening."[97]

Over the course of twenty-seven minutes, Reagan drove home his arguments with a series of simple but evocative examples. Pointing out that welfare spending was now "ten times greater than in the dark depths of the Depression," he explained that if we divided the $45 billion welfare budget among the nation's nine million poor families they would each receive $4,600, an amount that combined with their present earnings would "eliminate poverty." Yet, because of bureaucratic inefficiency, direct aid to the poor was running only about $600 per family. Government ineptitude also extended to its handling of social security. For the same money that he paid in social security taxes, a twenty-one-year-old could buy an insurance policy that would guarantee him $220 a month at sixty-five as compared to the $127 payment he would receive from Uncle Sam.

Reagan assailed those who sought to appease the Soviets and called for a foreign policy "based upon what we know in our hearts is morally right." Laying the foundation for his later talk of an Evil Empire, he warned we "cannot buy our security, our freedom from the threat of the bomb by committing an immorality so great as saying to a billion now in slavery behind the Iron Curtain, 'Give up your dreams of freedom because to save our own skin, we are willing to make a deal with your slave masters.'" Confronting Khrushchev was far less dangerous than believing that "he will forget his evil ways and learn to love us." Peace was preferable to war, but each of us needed to "have the courage to say to our enemies, 'There is a price we will not pay.'"

Building toward an almost apocalyptic ending, Reagan closed by invoking FDR, Abraham Lincoln, and Barry Goldwater in successive sentences. "You and I have a rendezvous with destiny. We will preserve for our children this, the last best hope of man on Earth, or we will sentence them to take the last step into a thousand years of darkness . . . [Goldwater] has faith that you and I have the ability and the dignity and the right to make our own decisions and determine our own destiny."

The power of The Speech lay less in what Reagan said than how he said it. Like the best preachers, he won over his audience with a reassuring voice that mixed calm certainty with a passionate call to action. He spoke not as a conservative, not as a Republican, but as a reasonable citizen disgusted by the incompetence of our government. No sensible man or woman would run their business the way federal officials ran our government. If they did, they would soon be out of business, which is precisely what Reagan urged his citizens to do: replace the bloated bureaucrats with a new administration that could do the job.

New York Times reporter David Broder hailed Reagan's televised address as "the most successful national political debut since William Jennings Bryan electrified the 1896 Democratic convention with the 'Cross of Gold' speech." The Hollywood Republican succeeded in inspiring the faithful and converting the uncertain. "Tens of thousands of active conservatives wrote to Reagan, to the Republican Party, to their local papers, and to anyone else who might listen," recounted Houston-based conservative and future Reagan campaign manager Tom Reed. "They proclaimed The Speech as the best thing that happened in 1964."[98] Leaders at Goldwater headquarters reported that the speech generated an additional $8 million in campaign donations.

Barry Goldwater was defeated so badly on Election Day that commentators declared the conservative movement dead. They were wrong. After The Speech, Reagan emerged as the right's new hope. The calm actor was everything the bristly Goldwater was not: personable, self-effacing, and eternally optimistic even in the face of the Soviet menace. What Reagan's critics saw as his inability to venture beyond a few simple ideas, his supporters saw as his strength. He knew how to stay on message, how to seize on a few basic concepts and repeat them over and over until even the most unsophisticated voter could understand them. "We're going to rise up from this defeat," he told a cheering group of 700 Young Republicans on November 7, "and start the second round of our struggle to restore the republic."[99] Reagan was now the hottest Republican in America. A few days after the election, enthusiastic conservatives in Owosso, Michigan, formed a Reagan for President Club, while their southern California compatriots proudly placed "Reagan for Governor" bumper stickers on their cars.[100]

In early 1965, a small cadre of wealthy conservative businessmen known as the "Los Angeles Elders" put up the seed money for Reagan to test the political waters. Led by longtime friends Cy Rubel, chairman of Union Oil; Holmes Tuttle and his associate, Ed Mills; and oil entrepreneur Henry Salvatori, the group believed Reagan was the one man who could unite the party, undo the New Deal, and reestablish a business-friendly government. Quitting his job as host of the popular television show *Death Valley Days*, the actor spent the next several months delivering speeches denouncing Medicare, championing individualism over collectivism, opposing the Civil Rights Act, and vilifying liberals who attempted to appease the Soviet Union. By late April, a Field poll revealed the popular conservative had established a commanding lead over his three moderate gubernatorial rivals,

Senator Thomas Kuchel, former Governor Goodwin Knight, and San Francisco Mayor George Christopher. On June 1, a *Washington Post* headline declared, "Reagan Is the Candidate to Beat."[101]

With registered Democrats outnumbering Republicans by a three-to-two margin, Reagan needed to follow Murphy's example by maintaining his conservative base while attracting moderate Republicans, disgruntled Democrats, and independents. To that end, he hired political consultants Stu Spencer and Bill Roberts. Longtime Republican moderates, the pair had run Nelson Rockefeller's quixotic California presidential primary campaign. When they took him on, Rockefeller was 30 percentage points behind Goldwater; on primary day, he finished 3 percent behind his conservative rival. Reagan was a more ideologically devout conservative than Murphy, and his inner circle included four men of similar beliefs but diverse backgrounds: Bill Clark, a rancher and small-town lawyer from Ventura County; Ed Meese, a prosecuting attorney; Lyn Nofziger, a reporter with the Copley Press; and Tom Reed, a former scientist at Lawrence Livermore National Laboratory, who went on to become a high-tech businessman. The four argued policy with Reagan but remained committed believers, as Reed remarked, in his "fundamental values, in his ability to articulate them and in his mission to accomplish nothing less than the salvation of the free world as a result."[102]

With Spencer and Roberts pushing him toward the middle and his inner circle urging him to hold fast to his core values, Reagan soon found himself in the midst of the 50.1 percent dilemma that has divided political activists throughout the century. Pragmatists argue that compromise is necessary because you cannot effect change unless you win 50.1 percent of the vote; ideologues argue that if you compromise too much any subsequent electoral victory is hollow for too many principles have been sacrificed to effect significant change. Fearing Spencer and Roberts would move him too far to the center, CRA president Cyril Stevenson Jr. reminded the political hopeful, "Your entire excuse and strength for running comes from the grassroots conservative movement."[103] What Stevenson and many reporters did not understand was that Reagan moved toward the center not simply to win an election but to achieve an overwhelming mandate for change. Only by building a broad coalition of conservatives and disgruntled moderates could he hope to inaugurate a radically new approach to government.

Reagan was willing to do the work needed to be successful, but like Murphy, he did it in a different way than most traditional politicians. Scholars rightly point to the Kennedy-Nixon debates as a turning point in American politics. Yet the televised events were only a small part of the candidates' overall strategy. Reagan ushered in a new era of politics by placing television at the center of his campaign, preferring carefully orchestrated media appearances to traveling on the road. This became evident on January 4, 1966, when he bypassed traditional news conferences and announced his candidacy in a carefully staged television appearance. Drawing on themes raised in The Speech, he laid out a message of fear and reassurance that he repeated throughout the campaign: High taxes were depriving hard-working Americans of the fruits of their labors and forcing elderly folks to sell their homes. If elected, he would solve the problem with a tax moratorium on homes owned by retired citizens and a call to state legislators to cut taxes. City streets had become "jungle paths after dark," and crimes of violence in California were more than the combined totals of New York, Pennsylvania, and Massachusetts. If elected, he would solve the problem by restoring power to local police and eliminating police review boards that created "unnecessary interference" in fighting crime. After citing more examples, he looked straight into the camera and reassured voters that "our problems are many, but our capacity for solving them is limitless."[104]

Politicians in both parties greeted Reagan's candidacy with derision. Republican rival George Christopher dismissed the fifty-four-year-old candidate as "just an actor with one speech." Two-term Democratic incumbent Pat Brown wanted Reagan as his opponent because he thought the liberal Christopher would be a far tougher rival than the politically inexperienced conservative. What Brown and others failed to realize was that Murphy's victory signaled the maturation of media politics in California, and candidates who knew how to use television had a tremendous advantage over those who did not. Democratic fundraiser Manning Post, who understood this sea change in electoral life, warned Brown that Reagan was a highly dangerous opponent. "He's the guy with the white hat. He's the Shirley Temple of the male set. This sonofabitch is going to beat the shit out of you . . . because the first thing you've got to have in politics is recognition, that's what you pay all the money for. . . . You take an actor who had the image of a good guy; man, you can't overcome it. You just can't make him a bad guy anymore."[105]

During the next eleven months, Reagan set out to transform state politics by building coalitions, "rainbow committees" as Reed called them, with conservatives and moderates in both parties. His greatest challenge lay in convincing the nonconverted that he could represent their interests better than any other candidate. In a brilliant strategic move, he turned what his opponents claimed was a weakness, his political inexperience, into an asset. "I am not a politician," he told voters. "I am an ordinary citizen with a deep-seated belief that much of what troubles us has been brought about by politicians. If we ordinary citizens don't run government, government is going to run us." Knowing how tough it was to convince people to abandon long-standing partisan loyalties, Reagan reminded Californians, "I am an ex-Democrat who found I could no longer follow the philosophy of the leadership of that party." He welcomed support from those who preferred principles to labels and pledged to replace Lyndon Johnson's ineffective bureaucratic Great Society with the Creative Society "in which the people themselves have the strength and the ability to solve the problems that confront us."[106]

At a time when Americans were growing increasingly angry after two summers of race riots and several years of protests on college campuses, Reagan offered voters a moralistic social vision that crossed party lines. Preaching a politics of resentment that appealed to the kind of working- and middle-class white ethnics he had come to know during his GE tours, he denounced welfare regulations that encouraged "divorce and immorality"; he railed against "sexual orgies" at Berkeley "so wild I cannot describe it to you"; he condemned "arson and murder" in Watts; and, finally, he called for a "moral crusade" aimed at closing "the morality and decency gap." Far from being a Goldwater-like messenger of doom, Reagan also offered a vision of a happier America. "Join me in a dream of a California whose government isn't characterized by political hacks and cronies and relatives," he urged a group of college students, "an administration that doesn't make its decisions based on political expediency but on moral truth. . . . [This is] a dream you can believe in—it's a dream worthy of your generation. Better yet, it's a dream that can come true and all we have to do is want it badly enough."[107]

On June 7, 1966, in the heaviest primary turnout in state history, Republicans selected the former actor as their overwhelming choice to oppose Governor Pat Brown, who fended off a challenge from conservative Los

Angeles Mayor Sam Yorty. Not only did Reagan defeat Christopher 1,419,623 to 675,683, but he captured all but five of the state's fifty-eight counties. Taking no time to bask in his victory, Reagan lined up endorsements from Dwight Eisenhower, California's Republican congressmen and -women, and many of Goldwater's key financial and political backers. He also secured the support of Brown's opponent Sam Yorty and other conservative Democrats who formed Californians for Reagan. Pleased with his success in coalition building, Reagan wrote George Murphy in August, "We do have the party glued together, if only we can keep some of the kooks quiet."[108]

Success does not necessarily command respect. The question of whether the personable actor was really a leader of the conservative movement or simply a talented figurehead haunted Reagan throughout the campaign and in the forty years after his election. Reading through oral histories and memoirs of friends and political allies, one comes away with a sense that Ronald Reagan was very much his own man: an independent thinker who, while no political genius, was smart enough to fashion a compelling worldview and convey it to a mass audience in a highly appealing fashion. Reagan rarely asked aides to write his speeches; they supplied him with ideas and facts that he put into his own words. Apparently, he had a photographic memory and the ability to turn a phrase without a prepared text. Neil Reagan recounts how when his brother was set to deliver his first major campaign speech "talking about the Central Valley Water Project, which means acre-feet of water figures, money figures, time figures, everything else," reporters were incredulous when they discovered he only had a few index cards rather than a prepared text. "He'll never be governor," *Los Angeles Times* reporter Carl Greenberg told Neil. "In this one speech, tonight, he can cut his throat a thousand times by saying the wrong things and having the wrong figures, having the wrong dates." Reagan spoke flawlessly for thirty minutes and nailed every fact. When the speech was over, an astonished Greenberg confessed to Neil, "I would never have believed it if I hadn't seen it."[109]

Good actors know how to deliver lines, but Reagan truly believed what he said. His speeches conveyed a sincerity that won him many admirers (see fig. 4.5). According to a survey taken in September 1966, 70 percent of respondents listed his personality and speaking ability as his most outstanding qualities as a candidate. As for his weaknesses, 71 percent pointed to his

FIGURE 4.5 Campaigning for governor, Reagan promised a clean sweep in statewide elections, September 30, 1966.
SOURCE: ASSOCIATED PRESS

inexperience in government as his greatest shortcoming. On the other hand, 49 percent of respondents agreed that Governor Brown's weakest point was that he had been in office too long.[110]

By the time both candidates launched their official campaigns shortly after Labor Day, Reagan held a narrow 45–41 percent lead. Although his lead had shrunk since the spring, the good news was that 21 percent of Reagan's support came from Democrats. During the next two months, while Brown pounded the flesh in traditional campaign style, Reagan played to his strength by making television appearances that targeted crossover voters in Southern California. Like Murphy, he also benefited by having his old films run on late-night television. As one reporter quipped, "Anyone staying up late enough can't escape seeing an old Ronald Reagan movie on TV."[111]

Although he preferred television, Reagan still hit the campaign trail when needed. With union leaders committing their organizations to Brown, the

Republican reached out to rank-and-file members. Judging from popular responses, Reagan's efforts proved successful. An Orange County union member's wife told him that despite instructions "from their San Francisco headquarters," there is "strong feeling running in your favor." The Brown forces grew increasingly concerned as letters poured in from longtime party loyalists warning, "We may be Democrats, but find more and more the Conservative view is the American way."[112]

Reagan's media skills proved invaluable in the closing weeks of the campaign. During the course of three televised debates held between September 11 and October 3, he succeeded in putting his far more experienced opponent on the defensive. He parried Brown's efforts to portray him as an extremist by turning the tables and blasting the state's Democratic Central Council as a group of "militant left-wing radicals" who wanted to abolish HUAC and recognize Cuba and Red China. Reagan was the Rachmaninoff of the political world, playing endless variations on themes raised in The Speech. "Americans are really conservatives," he told television audiences. "They pay their bills; they don't run big debts." He told them that this "country was created by ordinary citizens, not by politicians, to be run by ordinary citizens." He told them that something was wrong when the "five dollars you saved twenty years ago will only buy you $1.85 of groceries today." Finally, he attacked Brown for his inability to curb racial violence, campus insurrections, welfare spending, and a state budget that was out of control. Struck by the telegenic contrast between the two candidates, ABC producer Peggy Wheadon observed how Brown "sometimes gropes for a word" while Reagan "always has the word at the tip of his tongue and goes right on. Brown never smiles; Reagan has that beautiful smile."[113]

During the closing weeks of the campaign, Hollywood stars rallied behind their favorite candidates. Frank Sinatra led a bevy of actors that included Gregory Peck, Gene Kelly, and Henry Fonda in support of Brown, while the Reagan forces included Pat Boone, Andy Devine, Chuck Connors, and teenage television heart-throb Ed Nelson. Yet, few movie stars of the time understood what Reagan was achieving. "Reagan's living in that Disneyland out there," liberal actor Robert Ryan derisively remarked in July 1966, "that land of enchantment, as if it were a hundred years ago. Things are pretty complicated today, but Reagan makes them sound simple, and people like that. 'Thank God,' they say when they hear him speak about how simple things are." What Ryan saw as Reagan's fatal flaw, others saw as his strength. A California poll taken in the fall of 1970 showed that what voters liked most about Reagan "was not what he said but how he said it." As one reporter explained, "He holds out the hope that all those troublesome problems that make the evening news so unpleasant will solve themselves."[114]

As Election Day drew closer, endorsements from the *Los Angeles Times* and the ten California newspapers that comprised the Copley chain buoyed the Reagan camp. The only sour note came when Senator Thomas Kuchel refused to back his party's candidate. On November 4, three days before the election, Reagan led Brown by a 46 to 41 percent margin, with a critical 13 percent of the voters still undecided.[115]

On Tuesday, November 8, a curious nation turned its attention to California wondering whether a former movie star could play a new role as governor of the country's second-largest state. Reagan crushed his opponent, garnering 3,742,913 votes (57.7 percent) to Brown's 2,749,174 (42.3 percent). The popular candidate captured fifty-five of the state's fifty-eight counties, received one million Democratic votes, and led his party to a sweeping victory by winning five of six statewide offices, twelve additional seats in the assembly and senate, and narrowing the state's Democratic congressional margin from an eight- to two-seat difference. The former actor had proven himself the Great Uniter as well as the Great Communicator.[116]

Reagan achieved the sweeping popular mandate he needed to advance the conservative revolution. "The New Deal era, begun with the election of Franklin D. Roosevelt in 1932, was over," remarked Northern California campaign manager Tom Reed. "Big government and unauthorized wars were repudiated by the voters all across America, but especially so in California. . . . One epoch had ended and another had begun."[117]

Goodbye to Hollywood

On January 1, 1965, George Lloyd Murphy traded a life in show business for a career as a United States senator. Although not always taken seriously by his Senate colleagues, the self-professed "dynamic conservative" emerged as the most popular speaker on the Republican fundraising circuit. During his first eighteen months in office, he delivered 207 speeches in twenty-nine states and raised $2 million. "George is the hottest thing in the party right now," observed one party strategist. Conservative leaders even talked of running him for vice president in 1968. Like his friend Ronnie, he fought to alter the course of American politics. There "is a valiant little band of us here in Washington," he wrote Hedda Hopper in September 1965, "who are determined to save the republic and restore the kind of government which made ours a great nation." Murphy established himself as one of the Senate's leading conservatives, speaking out against the Communist menace and attacking Lyndon Johnson's Great Society and War on Poverty as "ill-conceived programs that just haven't worked."[118]

The senator's prospects for political advancement took a downward turn when the removal of a cancerous throat tumor in August 1966 reduced his voice to a raspy whisper. The man who rose to office on his charm and wit was never again able to speak to large groups without using a microphone and amplifier. Murphy continued fighting for the conservative cause, but his political career ended six years later when a scandal cost him his reelection bid. His credibility with California voters suffered a fatal blow after Democratic rival John Tunney revealed that Technicolor Corporation president Patrick Frawley kept Murphy on the payroll during his Senate term. The *Los Angeles Times* refused to endorse him, explaining that a "senator must be above suspicion." On November 3, 1970, Tunney defeated Murphy 3,496,558 to 2,877,617 votes.[119]

After leaving the Senate on January 2, 1971, Murphy joined a Washington public relations firm; nine months later, he set up his own company representing clients such as Chiang Kai-Shek and the Taiwanese government. The loss of his Senate seat paled in comparison to the death of his wife, Julie, in September 1973. George flew home every other weekend while the Senate was in session to visit his arthritic bedridden spouse; but after she died, he moved to Washington to tend to his new business. In June 1982, Murphy married former model Bette Blandi and moved to Palm Beach, Florida, but still maintained his Washington venture as well as his involvement with conservative groups. On May 3, 1992, the eighty-nine-year-old actor-politician stopped dancing and charming forever. Ronald Reagan praised his longtime friend who had succumbed to leukemia as "a wonderful man and he and I got very close together in those terrible days in Hollywood when there was a Communist threat in the film business."[120]

Reagan's postelection story is familiar to most Americans. Winning the California governorship was the first step toward achieving a larger goal. "The real objective," explained Tom Reed, "was nothing less than political revolution in Washington." Shortly after taking office on January 2, 1967, Reagan's inner circle began planning a potential presidential run in 1968. By the middle of 1967, they were forging "a bottom-up organization by energizing most of those who had pursued and corralled the Goldwater delegates in 1964." As part of his coalition-building strategy, Reagan courted the Republican leadership base, attending national governors' conferences and meeting with key senators and Republican Party Chairman Peter O'Donnell. Party leaders remained skeptical that he could win, but Reagan entered the presidential primaries to promote the conservative cause. Disappointed their man did not secure his party's nomination, Reagan's advisers nevertheless welcomed Richard Nixon's victory as "a key step in ending the New Deal and welcoming the conservative/Reagan era."[121]

Reagan was easily reelected governor in 1970, ran against Gerald Ford in the presidential primaries in 1976, and finally achieved his goal of becoming president of the United States in 1980. Although he never fully succeeded in dismantling the New Deal, he led the biggest assault on it in history, creating a counterideology to the role the federal government should play in American life. Reagan failed in one key respect: instead of reducing the size of big government, his military spending policies created the largest budgets and deficits in U.S. history. Nevertheless, before the Great Communicator died on June 5, 2004, he knew that he and his longtime friend George Murphy would go to their graves having played the roles of a lifetime.

George Murphy and Ronald Reagan left an indelible impact on electoral politics by paving the way for the modern-day 24/7 media-infused world in which image is as important as content—a lesson that Charlton Heston and Arnold Schwarzenegger would later absorb and use to great effect. Murphy and Reagan brought politics into the new age of television and changed the ways in which candidates communicated with voters. In his 1968 article, "Ronald Reagan: A Republican Messiah?," Robert Kaufman observed how television now demanded a "more professional performance, and in any election with a large electorate some know-how in the uses of the medium now is considered an essential tool for candidates." There was hardly a politician, he concluded, "who doesn't wish for half the 'on-camera' talent and polish displayed by Ronald Reagan."[122]

The election of Murphy and Reagan opened the doors for other Hollywood stars to be taken seriously as political figures. The lines between politics and entertainment were blurring and party leaders could no longer
dismiss actors who wished to run for office. Showmanship mattered, and
men and women who spent their lives in front of the camera had a distinct
advantage over their rivals.

While conservatives worked to change the nature of federal government
during the 1950s and 1960s, movement activists on the left were quietly
building coalitions aimed at changing race relations and challenging what
they viewed as the nation's imperialistic policies. Once again, two of the central figures in the movement came from Hollywood. Like Murphy and Reagan, Harry Belafonte and Jane Fonda used their celebrity and media skills to
mount political crusades they hoped would alter the course of American life
and politics.

POLITICS IN BLACK AND WHITE: HARRY BELAFONTE

When Harry Belafonte walked into the basement of Harlem's Abyssinian Baptist Church in March 1956, little did he suspect that his life was about to change. Politicized several years earlier by Paul Robeson and W. E. B. Du Bois, Hollywood's hottest black star was suspicious of pompous black leaders who had failed to support his outspoken radical mentors. Yet, the young minister he met that day asked him to risk everything on behalf of his political beliefs. After recounting the progress of the Montgomery Bus Boycott launched on December 1, 1955, the Reverend Dr. Martin Luther King Jr. quietly told the twenty-nine-year-old actor, "We are caught up in a struggle that will not leave us. . . . I have no idea where it's going, and I don't quite know why I've been anointed to play the role I'm playing, but I accept it . . . and I'd like to ask you if you will serve in this mission as an ally to my needs."[1]

Meeting King was like being hit by a bolt of lightning. Impressed by the Reverend's humility and steely determination, the young radical agreed to help. Over the next twelve years, Belafonte often put his career on hold to serve as the civil rights movement's leading fundraiser and one of King's closest confidants. Together, the two men fought to change race relations in America.

Books about civil rights celebrate the achievements of Martin Luther King Jr., Ralph Abernathy, Bayard Rustin, and Stokely Carmichael but they rarely mention Harry Belafonte, who sat at the table with all of them. While George Murphy and Ronald Reagan served as highly visible spokesmen for the conservative movement, Belafonte preferred to "remain under the radar," as he put it, because he wanted to keep the spotlight on the movement and its leaders rather than on a movie star. Despite his absence from many historical accounts, Belafonte remained at the epicenter of the civil rights movement during its most important years. "It would be hard to say that Thurgood Marshall or Martin Luther King has made a stronger assault against the Jericho walls of segregation," observed one scholar, "than Jackie Robinson or Harry Belafonte."[2]

Like Murphy and Reagan, Harry Belafonte and Jane Fonda (the subject of the next chapter) used the power of their celebrity to fight what they viewed as dominant systems of American power that led to inequality at home and imperialism abroad. Believing the forces of capitalism were far too powerful for any one group to overturn, both struggled to build coalitions that collectively might succeed in generating radical change. Their stories appear in successive chapters, for while Murphy's and Reagan's political lives intertwined from the 1940s to the 1960s, Belafonte and Fonda represented sequential aspects of left movement politics. Beginning in the early 1950s and continuing through the 1980s, the two stars, though acting independently of one another, attacked racism, promoted civil rights, opposed the war in Vietnam, and struggled for women's rights and greater social and economic justice.

Movement politics on the left took many forms: marches, mass demonstrations, picket lines, sit-ins, voter registration drives, and electoral politics. While Murphy and Reagan relied on innovative uses of television to further their goals, the multitalented Belafonte used film, music, television, and concerts as weapons of political change. "There's a lot more to revolution than burning down the barricades," he observed, "and major social change is not always achieved by the front line troops."[3]

Harry Belafonte differed from the stars discussed in previous chapters in that he was politically active before his career took off. He was never part of the studio system or Hollywood's inner circle. Consequently, he used his stardom to serve his politics. During the 1950s and 1960s, the Harlem-born star was the most important left movement celebrity in the country. His striking good looks and breathtaking smile led *Modern Screen* to anoint him "Hollywood's first Negro star." His first two films, *Bright Road* (1953) and *Carmen Jones* (1954), thrust him into the public limelight at the same time his singing career was taking off. His *Calypso* album (1956), which featured "The Banana Boat Song" (known as "Day-O"), was the first record album to sell one million copies.[4]

Thinking of himself as an actor first, Belafonte wanted to make movies that would change the consciousness of a nation. When Hollywood studios proved too timid to move beyond racial stereotypes, he opened his own production company—the first modern black star to do so—and made films that offered audiences markedly different ways of looking at race. Politics, not money, is what drove Belafonte; but money made it possible to be political. Earning $750,000 in 1957 ($5.7 million in 2009 dollars) and over $1 million in 1958 and 1959 ($7.4 million in 2009 dollars) freed him to make polemical films without worrying about profits.[5]

While Murphy and Reagan turned to politics after their Hollywood careers faded, Belafonte gave up the screen at the height of his career in 1959 and spent the next decade as Hollywood's central figure in the civil rights movement. Serving as Martin Luther King Jr.'s liaison with Attorney General Robert F. Kennedy, he also helped organize the Hollywood March on Washington in 1963, mediated between contentious civil rights groups, promoted Pan-Africanism, opposed the Vietnam War, and, as Coretta Scott King remarked, remained one of her husband's two "most devoted and trusted friends."[6]

Ironically, Belafonte never intended to join the movement; the movement came to him. He wound up devoting his life doing something he often found burdensome, but felt compelled to do. His political involvement cost him a marriage and his health and earned him a reputation as a troublemaker.

FROM HARLEM TO HOLLYWOOD

Born in Harlem on March 1, 1927, Harold George Belafonte Jr. entered a world marked by poverty and racism on one hand and a vibrant political and cultural legacy on the other. During the 1920s, Harlem emerged as what black writer James Weldon Johnson called "the intellectual and artistic capital of the Negro world." The Harlem Renaissance produced literary and cultural figures who celebrated the rise of the "New Negro," men and women fiercely proud of their African heritage. Harlem was also home to Marcus Garvey, whose United Negro Improvement Association advocated black economic independence and encouraged kinsmen to return to Africa where they would be treated with dignity. Although federal authorities deported Garvey several months after Harry's birth, the young boy grew up listening to his mother praise the radical leader who came from the same Jamaican town. Committed to political change, Melvine Belafonte talked to her son about men like Garvey and radical actor-singer-activist Paul Robeson. "Don't be like your Uncle Lenny," who was a bootlegger and ran Harlem's numbers racket, she implored her son. "Be like Paul Robeson."[7]

Born in a highly race-conscious nation, Belafonte's self-identity was complicated by the fact that his Martinique-born father, Harold, and Jamaican-born mother, Melvine Love Belafonte, each came from mixed-race backgrounds. His paternal grandfather was a white rancher and his maternal grandmother a blond, blue-eyed Englishwoman. Melvine came to New York at age fifteen hoping to find a better life, but she barely eked out a living working as a domestic in the homes of white families. His father, a chef on British merchant vessels, left his family for a white woman when Harry was six, forcing the Belafontes to move into a six-room tenement flat that they shared with four other families. Melvine struggled to raise her children in a neighborhood where 60 percent of the population was unemployed, and only 14 percent of the poor were able to obtain relief. Pent-up anger among Harlemites sparked a massive riot on March 19, 1935, which left 4 people dead, 30 hospitalized, and 100 wounded.[8]

Hoping to provide her fatherless sons with a safer environment, Melvine sent eight-year-old Harry and his brother, Dennis, to live with her family in Kingston, Jamaica. Over the next five years, Belafonte observed the effects of colonialism, poverty, and racism. His Jamaican relatives were poor plantation laborers who worked for wealthy British absentee landowners. The youth's cultural and political education came in the form of songs and stories about Africa. Many of the jaunty calypso tunes he learned, and later popularized in the United States, contained politically charged lyrics calling for resistance against myriad foreign oppressors. "The Gold in Africa" and "Ethiopian War Drums" blasted fascist Italy for attacking Ethiopia in 1935 and urged blacks to "take a gun in your hand to defend the Ethiopian war."

Other songs demonized Hitler and defended the Loyalists fighting fascists in the Spanish Civil War.[9]

When Germany invaded Poland in September 1939, Melvine, fearing Hitler's imposition of Nazi rule over British colonies, brought her children back to Harlem. The return was not a happy one. Belafonte's undiagnosed dyslexia made him an object of mockery at school, where teachers and fellow students judged him as slow and diffident. Alienated and facing an uncertain future, the troubled seventeen-year-old dropped out of high school and joined the U.S. Navy in 1944. When he scored high on an IQ test, the Navy sent him to its Storekeeper School in Hampton, Virginia.

His years in the Navy proved an eye-opening experience. In addition to discovering the world of Southern racism, he met a diverse array of black soldiers—artists, musicians, poets, and writers—who encouraged him to read books by black intellectuals such as W. E. B. Du Bois. Shortly after arriving at Hampton, he also met Frances Marguerite Byrd, daughter of a well-to-do African American family, who was studying psychology at nearby Hampton Institute. When the Navy discharged him in 1945, Harry moved back to New York where he worked as a janitor while Marguerite completed a Ph.D. in child psychology. Three years later, the couple married.

Like many black servicemen, Belafonte hoped a nation that had defeated fascism abroad could now attack racism at home. Reading Du Bois and other black writers convinced him that the United States could bring "democracy and progressive change to 'oppressed colonial people'" throughout the world. How the nation would do so and what role he would play in fostering change was unclear. After attending a performance by the American Negro Theater (ANT), the veteran decided that the stage was his path. Theater, he discovered, "moved people. It could inspire. It sang magically."[10]

Volunteering as a stagehand, Belafonte soon began playing a number of small parts in ANT performances and forged a lifelong friendship with three of the company's aspiring actors, Sidney Poitier, Ruby Dee, and Ossie Davis. Using funds from the GI Bill, he enrolled in the Dramatic Workshop at the left-oriented New School for Social Research, where his classmates included Marlon Brando, Tony Curtis, Elaine Stritch, and Paddy Chayefsky.

Belafonte's first transformative political moment came in 1947 when he became friends with Paul Robeson, the nation's most outspoken black performer. A former all-American football player at Rutgers and graduate of Columbia Law School, Robeson spurned lucrative careers as a professional football player and lawyer for a career on stage and a lifetime of political acti-vism. While living in England between 1927 and 1939, he embraced socia-lism, African nationalism, and, after traveling to Moscow in 1934, the utopian goals of the Soviet Union. When he returned to the United States in 1939, the black radical established himself as a leading spokesman for racial equality and numerous left causes. Robeson's criticism of Truman's Cold War policies and praise of the Soviet Union's progressive stance on racial equality led the government to revoke his passport in 1950. J. Edgar Hoover called him the most dangerous black man in America, and Adolphe Menjou told HUAC that he defined a Communist as "anyone who attends any meeting at which Paul Robeson appears—and applauds."[11]

Robeson first met Belafonte after seeing him perform in Sean O'Casey's *Juno and the Paycock*, a story of British repression in Ireland. Robeson befriended Harry and Sidney Poitier, and the three men frequently took long walks through Harlem—then a bastion of Communist Party activism—or met at a bar on 125th Street and Fifth Avenue where they talked politics and revolution. Belafonte and Poitier admired Robeson's fearlessness and devotion to equality. Insisting "black people would never get their freedom under capitalism," Robeson urged both men, and friends Ossie Davis and Ruby Dee, to use their art as a tool of social change. Belafonte did and joined his mentor in campaigning and performing for Progressive Party presiden-tial candidate Henry Wallace in 1948. "As we went through those campaigns and sang at all rallies, my career began to unfold." Belafonte discovered that crowds loved his singing, which was then followed by talks from Robeson and Du Bois. "It was Robeson," he insisted, "who gave me the backbone to use my art to reach people."[12]

Davis, Dee, and Belafonte emerged from their early political years as rad-icals who, as Davis put it, were "part and parcel of a worldwide struggle against capitalist exploitation." The young trio, none of whom had yet launched their careers, saw themselves as "Black revolutionaries" fighting "to liberate the workers and save the world." The main question was where to channel their political energy. As Davis explained, "We wanted leaders who knew about revolution, the class war, and the dictatorship of the prole-tariat to take charge of the Struggle."[13]

Belafonte's first career break came in January 1949 when he performed at the Royal Roost jazz club in midtown Manhattan, where his backup band consisted of Charlie Parker, Miles Davis, Max Roach, and Tommy Potter. Although his singing career took off over the next several years, he hated performing pop songs whose vapid lyrics held little meaning for him. Thinking back to the politically edgy calypso tunes he learned in Jamaica, Belafonte traveled to the Library of Congress to research and learn folk songs and traditional ballads, music he felt spoke to the condition of blacks and working people. He also met with dockworkers and cotton pickers "to pick up their manners and problems."[14] In 1953, he released his first single, "Matilda," which became an immediate hit. Three years later, his *Belafonte* and *Calypso* albums both reached number one on the record charts. His new repertoire proved extraordinarily popular and Belafonte soon played at major venues in Las Vegas, Miami, and Los Angeles, where he became the first black performer at the famous Coconut Grove nightclub.

With his light bronze-colored skin, good looks, and taut muscular body, the 6' 1," 175-pound charismatic singer exuded a "visual magnetism" that made him the first black sex symbol of the 1950s (see fig. 5.1). When Belafonte walked out on stage in his signature tight silk pants, dark sunglasses,

FIGURE 5.1 Harry Belafonte was the first black matinee idol of the 1950s.
SOURCE: PHOTOFEST

and tailored bullfighter shirt open to the waist, he oozed self-confidence and, as one reporter noted, "an electrifying air of sexiness."[15]

At a time of rampant racism, Belafonte proved the most radical star of all: a black entertainer who appealed to all races, sexes, ages, and classes. "Negroes and whites both fell under his 'Valentino-like' spell," remarked one journalist. And while girls were "certainly wild about Harry," men saw in him "something of the he-man qualities of Clark Gable." During a 1959 concert in Pittsburgh, observed *Time*, Belafonte "packed the hall with steelworkers, symphony patrons, bobby-soxers and school children." As one radio disc jockey noted, "I can play Belafonte and not lose any part of my audience."[16]

Success did not diminish Belafonte's political activism. During the early 1950s, he walked picket lines protesting the arrest of W. E. B. Du Bois, sang at union gatherings, and worked with a number of surviving Popular Front organizations. He joined the Young Progressives of America (a successor to the defunct Young Communist League), raised funds for Robeson's *Freedomways* magazine, and held office in the Committee for the Negro in the Arts, a group led by Robeson and Du Bois. In 1956, after meeting King, he also took up the cause of civil rights.[17]

Like Charlie Chaplin and Edward G. Robinson, Belafonte soon learned that activism had its costs. The first casualties were his health and marriage. The singer was plagued by chronic laryngitis and in 1956 was operated on to remove nodes and widen his vocal chords. Worse yet, his relationship with Marguerite was marked by tensions from the start, for her status-conscious parents never accepted their high-school dropout son-in-law. During the first several years of their marriage, the couple lived mainly on her $3,600-a-year income. Once he became successful, his wife and mother-in-law wanted him to settle down, become a more stable breadwinner, and spend time with daughters Adrienne (born in 1950) and Shari (born in 1954). Yet Belafonte was compulsively drawn to politics. He was "always ready to get up and deliver a soap-box speech on civil rights," Marguerite grumbled. "He used to say, 'If it is necessary to fight—fight.'" Belafonte tried dealing with his problems by entering psychoanalysis, but tensions continued and the couple divorced in 1957. As he confessed to a reporter that year, "Success was traumatic for me. Here I was, a Negro, being accepted by people of all denominations, in all walks of life, by millions as a performer and an artist. Yet in my personal life, I was nowhere, not ready for it."[18]

Despite his pleasing public persona, the private Belafonte could be extremely difficult. When Sidney Poitier first met him in the late 1940s, he found the Navy veteran "proud, arrogant, good-looking, [and] intensely political." Belafonte could "be the worst S.O.B. that God created," Poitier explained. "But if he's there for you, he's there for you all the way." Belafonte knew he was impatient, especially with white employers who viewed him as an uppity black man who should be grateful for his success. Marguerite begrudgingly admired his political commitment but complained that his diffident attitude prompted many club owners to stop hiring him. Yet his anger often came from frustration with those who did not understand his fierce desire to improve racial conditions. Television director Don Medford understood and explained how the star's "hard core hostility" gave "a demon drive to Belafonte's career and immense conviction to his work." Black reporters, however, found him "so affable and outgoing that you forget for a moment that basically he is a resolutely serious man, one of the country's most militant fighters for human rights."[19]

Although his family life proved problematic, Belafonte's singing success was paralleled by his rising fortunes as an actor. He appeared in several television variety shows in 1951 and made his Broadway debut in December 1953, costarring with Hermione Gingold in *John Murray Anderson's Almanac.* Several months later, he won a Tony Award for his performance, the first African American to do so.[20] The Tony was gratifying, but his emerging film career more so. After seeing him sing in the spring of 1952, MGM's Dore Schary, the liberal Democrat who replaced Louis B. Mayer, signed the talented artist to costar with Dorothy Dandridge in *Bright Road.* In August 1952, Belafonte traveled to Hollywood to begin production. This was the opportunity of his dreams: the chance to portray black life in a dignified way to mass audiences throughout the world. Over the next seven years, the movie industry's hottest black star made four more films that he hoped would change the way Americans, black and white, thought about race. Hollywood, however, was not ready for Harry Belafonte.

Culture, Politics, and Race

Belafonte went to Hollywood determined to change a nation, not just to entertain it. "Celebrity and politics is very much a 20th century phenomenon," Belafonte observed years later, and he believed that movie stars could exert tremendous power "over people's minds and thoughts." He envisioned film as a powerful tool for reshaping national ideas about race. "There was a great reluctance on America's part to think black people are the most oppressed in the nation. Just relying on politics wouldn't have gotten us anything." But movies could. He arrived in Hollywood confident there "was still enough of the liberal community even in the wake of McCarthyism" to make progressive films about race. But he soon discovered that studios "were resistant to anything radical; to Hollywood it [movies about black life] seemed radical, to us it wasn't that radical."[21]

Belafonte began production on *Bright Road* in August 1952 well aware of cinema's potential to change racial attitudes. He remembered sitting in a movie theater in 1944 and being amazed as a white audience cheered when a black soldier killed a Nazi in *Sahara*. Yes, the man may have been a Nazi, but he was still a white man who died at the hands of a black man. Belafonte also understood that cinematic moments like these were rare. Before the 1950s, only a brief cycle of films—*Pinky* (1949), *Home of the Brave* (1949), *Intruder in the Dust* (1949), and *Lost Boundaries* (1949)—ventured beyond stereotypical portrayals of African Americans as anything other than slaves, domestics, or Pullman porters. The movie industry could hardly expect to offer progressive visions of race when it could not even integrate its own studios. Ruby Dee recounted how when she arrived at Fox in 1949 to shoot *No Way Out*, a liberal film in which Sidney Poitier played a doctor, the two leads were "immediately struck by the fact that we didn't see any black people working anywhere. No technicians, no grips, no electricians, no props people. We didn't see any dark skins in the makeup and wardrobe departments or as hairdressers. From the minute we entered the gate in the morning till the time we left, we were in an all-white world, and that reality was hard for us to ignore."[22]

Despite the efforts of progressives such as Dore Schary, the box-office crisis caused by the rise of television and lingering fears of HUAC heightened racial timidity in Hollywood. With Southern markets accounting for an estimated 20 percent of domestic sales, studio heads hesitated making any films that might offend white patrons. After all, they were in the money-making business, not the consciousness-raising business.

Belafonte's determination to have audiences see African Americans as people rather than as people of color is the common denominator running through his early movies. "If we do not begin to get a whole new set of visions and attitudes in our vocabulary," he explained, "we are going to be locked in the same places that we've always been in."[23] Like George Murphy, Belafonte understood the power of images. Yet unlike Murphy, he wanted to use the mass media to sell a race, not simply a candidate.

Bright Road is a small film about the everyday life of black teachers and children that could just have easily been about white teachers and children. Based on a story by West Indian Mary Elizabeth Vroman, the movie stars Dorothy Dandridge as the dedicated fourth-grade teacher Jane Richards who reaches out to a seemingly slow and diffident student, C. T. Young. The kind-hearted Richards discovers that the boy's inattentiveness stems not from a lack of brains but from poverty, hunger, and shame. His family is so poor they cannot afford lunch or decent clothing for their child. When Richards asks C. T. what he has against school, he replies, "I got nothing against school, but I got nothing for it." With the help of Belafonte, who plays school principal Mr. Williams, they turn C. T.'s life around and interest him in learning.

Belafonte is stiff in his first screen role—only coming alive when he sings "Suzanne"—and the exceedingly slow-paced film does not hold up over time. Nevertheless, it marked an important effort to break from stereotypical plots and roles for black actors. The nine- and ten-year-old black schoolchildren behave no differently than white kids of the same age. Audiences see that the problems black teachers and parents face are the same problems white teachers and parents face. By emphasizing the fundamental similarities between black and white family life, the filmmakers hoped to foster greater empathy and understanding among white audiences.

While such an approach might seem outdated today, it is important to remember that *Bright Road* appeared when segregation ruled the South and de facto segregation appeared nearly everywhere else. To suggest the fundamental sameness of black and white children in 1953 was a daring statement. Indeed, no major theater chain was willing to distribute a film starring a black man and woman. Black audiences, however, loved it and the Urban League honored *Bright Road* for its "contribution towards interracial cooperation."[24]

Belafonte and Dandridge teamed up the following year to make *Carmen Jones* (1954), a cinematic version of Oscar Hammerstein's stage adaptation of Bizet's *Carmen* and the first all-black studio musical since MGM's *Cabin in the Sky* in 1943. Shot in the months following the Supreme Court's landmark decision ending segregation, *Brown v. Board of Education* (May 17,

1954), the production generated controversy within the African American community over the wisdom of making an all-black film during the struggle for integration. Belafonte, who was praised for his starring role as Joe (Don José in Bizet's opera), defended the movie for making two vital contributions: it provided nonstereotypical roles for black actors and actresses, and its success at the box office "established the fact that pictures with Negro artists, pictures dealing with the folklore of Negro life, were commercially feasible." Belafonte saw the cinematic tale of love, lust, and jealousy as a human story, not a black story. He proved right. Even conservative columnist Hedda Hopper raved about it. "I got so excited I burned a big hole in the front of my dress. Yep, the film is that hot." The movie was a hit, setting box-office records in numerous cities and earning $3 million for the studio.[25]

Ironically, the film's male lead proved far more controversial than the film. The anti-Communist periodical *Counterattack* nearly derailed the budding star's career in January 1954, when it accused him of being "a Communist fronter." Calling him a close friend of Communist Paul Robeson, the editors listed Belafonte's suspect political activities: singing for the Distributive Workers Union ("a 100% follower of Moscow's line"), chairing the theater chapter of the Committee for the Negro in the Arts, and performing for numerous subversive organizations.[26] In being "named," Belafonte joined the ranks of other politically outspoken African Americans targeted by Red-hunters: Robeson; actors Canada Lee, James Edwards, and Ossie Davis; actresses Lena Horne and Ruby Dee; and pianist Hazel Scott.

Uncertain what to do, Belafonte turned to Robeson for advice. His radical mentor explained how following his run-in with HUAC his popularity and income declined so severely—from $104,000 in 1947 to $2,000 a year in the early 1950s—that he could no longer function as an artist. Knowing that his friends were not yet as famous as most of the Hollywood stars pursued by the publicity-conscious HUAC, Robeson cautioned Belafonte and Sidney Poitier "not to be too radical because he never wanted us to lose our credibility." Robeson urged them to use their growing popularity within the white community to work for integration. Heeding Robeson's counsel, Belafonte visited *Counterattack*'s editors and told them he was "not and has never been a member of the Communist Party and has never knowingly associated with any Communist front."[27] He admitted participating in the various groups they listed but without knowing that they were Communist fronts.

Counterattack's editors remained suspicious but removed his name from the blacklist at the request of Ed Sullivan. Anxious to get the singer on his popular television show, the powerful anti-Communist columnist and TV host asked Belafonte to meet with him to discuss the charges. "The morally elite thing to have done," Belafonte recounted in 1996, "would have been to tell him where to shove his show." But he did not. He gave Sullivan the same set of vague answers he gave *Counterattack*. That proved sufficient for the TV host, who booked him for several performances.[28]

Belafonte did not tell the editors or Sullivan the entire truth. Although he was not a member of the Communist Party, he certainly knew the radical orientation of the groups he joined and did not intend to retreat from political activism. It is unclear whether Belafonte's willingness to cooperate with *Counterattack* and Sullivan was a strategic decision that would allow future activism or a traumatic reaction to Robeson's fate. Throughout his life, Belafonte insisted on staying out of the political limelight in order to avoid the jealousy of civil rights leaders. While that was probably true, his decision may also have come from an unwillingness to surrender a potentially lucrative career. Belafonte knew what it meant to be poor and did not want to revisit that part of his life again. So he told the Red-hunters what they wanted to hear and got on with his life and politics.[29]

When Marge and Gower Champion asked him to tour Southern cities in the pre-Broadway run of *Three for Tonight* in 1954, Belafonte quickly agreed. "My motivation," he explained in a guest newspaper column, "was to help bring about as much as any one could a greater feeling of respect for my race. I was determined to face whatever conditions existed in order to go out there on stage and cause white Southern audiences to accept a Negro performer in a mixed cast."[30] The tour provided the New Yorker with firsthand knowledge of racial conditions in the South. A star on the stage, he was just another black man off it, forced to use segregated bathrooms, water fountains, restaurants, hotels, and airport lounges.

Over the next several years, Belafonte's skyrocketing success as a nightclub performer and recording artist earned him a financial freedom enjoyed by few politically active stars. His ability to sell out major nightclubs such as New York's Empire Room at the Waldorf Astoria and Los Angeles' Coconut Grove gave him unprecedented clout, which he used to break the color barrier in a number of major venues. When the New Frontier Hotel in Las Vegas offered him $12,000–$15,000 a week ($96,100–$120,000 in 2009 dollars) to perform in July 1955, he refused until they gave him and his accompanist a room in the hotel. In November, he became the first African American to play the Palmer House in Chicago, and in December he did the same for Miami's posh Eden Roc Hotel, where he demanded—and was granted—use of the same facilities as white guests. Only five years earlier, the singer needed six separate passes in order to move around Miami after the 9:00 P.M. curfew imposed on all blacks.[31]

While nightclubs allowed him to reach thousands, Belafonte hoped to raise racial consciousness by entering the homes of millions of Americans. One of the first African Americans to make regular appearances on television, he offered audiences an image of racial dignity that flew against stereotypes seen on shows like *Beulah* and *Amos 'n' Andy*. Between 1954 and 1957, he sang his popular calypso songs on *The Ed Sullivan Show*, *The Colgate Hour*, *The Jackie Gleason Show*, the *28th Annual Academy Awards*, and *The Nat King Cole Show*, and he made his dramatic debut on the Ronald Reagan–hosted *General Electric Theater*. The only controversial moment came in November 1958 when saboteurs in Montgomery, Alabama, cut the transmission cable of a local television station just as TV host Steve Allen was introducing his guest star.[32]

Belafonte's success as a recording artist propelled him to international fame. In 1957, his record albums sold more copies than Elvis or Frank Sinatra and the popularity of hits "Jamaica Farewell" and "The Banana Boat Song (Day-O)" earned him the title of "King of Calypso." As with all his cultural endeavors, Belafonte infused his songs with political meaning. "When I sing 'The Banana Boat Song,'" he explained to one reporter, "some people glimpse it as a fanciful little tale that charms and delights the listener. But for the singer, it talks about a human condition that was very real to me, very painful and extremely oppressive."[33]

Confident that cultural politics could heighten mass awareness, Belafonte also felt that social movements needed to exert constant pressure on politicians in order to force changes in government policies. To that end, he cemented ties with key leaders in the Democratic Party. In October 1956, after performing at several Democratic National Committee fundraisers, he held two private meetings with the party's presidential nominee Adlai Stevenson, in which they discussed ways of achieving greater racial justice. Pleased with their conversation, the singer filmed a television spot endorsing the Illinois governor. Belafonte also used his celebrity to attract people to the civil rights movement by performing at demonstrations and fundraisers around the country. At a Chicago gathering in May 1956, he promised that fame would never distract him from his larger goals. "I will rise or fall with my people who have been struggling so long for complete democracy."[34]

Belafonte kept his word. When in the fall of 1956 producer Darryl Zanuck offered him the starring role in *Island in the Sun*, based on Alec Waugh's hard-hitting novel about the legacy of slavery, colonialism, poverty, and interracial romance in the West Indies, he immediately accepted. Here was a role that explored issues of race, class, and the black islanders' pursuit of political independence. The film is set in the fictional West Indian island of Santa Marta, a British colony of 100,000, nine-tenths of whom are descended from slaves. Playing tough-talking labor leader David Boyeur, Belafonte actualizes on the screen the model of the "New Negro" envisioned by writers and activists of the Harlem Renaissance. Smart, articulate, and self-confident, Boyeur does not tolerate the patronizing attitudes of the island's white elite. He stands up to the colonial power structure and voices the islanders' determination to break free of racial and political oppression without ever losing his cool. The film moves back and forth between the story of local struggles for political independence and a series of interracial romances.

Belafonte embraced the project hoping that its onscreen militancy would serve as a role model for offscreen actions. Released in June 1957, the film appeared at a moment when African Americans in Little Rock, Arkansas, were preparing to integrate their public schools; when blacks in Africa were calling for freedom from colonial rule; and when Belafonte's marriage to a white woman, Julie Robinson, generated controversy within the black community. How timely, then, to hear Belafonte's labor leader tell an investigative reporter of the islanders' determination to break the shackles of colonialism and establish their own free nation. "What we want is equality," he explains. When the reporter asks him to identify the most important current problem, he answers without hesitating, "Race."

Island in the Sun was the first Hollywood film in which a black male lead was romantically involved with a white woman who was equally passionate for him. *Island*, Belafonte told a black reporter, is the "most important sociological film ever made. This could open the way for other Negroes to play better and more advanced parts."[35] Indeed, the movie appeared a year after the Production Code Administration eliminated its long-standing prohibition against miscegenation. Woven into the story of the island's upcoming elections is a romance between Belafonte and Joan Fontaine, who plays Mavis Norman, sister-in-law of aristocratic plantation owner and political candidate Maxwell Fleury (James Mason). Another interracial relationship involves secretary Margot Seaton (Dorothy Dandridge) and the governor's aide, Dennis Archer (John Justin).

Boyeur finds himself torn between love and the struggles of his people. Colonial elites, he tells Norman, think of him as "an upstart, a nobody who has gotten control of the union; a dangerous man who should be watched, carefully." When the two stand on a hillside, watching the plane carrying Seaton and Archer as it leaves for England, the blond actress suggests that they too could fly away to Europe. But Boyeur cannot abandon his home. "My skin is my country," he tells her. "Here's my world. These are my people and this is where I belong." "You're like a rock," Norman laments as she walks away. Boyeur calls out that his people finally have hope and power. "And I have to show them how to use it." The movie ends with the heartsick labor leader alone on a cliff, head bowed, knowing that the cause is greater than the individual—just as Belafonte felt off the screen.

According to *Look* magazine, *Island in the Sun* established Belafonte as "the first Negro matinee idol in our entertainment history." Yet, the charismatic star wound up profoundly disappointed with the final product. Fearing box-office losses, producer Darryl Zanuck eliminated explicitly romantic scenes between the two leads, including a shot of Fontaine gazing lovingly into Belafonte's eyes and touching his shoulder as he wraps his arms around her waist. In the final version, the black star never touches his white costar, and the film's steamiest moment comes when they drink out of the same coconut. According to Fontaine, Zanuck cut the scene in which they kiss because he "felt that it was too soon to tackle the race question with honesty."[36] Worse yet from Belafonte's point of view, Zanuck toned down the novel's controversial politics. In Waugh's book, the labor leader is a fighter for class and racial rights, yet we rarely see or hear him do so in the film. Although the novel focused on the longtime exploitation of island workers, the film only briefly mentions the islanders' economic problems and opposition to colonialism.[37]

Belafonte considered the film hopelessly bland, but many groups around the country viewed it as one of the most dangerous movies ever made. At the time of its release, twenty-eight states still prohibited interracial marriage. Memphis censors banned *Island in the Sun* on the grounds it offered "a depiction of miscegenation offensive to moral standards and no good for either White or Negro." South Carolina legislators threatened to pass a bill imposing a $5,000 fine on any theater that ran it, while Florida Klansmen picketed a Jacksonville theater with signs proclaiming "A TICKET TO THIS SHOW IS INTEGRATION." Protests also extended north to Minneapolis, where concern that the movie would lead to "teenage Negro-white dating and petting parties" sparked a campaign to stop local theaters from running it. An upset Joan Fontaine told reporters of receiving hate mail. "I never realized when I took this role there would be such a furor. Most of the letter-writers termed me unprintable, filthy names." She noted that hate mail came from New Jersey, Ohio, and Pennsylvania, as well as from Southern states.[38]

Despite or perhaps because of the controversy, the Twentieth Century–Fox production did very well at the box office and secured Belafonte's reputation as a bankable star. Success did not diminish his anger. Soon after its opening, Belafonte criticized Zanuck for caving in to Southern pressure by asking him and Fontaine not to refer to each other in any public statements about the movie. Fox Studios, he told the press, got frightened by "a small group that makes a big noise in an empty tin can but it sounds like a tremendous armada." The only praise he offered was for the film's "portrayal of a Negro on a completely equal social level with a white man." Belafonte's unprecedented criticism led columnist Louis Sobol to observe, "The film colony could not recall any star rapping his own picture—especially a picture bearing the stamp of Darryl Zanuck. 'Belafonte's through in pictures,' is Hollywood's opinion."[39]

Hollywood was not through with Belafonte, but Belafonte was through with Hollywood. The studios, he insisted, lacked artistic and political integrity. "I've found censorship and . . . fear the predominant factors both in television and motion pictures whenever it comes to subject matter involving Negroes," he told a reporter in July 1957. "If I were a white artist I could make many motion pictures and TV spectaculars," but studios "never give stories of Negro life a chance to bloom—everybody is afraid someone might be hurt."[40]

Belafonte earned a reputation as a difficult and angry actor because he turned down so many projects for political reasons. "Anyone who came to me with a movie that was fraught with benevolent paternalism and still incapable of seeing black people as some neuter object," he explained, "got really pissed" when "you brought this to their attention, especially if they expected you to do it." When Samuel Goldwyn offered him the starring role in *Porgy and Bess* in 1957, the actor refused because he felt that Catfish Row, with its pimps and pushers, presented blacks in an undignified light. As he told one black periodical, he would "never play any role which demands that he spend all his time on his knees."[41] Over the next several years, he rejected starring roles in *Lilies of the Field* (1963)—because it was "just a token placement of a black character that made no real sense"—*Guess Who's Coming to Dinner* (1967), *To Sir, with Love* (1967), and *Shaft* (1971). Belafonte's uncompromising position created tensions with the more accommodating Sidney Poitier, who accepted many of the parts he turned down. Never as publicly outspoken as his militant friend, Poitier told a reporter in the late 1950s, "I have no politics, but I am a Negro. For this reason I try to do and say nothing that might take a step backward."[42]

Belafonte's anger over Hollywood's reluctance to deal with racial issues in a frank manner, especially interracial romance, was personal as well as political. In April 1957, two months prior to *Island in the Sun*'s release, he generated national controversy by marrying a white Jewish woman, Julie Robinson. A graduate of New York's infamous Little Red Schoolhouse, Robinson shared Belafonte's radical politics and commitment to racial justice. She spent six years dancing in the otherwise all-black Katherine Dunham Company and staying in the same segregated hotels as the rest of the troupe. In an article he wrote for *Ebony*, Belafonte explained that he did not marry her "to further the cause of integration. I married her because I was in love with her."[43]

Being in the public eye turned a private matter into a heated public debate, something the star loathed. Letters to *Ebony* reflected divided views within the African American community. While some argued "we would do well not to make an issue of interracial marriage so often in our magazines," others condemned the star for abandoning his wife and children for the white dancer. Criticism was so intense that *Life* magazine ran a feature story about Belafonte in May 1957 entitled, "I Wonder Why Nobody Don't Like Me."[44]

Refusing to be constrained by public criticism of his personal life or the fears of white studio heads, in August 1957 Belafonte opened the first modern black film company, HarBel Productions, with the dual goal of making progressive films and integrating the movie industry by training young African Americans in all aspects of production. Belafonte saw film as a powerful weapon in the hands of a black artist, albeit an often reluctant one. "I haven't wanted to become a symbol but I have," he explained. "And, since I want to work, I at least want to do pictures I consider worthwhile and the film industry is not really geared toward pictures of this sort."[45]

Dramatic changes in the structure of the postwar film industry made Belafonte's new venture possible. The breakup of the studio system following the Paramount antitrust decision in 1948 led studios to cut costs by ending long-term star contracts (freeing actors to be more political) and striking deals with independent companies to produce films which studios would then distribute. In 1949, only 20 percent of the 234 major studio releases were independently produced; by 1957, independents accounted for 58 percent of Hollywood's 291 releases. Hoping to achieve greater profits by doubling as stars and producers, many actors created their own independent production companies in the 1950s. Few stars, however, organized companies with as explicit a radical agenda as Belafonte, for few were willing to place politics ahead of profits.[46]

Like Charlie Chaplin, whom he considered "the supreme working-class hero," Belafonte felt that film allowed him "the opportunity to say a number of things I'd never be able to express just talking." Yet unlike Chaplin, whose cinematic politics were highly personal, Belafonte linked his cinematic efforts to the goals of the civil rights movement. He wanted to alter stereotypes by making movies in which roles for black and white actors were interchangeable. "I'd like to be in a Cary Grant type of picture—something light and frothy," the intense actor told a startled reporter. "I'm not talking about the *Amos 'n Andy* kind of thing, but something more sophisticated—about an average guy with an average job in an average situation, but one filled with humor. I think it would be just as commercial, and contribute just as much to social advancement for the Negro to be seen in light and pleasant roles for a change."[47]

Belafonte did not make a comedy until the 1970s, but he developed a series of eclectic film projects that included the life story of black Russian poet Alexander Pushkin; a science-fiction drama about a nuclear holocaust; a crime caper; a story on the Montgomery Bus Boycott in which he would star as Martin Luther King Jr.; and an account of the Little Rock integration struggle. He also hoped to make a movie about Hannibal the Great, the North African leader who conquered Spain, and a Western about the post–Civil War black migration. Belafonte was confident that success at the box office would "prove that Hollywood's fears about showing the Negro out of type have been misplaced and that others will follow suit and create more jobs for Negro performers."[48]

Belafonte used cinema as a weapon of propaganda as well as entertainment. People who never listened to civil rights speeches paid their hard-earned money to see similar messages in HarBel films. Over the next two years, Belafonte turned out two pictures—*The World, the Flesh, and the Devil* (1959) and *Odds against Tomorrow* (1959)—that he hoped would open minds. Both films feature racial themes but they are not fundamentally about race. As he told reporters, "I intend to show the Negro in conflicts that stem from the general human condition and not solely from the fact of his race." Belafonte's characters offered audiences models of secular, tough-minded, independent yet flawed men who took crap from no one. The main protagonist in *Odds against Tomorrow*, Belafonte observed, "demanded his dignity by just his presence. . . . No black guy ever talked to white guys that way in films."[49]

In September 1957, Belafonte partnered with independent producer Sol C. Siegel to make *The World, The Flesh, and the Devil*, which MGM agreed to distribute. HarBel put up $250,000 of the feature's $1.4 million budget in exchange for one-third of its profits. Dealing with racial issues, his film also focused on a key left concern of the 1950s: the threat of nuclear war. On November 15, 1957, the National Committee for a Sane Nuclear Policy placed a full-page ad in the *New York Times* warning, "WE ARE FACING A DANGER UNLIKE ANY DANGER THAT HAS EVER EXISTED."[50] Five months later, Belafonte began shooting a film about the aftermath of a nuclear catastrophe that destroys most of civilization. Based on Matthew Shiel's 1901 novel *The Purple Cloud*, the oddly titled *The World, the Flesh, and the Devil* opens with Belafonte playing Pennsylvania mining engineer Ralph Burton, who survives a nuclear catastrophe and gradually makes his way to New York City where the only other survivor he meets is Sarah Crandall, played by blond beauty Inger Stevens.

After radiation poisoning devastates the world, it is an ingenious black man who begins the impossible task of reconstructing civilization. The political metaphor was subtle but clear: if blacks could reconstruct the world, they could overcome racial inequalities. Burton finds food, clothing, and housing for the couple, rigs up a generator to power the deserted city, and tries to reach other survivors by broadcasting messages on a radio station transmitter. The engineer is too concerned with survival to think about sex, so much so that the pair—despite Crandall's objections—maintain separate residences. An hour into the movie, a boat pulls into the New York docks and out crawls a nearly dead Benson Thacker, played by Mel Ferrer. The film takes a melodramatic turn as the two men vie for Crandall's affection. Crandall loves Burton, but he is too obsessed by their racial differences to express his feelings. When Crandall talks about love and marriage, Burton curtly reminds her that despite the nuclear catastrophe, he is still "colored," "a Negro," a "nigra" or "nigger," and that in any other situation she would never give him the time of day. The jealous Thacker starts a gun battle with his rival that Burton wins; but our hero puts down his weapon rather than kill him. The film ends with Burton finally taking Crandall's hand and they walk off together, a happy couple until they stop and ask Thacker to join them. As the three walk off together holding hands, an intertitle flashes on the screen: "THE BEGINNING."

Belafonte delivers a powerful performance, holding the screen by himself for the first half hour. The scenes of the deserted city, especially of an abandoned, auto-clogged Lincoln Tunnel and Washington Bridge are hauntingly beautiful. Yet the film ultimately proved as racially timid as *Island in the Sun*, a fact Belafonte blamed on Sol Siegel and "Hollywood studio chicanery." Soon after filming began, Siegel accepted a position as head of production for MGM and used his power as coproducer and studio distributor to tone down the interracial romance. Other than cutting her hair, Burton does not touch his white girlfriend until the last scene. Belafonte was so upset that at one point he walked off the set. When asked by a reporter if he thought the film shied away from controversial racial themes, Belafonte responded, "Not only do I agree, but I said as much to Sol Siegel while we were making the film. And the protests of Inger Stevens and Mel Ferrer were even stronger than mine. But it didn't do any good." Belafonte's power as coproducer was weakened when, at the outset of production, his name resurfaced on yet another blacklist. "The first thing they [Siegel and MGM] talked about was a loyalty agreement. We worked all that out, but it was a struggle."[51]

Despite his disappointment, critics praised the actor and the film. *Boxoffice* magazine hailed it as a "revolutionary picture" and spoke glowingly of Belafonte's portrayal of "a proud, and intelligent, mechanically proficient Negro." They also extolled him as "one of our most astute dramatic stars" and "as an actor to be reckoned with." Unhappy with the film's ambiguous ending, the *Saturday Review* sarcastically quipped that "segregationist Southerners and the South African government will be heartened to know that even in a relatively empty world the race problem continues." Despite the periodical's sarcasm, angry Southerners boycotted theaters showing the controversial film.[52]

Determined not to make the same mistake twice, Belafonte signed a six-picture distribution deal with United Artists that gave him total control over all aspects of production, making him the first African American to obtain such an agreement. For his initial picture, *Odds against Tomorrow* (1959), HarBel put up $274,000 of the $1.3 million budget and took 50 percent of the gross. Setting up production headquarters in the Bronx, far away from Hollywood eyes and interference, Belafonte brought in a number of leftists to work on the film. He secretly hired blacklisted writer Abe Polonsky to do the screenplay (which was credited to John O. Killens), longtime antifascist Robert Wise to direct, and leftists Robert Ryan, Ed Begley, and Shelley Winters to costar. Ryan, who spent most of his career playing bad guys, was one of Hollywood's most fearless activists. Refusing to be silenced by HUAC investigators, he insisted in 1952 that if an actor "believes enough in a cause, he should speak up for it, no matter his position." He took the role in *Odds* because he believed the film would make a "distinctive contribution to the process of making democracy complete."[53]

With a score written by Modern Jazz Quartet's John Lewis and a stylish film noir look, the movie's tone and characters are closer to Miles Davis than to Martin Luther King Jr. Belafonte wanted *Odds* "to change the way America was doing business, and in that climate Abe and I then saw the opportunity to put a point of view on the screen." The tension-laden plot focuses on three men who plan to rob a bank in upstate New York. Belafonte plays nightclub performer Johnny Ingram, Begley ex-cop David Burke, and Ryan ex-con Earl Slater. While Belafonte's hip singer was no Cary Grant, the actor kept his pledge to break away from caricatured roles. "The character I play is not thrown in for a racial thesis," he told the *New York Times*, "but because the bank robbers . . . need a Negro who can enter the bank as a colored delivery man."[54]

Fundamentally a heist film, *Odds* nevertheless delivers a strong message about the destructive power of hate. When Ryan's racist Southern ex-con meets Belafonte's gambling-addicted singer, he angrily tells mastermind Burke (Begley), "You didn't say nothing about the third man being a nigger."

Racism is a two-way road to destruction in this film, for Ingram's loathing of whites equally diminishes him. When he walks in on an integrated PTA meeting at his ex-wife's upscale apartment, he disparagingly refers to the group as "your ofay friends who are going to save the world." Later on, the bank robbery goes wrong and the cops shoot Burke. Instead of trying to escape, Slater and Ingram start shooting at each other. The final scene has the two criminals running up a gas tower. Oblivious of the dangerous setting, they fire at each other and the tanks explode. When an ambulance attendant finds the two charred bodies and asks the police chief, "Which is which?" the cop replies, "Take your pick." The film ends with the camera focusing on a road sign, "STOP. DEAD END." Explaining the ending to the press, Belafonte remarked that unlike the weak conclusion in *The World*, "No brotherly love saves everybody here. Their hatred destroys both of them." Despite opening to positive reviews, the film only managed to break even during its initial run.[55]

Belafonte's rising screen success led him to take a more active role in the civil rights movement. The actor was part of a circle we might call "Hollywood's African American left," men and women—such as Belafonte, Davis, Dee, Poitier, and Lena Horne—committed to fighting racism. In May 1957, he and Julie joined King, Roy Wilkins, and A. Philip Randolph in the Washington Prayer Pilgrimage to celebrate the third anniversary of the *Brown v. Board of Education* decision. A year later, screenwriter Abe Polonsky noted how even in the midst of working together on the screenplay of *Odds against Tomorrow*, Belafonte was constantly preoccupied with movement struggles and "goes on all time with [his concerns about] Negroes."[56]

The difficulties of participating in movement events while starting a film company, maintaining a singing career, absorbing criticism for marrying a white woman, and suffering through several eye operations took its toll on the normally energetic star. Reluctant to devote so much of his life to racial struggles, the young radical nevertheless felt compelled to do so—and now felt resentful. As he confided to Ossie Davis in the summer of 1958, he was tired of fighting all the time; he wanted to quit the movement and get on with his life. Davis responded by writing his friend a frank letter that reviewed the racial struggles of the past decade and sounded a call to action. "Any Negro young or old might have been fully justified at the end of WWII in believing that the millennium had come and a better life for him and his people was at hand." But they soon discovered "fascism and racism were not

dead: they were happening here. . . . Which of us did not feel impelled to
fight back with everything we could? And if the weapons we found in our
hands to fight with were placed there by communists, who can blame us:
who the hell asks questions when he finds himself in a fight for his life!"
Their ultimate commitment was never "to the Left for the sake of the Left"
but "to the cause of negro liberation."[57]

The left leadership of the 1930s and 1940s, Davis insisted, was no longer
appropriate. Martin Luther King Jr. and his massive black following had rendered old patterns of power obsolete. Yet King's rapid rise had also "brought
on a grave crisis among the Negro powers-that-be: all the old heads see
themselves and their preferred positions threatened by this young black tor-
nado from the sidewalks of Montgomery, Ala; and each is moved to do what
he can to cut King down to size and so eliminate the threat he represents."
Remarking that "Negro Nationalism, in its broadest aspects now becomes
the only legitimate vehicle of revolution and change possible in this country," Davis concluded his letter with an inspiring appeal to his friend:

> And it is in the very center of this movement that you belong, Harry, as do
> the rest of us. It needs us as we need it. It is a great big, black umbilical, and
> to cut yourself off from it would be to perish. You say you are tired! Of
> course you are! So why don't you take the hell off—you and Julie? This is
> no minor upheaval . . . this movement is not in such dire straits that any of
> us must stand watch by the barricades through the night. It will take King
> at least five years to consolidate his position as spokesman for this "third
> phase" of the American Revolution which began in 1776 and has not
> been finished yet. So cool it; rest yourself; take a vacation; go abroad, to
> Africa, to Asia, to Europe—help tie the scattered threads of aspiring black
> men together; become an international spokesman for the New Negro in
> America if you will . . . or if you want to just keep your mouth shut except
> for singing: either way you serve the cause. Being the best of what you are
> is all that counts. None of us owes anything now to Marx, to the left, or to
> communism: our supreme obligation is to Negro Liberation . . . whatever
> the red flag stood for yesterday; it is the black flag under which mankind
> will take its next step forward.[58]

Belafonte took his friend's advice. In August 1958, he, Julie, and their
young son David went on a month-long European singing tour where, in

addition to captivating audiences, he spoke out about racial struggles at home. "Justice will prevail," he told reporters in Rome, and "America will survive [Arkansas Governor Orval] Faubus in the same way Europe survived Hitler." His faith in white liberals was shaken when upon his return he found it impossible "to rent an apartment in the liberal center of the United States," New York City. Landlords saw him first and foremost as a black man. Belafonte responded by buying his own building on West End Avenue.[59]

Over the next few months, the emotionally recharged star became increasingly involved in movement struggles. In October 1958, he joined Coretta Scott King, A. Philip Randolph, Jackie Robinson, and several thousand black and white students in a Youth March for Integrated Schools in Washington, D.C. He also led a delegation of five white and six black students to the White House to present President Eisenhower with a petition demanding greater federal efforts to promote school integration. After their request to see the president was turned down, the indignant star declared that Eisenhower's refusal "will have far-reaching meaning to millions" not just in the United States but also in Africa, Asia, and Europe.[60]

When *Odds against Tomorrow* was released in November 1959, the thirty-two-year-old reigned as the highest-paid black entertainer in history. He took in $140,000 for four weeks at the Riviera in Las Vegas, $100,000 a year (for ten years) from his recording deal with RCA, and over $150,000 for film work. Success led him to form an expanded parent company, Belafonte Enterprises, that looked after his various ventures: HarBel (for films), Belafonte Presents (his concert and TV company), and three separate music publishing firms. Happy with his work, he grew increasingly frustrated by the slow pace of racial change. "Making money is not all I'm interested in," he explained. "I want to use my talent to fight for the freedom of my people."[61]

In 1959, at the peak of his career, the charismatic star left Hollywood for eleven years to fight for the civil rights movement.

MOVEMENT MAN

Harry Belafonte was the rarest of Hollywood stars: a committed radical. For him, radicalism meant seeing capitalism, racism, and imperialism as interlocking systems of oppression so powerful that no one individual or organization could hope to overturn them. Influenced by the Popular Front groups of the 1930s and 1940s, he believed the only way to crack these dominant systems—especially the power of white segregationist America—was by forging coalitions with as many like-minded people and groups as possible, be they liberal, radical, or conservative.

For the next decade, Belafonte played three key roles within the civil rights movement: coalition builder, fundraiser, and strategist. Far from being a unified struggle, the civil rights movement was marked by numerous political and personal divisions, rivalries that threatened its overall success. Powerful entrenched forces that could easily defeat a fragmented opposition would have a tougher time against a united mass movement. Building effective coalitions, he believed, meant putting one's ego and personal politics to the side and staying focused on what needed to be done: working together to achieve racial equality.

Practicing what he preached, Belafonte emerged as one of the few activists trusted by all groups. Working primarily with Martin Luther King Jr. and the Southern Christian Leadership Conference (SCLC), Belafonte also allied himself with—and mediated differences between—the Student Non-Violent Coordinating Committee (SNCC), the Congress of Racial Equality (CORE), the National Association for the Advancement of Colored People (NAACP), and the Black Panthers to promote racial equality and pressure federal and state bodies to enforce civil rights legislation.

In the years after their initial meeting in 1956, Belafonte (and later Julie) grew increasingly close to Martin and Coretta Scott King. They participated in rallies and socialized with the couple when they traveled to New York. "Between Harry and Martin," observed Sidney Poitier, "there was an almost invisible electricity, and a mutual respect and admiration that gave their robust friendship a flavor that at times seemed almost mystical" (see fig. 5.2). Freed from the burdens of filmmaking, Belafonte quickly established himself as the movement's chief fundraiser and, as Coretta remarked, "one of our truest friends." Poitier, who lived four blocks away, recounted how Belafonte turned his spacious ten-room apartment into "a beehive of civil rights activities. Civil rights leaders, moderates, radicals, headliners, planners, strategists, fund raisers, were coming and going nearly all the time."[62]

From their first meeting on, and especially after 1959, King used his friend's celebrity to attract people to rallies and benefit concerts who might not otherwise have listened to the messages of civil rights leaders. Equally

FIGURE 5.2 Belafonte and his
friend Martin Luther King Jr.
SOURCE: PHOTOFEST

important, he relied on Belafonte to raise money to sustain the movement. Unlike George Murphy and Ronald Reagan, who received financing from wealthy conservatives, Belafonte served as one of the civil rights movement's leading financiers. Whenever the movement needed money, King asked his friend to go out on tour. The popular singer took only what he needed for his family and turned the rest of the money over to King. While his fundraising efforts and personal contributions stemmed largely from his generosity and commitment to the cause, guilt may also have played a role. Once Belafonte became famous, he found it hard to reconcile his anticapitalist radicalism with his sudden wealth. Whatever the reason, without his fundraising efforts, the SCLC might have suffered a slow death.[63]

In January 1960, after an Alabama grand jury indicted King on tax falsification charges that could have kept him in jail for a decade, the civil rights leader telegrammed Belafonte, Poitier, and Roy Wilkins for help. Meeting at Belafonte's apartment with black activist Bayard Rustin, they immediately set out to raise $200,000 to fund King's Alabama defense team and the SCLC's voter registration drive. Belafonte used his long-standing ties with left labor leaders such as Moe Foner to forge coalitions with the New York Central Labor Council, which agreed to stage a huge demonstration and fundraiser in the garment district. Belafonte persuaded several of his friends—Poitier, Dorothy Dandridge, Sarah Vaughan, and Odetta—to perform at a concert that May. A month later, he split the proceeds from a one-man show in Los Angeles between the King defense fund and Hollywood for SANE, which was cochaired by his friend Robert Ryan. By the end of July, Belafonte had raised $85,000, a considerable achievement given that the SCLC's entire budget for 1960 was $65,000. "Harry Belafonte has stirred the cultural forces as never before," King's closest adviser Stanley Levison wrote him, "and they should become a new and increasing source of strength" (see figs. 5.3 and 5.4).[64]

Over the course of the decade, Belafonte played a key role in building the movement's cultural side. King was more interested in Belafonte the

FIGURE 5.3 Belafonte sings at a fundraiser for King's defense team and for the SCLC voter registration drive in New York City's Garment District in May 1960.
SOURCE: BISON ARCHIVES

FIGURE 5.4 In 1960, Belafonte joined protesters picketing a Woolworth's in Massachusetts to support SCLC efforts at desegregation.
SOURCE: BISON ARCHIVES

singer than Belafonte the actor, for he saw music as a central component in forging a shared culture. King "knew how powerful songs could be," Belafonte explained. "When he came into the movement and saw the power of song . . . he came to see the incredible power of culture. When he discovered 'We Shall Overcome' and decided it would be the song of the movement, it was almost as if you've given them the power to vote." The recording star's frequent appearances at rallies, especially in the South, lifted the spirits of embattled activists who often sang along with him. "Freedom songs are the soul of the movement," King wrote in his 1963 book *Why We Can't Wait*. "These songs bind us together, give us courage together, help us march together."[65]

Belafonte's cultural work also extended to television, where he produced and starred in a number of shows. In June 1960, he solidified his role as a national cultural force when he became the first African American to win an Emmy Award for his television show *Tonight with Belafonte*. Over the next several years, HarBel's television wing received Emmy nominations for its 1966 *The Strollin' Twenties* (written by Langston Hughes and starring Sidney

Poitier, Diahann Carroll, Sammy Davis Jr., and Duke Ellington) and its 1967 *A Time for Laughter: A Look at Negro Humor in America* (featuring Richard Pryor, Redd Foxx, Moms Mabley, and Pigmeat Markham).[66]

Belafonte's fame also attracted the attention of presidential hopeful John F. Kennedy. One night in late May 1960, Kennedy dropped by the activist's apartment unannounced and asked him to organize black performers on his behalf. During their three-hour conversation Belafonte bluntly told the Massachusetts senator that he had no record of supporting civil rights and therefore held little appeal to black voters. If Kennedy wanted to forge "an alliance that will make the difference," he needed to establish close ties with Martin Luther King Jr. When the Democrat asked, "Why do you see him as so important?" Belafonte explained that King was the leader of a movement and not just an isolated celebrity.[67] Loathing Richard Nixon for his Red-baiting, Belafonte promised to support Kennedy if the vice president received the Republican nomination.

Immediately after Kennedy left, Belafonte called King and recounted their conversation. The actor urged his friend to get to know Kennedy; the senator was naive and unschooled on civil rights but he was smart and a quick study. King got the same advice from Harris Wofford, a white lawyer whom Bobby Kennedy assigned to recruit the black vote. On June 23, 1960, as per Belafonte's suggestion, Kennedy and King met at patriarch Joseph Kennedy's New York apartment. Belafonte kept his promise and joined the Hollywood for Kennedy committee. The two appeared together in a campaign film that showed them walking down a Harlem street and into the apartment of a black family where they all engaged in a conversation about "civil rights, about foreign policy, about the economy of the country, and about things that will happen." After JFK answered their questions, Belafonte turned to the camera and said, "I'm voting for this Senator. How about you?"[68]

Kennedy's election gave King, Belafonte, and the movement a sympathetic ear in Washington. In March 1961, the president appointed Belafonte to the Peace Corps' National Advisory Committee. More importantly, Belafonte served as King's liaison to Attorney General Robert Kennedy, a man the star believed was unsympathetic to civil rights. Belafonte was also suspicious of Kennedy because of his earlier work with Senator Joe McCarthy. "When Bobby was appointed Attorney General," Belafonte recalled, "most of us greeted it with horror. But Dr. King convinced us, 'Go win him, find his moral center that can be appealed to.' He pointed out that Bobby was the Attorney General and we needed to work with him."[69]

King was right. Bobby proved more empathetic than Belafonte initially thought, and the two struck up a friendship. The attorney general worked closely with King in planning a massive voter registration drive during the summer of 1961. When SNCC voiced its reluctance to abandon their direct action sit-ins, Belafonte invited Stokely Carmichael and a group of leaders to Washington where he was performing that June. He convinced them to trust the Kennedys and adopt the voter registration plan; he also gave them $10,000 to get the project started. "Folks were just overwhelmed," Carmichael wrote in his autobiography, "and I believe that marked the beginning of Brother Belafonte's long relationship—as adviser, benefactor, and big brother—to the young freedom-fighting organization." The following April, a grateful attorney general hosted a reception for Harry and Julie Belafonte at the Department of Justice.[70]

Belafonte was a true movement man, which meant he worked with a wide variety of civil rights groups to build and expand the struggle. In addition to devoting time and money to the SCLC, SNCC, and CORE, he donated 20 percent of his income to the Belafonte Foundation of Music and Arts, an organization created to support young black artists. Belafonte was especially taken with SNCC, whose members were younger and more radical than their SCLC counterparts, and they with him. In September 1961, he performed at their annual meeting in Nashville; a month later, when 122 SNCC Freedom Riders were arrested in Mississippi, he sent $5,000 to bail them out. Belafonte also mediated ongoing tensions between the more cautious SCLC and the increasingly militant SNCC, whose leaders disparagingly referred to King as "De Lawd."[71]

Belafonte's fundraising proved crucial to sustaining the movement in the face of local repression. Southern law enforcement officials hoped to discourage civil rights demonstrations by arresting and jailing participants. Activists remained willing to protest so long as they knew they would be bailed out quickly; however, without sufficient money for bail bonds, the prospect of facing long stays in hostile Southern jails would have seriously curtailed future demonstrations. With revenues barely covering operating expenses, the SCLC and similar organizations desperately needed outside support. This became painfully clear during a series of dramatic protests in Birmingham, Alabama, in April and May 1963.

Defying a court order by leading a demonstration through the streets of what he called "the nation's most racist city," King was arrested by arch-segregationist Sheriff Eugene "Bull" Connor, who kept him in solitary confinement and denied him access to a lawyer. The demonstrations continued and Connor garnered national attention as television cameras showed police attacking peaceful protesters with German shepherds and high-pressure fire hoses, and then jailing hundreds of nonviolent youths.

After spending more than $20,000 in bonds for seventy-one activists, the SCLC ran out of money. Without more funds, the Birmingham protest would be lost. King recalled how SCLC lawyer Clarence Jones visited him in jail and spoke "a few words that lifted a thousand pounds from my heart: 'Harry Belafonte has been able to raise fifty thousand dollars for bail bonds. It is available immediately. And he says that whatever else you need, he will raise it.'" Belafonte also called a worried and financially strapped Coretta Scott King, who had just given birth to the couple's fourth child, and told her to hire a secretary and nurse at his expense. He then telephoned Bobby Kennedy and asked him to intervene on Martin's behalf. "It would be hard," the civil rights leader wrote later that year, "to overestimate the role this sensitive artist played in the success of the Birmingham crusade."[72]

Buoyed by the success of the Birmingham campaign, the SCLC leader decided to hold a massive March on Washington for Jobs and Freedom on August 28, 1963. He asked Belafonte to help publicize the event by getting a large Hollywood contingent to participate. Preferring to remain behind the scenes, the actor convinced old friends Marlon Brando and Burt Lancaster to work as co-organizers. To attract the attention of conservative Americans, he also asked Charlton Heston to serve as co-organizer. "Charlton Heston was a big player for Middle America," he explained. "We had a lot of other celebrities, but his participation was critical to the constituency he represented. These people would have to take a second look [if Heston was involved]." The actors sent a delegation of over fifty stars, many of whom appeared on the platform with King as he delivered his memorable "I Have a Dream" speech to a crowd of over 250,000 (see fig. 5.5). As a pleased Belafonte later observed, "It was the first time Hollywood had come in such numbers, in such a group since the

FIGURE 5.5 Sidney Poitier, Belafonte, and Charlton Heston led the Hollywood contingent in the March on Washington in August 1963.
SOURCE: NATIONAL ARCHIVES

time they came to Washington [in 1947] with the First Amendment, when they got crucified."[73]

Happy to yield center-stage to others, Belafonte also knew when to use the power of his celebrity to inspire the movement's rank-and-file members, even if it meant putting himself at risk. In early August 1964, as government authorities were unearthing the bodies of slain civil rights workers Michael Schwerner, James Chaney, and Andrew Goodman, Belafonte and Sidney Poitier flew to nearby Greenwood, Mississippi, with $60,000 in cash to bail out volunteers participating in the Council of Federated Organizations' (COFO) Freedom Summer campaign aimed at registering black voters. Mississippi was arguably the most dangerous place for a black man in 1964, but the two stars felt their presence would boost the morale of embattled volunteers. As they drove to town, a car filled with Klansmen tried to bump them off the road. The SNCC's Stokely Carmichael reassured his nervous passengers that the Klan had "come to start some trouble. But don't worry— if they've got cannons, we've got cannons, so be cool."[74]

When they arrived at COFO headquarters, ebullient civil rights workers started singing Freedom Songs with the celebrities. The power of song was so great that when Harry sang "Day-O," Klansmen standing outside joined in the chorus. As Belafonte talked to the group about his dedication to the movement and held up the black satchel containing the money, shots rang out; the windshield of a staff car parked outside the building had been cracked by bullets. That night, neither star slept well. They saw someone hiding near the chicken coop outside their farmhouse room and feared the worst. Poitier remembered how they covered their unease with banter, "but every time we heard a twig crack outside we would stop talking and listen." Belafonte dealt with his anxiety by telling spooky stories that had Poitier "falling out of the bed laughing." At 4 A.M. they heard a car pull up outside and then finally drive off. In the morning, four armed SNCC guards who spent the evening outside their room told the pair that they had the car in "their cross hairs" the entire time.[75]

Belafonte traveled to Mississippi with a second agenda: to promote Pan-Africanism. Influenced by Du Bois' writings and the African independence movements of the mid-1950s, Belafonte saw struggles for racial justice as international battles that linked people of color throughout the world. In 1959, he launched Project Airlift Africa with Poitier and baseball star Jackie Robinson. The trio hoped to link activists on the two continents by bringing several dozen African students to study at American universities. Five years later, worried that Carmichael and his coworkers "had been on the front lines so long and had endured so much, been doing so much, that I feared burnout," Belafonte paid to fly ten SNCC activists to the Republic of Guinea to meet its visionary anticolonial leader, President Sékou Touré. The September trip, notes one historian, "had a profound impact on the SNCC delegation," as Touré, an advocate of African socialism and nonalignment in the Cold War, encouraged them to take a broad view of their mutual goals and forge a closer relationship between American and African activists.[76]

Belafonte faced his greatest challenges between 1965 and 1968, as discontent with the government's failure to pursue meaningful racial change, coupled with deadly race riots in the summers of 1964 and 1965 and growing opposition to the war in Vietnam, created deep rifts within the civil rights movement. The SNCC's young radical leaders grew impatient with King's failure to confront the white power structure. Bayard Rustin suggested that the SCLC break with SNCC, but King once again asked Belafonte to mediate. Meeting with the singer in Atlanta, the two organizations reached a general accord on all issues save SNCC's refusal to ban Communists from the movement. Belafonte sympathized with SNCC radicals, whom he saw as the "voice of noncompromise," and continued raising money for them. The success of King's three-week-long Selma-to-Montgomery march for voting rights in March and April 1965, and Congress's subsequent passage of the Voting Rights Act, blunted criticism for a while. Yet, like SNCC, Belafonte wanted King to move further to the left.[77]

The emergence of the antiwar movement in the mid-1960s threatened to undermine the civil rights struggle. Radical activists like Belafonte and SNCC saw the two battles as linked, but more cautious leaders feared outspoken opposition to the Vietnam War would undermine public support for their cause. As the U.S. military buildup in Vietnam intensified following the deployment of Marines in the spring of 1965, antiwar sentiments grew more pronounced. In July 1965, three months after the radical Students for a Democratic Society (SDS) organized a massive antiwar demonstration in Washington, Belafonte began speaking out against the war, one of the first movie stars to do so. "We seem to have a grand design for being in all the wrong places at the wrong time," he told reporters. "Johnson is a sick man. . . . He lied . . . about what he would do. Patriotism now has a whole different meaning to me than I was taught on the battlefields in WWII." Voicing his support for upcoming antiwar protests in Washington and Detroit, he also attacked the still-active House Un-American Activities Committee's request for $50,000 to investigate civil rights groups. "The 'enemy,'" he insisted, "is not communism, but those who refuse to deal on a human level because they have greed all over their faces."[78]

On January 6, 1966, SNCC became the first civil rights organization to formally oppose the war. Linking the persecution of blacks at home to American imperialism abroad, SNCC leaders noted how "16% of the draftees from this country are Negroes called on to stifle the liberation of Vietnam, to preserve a 'democracy' which does not exist for them at home."[79]

Belafonte sympathized with SNCC and SDS, organizations *The Nation* magazine described as comprised of "indigenous radicals: tough, democratic, independent, creative, activist, unsentimental." Urban League head

Whitney Young, however, repudiated any group that "adopted black power as a program, or, which [tied] in domestic civil rights with the Vietnam conflict." An equally concerned Roy Wilkins distanced the NAACP from SNCC's strident antiwar statements. King's support would be crucial to any potential alliance between the two movements.[80]

King's decision to accompany Belafonte to Europe on a fundraising tour in March 1966 proved a critical moment in left politics. Shortly after arriving in Paris, Belafonte asked French unionists and movie star Yves Montand to organize a special benefit for King. In three days, the group arranged a massive concert at the Palais des Sports and persuaded a number of European stars to participate. "The State Department went ape shit," Belafonte recalled. "I guess all this showed the power of celebrity and what it can do." As popular in Europe as he was in the United States, Belafonte's tour raised $100,000 ($661,000 in 2009 dollars). Equally important, King joined him on stage and spoke out against the war and U.S. support of apartheid in South Africa. A furious American Ambassador to France Charles Bohlen scolded Belafonte, telling the singer that he and the Reverend "should keep our movements within the national boundaries of the United States."[81]

King returned from Europe determined to join Belafonte, SNCC, and other left groups in opposing U.S. involvement in Vietnam. In April, he convinced the SCLC board to pass a resolution condemning the war, and in August, two months after the shooting of Mississippi civil rights worker James Meredith, the organization called for the immediate and unilateral deescalation of the war. The SNCC and CORE reacted even more strongly to the attack on Meredith and demanded that black activists operate independently of white liberals. As Stokely Carmichael told a crowd at a Mississippi rally, "What we gonna start saying now is Black Power!" Urban League and NAACP leaders immediately dissociated their organizations from SNCC, CORE, and the Panthers, something Belafonte was unwilling to do. Looking beyond what many saw as their intimidating rhetoric and garb, the singer praised the Panthers for their dedication and "inordinate level of intelligence."[82]

Belafonte's activism attracted the attention of the FBI, which saw him as a dangerous radical influence on King and the SCLC. J. Edgar Hoover hated King and began tapping his phones in the mid-1950s. In the early 1960s, he ordered agents to tap Belafonte's phone. Always looking for ways to undermine the civil rights campaign, the FBI chief told Presidents Kennedy and Johnson that SCLC adviser Levison was a Soviet agent and that the movement was riddled with Communists. He also blamed Belafonte for King's leftward shift, insisting that because of the singer's "pressure on him, King is beginning to think like SNCC."[83]

In early 1967, King delivered a series of antiwar speeches at demonstrations in Chicago, Los Angeles, and New York, where his April 4 address, "Beyond Vietnam: A Time to Break the Silence," linked the war to the destructive interests of American imperialism and unbridled capitalism. Denying his critics' charges that "peace and civil rights don't mix," the black leader declared the war an enemy of impoverished blacks and whites. Politicians, he explained, will "never invest the necessary funds or energies in rehabilitation of its poor so long as adventures like Vietnam continued to draw men and skills and money like some demonic destructive suction tube." King urged citizens to raise their voices "if our nation persists in its perverse ways in Vietnam." Defending the Reverend from the attacks that followed the speech, Belafonte insisted that the "right wing conservative forces would stop at nothing to create the image of him as a treasonous, unpatriotic, ungrateful man who was not only betraying his country, but his own people and their cause." King, Levison, Carmichael, and other leaders soon met at Belafonte's home and, at the singer's urging, agreed to suspend mutual criticism and cooperate on common goals.[84]

Belafonte spent much of 1967 and 1968 working for the antiwar and civil rights movements. He also began forging alliances between black power leaders in the United States and Africa. The Pan-African group, he told the press, would "counterbalance the right-wing campaign of support for white supremacy regimes in South Africa" and "encourage more radical solutions to the urban problems of the nation as Negroes use their voting majority to exercise real control over the big cities in the years ahead." The entertainer organized a series of fundraising concerts and solicited donations from movie and recording industry friends with the idea of mobilizing all minorities—Native Americans, Mexicans, Puerto Ricans, Appalachians, and blacks—in a common struggle to stop the war and promote economic and racial justice.[85]

Merging entertainment and politics, Belafonte used television to inform audiences about the goals of the antiwar and civil rights movements. When NBC executives asked him to host *The Tonight Show* while

Johnny Carson was vacationing February 5–9, 1968, he agreed on the condition that he could invite anyone and talk about anything. The network consented and Belafonte exposed the country to a raft of African American entertainers rarely seen on popular (largely white) late night shows—Lena Horne, Aretha Franklin, Diahann Carroll, Sidney Poitier, Bill Cosby, and Nipsey Russell—as well as left-leaning white stars such as Paul Newman, Robert Goulet, Pete Seeger, and the Smothers Brothers. "I like TV," he told one reporter, "there are things I feel should be better known to more people and TV is the way to reach them." Taking advantage of the rare opportunity, Belafonte also brought Senator Robert Kennedy and Martin Luther King Jr. onto the show. The host grilled Kennedy about his positions on Vietnam and government reductions in poverty programs. When King appeared several nights later, the two friends discussed the peace movement and the SCLC's Poor People's campaign planned for the spring.[86]

The weeklong shows proved a great hit and led the *New York Times* television critic to observe, "The presence of Mr. Belafonte, who concurs in the belief that being an entertainer does not preclude a lively interest in social problems, demonstrated anew the cross-fertilization of show business and matters of more serious moment." Alfred Duckett told the *Chicago Daily Defender*'s largely African American readers that watching Belafonte, "I found out there is one more form of Black Power that I never thought about before. The power of being so big that you can take over such a giant show and do it better. . . . The power to joke about The Problem without being bitter but getting the message through."[87]

Belafonte's role as movement leader came to a temporary halt on April 4, 1968, when James Earl Ray assassinated King in Memphis, Tennessee, as he prepared to lead a march of sanitation workers protesting low wages and poor working conditions. As the grieving widow prepared for the funeral, she asked two men to sit beside her at the graveside, her father and Harry Belafonte. "I wanted Harry," she wrote in her autobiography, "because of what Harry had meant to Martin and to me all these years." King's death, Belafonte assured the press, did not mean the death of the movement. "New leaders obviously are going to come. There's going to be a new wave of need for revolt, a new wave of demand and that it would even be global." Yet, four months later, after helping Coretta Scott King settle her affairs, and shattered by the assassination of Bobby Kennedy, an exhausted Belafonte talked of taking his family to Africa and retreating from politics. "The assassinations of John Kennedy, Martin Luther King Jr., and Robert Kennedy," he explained, "put a hole in the political soul of America. People just backed away because the price was too severe."[88]

Heartbroken by the loss of his close friend and worn out by the constant pressure of raising money for the movement, Belafonte snapped. As he explained in August 1968, he wanted to "stop answering questions as though I were a spokesman for my people. I hate marching, and getting called at 3 A.M. to bail some cats out of jail, or sitting on panels and talking to reporters about America's racial problems."[89]

In the years after King's death, the Hollywood left increasingly turned its focus from civil rights to the Vietnam War, which seemed a larger, broader issue. With Belafonte's temporary retreat from the political arena, the most visible antiwar star was no longer a black man, but a white woman with a long Hollywood pedigree, Jane Fonda.

CITIZEN OF THE WORLD

Despite his initial depression over the death of the man he talked to "every day for ten years," Belafonte soon resumed his activism. After a decade's absence from Hollywood, he once again strove to make progressive films that challenged racial stereotypes. Fulfilling his earlier fantasy of playing against type, he cast himself in a Cary Grant–like role as a black Jewish angel in the comedy *The Angel Levine* (1970), a Belafonte Enterprises production that costarred former blacklisted actor Zero Mostel. Two years later, he realized his dream of writing African Americans into the history of the American West by producing and starring in *Buck and the Preacher* (1972) with Sidney Poitier and Ruby Dee. Based on the true story of the post–Civil War black migration, the film mixes comedy with the militant spirit of the Black Power movement to tell the tale of an ex–Union Army soldier (Poitier) and con man (Belafonte) who battle white vigilantes as they lead a group of freed slaves to a better life in Colorado. "We wanted Black audiences to see that the heroes of that period were others than the 'bad niggers,' and the malcontents," Poitier told reporters.[90]

After appearing with Poitier in the very funny *Uptown Saturday Night* (1974), Belafonte once again found himself frustrated with the dominant trends of Hollywood. Disgusted with Blaxploitation films such as *Shaft* (1971) and *Superfly* (1972), he decided it was impossible "to hammer away at Hollywood as an independent institution, because it was really linked to so much that was just America." As he told one reporter, "I've had the opportunity to do the 'Super Flies'... the 'Nigger Charlies,'" but he would not take the parts "because I find them anti-black. I find them anti-woman. I find them demeaning."[91]

After King's death, Belafonte never again played the same central role in any one organization. Without King, the movement never gained another charismatic leader who could unite feuding civil rights groups. Belafonte could have assumed a key leadership position, for the charismatic star was the one person trusted by most groups. But he was reluctant to do so. He never wanted to become a movement symbol like Ronald Reagan or Jane Fonda. Political activism had doomed one marriage; he did not want it to kill another. As early as 1957, reporters observed how he seemed "weighed down by his own sense of responsibility as a Negro." Thirty-seven years later, when asked whether he enjoyed being an activist, Belafonte responded, "No. It's sucked up most of my life."[92]

Participating in political movements on the left, Belafonte discovered, could be a frustrating and often lonely experience. Attacking capitalism, racism, and imperialism proved far more difficult than Murphy and Reagan's efforts to overturn the New Deal. After all, if Southerners proved unwilling to accept Reconstruction following a deadly Civil War, why would they accept racial equality and integration just because the Supreme Court ordered it? Nor did Belafonte ever get as much help from Hollywood as he had hoped. Few stars proved willing to endanger their lucrative careers by committing themselves to long-term movement struggles. "People have had to constantly make choices between real social commitment to the ideals of the Bill of Rights and humanity in general," Belafonte observed, "and how to deal with that in the face of outrageous acquisition of material power and material goods."[93]

No longer anchored in a single movement, Belafonte turned to global activism and shifted his political focus from the national to the international and from film to music. Continuing his efforts to forge a "creative coalition between the black people of the U.S. and the black people of Africa," he spent several decades promoting Pan-Africanism and fighting apartheid. In 1985, he and Michael Jackson made an international splash by bringing together forty-five performers to record "We Are the World," a project that raised millions of dollars for African famine relief. Eschewing the feel-good rhetoric that surrounded the project, Belafonte told the press, "If the people over there were of another color there would have been a much swifter response to the situation . . . but unfortunately, death among peoples of color is an accepted state."[94]

As he grew older and more impatient with the snail-like pace of meaningful change, Belafonte became increasingly outspoken in his radical critiques of U.S. policies. The man who now considered himself a "citizen of the world" and accepted "no borders" made national headlines in October 2002 when he attacked President George W. Bush's handling of the war in Iraq. Belafonte leveled especially harsh criticism at Secretary of State Colin Powell and National Security Advisor Condoleezza Rice, comparing them to plantation slaves who "come into the house of the master." A few years later, he led a delegation of activists—which included actor Danny Glover, United Farm Workers' leader Dolores Huerta, and academic Cornel West—to meet with Venezuela's President Hugo Chavez. Calling President Bush "the greatest terrorist in the world," Belafonte told the Socialist leader, "We respect you, admire you, and we are expressing our full solidarity with the Venezuelan people and your revolution."[95]

Like Edward G. Robinson, Belafonte discovered that if you live long enough you are likely to receive a wide range of awards. Honored with the Kennedy Center Honor for lifetime achievement in the performing arts in 1989, the radical activist was especially moved when surprise guest Archbishop Desmond M. Tutu of South Africa appeared on stage and told his friend, "You have worked with consistent zeal in your opposition to the madness of apartheid. When the true history of Africa is written, your name will be written in gold." In 1995, *Ebony* magazine named Harry Belafonte as one of the top "50 Who Changed America."[96]

The Harlem-born radical remains pessimistic about American politicians' tolerance of racism and imperialism, but optimistic about the potential for change from below. "Yes, I'm proud that Barack Obama is president," he told a group gathered to celebrate the fiftieth anniversary of SNCC in April 2010, "but I find nothing [in his policies] that speaks to the issue of the poor. I find nothing that speaks to the issue of the disenfranchised." Ordinary citizens would once again have to be the ones to force widespread democratic change. "It is up to us to be proud of who we are," he told *Democracy*

Now radio listeners, "proud of being liberals, proud of being progressives, proud of being gay, proud of being black, proud of being women, proud of being workers, proud of being young, and know that we can shape the future. Each and every one of us has that task."[97] His friend Martin could not have said it better.

MOVEMENT LEADER, GRASSROOTS BUILDER: JANE FONDA

As the nation's attention shifted toward ending the war in Vietnam, Jane Fonda supplanted Harry Belafonte as Hollywood's dominant movement leader. Known for her work in the antiwar movement, her political activism continued long after the war's end. For nearly twenty years, the Oscar-winning actress used her fame and money to build grassroots organizations that served as prominent left voices in American politics. Yet Fonda's path into movement politics was almost the opposite of Belafonte's. He was politically sophisticated before he joined a movement; she entered movement politics as a political naïf and grew savvier during the course of her activism. He tried injecting politics into his movies early in his career and then, frustrated, left Hollywood to join the civil rights campaign; she got involved in movement politics and then brought her politics to the screen by founding her own company and making *Coming Home* (1978), *The China Syndrome* (1979), *Nine to Five* (1980), and *Rollover* (1981). He preferred keeping the public's focus on the movement rather than on the celebrity-activist; she operated in a highly visible manner and earned the enmity of many conservatives.

Despite their different trajectories, Fonda proved to be a more hands-on activist than either Belafonte or conservative movement stars George Murphy and Ronald Reagan. Belafonte joined ongoing movements, while the two Republicans served as key spokesmen but not as central figures in building the foundations of grassroots conservatism. Fonda went a step further, working as an organizer as well as an activist. While Belafonte focused primarily on racial justice, Fonda, like Reagan, tackled a wide range of issues. Aided by her mentor and husband, Tom Hayden, she set out to build broad-based movements that sought to transform American life. The Indochina Peace Campaign (IPC) and the Campaign for Economic Democracy (CED), which she and Hayden founded in 1972 and 1976, respectively, mobilized citizens to oppose American imperialism, challenge corporate dominance of the economy, alter energy policy, promote women's rights, and restore democracy at the local and state levels.

From provocative sex symbol in *Barbarella* (1968) to antiwar firebrand and bumper-sticker icon ("I'M NOT FONDA JANE" stickers still adorn the cars of many conservatives), the former "Miss Army Recruiter" of 1959 was the most controversial and hated movie star of her generation—especially after newspapers printed a picture of her sitting in a North Vietnamese anti-aircraft gun in 1972. She was harassed by federal agencies, denied an appointment to the California Arts Council because of her "traitorous" antiwar politics, and avoided by liberal politicians who feared being associated with "Hanoi Jane." Even Republican loyalists like entertainer Sammy Davis Jr. complained, "What's happened to Jane Fonda smacks of McCarthyism—of prejudice of the worst kind."[1]

Fonda's opposition to the Vietnam War and participation in many left-oriented struggles helped usher in the current era of celebrity politics, with all its negative connotations. *Newsweek* and *Penthouse* disparagingly labeled her the "Cause Celeb" and "Queen Mother of celebrity politics," while conservative intellectual William F. Buckley Jr. mockingly dubbed her "Secretary Fonda," a snide reference to Chinese Communist Party Secretary/Chairman Mao Zedong. No male star of the era received such widespread criticism. "She didn't deserve the hatchet job they did on her," remarked former Democratic senator and presidential candidate George McGovern. "But they wouldn't have done that hatchet job if she wasn't effective."[2]

Certainly Fonda herself was responsible for some of the negative press. Her entry onto the political scene was marked by two problems: her lightweight cinematic image as a sex kitten and the many early gaffes she committed that undermined her political credibility. Even though she went on to become a serious grassroots organizer, she never shook off her image as an uninformed celebrity who did not know what she was talking about. Instead of taking her radical critiques seriously, misogynistic articles, such as *Life* magazine's "Jane Fonda Non Stop Activist: Nag, Nag, Nag," dismissed her as a whining woman who believed "all causes fit together into one complaint about society."[3]

Fonda's story illuminates the dual aspect of celebrity politics: why it mattered and why it threatened its participants. She demonstrated that celebrities could use their star power to draw attention to controversial political issues and bring people into mass movements aimed at restructuring American life. Her subsequent vilification revealed how the public often viewed such activism, especially left activism, with suspicion and cynicism. Nevertheless, Fonda's steadfast devotion to movement politics in the face of scathing and often sexist attacks encouraged other women to emerge from the shadows of a male-dominated Hollywood and speak out on behalf of a wide range of progressive causes. In addition to her work with the IPC and CED, she nurtured young stars such as Rob Lowe, Rosanna Arquette, and Alec Baldwin and fostered their political activism by founding Network in 1985.

Perhaps most important, her success at the box office showed that a talented actor could be a radical activist without necessarily losing an audience. Americans may have hated her politics, but they loved her movies. By the end of the 1979–1980 season, Fonda reigned as Hollywood's most bankable female star. Moreover, despite her early political missteps, she still garnered a great deal of public respect. The 1980 *World Almanac* ranked her as the nation's fifth most influential woman. But the actress paid a high price for her activism. To this day, conservatives continue to denounce her, Internet sites sell dozens of "hate Fonda" items, and Naval Academy plebes end their evening by responding to a round of ritualistic "Good Night" shouts with a last plebe yelling, "Good Night, Jane Fonda," and the entire company answering, "Good night, bitch!"[4] Her story is both a lesson and a warning about the rewards and perils of left-wing movie star activism.

FROM HOLLYWOOD TO HANOI

Jane Fonda was born on December 21, 1937, into a family filled with political and emotional conflict. Her father, actor Henry Fonda, was a liberal Democrat whose "heart was with Roosevelt and the New Deal," while her mother, wealthy socialite Frances Seymour Brokaw Fonda, cast her loyalties "with the elite," many of whom worried about "that man in the White House." Best known for his compassionate performance as Tom Joad in *Grapes of Wrath* (1940), Henry was an emotionally detached parent, prone to anger and black moods. Jane spent her childhood trying to stay in what one reporter referred to as "her pathologically cold father's good graces." Hoping to please her father, she grew up learning to see herself "through the eyes of men" and to accommodate "them on the deepest invisible level."[5]

Jane's relationship with her mother proved even more problematic. Frances met Henry in 1936 and the two married several months later. Jane was born the following year and brother Peter two years later. Suffering from mental illness, Frances resented Jane's birth, fearing it would make her seem older and less attractive. She reacted by disappearing for long periods. When the family moved to Connecticut to allow Henry to star in the Broadway play *Mister Roberts*, Frances left again, this time confined to a mental institution. The Fondas' marriage fell apart and the couple divorced. A year later, on her forty-second birthday, a severely depressed Frances committed suicide, leaving behind her distraught twelve-year-old tomboy daughter Jane. "We never discuss it," she told columnist Rex Reed years later, "but it affected our lives more than we will ever realize. I kept my emotions inside." Scarred by her childhood traumas, Jane suffered from bulimia from the age of twelve to thirty-five.[6]

Insecure and suffering bouts of depression throughout high school, Fonda entered Vassar College in 1955. After leaving school in the summer of 1957 and spending the next two years in Paris, where she met French film director Roger Vadim, Fonda moved to New York and enrolled in Lee Strasberg's Actors Studio. His students included people active in liberal and left politics during the 1960s and 1970s: Paul Newman, Joanne Woodward, Anne Bancroft, Dustin Hoffman, and Sally Field. Fonda's big break came in the spring of 1959 when director Joshua Logan cast her to costar in *Tall Story* (1960). Jane impressed actor Tom Laughlin as someone yearning to do something important, someone "a little naïve" but with "a tremendous intellect that was just going crazy for something to latch onto."[7]

Over the next four years, she appeared in five more films as well as several Broadway plays, earning praise as a "gifted and appealing young actress." In 1963, Roger Vadim asked her to return to Paris to star in his remake of the sex farce *La Ronde*. She remained in France for the next six years, eventually marrying and having a child with the French director.[8]

Just as his friendship with Paul Robeson changed the course of Harry Belafonte's life, so too did Fonda's relationship with Vadim and his circle of left intellectuals alter her political trajectory. This period also marked the beginning of her dependence on a series of mentors—usually men—who served as her political guides. A womanizing radical who had married Brigitte Bardot and fathered a child with Catherine Deneuve, Vadim was close friends with many of France's intellectual left: Jean-Paul Sartre, Simone de Beauvoir, Albert Camus, Simone Signoret, and Yves Montand. An eye-opening trip to Moscow in 1964 led Fonda to question, as Vadim noted, "the readymade ideas she had acquired in America and had taken for granted." Upon her return, Fonda began attending anti–Vietnam War rallies with Elisabeth and Roger Vailland (members of the French Communist Party) and actress Signoret, a feminist as well as a radical.[9]

As her friends talked to her about the evils of colonialism and the atrocities American forces were committing in Vietnam, Fonda's initial reaction was disbelief. "I had grown up with this Second World War father-fighting-in-the-Pacific notion that we were on the right side and that it was just inconceivable that we were doing this." She changed her mind after meeting a number of American soldiers in Paris. Some left the army after serving in Vietnam; others deserted and sought shelter in the City of Lights. "When the soldiers said 'We're torturing, we're murdering. Here's a book, if you don't believe us, read this.' That just turned my life around. I didn't know how to process this." Pregnant and not working, she began reading about events in Southeast Asia and discussed them with Signoret.[10]

The spring 1968 uprising in Paris hastened Fonda's politicization. She watched as 10,000 students battled with police for fourteen hours on May 6, tearing up streets, overturning cars, and setting up barricades. She also received political tutoring from radical actress Vanessa Redgrave, who convinced her to make a speech on behalf of the striking unions. Confined to bed in France during the first three months of her pregnancy, Fonda watched television coverage of the war's devastation: scenes of bombers destroying schools, hospitals, and churches. She watched antiwar protestors descending on the Pentagon and the 1968 Chicago Democratic Convention. In the aftermath of the summer riots that followed Martin Luther King Jr.'s assassination, she also began reading about civil rights struggles.

These events left Fonda with an intense desire to participate in political change, but unsure how to do so. "God," she remembered thinking, "it was like standing on shifting sand. Everything could change—for better or worse. Don't I want to be part of the change? I don't want to just live here, living the life of a somewhat hedonistic movie star. I'm being called here." After giving birth to her daughter Vanessa in 1969, named in honor of Redgrave, she returned to the United States to make *They Shoot Horses, Don't They?* Hailed by Albert Camus as the "first existential novel to come out of America," Horace McCoy's 1935 book offered a scathing critique of American capitalism during the Great Depression. The Sidney Pollack–directed film about impoverished couples who take part in a marathon dance contest marked a turning point in her cinematic career. "It was the first time as an actress that I had made a movie that was about broader social issues," she explained. "God, it felt good, it felt so good that I said I don't want to do anything else. This is what art is supposed to be, this is what I'm supposed to be doing. I had these new thoughts and new ideas. I had to learn more and deepen them, and then express this through my work. That's when I left Vadim."[11]

During production, Fonda talked politics with Al Lewis, who had starred as Grandpa in the popular television series *The Munsters* and would later run for governor of New York on the Green Party ticket. Lewis told her about the activities of the Black Panthers and mutual friend Marlon Brando's involvement with the organization. Subsequent conversations with Paul Newman and Joanne Woodward confirmed that there had been a dramatic change in the civil rights movement while Fonda was in France. The nonviolence that had been at the core of the movement was eroding as many African Americans grew impatient with the slow pace of change.[12]

In early 1970, Fonda moved back to Los Angeles and, displaying the enthusiasm of a recent convert, plunged herself into a wide variety of causes without being fully informed. During the next two decades, her activism fell into two stages: from 1970 to 1972, she was a freelance radical who often hurt causes as much as she aided them; and from 1972 to 1986, she became a more knowledgeable movement organizer and political filmmaker. As in France, she initially relied on a series of mentors to guide her through the intricacies of movement politics. Fred Gardner, founder of the GI coffeehouses, and radical attorney Mark Lane urged her to travel around the country to see what was going on. After reading about the recent occupation of Alcatraz Island by Native Americans, Fonda spoke at several Native American protests, including at Fort Lewis near Seattle where military police arrested her when protesters tried to reclaim a portion of the base.[13]

Although many people today associate her with the antiwar movement, it would be a mistake to see Fonda as one of its leaders. By the time she returned from Europe the movement was well underway. "She was never part of the central movement leadership that included people such as Rennie Davis, Dave Dellinger, Tom Hayden, and Abbie Hoffman," reflected James Lafferty, one of several national coordinators of the National Peace Action Coalition. Like the civil rights crusade, the antiwar campaign was not a single entity but a diverse grassroots movement composed of numerous coalitions whose politics ranged from the liberal center to the far left, and whose members included clergy, veterans, pacifists, trade unionists, students, and businessmen. As the movement grew so too did the size of its demonstrations. In April 1965, the radical Students for a Democratic Society drew 20,000 people to their protest in Washington, D.C. Two years later, the National Mobilization Committee Against the War sponsored rallies in New York and San Francisco that drew several hundred thousand marchers. In November 1969, half a million citizens converged on Washington, D.C., to voice their opposition to President Richard Nixon's policies.[14]

A late recruit to the movement, Fonda became active after public opinion began turning against the war. In June 1965, a Gallup poll showed that only 12 percent of those surveyed favored withdrawing our troops. Public opinion turned against the war in early 1968 after the North Vietnamese army's Tet Offensive attacked more than a hundred cities and towns, including a daring raid on the U.S. embassy in Saigon. Lyndon Johnson grew so despondent with the growing opposition to the war that in March 1968 he declared he would not run for another term. Seizing on massive public discontent, Richard Nixon won the presidency that year on a platform promising a secret solution that would bring "peace with honor." He achieved neither during his first term. Instead, he increased the bombing of North Vietnam and expanded the war into Laos and Cambodia.[15]

Fonda focused on the issue that first grabbed her attention in Paris: protecting GIs who opposed the war. Accompanied by Elisabeth Vailland, she embarked on a two-month cross-country trip in April 1970, stopping along the way to attend antiwar rallies and visit coffeehouses run by civilian activists for antiwar GIs. Located near major bases, the coffeehouses offered soldiers a place to relax, discuss the war, and learn more about their legal rights. Following the U.S. invasion of Cambodia and killing of students at Kent State and Jackson State universities, Fonda spoke at demonstrations in half a dozen cities. She also got arrested and/or detained for distributing antiwar literature outside forts in Colorado, Maryland, and Texas. "I took off on that trip a liberal," she explained, "and I ended up a radical."[16]

During these early months of activism, Fonda proved more important at generating publicity than creating new strategies. "She was tangential to the movement's core leadership," insisted antiwar leader Lafferty, "but her name and celebrity were important in drawing public attention to the cause." Although numerous studio executives were personally against the war, their fear of box-office backlash led them to back off producing any film critical of the war effort. John Wayne's 1968 prowar feature *The Green Berets* (made with the cooperation of the Johnson administration) was the only major production to come out at the height of the war. Antiwar films such as *The Deer Hunter* (1978) and *Apocalypse Now* (1979) only debuted long after the war's end.[17]

With prowar forces garnering support from John Wayne, Bob Hope, and Charlton Heston, it is not surprising that left activists welcomed Fonda's involvement. After all, the Fonda name resonated with a wide variety of Americans. Henry was popular with an older generation, while her brother, Peter, who produced and starred in *Easy Rider* (1969), emerged as a counterculture hero to a youth generation strongly opposed to the war.

Personal issues played a vital role in Fonda's budding politicization. Growing up insecure and in need of male approval, she found meaning and fulfillment by participating in movement politics. Her insecurity proved a boon to the antiwar movement. She worked tirelessly at whatever tasks needed to be done—from stuffing envelopes to speaking at mass demonstrations—and rarely acted like a star. But she was a star, and her celebrity helped focus national attention on the antiwar movement, especially as public opinion turned against U.S. involvement. Black stars, even ones as famous as Belafonte, simply did not generate the same publicity as white stars, especially young and beautiful white women who were considered Hollywood royalty.

Fonda may have felt a calling, but she was not prepared to preach. Conservative activists such as George Murphy and Ronald Reagan worked in the political trenches perfecting their positions long before they became visible spokesmen for their cause. Fonda was an actress, which meant she could learn her lines quickly. But that did not mean she always understood them. During her initial stage of activism her enthusiasm often outpaced her knowledge. Consequently, she often spoke in clichés and committed gaffes that undermined her effectiveness and hurt the movement.

During an appearance on ABC's popular *Dick Cavett Show*, after raising a clenched fist in a Black Power salute, Fonda embarrassed herself by making numerous factual errors about American history and the United States' involvement in Vietnam. Native American activist and singer Buffy Sainte-Marie appreciated Fonda's sincerity but noted that she had "unintentionally blown a couple of our most important issues by not understanding the problems and diverting the press away from our issues." The actress generated widespread mockery when she held a press conference for Black Panther leader Huey Newton in her posh Manhattan penthouse, where he delivered a blistering diatribe against the government while sitting in an expensive antique French chair. Even her father belittled her political work. "She won't accomplish anything worthwhile," he told the press in May 1970. "She's like a zealot on a crusade and she won't be satisfied until she gets herself burned at the stake."[18]

Fonda's zealotry came from a sense of rage, she explained in 1972, "that people feel when they've been lied to and suddenly realize it. Rage of someone who was . . . very idealistic about my country and was very angry about the deception." Several years later, she would refer to these earlier times as her "extreme sectarian period." She wanted to impress other radicals, so she tried too hard and made mistakes, all the worse as the media turned her into a key spokesperson for the movement. "What got me into so much trouble," she reflected, "was this attitude that, 'I'm not left enough, I'm not militant enough.' More rhetoric came out of my mouth during this time—I didn't even know what the words really meant. I was trying too hard to prove my credentials, to prove that I was sincere. It was very bad, both for me and the movement."[19]

Despite her early mistakes, Fonda succeeded in politicizing the previously apolitical. After hearing her talk about the Vietnam Veterans Against the War (VVAW) on the *Dick Cavett Show*, veteran Ed Damato joined the VVAW and went on to become its president. Former Marine Scott Camil went to hear her speak at the University of Florida just "to see what a movie actress looked like"; but after listening to her, he too joined the VVAW and soon became its southeast coordinator. Fonda's steadfast if flawed dedication also inspired a number of Hollywood figures. *Easy Rider* producer Burt Schneider, whom she introduced to local Panthers and antiwar activists, admired her refusal to "take things lying down. She put her commitment to the test and accepted the consequences."[20]

On the other hand, Fonda's cinematic image at the time undermined her political credibility. The roles left and right activists play on the screen can influence what audiences think about their offscreen pronouncements. "John Wayne had no more inherent moral authority to speak about the war than Fonda," observed reporter Ronald Brownstein, "but he had an easier time pushing his views because he had played war heroes for so long that many Americans confused him with the genuine article." The parts Fonda played in her first sixteen films hardly inspired audiences with a sense of her gravitas: prostitute, adulteress, mistress, ingénue. The actress would be haunted for the rest of her life by her star turn in Roger Vadim's soft-porn science-fiction fantasy *Barbarella: Queen of the Galaxy* (1968). Fonda plays a forty-first-century government agent searching for evil scientist Durand-Durand whose "positronic ray" threatens to destroy earth. Each time a man rescues her from a life-threatening situation, Barbarella, ever the sex kitten, repays them by making love. Vadim dresses her in revealing skintight outfits and black leather boots and frequently shows viewers her naked breasts. "People found it very difficult to reconcile this image that they had of me on the screen with the person they heard talking about Vietnam," she lamented several years later. Even her supporters tried attracting larger crowds by advertising her talks with banners reading "COME HEAR BARBARELLA SPEAK."[21] No male star was ever so widely mocked for showing off his body.

Fonda's impact can also be judged by the reactions of her opponents. Although many radical leaders minimized her contributions to building the antiwar movement, Fonda's participation was serious enough to attract the attention of the FBI, CIA, National Security Agency, Defense Intelligence Agency, and Secret Service—several of which placed her under close surveillance. The government feared the power of movie stars to sway public opinion; they were scared of what might happen if millions of citizens followed the political urgings of popular fantasy figures. In late 1970, the Bureau officially labeled Fonda "a Marxist," which meant she was considered as "potentially dangerous." J. Edgar Hoover hated the radical actress and worked with other federal agencies in conducting a series of illegal operations that included stealing her bank records and having her arrested on trumped-up drug charges at a Cleveland airport. President Nixon was so obsessed with her case that he ordered the FBI to send her files to the White

House. "What [Soviet Premier Leonid] Brezhnev and Jane Fonda said got about the same treatment," an aide later recalled.[22]

Ironically, while conservatives vilified her in later years for allegedly disrespecting soldiers, Fonda focused her early efforts on defending GIs who criticized the war effort. In the summer of 1970, she moved to Detroit to help coordinate and fund the Winter Soldier hearings, a name taken from Tom Paine's distinction between what he called the "sunshine patriots" of the American Revolution and the committed "winter warriors" who fought with George Washington at Valley Forge. Organized in response to the military's decision to place sole blame for the November 1968 My Lai massacre on Lieutenant William Calley, the Winter Soldier hearings took testimony from 105 veterans—including young lieutenant John Kerry—who described atrocities they had seen or committed in Vietnam. My Lai, they insisted, was not an isolated event but part of the chaos and death that characterized a war out of control. Breaking out in tears as they spoke, veterans recounted gruesome incidents of raping women, burning villages, and torturing captured Vietcong by cutting off ears and heads. "To have soldiers who had fought in Vietnam tell us what was really going on had a positive educative and propaganda effect," noted James Lafferty, then head of the Detroit Coalition to End the War in Vietnam Now. "Jane's involvement brought public attention to the hearings, something that might not have occurred without her highly visible presence."[23]

Fonda's commitment grew so intense during those summer months that she considered giving up acting to work full-time as a political activist. Ken Cockrel, a Detroit attorney and member of the League of Revolutionary Black Workers, dissuaded her by explaining, "Jane, movement activists and members of collectives are a dime a dozen. We don't have anyone in the movement who is a movie star. We need you to be a movie star." Taking Cockrel's advice to heart, Fonda thought, "He's absolutely right. My success as an actress will be part of what I can do for the movement. For one thing, it could show that you could have a career and be part of the movement at the same time."[24]

Fonda's political engagement brought a new maturity to her screen presence. In July 1970, she spent her days shooting *Klute* (1971) and nights working on behalf of antiwar organizations (see fig. 6.1). In the film, Fonda plays prostitute Bree Daniels, a complex and intelligent woman who wants to leave the sex trade and work as a model or actress. The star's research into the

FIGURE 6.1 Fonda addressing an antiwar rally in San Francisco, August 24, 1972.
SOURCE: ASSOCIATED PRESS

lives of prostitutes drew her into the burgeoning women's movement. "I began to realize that this particular revolution is not only their revolution," she explained, "it's my revolution." *Klute* was a hit and reviewers who had been critical of past performances now called her "one of the best actresses around."[25] Her peers agreed, awarding her an Oscar for Best Actress in April 1972.

When production ended, Fonda and *Klute* costar Donald Sutherland organized a left alternative to the patriotic USO shows that Bob Hope brought to American military bases throughout the world. Sutherland and his wife, Shirley (whose socialist father headed Canada's New Democratic Party between 1961 and 1971), were outspoken supporters of the antiwar and Black Panther movements. In March 1971, after recruiting actors, singers, comedians, and writers, the two stars premiered their FTA Tour (the initials standing for "Free the Army" or "Fuck the Army" depending on the venue) to a packed coffeehouse just outside of Fort Bragg, North Carolina. When the Pentagon and State Department denied them permission to perform on military installations in the United States and Southeast Asia, the FTA took their array of skits, songs, and comic riffs to public venues near bases on the mainland, in Hawaii, in the Philippines, and on Okinawa.

Fonda and Sutherland designed the show, which played to an estimated 64,000 soldiers during a nine-month period, "not only to support the soldiers' antiwar sentiments but to call attention to the way soldiers were dehumanized in the military." The troupe's most popular skit had Fonda, playing Pat Nixon, rushing to tell her husband (played by Gary Goodrow) that a mob was about to storm the White House. When Nixon asks her to call in the Army, Pat responds they can't because "it *is* the Army!"[26]

As Fonda's political confidence grew, she began displaying a sectarian self-righteousness that alienated other activists. "Within the movement," observed one reporter, "she began denouncing other radicals as Trotskyite" which usually meant "people whose views did not coincide with her own." The FTA director Alan Myerson, whom Fonda fired for his "bad politics," insisted that she "only understood ideology; she lacked humanity." However, Myerson found her changed after returning from North Vietnam in 1972. "She had stopped ideological posturing. She was in love with Tom Hayden. For the first time, I found her to be natural."[27]

As Myerson suggests, Fonda's political life changed as a result of her relationship with Tom Hayden. Raised in the Detroit suburbs by a liberal Democratic mother and a conservative Republican father, Tom frightened both parents by participating in a series of increasingly radical activities. After graduating from college in 1961, he traveled south to work full-time on voter registration drives; he also helped launch Students for a Democratic Society (SDS). He then spent four years in Newark, New Jersey, organizing welfare and renters' rights groups, and soon he emerged as one of the country's leading antiwar spokespersons. Hayden gained national attention in 1968 when he, along with seven other radicals known as the Chicago Eight, was tried for crossing state lines to incite a riot.[28]

When he met Fonda, the often pugnacious Hayden was living in a rundown apartment in Venice Beach and teaching a class on Vietnam at Pitzer College in Claremont, California. The actress and the activist had crossed paths at a number of antiwar rallies, but now, living in the same city, Fonda was drawn to the more experienced radical. Not only did she find him "a powerful public speaker who could capture people's seemingly disconnected, confused feelings and weave them into a coherent vision they could identify with," but he was the first leftist she met who took movies seriously. Deeply in love and three months pregnant with his child, Fonda married Hayden in the living room of her Laurel Canyon home in January 1973.[29]

After the actress received an invitation from North Vietnamese officials in May 1972 to visit Hanoi, Hayden urged her to go, arguing that her celebrity would draw attention to the cause. Since 1965, over 200 Americans had traveled to North Vietnam, usually on peace or fact-finding missions. Hayden went there in 1965 and again in 1967, when he brought back the first three American POWs released by the North Vietnamese. Fonda arrived in Hanoi on July 12, 1972, with a specific agenda: to deliver 200 letters to American POWs and to photograph the damage done to the country's vital dike system as a result of carpet bombing around the Red River Delta, home to 15 million peasant farmers. Although the Nixon administration denied bombing the dikes, Swedish Ambassador Jean-Christophe Oberg insisted he had seen the extensive damage caused by American warplanes. If the dikes collapsed they would flood the region, killing thousands of civilians, ruining rice crops, and creating widespread starvation.

During the next two weeks, the famous guest visited villages and schools in outlying rural areas, inspected the dike system, and met with American POWs. Fonda often found herself jumping into roadside holes when caught in the middle of American air raids. After filming the damaged dikes, the Hollywood star agreed to record four radio appeals to American soldiers, especially bomber pilots flying at high altitudes. In her first address, Fonda described what she had seen in Hong Phong village, where Pentagon spokesmen claimed only military targets were hit. She told the pilots they were being lied to. The areas they were bombing contained no military targets, only peasants. "They are similar to farmers in the Midwest many years ago in the United States. Perhaps your grandmothers and grandfathers would not be so different from these peasants."[30]

In subsequent addresses, she told pilots about bombs that damaged hospitals and also of the devastating effects of napalm that left its victim "living as a mutilated person, forever in physical pain." Blaming a deceitful administration, not the soldiers, she warned, "Nixon is continuing to risk your lives and the lives of American prisoners of war under the bombing in a last desperate gamble to keep his office come November. . . . The people back home are crying for you. We are afraid of what must be happening to you as human beings. For it isn't possible to destroy . . . without having done damage to your own souls."[31]

Following her first broadcast, Fonda met with seven American POWs who talked about their experiences. The next day, she went on Radio Hanoi and reported that the pilots believed they were "bombing military targets" and were shocked to discover otherwise. "They asked me to bring messages back home to their loved ones and friends, telling them to please be as actively involved in the peace movement as possible, to renew their efforts to end the war."[32]

Fonda remained confident that meeting so many soldiers at coffeehouses and rallies made her sensitive to the POWs' concerns. What she did not realize was how easily North Vietnamese government officials could manipulate her. On the last day of her trip, she traveled to an anti-aircraft military installation where she was greeted by musicians and soldiers who sang songs about freedom and liberty. When photographers asked their naive guest to sit on an anti-aircraft emplacement, she donned a hard hat and laughed along with her hosts as they took photos (see fig. 6.2). Fonda's festive mood

FIGURE 6.2 Fonda sitting in North Vietnamese anti-aircraft gun, July 1, 1972.
SOURCE: ASSOCIATED PRESS

quickly disappeared when she realized what was happening. "Oh my God," she thought. "It's going to look like I was trying to shoot down U.S. planes!" She begged the photographers not to publish the pictures. They assured her they would not, but they did. One of the pictures hit the newswires within twenty-four hours and sparked an outpouring of anger at home. The photo, which along with the radio broadcasts earned her the sobriquet "Hanoi Jane," would haunt her forever. Whatever her intentions, these weapons were being used to shoot down American planes. "That two-minute lapse of sanity," she confessed in her autobiography, "will haunt me until I die."[33]

Fonda returned home in late July to mixed responses. After seeing her footage of the damaged dikes, United Nations Secretary General Kurt Waldheim appealed to the White House to stop the bombing. Nixon responded by asking UN Ambassador George H. W. Bush to tell Waldheim to stop repeating Fonda's lies. After meeting the UN head and viewing the footage, Bush told the press, "I think the best thing I can do on the subject is to shut up." That August, ten U.S. senators sponsored a resolution demanding that the "United States shall not bomb or otherwise attack by air or sea the dams, dikes, or hydraulic systems in North Vietnam."[34] Frustrated by the president's refusal to honor his pledge to end the war, the Senate also passed an amendment calling for American troops to be withdrawn over the next three months. The enormous publicity generated by her visit allowed Fonda to accomplish her goal: the United States stopped bombing the dikes in August.

But Hanoi Jane paid a high price for her activism. Conservative critics used her trip to shift attention away from the war and warn off other movie stars from going public with their antiwar activities. They blamed a woman for a failed man's war. White House officials placed her on Nixon's secret "enemies list" and asked Attorney General Richard Kleindienst to charge her with treason. When the Justice Department head refused, arguing that her visit broke no laws, the House Internal Security Council (an updated version of HUAC) opened their own hearings in September. The committee charged Fonda with treason for giving "aid and comfort to the enemy," but explained there would be no further prosecution because it did not want to give her martyr status.[35]

Over the next several months, Fonda encountered a campaign of intimidation and vilification not seen since the early days of HUAC. Legislators in Maryland, California, Ohio, Colorado, and Indiana introduced bills censuring the actress and banning her and her films from their states. One Maryland official even suggested she be "sentenced to death" for treason. The Veterans of Foreign Wars denounced the actress as a "traitorous meddler in official government." American Liberty League representative Art Jaskjy warned, "you are now destined for assassination" and "one day a shot will ring out ending your life." The *Los Angeles Times* even printed a letter calling for donations to "the Jane Fonda, Ramsay Clark assassination fund."[36]

Ironically, the FBI was the only government agency to give Fonda a clean bill of political health. Shortly after her return from Hanoi, the agency turned her files over to an internal panel of three agents who were asked whether a clandestine investigation should be continued. All three agreed that the Bureau had no reason to continue spying on her. "There are more dangerous characters around needing our attention," the panel concluded, and "these investigations should be closed. The basis for investigation appears to be—pick someone you dislike and start investigating."[37]

Building a Movement

Following her return from Hanoi in July 1972, Fonda began a new stage in her political evolution. No longer content with simply being another participant, she teamed up with Tom Hayden to become a movement leader and grassroots builder. Like Harry Belafonte, she believed organized movements could wield far more power than even the most dedicated individuals. Over the next two decades, the couple launched the Indochina Peace Campaign (IPC) and, following the war's end, the Campaign for Economic Democracy (CED). Taking her politics directly to the screen, she also produced and starred in a series of movies that dramatized many of the issues raised by the IPC and CED. Far from being a junior partner or celebrity tagalong, as her critics suggested, Fonda, insisted Hayden, "was absolutely central" in the "planning, thinking, details, strategy, and tactics" of both organizations.[38]

After years of toiling on a variety of radical causes, Hayden and Fonda set out to build a long-lasting grassroots movement. Both saw an important difference between an antiwar movement that mobilized citizens around a single issue—and died out when the war ended—and a more ambitious organization that sought to remedy the inequalities of American life by radically altering the basic structures of power. Recognizing that Fonda wanted to accomplish things quickly, Hayden urged patience. Tom "taught her right off," explained Peter Fonda, "that you don't have to achieve revolution over-night. That was Jane's problem all along, trying to change people and getting frustrated when they failed to change purely on her say-so."[39]

Founded in June 1972, the IPC pursued three tasks: exposing Nixon's escalation of the war, opposing American imperialism in Southeast Asia, and laying the groundwork for a continuous left presence in American life by bringing activists into the mainstream of political power. One of the key problems of the antiwar movement, the IPC's founding document stated, was "its failure to steadily reach out to more and more Americans and edu-cate them about the war." Radicals could no longer afford to "talk only to ourselves" but needed to build broad-based coalitions throughout the coun-try. To that end, the IPC worked with an array of unions, churches, politi-cians, PTAs, YMCAs, farm workers, veterans' organizations, and other antiwar groups.[40]

The IPC operated at two levels. Local chapters focused on recruiting and educating citizens through a series of meetings, talks, newsletters, and films, while the two founders—operating out of their headquarters in Santa Mon-ica, California—worked on more highly publicized national events. In fall 1972, as Senator George McGovern ran against President Richard Nixon on an antiwar platform, Fonda and Hayden embarked on a two-month-long, ninety-five-city speaking tour to support the Democrat and raise public awareness about the antiwar movement. Accompanied by singer Holly Near, former POW George Smith, and occasional appearances by Daniel Berrigan, Frances FitzGerald, Pat Ellsberg, David Dellinger, and other anti-war figures, the IPC entourage averaged four appearances a day. While many attended gatherings in order to catch a glimpse of the controversial movie star, they left better informed than when they entered.[41]

By the time the tour ended on November 6, the antiwar group succeeded in speaking to over 160,000 people and generating twenty-five new IPC chapters. Although disappointed with the outcome of the presidential elec-tion, Fonda emerged from her travels a more compelling speaker. Frequent appearances on TV and radio allowed her to perfect her political messages and delivery style. In subsequent months, she repeatedly won over often-suspicious audiences by delivering a personal speech that described her transformation from movie star to antiwar activist, and from sex object to feminist. "I was in prison," she confessed to a Philadelphia audience. "My mind was behind bars and you know what I looked like—Barbarella."[42]

On January 27, 1973, representatives of the United States, South Vietnam, and North Vietnam signed the Paris Peace Accords. On March 29, the last remaining American combat troops left Vietnam. As most antiwar groups disappeared following the withdrawal, the IPC launched a new campaign aimed at halting the war in Cambodia and Laos. "Over 80,000 civilians have been killed," Fonda told reporters, "over one million refugees created and over 300 people are still being killed daily in Cambodia." During the next two years, the IPC raised public awareness about ongoing tragedies in Southeast Asia by sponsoring national speaking tours, distributing over a million educational pamphlets, producing a film (*Introduction to the Enemy*), and working with domestic and international peace groups.[43]

Fonda played an integral role in the organization's seven-person leadership cadre, planning strategies as well as giving speeches. "Jane wasn't on a soapbox," observed former blacklisted actress Lee Grant, who was living in Malibu at the time, "but was a real original thinker and talent." The IPC recruiting efforts paid off as it established new branches throughout the country, especially in powerful electoral states such as California, Ohio, Michigan, Illinois, Pennsylvania, and New York. Hayden and Fonda even persuaded several dozen congressional aides to join the IPC.[44]

The birth of their first child on July 7, 1973, Troy (named after Vietcong hero Nguyen Van Troi) O'Donovan Garrity (Hayden's mother's maiden name), did little to slow the couple down. Fonda spent six weeks in Washington that summer lobbying Congress to end all military funding and arms shipments, occasionally interrupting her efforts to breastfeed Troy. Attacked by leftists who accused her of hypocrisy for living a movie-star lifestyle, the actress sold her Laurel Canyon home and moved her family into the second floor of a rundown $45,000 two-family wood-frame home in Santa Monica that her father dubbed "The Shack." Fonda was probably the only Hollywood star whose bedroom furniture consisted of a mattress thrown on the floor.

Despite its efforts to reach beyond a single issue, the IPC dissolved shortly after the fall of Saigon in April 1975. Fonda's work with the IPC earned her the admiration of previously skeptical citizens. Two years earlier, despite the furor over her trip to Hanoi, a Gallup poll listed her as one of the most admired women in America. Experienced activists such as Stanley Sheinbaum, who headed fundraising efforts for Daniel Ellsberg's defense in the Pentagon Papers trial, praised her as "a mainstay of the movement, not always as effective as we would have liked, but she was a key player. She was a movie star, she was beautiful, she was very articulate, and she had a good political head on her shoulders." More importantly, Fonda succeeded in drawing new people into the antiwar movement. Members of the IPC's Downey (California) chapter insisted the group could "trace its beginning to a speaking engagement by Jane Fonda at a community college over a year ago."[45] She even managed to earn the respect of her often-estranged father, who held a fundraising benefit for the IPC in March 1974 following the Broadway opening of *Clarence Darrow*, in which he starred.

Despite her newly minted respectability, Fonda remained a lightning rod for conservatives. Members of the Young Americans for Freedom and the Young Republicans hung her in effigy when she came to talk at the University of Southern California in April 1973. "Does Jane Fonda know how much we loath her and wish she'd shut up?" a reader wrote the *Los Angeles Herald-Examiner* the following month. "What does she think about being the most hated woman in America?"[46]

Fonda fought back by filing a lawsuit against the Nixon administration in 1973 to compel various government agencies to stop illegal surveillance operations against her. The actress settled the case in 1979 when the FBI admitted to a series of illegal operations aimed at smearing her reputation and impairing her political work. During the course of the trial, the CIA, State Department, Internal Revenue Service, Treasury Department, and White House all confessed to keeping files on her—and 1.5 million Americans—and conducting a number of unconstitutional investigations. Fonda's suit sparked a Senate investigation (known as the Church Committee) into abuses by the intelligence community and succeeded in altering privacy rights and government surveillance policies for the next three decades.[47]

In later years, Fonda insisted that activism helped her career by deepening her humanity and making her "a better actor," but in the short run, she found herself "graylisted" because of her antiwar work. With conservative groups organizing boycotts and several state legislatures threatening to ban her movies, studio heads saw her as box-office poison. "Many executives were against the war," she reflected a decade later, "but when it came down to spending millions on a film with Fonda's name, it was too much of a risk, so I wasn't getting many offers." As one blunt studio head allegedly remarked after the Hanoi firestorm, "The bitch will never be allowed inside my gates again."[48]

Unable to get the kind of meaty roles she wanted, she made films whose politics she admired. After finishing *Klute*, she returned to Paris to shoot

Tout Va Bien (1972) with Marxist French New Wave director Jean-Luc Godard, "the only person I've ever met," she insisted "who's truly revolutionary."[49] She followed that with a series of small productions: *FTA* (1972), a filmed version of her antiwar tour; *Steelyard Blues* (1973), a comedy about blue-collar life in the midst of the counterculture rebellion; *A Doll's House* (1973), Henrik Ibsen's play about the destructive effects of sexism; and *The Blue Bird* (1976), a Russian-American production based on a children's fairy tale. In 1974, she founded her own production company, IPC Films, and narrated its first release, Haskell Wexler's *Introduction to the Enemy* (1974), a documentary about the struggles of the North Vietnamese people. All these films (save *Klute*) were box-office failures.

In 1976, with her career in limbo, the war over, and the IPC dissolved, Fonda turned her attention to another ambitious goal: helping Hayden win a seat in the U.S. Senate. With Nixon resigning after the Watergate scandal and the Republican Party in disarray, the opportunity to refashion American government seemed greater than at any time since the New Deal. In April 1976, Hayden declared he would run in the Democratic primaries against liberal incumbent John Tunney. "The forces of left and center," he explained in a letter to the former IPC faithful, "have never in 30 years lacked a vision and program as they do now." Many radicals denounced his entry into electoral politics as a sellout of his earlier principles, but Hayden argued that the only way to create major changes in the American state was by fighting on several fronts. By bringing movement politics into the mainstream of power, he hoped to restore "democratic participation" to a government whose legitimacy had been called into question. As Hayden confidant and former radical Weatherman Andy Spahn explained, "We were interested in systematic change, in changing political alignments and power structures."[50]

The IPC's earlier efforts to foster a new generation of activists paid off as many of its workers flocked to Hayden's campaign. "They gave me a constructive outlet for my energy," Spahn recounted, and "brought in a whole group of people who were outside the political system." Hayden's Senate campaign also marked another key moment in Fonda's political evolution. "Jane's politics changed as we became more involved in electoral politics," Spahn recalled. "Jane was committed to building an organization and a movement" and to that end she "endorsed Democratic candidates" that she "never would have several years earlier." Campaigns, however, cost a great deal of money. Since Hayden had no personal wealth, his wife helped finance his primary run by starring in *Fun with Dick and Jane* (released in 1977), a satire in which a recently fired aerospace company executive (George Segal) and his wife (Fonda) maintain their upwardly mobile lifestyle by robbing banks, supermarkets, and phone companies. The film was a box-office hit and led Columbia Pictures to proclaim, "America Loves Jane Fonda Again."[51]

During production breaks, Fonda traveled around the state talking with voters about Hayden's determination to restore democracy to American government. The candidate's wife and largest donor (she gave over $500,000) called on her Hollywood friends to donate their time and money. Despite Hayden's efforts to reach the unconverted, the often-surly candidate never excited California voters in the way charismatic conservatives like Murphy and Reagan had several years earlier. Reviled by his opponents as a combination of Marx and Lenin, Hayden lost his primary battle to incumbent Tunney, garnering 37 percent of the vote. Putting a positive spin on defeat, Fonda saw the campaign as the first step in expanding their political base. After all, she observed, "1.2 million Californians had cast their votes for a New Left radical, cofounder of SDS, and co-conspirator of Chicago."[52]

Following Hayden's defeat, the couple returned to grassroots organizing by founding the CED. Begun as a California-based organization, CED hoped to transform itself into a national movement. Economic democracy, Fonda told the press, meant restructuring government responsibilities in radical ways by creating "a different mix of private and public ownership." At a time of inflation and high unemployment, when multinational corporations were taking jobs overseas, and when reliance on foreign oil and nuclear energy jeopardized the nation's well-being, CED aimed to alter the relationship between government, citizens, and corporations.[53]

Laying out a farsighted agenda, CED called for the creation of a solar energy industry that would replace oil and nuclear power, create new jobs, and protect national interests by freeing the United States from dependence on Middle East oil. The group also moved to limit the power of corporate America by requiring companies to put public representatives on their board of directors. "We call ourselves a democracy," Fonda explained, "yet in the area of the economy huge corporations have more weight, have more say so and more power even than our elected officials." The group also pressed for rent control reforms in California that would restrict the rights of individual capitalists. Taken collectively, CED's policies challenged the most sacred of all American principles: the sanctity of private property. By limiting property and corporate rights in one or two areas of the economy, the government would set precedents that could lead to more radical changes later on.[54]

Like Ronald Reagan, Fonda came to understand the importance of language in swaying the unconverted. Consequently, she and Hayden defended their agenda by using "democracy" as their rallying cry. Harkening back to the legacy of the Founding Fathers rather than Castro, Mao, or Marx, Fonda no longer referred to herself as a revolutionary but as a "progressive" Democrat. "I think I am quintessentially American," she told a Chicago reporter. "I'm hard working; I feel a commitment to my country. . . . I'm moral."[55] Whatever rhetorical devices they used to justify their actions, the couple pursued an agenda as radical to the left as Murphy's and Reagan's ideas were to the right.

Fonda and Hayden fought to push the Democratic Party further to the left by working to elect candidates sympathetic to their agenda. "It's now possible for people who represent the politics of the sixties movements to begin to take political power," the actress explained. "We're not interested in being protestors for the rest of our lives." The group adopted a strategy remarkably similar to that used by California conservatives in the early 1960s. They organized grassroots chapters that worked with coalitions of progressive groups to seize control of local Democratic Party committees. The strategy worked. In addition to securing eleven seats on the Orange County Democratic Central Committee, CED helped elect a mayor and several council members in Berkeley and Oakland, and two city council representatives in Santa Monica, who in turn passed one of the nation's most progressive rent control measures.[56]

Over the next several years, Fonda traveled around the state bringing CED's message to a wide range of community, religious, civic, business, and political groups. Drawing on her skills as an actress, she proved a highly effective speaker. "She had an ability to reach people," noted one former coworker, "to address issues in a way that moved people." By September 1979, the organization's membership rose to 7,000 people and thirty chapters that spanned the state from San Diego to Humboldt County. Working closely with Governor Jerry Brown, State Senator David Roberti, and local politicians, the group succeeded in turning ideas into laws and securing seventeen ballot-box victories. "Four years ago there was a fair amount of animosity toward CED," southern California Democratic Party chair Peter

Kelley told a reporter in September 1982, "however, the times have caught up with the Haydens."[57]

The Campaign for Economic Democracy would not have happened without Fonda's largesse. Although members paid modest dues, Fonda provided the organization with the bulk of its finances. An exercise fanatic long before it became fashionable, she created "Jane Fonda's Workout" in 1979—and its ancillary array of books and videotapes—as a way of raising money for CED. A sign inside her Beverly Hills Workout facility openly declared, "Profits from 'The Workout' support the Campaign for Economic Democracy in its efforts to promote alternative sources of energy, stop environmental cancer, fight for women's rights, justice for tenants, and other causes related to environmental protection, social justice, and world peace." By the mid-1980s, her business had generated $17 million for CED.[58] In addition to her financial contributions, Fonda also did the day-to-day grunt work—answering telephones, walking precincts—that most liberal stars shied away from.

The group represented only part of Fonda's involvement in building a movement culture. The actress set out to do something no other star had ever done at the peak of their career: dramatize controversial movement issues on the screen while simultaneously promoting them off the screen. Chaplin and Belafonte made political films but never explicitly linked them to ongoing political movements. As Fonda grew more politically sophisticated, she saw the need to fight on two fronts simultaneously: political films and grassroots organizing. "On the one hand," she observed, "films can put out powerful images and messages that have a deep impact on the people; on the other hand, they are only images, not actions in themselves."[59] She set out to marry images to actions.

Dramatizing Movement Politics

Fonda and producer Bruce Gilbert, a former antiwar activist, founded IPC Films in order "to make the kind of movies which Hollywood should have been turning out but wasn't." Drawing on her experiences in the antiwar and women's movements, her films revealed how previously apolitical people could transform their lives and the nation through activism. The main characters in her first three films are initially apolitical; they become political when specific events in their lives make them understand they can no longer remain silent about the problems they see. Ordinary people in Fonda's films surprise themselves by doing extraordinary things.[60]

Fonda presented her politics in the form of entertaining movies that were neither too preachy nor overtly radical. "I wanted to make films that were stylistically mainstream," she explained, "films Middle America could relate to: about ordinary people going through personal transformation." As she told one reporter, "I don't want to play liberated women, roles where people say, 'Oh, that's Jane Fonda, that's the way she perceives herself.'" Instead she wanted to play "the antithesis of what I feel—a prowar or apolitical kind of woman existing in a situation most average people live in," so she could help "clarify the situation for other women."[61]

Despite her controversial past, the financial success of *Fun with Dick and Jane* (1977) and *Julia* (1977) revived her reputation with studio executives who were now eager to finance and distribute IPC productions. *Coming Home* (1978) is an emotional tour-de-force with a compelling political strategy. Inspired by her friendship with Marine veteran and paraplegic Ron Kovic, the subject of Oliver Stone's *Born on the Fourth of July* (1989), Fonda's film is less about whether the Vietnam War was wrong or right than how the government failed to care for severely injured veterans. *Coming Home* is a human story filled with a pathos that transcends left and right, Democrat and Republican.

Set during the height of the war, *Coming Home* combines her long-standing interest in Vietnam vets with her burgeoning commitment to feminism. Jon Voight plays Luke Martin, an embittered Marine sergeant who returns home a paraplegic. Fonda costars as Sally Hyde, the deferential wife of macho Marine Captain Bob Hyde (Bruce Dern). Following through on her determination to appeal to Middle America, she initially appears as a very unglamorous woman, a former high-school cheerleader who straightens her curly hair to look more conventional. The opening scenes show her to be a traditional wife who is dutiful toward her husband, dutiful toward sex, dutiful toward everything but her own feelings.

After her husband is sent to Vietnam, Sally volunteers at the local VA hospital, a decision that changes her life. For the next hour, the film reveals the difficulty of rehabilitating from major wartime injuries and the woefully inadequate staffing of VA hospitals. The movie exposes the hypocrisy of politicians who readily send men to war but do little to help when they return severely injured. As one paralyzed African American vet complains, "They don't ask how are you, they don't tell you anything about how to manage your finances, how to go back into society, they don't tell you anything about your sex life." As Sally becomes friends with the veterans, she grows angry at the government's callous mistreatment of its wounded heroes. "You've done your duty, you've served your purpose," she tells them, "so they just toss you into the heap like used Kleenex or something."

As Sally falls in love with Luke, we see the deep interconnection between personal and political transformation. Her work at the VA and affair with Luke alter her life. She buys a used Porsche and lets her hair grow out to a curlier, hipper look. As her political awareness evolves, she abandons her docile ways and becomes more assertive in confronting authorities and standing up for her beliefs. She also allows herself to enjoy sex for the first time in her life. For Sally, feminism and women's liberation are not about demonstrations or political statements. They are about awakening to a greater inner sense of who she is rather than how others define her. It is a realization that is both exhilarating and frightening.

Luke also goes through a political metamorphosis from gung-ho patriot to antiwar spokesman. As he tells an auditorium filled with draft-age students, he used to be captain of his high-school football team and supported the war. "And now I'm here to tell you that I have killed for my country, and I don't feel good about it, because there is not enough reason to feel a person die in your hands or to see your best buddy get blown away." Unashamedly crying, he confesses, "there is a lot of shit I did over there that I find fucking hard to live with." No one, he explains, should go to Vietnam out of blind patriotism. "I'm telling you there is a choice to be made here."

When Sally's husband returns from Vietnam, FBI agents tell him about her affair. The Bureau had secretly tailed the couple after Luke protested conditions in the VA hospital by chaining himself to the gates of a Marine recruiting depot. Hyde listens to the agents, but after serving in Vietnam he is no longer the same man. Several months earlier, during a brief furlough visit with Sally in Hong Kong, he told her about the daily horrors he witnessed. "My men are chopping heads off," and his lieutenant wanted to put them on a pole "to scare the shit out of the Viet Cong." The actual experience of combat proved far different from the patriotic ideology he once believed. Unable to cope with wartime atrocities and devastated by his wife's affair, Hyde walks into the ocean determined to commit suicide. As he does, the camera cuts to Sally pushing a grocery cart into the market—and then the screen goes blank as the soundtrack plays the Rolling Stones' "You're Out of Time."

Coming Home was a tremendous success. Fonda and Voight won Best Actress and Best Actor Oscars, while its writers won Oscars for Best Screenplay. The movie proved equally popular with audiences, earning $13.5 million. More importantly, producing a box-office hit allowed Fonda to shape the way millions of Americans looked at the meaning of Vietnam. "We knew there was going to be a cultural battle of ideas to interpret" the war, explained coproducer and former Berkeley radical Bruce Gilbert, and "we wanted our film to be out there as a cultural expression and to hopefully help people learn some lessons from the Vietnam War." In a town that still remembered McCarthyism, Fonda demonstrated that outspoken political activism did not necessarily diminish box-office power. The unrepentant leftist finished 1978 as Hollywood's eighth most bankable star and its second leading actress.[62]

Buoyed by success, Fonda set out to publicize the dangers of the poorly regulated nuclear energy industry in an entertaining fashion. During the shooting of *Coming Home*, actor Michael Douglas sent her the script for *The China Syndrome*, the fictional story of a near meltdown at a California nuclear plant. The film, she recounted, "dovetailed perfectly with what the Campaign for Economic Democracy was all about: blowing the whistle on large corporations that were willing to risk the public's welfare to protect their profits."[63]

Like *Coming Home*, *The China Syndrome* (1979) is about the politicization of ordinary people who rise up to oppose authorities they never previously questioned. The film focuses on three key characters: Kimberly Wells (Fonda), an apolitical television newscaster; Richard Adams (Michael Douglas), an irreverent cameraman who pushes her to discover the truth; and Jack Godell (Jack Lemmon), the engineer who runs the Ventana Nuclear Power Plant owned by the fictitious California Gas and Electric Company (CG&E). Wells and Adams are sent to do a puff piece on the plant—which CG&E insists is the most efficient way to meet the nation's energy needs—and wind up filming a near meltdown caused by an earthquake. Government regulations require the plant to shut down for a few days, but company officials convince the TV station not to run the potentially damaging footage. Fonda's character is neither a feminist nor a radical. Even though Wells observed the panic in the nuclear control room, she is too concerned about her career to make waves. Politics is for other people.

The cameraman and the engineer emerge as the real heroes of the film. Worried that the network is stonewalling the truth, Adams (Douglas) steals his footage and takes it to a physicist and a nuclear engineer who, after viewing the film, tell him and Wells "you are probably lucky to be alive. For that matter, we might say the same for the rest of Southern California." The footage revealed a failure of the water system to cool the nuclear core, a failure that came close to the China Syndrome. When the core is exposed, the fuel heats up so much that it will melt down through the bottom of the planet, theoretically all the way to China, and send clouds of radioactivity into the atmosphere. "The number of people killed depends on which way the wind is blowing," the scientists warn, "rendering an area the size of Pennsylvania permanently uninhabitable, not to mention the cancer that would show up later."

In the meantime, Godell (Lemmon) discovers that a corrupt inspector falsified the water-cooling system's X-ray reports. When he demands a thorough reexamination, his bosses explain it would cost fifteen to twenty million dollars; they order him to return to work and shut his mouth. This is Godell's politicizing moment. He has found a serious problem but his supervisors care more about saving money than saving lives.

The remainder of the film turns into a thriller as viewers wonder whether the reporter, the cameraman, and the engineer can stop the faulty plant from going back on line. Fonda interrupts the straight-ahead narrative at one point for a moment of political education. The camera cuts to a public licensing hearing for a new nuclear facility at Point Conception. Fonda uses this opportunity to explain CED's arguments against nuclear power. Those speaking at the hearings are not radicals but ordinary men and women concerned about public safety. A housewife with six grandchildren tells the federal bureaucrats that she is frightened about nuclear energy and wants to know what will happen in case of a nuclear accident. Another citizen complains that the country "is proceeding with the building of nuclear plants and yet we do not have a program for the safe disposal of nuclear wastes."

Fonda encourages grassroots activism with scenes of men and women—old and young—picketing outside the government hearings. As reporter Wells reviews her notes, we see protesters in figure 6.3 carrying signs with slogans promoting CED's agenda: "ACTIVE TODAY OR RADIOACTIVE TOMORROW," "STOP NUKES," "NO NUKES," and, in a more specific plug for her organization, "C.E.D. WESTSIDE CAMPAIGN FOR ECONOMIC DEMOCRACY."

FIGURE 6.3 Fonda brought her activism to the screen in this scene from *The China Syndrome* (1979), where protestors carry CED signs. SOURCE: PHOTOFEST

The main characters wind up doing the right thing, even though it costs Godell his life. After the utility company ignores his warnings about a possible meltdown, the engineer locks himself in the control room and agrees to tell the truth on a live television report. That never happens. A CG&E-ordered SWAT team breaks down the door and kills him. The company's PR man explains that Godell was "an emotionally disturbed employee" who "had been drinking." However, before they can sweep the incident under the rug, the engineer's best friend and coworker (Wilford Brimley) goes on the air. Politicized by what he just witnessed, he tells the press that Godell was a hero who tried to expose the truth and died for it. A few minutes later, Wells confirms that Godell was about to present evidence proving the plant should be shut down. In the final scene, after a distraught Wells takes a moment to compose herself, the TV station cuts to a commercial for microwave ovens.

The film opened on March 16, 1979, to considerable opposition from the nuclear power industry. General Electric withdrew its sponsorship of the *Barbara Walters Show* after she interviewed Jane Fonda, while a Southern California Edison Company executive (the real life counterpart to CG&E) insisted that the movie "hasn't any scientific credibility and is, in fact, ridiculous." The film's fortunes took a fortuitous turn on March 28, when a near-meltdown of the Three Mile Island nuclear plant forced the evacuation of residents near Harrisburg, Pennsylvania, and the closure of five other nuclear plants. *China Syndrome* became the number-one box-office hit, grossing $25.8 million, and brought Fonda her fifth Oscar nomination. As CED hoped, the film's political impact extended well beyond its initial theatrical run. In January 1984, the *Wall Street Journal* attributed the considerable slowdown of nuclear expansion to *China Syndrome*'s ability to shake "public confidence" in the industry.[64]

Hoping to leverage Fonda's growing popularity, CED launched an ambitious thirty-two-day, fifty-two-city national tour in September 1979 aimed at expanding their membership and mobilizing citizens to support rent control, health care improvements, and better working conditions (see fig. 6.4). Knowing that people would come to rallies to see a "movie star," Fonda used the opportunity to attack banks, utilities, multinational corporations, and the Carter administration's energy policy. Distinguishing CED's agenda from liberals who dole "out money to deal with the symptoms of the problem, rather than their fundamentals," she insisted that their organization was

FIGURE 6.4 Several months after the opening of *The China Syndrome*, Fonda and Tom Hayden address an antinuclear rally in New York City, September 23, 1979. SOURCE: ASSOCIATED PRESS

attempting to bring about "changes in government policy that would get at these fundamentals." The Edison Electric Institute found CED's attacks on the nuclear industry so threatening that they sent a "truth squad" team of two engineers to follow Fonda and Hayden and question their stance at rallies.[65] The tour succeeded in attracting 2,500 new members to CED and providing Fonda with the subject of her next film: the harassment and exploitation of working women.

Since the mid-1970s, Fonda grew increasingly interested in feminism and battling for gender equality. The Civil Rights Act of 1964 declared sexual discrimination at the workplace illegal, but it was one thing to pass a law and quite another to enforce it. In 1966, a group of female activists formed the National Organization of Women (NOW) with the goal of achieving "equal rights in partnership with men." Membership rose from 1,000 in 1967 to 40,000 in 1974. Fonda was a late but devoted addition to the cause. As she reflected several decades later, "Feminism saved my soul because I could begin to understand why my life has gone the way it has, why I have done the things I have done, why my mother chose to kill herself. That all came through my activism."[66]

Determined to share that sense of personal empowerment with women throughout the nation, she made several movies during this period that portray strong female characters. In *Comes a Horseman* (1978), she plays a Montana rancher forced to fight off rapacious land barons and oil tycoons. In *The Electric Horseman* (1979), she teamed with Robert Redford to tell the story of a tough television reporter (Fonda) and ex-rodeo star who fight corporate greed and the destruction of the environment. Even Neil Simon's comic *California Suite* (1978), in which the forty-year-old actress wore a skimpy bikini, sent a positive message to women: exercise could make you feel better about your life. "Getting fit is a political act," she insisted. "You can't be liberated when you remain a slave to bad physical and nutritional habits."[67]

Fonda followed these features with IPC's first comedy, *Nine to Five*. Her most successful movie in terms of both box office and political impact, *Nine to Five* was a direct result of CED's efforts to help organize women workers. During an earlier stopover in Boston for the opening of *Coming Home*, the actress reconnected with Karen Nussbaum, a friend from the antiwar days who had founded Working Women 9 to 5, a national organization that represented female clerical workers. Nussbaum regaled Fonda with stories of sexual harassment at the workplace, of women training men who then became their supervisors, and of female clerical workers paid so little by wealthy banks that they were eligible for food stamps.[68]

Disturbed by what she heard, Fonda decided to make a film about the intersection of class and gender at the workplace. Few people who heard her political harangues in the early 1970s would have thought the actress capable of making a successful political comedy. But *Nine to Five* is a highly entertaining, if sometimes silly, revenge fantasy about three very different women who rise up against their sexist, incompetent boss (Dabney Coleman). The film's slapstick plot exposes the hardships faced by working women. Fonda plays the mousy Judy Bernly who enters the workplace for the first time following her divorce and is far too timid to protest her ill treatment. Dolly Parton delivers a funny performance as Doralee Rhodes, the busty executive secretary who has to deal with the constant sexual advances of her boss and the disdain of coworkers who wrongly assume she is sleeping with Coleman. Lily Tomlin, the film's central figure, plays Violet Newstead, the brilliant office manager and single mother who fumes as the men she trains steal her ideas and get promoted over her. Despite their anger, none of the women can afford to quit their jobs. The three come to recognize their common plight and through a series of comic turns wind up kidnapping Coleman and instituting office reforms right out of Working Women 9 to 5's national agenda: equal pay for equal work regardless of sex, flexible hours, in-office daycare centers, more minority hiring, and promotions for capable secretaries.

Nine to Five opened on December 19, 1980, and went on to become IPC's biggest hit, grossing over $103 million and spawning a hit record (the film's theme song written by Parton) and a television series. Working women loved being the heroines of their own entertainment and told reporters how events on the screen mirrored their experiences in the office. The movie also aided the national organizing efforts of Working Women 9 to 5. Before *Nine to Five*, Nussbaum explained, "we had to argue that women's work was plagued by discrimination. The movie put an end to that debate . . . the audiences recognized it and laughed at it. Now the debate could shift to what we should do about it." The film created so much excitement among office workers that Nussbaum traveled to twenty cities building what she called "the movement behind the movie." With Fonda joining her on a number of stops, membership rose from 8,000 people in twelve cities to over 10,000 members in twenty-five cities. In 1981, Nussbaum founded District 925 as a national affiliate of the Service Employees International Union, and proceeded to win 24 of 26 certifying elections.[69]

Fonda took a break from political filmmaking to produce *On Golden Pond* (1981). Starring Henry Fonda, Katharine Hepburn, and herself, the film depicted what for Jane were the all-too-real tensions between an estranged father and daughter. Opening in December 1981 to strong reviews and eventual Oscar nominations for its stars, the movie helped soften Fonda's public image and earned over $119 million. That same month, the actress-producer also premiered IPC's first box-office flop, *Rollover* (1981). Made at a time of skyrocketing oil prices and widespread bank failures, the film visualizes CED's attacks on the dangers posed by U.S. dependence on foreign oil and the growing power of Middle Eastern oil magnates.[70]

Unfortunately, the movie is a mess. The first twenty minutes of the plot are difficult to understand, the pacing is deadly, and Fonda and costar Kris Kristofferson are miscast. Fonda plays a former actress who takes over her husband's chemical company following his death, while Kristofferson plays a financial troubleshooter who is hired to help a bank from going under. In the course of borrowing $500 million from Arab investors, the couple uncover a plot by wealthy Saudi oil sheiks to wreck the world economy. With help from greedy American financiers, the Saudis withdraw all their investments from American banks, plunging the world into chaos and putting the OPEC nations in a position of unprecedented power.

Twenty-six years later, Fonda insisted that *Rollover*, for all its faults, "was kind of prescient. It was about how indebted we were to Arabs who could pull the rug out from under us." At the time, the film proved as inert at the box office as it did on the screen, grossing only $6 million. Yet, those willing to look beyond the film's immediate problems heard that the only way to be a truly independent republic is to halt our dependence on foreign nations for essential goods. For Fonda and CED, that meant using solar energy as a way to wean the nation off oil and dependence on the Middle East.[71]

Taken collectively, the success of IPC's feature films proved that Fonda's offscreen politics did little to diminish her star presence. She finished the 1979–1980 season as the nation's top-ranking female box-office star, and by the end of 1982 her IPC productions grossed over $340 million. The publication of *Jane Fonda's Workout* in 1982 marked a further contribution to her feminist ambitions. In her autobiography, Fonda told of receiving poignant letters testifying to the transformative impact of her book and workout salons. Women wrote her about "the weight they had lost, self-esteem they had gained, how they were finally able to stand up to their boss or recover from a mastectomy, asthma, respiratory failure, diabetes."[72] Fonda also spoke to the press about her painful twenty-three-year battle with bulimia, a battle that only ended when she became pregnant with her second child, Troy.

Despite her success, or perhaps because of it, Fonda remained a lightning rod for conservatives who continued to vilify the activist for her 1972 visit to Hanoi. In July 1979, California state senators, by a 28–5 vote, vetoed her appointment to the State Arts Council by insisting that she had committed "an act of treason" by "giving aid and comfort to the enemy" during the Vietnam War. The public, however, seemed far more willing to embrace the star than her industry colleagues did. A 1980 poll conducted by the *World Almanac* listed her as the nation's fifth most influential woman.[73]

Over the next several years, Fonda alternated between political work on and off the screen. The CED continued working with community groups on specific issues while also trying to move the Democratic Party further to the left. As membership rose from 7,000 in 1979 to over 12,000 in 1982, the organization succeeded in electing sixty CED-backed candidates to office, including Tom Hayden, who won a bitterly contested seat in the state assembly in November 1982. Contributing $30,000 a month to support CED and Hayden's campaign, Fonda served as a key political strategist as well as financier. As campaign manager Michael Dieden told the press, "There is not a political decision that this campaign or Tom personally makes that Jane does not play a role in."[74]

Dependent on males for most of her life, Fonda grew increasingly independent as Hayden moved to Sacramento to serve in the state legislature for the next seventeen years. In the spring of 1984 she stopped channeling all profits from the Workout to CED and took control of her corporate earnings "so that I can have more latitude in the ways I use the money." Feeling more self-assured than ever before, Fonda spoke out on a wide range of issues: from prochoice to calls to boycott South Africa until its government ended apartheid. Despite continued attacks from right-wing groups, the actress refused to back down. "The role of an artist," she told a reporter in February 1984, "is to be controversial, to shake people up and make them think with new parts of their minds."[75]

Hoping to build a movement that would last long after they retired, Fonda and Hayden recruited some of Hollywood's brightest young stars into a new organization they called Network. In September 1985, the couple invited several dozen actors to their home, including members of the so-called Brat Pack—Tom Cruise, Rob Lowe, Judd Nelson, Eric Stoltz, Daphne Zuniga, and Rosanna Arquette. "Celebrities tend to see other celebrities as their peers," Hayden observed. "They would generally follow and were interested in what Tom and Jane were doing. The potentiality was endless." Appealing to self-interest as well as selflessness, she explained how activism would deepen their ability as actors. She also emphasized the difference they could make in swaying voters. "People know us and in some instances like us because of what they see on TV or on the screen. They want to hear what we have to say, and if we say it right and we know what we're talking about, we can persuade other people to join the cause." Ending on an emotional note, she explained how being an activist meant "we will die having made a difference if we can plant our flag in something that matters broader than us and our careers."[76]

Fonda's appeal worked. By creating Network, explained Marge Tabankin, former head of Vista under President Carter, Jane and Tom "took responsibility for politicizing a whole young generation of Hollywood people." The Network activists, in turn, attracted the attention of thousands of fans. When they traveled to Sacramento to promote a clean water initiative, Hayden marveled how the group brought "5,000 people out into the streets" and "created a huge motivation for young people to get involved when the celebrities were gone."[77]

Over the next several years, the young stars—whose ranks expanded to include Meg Ryan, Sarah Jessica Parker, Alec Baldwin, Demi Moore, Marlee Matlin, Michael J. Fox, and Mary Stuart Masterson—traveled to the Soviet Union to promote arms control, protested nuclear testing in Nevada's deserts, opposed conservative jurist Robert Bork's nomination to the Supreme Court, raised money for the anti-apartheid movement, and worked with Hayden to push the Democratic Party in a more progressive direction. Network "eventually grew so big," a pleased Hayden reflected, "it became a Democratic Party department and various Hollywood people duplicated the same thing."[78]

As Fonda's commitment to feminism grew stronger in the mid-1980s, she encouraged other female stars to speak out on behalf of important issues, thereby elevating the visibility of Hollywood women. In May 1985, she persuaded Jessica Lange and Sissy Spacek, stars of three recent films about strong rural women battling adversity, to testify before a special Congressional Farm

Task Force Committee about the plight of the American farmer. "The reason we are here," Fonda told the task force, "is to underscore the gravity of the crisis that is leading to the bankruptcy, humiliation, and banishment of farmers from their lands at a rate not seen since my father made *The Grapes of Wrath*." Following her lead, Lange and Spacek decried the administration's farm policies as uncaring and insensitive toward hardworking rural Americans. Although conservative columnists mocked the testimony of the three decidedly nonrural women, the trio succeeded in bringing national attention to an issue the Reagan administration was trying to sweep under the rug. Drawn to a hearing that would otherwise have received little notice, reporters outnumbered members of Congress by a 5 to1 margin.[79]

Far from harming her public image, Fonda's steadfast activism earned her the admiration of more and more Americans. In September 1985, a Gallup poll listed her as the third most influential woman in the country, while a U.S. News–Roper poll named her the number-one heroine among young Americans. These results are especially impressive given they came at the height of the conservative backlash against feminism that marked the Reagan era. But after fifteen years of intense political work, the exhausted star decided to pull back and focus on her career. Although she never made another IPC film, many of her subsequent roles explored provocative issues: church politics (*Agnes of God*), alcoholism (*The Morning After*), and adult illiteracy (*Stanley and Iris*).[80]

As Fonda's public standing rose, so too did attacks from her critics. In April 1984, she tried to win over Middle America with a heartfelt apology for her past mistakes. She confessed to making errors "in the way that I spoke, [and] how I tried to reach people" during the Vietnam War era. Since then, she tried "to show people a side of me that perhaps wasn't as apparent or that they didn't see, or that I didn't have time to show in those days." Yet she also realized that "there's a certain portion of those people who will never forgive me, ever."[81]

Fonda underestimated the sheer hatred people felt for "Hanoi Jane." Throughout the 1970s and 1980s, veteran and conservative organizations attacked her character, picketed her films, and even called for a boycott of her Workout clothing line. "There's a reservoir of bad feeling for Jane Fonda," an American Legion member remarked in July 1984. "We think she's a traitor." Critics accused her of turning "this country against its own veterans." Conservatives also attacked politicians linked to the "Red" actress. When Missouri Senate candidate Harriet Woods accepted a $2,000 campaign contribution from Fonda in 1986, her opponent ran provocative ads showing Jane sitting in a North Vietnamese anti-aircraft gun and condemning "Hanoi Harriet" for associating with traitors. Woods insisted that the vilification campaign "helped to keep me from mainstreaming myself" and led to her defeat. South Dakota Senate hopeful Tom Daschle faced similar attacks for inviting Fonda to testify at the Farm Task Force Committee hearings. The Democrat won but Republican campaigners came away convinced that "Fonda was our single best negative. . . . Jane comes with instant baggage, and you don't need to explain to voters who she is."[82]

In light of the fact that similar attacks persist to this day—including a doctored photo used in the 2004 presidential campaign showing Fonda and John Kerry together at an antiwar rally in the 1970s—it is worth spending a moment to explore the charges against her. Just as the left vilified Ronald Reagan for testifying as a friendly witness before HUAC when in fact he was not quite as friendly as his critics suggested, so too has Fonda been wrongly accused of hostility toward Vietnam-era soldiers. Her enemies have rewritten the past to equate opposition to the war with disrespect toward soldiers. Nothing could be further from the truth. Fonda began her activism by working with veterans' rights groups throughout the country, touring military bases on their behalf, and eventually making a film dramatizing the government's shameful neglect of injured GIs. Yet because of her 1972 trip to Hanoi, her critics consistently, and mistakenly, portray her as anti-GI and anti-American.[83]

Fonda's vilification also has as much to do with sexism and misogyny as it does with her first visit to North Vietnam. Right-wing hostility toward the activist increased after the release of the extraordinarily popular *First Blood* in 1982 and *Rambo: First Blood Part II* in 1985. Sylvester Stallone's mythic character demonstrated how one tough man could do what the military leadership could not: save soldiers from death at the hands of the North Vietnamese enemy. Conservatives embraced the film and blamed soft politicians for our defeat. If only our leaders had been like Rambo we could have won the war. In looking for enemies to blame, who better than Barbarella? Conservative critics attributed our defeat to the feminization of American culture and subsequent loss of our warrior ethos. It is not surprising that a woman emerged as the most hated figure of the antiwar movement. Although conservatives despised Tom Hayden, at least he was a man who understood politics. Fonda was a woman critics accused of knowing nothing: a brainless bimbo who shamed America and contributed to the loss of spirit that led to the loss of a war. Women who criticized our participation were "bitches"; men who supported it were "patriots."[84]

Although attacks against "Hanoi Jane" continue today, the actress reached a cathartic resolution while shooting *Stanley and Iris* in the summer of 1988. When veterans in Holyoke, Massachusetts, learned that Jane Fonda would be filming in nearby Waterbury, Connecticut, they pressured local officials to pass a resolution letting her know she was not welcome. As Clayton Hough Jr., who lost both legs in Vietnam, explained, "She seemed to choose the other side: wearing their clothes, sitting behind anti-aircraft artillery. . . . We've heard other people atone for her but we've never heard her say she made a mistake." Equally miffed Waterbury veterans sold 6,000 "We're Not Fond'a Hanoi Jane" bumper stickers in the weeks before her arrival and picketed the set during the first days of shooting.[85]

Hoping to mend fences, Fonda held a tearful four-hour private meeting with twenty-six hostile veterans. After explaining her opposition to the war, she apologized for any pain she may have caused and agreed to do several fundraisers for veterans' organizations. The meeting did not resolve all bitter feelings, but it proved therapeutic for both sides. "She told us there would be some things that she would go to her grave regretting," reported Frank McCarthy, president of Vietnam Veterans Agent Orange Victims Inc. "I still can't forgive her, but if she helps us, I'll respect her."[86]

Following the meeting, Fonda attended a Vets Who Care "Evening of Stars" event along with costar Robert De Niro and raised $28,000 for the handicapped children of Agent Orange victims. She also helped raise $10,000 for the Literacy Volunteers of Waterbury. These generous acts helped soothe angry feelings and reduce the number of demonstrators at the movie set. National groups proved less forgiving. Several weeks earlier, Fonda issued a highly public apology during a televised *20/20* interview with Barbara Walters. She referred to her infamous anti-aircraft gun photo as "a thoughtless and careless thing to have done" and added, "I'm very sorry that I hurt them [veterans] and I want to apologize to them and their families." The 13,400 delegates to the Veterans of Foreign Wars convention remained unmoved and passed resolutions in August condemning her "many treasonable actions" during Vietnam and demanding that Congress try her for treason.[87]

The Connecticut meetings marked Fonda's end as a movement leader. As her film career and Hayden's political career grew more demanding, her private life began disintegrating. Despite constant Red-baiting, Hayden won reelection to the state assembly from his Santa Monica district in 1984, 1986, and 1988 by increasingly greater margins. To meet his demanding legislative schedule, he took an apartment in Sacramento, returning home on weekends whenever possible. "If Jane and I have one evening at home alone," he quipped, "it is a scheduling mistake by the staff." The constant separations and rumors of Hayden's infidelities exacted an emotional toll on the actress. In February 1987, with her self-esteem at a low point, the guru of fitness who had repeatedly denounced elective plastic surgery had her breasts enlarged. "I knew when I did it that I was betraying myself," she wrote in her autobiography, "but my self had shrunk to the size of a thimble."[88] The dissolution of CED and IPC Films in 1986 also contributed to her growing depression. Fonda Films took its place, but her movies would never again be wed to her politics in quite the same way.

On December 21, 1988, the night Fonda turned fifty-one, her husband announced that he was in love with another woman—Vicky Rideout, a speechwriter for presidential candidate Michael Dukakis. Although the couple managed to keep news of their separation out of the newspapers for nearly three months, their seventeen-year marriage was over. He moved to Sacramento full time, while she stayed in their Santa Monica home. Fonda pledged that the separation would not mean the end of her activism. "I was a political woman before I met Tom," she insisted. "I'll just be my own person now. My gut-level attraction is to grassroots organizations rather than Democratic Party politics. I don't want to lose my idealism." She kept that pledge for a short time by remaining on the steering committee of Campaign California, the grassroots organization that Hayden founded late in 1986 to replace CED.[89]

On December 1, 1989, Fonda filed for divorce. Like Harry Belafonte, heartbreak led her to retreat from politics and from the screen. Yet unlike the black actor who resumed both several years after Martin Luther King Jr.'s assassination, the famed actress disappeared from the world of movement politics for the next twenty-five years.

A Legacy of Activism

On December 21, 1991, Jane Fonda shocked supporters and detractors alike by marrying billionaire media magnate Ted Turner. After being devoted to movement politics for so many years, how was such a decision possible? As Hayden himself remarked years later, "You can't say it was a logical transition." The answer, as simple and clichéd as it may sound, is that she was only human. After a lifetime of pleasing men, she was drawn to a man who tried to please her. In her autobiography, Fonda recounts her initial efforts to stave off Turner's advances. "I have friends who are Communists," he reassured her. "Gorbachev is my buddy and so is Castro." Hoping for love, she moved to Atlanta, and two years later married him. However, after discovering that Turner was cheating on her, she left him. The couple divorced in 2001.[90]

Many Americans will always remember Jane Fonda for what she later confessed was her one moment of naiveté: sitting in a North Vietnamese anti-aircraft gun. That single image earned her the enmity of the right and criticism by the left. To this day, many lifelong radical leaders resent how her unthinking actions hurt the antiwar cause. "Her mistakes in North Vietnam," 1960s radical leader James Lafferty insisted in August 2010, "allowed her and the movement to become identified with the enemy. For those who favored the war, the iconic image of the antiwar movement was Jane Fonda sitting in a North Vietnamese anti-aircraft gun. In totality, her contribution to the antiwar movement was probably negative, and I say this as someone who admires her." Others, however, took a more positive view toward her legacy. "Fonda was crucial to broadening public awareness of the antiwar movement during Nixon's alleged de-escalation of the war," insisted George McGovern. "She and Tom brought public attention to the carpet-bombing campaign and 'Vietnamization' of the war from 1969 to 1973."[91]

A moment does not define a life. From 1970 to 1988, no Hollywood star, male or female, devoted as much time and money to reshaping American politics as Jane Fonda. Although she relinquished her position as a grassroots organizer following her split with Hayden, she left a legacy that influenced the course of Hollywood activism. The couple founded the IPC in 1972 with the idea of recruiting a new generation of activists who would maintain a left political presence well beyond the end of the war. Looking back thirty-five years later, she believes they succeeded. "We brought a lot of young men and women into the movement then and they are still there today." Although CED never evolved into the national movement she and Hayden had envisioned, it raised a series of progressive issues that remain central to liberal and leftist struggles during the Obama presidency: universal health care coverage, tighter regulation of corporations, and greater reliance on environmentally safe energy sources.[92]

Fonda's willingness to speak out regardless of the negative effects on her career encouraged other Hollywood women to do the same. As former United Artists president Paula Weinstein explained, "It was such a big thing to have a movie star of Jane's stature come out against the war and be that much of an activist." In 1984, inspired by Fonda, Weinstein joined with songwriter Marilyn Bergman, attorney Susan Grode, Columbia Pictures Television president Barbara Corday, and a handful of other successful industry feminists to organize the Hollywood Women's Political Committee (HWPC). Although Fonda acted as a participant rather than a leader, her impact on the HWPC was profound. When Lara Bergthold joined the group as its political director in 1992, she found that almost "everyone I knew had worked with them [Fonda and Hayden] or had been trained by them . . . [especially] so much of younger Hollywood." Indeed, the HWPC's initial manifesto reflected much of CED's thinking: "We are committed to an economic policy based on every citizen's full participation in our country's economic wealth."[93]

For the next thirteen years, the HWPC fought "for what is right, not for what is practical or pragmatic." In addition to raising millions of dollars for progressive candidates and causes, the group lobbied on behalf of environmental issues, equal rights for women, prochoice, and opposition to Reagan's policies in South Africa and Central America. During their heyday, explained Andy Spahn, who worked for the IPC and CED before becoming the Democratic Party's fundraiser in Hollywood, the HWPC "was the most dominant political force in Hollywood. They were certainly a counterforce to the right. They held the candidate's feet to the fire. They provided pressure to keep them on the left."[94] The group dissolved in April 1997 when they felt that money rather than issues had become the driving force in politics.

Fonda also influenced the subsequent activities of the young movie stars she and Hayden nurtured in Network. The organization collapsed soon after the couple's divorce, but many of its members continued fighting for progressive causes within the HWPC and in the Creative Coalition, founded in

1989 to protect First Amendment rights, fight for campaign finance reform, and promote public funding for the arts.[95]

After several years of marriage to Turner, during which she kept a low profile, Fonda returned to the political scene to support feminist causes. She spent much of the 1990s funding and working with a variety of prochoice and adolescent pregnancy prevention organizations. During the next decade, she promoted feminist issues in the United States, Africa, and Latin America while also pursuing social justice by working with the Los Angeles Alliance for a New Economy. In 2001, the woman raised as an atheist shocked her radical friends by announcing she had become a born-again Christian. Yet her religious convictions were closer to the beliefs of "progressive Christian" friends such as Jimmy Carter and Andrew Young; that is, they were closer to the quasi-socialism of the late-nineteenth-century Social Gospel movement than to the preaching of conservative evangelicals such as Pat Robertson and Jerry Falwell.

Fonda's political life came full circle on January 27, 2007, when she joined 100,000 marchers in Washington, D.C., to urge Congress to stop funding the war and pull our troops out of Iraq. "I haven't spoken at an antiwar rally in thirty-four years," she told the crowd. "Silence is no longer an option. I'm so sad we have to do this—that we did not learn from the lessons of the Vietnam War." Explaining that she had stayed away from antiwar rallies out of concern that the "lies spread about me" would hurt the movement, she praised the protesters "for the courage to stand up to this mean-spirited, vengeful administration." The soul of America, she assured the crowd, "is alive and well."[96]

Today she considers herself a radical and a feminist, though no longer a movement activist. "Liberal, as far as I'm concerned, is a bad word. It means wishy-washy. I think it's hysterical that liberal has become this 'Oh, my God! That person is a liberal?? Oh, my God!!!'" As for feminism, she insists it "is the most radical of all because it speaks to the mustard seed at the core, which is patriarchy. We're progressive because we're talking about what democracy is really supposed to really stand for." Despite the numerous "hate Fonda" Web sites that still appear on the Internet, she remains optimistic that ordinary men and women can still change the world. "Profound change can happen. You don't realize it until you've experienced that kind of transformation; once you do, you'll never be the same."[97]

Perhaps the most striking tribute to the former movement leader comes from her ex-husband, Tom Hayden. "She was a nonpolitical movie star of

Hollywood elites who suddenly joins a movement in 1969 and stays with it consistently for a period of twenty years, which is more than most social activists stay with it. That's a third or a fourth of a life."[98] During the course of those years, Fonda articulated a political vision of what the nation could be and then worked tirelessly at the grassroots level and on the screen to implement it. She showed how celebrities could bring attention to often unpopular causes. Yet her story also reveals the limits of fame untethered to political power. For all the positive changes she inspired, there was also a sense of failure, not just for her but also for the entire radical community. It would be the Reagan-led conservative movement, not the left, that dominated the resurgent Cold War and antifeminist politics of the 1980s. And it would be liberal-turned-conservative movie star Charlton Heston who helped conservatives gain a stronghold over American life and politics.

MOSES AND THE RED TIDE: CHARLTON HESTON

On August 28, 1963, after living under the shadow of McCarthyism for over a decade, a contingent of sixty Hollywood stars, which included Gregory Peck, Paul Newman, Joanne Woodward, Sammy Davis Jr., Kirk Douglas, and Marlon Brando, held hands and sang "We Shall Overcome" as they boarded a midnight flight to join Martin Luther King Jr. and several hundred thousand Americans for the March on Washington. The Hollywood March Committee was headed by Charlton Heston, an early civil rights sympathizer who in May 1961 picketed segregated lunch counters in Oklahoma City. "I suppose I was elected chairman," the star who played Moses in *The Ten Commandments* (1956) told a reporter, "because I'd gotten all those folks through the Red Sea." Forty years later, the man many thought of as Moses was still fighting battles for unpopular causes. Only this time, those causes—opposition to affirmative action, gun control, and excessive government—were ones embraced by conservatives.[1]

During the last three decades of the twentieth century, no two stars attracted more venomous responses to their politics than Jane Fonda and Charlton Heston. While Fonda was the most hated Hollywood leftist of the 1970s and 1980s, Heston was the most reviled conservative star of the 1980s and 1990s. Ironically, both were linked in the public imagination by a set of iconic images: Fonda sitting in the North Vietnamese anti-aircraft gun and Heston as Moses. The critical difference is that Fonda's enemies used that image against her, while Heston's supporters used his to legitimize a series of political causes. "I've attended more rallies and appeared before more public forums than anyone other than Jane Fonda," he boasted in 1982.[2]

Heston's ability to use his cinematic persona to further controversial causes signaled the rise of yet another kind of Hollywood politics, image politics—that is, where a star's screen image is so widely venerated that large numbers of Americans pay close attention to his or her political pronouncements. Image politics represents a leap of faith by the public: a belief that the image and the person are one and the same. Heston differs from the seven activists discussed in previous chapters in his ability, and the ability of his allies, to use his cinematic image to lend greater credibility to particular causes. When Charlie Chaplin shifted from visual politics to issue-oriented politics he did not assume the role of the Tramp; he spoke as himself. But for Heston, the image and the man merged into one: he was always Moses, always the savior, lawgiver, and patriarch.

Image politics is not inherently ideological but can be used to defend causes on the left or the right. Over the years, a handful of movie stars forged screen personalities that imbued them with a gravitas rare among their peers. The tough, determined personas of John Wayne and Clint Eastwood commanded respect from millions of conservatives, while the sensitive and thoughtful cinematic images forged by Gregory Peck, Sidney Poitier, and George Clooney endeared them to liberals. Yet, with the exception of Clint Eastwood, who served one term as mayor of Carmel, California, no star linked their cinematic image to their offscreen politics as successfully and for so long a period of time without becoming a politician as Heston. His role as Moses created a biblical aura that legitimized him and his politics. As one Los Angeles woman remarked during a contentious community hearing in April 1979, "How could you go against what Moses says?"[3]

Heston was more than Moses. From the mid-1950s to the mid-1960s, he portrayed so many famous people that film critic Pauline Kael crowned him the "All-Time King of the Historical Epic." "I've played thirteen historical figures," he observed, "all either saints or presidents, geniuses or generals." At a time when the Cold War and the civil rights movement led many Americans to question the nation's political direction, Heston remained an unambiguous hero who repeatedly won cinematic battles between good and evil. Beginning in the late 1960s, the muscular actor broadened his image—and showed off his buff body—by playing postapocalyptic heroes in films such as *Planet of the Apes* (1968), *The Omega Man* (1971), and *Soylent Green* (1973). As one reporter noted, Heston was the only man in Hollywood who could be thought of as God by millions of people while also being named one of *Playboy*'s "Sex Stars of the '70s."[4]

Like George Murphy and Ronald Reagan, Heston began his political life as a liberal Democrat and ended up a conservative Republican. He voted for Franklin Roosevelt, Adlai Stevenson, John F. Kennedy, Lyndon Johnson, and Hubert Humphrey. However, in 1972, disenchanted with the "radical" agenda of presidential candidate George McGovern, he became a leading member of Democrats for Nixon. When his friend Ronald Reagan ran for president in 1980, Heston was one of the first stars conservatives called on to raise money and win public support. Over the next twenty years, the iconic figure emerged as a spokesman for a variety of conservative causes. His heroic image was so widely admired that leaders from both parties, Democrats in the 1960s and Republicans in the 1980s, asked him to run for the Senate. Indeed, a 1996 public opinion poll found that Americans considered Heston to be one of the country's most believable celebrity spokespersons.[5]

Heston was aware of the political advantages of his image and used it to further his ideological positions, first on the left and then on the right. "My public identity gives me a chance to stand on a very tall soapbox," he boasted to one reporter. During the early 1980s, he attracted national attention by debating Central American policy with Ed Asner and nuclear policy with Paul Newman, debates the press referred to as "Star Wars" and "Moses versus Butch Cassidy." In the late 1990s, he served as the National Rifle Association's (NRA) most visible spokesman. Asked about the propriety of movie stars debating national issues, Heston responded, "I see nothing wrong with actors speaking out for causes—that's a fundamental right in our society. . . . The only obligation we have is not to make horses' asses of ourselves."[6] While his detractors characterized him in such equine terms, Heston's star persona greatly enhanced the NRA's respectability. In the two years following his election as president in 1998, NRA membership swelled from 2.9 million to nearly 5 million. Pundits credit gun owners in West Virginia—where Democrats outnumbered Republicans two to one—with tipping the state and therefore the presidential election in 2000 to George W. Bush. Rarely has a movie star had such a profound impact on national life.

BECOMING MOSES

Charlton Heston's path to Hollywood was markedly different from the seven previously discussed celebrities. He was not an immigrant like Charlie Chaplin, Louis B. Mayer, or Edward G. Robinson. He was not born into poverty like Harry Belafonte or into a home with an alcoholic father like Ronald Reagan; nor was his family plunged into financial hardship after the death of a parent, like George Murphy. And he certainly was not the child of a famous movie star like Jane Fonda. Heston's upbringing was by far the most typically American of the group. Raised in the Midwest, he grew up with the rugged, self-reliant values that characterize Middle America. Like many others, however, he suffered a series of childhood traumas that colored the rest of his life.

John Charles Carter was born in Evanston, Illinois, on October 4, 1924, to Russell Whitford Carter and Lilla Charlton Carter. The Carters soon moved to the small rural community of St. Helen, Michigan, where Russell worked as a lumber mill operator and their son attended a one-room schoolhouse with twelve other children. Heston's lifelong love for guns was born in the dense backwoods of Michigan where he spent many solitary hours trapping and shooting wild game with his .22 rifle. Lilla Carter, however, abhorred her "life of exile in the Michigan woods" and divorced her husband when John was ten. Lilla eventually married Chet Heston and moved the family to Wilmette, Illinois. A new town brought a new name, as Lilla's oldest son combined his mother's maiden name with his stepfather's surname. Charlton Heston enrolled in New Trier High School and then entered Northwestern University in the fall of 1941 on a drama scholarship.[7]

The aspiring star made his screen debut in 1941 playing the lead in a student-made silent production of Henrik Ibsen's *Peer Gynt*. More significantly, he fell in love with another drama student, Lydia Clarke. The romance was not reciprocated. The Wisconsin-born daughter of a high school principal initially found him "arrogant and conceited, and supremely self-confident."[8]

Only after they acted together did she change her mind, and even then, it took nearly two years before Lydia accepted his marriage proposal. After a year and a half of university, Heston enlisted in the Army Air Corps. The couple married in March 1944, and Heston spent the next two years as a radio operator on B-25 bombers and later as a control tower operator in Anchorage, Alaska.

After his discharge in March 1946, the Hestons moved to New York and looked for theatrical work. Several months later, the unemployed couple relocated to Asheville, North Carolina, where they codirected a community theater. Unwilling to give up their Broadway dreams, they returned to New York in August 1947, where Heston landed the male lead in Katharine Cornell's production of *Antony and Cleopatra*. With subsequent theater parts hard to come by, the young actor turned to television and played a number of dramatic roles on *Studio One*. Heston far preferred theater to television or motion pictures, but his television work attracted the attention of producer Hal Wallis, who hired him to star in William Dieterle's 1950 film noir *Dark City*. Gossip columnist Louella Parsons dubbed him "the hottest bet for movies in a long time."[9]

Just as John Wayne reigned as the ultimate Western hero and icon of American manhood, Heston emerged as the screen's leading hero of historical epics. Two years after *Dark City*, director Cecil B. DeMille cast him as the circus manager in *The Greatest Show on Earth* (1952). In 1953, he starred as Andrew Jackson in *The President's Lady*, the first of his many historical roles. Over the next three years, Chuck, as his friends called him, made six films, playing a variety of characters. After finishing *The Private War of Major Benson* (1955), he accepted DeMille's offer to play the part that would become the defining role in his long career, Moses.

In the mid-1950s, DeMille, the New England son of an Episcopal minister and Jewish mother, decided to remake his 1923 version of *The Ten Commandments*. He adapted it for a Cold War world that saw democracy and religious freedom threatened by the Soviet Union. One of Hollywood's leading conservatives, the imperious director was a die-hard Republican who supported the House Un-American Activities Committee's efforts to purge the movie industry of all Communist influence. DeMille envisioned his new version of *The Ten Commandments* as a Cold War story of good versus evil, God versus Godlessness, and freedom versus tyranny—in short, the United States versus the Soviet Union. To make sure audiences understood his intentions, the director appeared in the film's two-minute prologue and explained, "The theme of this picture is whether men ought to be ruled by God's law or whether they are to be ruled by the whims of a dictator like Ramses. Are men the property of the state or are they free souls under God? This same battle continues throughout the world today."[10]

Since the 1903 production *Moses in the Bullrushes*, many actors have played the Prince of Egypt. DeMille's 1923 version starred the thin and balding sixty-two-year-old Theodore Roberts, who looked like an ancient sage. Charlton Heston, however, was unlike any previous Moses. As we see in figure 7.1, at 6' 3" and 205 pounds, the blond-haired, square-jawed star was a muscular Moses who looked as though he could physically and spiritually defeat any evil oppressor. Passionate about tennis and physical fitness, Heston conveyed a clear sense of strength and control with his flat stomach, solid pectoral muscles, and firm biceps. Despite being enslaved, we see that Moses is still more muscular and his look far more determined than Pharaoh's elite guard. Heston was a powerful Moses for a perilous Cold War world in desperate need of leaders.[11] Like John Wayne, he offered audiences a vision of hypermasculinity as opposed to the softer, more sensitive male

FIGURE 7.1 Moses as a young and powerful prophet in *The Ten Commandments*.
SOURCE: PHOTOFEST

images of Marlon Brando and James Dean. And like John Wayne, he appealed to men as well as women.[12]

DeMille chose Heston, he told one reporter, "because he, more than any other of the scores considered, had the necessary qualities of strength, sincerity, and spirituality." He also selected the thirty-one-year-old actor because of his striking resemblance to Michelangelo's statue of Moses. "I had a sketch made of Charlton Heston in a white beard and happened to set it beside a photograph of Michelangelo's famous statue of Moses," DeMille explained in his autobiography. "The resemblance was amazing."[13]

The director saw Moses as more than just another part. He insisted that Heston *be* Moses. To that end, he gave him twenty-one books to read ranging from the Koran to Sigmund Freud's *Moses and Monotheism*. Heston also met with a Talmudic scholar from Chicago and spent time observing Michelangelo's *Moses* in Rome. Once production began, he felt as though he had indeed become the prophet. Before shooting scenes in Egypt or at Mount Sinai, the fully costumed star would wander off by himself for a half-hour, deep in thought as he soaked up the historic atmosphere. "I stood on the ground where he stood," the actor reflected, "breathed the air he breathed, and was almost overwhelmed by the thought that here Moses became the only man in recorded history to meet God face to face." Impressed by Heston's deep, booming voice, DeMille also had him play the voice of God in the famous Burning Bush scene.[14]

After two years of preparation and shooting, the film opened on November 8, 1956, to largely positive reviews. With the exception of *Time* magazine's critic, who insisted that the wooden Heston was "ludicrously miscast," the actor was widely praised for his portrayal. A gushing Hedda Hopper told the star and her readers, "You were never Heston. You were Moses from the beginning."[15] Despite its success, the Academy of Motion Picture Arts and Sciences snubbed the film. The movie's only Oscar was for Best Special Effects.

The public, however, loved the movie and its star. *The Ten Commandments* played to sold-out houses for months. Believing it would appeal to the country's sizeable Hispanic population, Paramount released a Spanish-subtitled version in Los Angeles, and later throughout the Southwest. By August 1959, the $13.3 million production grossed $83.6 million and was seen by approximately 98.5 million moviegoers throughout the world. It is hardly surprising that audiences continued to think of Heston as Moses for decades. Other than *Gone with the Wind* and *The Wizard of Oz*, few pictures have remained on the screen for as long a time as DeMille's biblical epic. After its initial run ended late in 1960, the film was rereleased in 1966 and 1975 and reissued in 70mm Super VistaVision in 1990. On television, ABC has broadcast *The Ten Commandments* annually since the late 1960s, and the advent of videotape and then DVDs brought the movie into millions of homes. In 2010 Paramount released a restored Blu-ray version of the biblical epic. Heston's popularity was so great and fan letters so numerous that he started writing his own newsletter in 1956, and continued doing so until 1971.[16]

Despite the film's success, Heston remained unwilling to give up his theatrical career. This meant leading a simple life and carefully guarding his earnings. After touring the country promoting *The Ten Commandments*, the former Northwestern thespian played the lead in *Mr. Roberts* at New York's City Center Theater for $85 per week. For the next several years, Chuck and Lydia rented modest apartments in New York and Los Angeles, where they raised their young son, Fraser, who was born on February 12, 1955. The star's only extravagances were purchasing a new Corvette and taking time to hunt at his parents' Lake Michigan home.

Heston spent the next three years making five big-budget films—most notably *Touch of Evil* (1958) with Orson Welles; *The Big Country* (1958) with William Wyler; and *The Buccaneer* (1958), where he again played Andrew Jackson. In 1959, he cemented his image as Hollywood's leading biblical hero by starring in *Ben-Hur*, an epic tale of political, social, and religious turmoil during the time of Christ. Director William Wyler put Heston's athleticism and sculpted body to use by casting him as the muscular Judah Ben-Hur, a Jewish prince whom Roman authorities exiled as a galley slave when he refused to help them crush the rebellion in Judea. *Ben-Hur* is another Cold War parable in which the evil Roman Empire serves as a substitute for the godless Soviet Union. In the course of the film, we watch the enslaved but buff Heston battle Macedonian invaders, save the life of Roman consul Quintus Arrius, and join the resistance fighting the Roman oppressors.

Ben-Hur opened in New York on November 18, 1959, to an unprecedented marketing frenzy. Men, women, and children bought Ben-Hur swords, helmets, gowns, towels, T-shirts, candy bars, and even miniature chariot arenas. Audiences mobbed movie theaters for months to see the action-packed widescreen extravaganza. Costing $15 million to produce, the film earned $47 million by the end of 1961 and $90 million worldwide by January 1989. Like *The Ten Commandments*, *Ben-Hur* was rereleased several times in theaters, as well as being shown frequently on television. The cinematic epic won a record eleven Oscars, including a Best Actor Award for its star.[17]

Heston's portrayals of Moses and Ben-Hur turned him into Hollywood's premier "religious" star, an image he gladly promoted. "I won't say loftily that I found God by playing Moses and Ben-Hur," he told a reporter in September 1959. "But I understand mankind better through these men, and I am changed."[18] Six years later, he played his third biblical hero, John the Baptist, in *The Greatest Story Ever Told* (1965). Yet so far as audiences were concerned, Moses remained the defining role of his career. DeMille may have chosen the actor because of his resemblance to Michelangelo's sculpture, but for millions of devoted moviegoers, Moses came to resemble Charlton Heston.

Humorously referring to himself as "the [movie] industry's leading imitation Jew," Heston reinforced his cinematic image by participating in what we might call the "Moses Industry." In June 1959, he completed "Charlton Heston Reads the Five Books of Moses" for Vanguard Records, which he followed with an album of readings on the life and passion of Christ. A year later, Vanguard signed him to do a similar album of readings from the New Testament. His recordings proved so popular that Ed Sullivan paid the star $10,000 to read from the Bible on his 1959 Christmas show and brought him back again five months later.[19]

As the popularity of biblical epics faded in the early 1960s, Heston broadened his cinematic persona by playing heroic world leaders in a series of big-budget productions shot in exotic places around the world. In *El Cid* (1961) he is the courageous Rodrigo Diaz de Vivar (El Cid) who rescues Christian kingdoms of eleventh-century Spain from warring Moors. In *55 Days at Peking* (1963), his Major Matt Lewis protects European delegations under attack during China's Boxer Rebellion of 1900. After playing Michelangelo in *The Agony and the Ecstasy* (1965), he returned to his warrior's role in *Khartoum* (1966), starring as British general Charles Gordon. Heston also brought his historical image to television, playing Thomas Jefferson and Franklin D. Roosevelt and supplying the voice of George Washington.

Heston's sedate offscreen life reinforced his cinematic image, especially among Americans repulsed by what they saw as the decadent lives led by many Hollywood stars. A decidedly old-fashioned figure in a very hip town,

Heston did not attend Hollywood parties, did not drink in excess, and was never involved in any sex or drug scandals. "In the 1950s and early '60s," explained one journalist, "Heston was the anti-Brando, straight-forward and earnest and resolutely square." Throughout his life, the star's three great passions remained his family, tennis, and theater. Scarred by his parents' divorce, he enjoyed spending time with Lydia and their children, Fraser and Holly Ann, who was adopted in 1965. His family accompanied him on location as often as possible and they traveled to the Midwest each year to ski or visit his parents. He also proved a hands-on father, taking his children hiking, skiing, to the beach, or to ballet lessons. Lydia, who gave up theater to become a full-time mother, became an accomplished photographer who often took stills for her husband's films and publications.[20]

A physical fitness devotee, the actor's home included a pool, gym, sauna, and tennis court on which he held regular weekend matches with the likes of tennis stars Rod Laver, Pancho Gonzalez, Ken Rosewall, and Roy Emerson. "An actor's body is his crucial tool, like a concert pianist's Steinway," he wrote in his autobiography. "If it's out of tune, you don't do well." In between films and tennis games, Heston devoted himself to his last great passion: theater. From the 1950s to the 1980s, he tried to do a play every two or three years, often costarring with Lydia. "He was mediocre, but committed," remarked one theater director. "He wanted to prove he was a Shakespearean actor." Mediocre or not, he performed in *The Tumbler* with Laurence Olivier, *Macbeth* with Vanessa Redgrave, and *Long Day's Journey into Night* with Deborah Kerr and Bruce Dern.[21]

A happy man, Heston embraced his cinematic image and enjoyed the constant references to himself as Moses. Beginning in the 1960s, he used that persona to legitimize his participation in a variety of political causes. By 1963, he was done playing Moses. It was time to be Moses.

BEING MOSES

Like Edward G. Robinson before him, Heston remained too focused on his career to participate in political activities during his rise to fame. Other than doing dramatic readings at free speech meetings in the 1950s and supporting Adlai Stevenson in 1956, he refrained from partisan activism. Heston felt it was inappropriate for movie stars to speak out on political issues they knew little about. As he told Hedda Hopper in February 1952, "on any subject other than their work, [actors] should keep quiet." Too many stars "take a trip to Europe and come back and start discussing European recovery—it makes them look ridiculous." Eight years later, he remained convinced that the line between politics and entertainment should not be crossed. "A screen star pontificating on politics," he explained while shooting *El Cid* in Madrid, "is about the equivalent of a high school boy describing the charms of Sophia Loren; he's just in way over his head."[22] As his fame grew, Heston changed his mind and became involved in a wide range of issues, first on the left and then on the right.

Throughout his life, Heston's politics remained a jumble of ideological perspectives. A close reading of his journals, books, and public statements reveal him to be a political maverick—part libertarian, part liberal, part conservative, and part republican in the spirit of the Founding Fathers. This eclectic mélange of ideas was always present; they just revealed themselves differently at various points in time. His libertarianism fit well with his rural upbringing and conviction that individuals should be allowed to govern themselves. In a 1960–1961 interview, Heston stressed his belief in "the importance of the individual independence of man" and his fear of the government's "increasing encroachments" on citizens. One hundred years ago, he complained, "a man could do what he liked," but people's lives were now shaped "by the increasing network of rules and regulations. I'm not an anarchist, but I am afraid we are rapidly approaching a time when every breath we draw will be tagged and numbered, and assigned to us before birth."[23]

These pronouncements sound remarkably similar to Ronald Reagan's conservative views of the time, when he was denouncing Medicare and other government safety-net policies as socialism. Yet, in September 1966, though never registering with any party, Heston insisted that he had cast 80 percent of his votes for Democratic candidates. The Midwesterner tempered his libertarian streak with an equally passionate commitment to the eighteenth-century republican ideal of citizenship. Like his hero Thomas Jefferson, "as fearless a champion of freedom as ever walked the earth," he believed in the obligation of citizens to serve the republic. Actors had "both the right and the responsibility to function as conscientious citizens," and when injustice occurred they needed "to stand up and be counted." Heston considered himself a moderate, a citizen who followed the basic principles of the Constitution. "Moderates don't make themselves heard on public questions," he lamented. "It's too bad because moderates make a democracy work."[24]

The common denominator in these political pronouncements is not their ideological consistency but the fact that Heston's popularity meant he would be listened to by a wide swath of Americans. But first, there had to be something worth listening to. The 1960 presidential contest between Richard Nixon and John F. Kennedy marked the first time since the beginning of the Cold War that large numbers of liberal and left movie stars felt it was safe to reenter the political arena. But with memories of McCarthyism still hanging over the industry, few were willing to do so. "People in Hollywood are generally afraid to be active in politics," Republican Dick Powell confessed in September 1960. "This is especially true of some in television who believe that their sponsors would not want them to be identified with a political party."[25]

Heston had no such fear. While he urged actors to remain silent about complex issues they knew little about, he considered voting the obligation of every citizen. He attended the Democratic presidential convention in Los Angeles in July 1960 hoping that Adlai Stevenson would again capture the party's nomination, but when John Kennedy defeated the Illinois warhorse, he switched his support to the young senator. Heston's plans to campaign were cut short when he flew to Spain to begin shooting El Cid. Kennedy's subsequent election unleashed a wave of political activism not seen since the 1940s as Hollywood liberals spoke out on behalf of numerous causes.[26]

Few causes had greater need of a modern Moses than the civil rights crusade, and no biblical figure held greater meaning to liberation struggles past and present than the ancient Hebrew. During the eighteenth and nineteenth centuries, American slaves venerated Moses even more than Jesus. While the latter promised a better life in the hereafter, the former promised freedom in this lifetime.[27]

The political weight of Heston's Moses image became evident in May 1961, when he traveled to Oklahoma City to join a march calling for the integration of local restaurants (see fig. 7.2). Dr. Jolly West, knowing the power of his good friend's cinematic persona, asked him to come to Oklahoma on behalf of the cause. "I guess it's time I did something about this kind of thing besides deploring it at cocktail parties," Heston wrote in his

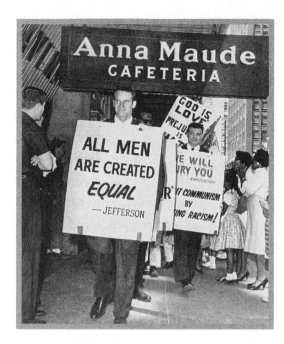

FIGURE 7.2 Heston picketing in Oklahoma City in May 1961. SOURCE: SPECIAL COLLECTIONS, USC

journal. Wearing a sandwich-board sign declaring, "ALL MEN ARE CREATED EQUAL," Heston joined West, African American physician Dr. Chet Pierce, and eighty black and white activists as they walked through downtown campaigning against segregation.[28]

One of the first white stars to march in a civil rights demonstration, Heston learned about the potent impact of celebrity. Local activists had been holding sit-ins in Oklahoma City since 1958 with only modest progress. But this time news of Heston's arrival "spread like wild fire" and drew large crowds who wanted "to get a quick glimpse of the star." Other than a few hecklers who shouted, "Go back to Hollywood, you Jew," the crowd was supportive, often rushing to shake hands with the recent Oscar winner. "Every step that Heston, West, and Pierce took," march organizer Clara Luper wrote in her memoir, "was adding tons of Freedom vitamins to our tired bodies that had been protesting for three years." Civil rights advocates across the country were equally heartened as photographs of "Moses" marching in the demonstration appeared in the nation's newspapers. The three major restaurants targeted by the marchers soon began admitting black patrons.[29]

Heston did not think about the personal consequences of his actions, but his employers did. Upon arriving in Oklahoma City, he received telegrams from anxious executives at MGM and Allied Artists urging him to reconsider his participation because they feared "alienating moviegoers." Yet marching in the demonstration marked a turning point in his belief in the liberating possibilities of political activism. "I suspect the next time I come to Oklahoma City," he told a reporter, "there won't be anything to demonstrate. The sentiments of the city are clearly in favor of desegregation."[30] Two years later, Heston cemented his public image as Moses by leading the Hollywood contingent participating in the March on Washington. As in Oklahoma, he did not initiate this leadership role; although he was a willing participant, others used his cinematic image to advance their political agendas.

No issue engaged Hollywood or the nation more fully in the summer of 1963 than civil rights. That July, leaders from the National Association for the Advancement of Colored People (NAACP) flew to Los Angeles hoping to end discrimination in the overwhelmingly white movie industry. At an emergency meeting of the American Civil Liberties Union's Arts Committee, Heston, Marlon Brando, Burt Lancaster, and Paul Newman urged colleagues to refuse to work in films that degraded or excluded blacks. "If every star gets together, and says 'that's it,'" Brando told the gathering of three hundred, "that could be the end of discrimination in our industry." Several days later, operating under threat of a national boycott, Hollywood producers and guilds met with NAACP national labor secretary Herbert Hill. As negotiations faltered, Martin Luther King Jr. joined the discussions. The civil rights leader proved highly persuasive and within a short time industry representatives agreed to a sweeping plan for integration.[31]

During a private breakfast meeting, King spoke to Heston (who was representing the Screen Actors Guild) about an upcoming march in Washington that he hoped would attract Americans of every race, religion, and background. Several months earlier, King had asked his close friend Harry Belafonte to generate national publicity by recruiting a large contingent of Hollywood stars. After enlisting longtime civil rights supporters Marlon Brando and Burt Lancaster, Belafonte called Heston, whom he had met in Rome in 1958 during the filming of Ben-Hur. Although Heston would later report that his peers selected him to head the Hollywood contingent because he had "gotten all those folks through the Red Sea," Belafonte offered another explanation. "Heston was not one of the original organizers. He was a figurehead who came on board. I had to ask him to do it."[32]

Belafonte wanted Heston to participate because his cinematic image made him one of the few celebrities who "would appeal to middle America." At the time, King was widely vilified among whites. Heartland citizens who might otherwise ignore the march, Belafonte reasoned, "would have to take a second look if Heston was involved." When the black activist asked Heston to serve as cochair with Brando and Lancaster, he refused. When Belafonte played upon Heston's ego by asking him to head the delegation and have the other two stars work under him, he agreed.[33]

Whatever the reason for his selection, "Moses" took his position seriously. Over the next several weeks, he planned strategy for the August demonstration with a core group whose members included Brando, Lancaster, James Garner, Paul Newman, Mel Ferrer, Tony Franciosa, Billy Wilder, and Tony Curtis. Heston proved a politically ambivalent head when his liberalism clashed with his libertarianism. Uncomfortable with collective action of any kind, the committee head feared that any violence in Washington would discredit all marchers and hurt the reputations of Hollywood participants. "I don't like to follow other men's drums," he wrote in his journal on July 31, "I like to walk by myself, but here I am, ass-deep in a complicated, emotionally charged group action, with ninety-seven people running off in forty-seven directions. The way to do this would be just to go to Washington by my damn self." When Brando suggested that the group chain itself to the Jefferson Memorial and lie down in front of the White House, Heston refused and demanded that they obey the law. Civil disobedience was not acceptable.[34]

Heston continued to worry about the possibility of bloodshed and political backlash. Not only might violence frighten neutral legislators into voting against the Civil Rights Act but also "participating celebrities would have exhausted their influence for good, and no longer be an effective force for integration." Heston's fears were well grounded. A Gallup poll reported that two-thirds of all Americans disapproved of the demonstration. "The general feeling," remarked the *Washington Daily News*, "is that the Vandals are coming to sack Rome." Despite his reservations, Heston believed the march would be an important step forward "in a gigantic revolution that has only just begun."[35]

After weeks of preparation, sixty stars flew from Burbank to Washington on August 28. Upon arrival, they boarded a bus to the Washington Monument and joined a crowd of 250,000 as they marched to the Lincoln Memorial. Earlier that morning, J. Edgar Hoover tried to derail the group by having FBI agents warn the stars of potential violence and urge them not to attend. No one listened. "Our job," Heston noted, "was to get as much ink and TV time as possible." And that they did. After holding a press conference, the Hollywood contingent joined the massive gathering and marched without carrying any signs or banners, as per Heston's instructions. When the group arrived at the Lincoln Memorial, a five-deep mob of photographers encircled Heston and asked the biblical star to pose in front of the other Great Liberator, Abraham Lincoln. Television crews took pictures of Heston, Belafonte, Lancaster, and Poitier, while Brando, Newman, and other celebrities answered press questions. In addition to local coverage by the major television networks, European media agencies broadcast the march via satellite (see fig. 7.3).[36]

The day's festivities began shortly after noon with songs by Peter, Paul and Mary—whom Harry Belafonte had asked to organize the singing

FIGURE 7.3 Heston, James Baldwin, and Marlon Brando at the March on Washington, August 1963.
SOURCE: NATIONAL ARCHIVES

acts—and additional performances by Bob Dylan, Joan Baez, Odetta, Marian Anderson, Mahalia Jackson, Pete Seeger, Josh White, Josephine Baker, and the Freedom Singers. Master of ceremonies Ossie Davis called on Charlton Heston, who, looking "serene and poised as one of his Bible readings," stepped up to the microphone and gave a brief speech written for him by black author James Baldwin. Although initially hesitant about delivering someone else's words, especially a figure "on the left fringe of the civil rights movement," a pleased Heston felt the speech was "very close to what I wanted to say." Belafonte then read a declaration of support endorsed by actors, entertainers, and writers, while Lancaster unfurled a petition signed by 1,500 Americans living in Europe. Their part of the day done, the Hollywood stars faded into the background as Dr. King stepped to the podium and mesmerized the crowd with his "I Have a Dream" Speech.[37]

For Heston, the day proved an extraordinary success. "I'll never forget it," he wrote in his journal, "and I'm proud to have been part of it." The march demonstrated "the strength of this country when our constitutional right to peaceable assembly can be exercised in such thousands, with such dignity and happy determination." Six months later, on February 10, 1964, the House passed the Civil Rights Act that had languished in committee; in June, it passed the Senate. On July 2, 1964, President Lyndon Johnson signed into law an act that provided "injunctive relief against discrimination in public accommodations," authorized the attorney general "to institute suits to protect constitutional rights in public facilities and public education," extended the Commission on Civil Rights, banned discrimination in federally assisted programs, and established the Equal Employment Opportunity Commission.[38]

Searching for the Political Promised Land

Despite the pride he took in his leadership role, the August demonstration marked the last time Heston participated in a civil rights march. Over the next few years, he slowly drifted to the right.

In 1967, as Americans argued about the war in Vietnam, Heston found himself on the same side of the political divide as a Fonda, only it was Henry rather than Jane. Initially opposed to U.S. policies in Southeast Asia, Heston changed his views after visiting Vietnam in January 1966. "I went out there colored by apprehensions and misgivings. I wasn't sure about what we were doing in the war," he told a reporter. "But I came back with much the same convictions as the privates and the generals."[39] In 1972, convinced that the Democratic Party had abandoned the legacy of FDR by nominating "radical" George McGovern, the actor joined Democrats for Nixon.

Heston's ideological shift from liberal Democrat to conservative Republican was not a sudden event, as it was for George Murphy. Rather, like Ronald Reagan, it took years and a variety of reasons to complete the transformation. In Heston's case, two factors proved crucial: the war in Vietnam and the leftward tilt of the Democratic Party.

Memory is a tricky thing. We often rewrite our past to accommodate our present. In Heston's 1995 autobiography, *In the Arena*, he recounts the moment when he first thought about becoming a conservative. During the summer of 1964, while shooting *The War Lord* in Northern California, he often drove by a large billboard with a picture of presidential candidate Barry Goldwater and a simple seven-word caption, "IN YOUR HEART, YOU KNOW HE'S RIGHT." Heston describes how one day, while staring at the sign, "I experienced a true revelation, almost an epiphany, like St. Paul on the road to Damascus. I looked at that photograph of Goldwater and said softly, 'Son of a bitch . . . he is right!' And I knew he was."[40]

Whatever he felt in his heart, Heston's brain and votes remained solidly Democratic, at least for another eight years. He endorsed Lyndon Johnson in 1964 and "rejoiced over . . . the election results." He also spoke out against California's most controversial issue that year, Proposition 14, the conservative-backed measure that would have restored racial discrimination in housing. Following Martin Luther King Jr.'s assassination in April 1968, Heston helped Coretta Scott King raise money for a King memorial center in Atlanta and then joined Sidney Poitier, Harry Belafonte, and Ruby Dee in narrating the Sidney Lumet and Joseph L. Mankiewicz documentary, *King: A Filmed Record . . . Montgomery to Memphis* (1970).[41]

It would be a mistake to overestimate Heston's liberalism or commitment to civil rights. He enjoyed being a political independent who made up his mind on an issue-by-issue basis. While a thoughtful man, Heston was not a deep political thinker. He supported moderate civil rights demands and believed in limited government intervention to promote equality of opportunity. However, he opposed civil disobedience on the grounds that only in dictatorships were such actions necessary; democracies could vote to remedy inequities. Heston failed to understand that racial equality was not possible when a significant percentage of white people refused to obey the new civil rights laws.[42]

During the 1960s and 1970s, Heston followed two political trajectories: one loosely rooted in a liberal Democratic tradition and the other emerging from the Louis B. Mayer–George Murphy–Ronald Reagan Republican trajectory. In January 1960, as actors prepared for their first major strike since the 1930s, Screen Actors Guild president Ronald Reagan asked Heston to join the executive board and then appointed him to the group's negotiating committee. The guild achieved a mixed victory: they won pension and medical plans but failed to persuade producers to pay them residuals for films shown on television. Although militant actors accused Reagan of forging a sweetheart deal with producers, Heston walked away "stunned by Reagan's negotiating skills." He was equally awed by the SAG leader's ability to remain calm and focused no matter how heated things became. "Hearing out a fierce assault from the studio people, he'd smile and say, 'Yes, that's a very good point indeed. But let me just say this . . .' and undercut them completely."[43] In later years, Heston insisted that he modeled his negotiating strategies, and eventually his politics, on what he learned from Reagan.

The guild's members proved equally impressed with Heston, electing him president for an unprecedented seven terms between 1965 and 1971. Heston rarely engaged in partisan politics during these years because he felt the need to remain politically neutral while serving in office. His long tenure as SAG president exposed him to the ins-and-outs of Washington politics and politicians. He lobbied legislators, testified before Congress, and served on President Johnson's Council on Youth Opportunity and the National Council for the Arts.[44] During these years, Heston broke his self-imposed nonpartisan rule on only two issues: the war in Vietnam and gun control.

In June 1965, the *Army Times* named Heston as one of the six movie stars American soldiers in Vietnam most wanted to see. Enormously flattered, he agreed to visit the wartorn country in January 1966. Like the skeptical reporter played by David Janssen in John Wayne's *The Green Berets* (1968), Heston went over to Vietnam with great "doubts, misgivings, [and] questions" about U.S. involvement in this remote but deadly war. Since he could not sing, dance, or tell jokes like most members of Bob Hope's USO contingents, he decided to visit troops in battle areas where the military generally refused to send entertainers. Hitching rides on helicopters and dressed in a tiger suit with jungle camouflage, the World War II veteran traveled with Special Forces to isolated outposts near Ba To, Pleiku, and Danang. Over the course of nearly two weeks, he visited two to twenty camps a day. He also managed a brief meeting with General William Westmoreland, head of American military operations. Among the many celebrities who traveled to Vietnam, few put themselves in as much danger as Heston.[45]

The SAG leader returned home publicly supporting the war. "He came back from Vietnam," his son Fraser explained, "with a profound admiration for people who were willing to put their lives on the line. Having been a soldier, he felt the need to support the troops." In July 1967, he joined Henry Fonda and Bob Hope in staging an Independence Day TV special "to explain U. S. goals in Vietnam." Unlike Henry's daughter, Jane, who questioned the economic motives behind the war, Heston insisted somewhat naively, "we are not functioning for our own benefit, not functioning for imperialistic motives but for altruistic ones." Hoping to raise soldiers' morale, he paid a second visit to Vietnam in September 1967 and returned home even more committed to Johnson's policies. That November, he shared his views with the president during a White House meeting. "Ah, what a heady feeling," he wrote in his diary, "to have the ears of the mighty, even if they're not listening."[46]

Heston's change of heart on Vietnam did not yet signal a permanent rightward shift. Television star Robert Vaughn, head of Dissenting Democrats (Hollywood's leading antiwar organization), still considered Heston a liberal and urged him to run for U.S. senator in February 1967. Despite their disagreements over the war, Vaughn and fellow Democrats saw Heston as one of the few actors who could attract moderate Republican and independent voters. But the biblical hero declined the invitation, explaining, "I am not interested in a political career." He was not prepared to leave Hollywood while still at the peak of his career. When Democrats again approached him to run for the Senate in 1969, Heston consulted with his wife and a group of friends that included conservative intellectual William F. Buckley Jr., former California Democratic Party head Paul Ziffren, and LBJ adviser Jack Valenti. Under no illusion about why he was courted, he understood that it was his image rather than his ideas that made him so attractive to party leaders. "I suppose from a politician's view," he wrote in his diary, "my qualifications to do the job aren't as important as my qualifications to get it, but that can't be a major factor for me." Once again, Heston declined. "I want to act," he wrote in his journal. "I know it's trivial, but there it is."[47]

Breaking with liberals on Vietnam, Heston allied with them on gun control. Following the murder of JFK, Lyndon Johnson struggled to pass a comprehensive gun control bill. In June 1968, after the assassinations of Martin Luther King Jr. and Robert Kennedy, actor Hugh O'Brian—who played law and order sheriff Wyatt Earp on the popular television show—courted gun loyalist support by recruiting stars with tough-guy images to endorse a bill restricting gun sales. Deeply affected by King's death, Heston agreed to help. However, when Johnson tried to pass a second bill imposing stricter control on gun sales and registration requirements, he demurred. Sounding a theme he championed thirty years later, the longtime hunter opposed "registering or confiscating all the firearms in private hands" on the grounds that "the Constitution establishes certain rights in this area not granted to citizens of other countries."[48]

Despite occasional forays into issue-oriented politics, Heston generally abstained from political activism while serving as SAG president. By the time his term ended in November 1971, dramatic changes within the Democratic Party hastened his turn to the right. Following Hubert Humphrey's defeat in 1968, antiwar activists demanded greater democratization of the party. Led by George McGovern, they wrested control of delegate selection from old party bosses and set new quotas for increased minority, youth, and female participation in the next convention. By 1972, the Democratic convention looked markedly different than in past years. Female and minority delegates tripled between 1968 and 1972, and the number of delegates under thirty rose tenfold. After rejecting Old Guard leaders such as Humphrey, Edmund Muskie, and Henry "Scoop" Jackson, Democratic delegates—80 percent of whom were attending a convention for the first time—nominated McGovern for president. They passed a platform calling for immediate withdrawal from Vietnam, nuclear disarmament, greater affirmative action, ratification of the Equal Rights Amendment, and other progressive measures.[49]

Disturbed by what they saw as the party's distinctly left agenda, a small group of liberal intellectuals, led by *Commentary* editors Irving Kristol and Norman Podhoretz, criticized Democrats for no longer championing the values they used to stand for, values that appealed to a broad spectrum of middle- and working-class Americans. While still favoring a welfare state and government regulation, they railed against what they saw as the moral and cultural excesses of 1960s counterculture: drugs, sex, student protests, radical feminism, and gay liberation. Believing the United States should use its power to promote democratic values around the world, they strongly disapproved of the party's opposition to the Vietnam War and its refusal to see the Soviet Union as a threat to democracy. These Cold War Democrats voted for Nixon and soon launched what socialist writer Michael Harrington dubbed the "neoconservative movement" (whose adherents became known as "neocons").[50]

For Heston, the 1972 convention laid the foundation for his later participation in what would come to be known as the "culture wars." He found the young Democrats too multicultural, too whiny, and too reliant on government helping individuals rather than people helping themselves. Although not formally aligning himself with the nascent neocons, Heston greeted McGovern's nomination with a sense of disgust. "I think many of his supporters are doomwatchers and the naysayers," he told the press. "I think this is a good country." He opposed the party's position on Vietnam, abortion, nuclear disarmament, and affirmative action. "He didn't view party loyalty as most important," his son Fraser noted. "It was more a question of political issues."[51]

Having stepped down as SAG's leader, Heston no longer felt compelled to remain politically neutral. Shortly after the Democratic convention, he wrote Nixon offering his support. The president took him up on his pledge and the actor received a phone call from another disgruntled Democrat, former Texas governor and Treasury Secretary John B. Connally, asking him to join the newly formed Democrats for Nixon. Heston agreed. Like the fledgling neocons, he embraced the Republican Party because he felt the Democrats had abandoned their legacy, not that he had abandoned his. Although he had not voted for Nixon in 1968, he wanted a president "who can be successful politically, and Nixon's demonstrated he can."[52]

Thrilled Republican leaders put him to work alongside GOP stalwarts John Wayne, Jimmy Stewart, Clint Eastwood, Rosalind Russell, Chuck Connors, and Desi Arnaz. In addition to appearing at rallies and fundraisers, Heston delivered national radio broadcasts criticizing the Democratic nominee for being motivated by a "deep feeling of national guilt." He also debated former U.S. attorney general and McGovern supporter Ramsay Clark about the treatment of POWs by the North Vietnamese.[53]

In the former Soviet Union, a person's status within the Communist Party could be measured by their placement on the May Day podium. The same held true for the Republicans. Nixon accorded the recent convert a place of honor at his inauguration by seating him between Health, Education and Welfare secretary-designate Caspar Weinberger and the Reverend Billy Graham and having him read the Declaration of Independence at the ceremony.[54]

Despite this signal honor, Heston never felt entirely comfortable with his choice of candidates. "I voted, with some misgivings," he wrote in his diary on Election Day, "but a wholer heart than I'd thought I'd have, for RMN. So, apparently, did almost everyone else." When Nixon invited him to a state dinner for Romanian President Nicolae Ceausescu in December 1973, Heston, though pleased to be part of yet another White House, bluntly told one Republican congressman, "I am not a Republican and I am not a Democrat. I am an independent."[55] Protestations aside, over the next decade the self-described independent changed his mind and his affiliation, much to the delight of conservatives throughout the nation.

Action Hero, Republican Activist

From the 1970s to the 2000 presidential election, no movie star activist exhibited more political contradictions than Charlton Heston. He spent the last four decades of his life refashioning his image on and off the screen, first as an action hero and then as a Republican activist. Although his offscreen politics steadily drifted rightward, his most successful films advanced issues at the forefront of progressive causes. The politics of three of his biggest hits—*Planet of the Apes* (1968), *The Omega Man* (1971), and *Soylent Green* (1973)—put him closer to Jane Fonda than to conservative stars such as Sylvester Stallone or Chuck Norris. Nevertheless, during the 1980s, Heston emerged as the Republicans' most important celebrity spokesperson, using his image to sell conservative causes and candidates to a wide range of Americans.

Biblical heroes are timeless, but they are not always good box office. Rather than remain a relic of the past, Heston reached out to a younger generation by recasting himself as a tough modern action hero: astronaut, quarterback, scientist, airplane pilot, and police detective. Though containing liberal messages, his films also appealed to conservatives. These were action-filled movies in which rugged, supermasculine individuals fought against mob rule and uncritical mass thinking. During the 1970s and 1980s, action stars such as Heston, Clint Eastwood, Sylvester Stallone, Chuck Norris, and Arnold Schwarzenegger supplanted Old Guard Republicans John Wayne, Jimmy Stewart, and Gary Cooper as the tough manly stars of the New Hollywood. Yet Heston's screen persona differed from those of Eastwood, Stallone, and Schwarzenegger. The latter three were loners; Heston's characters were tough leaders, men who guided others—albeit reluctantly at times—in the pursuit of justice.

Heston's three most political films—*Planet of the Apes, The Omega Man,* and *Soylent Green*—reflect his own complicated political sensibilities. Although the ideological messages of the films can be read as left-liberal, the highly individualistic solutions advanced by Heston's characters prove far more conservative. Set in the future, the three films deal with, respectively, discrimination and oppression, the devastating effects of germ warfare, and the problems of overpopulation and food shortages in an environmentally compromised world. Heston repeatedly plays a cynical postapocalyptic "Moses" who attempts to save humanity. Like the star himself, Heston's cinematic protagonists disdained the kind of collective action advocated by Harry Belafonte and Jane Fonda in favor of strong individualistic responses to crises—the kind of response that led him to march on Washington but refuse to engage in group protests. In short, he wanted to play characters like himself.

In *Planet of the Apes*, an allegory about race and intolerance in a postnuclear-war society, Heston stars as astronaut George Taylor, a cynic who is delighted to leave his flawed world behind and travel 2,000 years into the future. Taylor is an embittered idealist who decries the inhumanity of his own times and hopes to land in a world where man "no longer makes war with his brother" or keeps "his neighbor's children starving."[56]

Although playing a futuristic character, Heston remains the same kind of calm and self-assured leader that he portrayed in his biblical and historical epic films. He is the tough heroic figure any frightened person would look to if they wound up on a planet where intelligent but cruel apes rule over primitive Homo sapiens. With the future of humankind at stake, Heston ultimately triumphs over his oppressors, and he even performs his first nude scene. The film's stark ending blunts his apparent victory. As he rides along the beach on horseback with the human woman he has saved from the murderous apes, he is shocked to see the top half of a destroyed Statue of Liberty embedded in the sand. He suddenly realizes that he is not on a distant planet but has returned to earth. "Oh my God," he shouts out. "They finally did it. You maniacs. You blew it up. God damn you. God damn you all to hell."[57] Ironically, when Edward G. Robinson, Myrna Loy, and Robert Ryan warned of the dangers of nuclear war in the 1950s and 1960s, conservatives denounced them as Reds.

Planet of the Apes opened in February 1968 to favorable reviews and terrific box office. Costing $5.8 million to make, the film grossed $32.6 million and renewed Heston's appeal among a new generation of viewers. Three years later, he scored another hit with *The Omega Man*. This time he plays Colonel Robert Neville, a gun-toting Army doctor who emerges as the allegoric Jesus of the future. The 1971 release is set in 1977, two years after biological warfare between China and the Soviet Union destroys most life on earth and turns the majority of survivors into vampire-like creatures who cannot bear daylight. The film opens with a very cool Heston calmly driving a convertible through a deserted downtown Los Angeles, frequently pulling out his machine gun to kill wandering ghouls and then retreating home as night falls.

The Omega Man is a traditional action story with Heston repelling mutant attacks while trying to save a dying group of humans. After inoculating himself with an experimental vaccine, Neville discovers he can cure the remaining men and women on earth by injecting his blood into their veins. As one child asks him, "Are you God?" No, but he has graduated from Moses to Jesus. As he tries to bring the last bottle of his blood serum to his friends, the ghouls stop him with a spear through his chest and Neville falls into a fountain. Miraculously, he survives until morning when the humans find him. With his last ounce of energy, he hands over the serum. The final scene shows him dying, his blood flowing into the fountain and his arms spread out like Christ on the Cross. Once again, Moses-Jesus-Heston has saved humanity.

Soylent Green dealt with the abuses of class power and destruction of the environment long before it became fashionable to do so. Set in New York City in 2022, where 20 million of the dystopian city's 40 million residents are unemployed, the MGM production depicts a world where food is in short supply and overcrowding so severe that people sleep packed like vermin on staircases, fire escapes, and the floors of churches. Only the very wealthy can afford to live in apartments or eat real food. The vast bulk of civilization survives on tasteless high-protein food bars made by the Soylent Corporation. Heston plays another tough, cynical character, homicide detective Robert Thorn, a corrupt cop with a strong moral compass. After one of Soylent's directors is murdered, Thorn takes the case and, with the aid of his roommate (Edward G. Robinson), discovers a powerful conspiracy between the corporation and New York's political leaders. Police authorities demote the detective after he refuses to bury the case. When Robinson discovers that the Soylent Corporation makes their green wafers from the bodies of dead human beings, he goes to the city's Death Center to die. Arriving too late to stop him, Thorn discovers the horrific truth: "Soylent Green is people!" he yells out before the final cutaway.

Over the next several decades, Heston insisted that his appearance in these three films proved his continuing commitment to liberal ideals. He often parried his left critics by pointing to *Soylent Green* as evidence of his early interest in environmentalism and the dangers of overpopulation. As late as August 2007, one reviewer praised the movie for "trying to do for global overpopulation what Al Gore, in *An Inconvenient Truth* (2006) would do for global warming."[58] Despite the ambiguous politics of the three action films, Heston's heroes remained the secular reincarnation of Moses; his characters were the ones who saw the light, knew the truth, and could lead the masses.

Having renewed his fame as a modern action hero, Heston set out to become a modern political hero. His turn to activism coincided with his sense of financial security. "I seem to have managed to make a fortune acting for pay," he boasted in 1976. Like Ronald Reagan, who emerged as a dedicated conservative activist only after signing a lucrative long-term financial deal with General Electric, Heston's economic independence gave him the freedom to speak his mind on a wide range of issues. The man who, in 1952, cautioned actors to keep quiet on subjects other than their work now railed against those who felt that movie stars "should somehow be prohibited from expressing themselves or establishing positions of support for candidates."[59]

During the presidential elections of 1976, Heston once again moved into the Republican camp, but he pitched his tent with the party's moderates, supporting Gerald Ford over conservative challenger Ronald Reagan. That same year, he endorsed moderate congressman Alphonzo Bell in his unsuccessful bid to wrest the Republican senatorial nomination away from conservative former San Francisco State University president S. I. Hay-akawa. Heston also maintained liberal positions on environmental and arts-related issues. In October 1978, he campaigned for California's Proposition 5, the "Clean Indoor Air Act." Several years later, when President Reagan asked him to cochair a task force on the future of the National Endowments for the Arts and the Humanities, Heston surprised his liberal critics by persuading his old friend to fund both organizations at a much higher level than the chief executive initially intended.[60]

Heston's transition from liberal independent to conservative Republican accelerated during the next decade. When Ronald Reagan ran for president in 1980, the action star campaigned on his behalf. As Heston's conservative sensibilities grew stronger after the 1972 Democratic convention, he found himself drawn to Reagan's views on the dangers of excessive government. Like Reagan, Heston believed that "a free market is a sign of a free society" and strongly endorsed his efforts at deregulating industry. Work prevented the actor from campaigning as much as he would have liked, but he proved a close enough ally to watch the November election returns with the Reagans at the Century Plaza Hotel. He also performed at the Inaugural Ball, reading a series of patriotic quotes "in his 'God voice,'" while a band quietly played "The Battle Hymn of the Republic" in the background.[61]

Despite his support of Reagan, Heston did not consider himself a conservative activist, nor had he registered as a Republican. As eclectic as Heston, the conservative movement of the post-1960s represented a mélange of groups and ideas: libertarians, free-market ideologues, corporate business leaders, neoconservatives, and the religious right. Rejecting the social liberalism and moral relativism of the counterculture, these disparate groups united around three basic principles: opposition to an overly active state, belief in a free and unregulated market, and protection of individual rights. The movement's fundamentalist wing also worried about the erosion of spiritual values, and many undoubtedly agreed with conservative intellectual Russell Kirk who argued that "a divine intent rules society" and that "political problems, at bottom, are religious problems." Agreeing with them on many points, libertarians objected to any effort by conservatives to impose their values on individuals. Life choices and lifestyles, libertarians insisted, must remain as unregulated as the marketplace.[62]

In 1980, Heston remained closer to libertarians and neoconservatives— whom Irving Kristol described as "liberal[s] mugged by reality"—than to the conservative movement's more ideologically rigid New Right and Christian Right wings. Although he shared the New Right's opposition to Communism, affirmative action, and the Equal Rights Amendment, Heston did not see the New Deal as state socialism, nor did he wish to end federal programs such as Medicare and Social Security or halt legislation to protect the environment. As for civil rights, he wanted the government to provide a climate for individuals to succeed on their own merits, but he opposed affirmative action policies that gave certain people—most notably women and minorities—unfair advantage over others. Like many libertarians, he stressed the centrality of individual responsibility. "My admiration for man," he explained in 1977, "is in terms of the extraordinary individual rather than the man in the mass, who I think falls infinitely short of what God must have had in mind."[63]

As Ronald Reagan and his allies fought to restructure American government and society, they needed all the help they could get for they proposed nothing less than overturning the policies of the most popular president of the twentieth century, Franklin D. Roosevelt. Heston served as a valuable advocate. Despite the presence of a former actor in the White House, Americans still associated Hollywood with liberal politics, and for good reason. The left had a much larger array of glamorous stars: Warren Beatty, Barbra Streisand, Robert Redford, Paul Newman, Shirley MacLaine, Marlon Brando, and the young actors in Network who continued the work begun by Jane Fonda and Tom Hayden. Yet, few of them exuded the same gravitas as Charlton Heston, especially with evangelicals who dominated the Christian Right.

In the two decades between Reagan's victory and George W. Bush's election in 2000, Heston emerged as the GOP's leading celebrity spokesperson. With the victory of the "Great Communicator" in 1980, television's role as a medium of political communication and partisan propaganda assumed unprecedented importance. The telegenic president showed that an appealing image and simple but powerful short messages trumped longer presentations of complex ideas. Heston was no Reagan, but his trustworthy image and ability to communicate ideas in a convincing fashion helped further the conservative agenda. "Organizations are eager to have me testify before Congressional committees," he explained shortly after the inauguration, "and the congressmen on those committees are eager to have me do so—because it is likely to get on the six o'clock news. That's a contribution I can make that most other people can't."[64]

Heston's first major appearance as a conservative spokesperson came in 1982 when he defended the administration's anti-Communist stance on Central America and its nuclear policies in a series of high-profile encounters with Ed Asner and Paul Newman. Throughout 1981–1982, Hollywood progressives, led by *M*A*S*H* television star Mike Farrell, attacked Reagan's support of the right-wing military regime in El Salvador and the Contra rebels trying to overthrow Nicaragua's leftist government. Ensuing debates in Congress and the media often left the public confused as to whether the Contras were "Freedom Fighters," as Reagan called them, or paramilitary death squads, as administration opponents argued. Conservatives and progressives also debated whether the United States should support the anti-Communist El Salvador government, which tolerated widespread human rights violations, or the insurgent guerrillas. When SAG president Ed Asner, star of CBS's popular *Lou Grant* show, held a press conference in February and presented a check for $25,000 to a group that bought medical supplies for leftist Salvadorian rebels, SAG conservatives launched an effort to recall their leader.[65]

In a highly publicized intervention—"GET DOWN, MOSES" blared one newspaper headline—Heston jumped into the fray, defending the administration's efforts to root out Communism. He also condemned Asner for failing to stipulate that he was acting as a private citizen and not on SAG's behalf in supporting "the Marxist rebels in El Salvador." The subsequent furor over Asner's actions proved so controversial that CBS canceled *Lou Grant*. Asner attributed his firing to "Heston and his all-star hit squad" and warned of a return to McCarthyism. Soon after, President Reagan sent his old friend a letter thanking him for his support and noting that the "battle goes on and there will be a struggle to win approval in the House of any meaningful help in Central America."[66]

Heston made headlines again in October 1982, and this time the incident was dubbed "Star Wars." Heston debated Paul Newman over a California ballot proposition that called for the president to suspend the development and deployment of all nuclear weapons (Proposition 12, the nuclear freeze initiative). In the weeks prior to the election, Heston met with State Department officials to discuss the government's position; he also made several television spots opposing the freeze. Hoping to mobilize conservative voters, he appeared on Pat Robertson's influential talk show *The 700 Club* where, echoing Reagan's mantra of fear and reassurance, he insisted that Proposition 12 would make the world a more dangerous place. When Newman told the press that the Soviets "kept treaties as well as anybody," Heston countered that if the liberal star had "taken the time to read a little history" he would know that the Russians "don't keep their treaties. You can't trust them."[67]

After campaigning for several weeks, the two men debated on ABC's *The Last Word* on October 30 to great media fanfare—and derision. "See what happens when we elect an actor President?" quipped television critic Howard Rosenberg. "We get nuclear policy debated on TV by Moses and Butch Cassidy." Local viewers took a very different view, for many found the celebrity debate quite informative. As one Costa Mesa woman wrote the *Los Angeles Times*, "I applaud the Fondas, Asners, Hestons and Newmans of America for their courage, their deep concern, and the time and energy they've given to becoming informed citizens."[68]

Although several reports suggested that Heston proved far more articulate than Newman, the debates did not dissuade California voters from passing Proposition 12; but anti-freeze leader Nick Sorokin insisted that Heston made the final vote a lot closer than expected. The pro-freeze force's 25-point lead in the polls rapidly shrunk after the actor made two anti-freeze television spots and then clashed with Newman on ABC. On Election Day, the freeze passed by a surprisingly narrow 52 to 48 percent margin. Heston's efforts elevated the star to even greater prominence among GOP leaders. His advocacy of Reagan's nuclear policies so impressed Department of Energy officials that, in a move right out of a James Bond movie, they granted him Q clearance—the nation's highest nuclear weapons top-secret rating. Between 1983 and 1989, he narrated six training films (shown only to those with proper clearance) dealing with various aspects of the U.S. nuclear program.[69]

Flattery also played a role in Heston's rightward drift. One should never underestimate the ego of a movie star, especially one whose glory days were behind him. The actor enjoyed his newfound political notoriety and spent the next several years traveling around the country campaigning for Republican candidates and promoting conservative positions on abortion, gun control, Communism, Central America, anti-union right-to-work laws, and Reagan's Strategic Defense Initiative, which he praised in a sixty-second television spot as "a peace shield" against Soviet missiles. In 1987, he finally registered as Republican, insisting once again that the "Democratic Party moved, I didn't." That same year, he completed his transition from neoconservative to full-blown conservative, jettisoning many of his earlier libertarian views. When asked by libertarian periodical *Reason* whether he believed in government proscribing certain forms of nonaggressive behavior, like alternative lifestyles or smoking marijuana, he proudly declared himself "a conservative" and responded that the "government not only has the right but the responsibility to take whatever draconian measures are necessary." Few libertarians would have agreed to such blatant government interference in individual lives.[70]

Heston soon found himself pursued by arch-conservatives Phil Gramm, Jesse Helms, and Newt Gingrich; by the National Conservative Political Action Committee, National Conservative Foundation, and Christian Coalition; and also by Reagan during his reelection campaign and George H. W. Bush during his presidential run in 1988. The movie star's presence at campaign rallies proved especially important in the wake of the Federal Election Campaign Act of 1971, which limited individual campaign contributions to $1,000 for any one candidate and $25,000 annually for all federal candidates. As the cost of campaigns skyrocketed—the average Senate hopeful spent six times as much in 1986 as in 1971—candidates sought out celebrities who could help them raise modest sums from large numbers of donors. Not surprisingly, Republicans turned to Heston.[71]

The conservative star proved popular on the campaign trail and as early as December 1984 party activists discussed running him for Senate in California. "I think people identify with his heroic roles," explained Republican state senator Ed Davis. "How can you beat a man who goes up on the mountain and talks to God?" Polls the following May showed him with greater name recognition than either Republican Senator Pete Wilson or Democratic San Francisco Mayor Dianne Feinstein. The conservative faithful were so enamored of their hottest celebrity star that Stuart Spencer, Reagan's chief strategist during his 1966 gubernatorial campaign, visited the outspoken actor in hopes of persuading him to enter the political arena. Heston demurred, once again explaining, "I would rather play a senator than be one." One year later he was touted as a possible presidential candidate.[72]

What lay behind Heston's refusal to run? Despite enjoying public attention, he was a very private man with only a handful of close friends. Heston was a man who knew himself and what he wanted from life; and he knew he did not want to make the sacrifices needed to be a politician. He had a happy marriage and enjoyed being with his children. Running for office was one thing, but serving in office would greatly reduce his time with his family, his time to play tennis (no small thing in his mind), and his time on stage and screen. He also understood that if he stopped being a star to become a politician, he would likely lose the public adoration he so craved and enjoyed. "I don't have what politicians call the 'fire in the belly' about doing that kind of work," he confessed to a reporter in September 1984. "You have to have it to do that kind of work." Heston enjoyed being a political star, but he enjoyed being a film and stage star even more. "He loved to act and didn't want to stop acting for four, six, or eight years," his son Fraser explained. "He also didn't want to leave California and move to Washington."[73]

GUNS, MOSES, AND THE NRA

During the course of his evolution into Hollywood's preeminent Republican, Heston and his allies repeatedly drew upon his biblical image to appeal to the party's expanding base of loyal conservatives, Evangelicals, Reagan Democrats, libertarians, independents, and gun enthusiasts. "It is inconceivable that he would be so warmly embraced as a conservative champion," Ed Leibowitz observed in a 2001 profile, "had he made his reputation in the kind of slimeball parts favored by Robert Mitchum or Peter Lorre, or if, like his fellow conservative Tom Selleck, he had merely been Magnum P.I." Heston sustained that image, and the Moses Industry, by appearing on television screens every Easter and issuing a new series of biblical books, recordings, and television shows throughout the 1990s. And just to make sure he would never forget the role that made him famous, he rose at 5:00 A.M. each day, waded into his pool, and recited either the death of Moses scene or Prospero's farewell from *The Tempest*.[74]

After playing charismatic leaders on the screen for so many years, Heston came to believe he *was* one and confidently assumed the role off the screen. He became the Moses of his own imagination, one who now wanted to reshape the body politic. Like Ronald Reagan, he understood the power of media images and used them effectively in televised political spots. Calling the printed word "almost primitive," he insisted that the "moving image is the most powerful tool or weapon to change and shape the way people feel about the world and themselves." Any movie star could read lines, but few could do it like Heston. Looking straight into the camera with his piercing blue eyes and rugged good looks, he spoke with a deep baritone voice and an air of assuredness that educated the faithful and made the skeptical want to believe. After Heston threw his support behind George H. W. Bush in 1988, one delighted supporter exclaimed, "We can't lose now. We've really got God on our side." Likewise, during Paul Coverdell's successful effort to unseat incumbent Georgia Senator Wyche Fowler in 1992, Heston visited a number of small towns carrying two mock stone tablets engraved with the "Top Ten Lies of Wyche Fowler."[75]

Heston's ability to affect national political life peaked with his leadership of the NRA. Fighting for the right to bear arms marked a return to the fond memories of a childhood where he found his greatest pleasure in the quiet solitude of hunting. As an adult, he so treasured his guns that he slept with a Colt .45 under his bed. The prospect of having the government limit or ban weapons was simply unthinkable. At an ideological level, gun control merged Heston's opposition to excessive government with his faith in the sanctity of the Second Amendment, which declared that "the right of the people to keep and bear Arms, shall not be infringed." The "driving motivation" behind his father's opposition to gun control, explained his son, Fraser, was his belief that "freedoms were very easy to give up and very hard to get back. He was conservative in the sense that he wished to conserve those ideals and those freedoms."[76]

Between 1982 and 1998, when the NRA elected him its president, Heston proved an effective advocate, campaigning for gun rights candidates on both sides of the aisle, lobbying Congress, and making media advertisements for the cause. Joining the organization in 1978, Heston turned activist in October 1982, when he appeared in what the press called "an effective" twenty-eight-minute television documentary aimed at defeating Proposition 15, a California initiative that would have imposed the nation's toughest restrictions on the sale and registration of firearms. After trailing in the polls, the "No on 15" forces outspent their opponents by a 3 to 1 margin in television and radio commercials and, with Heston's help, defeated the initiative by a 63 to 37 percent margin.[77]

Despite its success in California, the NRA suffered repeated setbacks as it refused to compromise on gun-related issues. The passage of the Brady Bill in 1993, named after the aide wounded during the failed assassination attempt on Reagan in 1981, signaled the organization's declining power in Congress. The NRA's image sank to its lowest point in the wake of the Oklahoma City bombing in April 1995, when executive vice president Wayne La Pierre sent out a fundraising letter calling federal agents "jack-booted government thugs" who loved to "harass, intimidate, even murder law-abiding citizens." The harsh words so angered former President Bush that he resigned from the NRA. Membership plummeted nearly 20 percent between 1994 and 1995, from 3.4 million to 2.8 million, as many gun owners worried that the organization had become too ideologically extreme. By July 1998, the gun lobby's influence had slipped so badly that a *Time* magazine article asked, "Can Heston's Celebrity and Rhetoric Revive the N.R.A?"[78]

Delivering the keynote address at its annual convention in May 1989, the group's most famous member boomed out a patriotic defense of the organization's uncompromising efforts to protect the Constitution: "I went to the war when they asked me to go. I pay my taxes, I contribute to charity, I vote in every election. Now, because I support the Bill of Rights, I am a zealot? Like hell!" With considerable theatrical flourish, he raised a 1866 Winchester rifle high over his head like the staff Moses used to part the Red Sea and boomed out, "So, as we set out this year to defeat the divisive forces that would take freedom away, I want to say those fighting words for everyone within the sound of my voice to hear and to heed. . . . From my cold, dead hands!" (see figs. 7.4 and 7.5). The last phrase proved so popular that NRA members plastered bumper stickers on their cars proclaiming, "I'LL GIVE UP MY GUN WHEN YOU TAKE IT FROM MY COLD DEAD HANDS."[79]

Heston's increasingly outspoken activism on behalf of conservative causes led the *Washingtonian* to ask in a September 1993 article, "Moses in '96?" While a run for the White House was not on the table, he accepted the position of NRA vice president in May 1997 and president the following year. Joyous executive board members told a reporter that Heston was "the only human being in the world who could automatically open doors and rebuild the gun lobby in the eyes of mainstream America."[80]

During his five terms as NRA president, Heston led an aggressive grassroots campaign to revive the organization and elect pro-gun candidates to every level of government. "Too many gun owners think we've wandered into some fringe of American life and left them behind," he explained in his May 1998 inaugural address, but he would help "win back our rightful place in the mainstream of American political debate." Sounding a theme he repeated throughout his presidency, Heston heralded the Second Amendment as "the first among equals . . . the one freedom that makes all freedoms defensible, possible, the one right that protects all the others." With a rhetorical flourish that excited convention delegates, he leveled a blistering attack on President Clinton, whom a year earlier he disparagingly compared to a

FIGURE 7.4 Heston as Moses raising his staff to part the Red Sea. SOURCE: PHOTOFEST

FIGURE 7.5 Heston imitated that famous gesture by raising a musket at the NRA convention, May 2000. SOURCE: ASSOCIATED PRESS

"welfare father, or deadbeat dad." "Mr. Clinton, sir, America didn't trust you with their health-care system, America didn't trust you with gays in the military, America doesn't trust you with our 21-year-old daughters. And we sure Lord don't trust you with our guns."[81]

As his passion for conservative causes rose, so too did the nastiness of his rhetoric, which contributed to the lack of civility in politics that he decried. His attacks, like the one on Clinton, took on an increasingly personal and often venomous tone. In May 1998, he questioned Barbra Streisand's patriotism, calling her the "Hanoi Jane of the Second Amendment" for producing a television movie about a New York woman who won a congressional seat after a crazed shooter killed her husband and five others on a commuter train in 1993. In an earlier speech that generated widespread criticism, Heston equated the ridicule faced by gun owners with Jews forced by Nazis to wear yellow stars. "There may not be a Gestapo officer on every street corner," he remarked, "but the influence on our culture is just as pervasive." He also offended a wide swath of Americans by denouncing "the fringe propaganda of the homosexual coalition, the feminists who preach that it's a divine duty for women to hate men, blacks who raise a militant fist with one hand while they seek preference with the other, and all the New-Age apologists for juvenile crime. . . . We've reached that point in time when our national social policy originates on Oprah. I say it's time to pull the plug."[82]

This aggressive rhetoric played well with the NRA faithful but it alienated former admirers of Heston. "In his liberal days," explained close friend and producer Walter Seltzer, "he was much more civil to people of the other persuasion." When Heston spoke at public gatherings, observed one journalist, he "assumes a tone he doesn't use in casual conversation, where in the main, he's gentle, grandfatherly. It's the inverse of Nixon, whose private utterances were filled with vulgar diatribes, but who, before an audience, kept these thoughts to himself." Even his longtime publicist left him after the star fell under the "cult-like influence of the National Rifle Association."[83]

As Heston's early liberalism faded, his harsh invectives against homosexuals, feminists, rappers, and leftists earned him a venerated place on former Ku Klux Klan leader David Duke's Web site. This was a far cry from the man who told a reporter in 1983, "My living depends on people not getting mad at me. No matter what, I've never felt a significant part of the audience was mad at me. . . . Of course, I may live to eat those words. . . . The trick is to state your views as moderately as you can."[84]

After years of temperate comments, why did Heston grow so mean and angry? The nomination of George McGovern prompted his initial turn to the right, but the culture wars of the 1980s and 1990s pushed him solidly into the conservative camp and unleashed his worst instincts. At their core, the culture wars represented a deep conflict of values between liberals and conservatives over the best way to deal with controversial issues such as abortion, homosexuality, gun control, censorship, affirmative action, women's rights, and the separation of church and state. Heston could never acknowledge that the world of the 1950s and early 1960s had changed. The America he grew up with, he insisted, was under assault: "Heaven help God-fearing, law-abiding, Caucasian, middle class, Protestant (or even worse *evangelical*) Christian, the Midwestern or southern (or even worse *rural*) hunter, apparently straight or admitted heterosexual gun-owning (or even worse *NRA-card-carrying*) average working stiff, or even worse still *male* working stiff, because not only do you not count, you're a downright obstacle to social progress."[85]

Standing up against what he saw as the contemporary Pharaohs of moral decline, Heston repeatedly spoke of a "collision between the principled and the unprincipled, in a ferocious final clash for our nation's soul"—a "cultural war" that was "raging across our land, storming our values, assaulting our freedoms, killing our self-confidence in who we are and what we believe." As a devotee of "Old Testament ethics," he bemoaned the way in which the "last two generations of American society has abandoned even the idea of greatness. The media, academe, the creative community, now extol the ordinary, enshrine the victim."[86] In short, the nation failed to venerate the kind of great historical men the actor had played for years.

For Heston, the bitter culture wars were not just about abstract ideas; they represented a personal challenge to his self-image and his entire cinematic career. In his mind, he had not changed; the rest of the world had. He defended the Constitution in the same way the epic heroes he played defended their people. "My affinity with these [great men]," he told one journalist, "made me a little disdainful of people who don't [honor their achievements]." Instead of being lauded by an admiring public, his opponents denounced him as a gun nut, sexist, racist, and homophobe. Worse yet, if contemporary Hollywood filmmakers could readily dismiss the "towering achievements" of men like Thomas Jefferson in favor of focusing on "his putative relationship with a slave-girl," then who could the children of America admire?[87] Not Moses. Not Andrew Jackson. Not Michelangelo. And certainly not Charlton Heston. On the other hand, conservatives venerated Heston as the savior of the NRA, the Constitution, and the nation.

Heston's battle with alcohol and cancer may also have contributed to his occasional vitriolic outbursts. Explaining that he gave up Scotch earlier, he confessed to the *National Enquirer* in July 2000 that he drank a lot of white wine on planes and at dinners, too much wine. "I wasn't slurring my words, I wasn't falling over," he explained, "but I realized it had become an addiction for me." His drinking worsened under the pressure of working for the NRA, campaigning for Republican candidates, dealing with Lydia's breast cancer in 1991, and recovering from prostate cancer in 1998. In May 2000, he entered an alcoholic rehabilitation center in Utah. After a short stay, the sober star resumed his political activities.[88]

As the millennium neared, the self-proclaimed "foot soldier" in the conservative revolution had moved as far to the right as Ronald Reagan, railing against political correctness, affirmative action, and a government that "has become bloated" and exercised "too much authority over the individual American citizen." He even recast Moses in his own political image. "Moses was a conservative," he told the *New York Times* in April 1998. "You don't mess around with Moses. He was an angry, harsh leader, not a friendly fellow. This is not Jesus." Not surprisingly, the Hollywood star emerged as a popular speaker at annual Conservative Political Action conferences (the "Noah's Ark of the right" as one columnist called them), appearing with the likes of Dick Cheney, George W. Bush, Jesse Helms, Ann Coulter, and Robert Novak.[89]

Despite the presence of Arnold Schwarzenegger, Bruce Willis, and Tom Selleck, *Nation* political correspondent David Corn insisted there was "only one conservative celebrity in Hollywood committed to serious partisan activism: Charlton Heston." Under his leadership, the NRA reestablished itself as a powerful force in American political life as its membership swelled from 2.9 million in 1997 to an all-time high of 4.5 million by 2000. In the months before the 2000 presidential elections, the NRA and the GOP once again turned to their faithful advocate to promote the cause. The ensuing campaign proved the high point of Heston's political activism. In May 2000, he stepped up to the podium at the NRA's annual convention and challenged his peers to defeat Al Gore in the same way their forefathers defeated the British king who attempted to steal their liberties. "When freedom shivers in the cold shadow of true peril," he warned, "it's always the patriots who first hear the call." Repeating the gesture that proved so successful a decade earlier, he held a replica of a Revolutionary-era musket high over his head and told the wildly cheering members, "So, as we set out this year to defeat the divisive forces that would take freedom away, I want to say those words again for everyone within the sound of my voice to hear and to heed, and especially for you, Mr. Gore: From My Cold Dead Hands!"[90]

The NRA poured over $20 million into their effort to elect George W. Bush and help Republicans maintain control of Congress, more than double its budget for any previous election. The organization spent over $1 million on a "Vote Freedom First" television and billboard campaign that targeted twelve key swing states. The gun lobby also aired a series of half-hour infomercials that featured Heston accusing Democrats of losing touch with rural, conservative values and urging gun owners to register to vote and join the NRA or risk having their weapons confiscated. In a commercial run during the Democratic National Convention, Heston blasted the Clinton administration as "the most anti-gun White House in history" and asked viewers, "Tell me, why are so few Democrats willing to defend constitutional freedom?"[91]

The NRA also launched an aggressive grassroots get-out-the-vote campaign similar to the one conservatives mounted on behalf of Ronald Reagan in 1980. Heston proved a powerful force on the campaign trail, attracting large crowds and cheers wherever he spoke. Learning from his friend Ronald Reagan, he used buzzwords like "freedom," "liberty," and "individual rights" to turn partisan attacks into patriotic defenses of core American values. After telling an enthusiastic group of 2,000 NRA members in Roanoke, Virginia, that Democratic candidate Al Gore "had the guts of a guppy," Heston implored the faithful to vote for Bush, reminding them, "When you pull the lever to vote freedom first, you are doing no less than our forefathers pulling the trigger against the tyrants at Lexington and Concord." The NRA faithful were so enamored of their president that they showed their true feelings about who they wanted in the White House with bumper stickers that read, "My President is Charlton Heston."[92]

As Election Day approached, Hollywood's star conservative embarked on a seven-day, sixteen-city get-out-the-vote tour through key swing states trying to mobilize gun owners to vote for Bush. In Nashville, after recounting stories about *Ben-Hur*, he told the starstruck crowd, "Freedom has never been in greater peril, or needed you more urgently to come to her defense."

In heavily Democratic West Virginia, he warned that a Gore-Lieberman administration would take away their hunting rifles. "If you turn on the car radio in West Virginia," several journalists reported, "you cannot escape those commercials of Charlton Heston sounding like God speaking for the National Rifle Association." For many swing state voters, a Hollywood celebrity proved more appealing than a Washington celebrity, for Heston's rallies outdrew Gore rallies when the two appeared simultaneously in the same city.[93]

On November 7, 2000, over 105 million Americans went to the polls and elected George W. Bush their president. Gore won the popular vote 50,999,897 (48.38) to 50,456,002 (47.87), but the former Texas governor won the decisive electoral college vote 271 to 266. Numerous pundits and politicians attributed the narrow Republican victory to Heston and the NRA's efforts in five swing states, especially West Virginia, Tennessee, and Arkansas. In West Virginia, where Democrats outnumbered Republicans two to one, gun owners helped give Bush the five electoral votes that put him over the top. "We said from the beginning," Heston told a reporter, "the NRA—*gun owners*—can win the election." Bill Clinton agreed, admitting that his administration's support of gun control measures cost Gore "at least five states" where the NRA had "a decisive influence."[94] Postelection data revealed that 48 percent of all presidential voters came from gun-owning households, up dramatically from 37 percent in the 1996 presidential election. Gun owners voted for Bush 61 percent to 36 percent, while those from households without guns backed Gore 58 to 39 percent.[95]

Republican leaders did not forget Heston's critical role in the election. Addressing the annual meeting of the Conservative Political Action Committee Conference in February 2001, a delighted Vice President Dick Cheney told the delegates, "The president and I would not be where we are today if not for the support of friends across America." The audience knew precisely whom he was talking about: the men who stood next to him on the podium, Charlton Heston and NRA executive vice president Wayne LaPierre. Two years later, as Heston prepared to step down as NRA president, Florida Governor Jeb Bush praised him for what was perhaps his greatest starring role. "Were it not for your active involvement," he insisted, "it's safe to say my brother may not have been president of the United States."[96] After eight years of being lost in the Democratic desert, Moses led his flock back into the conservative Promised Land.

Down from the Mountain

To Americans born after 1980, Charlton Heston is not the muscular star who played Moses and Ben-Hur, but the frail seventy-eight-year-old man in Michael Moore's 2002 documentary *Bowling for Columbine* (2002). Made in the wake of the tragic April 20, 1999, shootings in which two Littleton, Colorado, highschoolers killed twelve students and a teacher, Moore's Oscar-winning film portrays Heston as callously elevating gun rights over human rights. Visiting Heston's Beverly Hills home a few years after the shootings, Moore grilled the aging star with a series of questions he found hard to answer. When asked to apologize to the people of Columbine, Heston walked out of the room without responding. Moore chased after him holding an 8 x 10 picture of a little girl killed at Littleton and then left it at the front door. The filmmaker's criticism of gun violence may have been on target, but many viewers felt he went too far in attacking the doddering actor. Even Al Gore confessed to the *New Yorker*, "I really appreciate what [Moore was] trying to do, but I wouldn't have thought before seeing the movie that anyone could have aroused any sympathy in me for Charlton Heston. And yet he did."[97]

Two months before the film's release, Americans learned why Heston appeared less than sharp. In an August 9 news conference, he revealed that he suffered from a neurological disorder whose symptoms were consistent with Alzheimer's disease. In a poignant videotaped statement, he explained, "I can part the Red Sea, but I can't part with you, which is why I won't exclude you from this stage in my life. . . . If you see a little less spring to my step, if your name fails to leap to my lips, you'll know why. And if I tell you a funny story for the second time, please laugh anyway." Despite his condition, the NRA president pledged to finish his term and continue his political work. During the 2002 election season, he campaigned for Republican candidates in twenty-two states.[98]

But this was a different Heston than in the past, a visibly aged man who shuffled across a room with his upper body bent forward and had difficulty remembering his lines. Nevertheless, the old pro still knew how to excite a crowd. At an October rally in Manchester, New Hampshire, Heston responded to chants of "Do it Chuck" by holding a rifle over his head and defying his critics to pry it "from my cold dead hands." Outside the hall, gun-control advocates held candlelight vigils for the victims of the "Beltway

Sniper" who killed ten people and wounded four in a series of shootings between September 21 and October 20. Despite his disease, Heston's steadfast refusal to compromise on any part of the gun control issue, including mandating safety locks on triggers to protect children, inspired anger like that directed against Jane Fonda.[99]

In April 2003, too weak and forgetful to give a speech, Heston videotaped his final comments for the NRA convention. Several months later, the organization erected a ten-foot bronze likeness of Heston as the cowboy Will Penny (his favorite film role), holding a rifle at his side, in front of its Washington, D.C., headquarters. That same year, President George W. Bush repaid his ally by awarding him the Presidential Medal of Freedom, while the American Film Institute established the Charlton Heston Award to recognize his contribution to film and television.[100]

Heston disappeared from public life but his impact continued to be felt in a number of areas. During his tenure in office, he helped a declining NRA regain its political power and, in so doing, helped swing a presidential election. In May 2001, *Fortune* reported in its "Power 25" rankings that for the first time in four years, the NRA supplanted the American Association of Retired Persons as the most powerful lobbying group in Washington. Democratic politicians also learned from the preeminent practitioner of image politics. During the 2004 presidential campaign, John Kerry held photo-ops showing him shooting pheasants on a hunting trip. Running mate John Edwards also played up his hunting days in 2004 and again in 2008.[101]

On a Saturday night, April 6, 2008, Heston quietly passed away. President Bush hailed him as a "strong advocate for liberty," while Senator John McCain praised him as a devotee of civil and constitutional rights. Calling Heston "one of Ronnie's and my dearest friends," Nancy Reagan told the press, "I will never forget Chuck as a hero on the big screen in the roles he played, but more importantly I considered him a hero in life for the many times that he stepped up to support Ronnie in whatever he was doing." The *Los Angeles Times*'s film critic Carina Chocano preferred to remember him for his roles as a liberator of the oppressed. "Heston's signature heroes were not the triumphalist über-beings that actors like Arnold Schwarzenegger, Heston's late-century counterpart, would later embody. . . . They were downtrodden and oppressed, the strength of their convictions an equal match for the brute strength of his body." Even his African American critics proved generous. "Charlton Heston was a complex individual," remarked Earl Ofari Hutchinson. "He lived a long time, and certainly, there were many phases. The phases we prefer to remember were certainly his contributions to Dr. King and civil rights."[102]

For over fifty years, Charlton Heston had shown how movie stars could use their cinematic image for political ends—and, under the proper circumstances, even help decide a presidential election. Although he refused entreaties by Democrats and Republicans to run for office and never took his own activism beyond issue-oriented politics, Heston established a precedent that others would follow. In October 2003, Arnold Schwarzenegger rewrote the political rules when he drew on the power of his cinematic image to become governor of California, a victory he owed in part to the legacy of his conservative friend. Yet three years before the Austrian immigrant's victory, another Hollywood star, one whose politics and playboy image were virtually the opposite of Heston's, elicited national admiration and mockery by contemplating a run for the presidency of the United States.

PRESIDENT BULWORTH, OR, WILL MR. BEATTY GO TO WASHINGTON? WARREN BEATTY

The atmosphere at the Beverly Hilton Hotel was electric as 1,000 guests and a frenzied media mob of 200 reporters gathered in the main ballroom on September 29, 1999, waiting to hear the answer to the question on everyone's mind: Would Warren Beatty run for president of the United States? At 9:13 P.M., in a performance straight out of *Mr. Smith Goes to Washington*, the potential candidate strode to the platform and began addressing the audience in a nervous and quiet voice filled with "ums" and "ahs." Ten minutes into his speech, the Jimmy Stewart shyness was suddenly replaced by a strong, resonant voice that spoke passionately about the great disparities of wealth in America, about poverty, joblessness, the need for universal health care, and the destruction of democracy by big money interests. At 9:48 P.M. Beatty ended his speech with a plea for all Americans to "speak up for the people nobody speaks for."[1] It was a performance that could have won him an Oscar. The dynamic truth-speaking politician from *Bulworth* (1998) had come to life. More reporters turned out for the dinner than showed up for the candidacy declarations of political heavyweights George W. Bush and Al Gore.

Lionized in gossip columns for decades as Hollywood's number-one Lothario, political cognoscenti also knew the actor as a savvy politico who had taken celebrity politics to new heights. The liberals and radicals who attended the Americans for Democratic Action dinner that September evening saw Beatty as the left's answer to Ronald Reagan: a charismatic figure who knew how to present complex issues in an engaging and persuasive manner.

No star of his generation played a more central role in the worlds of film and electoral politics than Warren Beatty. Louis B. Mayer, Hollywood's first major practitioner of electoral politics, served as a power broker and state party leader. But Beatty took electoral politics to another level by operating as an inside player in the high-stakes world of presidential politics. After first venturing into the campaign circuit during Robert Kennedy's doomed presidential run in 1968, he served as George McGovern's chief fundraiser and media adviser in 1972, sharpening the candidate's communication skills just as George Murphy did for Dwight Eisenhower. Forging a close friendship with McGovern's campaign manager Gary Hart, he emerged as an integral part of the Colorado senator's inner circle, shaping his messages and media strategies during his 1984 and 1988 presidential bids.

Like Harry Belafonte and Jane Fonda before him, Beatty fought to achieve dramatic changes in the nation's political system. Frustrated with the limitations of electoral politics and the losses suffered by McGovern and Hart, he used the screen to bring his ideas to millions of Americans. At a time when American politics were shifting rightward, Beatty made movies— particularly *Reds* (1981) and *Bulworth* (1998)—about radicalism, race, and class inequalities that no other major star would have touched. "My political conduct has changed," he told a reporter in May 1998. "I now think of myself as a person who deals in mass media.... [Y]ou can say things in a movie. You can say black people are treated badly in the United States.... You can say rich people control politics. It's an oversimplification but it needs to be said."[2]

Disgusted with President Bill Clinton's shift to the right and disappointed by the unwillingness of Al Gore and Bill Bradley to move out of the middle, Beatty considered running for president in 2000 with the goal of forcing the party to restore a New Deal–like government that would create universal health care, rebuild public schools, limit campaign contributions by corporations, and address problems of racial inequality and disparities in wealth. "We don't need a third party," he repeatedly told political gatherings, "we need a second party."[3]

POLITICS, ACTING, LOVE

Few movie stars grew up as immersed in politics as Warren Beatty. At the age of six, he wanted to be president; at seven, governor of Virginia; and at nine, an actor. Born in Richmond, Virginia, on March 30, 1937, to high-school principal Ira Beaty and drama teacher Kathlyn (Tat) MacLean Beaty, Henry Warren Beaty (he would later spell it with two t's) grew up listening to stories about George Washington, Thomas Jefferson, and an earlier Warren Beaty who spied for the Confederate Secret Service. "There was a historic element to my childhood," he recounted, "that propelled me to certain interests in politics."[4]

Like George Murphy and Ronald Reagan, Beatty was raised in a Democratic household that admired Franklin Roosevelt and his New Deal. "I was brought up to believe that Republicans were the party of the rich and the Democrats were the party of the people." By 1948, the eleven-year-old boy found himself caught up in the drama of the Harry Truman–Thomas Dewey campaign. "I stayed up late at night listening to my tiny Westinghouse radio," he recollected. "I heard Harry Truman come to the floor of the convention after the Dixiecrats tried to disrupt things. I remember very clearly the excitement I felt when Harry Truman came into the convention and said 'We're going to beat the Republicans and make them like it!'"[5]

The parallels between Reagan and Beatty also extended to troubled relations with alcoholic fathers. Like John Reagan, Ira Beaty, a failed violinist, failed Ph.D. candidate, and failed educator, began binge-drinking out of frustration, causing a rift between father and son. Warren's mother, a former speech and drama teacher at Maryland College for Women, directed local theatricals and encouraged him and his older sister, Shirley, to participate in the arts. Shirley developed a passion for theater and would later win an Oscar, acting under a variant of her mother's maiden name, MacLaine. Warren made his acting debut at age five and performed in many of his mother's plays. He also proved to be a talented pianist, entertaining friends and family by age twelve.

When the Supreme Court rendered its *Brown v. Board of Education* decision in 1954, the seventeen-year-old high school student found himself caught up in the beginnings of desegregation. "By that time," he explained, "I was interested in politics as something more than horse races, personalities, crowds, rhetoric and drama." Warren was also a typical teenager, thinking about girls, sports, music, and "mostly about myself."[6] Joining his high-school football team in ninth grade, the 6' 1," 185-pound center garnered ten football scholarships by his senior year along with the attention of many older female students. Tired of sports, he gave up football in favor of studying acting at Northwestern University, Charlton Heston's alma mater. Beatty may well have been influenced by his sister, Shirley, who made her Broadway debut in the chorus of *Oklahoma* and soon was starring in her first feature film, *The Trouble with Harry* (1955).

Bored with college, Beatty dropped out after his freshman year and moved to New York City in the summer of 1956, where he worked in construction on the Lincoln Tunnel. His goal was to be accepted into Stella Adler's prestigious Studio of Acting—an ambition he achieved that October after charming Adler, who, having recently mentored Marlon Brando, adopted Beatty as her latest protégé. Moving into a $13-a-week room in an Upper West Side boarding house, Beatty supported himself by playing piano and singing at a nightclub on East Fifty-eighth Street. Wanting to make it on his own, he never told anyone that his sister was Shirley MacLaine, who became even more famous after the success of *Around the World in 80 Days* (1956).

His time with Adler marked a new phase in Beatty's political evolution. An accomplished actress, Adler had worked with the famed Group Theatre, a left organization that mentored emerging radical artists of the 1930s and 1940s such as Elia Kazan, John Garfield, and Clifford Odets. Talking politics with Adler and his new colleagues, Beatty felt the latent political feelings of his youth slowly come to fruition. "The Blacklist and McCarthyism entered our lives. I began to get kind of serious, and I moved to the left." Political awakening aside, the youthful actor found himself caught up in the excitement of New York and new career possibilities. "You should never underestimate the narcissism of people who are going into the theater," he explained.[7]

Beatty's first break came in March 1957, when he appeared on CBS's Sunday morning religious program *Lamp unto My Feet*. Hoping for a feature career, he headed to Los Angeles in May 1959. The only role he landed was playing a vain, rich high-school student in the popular television series *The Many Loves of Dobie Gillis.*

Returning to New York, the actor's career took off in the fall of 1959, when playwright William Inge cast him as the lead in his new Broadway production *A Loss of Roses.* Although the play did not do well financially, Beatty received rave reviews and an offer by director Elia Kazan to star with Natalie Wood in *Splendor in the Grass.* This proved a turning point for Beatty as an actor and future director. During the 1940s and 1950s, Kazan reigned as a towering figure of American stage and screen, directing Broadway plays and politically conscious films. The co-creator of the Actors Studio was also one of the most controversial figures of his time. When called to testify before the House Un-American Activities Committee (HUAC) in 1952, the disillusioned former Communist chose to name over a dozen people. Former friends and colleagues denounced him as a collaborator and argued that he could have kept silent, been blacklisted, and still earned a living directing theater in New York. The left community was especially angered when the director took out a full-page advertisement in the *New York Times* aggressively defending his decision to testify.[8]

Beatty considered the director an important mentor, but he remained troubled by Kazan's decision to testify. On the fourth day of shooting *Splendor,* he recounted, "We had a three hour conversation about it [HUAC] that I instigated. By the end of the three hours, I felt that it was very respectful of him to have spent the time."[9] Whatever their political differences, Beatty remained loyal to his mentor, even during protests at the 1999 Academy Awards over Kazan's being awarded an honorary Oscar.

Filming on *Splendor* began in April 1960 and by the time it opened in October 1961, Beatty was a rising star with several movie offers in hand. *Life* magazine hailed him as the "biggest new name in American entertainment," while the London *Daily Mirror* called the "handsome, moody, cocky, highly-talented extrovert," a "kind of Marlon Brando without the mumble."[10] Two months later, Beatty starred as a gigolo opposite Vivien Leigh in *The Roman Spring of Mrs. Stone* (1961), and followed that with *All Fall Down* (1962) and *Lilith* (1964).

During these years, Beatty received as much attention for his sexual activities as for his cinematic prowess. As Woody Allen quipped, "If I come back in another life, I want to be Warren Beatty's fingertips." Like Hugh Hefner and his pathbreaking *Playboy* magazine, Beatty showed men how to embrace sexuality free from the restrictive puritanical values of the 1950s and early 1960s. His reputation as a seducer misrepresented his relationship with women and detracted from his perceived intelligence. Women seemed to love Beatty and did not hold it against him that he had other lovers. His ability to make them feel they were really being listened to attracted a wide range of lovers who also appreciated his intelligence, seductiveness, and discretion. Columnists showed no such tact and eagerly publicized the young star's affairs with a bevy of beautiful actresses such as Diane Lane, Jane Fonda, Joan Collins (to whom he was engaged), Natalie Wood (who caused the breakup of his engagement), Leslie Caron, Brigitte Bardot, Faye Dunaway, Inger Stevens, Princess Margaret, Lee Radziwill, Candice Bergen, and Julie Christie (to whom he proposed).[11]

Beatty's supreme self-confidence and persistent refusal to discuss his private life earned him the enmity of gossip columnist Hedda Hopper who denounced him as "the latest incumbent in the line of arrogant, attractive, hostile, moody, sensitive, self-conscious, bright, defensive, ambitious, stuttering, self-seeking and extremely talented actors who become myths before they are thirty." That said, Hopper also declared him "the sexiest guy I ever met."[12]

Beatty's reputation as a "difficult" star grew when he turned down the lead role in *PT 109*, the film version of President John F. Kennedy's World War II experiences. After receiving bad reviews for *The Roman Spring of Mrs. Stone*, the young actor grew extremely cautious in his choice of projects and rejected seventy-five scripts over the next two years, including a personal request by Kennedy to star in the Warner Bros. film. Even a visit by press secretary Pierre Salinger failed to change his mind. "He told me there was nothing he would rather do than portray the President," Salinger recalled, "but he saw no future for the film because the script wasn't very good and it would get worse in the hands of [producer Bryan] Foy." Politics also figured into Beatty's final decision. The left-oriented star was reluctant to work with the conservative Foy, who in 1951 produced Warner Bros.' Red-baiting film *I Was a Communist for the FBI*, a movie the *New York Times* criticized for its "patriotic chest-thumping and reckless 'red' smears," and for implying that "people who embrace liberal causes . . . are Communist dupes."[13] Beatty's fears were well grounded; *PT 109* bombed at the box office.

Never one who liked taking orders from others, especially those he deemed less intelligent, Beatty organized his own production company in

February 1965, Tatira (which combined his mother's nickname, Tat, and his father's first name), to make the kind of films he wanted to do—and take the profits if they succeeded. Seven months after its founding, Beatty starred in Tatira's first coproduction, *Mickey One* (1965). In 1967, after making two films for other companies, the ambitious actor produced and starred in the film that altered the course of a moribund Hollywood and his own career, *Bonnie and Clyde*.

By the mid-1960s, the older men who ran the major studios had lost touch with a younger audience being politicized by urban violence, an increasingly militant civil rights movement, and an unpopular war in Vietnam. Unable to attract teenagers and twentysomethings with old-fashioned fare featuring the likes of Doris Day and Rock Hudson, box-office receipts plunged from $1.7 billion in 1948 to $964 million in 1966. The release of a series of edgy films, starting with *Bonnie and Clyde* and followed by *The Wild Bunch* (1969), *Midnight Cowboy* (1969), and *Easy Rider* (1969), brought baby boomers back into movie theaters. Opening in August 1967, *Bonnie and Clyde* was unlike anything young audiences had seen. Marked by an unprecedented level of graphic violence and sympathy for its antiheroes, Beatty's film follows 1930s Depression-era criminals Clyde Barrow, Bonnie Parker, and their odd gang as they graduate from petty crime to bank robbery to murder, becoming folk heroes in the process. Insisting that banks, not he, were the real criminals, Clyde scolds a Texas Ranger and suggests, "You oughtta be protectin' the rights of poor folks instead of chasin' after the likes of us." In the movie's famous final scene, Bonnie and Clyde die a gruesome but balletic death as police riddle their bodies with hundreds of rounds of bullets.[14]

Much to the consternation of his critics, Beatty updated the usually negative and unattractive image of gangsters to make them appear more glamorous and their violence more acceptable. As figure 8.1 suggests, by casting himself as Clyde and Faye Dunaway as Bonnie, Beatty succeeded in getting young audiences to identify with the good-looking couple as they exchange gunfire with police.

More than just another gangster tale, *Bonnie and Clyde* mirrored the violence and alienation that plagued the nation during the mid-1960s. Several weeks before its release, clashes between police and black residents in Newark and Detroit resulted in twenty-three and forty-three deaths, respectively. As antiwar protesters marched in the streets that summer and greater numbers

FIGURE 8.1 Beatty and Faye Dunaway as the glamorous gangsters in *Bonnie and Clyde* (1967). SOURCE: CINEMA/TV LIBRARY, USC

of Americans criticized the government for its racist and imperialist policies, it is little wonder that *Bonnie and Clyde*'s anti-establishment sentiments attracted large audiences. As one group of young radicals declared, "We are not potential Bonnie and Clydes, we are Bonnie and Clydes."[15]

Bonnie and Clyde marked Beatty's first efforts to express his politics on the screen. "I have an increasing anger toward issues of scope," he told a reporter, "anger mobilizes, and a crucial part of our problem is to get mobilized." Embracing an anti-authoritarian perspective similar to Charlie Chaplin's silent films, his movie evoked sympathy with the plight of ordinary people caught up in a web of circumstances beyond their control. The wayward couple, Beatty explained, "were symptomatic of an economic situation that existed during the Depression—the loss of identity in the formless morass of poverty, and the need for an adopted identity." When movie critic Bosley Crowther denounced the film for being too violent, director Arthur Penn responded, "We're in the Vietnamese War, this film cannot be immaculate and sanitized and bang-bang. It's fucking bloody."[16]

After opening to mixed reviews and modest box-office returns, Beatty persuaded Warners to rerelease it while he traveled around the country promoting the film, sometimes showing up in small towns and entering the projection booth to complain about the sound level or poor quality of the print. After this, his reputation as a control freak grew, as did his bank account. Beatty had agreed to reduce his acting fee in exchange for 40 percent of the box-office gross. The deal proved a windfall for the actor-producer. The movie netted ten Oscar nominations and Beatty earned nearly $13 million by 1971 ($68.8 million in 2009 dollars).[17]

Beatty was now rich enough to do anything he wanted. And what he wanted to do was participate in politics. Characterizing himself as a New Deal Democrat, he supported Lyndon Johnson's Great Society program but broke with the president over Vietnam. "People were dying in Vietnam," he told a reporter. "It was very hard in 1968 to go to a sound stage and find that more interesting than what was happening outside." When New York Senator Robert Kennedy entered the presidential primaries on March 16, 1968, determined "to end the bloodshed in Vietnam and in our cities" and "close the gaps between black and white, rich and poor, young and old," Beatty joined the campaign. Two weeks later, Kennedy's chances of victory skyrocketed when a despondent Johnson announced he would not seek reelection. Beatty hit the campaign trail determined to help Kennedy change domestic and foreign policy. Thousands of starstruck voters turned out to rallies "because he was Warren Beatty," JFK press secretary Pierre Salinger recounted, but they stayed to listen "because he really knew what he was talking about."[18]

When Sirhan Sirhan assassinated Kennedy at a Los Angeles rally on June 5, a heartbroken Beatty, seeing control of the White House as the only way to end the war in Vietnam, threw his support behind Vice President Hubert Humphrey. Even though Humphrey backed the war, Beatty saw Richard Nixon as a far greater threat to a potential peace. In August 1968, still basking in the fame of *Bonnie and Clyde*, he met with Humphrey at the Democratic convention to discuss appearing in the candidate's campaign documentary. With a self-confidence bordering on arrogance, the movie star told the presidential hopeful, "'Absolutely I will, but you have to break with the Administration on Vietnam, which I assume you're going to do.' And he [Humphrey] said, 'Don't worry, that'll be happening within the next week and a half.' And, of course, it didn't happen."[19]

Following Richard Nixon's eventual victory, Beatty left the political arena to shoot *McCabe and Mrs. Miller* with his new love interest, Julie Christie. Angered by Nixon's escalation of the war and broken promise of "Peace with Honor," Beatty returned to electoral politics in what would be one of the greatest supporting roles of his career: part of George McGovern's quest for the nation's highest office.

ON THE CAMPAIGN TRAIL

In the spring of 1971, at the height of his career, Warren Beatty walked away from the screen for eighteen months to work on George McGovern's presidential campaign. Serving as the candidate's communications adviser and chief celebrity wrangler, Beatty emerged as Hollywood's key figure in McGovern's inner circle, the first time a movie star held such a position since George Murphy did so for Dwight Eisenhower in 1952 and 1956.

This period in Beatty's life is unknown to most Americans because, like Harry Belafonte, he understood the importance of keeping public attention focused on the political leader. "In the times when I have been most active and able to matter in some way," Beatty explained, "my participation has been outside the public eye." During the first decade of his career, the press concentrated so much on Beatty's love life, writing about the seemingly endless number of women coming in and out of his penthouse suite at the Beverly Wilshire Hotel, that they often overlooked his sheer intelligence and commitment to political ideals. Indeed, a recent biography suggested that during his notorious bachelor days, Beatty slept with over 12,000 women. Had reporters paid closer attention, they would have noticed that his suite was filled with stacks of political books and magazines such as *The Nation*, *The Progressive*, *Harper's*, and *The New Republic*. McGovern noticed.[20]

The politician and the movie star first met during Robert Kennedy's campaign in 1968 and again in August 1970, when Shirley MacLaine hosted a fundraising dinner at her home. An early underdog who occupied the party's far left wing, the forty-nine-year-old former World War II war hero and onetime history professor faced a crowded field that included former Vice President Hubert Humphrey, Senators Edmund Muskie and Henry "Scoop" Jackson, former senator Eugene McCarthy, Alabama Governor George Wallace, former North Carolina governor Terry Sanford, and Congresswoman Shirley Chisholm, the first woman and the first African American to seek the

Democratic nomination. After finishing a surprisingly close second to Muskie in the Iowa caucuses and New Hampshire primary, McGovern suddenly seemed a viable candidate.[21]

The dramatic changes in party structure that pushed Charlton Heston into the Republican camp in 1972 opened up new opportunities for movie stars to play an unprecedented role in political life, especially at the presidential primary level. In 1968, Democratic Party bosses still exerted tremendous control over the selection of delegates and their presidential nominee. However, between 1968 and 1972, young party activists enacted structural changes in the organization of primaries and selection of convention delegates that put greater power in the hands of ordinary voters. Consequently, a movie star's value, observed reporter Ron Brownstein, "ascended once the candidates were forced to sell themselves directly through primaries to the public, whose affections were more malleable [than party leaders]." This was particularly so in small state primaries "where less than 100,000 people might vote," creating "a field small enough to the stars to play on meaningfully."[22]

Why would Warren Beatty want to work for George McGovern? At the core of Beatty's activism lay a tension between selflessness and selfishness, between commitment and ego that would mark his political life over the next three decades. As clichéd as it may sound, the actor felt a patriotic call to duty. "I believe in the Jeffersonian concept of government, that politics should not necessarily be a profession one goes into, like medicine or law." Beatty also believed that in times of crisis citizens had an obligation to speak what they felt was the truth. By 1971, "I had spent so much time involved in the pursuit of my own affairs, business and so forth, that it seemed very much in order for me to do something less selfish." Defeating President Nixon and ending the war in Vietnam "just seemed more interesting to me. It was about life."[23]

Beatty was certainly no selfless citizen-saint. Aware of the dangers of falling prey to the narcissism that beset many of his peers, he saw politics giving him a sense of balance that movies did not. "I was always aware that serious practical application in politics was in some way therapeutic for me," he observed. "It kept me with ballast in my existence that might have been lost without it, both socially and artistically."[24]

After their initial meeting, Beatty found himself drawn to McGovern's policies, candor, and sense of decency. His charisma, as Norman Mailer aptly put it, "was not of personality but of purpose." In addition to promising an end to the war, the South Dakotan demanded a 37 percent reduction in defense spending, ratification of the Equal Rights Amendment, greater rights for unions, and a guaranteed minimum income for the nation's poor. McGovern was unlike any politician the actor had ever met. Beatty especially admired his call "for the United States to live by its highest principles and ideals rather than engage in power politics and corrupt politics."[25]

The Hollywood activist was also impressed by McGovern's stand on the 50.1 percent debate: Is it better to stand fast behind core principles and risk losing an election, or is it better to compromise with the hope of winning 50.1 percent of the vote, getting into office, and enacting as much change as possible? The senator endorsed the former. "I would rather go down speaking out for what I believe in," he insisted, "than compromise my principles to get elected."[26] This was not politics as usual.

McGovern was equally drawn to Beatty. He felt the charismatic star was "a political realist" who could bring publicity, glamour, and fundraising skills to an uphill campaign in need of all three. "When we started," the candidate explained, "I was at 5 percent in the polls. The big front runners were Muskie and Humphrey. Very few people would have bet more than a dollar that I would win the nomination. I thought the endorsements he could bring in would be helpful. And indeed they were." McGovern spoke of the "ripple effect" that movie stars brought to his campaign. Beatty attracted other stars, he explained, who "in turn attracted public attention, which allowed me to bring my message to a larger public." Having Beatty and his famous friends support his candidacy also energized the daily life of the campaign. "It raised my morale and the morale of our workers, volunteers, and staff people," the self-professed movie fan admitted. "It gave us all a lift to have these celebrities involved."[27]

Ironically, Beatty's close association with the campaign helped the candidate in an unintended way. Critics believed McGovern's friendship with the infamous womanizer harmed his public credibility, but the senator felt quite the opposite. "There was some writing by columnists that I was too good, too decent, too nice to be President. Warren's reputation with women actually helped me by making me more human."[28]

Over the next year and a half, Beatty traveled around the country ringing doorbells, speaking at large public rallies and small private gatherings, recruiting stars, and raising money for the campaign (see fig. 8.2). By

FIGURE 8.2 Beatty campaigning for McGovern in 1972.
SOURCE: PHOTOFEST

spring 1972, *Newsweek* reported that McGovern had "all but cornered the celebrity market" with 252 endorsements as compared to 59 for Humphrey and 125 for Nixon. Beatty was so deeply involved in his political role that he turned down starring roles in *Butch Cassidy and the Sundance Kid*, *The Sting*, *The Way We Were*, *The Great Gatsby*, and *The Godfather*. He was on the road for such long periods of time and so focused on the campaign that it ultimately led to the breakup of his longtime relationship with Julie Christie.[29]

Marked by its youth, McGovern's inner circle included a campaign manager (Gary Hart), who was only four months older than the thirty-four-year-old movie star, and a twenty-one-year-old chief pollster (Pat Caddell) who had not yet graduated from Harvard. The group was leavened by forty-eight-year-old political director Frank Mankiewicz, Senator Bobby Kennedy's former press secretary and the son of screenwriter Herman Mankiewicz.

Meeting for the first time at a Beverly Hills dinner party held several months before the campaign, Beatty and Hart immediately struck up a friendship. The handsome, intellectually minded Hart, who graduated from Bethany Nazarene College and held degrees in divinity and law from Yale, had served as an attorney in the U.S. Departments of Justice and the Interior prior to joining forces with McGovern. Beatty and Hart admired each other's intelligence, passion for politics, and love of movies; they would often be on the phone at 2 A.M. discussing issues, strategies, and their personal lives.

Radical students proved less interested in listening to a movie star's positions on national affairs. After being booed and heckled by University of Wisconsin–Milwaukee students in September 1971, who yelled "What do you have in common with ordinary people?," an unnerved Beatty decided he would be more effective working behind the scenes. Shortly thereafter, he assumed the role of communications adviser and gadfly within McGovern's inner circle, offering advice on social justice, civil rights, workers' rights, and the problems of the poor. Most strategy sessions occurred in Washington, but Beatty had unlimited access to the candidate and senior staff, and he was encouraged to attend meetings when in the nation's capital. Hart considered him the campaign's most eclectic adviser. Stressing the importance of media in politics, Beatty wanted McGovern to spend "all the campaign money to get him on primetime television for half an hour."[30]

Beatty's acknowledged ego emerged when he proved unable to play a greater role in directing the campaign. As a producer and director, he was used to having people follow his commands and found it frustrating "to function in the confines of a national campaign that wouldn't do" what he said. When it came to communications strategy, however, the inner circle did follow his advice. McGovern insisted that Beatty's "main contribution was in helping me present my ideas to a larger public. He knew exactly what I was talking about and he urged me to enunciate it in a more effective way." Just as George Murphy and Robert Montgomery helped Dwight Eisenhower overcome a dull media persona, Beatty schooled the low-key candidate on how to reach an audience more effectively. The actor, Hart reflected, wanted McGovern to be "more dramatic, more emphatic, less droll, less low key, and more energetic." He "had an automatic eye for lighting and camera angles and all the things you would imagine a good director would have. For those of us who didn't understand these things, it was both amazing to see the directorial genius at work but also focusing on things that would never occur to us as important."[31]

Beatty also understood the centrality of ideas and urged McGovern to communicate his antiwar message more aggressively. "Several times he stood me up in front of a microphone and made me deliver lines," the senator explained. "He wanted more force, he wanted more punch lines. He wanted me to look into the mike and declare my ideas more forcefully. He coached me on body language."[32] The movie star also coached him on the importance of using makeup, especially when the candidate appeared pale and worn out after exhausting periods on the road.

Advice is cheap, but campaigns are not. Following a string of victories in Wisconsin, Massachusetts, and Nebraska, the McGovern forces felt confident they could sew up the nomination by defeating chief rival Hubert Humphrey in the upcoming June primaries in California and New York (Governor George Wallace dropped out of the race in May after an assassination attempt left him paralyzed). One problem stood in the way of victory: money. The McGovern campaign was always short of funds, mainly because of the candidate's refusal to accept donations from large corporations. "If you turn down the wealthy to whom you would be beholden," McGovern explained years later, "where else could you get the money?" The answer was Warren Beatty. "He was the single most important celebrity in raising money," McGovern recounted.[33] The actor spent much of late 1971 and early 1972 on the road raising funds for the candidate. As they looked ahead to the critical June 6 California showdown, the financially strapped McGovern forces realized they might have to drop out or greatly scale back their campaign.

Beatty's greatest contribution came on the eve of the California primary when he "invented" the political rock concert. He came up with the ingenious idea of organizing a mid-April political fundraising concert at the 17,000-seat Los Angeles Forum. A campaign favored by the young might save itself by appealing to the young for help. Using his considerable charm and refusing to take no for an answer, he persuaded James Taylor, Carole King, and Barbra Streisand (who had not sung publicly in two years) to perform. He also recruited his extensive array of celebrity friends—Jack Nicholson, Gene Hackman, Shirley MacLaine, Burt Lancaster, James Earl Jones, Goldie Hawn, Julie Christie, and others—to serve as ushers. The show sold out in eighteen hours and raised nearly $300,000. "I wouldn't have won the California primary and then the Democratic nomination," McGovern insisted, "without the efforts of Warren Beatty."[34]

The concert also signaled a new kind of relationship between musicians and politics. "Rock music," observed *Los Angeles Times* music critic Robert Hilburn, "for all its purported cultural and sociological importance in recent years, has remained apart from partisan politics." Musicians participated in voter registration drives, he observed, but not in campaigns. Beatty changed that.[35]

The concert proved so successful that Beatty organized four more—in Lincoln, Nebraska; San Francisco; Cleveland; and New York. The last, held at Madison Square Garden on June 14 and dubbed "Together for McGovern," reunited Simon and Garfunkel, Peter, Paul, and Mary, and Mike Nichols and Elaine May and featured thirty celebrity ushers. The five concerts raised over $1 million and over the next several weeks McGovern scored primary victories in California and four more states, winning enough delegates to secure the Democratic nomination.

That July, as the McGovern forces descended on Miami, they found a party deeply split between an older prowar faction that rallied around former Vice President Hubert Humphrey and a younger, more radical antiwar group that supported McGovern. Once the mainstay of post–World War II liberalism, Humphrey's defense of the Vietnam War put him on the same side as conservatives. Many of his allies drifted even further rightward and became identified with the wing of the party that would emerge as neoconservatives or Nixon Democrats. "These were traditional New Dealers who professed to hold socially progressive viewpoints," Gary Hart explained, "but for whom the confrontation of communism became more important than domestic human needs."[36]

Although hating compromise, Beatty felt that defeating Nixon and ending the war in Vietnam proved more important than ideological purity. He pleaded with McGovern's inner circle to heal the break with the party's more conservative wing by offering the vice presidential slot to Humphrey and reaching out to traditional power brokers such as Chicago Mayor Richard Daley and AFL-CIO President George Meany. Despite his vacillation on the war, Humphrey was still a New Deal liberal who supported the same core beliefs as Beatty: an activist state committed to fighting poverty and promoting civil rights. "I didn't see any point of going through that campaign and not making the tent as big as possible," Beatty reflected years later.[37]

When Ted Kennedy and Walter Mondale turned him down before the convention, McGovern decided to ask Humphrey. Beatty begged him not to do it by phone; it would be too easy for the wounded former vice president to decline such a request. The actor wanted the drama of McGovern addressing the delegates on national television and asking them to choose, while carefully orchestrating a behind-the-scenes "draft Humphrey" campaign. Beatty felt certain that if the delegates asked the Minnesotan to run for the good of the party, he would have done so. He was so determined to effect his plan that, unbeknownst to McGovern, he went to see Humphrey and spent four hours with him, finally getting him to agree that if convention delegates publicly called on him to accept the vice-presidential nomination, he would consent.[38]

Beatty rushed back to tell McGovern the news. Always a gentleman, the senator did not like the idea of using pressure tactics. Instead, he called Humphrey and asked him on the phone. As Beatty expected, Humphrey said no. McGovern then asked Missouri Senator Thomas Eagleton, who accepted. Unfortunately, the McGovern camp had not thoroughly vetted Eagleton. When it was revealed several days after the convention that his running mate had been hospitalized and given electric shock treatment for depression, Eagleton resigned and was replaced on the ticket by former Peace Corps director and Kennedy brother-in-law Sargent Shriver.

The November 7 election proved disastrous for Democrats. Deriding his opponent as the candidate of "Amnesty, Acid, and Abortion," Nixon won 61 percent of the popular vote and all the electoral votes save for Massachusetts and the District of Columbia (520–17). Beatty and the inner circle knew how to sell their candidate to young, antiwar, progressive Democrats. But they did not how to sell his platform of anti-imperialism, antiracism, profeminism, prochoice, and pro–gay rights to culturally conservative voters who found McGovern too radical. Nor did they know how to counter Nixon's accusations that his opponent was soft on Communism. McGovern proved unable to hold on to the traditional base of old New Deal coalition, white ethnics (Irish, Italians, and Jews), Southern whites, and labor unions, a coalition that began crumbling in the mid-1960s when debates over civil rights and the war in Vietnam drove many Democrats into the Republican camp.[39]

Despite his disappointment, McGovern walked away from the campaign impressed by his Hollywood friend. "His ideas were shrewd and his advice valuable," he told a reporter in May 1974. "He has a political maturity astounding for someone so inexperienced, the instincts of a man who has spent a lifetime in politics." McGovern was not the only one impressed by the movie star's political acumen. Less than a year after the election, a private opinion poll placed Beatty's name at the top of a list of potential candidates to succeed Ronald Reagan as governor of California.[40] The actor, however, decided to pursue his politics by returning to the screen.

Politicizing the Screen

"Warren couldn't stand Nixon," George McGovern bluntly declared.[41] Yet, there he was, a photograph of his smiling face hanging on the wall while a banner proclaiming "NIXON'S THE ONE" spread across the room of a 1968 election night party. Far from being an homage, the scene in Beatty's 1975 production, *Shampoo*, mocks the hypocrisy of the new president and his vice president Spiro Agnew. Hoping to accomplish on the screen what he could not do in the electoral arena, Warren Beatty returned to Hollywood with an eye toward reshaping the ways in which millions of Americans thought about a wide range of issues. Between 1974 and 1981, the highly selective star made only five films, three of which contained explicitly political themes: *The Parallax View* (1974), *Shampoo* (1975), and *Reds* (1981).

A perfectionist who reshot the same scene dozens and dozens of times until it was right, Beatty simply could not stand the uncontrollable nature of electoral politics. Consequently, rather than run for governor, he turned to an arena in which he could exercise far greater control. "Movies are more fulfilling than politics," he told a reporter in May 1974. "I can say what I have to say in films. In politics, I feel that compromise keeps you from it."[42]

Shot in the summer of 1973 during the Watergate hearings but not released until June 1974, *The Parallax View* is a cinematic exercise in political conspiracy and paranoia. Beatty teamed up with director Alan Pakula, fresh from his recent success with *Klute*, to make a film that asked viewers to think about "this strange secret society that America had become." One of several films to explore political surveillance and extralegal government activities during the 1970s, *The Parallax View* opens with presidential hopeful Senator Charles Carroll attending a Fourth of July celebration at a Seattle restaurant. In a scene right out of the assassination of Robert Kennedy, we see a "waiter" shoot Carroll dead, just as Sirhan Sirhan shot Kennedy. Unlike the real event at Los Angeles' Ambassador Hotel, we spot a second gunman, also dressed in a waiter's uniform, standing in the wings unseen by all except the movie audience. The film cuts to a scene in which a Warren Commission–like tribunal announces that after several months of investigation they have concluded that a single psychotic gunman assassinated Senator Carroll. They insist there was nothing political about the killing nor was there any evidence of a wider conspiracy.[43]

Taking the panel at their word, investigative reporter Joe Frady (Beatty) is skeptical when three years later his ex-girlfriend, newscaster Lee Carter (Paula Prentiss), informs him that six of the people at the reception have died in "some kind of accident." When Carter is killed, Frady begins an investigation and eventually infiltrates the Parallax Corporation, a secretive organization that hires out assassins to eliminate troublesome politicians and corporate leaders. The reporter foils Parallax's efforts to kill another presidential hopeful, Senator George Hammond. But Parallax sets Frady up to take the blame for a second successful attempt on Hammond's life. The film ends with the reporter's death and the appearance of a government tribunal that concludes Frady killed Hammond; they assure the public there was no evidence of any larger conspiracy.

The message of this dark political thriller is that the good guys rarely win. Frank Capra's 1930s world where Mr. Smith can go to Washington to achieve justice no longer held sway in the Nixonian world of political duplicity. *Parallax View*'s politics are broadly anti-authoritarian rather than pointedly partisan. Beatty and the filmmakers ask viewers to question the honesty of our government and the extraordinary power exercised by those hidden in the shadows of political life. The problem with contemporary politics was not just a few corrupt individuals but a compromised system. Given the imbalance of power between ruled and rulers, the film suggests that citizens must be constantly vigilant and question everything the government tells them. As *Newsweek*'s film critic lamented, our nation "has refused to pursue its political killers for fear of finding that they are not peripheral pariahs but are intimately connected to us and our way of life."[44]

Beatty followed *Parallax View* by using the screen to settle a score with the man he loathed more than any other politician, Richard Nixon. Political films come in all forms; some are explicitly ideological, others less so. *Shampoo* occupied the latter end of this spectrum. As Beatty explained to an interviewer in July 1975, "It is difficult to make a film that *doesn't* have political implications, either by omission or commission. A Disney cartoon has political implications—but whether it moves to the level of propaganda or not is another question. *Shampoo* does relate very much to apathy on the part of a certain stratum of affluence, although it is not as overtly political as films like *The Parallax View* or *The Battle of Algiers*."[45]

Shot between June and August 1974, as President Richard Nixon prepared to resign from office rather than face impeachment, *Shampoo* is a satire that mocks the sexual and political double standards of the time. Having put up $1 million of the film's initial $5 million budget, as well as cowriting and starring in it, Beatty exercised final say over all aspects of the production, from script to final cut to promotion. "Politics is constant compromise," he explained. "Art should never be." The film is set on the eve, day, and day after the November 1968 presidential election, the moment, Beatty explained, "when this country came face to face with the hypocrisies that *Shampoo* represents—the day we turned to each other and realized that we had elected Richard Nixon and Spiro Agnew as his number two."[46]

Released in March 1975, *Shampoo*'s plot revolves around Beverly Hills hairstylist and sexual adventurer George Roundy (Beatty). Beatty offers a portrait of a world filled with sexual hypocrisy: George lives with Jill (Goldie Hawn), whose best friend Jackie (Julie Christie) is having an affair with wealthy Republican businessman Lester (Jack Warden), who is married to Felicia (Lee Grant), who is having an affair with George. Despite their own duplicity, everyone gets enraged when they discover that their significant other is sleeping with someone else. This sexual merry-go-round asks viewers: In a world where everyone cheats, why should we expect Nixon to be any different?

The first explicit political reference comes twenty minutes into the film when Lester asks George to take his mistress to an Election Night party at a swank Beverly Hills restaurant. Gathered to watch the returns, no one pays attention to what is happening; politics is just part of the background, white noise for these rich Republicans. Beatty makes his most pointed yet subtle political comments in these quiet spaces. The camera cuts to the television screen and we hear Spiro Agnew declare, "Exactly what can a President do to affect the moral code of a country? The President can end the permissive attitude of an individual who decides for himself when to obey or break the law." This sounds great for the gathered faithful, but moviegoers knew that by the time the film was released the vice president had resigned from office in the face of criminal charges of extortion, tax fraud, bribery, and conspiracy. So much for obeying the law. Nixon, also gone from office by the film's release, is shown telling citizens, "We are restoring respect for the United States of America. Under our administration, the American flag will not be a doormat for anybody."

The next morning, Lester goes to George's apartment and accuses him of having an affair with his wife. They stop talking to watch Nixon on TV pledging "to bring the American people together. This will be an open administration, open to critics as well as those who support us. We want to bridge the generation gap." Lester listens and then responds, "God damn Lyndon Johnson. Maybe Nixon will be better. What's the difference; they're all a bunch of jerks. I wouldn't let 'em run my business, I can tell you that." A despondent Lester then confesses to George: "I don't know what's right or wrong anymore."

This is a Beatty moment, one where hypocrisy and confusion are clearly laid out for audiences. In Lester's world, as well as George's, no one sees themselves at fault. Beatty's aim is not to critique the so-called permissiveness of the sexual revolution but rather to critique the hypocrisy of Nixon and those like him who mouth platitudes in public while breaking them in private.

The film ends with George standing alone on a hillside watching Jackie, who has just turned down his marriage proposal, drive off in a Rolls-Royce with Lester. Money has trumped love. Despite its often clichéd characters, Beatty insisted that *Shampoo* was "not a frivolous movie. It's a movie about frivolous people, and not only exists as a comedy of manners, but there's also a rather sad undercurrent." That sadness comes out in the film's implicit critique of an apolitical generation so focused on pleasure that it cannot or will not oppose the larger conservative forces arrayed against them.[47]

Shampoo proved Columbia Pictures' biggest box-office hit ever, grossing over $30 million and earning Beatty between $6 and 8 million. Members of the Academy of Motion Picture Arts and Sciences awarded Lee Grant an Oscar for Best Supporting Actress and also handed out Oscar nominations to Beatty and Robert Towne for Best Original Screenplay.[48]

During the four and a half years between the release of *Shampoo* in March 1975 and the beginning of production on *Reds* in August 1979, Beatty intrigued politicians and the public alike as pundits speculated about whether he would run for office. As the 1976 elections approached, his name was floated as a possible Democratic vice presidential or even presidential candidate. A group of Humphrey supporters approached him about entering several primaries as a stand-in for a Humphrey–Ted Kennedy ticket or, when Kennedy declined to run, a Humphrey–Jerry Brown ticket. With Democrats in disarray and Ronald Reagan proving that a charismatic actor could win elections, Beatty considered putting his name on the ballot in

California, Ohio, and New Jersey; but he ultimately declined. Not all Americans took a potential Beatty candidacy seriously. "The idea of Warren Beatty keeping his options open for '76 insofar as politics is concerned is downright hilarious," a San Antonio woman wrote in *People* magazine. "I was appalled to learn that Beatty spent eight years of his life making *Shampoo*. What a waste! I really wonder what he thinks he could contribute to any office in four years or less."[49]

Given his charm and intelligence, it is hardly surprising that Beatty's political future became a popular topic of speculation. Former girlfriend Leslie Caron conjectured that if you woke Beatty up in the middle of the night, "before his defenses were up," and asked him what he wanted to be, "I think he would say, 'President.'" So why, then, did he refuse to run for office? Hollywood's most notorious seducer enjoyed the role reversal in which he was the one being courted, cajoled, and seduced. Yet Beatty also understood the difference between the skills needed to run for office and those needed to run a government. "I have a reasonable sophistication about politics," he told a reporter in March 1975, "but not about government. And they are two vastly different things." The "problem in this country," he explained, "is that we turn to people to administrate the government who aren't necessarily administrative personalities."[50]

During the course of his political activism, Beatty was continually torn between the call to public service and the desire to maintain control over his privacy. When asked in 1974 and again in 1975 why he would not run for governor or senator, he confessed, "I've been around campaigns a lot, and it's amazing to me—the insults that the candidate takes. I don't think I'm unselfish enough to be willing to weather that kind of crap for that length of time. The criticism never stops. I don't know if I have that kind of . . . generosity."[51]

By 1975 Beatty had established himself as a serious power player in party politics. With Gerald Ford tainted by the Nixon scandals, Beatty emerged as a sought-after figure by presidential hopefuls looking ahead to 1976. His newfound status, however, had less to do with his policy ideas than his success in raising money. The smell of much-needed funds led conservatives like Washington Senator Henry "Scoop" Jackson to meet alone with the star for an hour "to see if our positions on defense are as far apart as they were in the past." While in Washington promoting *Shampoo* in March 1975, Beatty was feted by Senators John Tunney and Alan Cranston and spent time with Ted Kennedy, Walter Mondale, Birch Bayh, Dan Inouye, George McGovern, and liberal

Republican Jacob Javits. Serving as a delegate-at-large to the 1976 Democratic convention, Beatty participated in Jerry Brown's thwarted presidential quest; he also worked with Common Cause, the American Civil Liberties Union, and the United Farm Workers on a variety of progressive issues.[52]

Beatty continued his pattern of alternating between political engagement on and off the screen for the next three decades. "I'm not an actor," the star explained to one biographer, "but a person who sometimes acts." Rumors that the forty-year-old star would run for the California Senate seat held by Alan Cranston were put to rest when he left the political arena in the summer of 1977 to begin production on *Heaven Can Wait*. Following its release in June 1978, the man *Time* magazine dubbed as "Mister Hollywood" turned to making the most politically ambitious film of his career, *Reds*—a three-and-a-half-hour epic that, as Beatty noted, "attempts to reveal for the first time just something of the beginnings of American socialism and American communism."[53]

The idea for *Reds* took hold during a 1969 trip to Moscow, where Beatty became interested in Harvard graduate and radical journalist John Reed, who wrote *Ten Days That Shook the World*, an account of his experiences during the Russian Revolution. Considered a hero by the Soviets, Reed is the only American buried in the Kremlin Wall. The romantic visionary's story intrigued Beatty because it posed a question that plagued him for years: "The abdication of your personal life for a political life and whether it's fruitful, and if it is, how fruitful is it? How much do you have to give up?"[54]

Over the next several years, Beatty spent time at Harvard reading through Reed's papers, interviewing people who knew him, and working on a screenplay, first alone and then with British writer Trevor Griffiths. When Paramount chairman Barry Diller passed on *Reds*, exclaiming, "We're not making a picture about communists. We're not glorifying them," Beatty got a reluctant commitment from Paramount studio president Charlie Bluhdorn. In Hollywood you are only as good as your last hit, and Beatty's last three productions proved box-office gold. *Heaven Can Wait*, the sixth top-grosser of 1978, earned $60 million for Paramount and led them to take a chance on the star's new film. With funding in hand, Beatty began production in August 1979.[55]

Beatty was not just making a movie; he was engaged in a battle for control of the mind's eye—that is, the first image that pops into one's mind when a name or word is mentioned. When it comes to shaping public opinion, movies matter most about the things people know the least. Many Americans got their first glimpse of what a Communist or revolution looked like by watching movies. Whether they thought of these people and their ideas as good or bad might well be determined by what they saw and heard on the screen. By reshaping the ways in which Americans looked at radical politics, Beatty hoped he could reshape the ways they thought about radical politics. Citizens might be willing to consider left ideas if they associated "radical" with Warren Beatty rather with than the usual conservative-generated image of an unattractive, wild-eyed, violent activist. As producer Lawrence Bachmann observed, filmmakers are more likely to change attitudes by appealing to emotions than to intellect. "Documentaries convert the already converted. Fictional films convert the unconverted."[56]

As producer, director, cowriter, and star, Beatty exercised total control in translating his political vision to the screen, often to the consternation of a cast forced to shoot upward of eighty takes to get a scene "Beatty perfect." The director-star began his effort to reshape public opinion by getting audiences to identify with lead characters they found physically attractive. Republicans and independents would go to see *Reds* not because they were interested in John Reed or Communism but because they were drawn to Warren Beatty and his bevy of stars. To make his film as appealing as possible, he cast himself as Reed, Diane Keaton as feminist journalist Louise Bryant, Jack Nicholson as playwright Eugene O'Neill, Maureen Stapleton as anarchist leader Emma Goldman, and Edward Herrmann as the *Masses* magazine editor Max Eastman. To give *Reds* a sense of truth, he also interspersed the testimony of thirty-one "expert witnesses" who discuss the era's larger political context and recount their memories of Reed, Bryant, and their circle.

Keenly aware of the power of the visual, Beatty presents his politics in the popular form of a narrative melodrama filled with action, violence, and romance. As we see in figure 8.3, he made his political points more appealing by setting the love story between Reed and Bryant in the middle of the Russian Revolution. As played by Beatty, Reed is not the crazed radical usually depicted in conservative film. Rather, he is a man who remains calm and idealistic even when surrounded by wartime troops; he is a man who looks beyond the immediate moment toward a brighter future.

Reds's plotline takes us from the couple's initial 1916 meeting in Portland to their life together among the radical intellectuals of Greenwich Village, their journey to Russia on the eve of revolution, the disheartening experiences

FIGURE 8.3 Beatty as John Reed and Diane Keaton as Louise Bryant find themselves in the middle of the Russian Revolution. SOURCE: PHOTOFEST

of early Soviet rule, and, finally, the thirty-two-year-old Reed's untimely death in October 1920. During the course of their tumultuous romance, viewers are introduced to many of the same people who energized Charlie Chaplin during his first visit to Greenwich Village: Eastman, Floyd Dell, Big Bill Haywood, Lincoln Steffens, Margaret Sanger, and Eugene O'Neill. We are privy to their conversations about birth control, poverty, war, syndicalism, revolution, and the importance of reading Marx and Engels. We hear radicals debate the wisdom of the American entry into World War I (a war Reed insists is being fought to enrich wealthy capitalists); once war is declared, we see the Socialist Party split apart over whether to support or oppose the American war effort.

Beatty soon moves us to Russia, where Bryant and Reed have traveled to observe the imminent workers' revolution. He humanizes the causes of the revolution by showing long lines of hungry people hoping to obtain a scrap of food; we see how poverty, despair, and repression drove many previously apolitical Russians to rebel against the czar. We also meet the key people who led the October 1917 revolution—Vladimir Lenin, Leon Trotsky, and Grigory Zinoviev—and listen to their hopes for a better future. When the couple return home after the revolution, they experience the repression of America's first Red Scare, the period between 1919 and 1921 when Constitutional rights were violated and personal liberties trampled as thousands of Socialists and Communists were arrested, jailed, or deported for their political beliefs.

Expelled from the Socialist Party because of his Bolshevik sympathies, Reed helps organize the Communist Labor Party of America and returns to Russia in 1919 as their representative to the Third International meeting of the world's Communist parties (Comintern). Far from idealizing events, Beatty shows the Russian Revolution and its aftermath in all its complexities—its utopian aspirations as well as its repressive realities. We see the arrogant authoritarianism of party leaders and hear Reed denouncing them for killing the true spirit of revolution. Frustrated by the revolution's undemocratic turn, Reed laments, "It's not happening the way we thought it would. It's not happening they way we wanted it to. But it's happening." No other major Hollywood film has ever debated the merits and drawbacks of revolution in such serious fashion.

The film ends with Bryant returning to Russia only to find that her lover has fallen deathly ill. Years of poor health, exacerbated by time spent in a Finnish prison, have left him quite fragile. Reed enters a hospital, with Bryant at his side, and dies.

An explicitly left film made at the height of the Cold War, *Reds* opened to critical acclaim on December 4, 1981. Calling it "one of the most audacious and unexpected political acts in my lifetime," author Kurt Vonnegut praised Beatty's courage in making a movie about Communist sympathizers. "He might as well have gone over Niagara Falls in nothing but his Jockey shorts and a football helmet." The actor smiled when, after a special screening at the White House, Ronald Reagan, whom he first met in 1957, suggested that *Reds* could have used a happier ending. Unexpected praise came from columnist William Buckley Jr., who urged fellow conservatives to see the film. Buckley admired Beatty's frank depiction of Reed's disillusionment "with a despotic and impenetrable Soviet bureaucracy" and added that it would be good to play it "before those full-throated naïfs who march to revolutionary songs even as so many Russians did before experiencing the Gulag."[57]

Reds did relatively well at the box office and for a few weeks in early 1982 reigned as the nation's number-one attraction. Audience reception anticipated the current Red State–Blue State divide, with the film playing well on the coasts and poorly everywhere in between. Pacific Theaters' vice president Robert Selig noted how moviegoers in many cities "did not want a story of an American who is a Communist sympathizer." Despite the cool response in conservative areas, *Reds* went on to make a modest profit, garner twelve Oscar nominations, and win Academy Awards for Best Director and Best Supporting Actress. Beatty became the only Hollywood figure to twice be nominated in four categories in a single year: producer, director, actor, and cowriter (honors he also received for *Heaven Can Wait*). In 2006, *Time* film critic Richard Corliss named *Reds* the top political movie of the 1980s.[58]

Movie fans would have to wait another six years for his next film as Beatty once again returned to the electoral arena.

THE INNER CIRCLE OF PRESIDENTIAL POLITICS

During Gary Hart's presidential bids in 1984 and 1988, Beatty went beyond the roles of fundraising and media advising and entered the candidate's inner circle, discussing policies, going over speeches, and planning strategy on a regular basis. Louis B. Mayer had been a presidential power broker, George Murphy a media strategist, and Charlton Heston an iconic figure to trot out during campaigns. But Beatty operated at the highest political level, advising a candidate on how to win the presidency. And he did this with as little media attention as possible.

The friendship forged in 1972 persisted over the next decade as Beatty helped Hart win election to the Senate in 1974 and reelection in 1980. Beatty and Hart considered each other peers. "I wasn't a Kennedy or a half-generation older Senator," Hart explained. "We were the same age; we had similar family backgrounds and religious backgrounds." Hart stayed with Beatty whenever he was in Los Angeles, a habit he continued during the 1984 and 1988 campaigns, much to the concern of staffers who feared the actor's playboy reputation would besmirch the married politician. His advisers were not wrong. In the Age of Reagan, when "family values" occupied a prominent place in the culture wars, having a presidential candidate staying with the most notorious womanizer in Hollywood was not a good idea—especially when Hart, who had separated from his wife, Lee, several times and was suspected of having numerous affairs, told the press in 1972 that he believed in open marriage. The two men shared a certain naiveté that they could do as they pleased on the sexual front without consequences.[59]

When Hart decided to seek the 1984 Democratic presidential nomination, Beatty, flush from the success of *Reds*, left Hollywood to help him. In November 1982, the young senator was still a relative unknown who barely received 1 percent in the polls, trailing Walter Mondale, John Glenn, and Jesse Jackson. His immediate task was to raise money and visibility, problems Beatty could help solve. Working with Orion Pictures executive Mike Medavoy and Twentieth–Century Fox owner Marvin Davis, Beatty emceed a dinner at the Fox studios that raised $100,000 to jump-start the campaign; several months later, he mounted another event that netted $50,000. On February 17, 1983, Gary Hart officially entered the race.[60]

Beatty proved far more important than just a fundraiser. "What he did was play the role of cardinal, of senior close friend [to Hart]," noted veteran political operative John T. McEvoy, "with an aplomb and effectiveness I've not seen in other presidential campaigns, and I've been in four of them." As with McGovern, Beatty proved most valuable in guiding the candidate's media strategy, gauging the public mood, and working with Hart to shape messages and speeches that would excite voters. "I feel my activism was no more in '84 than in '72," Beatty reflected. "It's just that that people were more onto me and thought of me a little more of a grown up [in '84]." Beatty had in fact deepened his political knowledge by spending time on the board of the Center for National Policy, a Democratic policy think tank created after Reagan's election.[61]

Beatty's motives in helping Hart were both ideological and self-serving. Primarily, he wanted to defeat Reagan and undo the conservative revolution. He and Hart were both committed to reversing what they saw as the disastrous effects of Reagan's laissez-faire policies. At the same time, Beatty loved the idea of having a close friend in the White House and knowing that he helped put him there.

Despite their friendship, the two men clashed over political visions for the future. Hart was trying to remake the Democratic Party in ways Beatty did not always like. Unhappy with Republicans who wanted a return to the pre–New Deal era and with Democrats who never moved past the New Deal, Hart promised "new ideas for a new generation." As he explained, "I was trying to transform the Democratic Party beyond the New Deal, not abandoning it but adapting liberal and progressive policies toward the age of globalization, information, and a whole lot of other revolutions going on." He called for nuclear arms control, curbing defense spending, and reshaping the economy through tax reform. "Warren tried to produce and direct my campaign, for which he was very helpful," Hart noted years later. "He just couldn't write my script because he wanted me to go in a direction I didn't want to pursue. Warren operates on a very much traditional left-right plane and I operate more on a future-past plane. To the degree that he weighed in on ideology, he wanted me to be further left in a traditional sense."[62]

An unrepentant New Dealer, Beatty advocated a return to an activist federal government, particularly on matters of race and poverty. Hart did not disagree with Beatty's ideas, but he found them unpractical for anyone who preferred winning an election to mounting a noble fight. "We were now in the age of Reagan," the senator explained. "Democrats had been tainted as far left as Reagan could do and so you weren't going anywhere in the electorate at large by being far to the left."[63] Hart stood on the other side of the 50.1 percent divide taking a position unlike McGovern's: get elected and then change the system. Beatty, however, pressed for a more principled campaign. Unlike Hart, he could stand on principle because he ultimately had little to lose. No matter what happened in November, he was a movie star who could return to his day job.

Although Beatty continued pushing his friend to the left, his greatest contribution came in schooling Hart on how to convey his ideas to a mass electorate. By 1984, the Oscar winner saw himself not just as a media consultant but also as a skilled producer and director who could transfer his cinematic prowess to the political arena. "A producer," observed writer-director-producer Jon Boorstin, "has to line up many different kinds of people and get them working for a common goal. Warren certainly knew how to put things together."[64] Beatty saw voters as similar to movie audiences and elections as similar to the release of a new film. In both instances, you needed strategies aimed at luring voters/audiences to your side.

In the year before the primaries, the two men spent a great deal of time in Beatty's Mulholland Drive kitchen discussing the best way to present ideas to voters. Beatty urged his friend to be more like the Great Communicator, Ronald Reagan. As Hart recounts, "His main advice was always 'Try to simplify.' He kept saying, 'I don't understand, I don't understand'. I hear him in my sleep saying, 'I don't understand.' He'd say, 'What do you think we ought to do about the economy?' I'd say, 'I think there are four major things.' I'd get to about two or three of them and he would say, 'No, no, no. I don't understand.' And this went on and on and on. He'd ask, 'Why not just cut the defense budget?' 'Well, that hasn't served Democrats very well, so what we need to do is fundamentally reform military institutions. Let me tell you how we'd do that.' I'd get to point number two and Warren would say 'No, no, no, no. Nobody's going to understand that. You got to make it simple. Why not eliminate all these weapons?'"[65]

Beatty understood that Reagan had used the media to transform politics into short sound bites and he wanted Hart to do the same. Any time Hart took longer than fifteen or thirty seconds to answer a question, "Warren would start shaking his head and saying 'I don't understand what you're talking about.' He said it a hundred times. He would not agree to policy prescriptions." Yet Hart thought Beatty was urging him to be too simplistic. "I tried to explain to him that I'd won two senatorial races and made a huge breakthrough in the presidential race so I knew a little bit what I was doing. I don't recall making a major change in policy because of Warren, but he was helpful in getting me to be a little more demonstrative and less cerebral."[66]

As expected, former Vice President Walter Mondale won the Iowa caucus in January 1984, but Hart polled a surprisingly strong 17 percent. Two weeks later, surprise turned to shock as Hart won the New Hampshire primary, defeating the frontrunner 37 percent to 28 percent, with astronaut-turned-Senator John Glenn finishing a distant third at 12 percent. By the third week in March, a Gallup poll had Hart leading Reagan 52 percent to 43 percent. Momentum continued to grow as Hart captured eight caucuses and primaries to Mondale's three. Yet, because Mondale won many larger states, he led in the crucial delegate count. Beatty decided it was time to travel with the candidate and play a greater hands-on role.[67]

Beatty became a pivotal figure in the campaign, advising Hart on speeches and media strategy and generally keeping him calm and focused. Impatient with a politics-as-usual approach, the actor did not think like conventional advisers. "Warren deals in a world of big ideas because he is trying to get big audiences to watch his products," explained Hart speechwriter Mark Green. In "meetings he would sometimes come up with ideas you could call 'Hail Mary' passes, some of which were great and some of which were a little far out." While some advisers were taken aback, Hart always appreciated his advice, even if he did not always act on it. "I always liked to talk to him," the senator reflected years later, "to get a sense of public mood, cultural currents and how they might influence visceral feelings about politics, about leaders, about issues."[68]

Learning from Reagan, Beatty pressed the photogenic candidate to communicate with voters through more television spots. As the campaign headed to the crucial April 3 New York primaries, Hart agreed to do a thirty-minute TV broadcast. A blizzard that night forced the candidate to arrive at the studio late, with only one copy of a speech that was twice as long as time permitted. With airtime approaching, Beatty calmly raced through cutting it as a good director would a script; he kept cutting and rewriting even as Hart was speaking on the air. Afterward, Beatty refused to have his picture taken; he wanted all publicity focused on the political hopeful.[69]

Hart lost New York and though he went on to win eleven primaries to Mondale's seven, he still trailed in the delegate count. Running on a campaign heralding "New Ideas," Hart proved unable to overcome Mondale, who, quoting a line from a popular Wendy's hamburger commercial, repeatedly mocked his rival by asking, "Where's the beef?" Perhaps the candidate had listened too much to his Hollywood friend; Democratic voters were apparently more interested in policy details than Beatty had thought. Mondale eventually captured all the superdelegates and secured the party's nomination that July. Despite his defeat, Hart ran the closest primary campaign since 1972, losing the popular vote to Mondale by a margin of 6,952,912 to 6,504,842.[70]

Beatty's role in the presidential campaign fueled speculation about his political career. "Warren is bright, capable, intelligent, personable, and very knowledgeable in the field of politics on the local as well as the national level," remarked one reporter who asked readers to consider the idea of "Congressman Beatty. Or how about Senator Warren Beatty?" But this was not going to happen. Reluctant to surrender his privacy and knowing that he was ill-equipped to govern, Beatty preferred to remain behind the scenes helping others. When California Supreme Court Justice Rose Bird came under attack by conservatives, Beatty served as keynote speaker at a San Francisco fundraiser in July 1985. Seven months later, he agreed to organized four fundraisers to help Hart speechwriter Mark Green's New York senatorial run.[71]

Continuing his pattern of alternating between filmmaking and political activity, Beatty spent most of 1985 and 1986 developing several movie projects: a biographical portrait of eccentric industrialist Howard Hughes, a remake of the 1939 tearjerker *Love Affair*, a gangster film about mobster Bugsy Siegel, and a live-action production of comic-strip detective Dick

Tracy. He put all these on hold to work with writer-director Elaine May and close friend Dustin Hoffman in an oddball comedy about two dreadful lounge singers who get caught up in a CIA plot to suppress an Islamic revolution in the fictional North African country of Ishtar. Released in May 1987, Ishtar proved an epic flop: the $55 million film grossed only $14.4 million in domestic box office and was widely ridiculed in the press.[72]

Distraught over the death of his father in January 1987, Beatty was in the midst of promoting the ill-fated Ishtar when Gary Hart decided to enter the political arena again. Beatty alternated between spending time in the editing room and traveling to Washington to meet with his friend. "I talked to Warren a lot about it and he encouraged me to run," Hart recollected. "He liked the drama of it and felt that I could possibly make some very dramatic breakthroughs." The drama would revolve around selling Hart's progressive agenda to voters: a massive arms-reduction treaty with the Soviet Union; major reforms in education and health care; a shift in the tax system from income to consumption; new taxes on imported oils; substantial changes in the military; and infrastructure renewal programs that would modernize the nation and create hundreds of thousands of new jobs.[73]

The two friends had remained in close touch since the previous campaign. Beatty even loaned Hart $265,000 to buy 135 acres around his home—named "Troublesome Gulch"—to secure his privacy. In March 1987, an ABC News–Washington Post poll ranked Hart as the top Democratic hopeful. Calling on Pat Caddell to run his polling operations and Beatty to provide media strategy and general advice, the former senator announced his candidacy on April 13, 1987. Beatty's role during the early days of the campaign had less to do with influencing Hart's policies than trying to get him to be more demonstrative and less cerebral in selling ideas. Hart may have been "one of the most intelligent figures of contemporary American politics," as New York Times reporter E. J. Dionne declared. But Beatty believed brains did not always win elections.[74]

Despite his early frontrunner status, Hart's campaign was plagued by missteps from the start. Federal marshals raided his first Los Angeles fundraising event and seized all donations in order to pay off his $1.3 million 1984 campaign debt. Worse yet, when rumors began circulating that he was having a series of extramarital affairs, the candidate challenged the press: "Follow me around. I don't care. I'm serious. If anybody wants to put a tail on me, go ahead. They'll be very bored." The Miami Herald took up the challenge and on May 3 reported that a young woman spent the night at Hart's Capitol Hill home. Several days later, after he denied the charges, the *National Enquirer* ran a picture of twenty-nine-year-old Donna Rice, an aspiring actress and University of South Carolina Phi Beta Kappa, sitting on Hart's lap in a yacht—unforgettably named *Monkey Business*—berthed in a Bimini island harbor. That image would haunt him forever.[75]

When the scandal broke, many supporters defected but Beatty implored him to remain in the race. He and Caddell suggested he hold a press conference, admit his wrongdoings, announce his wife had forgiven him, and then refuse to answer questions about his personal life. The actor was convinced the scandal would blow over. But when Hart learned the *Washington Post* was about to publish more information about his affair with Rice, he admitted his "damn fool mistake" and withdrew from the race on May 8, 1987. Beatty was furious that "sexual McCarthyism" deprived the nation of the only political visionary in the field; he was also angered that instead of focusing on "important public positions on public issues," the press dwelled on the "more accessible soap-opera level of crap."[76]

Unwilling to allow Hart to fade away, Beatty urged him to reenter the race. "If you think you can contribute to public life," he told Hart that summer, "you have an absolute obligation to run despite it being painful." The media, however, continued mocking the candidate and his friend. "For Hart to turn to an unabashed Don Juan like Beatty for advice in a matter involving a sexual indiscretion," quipped *Newsweek*, "seemed a bit like hiring Dom DeLuise as a personal nutritionist." Hart preferred Beatty's advice to *Newsweek*'s and reentered the race in December 1987. Standing on the steps of the New Hampshire statehouse, he told the press, "Let the people decide . . . the voters are not dumb." With wife, Lee, at his side, he added, "We are ready for anything."[77] The announcement was greeted with derision. Unable to garner significant support, Hart once again withdrew. Sex had trumped policy.

With the culture wars at their height, Beatty's association with Hart may have ultimately done more harm than good. Hart's sexual conduct reaffirmed what many conservatives saw as the sharp divide between the values of Hollywood "libertines" and those of "mainstream" America. "The worst thing that ever happened to Gary Hart," remarked Robert Redford, "was getting into 'The Hollywood Set.'" Redford had supported Hart early in 1984, but as rumors of the candidate's affairs mounted, he left the campaign. It was one thing for a bachelor like Beatty to be seen as a womanizer, but quite another for a married man like Hart. The political and sexual hypocrisy that Beatty mocked in *Shampoo* destroyed Hart in 1988.[78]

A disappointed Beatty went on to support Democratic nominee Michael Dukakis, but the Massachusetts governor was not especially interested in Beatty or other Hollywood stars. "It's fun to meet folks you've seen on the screen," Dukakis reflected years later, "but as you get closer to the election, you need to appeal to people who will elect you." Unable to excite the electorate, Dukakis was crushed by George H. W. Bush, who garnered 426 electoral votes to the Democrat's 111. "Gary Hart's tragedy was even greater than Clinton's," lamented his national finance director Andy Spahn, who had worked closely with Jane Fonda and Tom Hayden. "Hart came from progressive politics, Clinton didn't. He was going to be the first of our generation to be elected president. We believed he was better prepared to govern than anyone else on the political landscape. Unfortunately, he was not better prepared to run."[79]

Disappointed, Beatty returned to Hollywood and began preparations on *Dick Tracy* (1990) and *Bugsy* (1991). As he did, he also began planning his most explicit cinematic critique of American politics, *Bulworth*, a film that led many to urge the actor to run for the presidency of the United States.

Bulworth Politics

The day no one thought would ever happen finally happened on March 12, 1992. Warren Beatty got married. Hollywood's most famous bachelor met Annette Bening while casting the female lead for his film about Las Vegas mobster Bugsy Siegel. Lunching at a pizzeria near his home, Beatty claimed he knew within thirty seconds that "she would change my life." Born in Topeka and raised in Wichita and San Diego, Bening came from a conservative, middle-class, churchgoing Republican family. After studying acting at San Francisco State and the American Conservatory Theater, she got her first major feature role in *Valmont* (1989) and her first Oscar nomination for her performance in *The Grifters* (1990). When she met Beatty, she was in the process of divorcing her estranged husband, actor-director Steven White.[80]

Filming on *Bugsy* began in January 1991 and the two soon became a couple. Having an affair was nothing new for the infamous womanizer. But this was different. Beatty was finally ready to become a father. When the couple announced on July 16, 1991, that they were expecting a child together, the *Washington Post* humorously declared it "a watershed moment in the history of American civilization."[81] On January 8, 1992, Annette gave birth to baby girl, Kathlyn, named after Warren's mother; the couple married two months later, just two weeks shy of his fifty-fifth birthday. Two years later, son Benjamin was born; by April 2000, Isabel and Ella had joined the family.

Beatty's delight at being a father did not alleviate his frustration with the state of contemporary politics. As he told Norman Mailer in a November 1991 interview, the "Democratic Party practically doesn't exist with its own set of principles now" but devoted itself to "doing patchwork nonsense, junior-Republican silliness." Sounding like German sociologist Max Weber, Beatty spoke about the need for a charismatic leader who could reinvigorate the party. "We need someone who can come along and truly speak to the people . . . a citizen willing to confront public opinion and enlighten it." He speculated that if "a person were to attack all those hypocrisies out there with short words and, as you say, real emotion, yes, I do believe they would change the dialogue—and they would, of course, lose the election."[82] Seven years later, that person would come along in the form of the fictional Senator Jay Bulworth.

Disturbed by the growing disparity of wealth and what he perceived as the failures of the Clinton administration, Beatty made a black comedy for Twentieth Century Fox that he hoped would get the Democratic Party to stand for something other than winning elections. He wanted nothing less than a paradigm shift in American politics: a rejection of antigovernment policies and a return to an activist state that would promote the interests of citizens over corporations. "In movies you can get people to listen to what you have to say," he explained, "in a way that politics—the art of the possible—doesn't always achieve."[83]

Beatty knew that a studio owned by conservative media mogul Rupert Murdoch would never knowingly approve such a radical film, so he never told them the full story. As far as Fox executives were concerned, the movie was about a politician who hires a hit man to kill him, falls in love, and then tries to call off the hit. "This picture was made in complete stealth," he told *Newsweek*. "The stealthier it got, the healthier I got." Fox had little say in the matter. In exchange for backing out of *Dick Tracy* (which was later produced by Disney), the studio gave the actor-writer-director complete control to do whatever he wanted so long as he remained under a $32 million budget.[84]

Senator Jay Bulworth is a cinematic surrogate for its star, a charismatic leader who speaks the truth no matter what the consequences. Bulworth was what he hoped President Bill Clinton would be. Disappointed he could not move Gary Hart further to the left, Beatty was disgusted by Clinton's shift to the right. Who would have thought that welfare would have ended under a Democratic president or that a Democratic leader would plan to win elections by adopting Republican platforms? "Clinton represents to Warren the epitome of Democrats saying winning comes first, principles come second," explained co-screenwriter Jeremy Pikser.[85]

Shot in 1997, in the midst of the Clinton–Monica Lewinsky scandal, and premiering on May 15, 1998, *Bulworth* is a blistering attack on the vacuity of party politics and the ways in which money has corrupted the political process. It is Beatty's fantasy about the issues he would raise if he were running for office. The film opens in March 1996, as California Senator Jay Bulworth (Beatty) enters the final weekend of his primary reelection campaign. As the credits roll he watches a series of banal campaign ads in which he mouths Clinton-like platitudes, "We stand at the doorstep of a new millennium," and then goes on to make statements denouncing welfare and affirmative action. The camera pans his office and we see photos of him and his earlier heroes: Martin Luther King Jr., Malcolm X, Rosa Parks, Thurgood Marshall, Huey Newton, and Robert Kennedy. Bulworth is in tears and falling apart. He has not slept or eaten for three days. He is disgusted with his betrayal of his earlier liberal values. A meeting with an insurance industry lobbyist confirms that. In return for killing a bill requiring insurance companies to provide affordable policies to the poor, Bulworth gets a $10 million life insurance policy. Senator Bulworth then calls in Vinnie the mobster and arranges for someone to kill him so that his family can collect the money.

In the next scene, Bulworth visits a black church in South Central Los Angeles, while constantly looking around for his assassin. He starts with the usual clichés and then suddenly stops. The prospect of death frees him to speak the truth that many Democrats think but no Democrat would ever say. When an angry parishioner asks why he has not fulfilled his pledge to help rebuild South Central, he smiles and tells her that he, Clinton, and George H. W. Bush told them what they wanted to hear and then after the elections "we pretty much forgot about you." When another woman asks why he has not come out for the pending insurance bill, he responds, "Well, because you really haven't contributed any money to my campaign, have you?" The crowd boos and Bulworth's aides are dumbfounded. When yet another astonished congregant asks, "Are you sayin' the Democratic Party don't care about the African-American community?" Bulworth blithely tells her, "Isn't that obvious? You got half your kids out of work and the other half are in jail. Do you see any Democrat doing anything about it? Certainly not me! So what're you gonna do, vote Republican? Come on! Come on, you're not gonna vote Republican! Let's call a spade a spade! I mean—come on! You can have a Billion Man March! If you don't put down that malt liquor and chicken wings, and get behind someone other than a running back who stabs his wife, you're never gonna get rid of somebody like me!" In the following scene, he chastises wealthy Beverly Hills Jews for caring only about Israel and for making films "that aren't any good."[86]

Instead of doing more campaigning, Bulworth spends the evening with three African American women—among them costar Halle Berry—who take him to a club where they smoke dope and dance the night away. The next morning the energized candidate heads off to give a speech to wealthy donors and lobbyists. He begins with his stock speech—"We stand on the doorstep of a new millennium"—but stops and starts rapping out a song, "Big Money, Big Money." Smiling at the gathered bankers, oil and insurance lobbyists, and HMO representatives, he raps:

> One man one vote
> Now izzat really real?
> The name of our game is
> Let's make a deal.
> Now people got their problems
> The haves and the have-nots.
> But the ones that make me listen
> Pay for 30-second spots! ... [Chorus, "Big Money, Big Money"]
> We got factories closin' down
> Where the hell did all the good jobs go?
> Well. I'll tell you where they went—
> My contributors make more profits
> Hiring kids in Mexico.
> Yo, everybody gonna get sick someday
> But nobody knows how they gonna pay
> Health care, managed care, HMOs

Ain't gonna work, no sir, not those
'Cause the thing that's the same in every one of these
Is these motherfuckers there, the insurance companies!
Yeah, yeah
You can call it single-payer or Canadian way
Only socialized medicine will ever save the day!
Come on now, lemme hear that dirty word—Socialism!

Liberated from politics-as-usual, Bulworth spends time with Nina (Berry), her family, and drug lord L. D. (Don Cheadle) who offer him an African American view of the nation's failures. They explain how the closing of factories and lack of decent jobs has destroyed hope. "How a young man gonna take care of his financial responsibilities workin' at a motherfuckin' Burger King?" L. D. asks. "He ain't." When Nina, who has fallen in love with Bulworth, confesses she is the assassin, he tries to call off the hit. In the meantime, Senator Bulworth continues speaking the truth, no longer caring about elections. He goes on television dressed as a rapper in a cap, sunglasses, orange top, and shorts and tells his interviewers, "Republicans, Democrats, what's the difference. It's a [rich guys'] club." He tells them the idea that corporations are more efficient than government is a myth. "You want to know why the health care industry is the most profitable in the United States? Because the insurance companies take twenty-four cents out of every dollar that's spent. Government takes three cents out of every dollar for Medicare."

When in yet another Election Special newscasters ask about his use of profanity, Bulworth criticizes the TV networks for giving little free time to candidates who criticize corporate America (think George McGovern). Without big money, no candidate can hope to win. Class, not race, is the central issue in American politics; ordinary whites, he insists, have more in common with blacks than they do with rich people.

One of the film's most interesting messages is that Bulworth/Beatty holds citizens responsible for ensuring that democracy works. It is not enough to blame corporate greed or corrupt politicians. We need to ask ourselves: What are we doing to fight back? As he tells L. D. in one of his many raps, "There's a time when every homey / Got to risk his life / For the thing that he believe in / And he got to preach it right."

In addition to his political raps, Beatty delivers his messages with a series of images that flip the usual relationship between black and white, rich and poor, and hip and square. The self-loathing politician in figure 8.4 who is brought to tears by knowing that he has sold out his earlier liberal ideals is transformed by the political and sartorial education he receives from the men, women, and children he meets in South Central Los Angeles. His new rapper's guise (fig. 8.5) frees him from the political clichés he came to loathe. Liberated from politics as usual, he returns to his more traditional suit-and-tie attire, stands before the American flag, and, as we see in figure 8.6, aided by a flask of alcohol, tells the people the truth.

So what happens when a politician finally speaks the truth? Bulworth entered the primaries behind in the polls and headed for defeat. But his blunt talk gains him new admirers and on Election Day an energized electorate gives the truthteller a 71 percent majority. Even more surprising, Bulworth receives a significant number of write-in votes for president: 15 percent of the Democratic vote and 8 percent of the Republican vote. Political pundits across the nation are astounded and one television commentator concludes, "Bulworth Democrats agreed on one thing, that leading is more important than winning." Unfortunately, even though Nina decides

FIGURE 8.4 Beatty as the self-loathing Senator Jay Bulworth. SOURCE: CINEMA/TV LIBRARY, USC

FIGURE 8.5 Senator Bulworth transformed after his stay in South Central Los Angeles.
SOURCE: CINEMA/TV LIBRARY, USC

FIGURE 8.6 Bulworth regains his confidence when he assumes the role of a truthtelling, white-rapper politician.
SOURCE: CINEMA/TV LIBRARY, USC

not to kill her new love, the infuriated insurance lobbyist who gave Bulworth the $10 million policy shoots him dead. America would have to wait for another savior.

Not caring about box-office profits liberated Beatty to make the starkly polemical film he wanted, one that was generally well received by critics and earned him and Jeremy Pikser an Oscar nomination for best screenplay. The executives at Fox were less thrilled. Distributed by a company whose head, Rupert Murdoch, was an arch-conservative, Beatty insisted that Fox never knew "what to make of the movie, in that it has an underlying theme that is anticorporate, that the greatest danger to democracy is big corporations." The studio tried to bury the film by opening it against projected blockbuster *Godzilla*. "I had complete artistic control," Beatty explained, "but no marketing control at all." Here was a rare instance when studio politics trumped box-office concerns. *Bulworth* opened to $10.5 million business in the first week, but by the end of 1998, the poorly distributed production grossed only $26.5 million; it would take several more years to break into the black.[87]

Despite Fox's hostility, Beatty used his publicity tour to promote *Bulworth*'s critiques of campaign finance reform, class inequities, and the failures of the Democratic Party. As he told a March 1999 symposium on Hollywood and politics, "It takes money to be heard. The underbelly of this country isn't being heard . . . and the disparity of wealth does not decrease, it increases. My beliefs—even though I am a pampered, rich Hollywood cultural plutocrat—are to articulate something on behalf of those people." The outspoken actor saved his greatest scorn for the Democratic National Committee, which he accused of becoming the "Republican Party Lite." Beatty's desire for campaign finance reform led to a friendship with Republican Senator John McCain, who was then committed to the same goal. Their mutual bond even led both families to spend time together.[88]

As the 2000 presidential primaries approached, Beatty sarcastically characterized party frontrunners Al Gore and Bill Bradley as "good decent liberal Republicans." The movie star still considered himself a Democrat, but he was now a "Bulworth Democrat." That declaration proved good enough for another Bulworth Democrat, recently converted former Republican Arianna Huffington. In an August 10, 1999, *Los Angeles Times* column, "Put 'Bulworth' in the White House?," she floated the idea of Beatty running an outsider's campaign in much the same way as Ross Perot and Jesse Ventura had done several years earlier. "If indeed we need a Bulworth," she told readers, "there is no better Bulworth, some say, than Bulworth himself: Warren Beatty." Journalist and former LBJ White House Press Secretary Bill Moyers endorsed her sentiments. As he told Huffington, "It took an actor to dramatize for conservatives the ideas that changed politics in the early '80s. Perhaps another actor can help all Americans see how private money is overwhelming public life. If Warren can speak the truth to power on the stump as well as he did in *Bulworth*, he can change politics, too."[89]

Intrigued by Huffington's column, Beatty quickly assembled an inner circle capable of running a campaign aimed at sparking a national debate about the role of government in people's lives. Reaching out to friends like pollster Pat Caddell, he also discussed matters with a number of left-leaning politicos: Steve Cobble, former political director of the Rainbow Coalition; Robert Borosage, who worked for progressive advocacy groups; Ellen Miller, who headed the Public Campaign, a Washington-based group working to change campaign finance laws; and Bill Hillsman, who created the ads that helped elect wrestler-turned-Governor Jesse "the Body" Ventura.[90]

Beatty came away from the meetings convinced he could capture the public's imagination. Learning from Gary Hart, he immediately identified the "meat" of his platform: campaign finance reform. This was the one issue that could drive all other reforms. Only by undermining the power businesses and corporations exercised over politicians in both parties could progressives hope to revive democracy. Articulating the same issues as Jay Bulworth, Beatty called for universal health care and policies aimed at lifting 35 million Americans out of poverty.

As Beatty expected, media outlets were soon filled with stories about his potential presidential bid. The would-he-or-wouldn't-he speculation reached a fevered pitch on a warm Wednesday evening in September 1999, when he accepted the Eleanor Roosevelt Award at the annual Southern California Americans for Democratic Action (ADA) dinner. The assembled horde was hoping to hear him declare his intention to run for the presidency. Shortly after 9 P.M., Beatty walked to the stage and began speaking in an unusually quiet voice and slumping body. Veteran *Los Angeles Times* political reporter Ronald Brownstein suggested that Beatty was "nervous at first." He was wrong. It was all an act, perfectly scripted and choreographed by a master performer. He was working the crowd. Speaking in a soft voice meant people had to pay closer attention to his words.[91]

Ten minutes into his speech, Beatty pulled himself up to his full 6' 1" and, adopting a populist rhetoric aimed at raising audience emotions, spoke about the rampant alienation in American society. He called for citizens to rise up and demand their rights—their rights to health care, to a decent standard of living, and to an activist government that would protect all Americans. Yet none of these reforms would happen until Congress initiated campaign finance reforms. "The primary cancer in this sick system," he insisted, "the big money in politics, has so metastasized into every area of government that we can't afford any longer to ignore that the life of the patient, American democracy, is in mortal danger of expiring." He urged Congress to enact a $3.50 tax per person to finance all campaigns and then eliminate other forms of outside financing. Noting that candidates from both parties raised money from the same corrupt sources, Beatty told the audience, "We don't need a third party. We need a second party."[92]

Beatty left the podium to enthusiastic applause and disappointment that he had not declared his intentions. But the potential candidate was far from disappointed. A master of the dramatic, Beatty's reluctance to declare his intentions was strategic; so long as he was a potential presidential candidate, he could attract the national bully pulpit that he would never get as an actor. "Because of Warren," explained delighted ADA president Lila Garrett, "the liberal agenda is suddenly warming up!" The African American press praised him for being the only Democrat willing to talk about the "negative effect of the prison industrial complex, privatization of prisons and welfare, child poverty rates, universal health care, and the disparity in our prosperity."[93]

Over the next several weeks, the potential candidate continued to draw national attention. Speaking at Harvard University, he teasingly suggested that he might run in a select number of primaries. When asked by a CNN/USA Today/Gallup poll of October 8–10, 1999, whether they would view Beatty as a serious candidate if he decided to run for president, 13 percent responded "Yes." While certainly a low figure, it was higher than the initial polling figures for McGovern in 1972 and Hart in 1984. A Beatty candidacy was no more far-fetched than that of Republican hopefuls Steve Forbes, Elizabeth Dole, Gary Bauer, and Pat Buchanan—four of the five top finishers in the GOP Iowa straw poll, none of whom had ever been elected to office. The Reform Party, which helped long-shot Jesse Ventura win the Minnesota governorship in 1998, thought well enough of Beatty's chances to court him as its possible presidential nominee.[94]

While winning the Democratic nomination was implausible, a campaign aimed at pushing the party and its candidates further leftward was possible. Anthony York, writing in Salon.com, noted how religious leader Pat Robertson's 1988 presidential bid galvanized religious conservatives and sparked the creation of the Christian Coalition. Beatty hoped he could reinvigorate the Democrats in a similar way.

But Beatty never took the challenge to pursue the greatest role of a lifetime: as leader of the free world. On January 3, 2000, he announced that he would not run for office. This was the moment when he could have said and done all the things he urged Gary Hart to do. Yet few of those who knew the actor thought he would run. First and foremost, he was a perfectionist who could not make the quick decisions required of the chief executive. Anyone who agonized over getting a movie scene right, and forced his crew to shoot dozens of takes, was not someone who could operate in a high-pressured world where immediate, potentially life-altering judgments were needed.

Beatty was also reluctant to relinquish the privacy he so craved. As a movie star, he could decline to answer questions and refuse to appear in public. But as a politician, he would have to answer questions, take abuse, and keep smiling. The first thing candidate Beatty would have to learn, Arianna Huffington observed, is "to get comfortable with ridicule. It's not clear that Beatty is willing to do that." The actor was also unwilling to give up his family life. "Had I not had three children and a fourth on the way," he wistfully reflected, "it could have been very interesting to go to New Hampshire and get a surprising percentage of the vote."[95]

Finally, as Beatty had remarked many times in the past, he ultimately did not want to govern. He did not want to give up his privileged life to battle with legislators. As producer Jon Boorstin observed, "If you're a struggling senator and become president your life gets better. If you're a movie star it gets worse."[96]

Although many were disappointed, Beatty withdrew feeling he had accomplished what he set out to do. "Celebrity and fame are part of an actor's capital; you can use it to speak out, but you also need to be extremely judicious as to how you use it and steadfastly avoid abusing it," he reasoned. "I thought it would be good to have these things said by someone who could attract a lot of attention." Yet knowing he would not seek the presidency, he refused to enter the primaries just to make a point. "If you think that you are going to run for an office, you should run for an office."[97]

Unwilling to support Democratic nominee Al Gore, Beatty endorsed Green Party hopeful Ralph Nader. This decision raises a question about Beatty's seeming lifelong vacillation between compromise and principle. He was willing to compromise by supporting Hubert Humphrey in 1968, despite the latter's prowar stance, yet he stood on principle when he refused to support Gore or Bradley in 2000. Did this signal a transformation in his politics? Not really. Like Charlton Heston, Beatty insisted he had remained consistent over the years; it was the party that changed. As he told one group in November 1999, "I'm whatever a liberal from the '60s should have turned into by now."[98] Compromising to defeat Nixon in 1972 was worth it because Humphrey was a New Deal liberal. By 2000, the Democratic Party no longer represented those earlier ideals. Beatty was unwilling to compromise because he saw the men he would compromise for—Gore or Bradley—as liberal Republicans rather than progressive Democrats.

In the end, the movie star was unwilling to risk the unknown. Nevertheless, he succeeded in keeping the idea of a left-liberal Democratic Party alive in the public imagination if not at the ballot box. The attention his potential candidacy received, observed political consultant Marge Tabankin, "showed what a hunger there was for someone a little bit outside the box of the Beltway."[99] No candidate wanted to tell the truth; no candidate wanted to be a Bulworth, not even Warren Beatty.

LOOKING BACKWARD, MOVING FORWARD

On June 12, 2008, the American Film Institute honored the longtime star with its Thirty-sixth AFI Life Achievement Award, the "one foot in the grave award," quipped Dustin Hoffman. The usual array of Hollywood celebrities took the stage at the Kodak Theatre to pay tribute, including Hoffman, Jane Fonda, Jack Nicholson, Diane Keaton, Al Pacino, Shirley MacLaine, Don Cheadle, and Halle Berry; Barbra Streisand and Gene Hackman appeared in prerecorded segments.[100]

The presence of so many Hollywood A-listers was not surprising. Far more remarkable was the appearance of four former presidential candidates and one former president: George McGovern, Gary Hart, Jerry Brown, John McCain, and Bill Clinton—four Democrats and one Republican. Each paid tribute to their friend's political work. Hart thanked Beatty for his "personal generosity to me," while McGovern facetiously remarked that "Richard Nixon would have been much better off if we'd been elected" in 1972. Although Fox News dubbed the evening the "Hollywood Left-Fest," Republican John McCain told the gathering that he respected Beatty not just "as a filmmaker or as an actor, but as an involved, intelligent and politically active citizen. Although Warren and I are clearly of different political parties, I admire him for what he truly believes." The evening's star presenter, Bill Clinton, recounted how Beatty helped him swing the 1972 Arkansas delegation to McGovern. Warren was "the reason we won on the first ballot."

After nearly two hours of praise and ribbing, it was time for the honoree to receive his award. As he walked to the Kodak stage, the orchestra paid homage to Beatty's dual role as actor and activist by playing the Communist anthem, "The Internationale," the theme song from *Reds*. After thanking the AFI and his many gathered friends, Beatty ended his speech by declaring, "I am still an old-time, unrepentant, unreconstructed, tax-and-spend, bleeding-heart, die-hard liberal Democrat. I was a liberal when it was fashionable, I was a liberal when it became unfashionable, and I'm still a liberal when it's coming back in style." As he stepped off the stage to a thunderous round of applause, AFI ushers handed out red, white, and blue buttons reading, "WARREN BEATTY FOR PRESIDENT."

Assessing legacies is usually reserved for those who are dead or past their prime, and Beatty is decidedly neither. After 1999, his name frequently surfaced as a possible California gubernatorial candidate, someone with enough cinematic heft and political savvy to challenge Arnold Schwarzenegger, a politician he criticized for pursuing a "reactionary right-wing agenda."[101]

Any movie star, left or right, willing to risk his or her career to engage in the political life of the nation is worthy of admiration. The most committed true believers became movement activists, a sacrifice Beatty was ultimately unwilling to make. George Murphy, Ronald Reagan, Harry Belafonte, and Jane Fonda all spent decades fighting for their cause. They did not simply float in and out of campaigns like Beatty, but participated in the daily grind that saps the energy of all but the most resolute. Fonda may have failed in many ways, but she had an important influence on the antiwar and economic justice movements of the 1970s and 1980s, the kind of mass movement influence that Beatty never exerted.

On the cinematic front, all three leftists formed production companies with the goal of putting their politics on the screen. But while Beatty's films reflected his personal politics, Belafonte and Fonda linked their films to the movement struggles in which they engaged. Such comparisons, however, are somewhat inequitable because Beatty was never as radical as Belafonte and Fonda. He did not challenge the state as they did. Rather, he wanted to reform it and restore an activist federal government that would serve the interests of citizens rather than corporations.

Yet, to be fair, leaving the movie industry for the political arena would have entailed a greater sacrifice for Beatty than the other stars. Neither Murphy nor Reagan ever approached Beatty's level of stardom; only Fonda did. By the time the two conservatives turned to politics, they did not have major careers to sacrifice. Moreover, Beatty was a significant filmmaker. Fonda and Belafonte were stars and producers, but Beatty was also a gifted director and screenwriter. As far as Gary Hart is concerned, Beatty had "an important impact on American politics, but more through his films than support for candidates." Indeed, the movies he made from the 1960s through the 1990s represent a notable body of political thought. His films alerted citizens to the dangers of government deception, hypocritical politicians, and rampant political corruption, while also providing an entertaining look at what radical leaders of the past had tried to achieve and what determined men and women might still accomplish.[102]

Beatty's story reveals some of the promises and pitfalls of Hollywood's involvement in American politics. In terms of influencing the course of electoral politics, his closest peer was George Murphy. Both men understood the importance of a politician's image and communication skills and advised presidential hopefuls on how to use the media to their greatest advantage. In 1999 Beatty even contemplated employing that advice to run a different kind of presidential campaign, a "media-dependent campaign" that would, as one reporter noted, rely on the "opportunities presented by the Internet and the proliferation of cable channels and new media."[103]

Ironically, Arnold Schwarzenegger adopted that approach in the 2003 California gubernatorial recall election. Not only did he employ the kind of media strategy Beatty contemplated, he also followed the advice Beatty gave Gary Hart: reduce longwinded policy statements into short dramatic statements that voters would understand. Only in the Republican's case, he showed what could happen if that advice was taken too far: he offered short sound bites that offered populist diatribes against government and humorous references to his films but few substantive policy ideas. Schwarzenegger succeeded in making politics entertaining, but California voters would soon question the costs.

GOVERNOR ARNOLD AND THE AGE OF CELEBRITY POLITICS: ARNOLD SCHWARZENEGGER

The 2003 California recall and gubernatorial election looked like a flashback to the 1960s. An actor with seemingly no political experience was trying to win a major office. Columnists breezily compared Arnold Schwarzenegger to movie-stars-turned-politicians George Murphy and Ronald Reagan. Such comparisons were inaccurate. Murphy and Reagan spent several decades toiling in the political trenches and perfecting their ideological messages before running for office. Arnold, as he liked to be called, was a relative newcomer. Although he campaigned for George H. W. Bush in 1988 and 1992, he had no deep ties to the Republican Party infrastructure. If history was any guide, he should have lost the special election to entrenched party stalwarts such as Republican State Senator Tom McClintock or Democratic Lieutenant Governor Cruz Bustamante.

But Schwarzenegger defied history, and in so doing elevated celebrity politics to unprecedented heights. Throughout the twentieth century, Democrats and Republicans used movie stars to attract crowds to political rallies and bolster the fortunes of party candidates. Schwarzenegger took this a step further and showed that the power of modern celebrity was so great that a movie star could be elected to high office without the benefit of an established party network or precise ideological message. "When you have name recognition like him," noted one NBC executive, "you can go directly to the people."[1]

Schwarzenegger's story reveals how dramatic changes in the entertainment industry transformed American political culture. His electoral success was made possible by the explosion of 24/7 entertainment media—*E!*, *Access Hollywood*, *Entertainment Tonight*, and a slew of gossip magazines, tabloids, and Web sites—that paved the way for a new era of celebrity politics. The Austrian immigrant was not the first political figure to use popular shows to reach voters. John F. Kennedy and Richard Nixon appeared on *The Jack Paar Show* during the 1960 presidential campaign, and Bill Clinton played saxophone on *The Arsenio Hall Show* in 1992. Yet these occasional media appearances were peripheral to the candidates' main focus. Political hopefuls saw newspapers and serious television talk shows such as *Meet the Press* as far more important in disseminating their campaign messages.

Schwarzenegger differed from other politicians in his innovative use of celebrity and media to forge a political career. He understood that these seemingly lightweight venues offered new ways of engaging and mobilizing voters. During his gubernatorial run, he shunned traditional news outlets and placed entertainment shows at the center of his campaign. He announced his candidacy on *The Tonight Show*, publicized it on *Oprah*, and made speeches that used lines from his movies—like promising voters that politicians who were not doing their job would be told "*Hasta la vista*, baby."[2] Instead of talking policy to reporters from the *Los Angeles Times* or *Wall Street Journal*, he preferred television interviews with Larry King, Jay Leno, and Sean Hannity. Although the political establishment mocked his candidacy as yet another instance of wacko Hollywood politics, the people of California thought enough of Arnold to elect him governor of the state with the fifth-largest economy in the world.

Schwarzenegger is best understood as a Republican celebrity rather than Republican activist, someone who brought glamour and image to the GOP rather than ideology. His political trajectory was closer to that of Charlton Heston than to Murphy or Reagan. Like "Moses," he was a major box-office star who used his cinematic persona to craft a political persona. Yet unlike Heston, who maintained a singular heroic image over the course of his career, Schwarzenegger altered his image to fit the Republican zeitgeist: a powerful action star whose films articulated messages of fear and reassurance during the Reagan era, and a more sensitive family-friendly hero during the more moderate conservatism of George H. W. Bush. While political focus groups in May 2001 favored his image as a "caring, compassionate" man, his action hero persona made his later campaign promises to be tough with liberal politicians highly credible.[3]

Arnold Schwarzenegger was the perfect actor to usher in the new age of celebrity politics because he was a celebrity before he was a movie star. Rising to fame as the six-time Mr. Olympia, five-time Mr. Universe, and one-time Mr. World, the Austrian bodybuilder's fame was further enhanced by marrying into the closest thing Americans have to political royalty: the Kennedy family. Despite his image as a muscle-bound action hero, Schwarzenegger was no political naïf. Embracing Richard Nixon and the Republican Party shortly after arriving in 1968, he was mentored in the intricacies of party politics and public service by his wife Maria Shriver, his in-laws Eunice and Sargent Shriver (George McGovern's running mate in 1972), and Maria's uncle, Senator Ted Kennedy. "The joy in public office is a tremendous idea," he told *Gentleman's Quarterly* in 1986. But if he ever ran he would aim higher than Clint Eastwood, mayor of Carmel, California. "I'd go after something major—like governor of California."[4]

Celebrity helped Arnold Schwarzenegger realize his dream, but it did not ensure he would be an effective leader. His campaign and subsequent years in office point to the limitations of turning politics into entertainment without offering the complex but perhaps "boring" policy statements that allow voters to select the candidate most capable of governing. Schwarzenegger's story reveals the thin line between using celebrity to energize or trivialize politics.

SEARCHING FOR FAME

Think of Arnold Schwarzenegger's life as a four-act play that focused, successively, on the pursuit of fame, cinematic stardom, positioning himself for a potential political career, and finally running for office. "Arnold has a big vision and thinks long term," observed longtime friend and adviser Bonnie Reiss. "At each point in realizing that vision, he is driven by the desire to be the best of the best of the best." Shortly after arriving in New York in 1968, the twenty-one-year-old bodybuilder laid out his master plan: he would be a millionaire by the time he was thirty, a movie star by thirty-one, husband of someone rich and famous soon afterward, a regular visitor to the White House, and then a successful politician. Boastful fantasies are nothing new in Hollywood. Yet, Schwarzenegger actually achieved all of this. Through body-building he quite literally turned himself into the ultimate self-made man.[5]

Just as the early lives of Louis B. Mayer and Edward G. Robinson were shaped by encounters with antisemitism in Eastern Europe, Schwarzeneg-ger's political path was influenced by growing up in a socialist-dominated town in post–World War II Austria. Arnold Alois Schwarzenegger was born on July 30, 1947, in the small village of Thal near the town of Graz—part of the province of Styria, whose southern portion was occupied by British troops and northern portion by Soviet troops during Austria's postwar par-titioning. His father Gustav joined the Nazi Party in 1938, volunteered unsuccessfully for the *Sturmabteilunger* (storm troopers) in May 1939, and served as a master sergeant in the German military police. After being wounded on the Russian front in 1943, he was sent home. Cleared of any possible war crimes during de-Nazification investigations in 1947, he moved to the small village of Thal and served as its police chief for fifteen years. Aurelia Jadrny was a young widow when she married Gustav in 1945 and soon bore him two sons, Meinhard and Arnold, whom she raised as Catho-lics. The brothers grew up in a rundown home with no indoor plumbing or toilets and with food scarce due to rationing.[6]

Gustav was a cold disciplinarian who beat his sons when he fell into one of his drunken rages. He wanted Arnold to become a policeman; Aurelia preferred that he go to trade school. But young Schwarzenegger's ambitions exceeded those of his parents. "Around the time of grammar school," he told a reporter in 1976, "I had this incredible desire to be recognized." Whenever he went to the movies or watched television he imagined himself on the screen. "I got the feeling that I was meant to be more than just an average guy running around, that I was chosen to do something special. At that point, I didn't think about money. I thought about fame, about just being the great-est. I was dreaming about being some dictator of a country or some savior like Jesus."[7] Bodybuilding proved the answer to his dreams and his ticket out of Austria.

The roots of Schwarzenegger's latter-day faith in individualism can be found in his adolescent experiences. Gustav encouraged his sons to play soccer but Arnold did not like sharing the credit with others if he did something special. By fifteen, he abandoned team sports in favor of bodybuilding, a far more individualistic endeavor in which one rose to the top based on singular ability and determination. Training with Karl Marnul, the reigning Mr. Austria, Schwarzenegger developed into one of the country's best young bodybuilders. Entering the army at eighteen, he went AWOL during basic training to compete in, and eventually win, the junior Mr. Europe bodybuilding contest in Stuttgart, Germany. Upon completing his service in October 1966, he left Austria to train in Munich. "It's not big enough, it's stifling," Schwarzenegger wrote of his native land. "Even people's ideas were small. There was too much contentment, too much acceptance of things as they'd always been."[8]

Arnold's frustration with Austria was political as well as personal, for politics was as much a part of his early life as bodybuilding. His closest training partner was Karl Gerstl, whose half-Jewish father Alfred was a city councilman and prominent member of the conservative People's Party. Alfred Gerstl was a staunch anti-Nazi who fought with the Resistance during the war. He invited Arnold, who considered him a "second" father, to join the small group that met at his home to discuss the pressing political issues of the day. Just as Louis B. Mayer schooled many of MGM's young stars in the intricacies of Republican politics, so too did Alfred explain the limitations of Socialism and Communism to his son's friend. Like Schwarzenegger, he too would go on to star in the arena of his passion, serving as a senator and twice as president of the *Bundesrat* (the Austrian Senate).[9]

Gerstl remained one of Schwarzenegger's political mentors for decades and helped shape his loathing of Socialism and welfare state policies. The economic philosophy Gerstl (and later Schwarzenegger) espoused was part of an Austrian tradition most prominently articulated by Ludwig von Mises and his famous disciple Friedrich Hayek. The latter's *The Road to Serfdom* (1944), which influenced conservatives from Milton Friedman to Ronald Reagan to Glenn Beck to Tea Party activists, was a best-selling polemic against the dangers of state-run economies. Hayek argued that direct government intervention in the economy, whether by Nazis, Communists, or New Dealers, would lead to tyranny by subverting the personal freedom of citizens and turning them into serfs of the state. Hayek heralded the virtues of a free market system, and, as one scholar noted, elevated "individual liberty above all other values."[10]

Schwarzenegger, like Gerstl, loathed the effects of socialist central planning. He hated living in a society where eighteen-year-olds were already planning when they would retire and take their state pension; he disdained a central government that thwarted local autonomy and destroyed individual ambition. Like his mentor, he preferred a free enterprise system in which ambitious people were allowed to profit from their success. "It is not very astonishing, not very surprising that he would think about a political career," a childhood friend explained years later. "He grew up around all these people who were involved. To go into politics would be almost like coming back to his roots."[11]

The key to understanding Arnold's success in so many endeavors—bodybuilding, film, and politics—is to appreciate the laser-like focus he brought to achieving his ambitions. As one close friend explained, when Schwarzenegger set a goal, "everything else is forgotten; nothing else enters his mind." While living in Munich, he spent weeks lifting weights and sculpting his muscles until they were perfect. Turning his 6' 2," 240-pound body into a work of art, the nineteen-year-old won the heavyweight division of the International Powerlifting Championship in 1966 and finished a surprising second in the Mr. Universe contest that same year. The next year, after winning the amateur Mr. Universe title, he announced his long-term goals: "I want to win the Mr. Universe title many times. . . . I want to go into films. . . . I want to be a billionaire. And then I want to go into politics."[12] The best place to achieve those dreams, he believed, was in the United States. When pioneering bodybuilding entrepreneur Joe Weider—who made his fortune selling magazines, workout equipment, and nutritional supplements—offered to bring him to the United States, the Austrian jumped at the opportunity.

By the time he arrived in Los Angeles in 1968 and settled in at Gold's Gym on Venice Beach, the self-proclaimed "Billy Graham of the muscle set" was an international star, albeit one unknown to the American public.[13] Schwarzenegger had already won two world championships and over the next several years established himself as the greatest bodybuilder in the sport's history. After a single defeat in 1969, the Austrian Oak, as he was known among his peers, never lost another contest. By the time he retired from competition in 1976, Schwarzenegger had transformed bodybuilding into one of the country's fastest-growing sports.

Schwarzenegger wanted wealth as well as fame, and he proved as shrewd a businessman as he was a bodybuilder. Soon after arriving, he enrolled in English and business classes at Santa Monica College, the UCLA Extension, and the University of Wisconsin–Superior (through a correspondence course). Barely speaking English in 1968, Arnold went into the bricklaying business with fellow bodybuilder Franco Columbu, building walls during the day and their bodies at night. He also opened Oak Productions with an eye toward a potential film career. Schwarzenegger slowly forged a financial empire by appearing at bodybuilding competitions, endorsing food and vitamin supplements, and selling a range of T-shirts, posters, weight-training belts, training seminars, bodybuilding records, books, videos, and pamphlets such as "How Arnold Builds His Chest Like a Fortress." Less than two decades after setting foot in America, Schwarzenegger was a key investor in over $34 million worth of real estate.[14]

For all his success, Schwarzenegger craved more than just money or being the world's leading bodybuilder. He wanted to be a major celebrity. For Arnold that meant becoming a movie star, even if it meant lowering his income. Relying on experts to teach him what he needed to know, he hired an acting coach and publicist. His first role came in the easily forgettable *Hercules in New York* (1970), in which he starred under the name Arnold Strong. After several guest appearances on television, Schwarzenegger's acting lessons finally paid off. In *Stay Hungry* (1976), which starred Jeff Bridges and Sally Field, he played bodybuilder Joe Santo, who was training for the upcoming Mr. Universe contest. The young actor's undeniable charm earned him strong reviews and a Golden Globe Award for the Best Male Acting Debut.

Stay Hungry got Schwarzenegger noticed, but *Pumping Iron* (1977) put him on the path to stardom and made him the darling of New York's hipster scene. Based on a book of the same title written by Charles Gaines and George Butler, the documentary follows Arnold as he trained for the 1975 Mr. Universe contest in Pretoria, South Africa. Schwarzenegger lights up the screen with a 1,000-megawatt smile, charismatic presence, and sense of humor that leads even his fiercest opponents to admire the man.

Released in January 1977, *Pumping Iron* elevated him to celebrity status. With the help of publicist Charlotte Parker, Schwarzenegger hobnobbed with the likes of Andy Warhol, Jamie Wyeth, Barbara Walters, and Jackie Onassis. "The intellectual world of New York is falling on its knees in front of me," he boasted after the premiere.[15]

Whatever he may have thought, Schwarzenegger's initial celebrity revolved around his body rather than his intellect or acting abilities. Beginning in 1974, when the *Los Angeles Times* dubbed him the "Babe Ruth of

Bodybuilding," images of his massive, almost cartoon-like physique flooded mainstream media outlets. Boasting a 57" chest, 31" waist, 22" biceps, and 28" thighs on a 6' 2", 235-pound frame, Schwarzenegger was hailed by the *New York Times* and *Chicago Tribune* as arguably possessing "the world's most perfect male body," a body they and other newspapers repeatedly featured posing in classic bodybuilding fashion in their daily columns.[16]

Having achieved fame as a bodybuilder and minor movie star, the Austrian immigrant turned to fulfilling his other youthful ambitions. His interest in American politics was piqued shortly after arriving in 1968, when he had a friend translate the televised speeches of presidential candidates Richard Nixon and Hubert Humphrey. The twenty-one-year-old found the Democrat too attached to an activist central government, an ideology similar to the Graz Socialists he loathed. "I like Nixon," he told his friend, because of his support "for a strong economy and free enterprise." If this is what Republicans stood for, then he would happily support the GOP.[17]

Whatever his childhood fantasies, few would have predicted that the poor boy from Thal would marry into America's most celebrated liberal political family. But Schwarzenegger was always lucky. When actor James Caan dropped out of the Robert F. Kennedy Pro-Celebrity Tennis Tournament in August 1977, the bodybuilder's publicist secured him an invitation to the star-studded event. What no one could have predicted was his fateful encounter with Kennedy's niece, Maria Shriver. The *Pumping Iron* star and the recent Georgetown University graduate immediately hit it off, so much so that she invited him to fly back with her to the Kennedy compound in Hyannis Port, Massachusetts. Shriver found herself attracted to his intelligence, humor, irreverent nature, and physique. "Everyone assumed that I was supposed to marry someone like a John Kerry," she explained, "some preppy that had gone to Harvard or Yale." Her mother Eunice knew Arnold was no John Kerry when he told her that Maria had "a great ass."[18] She laughed and the new boyfriend spent the weekend playing sports and offering advice about exercise to the extended family.

Over the following months and years, the Austrian became close friends with Eunice and Sarge (Sargent Shriver, Maria's father), who quickly discovered his interest in politics. Having spent parts of 1934 and 1936 as an exchange student in Germany, Sarge spoke to his daughter's boyfriend in German about his own decidedly liberal views on government and impatience with bureaucracy. Shriver found the bodybuilder so fascinated with

American politics that he called him "the sponge" because, as Arnold recollected, "I would go in there and pump him for information for hours."[19]
Eunice proved equally vital in laying the groundwork for a potential political
career. She explained how her brother Jack insisted that the best way to gain
national exposure was by focusing on one issue and building a career upon
it. Following his advice, she founded the Special Olympics in 1962, turned
it international in 1968, and made it her life's work until her death in 2009.

Although Schwarzenegger soon turned his attention to his film career, he
also heeded Eunice's advice and entered public service by involving himself
with children's physical fitness. Far from being a perfunctory celebrity who
showed up and then disappeared when the cameras did, the bodybuilding
champion spent the next two decades organizing fitness workshops throughout the country; he also served as the national weight training coach for the
Special Olympics. None of this was totally selfless, for Schwarzenegger
always had his eye on the future. "I could sense his political ambition, even
though he never overtly talked about it," publicist Charlotte Parker observed
in the early 1980s, so much so that she called her client "governor."[20]

The political career, however, would have to wait. Schwarzenegger was
famous, but he wanted to operate on a far bigger stage by becoming a major
movie star. Such a goal seemed ludicrous to film critics such as Molly Haskell
who dismissed him as a "muscle-beach male bimbo." Yet Arnold was a man
with a long-term vision and the persistence and intelligence to do whatever
he needed to attain it. If people wanted to think he was dumb, that was fine
with him. "Then they expect the worst, and anything you do well is a big plus
for you."[21] Schwarzenegger soon proved his critics wrong.

CONSERVATIVE ACTION HERO

For many years, the Austrian immigrant who became a citizen in 1983 was a
Republican in spirit rather than action. Other than donating money to candidates and attending the party convention in 1984, he did not participate in
partisan politics until 1988. This was not because he lacked political ideas,
but because during the second act of his life he focused on building his screen
career and did not want to risk alienating his audience. "When you promote
a movie," Schwarzenegger explained, "you want to win over everybody. You
try not to make political speeches. No matter what you say, there's a percentage out there that is against it. So why turn them off?"[22] Nevertheless, as

his films grew more successful at the box office, they also grew more explicit in engaging many of the controversial issues of the 1980s and 1990s.

More than any other star of his generation, including conservative action heroes Sylvester Stallone and Chuck Norris, Schwarzenegger's movies reflected the Republican zeitgeist of his times. Instead of honing his ideological messages by speaking to political groups, Schwarzenegger preferred to do it on the screen, offering the same kinds of messages over and over again until they became part of his cinematic persona and an integral part of American popular and political culture. The box office is the ballot box of the film world; it is the place where fans vote whether they approve of a star. During the 1980s and early 1990s, Americans voted for Arnold in astounding numbers. His films grossed over $1 billion in the 1980s and were among the most watched movies throughout the world, so much so that the National Association of Theater Owners voted him the "International Star of the Decade."[23]

Beginning with *Conan the Barbarian* (1982), his cinematic work reveals a marked political evolution from simple conservative tropes to more explicit political messages that reinforced many Reagan- and Bush-era policies. At the core of his collective cinematic ideology are four themes that made him popular with conservatives and libertarians: a staunch faith in individualism, suspicion of excessive government, fear of Communism, and an unflinching commitment to law and order. While no one Schwarzenegger movie was likely to shape the consciousness of viewers, the constant repetition of similar political messages over and over again eventually made them seem normal, natural, and true. Given the staggering popularity of his films, we need to take their collective meaning seriously. Republicans did, and they wanted Schwarzenegger in their camp long before he turned to party politics.[24]

Of course, there were limits to his initial political dedication. Unlike Charlie Chaplin, Harry Belafonte, Jane Fonda, and Warren Beatty, Schwarzenegger did not open his own production company in order to put his politics directly onto the screen. During the early years of his career, his desires for financial success trumped any need to make explicit political statements. Actors cannot always choose films that reflect their political leanings, but as Schwarzenegger's popularity rose, he exerted greater control over his choice of films and the content of scripts. During his peak years from 1982 to 2003, he starred in more movies (23) than Fonda (8), Beatty, (7), and Belafonte (2) combined, and many of those films popularized ideas favored by conservatives.

In rising to stardom, Schwarzenegger applied the same intense focus to his budding film career as he did to bodybuilding. However, his body and thick accent made his cinematic journey far more difficult. After appearing in two feature-length bombs—*The Villain* (1979) and *Scavenger Hunt* (1979)—he starred as Mickey Hargitay, Jayne Mansfield's bodybuilding husband, in the TV movie *The Jayne Mansfield Story* (1980). Undaunted by his previous failures, he told everyone on the set, "I'm going to be a big star." As producer Joan Barnett recounted, "We all used to say, 'OK, Arnold,' and shake our heads. It turned out he was right."[25] During shooting, director John Milius contacted Barnett and asked to see footage featuring Schwarzenegger, whom he was considering for the lead in *Conan the Barbarian*. He got the part that launched his career as a leading action hero and GOP star.

Timing played an important role in Schwarzenegger's success, for *Conan* appeared at a moment when many Americans were searching for heroes who could eliminate the bitter taste of defeat that characterized the post-Vietnam era. Ronald Reagan proved that timing is indeed everything. He was an action-star president compared to the more contemplative Jimmy Carter. Twenty minutes after he was sworn in as president on January 20, 1981, Iranian militants released the fifty-two hostages they held hostage since November 11, 1979. Even though Carter laid the groundwork, Reagan carefully staged events so that he got the credit and entered office with the aura of a man who got things done.

During the 1980s, Schwarzenegger reigned as the leading cinematic purveyor of heroic myths. "Fantasy-adventure is what people want to see in these difficult times," he explained in April 1982, and "people are starved of heroes." Unlike action-hero rivals Stallone and Norris, whose early films focused on Vietnam, three of Schwarzenegger's first four feature films of the 1980s were set in a mythical past, thereby allowing viewers to tease out their conservative messages rather than hitting them over the head. Based on 1930s pulp stories written by Robert E. Howard, *Conan the Barbarian* (1982), *Conan the Destroyer* (1984), and *Red Sonja* (1985) are morality plays as well as action stories that resurrect the idea of "Good Wars," or at least Good Warriors. They promoted an aggressive militarist culture that marked a sharp departure from the nonconfrontational approach favored by the Carter administration. Taken collectively, they, along with *The Terminator* (1984), offer dire warnings of what happens when tyrants are allowed to rule unopposed: freedom is lost and replaced by fear and death. Indeed, they echo the same message as

Reagan offered in his famous 1964 speech, "A Time for Choosing." Americans had to protect "individual freedom consistent with law and order" or risk sinking "down to the ant heap of totalitarianism."[26]

Conan was Schwarzenegger's political training film, a movie with someone else's politics, but that someone was writer-director John Milius, one of Hollywood's most conservative and talented Cold Warriors. In addition to penning several of Clint Eastwood's Dirty Harry screenplays, he also wrote and directed *Red Dawn* (1984), which depicted a Soviet invasion of the United States.

With his bulging muscles and cartoon-like body, Schwarzenegger's Conan resembled ancient Greek gods and demigods such as Hercules, fundamentally good but flawed mythic figures who are beyond politics and political labels. Conan is the reluctant hero who rises up to conquer oppressive authority and protect individual freedom. In this instance, the ruthless tyrant Thulsa Doom (James Earl Jones) kills Conan's parents, destroys his village, and enslaves the young boy. In this, as well as in *Conan the Destroyer* and *Red Sonja*, Schwarzenegger uses his sword to defeat despots, preserve liberty, and restore justice to a world gone awry. Such messages of individual courage are long-standing elements of American heroic film that go beyond simple labels of left and right. However, the emphasis on militarist solutions pushed Schwarzenegger's films into the conservative camp.[27]

Conan the Barbarian also mirrors right-wing antipathy toward the 1960s counterculture by portraying Doom as the leader of a mindless hippie-like cult of young men and women who carry flowers in their hands, engage in orgies, and happily jump to their deaths when ordered by their leader. Although Milius was the originator, it was Schwarzenegger who brought these politics to life.

Opening to mixed reviews, the $20 million Universal Pictures release proved enormously popular at the box office, grossing somewhere between $69 and $100 million worldwide ($153 to $222 million in 2009 dollars) depending on whose figures you use. Equally important, Milius's story attracted a heavily male audience, people who voted Republican in greater numbers than women.[28]

It would be a mistake to group Schwarzenegger with most conservatives of his time, for he proved a highly idiosyncratic Republican. Ideologically, he seemed closer to Charlton Heston's libertarianism than to Ronald Reagan's strain of conservatism. His politics favored the individual over the collective citizenry, and local autonomy over federal control. He wanted government to get out of the way and allow people to fulfill their destiny or fail in the attempt. "This idea of having Washington dictate down to the community rather than going the other way," he told a friend while listening to Hubert Humphrey in 1968, "this is something I have seen firsthand in Austria growing up under socialism, and it doesn't work."[29] Although his views on government were in sync with most conservatives, when it came to social issues such as abortion, marijuana, and same-sex marriages, he took positions closer to libertarians and liberal Democrats.

Differences aside, the Austrian immigrant saw himself as closely aligned with Reagan's Cold War agenda. Over the next several years, his films reinforced Reagan's mantra of fear and reassurance: we live in frightening times filled with evil, violence and danger, but heroes like Arnold—or Reagan—will always be there to save us.

The Terminator (1984), Schwarzenegger's next blockbuster hit, proved far more in tune with Reagan's policies than the simpler anti-authoritarian *Conan*. On March 23, 1983, the president announced his "Star Wars" missile defense program (Strategic Defense Initiative) designed to shield the United States from a possible nuclear attack by the Soviet Union. A year and a half later, Schwarzenegger visualized those fears in his most famous role of the 1980s, the cyborg robot killer in *The Terminator*. Although he plays a villain for the first and only time in his career, the film's overall message jibes with Reagan-era warnings about the need to be vigilant and to anticipate the actions of our enemies. The stakes in this film are nothing less than the survival of civilization.

Set in Los Angeles in 2029, this Cold War allegory depicts an Evil Empire that destroys most of mankind by launching a worldwide nuclear attack, only in this instance the Evil Empire is Skynet, a highly advanced Defense Department computer system gone awry—suggesting that an unmonitored federal government can be as great a danger as an uncontained Soviet Union. The film's heroes are part of the future resistance movement, "freedom fighters" as Reagan would call them, who defend humans against the machines. With the resistance on the verge of victory, the Skynet computers send a cyborg Terminator (Schwarzenegger) back to 1984 to assassinate Sarah Connor before she can give birth to her son, John, who grew up to head the resistance movement. The adult John Connor, in turn, sends one of his soldiers, Kyle Reese (Michael Biehn), back in time to protect his mother from the mechanized assassin.

Arnold is a great villain who wears a black leather jacket and dark shades, drives a motorcycle, blows away dozens of people with Uzis and shotguns, and utters memorable lines such as "I'll be back" (a signature quip that he has repeated throughout his career). The film's political message echoes the era's leitmotiv of fear and reassurance: our enemies are real and there is much to be afraid of, but with the presence of heroic individuals (in this instance Kyle Reese and Sarah Connor, who best the Terminator), we can defeat evil and restore justice. Even agencies of law and order such as the police prove incapable of stopping the Terminator. Individuals, not government, are the ones who save civilization. If this all seems simplistic, it was. But simplicity was the hallmark of Reagan's success, and the popularity of *The Terminator* and the Conan films meant that Schwarzenegger's cinematic politics were watched by millions of moviegoers.[30]

Box office was only one measure of the action star's impact. By building a sense of irony and self-mocking humor into his cinematic persona, Schwarzenegger's movies appealed to a far broader political spectrum than those of Hollywood's more didactic conservative stars. As one film critic observed in 1985, Schwarzenegger proved "an enormously likable hero, free from the bullish swagger of such flag-waving hunks as Chuck Norris or Sylvester Stallone." Not surprisingly, President Reagan confessed to loving the action hero's cinematic bravado.[31]

The success of *The Terminator* fueled Schwarzenegger's political fantasies. By this point in his career, money had become a secondary issue. With a net worth of at least $25 million in 1989, he did not need to depend on his film career. His ego and ambition now had other targets. Like Warren Beatty, Schwarzenegger never defined himself as an actor but as a man who sometimes acted. And like Beatty, he had long fantasized about running for office. As early as the fall of 1979 he told University of Wisconsin students how after "the movie bit, I would like to try politics." Five years later, friends predicted he would leave acting to become a producer or politician. "Maybe he'll run for the assembly or the state senate in California," one pal told a reporter, "but I think he's kind of always had the governorship of California in the back of his mind. He's a born politician."[32]

Unwilling to leave the movie business until he had realized his dreams of megastardom, Schwarzenegger began integrating contemporary political issues into his subsequent action films. South America, the arena for Reagan's real-life battles against Reds, is the setting for *Commando* (1985) and *Predator*

(1987). Both films implicitly endorse the kind of controversial Central American policies that prompted the bitter public exchanges between Charlton Heston and Ed Asner in 1982. In *Commando*, Colonel John Matrix, whose commando unit previously overthrew the government of a South American dictator. The film legitimizes a political situation that was anything but legitimate. In September 1973, the United States backed a coup d'état that overthrew the democratically elected government of Chilean President Salvador Allende, a man deemed dangerous by the U.S. government because of his Marxist background and support by his country's Communist Party. *Predator*, released seven months after the Iran-Contra Affair, also portrays Central America as a dangerous region plagued by drugs, dictators, and Communists. Schwarzenegger again plays a commando leader who, with the assistance of former wrestler and future Minnesota governor Jesse Ventura, is sent to rescue a cabinet minister kidnapped by Soviet-financed guerrilla forces in an unnamed Central American country. Both features proved box-office hits, grossing $57.5 million and $98.2 million, respectively.[33]

The action hero's next film warned audiences about the dangers of centralized state authority. Set in 2017, *The Running Man* dramatizes the perils citizens face when government regulation gets so strong that it turns the United States into a fascist nation. Political leaders respond to the collapse of the world economy by dividing the country into paramilitary zones and imposing total censorship on all forms of art, music, and communications. The opening crawl explains that "No dissent is tolerated and yet a small resistance movement has managed to survive underground"—a group just like the anti-Nazi Resistance that Alfred Gerstl described to young Arnold many years earlier. Schwarzenegger learned his lessons well, for in this film he plays a federal police officer who is jailed for disobeying orders to shoot hungry men, women, and children who are demanding food. The film suggests that the ultimate danger we face is not from nuclear war, but from the perversion of democracy by an all-too-powerful state—a message that undoubtedly appealed to the left as well as the right.

Conan the Republican

With his fame and career secure, Schwarzenegger began the third act of his life by starting a family, increasing his public service activities, and entering the contentious world of partisan politics. On April 27, 1986, national media

attention turned to the celebrity marriage of the year. After a nine-year relationship filled with rumors of the groom's frequent womanizing, thirty-
eight-year-old Arnold Schwarzenegger and twenty-nine-year-old Maria
Shriver were wed at the Kennedy compound in Hyannis Port, Massachusetts.
Fathering four children with Maria between 1989 and 1997, the action star
also became a Republican celebrity, campaigning alongside George H. W.
Bush in 1988 and serving the party on and off the screen. Bush considered
his new friend such an important GOP asset that he affectionately dubbed
him "Conan the Republican."[34]

Throughout his life, Schwarzenegger proved an idiosyncratic Republican. He was never a grassroots activist with connections to the party apparatus like Louis B. Mayer, George Murphy, or Ronald Reagan; nor was he
an ardent conservative spokesman like Charlton Heston. Schwarzenegger
was preeminently an individualist ideologue. As one friend noted, "He felt
that everyone could pull themselves up by their own bootstraps." His individualist philosophy also dovetailed with libertarian ideas. During the
1980s he attended a number of political forums, gave a talk, and cochaired
events sponsored by the libertarian Reason Foundation, which was based
in Southern California.[35]

Given his eclectic politics, why were Republican Party leaders so anxious
to embrace him? For two reasons: his celebrity and his unwavering commitment to free market ideology. Schwarzenegger may have kept his personal
politics quiet during his rise to stardom, but that did not mean he lacked a
well-conceived ideology. Schooled in free market thought during his youth,
his economic philosophy crystallized in January 1980 after watching Nobel
Prize–winning economist Milton Friedman's *Free to Choose* television series
on PBS. "It expressed, validated and explained everything I ever thought or
observed about the way the economy works," he told the *Wall Street Journal*.
A year later, Schwarzenegger visited the former economic adviser to Barry
Goldwater, Richard Nixon, and Ronald Reagan at his San Francisco home.
Friedman came away from their discussions with a "very favorable impression about the quality of his intellect." The economist also "sang his praises"
to Ronald Reagan and Secretary of State George Shultz.[36]

The two men struck up an enduring friendship. When Friedman asked
him to film an introduction to an updated *Free to Choose* series in 1990,
Schwarzenegger agreed. During the course of his remarks, the actor laid out
his ideology more thoroughly than he ever did on the campaign trail. "Being

free to choose," he told the television audience, means being "free to live your own life, pursue your own goals, chase your own rainbow without the government breathing down on your neck or standing on your shoes." While living in the United States, he discovered the "more the government interfered and intervened and inserted itself into the free market, the worse the country did. But when the government stepped back and let the free enterprise system do its work, then the better we did, the more robust our economy grew, the better I did, and the better my business grew, and the more I was able to hire and help others."[37] In sum, he was describing the pathway of his own success, and he believed in its universal application.

When Vice President George H. W. Bush asked the actor to join him on the campaign trail in November 1988, he did so because of the star's image rather than his ideology. Bush had been plagued by severe image problems ever since Newsweek put him on its October 19, 1987, cover with the caption, "Fighting the 'Wimp Factor.'" Ironically, Bush was anything but a wimp. During World War II, he distinguished himself by flying fifty-eight combat missions and received the Distinguished Flying Cross for completing an operation despite being hit by anti-aircraft fire.[38]

Fortunately for the vice president, Lee Atwater, his take-no-prisoners campaign manager, understood the vital role celebrities played in attracting voters and began surrounding the candidate with "manly" stars. He invited former martial arts champion and action star Chuck Norris to travel with Bush to California's blue-collar Central Valley. "Everywhere we went there were scores of people with Chuck Norris sweatshirts on," Atwater told reporter Ron Brownstein. "They didn't care about politics. Some of them never voted. But they were going to vote." Celebrities with the right kind of image, Atwater discovered, could "bring in people from their own followings that are not typically prone to care about politics one way or the other."[39] Here was an example of the sheer power of movie stars to shape the political landscape: they could get people who cared little about politics to vote.

On the eve of the November elections, Bush turned to another star to toughen his image. On November 3, Arnold Schwarzenegger traveled to Columbus, Ohio, where he introduced the vice president at a campaign rally. The appearance proved so successful that Bush asked the action star to accompany him to events in Illinois and New Jersey (see fig. 9.1). During the flight, they talked about a wide range of issues, including the dreadful state of American physical fitness.[40]

FIGURE 9.1 Schwarzenegger campaigns with Vice President George H. W. Bush at a Chicago rally, November 3, 1988. SOURCE: ASSOCIATED PRESS

At ensuing rallies, Schwarzenegger developed a rhetorical style that he used to great effect during his 2003 gubernatorial run. He discovered he could excite audiences by delivering popular lines from his films. Introducing the vice president as "the real American hero," the Hollywood star told a crowd of 10,000 in Columbus, "I only play the [destructive] Terminator in my movies. But when it comes to the American future, Michael Dukakis will be the real Terminator." At subsequent rallies, the actor continued drawing on popular culture references to make political points. "I saw them [Reagan and Bush] take over an economy that looked like Pee-Wee Herman," he told one wildly cheering crowd, "and I saw them turn this economy around to make it look like Superman." Growing increasingly comfortable with the star, Bush quipped that Maria's husband now had to return home and "take the heat from his own in-laws."[41]

On November 8, 1988, Americans elected George H. W. Bush their forty-first president by a wide margin. Schwarzenegger may not have played a decisive role in Bush's victory, but his presence certainly helped. "A Presidential campaign is 90 percent marketing," explained Marty Kaplan, who served as Walter Mondale's deputy campaign manager during his 1984 presidential run. "The idea that we are having a conversation about the issues of the day [in a presidential campaign] only lives in civic classes, but then I forgot there are no civics classes." Schwarzenegger accomplished what Bush needed most. Along with Chuck Norris and Charlton Heston, observed columnist Maureen Dowd, he helped "assure voters that Mr. Reagan and Mr. Bush were not, as Mr. Norris put it, 'wimps.'"[42]

During the next four years, Schwarzenegger's increased political visibility was paralleled by a significant shift in his cinematic persona. His age, evolving relationship with the president, and life as a new father (Katherine was born in 1989, Christina in 1991, Patrick in 1993, and Christopher in 1997) led him to make several films that reflected the president's call for "a kinder, gentler nation," one in which "compassionate" Americans would show their children "what it means to be a loyal friend, a loving parent, a citizen who leaves his home, his neighborhood and town better than he found it."[43]

There comes a moment in an action hero's career when he needs to send up his own image or run the risk of growing stale. John Wayne did it toward the end of his career, as did Clint Eastwood. "It's smart career management," observed movie critic and documentarian Richard Schickel, "playing to the almost unconscious dubiety of their fans, who eventually begin to wonder if the star is entirely muscle-bound." *Twins* (1988), *Kindergarten Cop* (1990), *Terminator 2: Judgment Day* (1991), *Last Action Hero* (1993), *True Lies* (1994), and *Junior* (1994) can be viewed as the action hero's effort to refashion and reinvigorate his career. Done "more for success at the box office than for political purposes," remarked one close friend, these films nevertheless reinforced Bush's politics while also building a more caring image for their star.[44]

Schwarzenegger had always been tough, but his new films revealed an endearing, self-mocking humor that broadened his appeal. "You've got to have a feeling for hipness," he told one reporter. "You milk certain lines. 'Hasta la vista, baby,' or 'I lied.' You go over the top. People love it. Kids love it. And you do some athletic stuff, some fitness, and people think you're cool."[45] Whether self-consciously political or not, here was the world's leading action hero suddenly shifting gears to make moves in line with the chief executive's political agenda.

By turning to family-friendly films and embracing Bush's compassionate conservatism, Schwarzenegger was following the Shrivers' advice to think about the long run and not just the moment. Looking ahead to the next act in his career, especially since he and Charlton Heston were often mentioned as possible candidates for higher office, the action star became more involved in child-oriented public service programs. Schwarzenegger's efforts in this regard were not simply a cynical positioning ploy. "On the one hand, working on behalf of children is selfless and altruistic," explained Bonnie Reiss, who met him in 1979 while she and Maria worked on Ted Kennedy's presidential campaign, "but it coincides beautifully with the shrewd strategic part of politics. It's a win-win situation."[46]

The Shrivers did more than just give advice. In January 1990, after months of lobbying by Eunice Shriver, Bush appointed her son-in-law chairman of the President's Council on Physical Fitness (see fig. 9.2). Schwarzenegger approached his new job with the same intensity he devoted to bodybuilding and acting. Charged with raising "the consciousness of all Americans on the importance of good health through physical fitness," he traveled to all fifty states and met with their governors to forge a legislative plan of action. When he left the post in 1993, nearly three-quarters of the states he visited had passed new legislation requiring more physical education in the schools. "Arnold Schwarzenegger denies political ambitions," *U.S. News & World Report* observed in November 1990. "But some think his crusade for fitness among American children is just a warm-up."[47]

FIGURE 9.2 The head of the President's Council on Physical Fitness kicks off the Great American Workout Month with Secretary Louis Sullivan, President Bush, and Barbara Bush in May 1990. SOURCE: GEORGE BUSH PRESIDENTIAL LIBRARY AND MUSEUM

Schwarzenegger returned to the screen with the 1990 Christmas-season release *Kindergarten Cop*. Mocking his earlier image, the hulking action hero who killed hundreds of villains in previous films is brought to his knees by a bunch of unruly kindergarteners. "They're pushing me around. They're walking all over me," he whines to his female partner. Playing a New York City narcotics detective working undercover in Oregon as a substitute teacher, Schwarzenegger cleverly links his new onscreen persona to his off-screen public service by having the kids engage in a series of physical fitness exercises designed to turn their "mush into muscles." The film ends with the tough law-and-order cop leaving the police force to teach kindergarten and hopefully start a family with the woman he saves from a murderer.

Halfway into the film, Arnold's character marches straight ahead like a drill sergeant with a group of kindergarteners trailing behind (see fig. 9.3). The humor in this scene, and throughout the film, comes from the contrast between Arnold's long-standing image as a fierce, violent action hero and his role here as the flummoxed teacher. Operating outside his usual cinematic personality and surroundings, his tough-guy attitude becomes a kind of delusion, one that makes him comically vulnerable rather than intimidating. *Kindergarten Cop*

FIGURE 9.3 Arnold brings his kinder, gentler image to the screen in *Kindergarten Cop* (1990). SOURCE: CINEMA/TV LIBRARY, USC

and similar family films allowed Schwarzenegger to transform and neutralize his warrior image while still using it to entertain audiences.

The star and recent father has a genuine rapport with the children, and the film opened as the number-one box-office hit. *Kindergarten Cop* is "hardly heavyweight politics," observed one critic, "but it is a good opportunity for lots of favourable publicity, and not a bad platform for a future political career."[48]

Over the next few years, Schwarzenegger solidified his role as a Republican celebrity by appearing at party fundraisers and campaigning for California gubernatorial candidate Pete Wilson. By 1991, as the GOP's popularity in California dwindled and national antipolitician rhetoric grew, media stories speculated that Arnold might be just the person to lead the party back into power. The *New York Times* anointed him the GOP's star of the future, while *M Inc.* ran a long feature that asked, "Schwarzenegger as Governor of California?"[49]

Despite his rising political visibility, Schwarzenegger was not ready to trade a successful screen career for a tenuous political one. In addition to his family-friendly films, he maintained his status as the world's leading action hero by starring in the highly violent *Terminator 2: Judgment Day*, which opened in July 1991 to a phenomenal $32 million in its first weekend. Unlike his previous incarnation, this is a more humane Terminator programmed to protect and take orders from a young boy, John Connor. Schwarzenegger's kinder, gentler Terminator has been sent back in time by the resistance to defeat a more technologically advanced unit, T-1000, dispatched by Skynet computers to kill John. The boy humanizes his new protector by teaching him slang phrases such as *"Hasta la vista,* baby" and "no problemo," as well as how to give a proper High Five. Schwarzenegger even manages to sneak in another "I'll be back." In the midst of its comic and action sequences, the film offers the same message as T-1: individuals, not the ineffective forces of government, are the only ones capable of saving civilization.

Terminator 2 plays to Christian evangelical sensibilities with an emotional final scene in which the Christlike T-2, knowing that his parts could be used to reconstruct more killing machines, sacrifices himself by willingly sinking into a boiling caldron of molten steel. The film ends with Sarah Connor speaking Reaganesque words of reassurance: "The unknown future rolls toward us, and I face it for the first time with a sense of hope. If a computer can learn the value of human life, maybe we can, too." In a column entitled

"A Warmer, Fuzzier Arnold," *Los Angeles Times* critic Caryn James called Schwarzenegger's cyborg the "most tenderhearted alien since E. T."[50]

No longer believing that his political activity would hurt his box office, Schwarzenegger joined Bush during the 1992 Republican primaries to help offset a challenge from right-wing commentator Pat Buchanan. Standing next to the president at a February 1992 rally in New Hampshire, the Terminator "stirred much more excitement than the liberator of Kuwait could evoke," the *Washington Post* observed. Employing lines and clichés from his films and bodybuilder persona, the popular celebrity told the screaming crowd to "go out there and help the President and pump up his vote." A big grin spread across his face as he borrowed a line from *Terminator 2* and urged voters to "send a message to Pat Buchanan: '*Hasta la vista*, baby.'" The muscular Republican then dismissed Bush's Democratic rivals as "a bunch of 'girlie-men.'" He delivered similar messages to equally excited crowds in Ohio and Georgia. That August, starstruck delegates to the Republican convention brushed past former President Gerald Ford to catch a glimpse of the actor, who led off the day's ceremonies with a "meet the Flag Salute."[51]

Celebrity, however, had its limits and could occasionally backfire. Since the 1930s, Democrats and Republicans had repeatedly sent movie stars on the campaign trail to attract crowds to rallies with the hope that once they heard the candidate's message they would vote for him or her. The Bush team added a new wrinkle: they utilized celebrities whose image would counteract the candidate's perceived weakness. The danger, however, was, and still is, that the star's persona could overpower and diminish the candidate. Schwarzenegger's appearances in 1992, suggested columnist David Broder, ultimately did more harm than good. "Bush normally looks and sounds like a vigorous leader, but next to Schwarzenegger he—like most mere mortals—seemed like a shrimp. And his message at the moment is notably limp."[52]

The action hero's effectiveness was further diminished by what many people saw as hypocritical attacks on violence in the entertainment industry by GOP leaders. After Vice President Dan Quayle denounced rapper Ice-T's "Cop Killer," Bush told party loyalists, "I stand against those who use films or records or television or video games to glorify killing law enforcement officers." The president apparently saw no problem campaigning alongside a movie star who killed seventeen police officers in *The Terminator*. Even Schwarzenegger questioned the wisdom of such attacks. After Quayle blasted television sitcom character Murphy Brown (played by Democratic loyalist Candice Bergen) for having a child out of wedlock, the actor phoned Bush policy adviser Jim Pinkerton and insisted that the speech would "destroy you in California."[53]

Bush's Gulf War victory was not enough to stave off rampant discontent with the poor state of the American economy. After promising no new taxes, his 1990 tax hike alienated core conservatives who always suspected him of being too moderate. On Election Day, Americans cast 44.9 million votes (43.0%) for Bill Clinton, 39.1 million (37.4%) for Bush, and 19.7 million (18.9%) for Reform Party candidate Ross Perot.[54]

Although Bush was out of office by the end of 1992, Schwarzenegger continued to remold his image and broaden his appeal among potential voters. *Junior* (1994) is the third film—alongside *Twins* and *Kindergarten Cop*—where a single image captures its humor: Arnold with a huge pregnant belly. Lest anyone think the action hero had gone too soft, *Total Recall* (1990) and *True Lies* (1994) resurrected messages of fear and reassurance. In the former, Schwarzenegger helps freedom-fighting rebels on a futuristic Mars colony overthrow their repressive government. *True Lies* blends his comic presence with Reagan-like warnings about enemies who would stop at nothing to destroy the United States. Instead of battling the Soviet Union, Schwarzenegger saves the nation from the "Crimson Jihad," a Middle Eastern terrorist organization that plans to set off nuclear bombs in a number of American cities.

Taken collectively, Schwarzenegger's films succeeded where Bush failed. He showed audiences—and potential voters—that he could be compassionate and tough. The only glitch in his upward trajectory came in 1990 with the publication of Wendy Leigh's controversial biography, *Arnold: An Unauthorized Biography*. The British author raised questions about Schwarzenegger's earlier use of steroids, his long history of treating women badly, his alleged antisemitism and admiration of Hitler, and his father's Nazi past. Asked by the actor to investigate the charges, Rabbi Marvin Hier of the Simon Wiesenthal Center reported that Gustav Schwarzenegger had joined the Nazi Party but had never committed any war crimes. Faced with a libel suit, Leigh eventually retracted her claims and Schwarzenegger survived the scandal relatively unscathed.[55]

By the mid-1990s, Schwarzenegger had achieved most of his adolescent fantasies. He had fame, a famous wife, and a fabulous movie career. But he now wanted to do something more important, more challenging than just being a movie star. What could be a greater challenge than to solve the problems of the nation's most prosperous state? That would happen in the fourth act of his life.

THE ROAD TO SACRAMENTO

To understand the actor's road to Sacramento, we need to backtrack a moment. The idea of a celebrity with little political experience being elected to office was not a novel one. Astronaut John Glenn and basketball star Bill Bradley (both Democrats) entered the U.S. Senate in 1975 and 1979, respectively, with far less political experience than George Murphy or Ronald Reagan. Residents of Carmel, California, elected Clint Eastwood their mayor in 1986, while Palm Springs voters chose singer–television star Sonny Bono as their mayor in 1988 and congressman in 1994. Former Senate Watergate attorney Fred Thompson costarred in several films during the 1980s and then served as a Tennessee senator from 1994 to 2002. Disgusted with politics as usual, Minnesota voters elected Reform Party candidate, former wrestler, and occasional Schwarzenegger costar Jesse "The Body" Ventura as their governor in November 1998.[56]

As Republicans shifted farther to the right following the 1994 midterm elections, Schwarzenegger found himself occupying an awkward position. Despite campaigning for Pete Wilson in 1994 and proudly hailing House Speaker Newt Gingrich as "our leader," he was never fully trusted by party conservatives. "In an earlier era, he would have been a Rockefeller Republican," observed Dan Schnur, who at the time worked as Wilson's press secretary. Republican Party loyalists were less than thrilled when he bypassed Mitt Romney to support Ted Kennedy's reelection bid in 1994 in Massachusetts. The actor found himself in another awkward position a year later when presidential hopeful Bob Dole attacked the entertainment industry for producing violent movies and records. "We have reached a point," Dole told Los Angeles business leaders in June 1995, "where our popular culture threatens to undermine our character as a nation." Denouncing Hollywood violence when the party's number-one star killed more people onscreen than any other action hero of the time precipitated outcries of hypocrisy from numerous quarters, especially when Dole singled out Schwarzenegger's violent *True Lies* as a "family friendly" film. Only later did the senator confess that he never saw the films he praised or condemned.[57]

Over the next several years, the movie star broadened his appeal among audiences and voters by alternating between family-friendly films and fear-and-reassurance action stories. In addition to law-and-order fare such as *Eraser* (1996) and his lighter *Jingle All the Way* (1996) and *Batman and Robin* (1997), he selected projects whose messages would appeal to the GOP's conservative base. In *End of Days* (1999), a film that catered to the Christian Right, the star plays a biblically named former cop, Jericho Cane, who thwarts Satan's efforts to rule the earth for the next thousand years. As director Peter Hyams told the press, "This is about the biggest action star of the past 20 years putting the gun down and saying the only thing that works is faith."[58]

In the midst of his cinematic endeavors, Schwarzenegger experienced a major life-changing moment. In April 1997, the forty-nine-year-old underwent elective heart surgery to replace a faulty aortic valve. Although they said he would recover without any changes to his lifestyle, medical experts also predicted the actor would require repeated replacement surgery as the current heart valve degraded. His sense of the fragility of life grew more acute a year later when his mother died. As he looked ahead to the future, the aging star contemplated new arenas of action and met with Bob White, Governor Pete Wilson's right-hand man, to discuss the political landscape. White explained that, with Democrat Gray Davis having replaced Wilson, California Republicans were in trouble and needed a new voice—Arnold's voice. Schwarzenegger responded that the GOP's problems were rooted in its inability to create a compelling storyline. Marketing a candidate, he insisted, was similar to marketing a movie; both needed a compelling concept to succeed. He promised he would think about running and creating a concept he might employ.[59]

In November 1999, Schwarzenegger tested his storyline by making his most explicit public statements about seeking higher office. "I feel there are a lot of people in politics that are standing still and not doing enough," he explained in a lengthy magazine interview. "And there's a vacuum. Therefore I can move in." When pointedly asked if he would run for governor in 2002, Schwarzenegger teasingly responded, "Could be."[60]

Schwarzenegger's interview revealed two themes that proved of signal importance in charting his path to Sacramento. First, he began positioning himself as an antipolitician populist (an old but often successful storyline); and second, the venue he selected to reveal his ambitions was not some "serious" political magazine, but the entertainment monthly *Talk*. Schwarzenegger was no fool. He knew that his positions on abortion, drugs, and gay rights, and his well-reported history of transgressive sexual conduct toward women, placed him on the fringes of his party, especially after he confessed to *Talk* that he took steroids and smoked marijuana during his weightlifting days.[61] If he was to have any chance for electoral success, he had to appeal to independents, libertarians, and crossover voters disgusted with politics as usual. This was the strategy his friend Jesse Ventura used to get elected as governor of Minnesota.

Schwarzenegger continued building his storyline in a second November interview in yet another celebrity-oriented magazine, *George* (run by John F. Kennedy Jr.). The born-again populist denounced both parties for putting partisan posturing ahead of effective governing. He attacked fellow Republicans for failing to articulate what they "really stand *for* rather than going from one convention to the next talking about what we're against—guys like [Pat] Buchanan going up there and speaking about, 'We are anti-gay and we're anti-lesbian and anti-immigration. We are anti-taxation and anti-federal government.'" Confessing that his party's handling of the Bill Clinton–Monica Lewinsky scandal made him "ashamed to call myself a Republican," he savaged GOP leaders for "wasting time" on a trivial sex scandal instead of telling the American people "how we're going to solve the problems of inner cities."[62]

Over the coming months, Schwarzenegger criticized ineffective partisan politics and suggested he would be a different kind of politician. For more than twenty years, government leaders had failed "to inspire people or make the adjustments necessary to help people," he told the *Los Angeles Times* in October 2000. "I've been asked so many times to run," that it led him to wonder, "Wouldn't it be great to just sit in an office where your full-time job is just to serve people?"[63]

On January 2, 2001, Arnold Alois Schwarzenegger began his pursuit of higher office. Unhappy with the direction of California politics, and especially its budget and energy crises, he met with Bob White to discuss a 2002 gubernatorial run. Just as Ronald Reagan had relied on many of Richard Nixon's inner circle of advisers during his first gubernatorial run, so too did Schwarzenegger pull together a team drawn from Pete Wilson's inner circle— especially George Gorton, who had managed most of Wilson's campaigns and helped Russian President Boris Yeltsin win reelection in 1996. The actor also sought advice from his wife, Maria, and from her best friend, liberal

Democrat Bonnie Reiss. A month later, the Schwarzenegger brain trust conducted their first poll. Governor Gray Davis beat the Republican actor by a wide margin of 59 to 30 percent, but 45 percent of those surveyed believed the state was headed in the wrong direction. Davis, they decided, was vulnerable. Flying into action, Schwarzenegger discussed a potential run with GOP state chairman Shawn Steel and California Secretary of State Bill Jones.[64]

Unfortunately for the ambitious Austrian, his nascent campaign was derailed by the publication of two articles accusing him of scandalous sexual behavior. "Arnold the Barbarian," which ran in the March issue of the entertainment monthly *Premiere*, alleged that the actor had "groped women, berated his pregnant wife in public, and engaged in extramarital liaisons." It also repeated stories that appeared in Wendy Leigh's controversial 1990 biography that recounted a long history of alleged sexually inappropriate behavior and drug use. The *National Enquirer* joined the fray by accusing him of extramarital affairs and reporting that his fourteen-year marriage to Maria Shriver was in trouble. Schwarzenegger denied the charges. However, on April 26, 2001, his office issued a press statement that the actor would not run but would focus on expanding his involvement with youth activities and preparing to shoot *Terminator 3*.[65]

After withdrawing from the 2002 gubernatorial race, Schwarzenegger and his team began laying the groundwork for a 2006 run. Anxious to see what political storyline proved most effective, his seasoned inner circle organized a series of focus groups to test his proposed campaign slogan, "The people come first," and to see which image proved most effective with voters: Arnold the tough action hero; Arnold the shirt-and-tie leader; or Arnold the caring, compassionate candidate. The focus groups chose the last and strongly endorsed his populist rhetoric. To gain more campaign experience, Schwarzenegger succeeded in placing an after-school funding initiative, Proposition 49 (known as the "Schwarzenegger Initiative"), on the November 2002 ballot and then traveled the state lobbying on its behalf.

Placing Prop 49 on the ballot represented Schwarzenegger's vision of action-star politics. A pragmatist more than an ideologue, Schwarzenegger's goal, explained Reiss, "was not to just talk about running for governor; his goal was to do something while he was contemplating a run." He saw the initiative as a win-win situation: it would help children while at the same time giving him valuable experience in running a statewide campaign. After years of preparation, Schwarzenegger launched his political career around an issue for which he had obtained positive public recognition. After working with the Bush administration, he went on to head the California Governor's Council on Physical Fitness and Sports, helped Danny Hernandez expand his inner city after-school programs, and created his own Inner City Games Foundation (ICGF). By 2003, the ICGF provided after-school, weekend, and summer programs for 200,000 children in 400 locations throughout the country.[66]

Over the next several months, the actor met with politicians, teachers, sheriffs, nurses, and other key interest groups to fashion a proposition that all would find acceptable. On November 5, California voters passed his initiative by a wide margin of 57 to 43 percent. The compassionate action hero achieved his first political victory and gained valuable insights into the day-to-day compromises needed to get things done.[67]

Schwarzenegger's pragmatism and populist rhetoric pushed him further away from the core philosophy of GOP conservatives. For Arnold, ideology mattered until it conflicted with real life. At that point, he switched gears and asked how to get the job done, even if the answer angered his erstwhile allies. In this instance, years of working with children and then meeting with advocacy groups during the Prop 49 campaign altered his long-standing opposition to any kind of welfare state policies. "I used to go around saying, 'Everybody should pull himself up by his own bootstraps, just like I did.' What I learned about this country is this: Not everybody has boots."[68]

However clever he may have been in planning his run, Schwarzenegger might not have reached the statehouse without an incredibly lucky break: the gubernatorial recall election of 2003. Elected governor in 1999, Gray Davis had the misfortune of presiding over the disastrous decline of the state's economy. In 2000, as the dot-com boom provided the state's expanding economy with over $17 billion in tax revenues, the liberal Democrat dramatically increased spending for schools, health care, and government hiring. However, when the legislature refused to raise taxes after the Silicon Valley crash in 2002, the state budget deficit swelled to $35 billion. Davis's problems were compounded as the deregulation of electricity approved by former Governor Pete Wilson and illegal maneuvers by the Enron Corporation led to skyrocketing energy costs. Davis's popularity plummeted even further when he approved granting driver's licenses to illegal immigrants and increased state revenues by tripling vehicle-licensing fees. By April 2003, his approval rating dropped to an abysmal 24 percent.[69]

Disgusted with California's failing economy and its lackluster governor, conservative activists gathered enough signatures by July 23, 2003, to hold a special recall election on October 7. The recall involved a two-stage process. The first ballot asked voters whether Gray Davis should be recalled. If a majority voted no, then everything else was moot. However, voters were also asked to select a candidate in case a majority voted to replace him. The 134 people who registered to run included well-known public figures such as Democratic Lieutenant Governor Cruz Bustamante, Republican State Senator Tom McClintock, former Los Angeles Mayor Richard Riordan, Republican-turned–independent columnist Arianna Huffington, former baseball commissioner Peter Ueberroth, and, to the amusement of Americans who already thought California was the land of crazies, porn star Mary Carey, *Penthouse* publisher Larry Flynt, and former child actor Gary Coleman. The media buzz, however, was focused on whether Arnold Schwarzenegger would be the 135th candidate.

Schwarzenegger kept everyone waiting as he pondered entering the race. Three factors allowed him to think he could steal the election from more experienced politicians: the absence of party primaries, the large number of candidates vying for office, and, most importantly, his innovative plan to rely on the entertainment media.

Given his stance on social issues, it is highly unlikely that Schwarzenegger could have won a regular Republican primary in a state dominated by conservatives. "His candidacy engendered excitement, but not political support," observed Dan Schnur, who ran Peter Ueberroth's brief campaign. "His credentials were too liberal for California Republicans and his anti-politician rap wouldn't have worked with core party activists." Hoping to get a Republican into the California statehouse, House Ways and Means chairman Bill Thomas urged Schwarzenegger to take advantage of this unique opportunity. The recall election, he told the actor, would enable him to bypass the traditional party apparatus and take his populist appeal directly to California voters.[70]

Schwarzenegger's celebrity proved essential in catapulting him to the top of the polls. In a field of over a hundred candidates, the superstar's fame distinguished him from all but a handful of rivals. Tom McClintock was loved and well known among the GOP's conservative faithful, but he, as well as Democrat Cruz Bustamante, had far less appeal among ordinary voters. In the current climate of antipolitician discontent, image mattered more than specific policies. As campaign analyst Tony Quinn explained, voters were "not looking for a 12-point plan dealing with water transfers. They just don't like the way the whole political class has run things."[71]

While all these factors proved important, the key to Schwarzenegger's eventual success lay in his ability to use entertainment media outlets to sell himself to voters. As late as early August, he was still not certain he would enter the race. Maria did not want him to run and a newspaper poll released the previous month showed the unannounced candidate trailing former Los Angeles Mayor Richard Riordan 21 percent to 15 percent.[72] In July, *Terminator 3: Rise of the Machines* grossed $44 million in its initial domestic weekend, his biggest opening ever. Schwarzenegger's box-office returns may have declined since his peak, but he still made studios a great deal of money. If he wanted to give up his film career, he had to decide before the August 9 filing deadline. Not even his closest friends could predict what he would do.

Schwarzenegger knew he could not win by running a traditional campaign. That became evident on the evening of August 6, when he announced his candidacy on *The Tonight Show with Jay Leno*. The dramatic announcement surprised even his inner circle. "Arnold faked us all out," Bonnie Reiss recounted. "Other than telling Maria that morning, he led us all to believe he wasn't going to run." In the course of eleven minutes and twenty-one seconds, Schwarzenegger set the tone for his campaign: a mix of humor, populist rhetoric, and references to his cinematic persona. Entering the race, he told Leno, "was the most difficult decision to make in my entire life except for the one in 1978 when I decided to get a bikini wax." Adopting a very Ronald Reagan–like rhetoric, he promised to root out special interest groups in Sacramento. "The people are working hard," he explained. "The people are paying the taxes, the people are raising the families, but the politicians are not doing their job. The politicians are fiddling, fumbling and failing." Paying tribute to California conservative icon Howard Jarvis's rallying cry, which the former tax revolt leader took from the film *Network*, the gubernatorial hopeful insisted, "We are mad as hell and we're not going to take it anymore." Shifting to his own cinematic turf, Schwarzenegger warned Democratic and Republican politicians, "Do your job for the people and do it well, otherwise you are *hasta la vista*, baby!"[73]

The candidate ended his television appearance by anticipating his critics' likely denunciations. "I know they're going to throw everything at me and they're going, you know, to say that I have no experience and that I'm a womanizer and that I'm a terrible guy." He was willing to suffer that abuse because "I want to clean up Sacramento. I want to go in there and reform the system so it's back in the people's hands. The people should make the decisions, rather than the special interests." After promising the audience, "I'm going to pump California up," the smiling actor walked off the stage to thunderous applause. Leno was equally pleased; his show drew its highest ratings in three years.[74]

Arnold Schwarzenegger was not the first candidate to use talk shows for political ends. As noted earlier, candidates had appeared on popular television programs since 1960. Forty years later, several presidential contenders hoped to win votes by appearing on Oprah, Rosie O'Donnell, Regis Philbin, Jay Leno, David Letterman, and MTV.[75]

Schwarzenegger, however, understood what many candidates and political pundits did not: The burgeoning entertainment media was not necessarily a debasement of politics, but an expansion of the venues in which political dialogue could occur, especially given the declining coverage of elections by mainstream media outlets. As the percentage of homes with cable programming rose from 6 percent in 1969 to 68 percent in 1999 (85 percent by June 2002 if we include satellite), Americans proved less likely to watch political news. When Nixon delivered a routine prime-time press conference in March 1969, it was shown on all three networks and watched by 59 percent of American television households. When Clinton held a similar press conference in April 1995, it drew a scant 6.5 percent of households. Likewise, the average presidential sound bite on network evening news shrunk from 42 seconds in 1968 to less than 7 seconds in 1996. This left candidates with precious little time to frame campaign messages.[76]

Audience surveys discovered that the greatest drop-off in political viewership occurred among people who expressed weak or no party affiliation and confessed to being uninformed about most political issues. A Pew Center Study in 2000 found that 6 percent of respondents said they watched network news with a remote control in their hand, turning to other stations when the story bored them. Political news often fell under that category. If politicians wanted to be heard, they had to present their message in a way that excited potential voters.[77]

Entertainment venues served to reenergize the political system, especially among younger voters turned off by politics as usual. These viewers
were far more likely to watch a candidate on *The Daily Show with Jon Stewart*
or *The Colbert Report* than on *Meet the Press* or the *Jim Lehrer News Hour*.[78]
By offering politicians a chance to spin their own stories over the course of
anywhere from five to thirty minutes, these less-than-hard-news talk shows
gave audiences a better sense of a candidate's likeability while also providing
candidates with more time to get their message out to the public than traditional news venues.

Bill Clinton discovered this truth in 1992 and it helped get him elected.
After being subjected to a barrage of negative mainstream news coverage in
early June, Clinton trailed Ross Perot and George H. W. Bush with a popularity rating of 29 percent. However, after appearing on ten talk shows that
month—including *Larry King Live*, *The Today Show*, *Good Morning America*,
and *The Arsenio Hall Show*—his positive rating shot up to 93 percent by the
end of July. Instead of trying to compress his message into ten-second sound
bites, the charismatic candidate took the opportunity to talk at length about
the problems facing education, jobs, health care, and welfare reform; he also
used expanded time slots to explain his tax plan and reasons for supporting
gun control.[79]

What distinguished Schwarzenegger from Clinton and others is that he
reversed the usual media constellation by putting entertainment outlets at
the center of his campaign and pushing traditional news outlets to the margins. In strategy meetings that followed *The Tonight Show* appearance, he
repeatedly told his advisers, "I'm a different kind of candidate. I'm not a traditional politician. I can't run a campaign like a traditional politician.
Remember the recall was a reaction against normal politicians." The person
who best understood this was Maria Shriver. No candidate had ever had a
more media-savvy wife. In addition to her Kennedy connection, she spent
over twenty years working in traditional network news—including stints as
co-anchor of *The CBS Morning News* and anchor of *NBC Weekend News*—
and on entertainment programs such as *PM/Evening Magazine* and *The
Today Show*. During the campaign she helped devise her husband's media
strategy and served as his most important senior adviser. Despite initial protests from Schwarzenegger's more experienced campaign staff, they eventually heeded her suggestion to "Let Arnold be Arnold."[80]

For Arnold that meant using his celebrity as a way to frame his campaign and sell it to voters. Twenty years of active involvement in creating marketing strategies for his films gave him valuable insights into how to reach audiences. He approached his gubernatorial bid as he would a major movie opening. That meant playing to those who knew him best and were most likely to be favorable to his candidacy: the entertainment media. His strength lay in milking the same media outlets he had relied on to market his films: appearances on Oprah, Howard Stern, Larry King, Jay Leno; and conversations with reporters from *Variety, Access Hollywood, Inside Edition*, and *E!* Other candidates may have wanted similar exposure, but only someone with Arnold's celebrity could get on these shows as often and for as long as he wanted. These entertainment venues, explained his communications director Sean Walsh, "gave us five, seven, eight minutes of unfiltered opportunities to get our message every day."[81]

Knowing that he did not have the same close relations with the mainstream press, Schwarzenegger avoided traditional meetings with newspaper editorial boards and question-and-answer sessions with reporters from the *Los Angeles Times, New York Times, Wall Street Journal*, and Sunday morning news shows. This did not sit well with the political intelligentsia of the media world, but they were not the ones voting in the recall election. "The Main Street media missed this completely," observed Republican media strategist Dan Schnur. "Because the Main Street media were so busy paying attention to themselves, they didn't even notice how much effort Schwarzenegger and his campaign were putting into reaching out to entertainment media."[82]

As a famous movie star, Schwarzenegger knew he did not need traditional news outlets to garner greater recognition. His celebrity would attract cameras and reporters wherever he went. His first formal press conference drew 160 journalists from around the world, more than usually attended a presidential candidate's formal declaration. The longtime star also knew how to control the media. Schwarzenegger avoided discussing specific policies and instead repeated his campaign leitmotiv: he would be an agent of change for the state's do-nothing status quo. In this last instance, he was following the advice Teddy Kennedy gave him early in the campaign: "Never get too specific with your proposals otherwise the press will go after you on every single detail."[83]

Schwarzenegger understood that celebrity alone was not sufficient to win an election. He needed to convince voters that he could actually govern the state. To that end, he recruited prominent advisers who represented a broad spectrum of ideological thought. To deal with California's rapidly declining economy, he created an economic advisory board cochaired by former Republican Secretary of the Treasury and Secretary of State George Shultz and billionaire economic guru and moderate Democrat Warren Buffett; he also brought in Reagan-era adviser Arthur Laffer, who, though discredited among economists, remained popular in conservative circles. Schwarzenegger expanded his inner circle to include Bob White, who had run John McCain's presidential campaign in 2000, and Landon Parvin, Reagan's former speechwriter. His advisers continued meeting with focus groups—especially self-identified independents and ticket-splitting Democrats—to see what positions would most appeal to them. Despite its antipolitician rhetoric, this was a highly professional and well-organized campaign.[84]

The action-star candidate also reshaped traditional campaign strategies by venturing outside conventional wisdom. Seasoned political consultants have long argued that only 50 percent of eligible voters will turn out for any election; among that group, 40 percent will vote Democrat and 40 percent Republican. Consequently, most campaigns focus on attracting the 20 percent of undecided voters. Schwarzenegger believed that he could reach the 50 percent who did not usually vote, and thereby win the election, by appearing on popular daytime and evening talk shows. He courted potential female voters by going on *Oprah* with Maria, who talked about how her husband brought her coffee in the morning and regularly drove their kids to school. Watching "a candidate interview on an E-talk show," observed one media scholar, "is likely to enhance a low-awareness viewer's regard for that candidate . . . [and] trump any more critical information about the candidates presented in traditional campaign coverage." Oprah certainly agreed. "Over the years," she told a reporter, "I have not found that interviewing politicians about the issues worked for my viewing audiences. I try to bring issues that people understand through their hearts and their feelings so they can make decisions."[85]

During the early part of the campaign, the candidate followed Teddy Kennedy's advice and relied on populist rhetoric rather than specific policy proscriptions. When an NBC News producer asked him what cuts he would

FIGURE 9.4 Like Ronald Reagan, Arnold promised to sweep out inefficient legislators during the California gubernatorial recall election. SOURCE: ASSOCIATED PRESS

make to ease the state's deficit, Schwarzenegger responded, "The public doesn't care about figures. I will be the people's governor."[86] Instead of discussing problems related to race, class, and immigration, he employed stunts such as holding a press conference on the steps of the state capitol with a broom in hand and promising to make a clean sweep of state government (see figs. 9.4 and 9.5). Nor did he care when the *Los Angeles Times* printed a series of responses to specific policy questions from the other major candidates, but left Schwarzenegger's column blank. He would appeal to voters on his terms, not theirs.

Schwarzenegger's campaign bore a number of similarities to George Murphy's senatorial run in 1964. Just as television viewers saw striking contrasts between the trim, smiling Murphy and the overweight, dour Pierre Salinger, Schwarzenegger's carefully orchestrated television appearances in 2003 offered a sharp contrast between the self-assured actor and the depressed-looking Gray Davis. And like Murphy, who benefited from his old films being shown on late-night television, the sales of Schwarzenegger's movies and books soared during the recall, giving him increased visibility throughout the state. Indeed, in the weeks prior to the July 2 opening of

FIGURE 9.5 Schwarzenegger's campaign was filled with crowd-pleasing stunts such as throwing T-shirts into the audience.
SOURCE: ASSOCIATED PRESS

Terminator 3, the actor did over fifty television interviews and appeared on six magazine covers.[87]

The political hopeful also received enthusiastic support from the tabloid press. The *Star* featured a bold headline, "VOTE SCHWARZENEGGER!" and a long story, "Arnold: A New American Patriot," which compared him to George Washington. Grocery stores stocked copies of *Weekly World News* and its story, "Alien Backs Arnold for Governor," while American Media released a special 120-page magazine titled *Arnold, the American Dream.*[88] Alien support proved less useful than backing by powerful conservative radio and television hosts such as Sean Hannity, who, though skeptical of Schwarzenegger's commitment to conservative ideals, felt he was the party's best chance to oust Democrats from the statehouse.

Schwarzenegger helped his cause by "winning" a ninety-minute televised debate on September 24 that featured the campaign's leading candidates:

him, Bustamante, McClintock, Huffington, and Green Party leader Peter Camejo. Once again, luck and personality played a key role. Tom McClintock, the GOP's most compelling candidate, failed to press the movie star on either his conservative credentials or his specific solutions to the state's economic problems. Schwarzenegger repeatedly turned the debate into a setting for quips rather than content. When Huffington accused him of failing to endorse laws that would close corporate tax loopholes, he pointed out that over the past two years the millionaire had paid only $771 in federal taxes and no state taxes. "Your personal income tax has the biggest loophole. I can drive my Hummer through it." When she shot back, "Completely hypocritical of Arnold," and later shouted, "Let me finish! Let me finish! You know, this is completely typical of the way you treat women," the moderator asked him to respond. The audience broke out into laughter when he retorted, "I would just like to say that I just realized I have a perfect part for you in *Terminator 4*."

John Feliz, McClintock's campaign manager, insisted that the reason Schwarzenegger "won the debate was because it wasn't about the issues, it was about Arnold Schwarzenegger." The clip shown on television the entire next week, Feliz noted, was not McClintock saying, "You don't know the budget deficit from a hole in the ground," or Peter Camejo saying, "You don't understand the tax structure." It was Arnold saying, "I've got a role in *Terminator 4* for you."[89]

Schwarzenegger's greatest opposition did not come from his electoral opponents, but from the *Los Angeles Times*. "California voters know more about Schwarzenegger as a bodybuilder and Hollywood action figure than they do about his public policy ideas," the paper warned readers on August 8. "To fill in the gaps, the state's media should doggedly question him in his views and not accept simplistic answers." On October 2, five days before the election and with Schwarzenegger leading his nearest opponent by 8 percent, the newspaper published allegations from six women accusing him of a long history of groping and sexual harassment dating back to his days at Gold's Gym. Although campaign aides labeled the charges as politically motivated, Schwarzenegger responded with a mea culpa, telling the public, "Yes, I behaved badly sometimes. Yes, it is true that I was on rowdy movie sets, and I have done things that were not right, which I thought then was playful. But I now recognize that I have offended people. And to those people that I have offended, I want to say to them, I am deeply sorry about that, and I apologize."[90] By being contrite rather than attacking his accusers, Schwarzenegger came off as an honest, if occasionally misguided, man.

Allegations of sexual harassment were followed by a brief uproar over comments the former bodybuilder made about Adolf Hitler twenty-five years earlier. While filming *Pumping Iron* (1977) Schwarzenegger voiced his admiration for the Nazi leader's oratory abilities and for "being a little man with almost no formal education, [who rose] up to power." Insisting the quotes were taken out of context, the star released a transcript of the interview that revealed how he followed those statements by adding, "But I didn't admire him for what he [Hitler] did with it [power]." As the longtime supporter of the Simon Wiesenthal Center (named after the famous Nazi hunter) then told the press, "I have always despised everything that Hitler stands for. . . . That's why I'm very adamant for the fight against prejudice and to never let that happen again."[91]

The accusations, subsequent apology, and explanation led to a brief drop in the polls, but the "Teflon Terminator," as he was dubbed by the media, quickly bounced back as Republicans and radio talk shows denounced the *Times* for injecting scandal and smut into the campaign. The newspaper reported losing thousands of subscribers because of its coverage of Schwarzenegger's tainted past.[92]

Although publicly avoiding specific policy statements, the candidate met regularly with scores of academic and political experts dubbed "Schwarzenegger University" by insiders—who educated him about the issues he would confront as governor. On October 1, after months of consulting with advisers, Schwarzenegger issued a Franklin Roosevelt–like plan for the first 100 days of his administration. In a dramatic piece of political theater, he told the cheering faithful gathered in the Sacramento Memorial Auditorium, "I'm not here to talk about campaigning. I'm here to talk about governing." If elected, he promised to repeal the tripling of the car tax, repeal a new law permitting driver's licenses for illegal immigrants, renegotiate state employee contracts and Indian gaming agreements, arrange a comprehensive audit of the state budget to cut waste, and call a special session of the legislature.[93]

Schwarzenegger followed this with several days of rallies that drew on his tough-guy cinematic persona to make political points. With crowds chanting "Arnold, Arnold," he offered clichés such as "This is hand-to-hand combat!

We are in the trenches. This is war." In Orange County, he arranged for a crane to drop a 3,600-pound weight on top of an old car and then yelled out to the crowd, "*Hasta la vista* car tax." At other rallies he promised to be known as "the Collectionator," because he would squeeze more money out of the federal government. Few supporters cared that their next governor had not voted in thirteen of the past twenty-one elections, or that his longest interview was an hour-long chat with Larry King. The faithful saw him as a man of action more than a man of ideas. "All he said was, 'I'll be back,' and that was enough," explained entrepreneur Gary Reynolds. "He has the ability to change the atmosphere. Sometimes it's not how much you say, but how you say it." Voters said the same thing about Ronald Reagan during his gubernatorial run in 1966.[94]

On October 7, California voters went to the polls and cast two sets of ballots. On the first, 55.4 percent of the nearly 5 million participants voted in favor of recalling Gray Davis. On the second ballot, 48.6 percent of the electorate selected Arnold Schwarzenegger to be the thirty-eighth governor of California; Lieutenant Governor Cruz Bustamante finished a distant second with 31 percent of the vote. Various exit polls revealed that he captured approximately 77 percent of the Republican vote, 46 percent of the independent vote, and 21 percent of the Democratic vote. He won all age cohorts, attracted a plurality of female votes, and even captured nearly one-third of the traditionally Democratic Latino vote.[95]

More importantly, Schwarzenegger's strategy of mobilizing people who usually refrained from voting appeared to work: 22 percent more people voted in 2003 than in the 2002 gubernatorial election, and the number of eligible voters going to the polls increased from 36 percent to 43 percent. As for the 50 percent who usually sat out elections, 7 percent of his supporters told exit pollsters that they rarely or never voted. But Arnold got them to the polls.[96]

The recall election was ultimately less a mandate for Schwarzenegger than a rejection of Gray Davis. The movie star had been right when he told voters the day before the election, "Tomorrow, it is all about the people versus the government, the politicians." Attracted to his celebrity, voters also understood his limitations; 63 percent felt the new governor had not sufficiently addressed critical issues facing the state. Nevertheless, the promise that Schwarzenegger would inaugurate a new kind of action-oriented politics led them to select him over his politics-as-usual opponents. Although numerous media pundits questioned the sanity of California voters, Golden State residents offered a different opinion. The recall and subsequent election, L. Vigor wrote in the *Los Angeles Times*, was "a great day for democracy" because California voters "have affirmed what Thomas Jefferson said two centuries ago. To be successful, a democracy needs a little revolution every now and then."[97]

THE GOVERNATOR

On November 17, 2003, having spent $22 million in sixty days, Arnold Schwarzenegger, or "the Governator" as many now called him, took the oath of office on the steps of the state capitol. With 130 television cameras and reporters from *E!, Access Hollywood, Entertainment Tonight,* and other entertainment shows covering an inauguration for the first time, the event seemed more like a movie premiere than a political swearing in. Over the course of twelve minutes, California's new chief executive delivered a speech that could have been written by Louis B. Mayer or Ronald Reagan. Combining the optimism of Mayer's Andy Hardy series with the hopefulness of Reagan's vision of America as "a shining city on a hill," Schwarzenegger boasted that anything is possible in this great land. "I see California as a golden dream by the sea," he told the crowd. "Perhaps some will think this is fanciful, but to someone like me, who came here with absolutely nothing and gained absolutely everything, it is not fanciful to see California as the golden dream. I have taken the oath to uphold the constitution of California, and now with your help and with God's, I will uphold this dream that is California."[98]

Unfortunately for California residents, God apparently had more important things to do than help Arnold Schwarzenegger. The actor's innovative use of celebrity proved sufficient to get him elected, but not to ensure that he would be an effective governor. Personality could trump policy during a recall, but not when it came to running an economically embattled state. In the months and years following his victory, Schwarzenegger discovered what Warren Beatty had been telling reporters for decades: there is a critical difference between running and governing.

Initially, it appeared as if Schwarzenegger could be a different kind of governor. His greatest success came during his first year in office when he dropped his antipolitician rhetoric and worked closely with the people he had denounced during the recall. The pragmatic chief executive brought Democrats and Republicans into his inner circle of advisers, consulted regularly with legislators on both sides of the aisles, and quietly struck bargains with a wide variety of "special interest" groups. This cooperative approach to governing worked as he achieved a series of victories that first year: he lowered the costs of workers' compensation insurance (then the highest in the nation) and succeeded in passing ballot initiatives that raised billions of dollars for schools and infrastructure while also requiring the legislature to balance the state budget. The populist governor achieved a 68 percent approval rating by March 2004 and proved so beloved that people talked about passing a constitutional amendment that would allow immigrants like Arnold to run for president.[99]

Success, however, went to the governor's head. Emboldened by his early victories, he resumed his action-star persona, told legislators what to do, and grew impatient when they refused to listen. He abandoned bipartisan alliances in favor of putting forth ballot initiatives favored by conservatives that bypassed the legislature and went directly to the people. Acting like a tough CEO might work in business, but it could not work in a political system where there were too many groups that did not have to answer to the governor or respond like they were his employees.

Rather than negotiate, Schwarzenegger went on the attack. In a July 2004 speech at the Ontario Mills Mall, he angrily accused legislators of selling out to unions and special interests. Employing the heated and often sexist rhetoric that proved so popular during the recall, he asked voters to "terminate" legislators who did not pass the budget he desired. "If they don't have the guts, I call them girlie men." Several months later, while speaking at the Republican National Convention, he again accused his critics of being "economic girlie men."[100]

Schwarzenegger's attacks played well with his supporters but not with the politicians who ran the system. He soon learned that populist candidates who position themselves as outsiders and attack politics as usual have a hard time governing once they get into office. Schwarzenegger's problems were compounded by the fact that he had no strong allies within the state's Republican Party. Conservatives may have supported him in the recall, but they did not trust him. Democrats proved even more suspicious of the new chief executive. And neither side of the political divide was willing to cut slack to a chief executive who derogatorily referred to them as "girlie men."

In all fairness, Schwarzenegger faced a series of structural problems that made it extraordinarily difficult for anyone to govern the state. Dealing with California's budget crisis proved the greatest challenge the new governor faced during his years in office. The expansive hiring and lucrative benefit packages granted by Gray Davis during flush times came to choke the state during the subsequent economic downturn. A constitutional amendment that required a two-thirds vote by legislators to raise taxes and the lingering effects of Proposition 13, which limited tax revenues from homeowners, made it nearly impossible for the governor to obtain the revenues needed to lower the deficit. Moreover, California's term limit law of 1990, which restricted citizens to three two-year terms in the legislature and two four-year terms in the senate, prompted even greater ideological polarization among legislators and left them with little incentive to cooperate with the other party or the new governor. Schwarzenegger's limited ability to dictate policy was made even harder by a referendum system that allowed wealthy interest groups to bypass the legislature and governor and present issues directly to the people.

Given these structural difficulties and operating without a strong political base in Sacramento, Schwarzenegger found it hard to deal with the various "special interest" groups he promised to confront. When legislators refused to bow to his demands, the "people's" governor called a special election in November 2005 and asked voters to approve four ballot measures he devised—two of them aimed at curbing spending and easing gridlock. His credibility suffered a major blow when the press reported that the outspoken enemy of all special interests had accepted $47 million from bankers, financial firms, entertainment industry groups, and real estate and construction companies to fund his gubernatorial campaign and ballot initiatives. That November, all four initiatives went down to defeat and Schwarzenegger's approval ratings plunged to 33 percent. At his state of the state address several months later, a duly chastened governor apologized to Californians and promised that he would "cut the warfare, cool the rhetoric, find common ground and fix the problems together."[101]

Schwarzenegger managed to win a second term in 2006, defeating state treasurer Phil Angelides, a man whose lack of charisma was exceeded only by the aptly named Gray Davis. However, the former actor's political inexperience ultimately prevented him from achieving the political revolution he had promised during the recall. It was one thing for a superstar to control what went into a movie script, but quite another for a governor to control a state legislature dominated by the opposing party. "This is a guy who can get any world leader, any CEO of any major company, on the phone in two seconds," observed former Davis speechwriter Jason Kinney. "But the 120 people in the state he has the least influence over are the [members of the] Legislature."[102]

After serving Californians for more than seven years, Schwarzenegger left office widely perceived as a failed governor and with little popular talk of running him for higher office. A Field poll released in July 2010 showed only 22 percent of voters approved his performance while 70 percent disapproved; these were even lower than Gray Davis's ratings. In the end, his political ambitions exceeded his political abilities. Warren Beatty understood this about himself and it was one of the reasons he never ran for office. As he told a Democratic gathering during Schwarzenegger's reelection campaign, "Government is not show business. Governing by show, by spin, by cosmetics, by photo ops, fake events, fake issues, and fake crowds is a mistake."[103]

Despite Beatty's admonition, Schwarzenegger should be credited for recognizing a fundamental truth about electoral politics. For democracy to work more effectively, politicians need to reach beyond the already interested and engage the 50 percent of the eligible electorate who rarely vote. Relying on the entertainment media does not necessarily trivialize politics. Entertainment and political ideas can, and have been, combined without degrading either. As early as 1913, radical filmmakers such as Frank E. Wolfe presented highly polemical messages in the form of melodramatic love stories that merged ideology and entertainment in an appealing fashion. Unfortunately, Schwarzenegger pursued the latter at the cost of the former.

For better and worse, Arnold Schwarzenegger represents the culmination of a relationship between movie stars and politics that began with Charlie Chaplin and continues today. Schwarzenegger proved a remarkably shrewd campaigner, but once in office he confronted the limits of celebrity politics and uses of entertainment media. As governor, he had to deal with the people he belittled or avoided during the recall: politicians and mainstream media. Celebrity got him elected but did not prepare him for overcoming California's many financial crises; instead, he deepened them. In the end, his story highlights the critical difference between a celebrity who knows how to win an election and a politician who knows how to work within the system. As Barack Obama showed in 2008 and John Kennedy before him, politicians who become celebrities have a better chance of governing effectively than celebrities who become politicians.

EPILOGUE

Rarely have the limits and power of celebrity politics been more evident than during the 2008 presidential campaign, as two candidates struggled to distinguish themselves from a pack of rivals. Fred Thompson believed that in a field of eleven Republican hopefuls, his fame and cinematic image could propel him all the way to the White House. Likewise, Oprah Winfrey hoped that her endorsement of Illinois' young but charismatic Senator Barack Obama would boost his prospects for defeating Democratic frontrunner Hillary Clinton.

In 2003, Arnold Schwarzenegger demonstrated that a hardworking movie star with a strong image and well-organized campaign team could, in the right circumstances, overcome the lack of deep party ties. Thompson attempted to take celebrity politics a step further by initially relying almost solely on the appeal of his tough cinematic persona. While never a star of Schwarzenegger's magnitude, the former U.S. attorney and two-term senator from Tennessee (1994–2003) appeared in more than two dozen feature films and television movies, playing a range of leaders: a U.S. president, CIA director, White House chief of staff, and rear admiral. Most Americans, however, knew him for his longtime role as tough-on-crime District Attorney Arthur Branch in the popular *Law and Order* television series.

At first Thompson's primarily celebrity-driven strategy seemed to work. He polled higher numbers in the months preceding his formal declaration than he did afterward. As a potential candidate, voters could indulge their fantasies of who he might be and what he might do in office. Newspapers and entertainment programs repeatedly referred to him as the "Law and Order" candidate. His rival Mitt Romney confessed that Thompson's image gave him a distinct advantage with voters. "He's a terrific guy and he's been putting bad guys away every week." In June 2007, though he had not yet declared his candidacy, the politician-turned-actor polled second (21 percent) to New York City Mayor Rudolph Giuliani (27 percent) and well ahead of Arizona Senator John McCain (12 percent). On September 5, 2007, while his rivals were debating policy in New Hampshire, Thompson went on the *Tonight Show with Jay Leno* and announced, "I'm running for president of the United States."[1]

Thompson, however, was no Schwarzenegger. The latter understood that image and celebrity were not enough to get him elected; he needed to run a well-organized campaign aimed at convincing voters that he could govern the state. "Hollywood Fred," as he was often called in the press, squandered his celebrity capital by shying away from the hard work and long hours required to run for high office. "The book on him is he's lazy," David Keene, president of the American Conservative Union, told reporters in June 2007. The *Los Angeles Times* reported how his precampaign days occasionally began at 8:15 A.M. and ended by 11:00 A.M. By November, his campaign imploded, torn apart by poor organization and the departure of his press secretary and communications director. By December, his ratings had dropped to 7 percent; a month later, he withdrew from the race. Unlike Murphy, Reagan, or Schwarzenegger, Thompson failed to convince voters that the man and the image were one and the same.[2]

Celebrity was not strong enough to overcome Thompson's weaknesses, but it helped Barack Obama secure a number of critical primary victories. In May 2007, he received the backing of the nation's most popular celebrity and occasional movie star, Oprah Winfrey. This was the first time the powerful media figure had ever endorsed and then campaigned for a politician. Movie stars had been supporting candidates since the 1920s, but Oprah had a gravitas and credibility that most of them lacked. Voters knew that she was a serious activist who had spent years using her TV shows, magazines, and blogs to improve people's lives. Now, instead of selling the books of her guests, she was selling a candidate. Polls released between July and September 2007 reported that 30 percent of respondents said they were more likely to vote for Obama because of her endorsement, while 60 to 70 percent claimed it made no difference; 3 percent said it would make them less likely to vote for the Illinois senator.[3]

What these polls did not reveal was Oprah's ability to reach the 50 percent of the electorate who do not usually vote, especially women. Over the years, surveys have shown that nonvoters feel they lack the information needed to make informed decisions. Surveys also report that women are less likely than men to know the positions taken by presidential candidates. Here is where Oprah's support made a significant difference: many of the 50 percent who rarely vote are Oprah's people. When compared to traditional news audiences, talk show viewers are less interested in politics and more likely to be young, female, and liberal. With a television show that draws eight million viewers each weekday (80 percent of whom are women), a magazine with a circulation of two million, a weekly newsletter sent to nearly a half-million, and 360,000 people who receive her Web site's daily "Oprah Alerts," Winfrey had the potential to educate and mobilize a huge part of the electorate usually ignored by campaign strategists.[4]

Oprah's endorsement did not automatically translate into votes for Obama. Pollsters pose the wrong question when t0hey ask if celebrity endorsements make people more likely to vote for a candidate. The better question is: Does a celebrity make voters more likely to pay attention to a candidate? Oprah did precisely that; her endorsement led viewers to listen to what Obama had to say. Once they no longer felt ignorant about key campaign issues, many wound up voting for him in the primaries and in the general election. A study by two economists concluded that Winfrey's endorsement gave Obama a boost of more than one million votes in the primaries and caucuses, nearly 1 percent of the total votes cast in the 2004 presidential elections. More importantly, the study conjectured that Hillary Clinton would have garnered more votes than Obama if not for Winfrey. In short, her power was great enough to help throw the nomination to her preferred candidate.[5]

Once Republicans nominated John McCain, it appeared that a fear-and-reassurance conservative would yet again defeat a young Democratic hopeful with star backing—and Obama would head down the same road as Gary Hart. That did not happen. The success of the Obama–Oprah connection marked a departure from the long-standing relationship between Hollywood and politics, one in which the left usually pursued causes while the right elected candidates. This new wrinkle leads us to return to the counter-intuitive statement raised in the book's introduction and ask: Why is it that the Hollywood right has been more successful in the world of electoral politics than the Hollywood left?

Arnold Schwarzenegger had a simple but profound insight before he decided to run for governor: to be successful a candidate or a party needs an effective storyline. Over the years, Republicans have offered voters better storylines than Democrats. Hollywood movies are about fantasies, especially hopeful fantasies. The Hollywood right achieved many of their victories by talking about a nostalgic Golden Age of America that never was. Reagan was victorious in part because he promised a new dawn for America, a return to an imagined past of simpler, better days.

The Hollywood left's storyline has been one of hope and guilt: hope of what the United States could be and guilt that we are not doing enough to achieve that vision. For the left, a better America means looking to the future rather than the past and doing more to expand rights and democracy for all Americans. In addition, their storyline envisions an active government as the best way to implement those ideals. Such a concept, however, plays to the brain rather than the heart and often lacks strong emotional appeal.

From Louis B. Mayer to Arnold Schwarzenegger, the Hollywood right has told a simple but compelling story of American triumphalism: America is the greatest nation in the world. What more do you need to know? Few citizens want to hear a Jane Fonda, Warren Beatty, or Sean Penn point out what is wrong with the United States. They like to hear about God, faith, country, and hope; and they want to be reassured that in frightening times our leaders can defeat all foes. The political stars of the Hollywood right understood this need and preached it to the electorate. Since the Cold War, their message of fear and reassurance has proved stronger than the left's message of hope and guilt. Both sides want a better world, but the right plays more to emotions and employs fear-mongering to sell its stories. Fear usually has a greater impact on voters than hope—but not always.

Since the 1930s, the Hollywood left has generally focused on issues and movements. However, as Barack Obama showed, if they decided to concentrate on electoral politics—and learn from Obama and from their conservative counterparts—they could be just as successful as the Hollywood right. The Illinois senator understood the importance of storyline and steered clear of unsuccessful narratives of hope and guilt. Instead, he shifted his party's mantra to hope and "change we can believe in." Despite losing the New Hampshire primary in January 2008, his supporters were buoyed by his new campaign slogan, "Yes, we can," and its accompanying storyline: "It was whispered by slaves and abolitionists, as they blazed the trail toward freedom. Yes, we can! By immigrants who traveled to a new land, workers who organized, women who reached for the vote. Yes, we can!" Several months later, after winning the support of the party's superdelegates, he laid claim to the Democratic nomination with a powerful exhortation: "You chose to listen not to your doubts or your fears, but to your greatest hopes and highest aspirations."[6] Obama's storyline appealed to the emotions and inspired millions of voters.

The Hollywood right's success in the electoral arena should not obscure the important impact the Hollywood left has had on political life. The latter preferred pursuing issues and movements of broad national importance rather than running for high office. And they often did so at times when many of those causes were highly unpopular. Despite encountering considerable opposition, the Hollywood left helped publicize the dangers posed by Hitler in the 1930s and 1940s, helped expand civil rights in the 1950s and 1960s, helped lead antiwar movements in the 1960s, 1970s, and 2000s, and helped advance social and political movements that advocated a more open and tolerant society during the late twentieth and early twenty-first centuries.

A number of factors help explain why most left stars focused on issue-oriented politics. Many of them had more successful careers than their right counterparts and did not want to give up their fame, wealth, and adulation for the contentious electoral arena. Murphy and Reagan never had to make that choice; they did not get seriously involved in movement politics until after their movie careers had ended. Ed Asner offers one explanation for why successful actors, left and right, shy away from public office. "Why would you leave a prominent position in show business to run for public office and be buried in the bullshit that occurs with being a politician? That's why Heston certainly would never do it and why Beatty wouldn't do it."[7] One could also add the names of John Wayne and Jimmy Stewart, two successful conservative stars who were asked, and refused, to run for office.

The right's success in the electoral arena can be attributed to structural forces as well as the actions of individuals. The left has always had to pursue a harder path, for it struggles to initiate reform while the right fights to maintain the status quo. The history of American politics demonstrates that it is easier to preserve the status quo than to inaugurate dramatic change. The 1830s, the Civil War, the Progressive Era, the New Deal, and the 1960s were marked by outbursts of reform and federal activism. But given our nearly 250-year history, these eras are infrequent; they were the exceptions and not the rule. There have been more years in which government has been dominated by a laissez-faire ideology than one calling for an activist state. Likewise, the Supreme Court, with some notable exceptions, has tended to favor the status quo. None of this is surprising when you consider that the Founding Fathers feared an excess of democracy and created a Constitution that would make radical change difficult to achieve.[8]

Like the stories they tell, the roles movie stars play can have an important impact on voters, and any actor who is considering a political career should carefully choose films that enhance a certain kind of image. Murphy's and Reagan's careers offer us a glimpse into why the "good guy" cinematic images of the Hollywood right allowed them to fare better with the voting public than their left counterparts. Both men were affable Midwesterners who represented the kind of entertainment values favored by those disgusted with stars whose politics seemed out of touch with ordinary Americans. The HUAC hearings and ensuing Red Scare left many citizens with a sense that "liberal" Hollywood had grown too radical and dangerous. Reagan and Murphy never achieved the stardom of a Charlie Chaplin, Edward G. Robinson, Jane Fonda, or Warren Beatty, but they proved far more appealing to cultural conservatives. For one thing, they were not Jews or leftists, two groups often seen as unduly critical of American politics. In 1964, many California voters still remembered Murphy as the nice guy who danced with Shirley Temple. Reagan had an equally wholesome quality and while he was certainly part of Hollywood, he belonged to its conservative, more Christian, anti-Communist wing.

Once they turned to political activism, both men used their good-natured cinematic image to reassure the public that they were not going to undermine the nation's "traditional" cultural foundation, something neither Fonda nor Beatty nor Harry Belafonte could easily do. In 1950, Reagan complained to *Silver Screen* magazine of being tired of playing "the good, the sweet, the color-less charmboy."[9] But that image served him well during the culture wars of the 1960s and 1980s, and the accompanying antipathy to a Hollywood that seemed out of touch with the values of Red-State America. Even Schwarzenegger's action-hero image was softened by his immigrant rags-to-riches storyline and his self-professed patriotism, something those on the left rarely declare. The growing importance of the "good guy" image in politics helped George W. Bush defeat Al Gore in 2000. Many voters preferred Bush because they saw him as a regular guy with whom they would want to have a beer.

After examining nearly a hundred years of Hollywood's history, one final question remains: Does the participation of movie stars and celebrities in political life strengthen or weaken democracy?

Radical activist Tom Hayden, who lived with celebrity politics during his marriage to Jane Fonda, sees movie star participation as a mixed blessing. "By playing to celebrity," he suggested, "you undermine democracy by turning citizens into fans. You turn critical thinking into adoration." On the other hand, stars "draw attention to issues, raise a lot of money, and get media attention." The appearance of several movie stars at a rally promoting a clean water initiative "created a huge motivation for young people to get involved when the celebrities were gone." Yet in the end, the radical democrat concluded that he "wouldn't want to build a left movement around a Hollywood left," for doing so "elevates stars to a kind of Papal role" and undermines a core principle of mass democracy: the people, not one figure, should decide a nation's path.[10]

Whether celebrity politics are good or bad for democracy can be debated. What remains true is that movie stars help expand democracy by getting people to pay attention to issues and then vote. There is something very wrong with democracy when political consultants regularly write off the 50 percent of nonvoters rather than try to mobilize them. Given the abysmal history of voter turnout since the middle of the twentieth century, movie stars have aided democracy by using their celebrity to get people off their couches and into voting booths. Arnold Schwarzenegger's presence in the 2003 California recall election generated 1.7 million more votes than in the regular gubernatorial election that occurred twelve months earlier.[11] If Oprah can increase voter turnout in presidential primaries by 1 percent, if Chuck Norris's participation at rallies helps turn nonvoters into voters, then movie stars and celebrities have succeeded in creating a more engaged electorate.

Politics in a democracy is a participatory activity and not just a spectator sport. The ten people profiled here worked hard to change the nation for the better and disproved assumptions about the shallowness of Hollywood politics. In many ways, their differences are less significant than their one common denominator: they were all passionate about improving the lives of millions of citizens. All ten had what they needed in life, at least insofar as material comforts and ego gratification. Political participation did not help their careers. Rather, they always had people telling them not to get involved. Although they may not have always succeeded in the ways they envisioned, they were willing to sacrifice their time and risk their livelihood to do what they felt was their right and their duty. At the very least, they tried to make democracy work by mobilizing people to engage in politics.[12]

With new forms of entertainment, new sources of news, and a new digital age to deliver them, we are on the threshold of a new political landscape in which movie stars and celebrities will have even more influence and politicians will have to become entertainers if they wish to reach a broader electorate. As Ronald Reagan once quipped, "I don't know how anybody can be in politics without being an actor." We have a long history of movie stars who became politicians, but now we have politicians who have turned themselves into celebrities. Sarah Palin hosted her own reality show, *Sarah Palin's Alaska*, on The Learning Channel; former House Majority leader Tom DeLay tried to resurrect his career with an appearance on *Dancing with the Stars*, which also featured Palin's daughter Bristol. And Fox News, long the leader of news infotainment, has established itself as the celebrity-politician channel. By September 2010, they signed four of the five likely Republican presidential candidates for 2012 as regular contributors: Palin, Mike Huckabee, Rick Santorum, and Newt Gingrich. Only Mitt Romney remained outside the fold.[13]

At their best, these politicians-turned–celebrity hosts could join movie star activists in helping to educate and expand the electorate. Yet it would be naive not to believe that their shows can just as easily trivialize complex issues and do more harm than good. Unfortunately for democracy, these commentators and programs are primarily focused on generating ratings and revenues. Consequently, they are far more likely to bypass the serious for the salacious, and bring heat rather than light to political discourse. Over two hundred years ago, the Founding Fathers warned that for a republic to survive it needed an informed citizenry. Conservative commentators have strayed far from the obligations of citizenship articulated by the Founding Fathers they so openly venerate. Instead of educating and finding common grounds of agreement, they offer inflammatory rhetoric filled with rumors and half-truths that pit right against left, and American against American.

Celebrity hosts and infotainment programs do not have to inflame or dumb down political discourse. From Jonathan Swift to Jon Stewart, pundits have used satire as a way to combine politics and entertainment without trivializing either. Americans today, especially eighteen- to thirty-year-olds, like their political information to be entertaining. This helps explain the popularity of programs that offer a knowledgeable mix of news and comedy, information and wit: shows such as *The Daily Show with Jon Stewart*, *The Colbert Report*, and *The Glenn Beck Show*, whose Web site proclaims it the "fusion of entertainment and enlightenment." Although Beck is often guilty of inflaming passions, he has also succeeded in getting his audience to read (or at least buy) serious works of political theory such as Friedrich Hayek's *The Road to Serfdom*. Moreover, he and Jon Stewart have crossed the line into political activism, and brought their viewers with them. Glenn Beck's "Rally for America" drew approximately 80,000 people to Washington, D.C., in August 2010; two months later, over 215,000 traveled to the nation's capital to attend Jon Stewart's "Rally to Restore Sanity."[14]

Looking ahead to the future, movie stars are more likely to bring greater sanity to political discourse than most news/entertainment show commentators. For one thing, they are not paid to be political; they leverage their celebrity for the public good, not for ratings or income. One may not like their politics, but we need to admire the intense preparation they bring to their activism. The movie stars examined in this book did not just spout off; they supported their ideas with serious preparation. Charlton Heston would thoroughly research a topic before speaking about it. Whether it was his debates with Ed Asner and Paul Newman or speeches on behalf of the National Rifle Association, his son Fraser recounted, "he did his homework. He didn't want to be a spokesman for someone else's political point of view." Likewise, the movie stars belonging to the Creative Coalition—a lobbying group that promotes First Amendment rights, arts advocacy, and public education—are given thick binders and run through mock interviews before they are allowed to speak on behalf of the organization. As the late Christopher Reeve explained, "[we] had to educate ourselves about important issues, and then use our talents as communicators to educate others."[15]

The ultimate responsibility for reinvigorating democracy lies not with politicians but with citizens themselves. Patriotism is not just about defending the nation during war or opposing what some see as misguided government policies. It is also about the everyday actions people take to make democracy work. We can blame whomever we want for the failures of our government and society, but it is up to every citizen to do something to change things for the better. Each one of us might ask, what have we done to fulfill our obligations as citizens? How much time have we devoted to political activism? All ten Hollywood activists profiled here used their charisma and emotional appeal as movie stars to make people believe in the possibilities of a better nation. They were leaders, not just followers. They did not simply bask in their fame and wealth; they worked as hard at their politics as they did at their screen careers. They spoke out on behalf of causes that were popular and unpopular, regardless of the consequences. They fit the Founding Fathers' model of citizen-statesmen in that they had a vision of the world they wanted to see and they were willing to work to usher in that change. And for that, they deserve our respect. If every citizen behaved like them, the United States would be a far better place.

NOTES

★

ABBREVIATIONS

AMPAS	Margaret Herrick Library, Academy of Motion Picture Arts and Sciences, Beverly Hills, California
Crocker Coll.	Harry Crocker Collection, Margaret Herrick Library, Academy of Motion Picture Arts and Sciences, Beverly Hills, California
CUOHP	Columbia University Oral History Program, Special Collections Department, Columbia University, New York
FBI Records	Federal Bureau of Investigation, Confidential Files, *Communist Activity in the Entertainment Industry: FBI Surveillance Files on Hollywood, 1942–1958*, ed. Daniel J. Leab (University Publications of America, Microfilms, 14 rolls)
Heston Coll.	Charlton Heston Collection, Margaret Herrick Library, Academy of Motion Picture Arts and Sciences, Beverly Hills, California
Hoover Papers	Herbert Hoover Papers, Herbert Hoover Presidential Library, West Branch, Iowa
Hopper Papers	Hedda Hopper Papers, Margaret Herrick Library, Academy of Motion Picture Arts and Sciences, Beverly Hills, California
IPC Records	Indochina Peace Campaign Records, 1940–1976, Wisconsin Historical Society, Madison, Wisconsin
LAT	*Los Angeles Times*
NYT	*New York Times*
PCA files	Production Code Administration Files, Margaret Herrick Library, Academy of Motion Picture Arts and Sciences, Beverly Hills, California
Robinson Coll.	Edward G. Robinson Collection, Cinema-TV Library, University of Southern California, Los Angeles, California
USC	University of Southern California, Los Angeles, California

INTRODUCTION

1. "Memorandum for Mr. Hoover," August 28, 1922, FBI subject file for Charlie Chaplin, 100-127090, Bureau of Investigation, Washington, D.C. Chaplin's file is reproduced in FBI Records, Disc 2 (of 43 disks), www.paperlessarchives.com, accessed June 15, 2005 (disks can be purchased from the aforementioned Web site). For surveillance of movie industry figures dating back to March 1918, see Steven J. Ross, *Working-Class Hollywood: Silent Film and the Shaping of Class in America* (Princeton, N.J., 1998), 326n66.
2. Peter Manso, *Brando: The Biography* (New York, 1994), 573; *LAT*, May 30, 1997.
3. William C. deMille, "Censorship: Lecture Notes," September 5, 1935, unpublished manuscript, box 2, William C. deMille Collection, Special Collections, New York Public Library.
4. Jackie Cooper, Oral History, June 1959, 85, series 3, vol. 4, Popular Arts Project, Columbia University Oral History Program; author notes from Creative Coalition meeting, September 30, 1999, Brentwood, California.
5. Prominent left activists include Gene Kelly, Betsy Blair, Melvyn Douglas, Helen Gahagan Douglas, Ossie Davis, Ruby Dee, Gregory Peck, Burt Lancaster, Paul Newman, Marlon Brando, Robert Redford, Barbra Streisand, Shirley MacLaine, Mike Farrell, Susan Sarandon, Tim Robbins, Danny Glover, George Clooney, and Sean Penn. The Hollywood right includes an equally impressive array of stars: Mary Pickford, Adolphe Menjou, Harold Lloyd, Ginger Rogers, Gary Cooper, Ward Bond, Robert Montgomery, Robert Taylor, John Wayne, Bob Hope, Shirley Temple, Sonny Bono, Bruce Willis, and Tom Selleck.

CHAPTER 1

1. William C. deMille, *Hollywood Saga* (New York, 1939), 196; "Report of Special Agent A. A. Hopkins," August 15, 1922, Los Angeles, FBI subject file for Charlie Chaplin, 100-127090, Bureau of Investigation, Washington, D.C. (hereafter, Chaplin, FBI files). Chaplin's file is reproduced in FBI Records, disc 2, www.paperlessarchives.com, accessed June 15, 2005.
2. W. J. Burns to Leon Bone, August 24, 1922, Chaplin, FBI files.
3. Emanuel Julius, "The Social Significance of Charlie Chaplin," *New York Call*, June 27, 1915.
4. Edward G. Robinson with Leonard Spigelgass, *All My Yesterdays: An Autobiography* (New York, 1973), 277.
5. Charles Chaplin, *My Autobiography* (New York, 1964), 14. Biographical information about Chaplin's early life is drawn from ibid.; Charlie Chaplin, *My Trip Abroad* (New York and London, 1922); Wes D. Gehring, *Charlie Chaplin: A Bio-Bibliography* (Westport, Conn., 1983); David Robinson, *Chaplin: His Life and Art* (New York, 1985); Harry M. Geduld, ed., *Charlie Chaplin's Own Story* (Bloomington, Ind., 1985); Jeffrey Vance, *Chaplin: Genius of the Cinema* (New York, 2003); Kevin J. Hayes, ed., *Charlie Chaplin Interviews* (Jackson, Miss., 2005). For an overview of his early films, see Harry M. Geduld, *Chapliniana: A Commentary on Charlie Chaplin's 81 Movies* (Bloomington, Ind., 1987); Vance, *Chaplin*.

6. Chaplin, *Autobiography*, 22. Autobiography is always a tricky source because subjects often alter their past to fit the present. I used only those quotes whose accuracy could be confirmed by information contained in the sources mentioned above in n. 5.

7. Ibid., 31.

8. Ibid., 134.

9. Dollar equivalencies are taken from www.measuringworth.com/ppowerus/, accessed May 8, 2010.

10. Charlie Chaplin Vertical File Collection, reel 2, side 2, 6, Margaret Herrick Library, Academy of Motion Picture Arts and Sciences, Beverly Hills, California (hereafter, AMPAS). Although *Kid Auto Races at Venice* appeared first, *Mabel's Strange Predicament* was actually filmed several days earlier.

11. For dollar comparison, see n. 9.

12. *Detroit News*, April 13, 1916, quoted in Charles J. Maland, *Chaplin and American Culture: The Evolution of a Star Image* (Princeton, N.J., 1989), 16; Minnie Maddern Fiske, "The Art of Charles Chaplin," *Harper's Weekly*, May 16, 1916.

13. Lucy France Pierce, "The Nickelodeon," *World Today*, October 1908, quoted in Gerald Mast, ed., *Movies in Our Midst: Documents in the Cultural History of Film in America* (Chicago, 1982), 51; *Moving Picture World*, October 30, 1908; *Chicago Daily Socialist*, December 17, 1909. For attendance figures, see U.S. Department of Commerce, *Historical Statistics of the United States: Colonial Times to 1970*, 2 vols. (Washington, D.C., 1975), 1:400–401; Steven J. Ross, *Working-Class Hollywood: Silent Film and the Shaping of Class* (Princeton, N.J., 1998), 7, 11. Figures for 1930 include multiple attendance by the same people.

14. For politics and radicalism during this era, see Michael McGerr, *A Fierce Discontent: The Rise and Fall of the Progressive Movement in America, 1870–1920* (New York, 2005); James Weinstein, *The Decline of Socialism in America, 1912–1925* (New Brunswick, N.J., 1987).

15. Walter Prichard Eaton, "Class Consciousness and the Movies," *Atlantic Monthly* 115 (January 1915): 50. The early uses of film for political ends are discussed in Kay Sloan, *The Loud Silents* (Urbana, Ill., 1988); Kevin Brownlow, *Behind the Mask of Innocence* (New York, 1990); M. Keith Booker, *Film and the Left: A Research Guide* (Westport, Conn., and London, 1999); Michael Slade Shull, *Radicalism in American Silent Films, 1909–1929: A Filmography and History* (Jefferson, N.C., and London, 2000); Ross, *Working-Class Hollywood*.

16. Transcript of "Charles Chaplin Interview," ca. 1966, reel 2, side 1, 49, folder 302, Charlie Chaplin Vertical File Collection, AMPAS (hereafter, Chaplin Vertical).

17. This discussion is drawn from my viewing of the entire opus of Chaplin's early films, which are readily available on DVD. For an excellent overview of these films, see Vance, *Chaplin*.

18. Max Eastman, *Heroes I Have Known: Twelve Who Lived Great Lives* (New York, 1942), 164, 192.

19. Mabel Normand, "From the Inside," *Photoplay*, August 1913, 102; also see *Los Angeles Citizen*, April 18, 1913. I am grateful to Rob King for bringing this material to my attention.

20. Harry Crocker, "Charlie Chaplin: Man and Mime," unpublished manuscript, 14, 15, Harry Crocker Collection, Margaret Herrick Library, Academy of Motion Picture Arts and Sciences, Beverly Hills, California (hereafter, Crocker Coll.). For the uses of celebrities during World War I, see Mary Pickford Scrapbooks, vols. 30–31 (War Bonds Tour), Mary Pickford Collection, Margaret Herrick Library, AMPAS; Craig W. Campbell, *Reel America and World War I* (Jefferson, N.C., and London, 1985); Maland, *Chaplin and American Culture*. For the best overview of the evolving relationship between movie stars and politics, see Ronald Brownstein, *The Power and the Glitter: The Hollywood-Washington Connection* (New York, 1990).

21. Chaplin, *Autobiography*, 215.

22. *Los Angeles Herald*, December 2, 1919; *LAT*, January 24, 1918. For a description of *The Bond*, see Vance, *Chaplin*, 94–97.

23. *LAT*, June 30, 1918; Chaplin, *Autobiography*, 225.

24. Vance, *Chaplin*, 173–174.

25. Crocker, "Chaplin," chapter 7, 22, Crocker Coll.; Chaplin, *Autobiography*, 350; for Charlie's wealth, see Chaplin, *Autobiography*, 288.

26. Upton Sinclair to Charlie Chaplin, August 18, 1918, Upton Sinclair Collection, Lilly Library, Indiana University (hereafter, Sinclair Coll.). For Sinclair's view of their early friendship, see "The Reminiscences of Upton Sinclair," Oral History Research Office, Columbia University, 1963, 2 vols., 2:206 (hereafter, CUOHP). The two men remained friends and corresponded through the 1960s. For Sinclair's involvement with film, see Ross, *Working-Class Hollywood*.

27. For an overview of the Red Scare, see Robert K. Murray, *Red Scare: A Study in National Hysteria, 1919–1929* (Minneapolis, 1955).

28. Eastman, *Heroes*, 160, 155.

29. Ibid., 163; *Variety*, November 14, 1919.

30. Author interview with Larry Bachmann, October 3, 2002, Beverly Hills, California; *NYT*, September 18, 1921.

31. Crocker, "Chaplin," chapter 8, 5, Crocker Coll.

32. Chaplin, *My Trip Abroad*, 101; *NYT*, December 6, 1921.

33. Chaplin, *My Trip Abroad*, 71; Chaplin, *Autobiography*, 280.

34. *New York Call*, October 21, 1921; *Literary Digest* 72 (January 28, 1922): 48.

35. Crocker, "Chaplin," chapter 13, 11. County tax rolls assessed Charlie's wealth at nearly $8 million in 1932. *LAT*, July 8, 1932.

36. R. M. Whitney, *Reds in America* (New York, 1924), 151. For the FBI surveillance of early radical filmmakers, see Ross, *Working-Class Hollywood*.

37. Americanism Committee quoted in Ross, *Working-Class Hollywood*, 129. Between April 1917 and 1929, nearly two-thirds of films dealing with labor-capital relations were hostile to radicalism, as compared to 34% before the war. For a closer look at the Hollywood–Washington connection and decline of labor and the left, see ibid., 115–142.

38. *Seattle Union Record*, February 22, 1923.

39. Cecil B. DeMille, *The Autobiography of Cecil B. DeMille* (Englewood Cliffs, N.J., 1959), 169. For examples of typical DeMille productions, see *Male and Female* (1919) and *Saturday Night* (1922). For a more thorough discussion of DeMille and cross-class fantasy films, see Ross, *Working-Class Hollywood*, 173–211.

40. [London] *Times*, September 3, 1925, quoted in Hayes, *Charlie Chaplin Interviews*, 83.
41. DeMille, *Autobiography*, 137.
42. Quotes from *NYT*, October 7, 1923.
43. Chaplin, *Autobiography*, 337.
44. deMille, *Hollywood Saga*, 287.
45. *NYT*, March 17, 1935.
46. Ibid., June 14, 1932.
47. "John Bull Hit by a Chaplin Pie," *Literary Digest* 109 (May 23, 1931): 10, quoted in Maland, *Chaplin and American Culture*, 128. For his economic plan, see *LAT*, June 27, 1932; for his views on the economy and government obligations, also see Robinson, *Chaplin*, 456–458; Chaplin, *Autobiography*, 338–365.
48. *LAT*, October 24, 1933; *NYT*, February 12, 1931.
49. Telegram, Chaplin to Sinclair, December 4, 1933, Sinclair Coll.; "Reminiscences of Sinclair," 2:307, CUOHP. As a foreign national, Chaplin could not have held any formal position in California government. For Sinclair's promise, see *NYT*, March 17, 1935.
50. For Chaplin's visit and reaction to the automobile plant, see Chaplin, *Autobiography*, 383.
51. Eastman, *Heroes I Have Known*, 174; transcript of "Charles Chaplin Interview," ca. 1966, reel 4, side 1, 14, folder 302, Chaplin Vertical, AMPAS; F. L. Herrron to Arthur Kelly (United Artists, N.Y.), May 4, 1937, in Banned Films Abroad, Production Code Administration file for *Modern Times*, Margaret Herrick Library, Academy of Motion Picture Arts and Sciences, Beverly Hills, California (hereafter, PCA files, AMPAS); *NYT*, February 18, 1936.
52. For Chaplin's friendship with émigré communities, see John Russell Taylor, *Strangers in Paradise: The Hollywood Émigrés 1933–1950* (New York, 1983); Anthony Heilbut, *Exiled in Paradise: German Refugee Artists and Intellectuals in America, from the 1930s to the Present* (New York, 1983); Otto Friedrich, *City of Nets: A Portrait of Hollywood in the 1940s* (New York, 1987); Saverio Giovacchini, *Hollywood Modernism: Film and Politics in the Age of the New Deal* (Philadelphia, 2001).
53. Quoted in Brownstein, *Power and the Glitter*, 60; Maland, *Chaplin and American Culture*, 164.
54. *New York Telegraph*, August 12, 1939. Alexander Korda, Ivan Montagu, and Konrad Bercovicci all claimed credit for inspiring Chaplin; Bercovicci sued his former friend for $6 million.
55. Karl Lischka Notes, "Storm over America," January 22, 1939, PCA files, *Confessions of a Nazi Spy*, AMPAS. For an overview of Breen, the PCA Code, and efforts to make antifascist films, see Steven Carr, *Hollywood and Anti-Semitism* (Cambridge, U.K., 2001); Steven J. Ross, "The Politicization of Hollywood before World War II: Anti-Fascism, Anti-Communism, and Anti-Semitism," *Jewish Role in American Life* 5 (2007): 1–28.
56. Dr. Georg Gyssling, Consul of Germany (L.A.) to Joseph Breen, October 31, 1938, PCA files, *The Great Dictator*, AMPAS; Chaplin, *Autobiography*, 397, 398.
57. *Seattle Jewish Transcript*, December 20, 1940; *LAT*, June 15, 1939. The money never went there because by the time the film opened the Vienna organization was

defunct. However, on July 28, 1940, it was reported that Chaplin was among many who had collectively deposited $6 million in a Milan bank to support Austrian Jews forced out of Austria. Maland, *Chaplin and American Culture*, 171.

58. *Confessions* was banned everywhere the Nazis could exert pressure. By August 1939, the film was prohibited in Germany, Italy, Japan, Holland, Norway, and Sweden. During the following year it was banned in eighteen more nations. Reports from foreign and domestic censors can be found in the "PCA Confidential Files of Reports from Local Censor Boards," PCA files, *Confessions*, AMPAS.

59. *New York Tribune* and *New York Daily Mirror* quoted in *Motion Picture Daily*, October 16, 1940; *Variety*, October 15, 1940.

60. *Motion Picture Herald*, October 19, 1940; *Hollywood Reporter*, October 15, 1940; *NYT*, October 20, 1940; *Hollywood Reporter*, October 15, 1940.

61. Walter W. McKenna to Senator Robert R. Reynolds, February 17, 1939, *The Great Dictator*, PCA files, AMPAS; Crocker, "Chaplin," chapter 15, 18–19, Crocker Coll; Gallup poll cited in Nancy Snow, "Confessions of a Hollywood Propagandist: Harry Warner, FDR and Celluloid Persuasion," in Martin Kaplan and Johanna Blakley, eds., *Warners' War: Politics, Pop Culture and Propaganda in Wartime Hollywood* (Los Angeles, 2004), 69.

62. *LAT*, September 16, 1941. A March 1947 FBI report listed Chaplin's descent as "Jewish" and noted that the British-born actor "Speaks with a Jewish accent." Report on Charles Spencer Chaplin, March 13, 1947, FBI Records, disc 2, www.paperless-archives.com, accessed June 15, 2005. For a fuller discussion of the Senate investigation, see U.S. Congress, Senate Committee on Interstate and Foreign Commerce, Subcommittee, *Propaganda in Motion Pictures: Hearings before a Subcommittee on Interstate Commerce . . . September 9–26, 1941* (Washington, D.C., 1942); Michael E. Birdwell, *Celluloid Soldiers: Warner Bros.'s Campaign against Nazism* (New York, 1999), 154–171; Carr, *Hollywood and Anti-Semitism*, 238–277.

63. "Charles Chaplin Interview," reel 1, side 1, 34, Transcript of Oral Interview, Charlie Chaplin Vertical, folder 302, AMPAS.

64. Chaplin, *Autobiography*, 408.

65. *Washington Post*, December 13, 1942; "Communist Activities: Charlie Chaplin," December 4, 1942, report included in P. B. Foxworth to J. Edgar Hoover, December 12, 1942, Chaplin FBI Records, disc 2, www.paperlessarchives.com, accessed June 15, 2005; also see *NYT*, December 4, 1942. For a report of Chaplin's earliest speeches, see *Everybody's*, June 17, 1942. For the Madison Square Garden speech, see Chaplin, *Autobiography*, 410–413.

66. *LAT*, December 22, 1942, June 3, 1942.

67. Harry Crocker, "Chaplin—City Lights," 11, unpublished essay; Harry Crocker, "Chaplin—Courage," 2, unpublished essay, Crocker Coll., AMPAS.

68. For a discussion of the Barry trial, see Robinson, *Chaplin*, 512–513, 517–528.

69. Name deleted to J. Edgar Hoover, May 28, 1946, Chaplin, FBI files, disc 2, www.paperlessarchives.com, accessed June 15, 2005; Frank Case (NYC) to Hedda Hopper, n.d.; and Esther Klooster to Hopper, February 10, 1944, box 4f, Hedda Hopper Papers, AMPAS.

70. Quoted in Robinson, *Chaplin*, 525.

71. *LAT*, May 10, 1947.

72. The film was banned in Memphis for making "murder a joke." *NYT*, June 11, 1947. For opening-night reactions and subsequent protests, see ibid., August 9, 1925, May 8, 1947; Vance, *Chaplin*, 274–279; *LAT*, March 14, 1982.

73. *NYT*, December 7, 1950. For boycotts of *Limelight*, see "Limelight," Chaplin Vertical, reel 3, side 1, 17–20; Vance, *Chaplin*, 295. For reactions to both films, see D. William Davis, "A Tale of Two Movies: Charlie Chaplin, United Artists, and the Red Scare," *Cinema Journal* 27 (Autumn 1987): 47–62.

74. Hedda Hopper to J. Edgar Hoover, April 7, 1947, box 10, J. Edgar Hoover, 1946–1965, Hopper Papers, AMPAS; *LAT*, June 13, 1947; Chaplin, *Autobiography*, 449.

75. *NYT*, October 3, 1952.

76. Ibid., April 20, 1947.

77. Crocker, "Chaplin," chapter 16, 8–9, Crocker Coll.

CHAPTER 2

1. *New York Herald Tribune*, December 1, 1957; Goldwyn quoted in Bosley Crowther, *Hollywood Rajah: The Life and Times of Louis B. Mayer* (New York, 1960), 6; also see Telegram: Herbert Hoover to Mrs. Louis B. Mayer, October 29, 1957, Post-Presidential Individual—Mayer (hereafter, PPI) files, Herbert Hoover Papers, Herbert Hoover Presidential Library, West Branch, Iowa (hereafter, Hoover Papers).

2. *New York Herald Tribune*, October 30, 1957; *Washington Post*, October 30, 1957.

3. Hayes, Bellamy, and Neilan are quoted in Scott Eyman, *Lion of Hollywood: The Life and Legend of Louis B. Mayer* (New York, 2005), 7; Anita Loos, Oral History, June, 1959, 24–25 (series 3, vol. 1, pt. 1), Popular Arts Project, Columbia University Oral History Program, Special Collections Department, Columbia University (hereafter, CUOHP).

4. Accurate information on Mayer's early life is hard to come by. The most useful biographical sources are Eyman, *Lion of Hollywood*; Crowther, *Hollywood Rajah*; Charles Higham, *Merchant of Dreams: Louis B. Mayer, M.G.M., and the Secret Hollywood* (New York, 1993); Neal Gabler, *An Empire of Their Own: How the Jews Invented Hollywood* (New York, 1989); and Irene Mayer Selznick, *A Private View* (New York, 1983). When Mayer's grandson Daniel Selznick asked Myron Fox why he destroyed his grandfather's papers, the estate executor explained, "I did it to protect your grandfather's memory. You know he didn't get past 8th grade. You know he didn't write English very well. We couldn't allow the impression to be given to people writing books that your grandfather couldn't compose a grammatically correct letter." Author interview with Daniel Selznick, October 11, 2006, Pacific Palisades, California.

5. Mayer quoted in Eyman, *Lion of Hollywood*, 39. For the growth of his early empire, see sources mentioned in n. 4; and Louis B. Mayer Publicity Sheet (mimeo), n.d., from Pete Smith, MGM Studios, Culver City, in L. B. Mayer Clippings file, Billy Rose Theatre Collection, New York Public Library for the Performing Arts; Gary Carey, *All the Stars in Heaven: Louis B. Mayer's M-G-M* (New York, 1981). For dollar equivalencies, see www.measuringworth.com/ppowerus/, accessed May 8, 2010.

6. Statistics are taken from *NYT*, November 11, 1920; David Bordwell, Janet Staiger, and Kristin Thompson, *The Classical Hollywood Cinema: Film Style and Mode of*

Production to 1960 (New York, 1985), 123; Richard Koszarski, *An Evening's Entertainment: The Age of the Silent Picture, 1915-1928* (New York, 1990), 104-106.

7. Barton W. Currie, "The Nickel Madness," *Harper's Weekly*, August 24, 1907, quoted in Gerald Mast, *Movies in Our Midst: Documents in the Cultural History of Film in America* (Chicago, 1982), 45. For the MPPA's political agenda, see W. J. Reynolds to Hal Roach, March 8, 1919, Motion Picture Producers' Association Files (henceforth, MPPA files), folder 2, Hal Roach Collection, Special Collections, University of Southern California Library.

8. Frank Garbutt to Hal Roach, April 30, 1921, MPPA files, folder 4, Roach Collection; also see I. G. Lewis to W. J. Reynolds, October 23, 1916; and W. J. Reynolds to D. Whiting, April 7, 1917, MPPA files, folder 1, Roach Collection; *LAT*, March 19, 1917.

9. For the wartime and postwar Hollywood–Washington connection, see Steven J. Ross, *Working-Class Hollywood: Silent Film and the Shaping of Class in America* (Princeton, N.J., 1998), 115-142. For Hays and the scandals, see "The Hays Office," *Fortune* 18 (December 1938), in Tino Balio, ed., *The American Film Industry* (Madison, Wis., 1976), 286; Budd Schulberg, *Moving Pictures: Memories of a Hollywood Prince* (Chicago, 2003), 300-305; Louis Pizzitola, *Hearst over Hollywood: Power, Passion, and Propaganda in the Movies* (New York, 2002), 198-200; Will Hays, *The Memoirs of Will H. Hays* (Garden City, N.Y., 1955).

10. Coolidge quoted in Robert H. Ferrell, *The Presidency of Calvin Coolidge* (Lawrence, Kans., 1998), 61; and Paul Carter, *Another Part of the Twenties* (New York, 1977), 175. For changing Republican politics during the early and mid-1920s, see John Early Haynes, ed., *Calvin Coolidge and the Coolidge Era: Essays on the History of the 1920s* (Washington, D.C., 1998); Robert K. Murray, *The Politics of Normalcy: Governmental Theory and Practice in the Harding-Coolidge Era* (New York, 1973); Ferrell, *Presidency of Coolidge*.

11. Robert W. Kenny, "My First Forty Years in California Politics, 1922-1962," 59, Oral History Program (hereafter OHP), Special Collections, UCLA (1964), 300/19. Party statistics can be found in James Gregory's introduction to Upton Sinclair, *I, Candidate for Governor: And How I Got Licked* (Berkeley and Los Angeles, 1994, originally published 1934), vii; Stanley D. Hopper, "Fragmentation of the California Republican Party in the One-Party Era, 1893-1932," *Western Political Quarterly* 28 (June 1975): 372-386. For an overview of California politics during this period, see Hopper, "Fragmentation of the California Republican Party"; Richard Dale Batman, "The Road to the Presidency: Hoover, Johnson, and the California Republican Party 1920-1924," unpublished Ph.D. diss., University of Southern California, 1965.

12. Author interview with Selznick. Production statistics are taken from *NYT*, November 11, 1920; business figures are from *LAT*, December 28, 1921. The rise of the studio system is discussed in hundreds of books and articles. The most useful recent works include Balio, *American Film Industry*; Janet Wasko, *Movies and Money: Financing the American Film Industry* (Norwood, N.J., 1982); Douglas Gomery, *The Hollywood Studio System* (New York, 1986); Thomas Schatz, *The Genius of the System: Hollywood Filmmaking in the Studio Era* (New York, 1988); Bordwell, Staiger, and Thompson, *Classical Hollywood*; and Koszarski, *Evening's Entertainment*.

13. For Mayer's initial involvement in local politics, see *LAT*, April 17, August 15, 27, September 5, 1924; for his work in the 1924 presidential campaign, see ibid., September 25, 1924.

14. Von Sternberg quoted in David Thomson, *The New Biographical Dictionary of Film* (New York, 2004), 578; Schulberg, *Moving Pictures*, 147; Mrs. Hollywood quote, *Los Angeles Herald Express*, November 27, 1954.

15. Author interview with Selznick. What little biographical information there is about Koverman is either wrong or incomplete. Various reports have her first appearing on the Los Angeles scene in 1924, 1926, or 1928. In fact, she was well entrenched in local and state politics by October 1920. During the early 1920s, Ida served as executive secretary of the Los Angeles Republican County Central Committee and the Republican Women's Federation of California. There is even confusion over Ida's maiden name. Her friend Hedda Hopper says she was born Ida Rynus. Film historian Cari Beauchamp says she was born Ida Brockaway. Hedda Hopper and James Brough, *The Whole Truth and Nothing But* (Garden City, N.Y., 1963), 265; Cari Beauchamp, *Without Lying Down: Frances Marion and the Powerful Women of Early Hollywood* (Berkeley and Los Angeles, 1997), 248. For Ida's engagement in Republican politics in 1920, see Ida Koverman to Ralph Arnold, October 8, 1920, Arnold to Koverman, October 26, 1920, in Ralph Arnold Papers, Huntington Library, San Marino, California. For an overview of her life and early political career, see sources mentioned above as well as Batman, "Road to the Presidency," 162–165; *Los Angeles Herald*, November 24, 1954; *Hollywood Citizen-News*, November 24, 1954; *LAT*, November 24, 1954; *Los Angeles Express*, November 25, 1954; *Los Angeles Herald Express*, November 27, 1954; *Hollywood Reporter*, November 29, 1954. Ida Koverman to W. C. Mullendore (Dept of Commerce): June 26, 1923, Hoover Papers. The single best account of Mayer's political life is Ronald Brownstein, *The Power and the Glitter: The Hollywood-Washington Connection* (New York, 1990), 19–47.

16. *LAT*, December 25, 1928.

17. Hopper, *Whole Truth*, 264; Selznick quoted in Brownstein, *Power and the Glitter*, 30.

18. For Hoover's changing position within his party and attitudes toward film, radio, and publicity, see John Braeman, "The American Polity in the Age of Normalcy: A Reappraisal," in Haynes, *Coolidge and the Coolidge Era*; Donald R. McCoy, "To the White House: Herbert Hoover, August 1927–March 1929," in Martin L. Fausold and George T. Mazuzan, eds., *The Hoover Presidency: A Reappraisal* (Albany, N.Y., 1974); Joan Hoff-Wilson, *Herbert Hoover, Forgotten Progressive* (Boston, 1975); David Burner, *Herbert Hoover, A Public Life* (New York, 1979); Ellis W. Hawley, ed., *Herbert Hoover as Secretary of Commerce: Studies in New Era Thought and Practice* (Iowa City, Iowa, 1981); Richard Norton Smith, *An Uncommon Man: The Triumph of Herbert Hoover* (New York, 1984).

19. Telegram, Herbert Hoover to Louis B. Mayer, September 8, 1924, Commerce Papers—Mayer, Louis B.; also see Telegrams, Mayer to Hoover, September 2, 6, 1924, Hoover Papers.

20. Herbert Hoover to the Secretary of State, September 23, 1924; also see Herbert Hoover to Henry C. MacLean, Commercial Attaché, Rome; Herbert Hoover to J. F. Butler, Acting Commercial Attaché, Paris; and Herbert Hoover to Hugh D. Butler, Acting Commercial Attaché, London, all September 24, 1924, Commerce

Papers—Mayer, Hoover Papers. For the FTC report, see Lawrence Ritchey to L. B. Mayer, November 21, 1925, Commerce Papers—Mayer, Hoover Papers.

21. Eddie Cantor, *Take My Life* (New York, 1957); Robert Slayton, *Empire Statesman: The Rise and Redemption of Al Smith* (New York, 2001). For Mayer's trips to Washington, D.C., see Samuel Marx, *Mayer and Thalberg: The Make Believe Saints* (New York, 1975), 102.

22. Conrad Nagel, Oral History, September 1958, 44–45, series 1, vol. 4, CUOHP.

23. *LAT*, October 27, 1928; see n. 5 for dollar equivalencies.

24. Higham, *Merchant of Dreams*, 149.

25. Selznick, *Private View*, 84. For Hearst's early political career, see David Nasaw, *The Chief: The Life of William Randolph Hearst* (Boston, 2000). The relationship between Hearst and Mayer is explored in Nasaw, *The Chief*, 82–86; Pizzitola, *Hearst over Hollywood*, 226–228; Brownstein, *Power and the Glitter*, 31–37.

26. In 1926, Mayer and Koverman asked the Secretary of Commerce to help obtain a favorable wavelength for a Chicago radio station jointly controlled by Hearst and Mayer. Hoover agreed "to arrange a satisfactory wave length for your proposed station" and quickly delivered on his promise. "This is very important," a jubilant Mayer telegrammed Ida, "as it will give me just the ammunition I need to enlist their [Hearst] support and friendship." Herbert Hoover to L. B. Mayer, January 2, 1926; Telegram: L. B. Mayer to Ida Koverman, December 2, 1927, Commerce Papers—Mayer; also see Hoover to Mayer, September 21, 1926, Commerce Papers—Mayer. For the Hearst-Mayer-Hoover alliance, see Nasaw, *The Chief*, 398; Colin Shindler, *Hollywood in Crisis: Cinema and American Society, 1929–1939* (London and New York, 1996), 60; Brownstein, *Power and the Glitter*, 31–34; Crowther, *Hollywood Rajah*, 137.

27. Democrats spent $903,908 in 1924 and $7.2 million in 1928. Roy V. Peel and Thomas C. Donnelly, *The 1928 Campaign: An Analysis* (New York, 1931), 47–51. For ownership statistics and the increased reliance on radio by both parties, see Paul Starr, *The Creation of the Media: Political Origins of Modern Communications* (New York, 2004), 354; Kathleen Hall Jamieson, *Packaging the Presidency: A History and Criticism of Presidential Campaign Advertising* (New York, 1996).

28. For Mayer's trips to Washington, see Telegram: Geo Akerson to L. B. Mayer, October 9, 10, 1928; Telegram: Mayer to Akerson, October 9, 1928, C&T—Mayer. For Walker's accusation, see *Washington Post*, July 11, 1928.

29. *LAT*, February 2, 1929; Bernice Miller to Bosley Crowther, July 8, 1958, Post-Presidential Individual—Crowther, Bosley, Hoover Papers; Ida Koverman to Lawrence Richey, January 28, 1929, C&T—Mayer. Hoover received 21.4 million votes (58.3%) to Smith's 15 million (40.8%). Peel and Donnelly, *1928 Campaign*, 170–171.

30. Edith Mayer Goetz quoted in Gabler, *Empire of Their Own*, 316; Marx, *Mayer and Thalberg*, 117.

31. "Hand Notes," April 24, 1929, PP-Secretary's—IK; Telegram: Lawrence Richey (Secretary to Hoover) to L. B. Mayer, January 9, 1930; L. B. Mayer to Lawrence Richey, September 13, 1929, and Richey to Mayer, October 5, 1929, Hoover Papers. For Hoover Jr., see Higham, *Merchant of Dreams*, 157.

32. For the Fox case, see Shindler, *Hollywood in Crisis*, 6–7; Eyman, *Lion of Hollywood*, 145–146. For letters requesting Hoover's help with screenplays and movie industry

jobs, see Lawrence Richey Memo Regarding M. F. Judell, November 21, 1931, and Concetta Yingarelli, December 1, 1931, Presidential Papers—Secretary's File—Mayer, Louis, Hoover Papers. For Mayer's use of patronage, see "Hand Notes," April 24, 1929, PP-Secretary's—IK; Telegram: Lawrence Richey (Sec to HH) to L. B. Mayer, January 9, 1930; L. B. Mayer to Lawrence Richey, September 13, 1929, and Richey to Mayer, October 5, 1929; Mayer to Richey, September 13, 1929, and Richey to Mayer, October 5, 1929; Memo: May 2, 1930: L. B. Mayer; Richey to Mayer, January 10, 1931; Note from Mayer, May 7, 1931; Note from Ida Koverman, June 8, 1931; Richey to Mayer, August 10, 1932; Memo August 6, 1932, Hoover Papers.

33. Versailles quote from Crowther, *Hollywood Rajah*, 124. MGM was also referred to as the Cadillac of the studios.

34. "Metro-Goldwyn-Mayer," *Fortune* 6 (December 1932), in Balio, *American Film Industry*, 266.

35. For Thalberg's role at MGM, see Marx, *Mayer and Thalberg*; Ethan Mordden, *The Hollywood Studio System: House Style in the Golden Age of the Movies* (New York, 1988); Mark A. Vieira, *Hollywood Dreams Made Real: Irving Thalberg and the Rise of M-G-M* (New York, 2008). For his membership in the Young People's Socialist League, see Donald Ogden Stewart, *By a Stroke of Luck! An Autobiography* (New York, 1975), 227. For studio profits, see Donald Crafton, *The Talkies: American Cinema's Transition to Sound 1926–1931* (Berkeley and Los Angeles, 1999), 207.

36. For Mabel's relationship with Louis and Ida, see Dorothy M. Brown, *Mabel Walker Willebrandt: A Study in Power, Loyalty, and Law* (Knoxville, Tenn., 1984), 45, 115, 153, 229–231.

37. For an overview of the Great Depression, see William Leuchtenburg, *The Perils of Prosperity 1914–32* (Chicago, 1993).

38. *LAT*, January 30, 1932. For Mayer's speech lessons, see Marx, *Mayer and Thalberg*, 52. Although Eyman is most explicit in discounting Mayer's political acumen, other biographers also minimize his commitment and knowledge. For his work with Hoover, see Telegram, Richey to Mayer, January 27, 1931, and Mayer to Richey February 9, 1931, PPI, Hoover Papers; *LAT*, October 26, 1931; Higham, *Merchant of Dreams*, 187, 195.

39. For Mayer's speeches and policy statements, see *LAT*, April 22, 1932; *Los Angeles Examiner*, June 11, 1932.

40. *Los Angeles Examiner*, June 22, 1932; for the split between Hoover and Hearst, see Higham, *Merchant of Dreams*, 201.

41. "Desert of dullness" quote from McCoy, "To the White House," in Fausold and Mazuzan, *Hoover Presidency*, 35; *Variety*, June 21, 1932. For descriptions of the convention, see [no city] *Illustrated News*, June 18, 1932; *Time*, June 27, 1932.

42. For exhibitor discontent over newsreels, see *Christian Science Monitor*, August 29, 1932.

43. *LAT*, October 11, 1932.

44. For campaign rallies, see *LAT*, November 3, 5, 6, 1932.

45. *LAT*, November 3, 1932.

46. Ibid., November 8, 1932. For Mayer's request, see Telegram: Ida Koverman to Lawrence Richey, January 19, 1933; Richey telegrammed back January 19, 1933,

approving the request. HH PP-Sec., Hoover Papers. For California voting statistics, see Kenny, "My First Forty Years," 82.

47. *LAT*, December 10, 1931. Statistics are taken from John Douglas Eames, *The MGM Story: The Complete History of over Fifty Roaring Years* (New York, 1976), 82, 100.

48. Author interview with Selznick; Mayer quoted in Crowther, *Hollywood Rajah*, 156. The disowning of the Goetzes is discussed in Hopper, *Whole Truth*, 91–92. For Mayer's family life, see Selznick, *A Private View*; Crowther, *Hollywood Rajah*, 154–158.

49. Crowther, *Hollywood Rajah*, 257. The Talmud actually says a man is judged from the shoulders up. For Mayer's sexual dalliances and Margaret's declining health, see Higham, *Merchant of Dreams*, 204–205, 245–248, 253–256; Eyman, *Lion of Hollywood*, 193–198; Schulberg, *Moving Pictures*, 381, 484–485; Carey, *All the Stars in Heaven*, 178–183; Diana Altman, *Hollywood East: Louis B. Mayer and the Origins of the Studio System* (New York, 1992), 222.

50. The best study of the 1934 campaign is Greg Mitchell, *The Campaign of the Century: Upton Sinclair's Race for Governor of California and the Birth of Media Politics* (New York, 1992); also see Upton Sinclair, *The Autobiography of Upton Sinclair* (London, 1963), 282–291; Upton Sinclair, "The Reminiscences of Upton Sinclair," CUOHP, 1963, 2 vols., 1:264, 2:132; introduction by Gregory in Sinclair, *I, Candidate*; Leo C. Rosten, *Hollywood: The Movie Colony, The Movie Makers* (New York, 1941), 134–138; Carey, *All the Stars*, 185; Brownstein, *Power and the Glitter*, 40–42.

51. The Merriam description is from Rosten, *Hollywood*, 135. For Sinclair's vote totals, see Gregory in Sinclair, *I, Candidate*, viii. For Haight's profile, see Mitchell, *Campaign of the Century*, 46–47.

52. Schenck quoted in Gabler, *Empire of Their Own*, 314; *Hollywood Reporter*, October 15, 1934. For stock decline, see *Time*, November 12, 1934; for movie industry salaries, see "Loew's Inc.," *Fortune* 20 (August 1939), in Balio, *American Film Industry*, 286; Gabler, *Empire of Their Own*, 316.

53. *Los Angeles Examiner*, October 8, 1934. For Mayer, Thalberg, and Sinclair, see Mitchell, *Campaign of the Century*, 30, 62.

54. Albert Hackett, Oral History, September 1958, 23–24, CUOHP.

55. For Mayer's request, see *NYT*, November 4, 1934. For Cagney's response, see Mitchell, *Campaign of the Century*, 359.

56. Marx, *Mayer and Thalberg*, 236; on the use of actors in newsreels, see *NYT*, November 4, 1934. A copy of *California Election News Nos. 1 and 2* can be found at the end of the Kino Video release of *Our Daily Bread*. All newsreel quotations are taken from my viewing of the surviving footage.

57. Crowther, *Hollywood Rajah*, 199.

58. *Hollywood Reporter*, October 27, 1934. For Rankin, see *NYT*, November 4, 1934; Mitchell, *Campaign of the Century*, 340.

59. Sinclair, *I, Candidate for Governor*, 141–142; *Time*, November 12, 1934.

60. *Variety*, November 6, 1934; also see Mitchell, *Campaign of the Century*, 505.

61. Marx, *Mayer and Thalberg*, 236; March-Thalberg exchange is from Kyle Crichton, *Total Recoil* (New York, 1960), 245–246. Election results are reported in Gregory's introduction, Sinclair, *I, Candidate*, x; Mitchell, *Campaign of the Century*, 617n.

62. *Hollywood Reporter*, November 5, 7, 1934.

63. Marx, *Mayer and Thalberg*, 201n. Poll results are reported in Rosten, *Hollywood*, 160. Directors supported FDR 8:1, actors 7:1, writers 5:1, laborers 8:1, agents 24:1, and executives 5:1.

64. Henry F. Pringle, "Yes, Mr. Mayer," *New Yorker*, April 4, 1936, 28.

65. Nice quoted in *LAT*, July 16, 1936; two subsequent quotes are from ibid., April 19, 1935; political salon quote is from Gabler, *Empire of Their Own*, 316. For Sullivan's talk, see *LAT*, December 5, 1933.

66. *LAT*, December 21, 1940; Ida Koverman to Lawrence Richey, April 14, 1948, PPI; Ida Koverman to Del Reynolds (Security 1st National Bank, LA), October 16, 1935, Hoover Papers. For examples of events Koverman held, see *LAT*, June 6, 1933, March 19, 1938.

67. Adela Rogers St. Johns, "The Reminiscences of Adela Rogers St. Johns," June 23, 1971, 15, CUOHP.

68. All quotes are from Robinson, *All My Yesterdays*, 193, 192. For political life in the Commissary, also see Richard J. Collins, Oral History, July 25, 1990, Number 474, Ronald L. Davis Oral History Collection, DeGolyer Library, Southern Methodist University (copy in Special Collections, Herrick Library, AMPAS).

69. *LAT*, May 24, 1964; Herbert Gold, "Nobody's Mad at Murphy," *NYT Magazine*, December 13, 1964; *Hollywood Citizen-News*, January 18, 1955.

70. Selznick, *Private View*, 26. For movie attendance and voting, see U.S. Department of Commerce, *Historical Statistics of the United States*, 2 vols. (Washington, D.C., 1975), 1:400, 2:1073.

71. Mankiewicz quoted in Eyman, *Lion of Hollywood*, 97. The visit of the Nazi editors is described in *Hollywood Now*, June 23, 1939; see Jack Warner Collection, Folder 3: Printed Materials—1939, Nazi Data, Warner Bros. Archives, University of Southern California. For Gabler, see *Empire of Their Own*. For the importance of foreign markets and Mayer's continued dealings with Germany, see Steven J. Ross, "The Politicization of Hollywood before World War II: Anti-Fascism, Anti-Communism, and Anti-Semitism," *Jewish Role in American Life: An Annual Review* 5 (2007): 1–28.

72. Loos, Oral History, 24; Crowther, *Hollywood Rajah*, 255.

73. Schulberg, *Moving Pictures*, 483.

74. Goldwyn quoted in Kevin Brownlow, *Behind the Mask of Innocence* (New York, 1990), xviii.

75. *American Weekly*, June 8, 1958; Wilder quoted in Gabler, *Empire of Their Own*, 215. For more on Mayer's involvement, see Peter Hay, *MGM: When the Lion Roars* (Atlanta, Ga., 1991), 164–165; Eames, *MGM*, 138.

76. *Love Finds Andy Hardy* is available on video. The other three films can be seen from time to time on Turner Classic Movies (TCM). The following analysis is drawn from my viewing of the series.

77. *Variety* quoted in David M. Considine, *The Cinema of Adolescence* (Jefferson, N.C., 1985), 13; Mayer quoted in Otto Friedrich, *City of Nets: A Portrait of Hollywood in the 1940s* (New York, 1987), 13. Eames calls the Hardy films "the most profitable series in Hollywood's history." Eames, *MGM*, 136. For Rooney as the top star and for cost and gross statistics, see Schatz, *Genius of the System*, 261, 268.

78. William C. deMille, "Great Pictures and the Men Who Have Made Them—Notes," October 4, 1935, unpublished essay, in William C. deMille Collection, Special

Collections, New York Public Library. For MGM's courtship of teenage viewers, see Jennifer Rosales, "MGM's Courtship of Youth, 1936–1946," unpublished senior thesis, University of Southern California, April 2005.

79. Special Oscar quote from Hay, *MGM*, 165; Dave Sendler, "Movie Star Robert Ryan Charges: 'Actors Are Unfit for Political Office!'" *Pageant*, July 1966, 23. Mayer also received Americanism Awards in 1940 from the American Legion and the Veterans of Foreign Wars. *Los Angeles Herald*, April 19, 1940; *LAT*, August 30, 1940.

80. *Los Angeles Herald Express*, November 27, 1954. Details about her final years are taken from newspaper sources mentioned in n. 15.

81. Hopper, *Whole Truth*, 272.

82. *Variety*, April 7, 1954.

83. *NYT*, October 31, 1957; Lillian Ross, *Picture* (Cambridge, Mass., 2002), 170.

CHAPTER 3

1. *NYT*, January 22, 1939; Walter S. Loebl to Edward G. Robinson, December 12, 1938, box 29, folder 9; T. Conden to Edward G. Robinson, December 12, 1938, box 30, folder 14-B, Edward G. Robinson Collection, Special Collections, University of Southern California (hereafter, EGR Coll.).

2. George Gallup and Claude Robinson, "American Institute of Public Opinion—Surveys, 1935–38," *Public Opinion Quarterly* 2 (July 1938): 388. The 1941 poll is quoted in Nancy Snow, "Confessions of a Hollywood Propagandist: Harry Warner, FDR and Celluloid Persuasion," in Martin Kaplan and Johanna Blakley, eds., *Warners' War: Politics, Pop Culture and Propaganda in Wartime Hollywood* (Los Angeles, 2004), 69.

3. Edward G. Robinson, "How the Reds Made a Sucker Out of Me," *American Legion Magazine*, October 1952, 11, 62–70.

4. For an overview of the Hollywood Ten, the blacklist, HUAC, and Hollywood politics during this era, see Thom Anderson, "Red Hollywood," in Suzanne Ferguson and Barbara Groseclose, eds., *Literature and the Visual Arts in Contemporary Society* (Columbus, Ohio, 1985), 141–196. Other key works include Gordon Kahn, *Hollywood on Trial* (New York, 1948); Carey McWilliams, *Witch Hunt* (Boston, 1950); John Cogley, *Report on Blacklisting*, vol. 1, *The Movies* (New York, 1956); Frank J. Donner, *The Un-Americans* (New York, 1961); Alvah Bessie, *Inquisition in Eden* (New York, 1965); Walter Goodman, *The Committee: The Extraordinary Career of the House Committee on Un-American Activities* (New York, 1968); Eric Bentley, ed., *Thirty Years of Treason* (New York, 1971); Dalton Trumbo, *The Time of the Toad* (New York, 1972); Stefan Kanfer, *A Journal of the Plague Years* (New York, 1973); Larry Ceplair and Stephen Englund, *The Inquisition in Hollywood: Politics in the Film Community: 1930–1960* (Garden City, N.Y., 1980); Victor S. Navasky, *Naming Names* (New York, 1980); Bernard F. Dick, *Radical Innocence: A Critical Study of the Hollywood Ten* (Lexington, Ky., 1989); Kenneth Lloyd Billingsley, *Hollywood Party: How Communism Seduced the American Film Industry in the 1930s and 1940s* (Rocklin, Calif., 1998).

5. Biographical information on Robinson's life was drawn from the Robinson Collection; the biographical files are at the Margaret Herrick Library, Academy of Motion

Picture Arts and Sciences, Beverly Hills, California (hereafter, AMPAS); Edward
G. Robinson with Leonard Spigelgass, *All My Yesterdays: An Autobiography* (New
York, 1973); Alan L. Gansberg, *Little Caesar: A Biography of Edward G. Robinson*
(Latham, Md., 2004); Edward G. Robinson Jr. with William Dufty, *My Father—My
Son: An Autobiography of Edward G. Robinson Jr.* (New York, 1958).

6. Dick Stout, "The Last Interview with the Late, Great Actor," *In Touch*, June 1974,
41; also see Victor Lasky, typescript of unpublished article, 7–8, box 30, folder 17,
EGR Coll.

7. Edward G. Robinson, "From Steerage to Stardom," ca. 1939 newspaper clipping,
Confessions of a Nazi Spy, Scrapbook book 21, EGR Coll.; Jaffe quoted in Gansberg,
Little Caesar, 12; *NYT*, January 28, 1973. He kept E as his first initial and G to
remind him of the family name.

8. Robinson quoted in Gansberg, *Little Caesar*, 22.

9. *Photoplay* 83 (May 1973): 73.

10. Robinson, *All My Yesterdays*, 81; *Los Angeles Express*, September 23, 1935. In the
late 1930s, he began collecting works by Daumier, Corot, Gauguin, Pissarro, Modi-
gliani, Delacroix, Seurat, and Chardin. The *LAT* insisted Robinson knew "more
about art than any other Hollywood screen player." *LAT*, May 31, 1936.

11. *NYT*, January 27, 1973. For salary figures, see *Motion Picture Herald*, August 9,
1941.

12. The Robinson-Hoover story is told in Ronald Brownstein, *The Power and the Glitter:
The Hollywood-Washington Connection* (New York, 1990), 74.

13. Edward G. Robinson speech, May 30, 1957, Edward G. Robinson to Eleanor Roosevelt, June 20, 1957, box 37, folder 3, EGR Coll.; Robinson quoted in *Variety*, January 29, 1973; Conrad Nagel, Oral History, September 1958, 44–45, series 1, vol. 4,
part 2, Popular Arts Project, Columbia University Oral History Program, Special
Collections Department, Columbia University (hereafter, CUOHP). Broadway's
left politics are discussed in Albert Maltz, "The Citizen Writer in Retrospective,"
1:230–259, February 1975, UCLA Oral History Program, Special Collections,
UCLA. For salary differentials between Broadway and Hollywood, see Ingrid Win-
ther Scobie, *Center Stage: Helen Gahagan Douglas, A Life* (New Brunswick, N.J.,
1995), 71.

14. George S. Kullen, "Little Caesar Joins the G-Men," *Screen Book*, June 1939, 97; Leo
C. Rosten, *Hollywood: The Movie Colony, The Movie Makers* (New York, 1941), 55.

15. Quotes are from, respectively, Nancy Schwartz, *The Hollywood Writers' War* (New
York, 1982), 10; Albert Hackett, Oral History, September 22, 1958, 22, CUOHP.
The rise of the Screen Writers Guild and Screen Actors Guild are discussed in
Schwartz, *Hollywood Writers' War*; David P. Prindle, *The Politics of Glamour: Ideol-
ogy and Democracy in the Screen Actors Guild* (Madison, Wis., 1988); Danae Clark,
Negotiating Hollywood: The Cultural Politics of Actors' Labor (Minneapolis, 1995).

16. Robinson, *All My Yesterdays*, 121. For the intriguing political journeys of Melvyn
and Helen Douglas, see Melvyn Douglas and Tom Arthur, *See You at the Movies: The
Autobiography of Melvyn Douglas* (Lanham, Md., 1986); Scobie, *Center Stage*.

17. For Hollywood's émigré community, see John Russell Taylor, *Strangers in Paradise:
The Hollywood Émigrés 1933–1950* (New York, 1983); Otto Friedrich, *City of
Nets: A Portrait of Hollywood in the 1940s* (New York, 1987); Saverio Giovacchini,

Hollywood Modernism: Film and Politics in the Age of the New Deal (Philadelphia, 2001); Rosten, *Hollywood*, 57.

18. Gallup and Robinson, "Surveys, 1935–38," 388; Edward S. Shapiro, "World War II and American Jewish Identity," *Modern Judaism* 10 (February 1990): 68–69.

19. Robinson, *All My Yesterdays*, 162–163; *NYT*, October 18, 1936, March 24, 1934; *New York World Telegram*, May 3, 1937. Adolphe Menjou accepted Hitler's personal invitation to attend the 1936 Olympics. Gansberg, *Little Caesar*, 74. During the presidential elections of 1940, Pickford sent Robinson and other stars a circular letter claiming "that Jews in New York are going to vote for Roosevelt as a group," a charge Eddie insisted was "wholly unjust and untrue and to use such premise as a means to draw other unwarranted conclusions must offend every good American." Edward G. Robinson to Mary Pickford, November 4, 1940, box 30, folder 14-B, EGR Coll.

20. Warner quoted in Friedrich, *City of Nets*, 50; photo of flyer in Steven Carr, *Hollywood and Anti-Semitism* (New York and Cambridge, U.K., 2001), 112; *LAT*, November 17, 1938. For fascist activities in Los Angeles and across the nation, see Neal Gabler, *An Empire of Their Own: How the Jews Invented Hollywood* (New York, 1989); Alan Brinkley, *Voices of Protest: Huey Long, Father Coughlin and the Great Depression* (New York, 1982); Carr, *Hollywood and Anti-Semitism*.

21. Leo Rosten, Oral History, June 1959, 46, 47, 1–2, CUOHP.

22. For a complete list of all donations made during this time, see *Testimony of Edward G. Robinson, Hearings before the Committee on Un-American Activities of the House of Representatives. Eighty-First Congress, Second Session, October 27, and December 21, 1950* (Washington, D.C., 1951), 3308–3320 (hereafter, Testimony of Robinson, HUAC, . . . October, December 1950). Dollar-figure conversions are computed by using www.measuringworth.comppowerus/, accessed May 8, 2010. I averaged the price indexes for 1939 and 1949 to find a median figure to compare to 2009 prices.

23. Philip Dunne, *Take Two: A Life in Movies and Politics* (New York, 1980), 109. For humanitarian efforts on behalf of Spain, see *LAT*, August 16, 1938. Other major groups included the American Youth Congress, the Abraham Lincoln Battalion, Writers' and Artists' Committee for Medical Aid to Spain, the National Lawyer's Guild, and the Motion Picture Democratic Committee. For an overview of the Popular Front, see Michael Denning, *The Cultural Front: The Laboring of American Culture in the Twentieth Century* (London and New York, 1997); Lester Cole, *Hollywood Red: The Autobiography of Lester Cole* (Palo Alto, Calif., 1981); Brownstein, *Power and the Glitter*; Ceplair and Englund, *Inquisition in Hollywood*.

24. For Mussolini and Riefenstahl, see *Los Angeles Examiner*, October 9, 1937; *NYT*, November 30, 1938. For the HANL mission statement, see *LAT*, January 7, 1937, August 16, 1938. League activities were regularly reported in the *LAT* and *NYT*. The best overviews of the HANL can be found in Michael E. Birdwell, *Celluloid Soldiers: Warner Bros.'s Campaign against Nazism* (New York, 1999); Donald Ogden Stewart, *By a Stroke of Luck! An Autobiography* (New York, 1975), 223–249; Cogley, *Report on Blacklisting*, 35–40; Dunne, *Take Two*, 109–111, 115–116; Gansberg, *Little Caesar*, 1, 74–76, 86–87; Giovacchini, *Hollywood Modernism*, 72–107. For HANL radio addresses, see "Melvyn Douglas Speech, Station KFWB, December 3, 1938," box 10, folder 4, Melvyn Douglas Papers, Wisconsin Historical Society, Madison, Wisconsin (hereafter, Douglas Papers).

25. Ella Winter, "Hollywood Wakes Up," *New Republic*, January 12, 1938, 276; *LAT*, October 24, 1937; Thalberg quoted in Gabler, *Empire of Their Own*, 338.

26. Dies quoted in Friedrich, *City of Nets*, 52; Robinson, *All My Yesterdays*, 13, 146. Sullivan told the press that Jews may have been worried about Nazis and Silver Shirts, but their concern "was not shared by any other agency." *NYT*, August 15, 1938. For an analysis of the Dies Committee, see D. A. Saunders, "The Dies Committee: First Phase," *Public Opinion Quarterly* 3 (April 1939): 223–238; Christine Ann Colgan, "Warner Brothers' Crusade against the Third Reich: A Study of Anti-Nazi Activism and Film Production 1933 to 1941," Ph.D. diss., University of Southern California, August 1985, 394, 487; Dunne, *Take Two*, 128–131.

27. *Los Angeles Examiner*, August 25, 1938; [No author], "American Institute of Public Opinion—Surveys, 1938–1939," 586.

28. For reports of the meeting, see *Los Angeles Examiner*, December 9, 1938. The Committee continued gathering signatures, doing dramatic readings of the Declaration of Democratic Independence, and recruiting organizations such as the American Legion, Los Angeles Central Labor Council, and the Congress on Industrial Organizations to take part in their programs. Their plans to produce newsreels were apparently sabotaged by Louis B. Mayer. Newspaper photographs of the signing can be found in *NYT*, January 1, 1939; for correspondence as well as more photographs, including ones in French newspapers, see Melvyn Douglas, Correspondence, box 11, folder 1, Douglas Papers.

29. Henry Bortin Jr. to Edward G. Robinson, December 10, 1938; Hyman Bloomfield to Edward G. Robinson, December 10, 1938, box 29, folder 9, EGR Coll.

30. Telegram, National Association of Southerners to Edward G. Robinson, December 21, 1938, box 29, folder 9; I. E. Schoening to Edward G. Robinson, December 13, 1938, box 30, folder 14-B, EGR Coll.

31. J. O'Connor to Edward G. Robinson and "Clique," December 9, 1938; Harwood Motley to Edward G. Robinson, January 21, 1939; *Our Sunday Visitor*, January 15, 1939, box 29, folder 10, EGR Coll.

32. Rosten, *Hollywood*, 134; D. Shea to Edward G. Robinson, December 10, 1938, box 29, folder 9, EGR Coll.

33. Edward G. Robinson to Professor D. R. Taft, December 22, 1938, box 29, folder 9, EGR Coll.

34. *New York American*, August 11, 1936. Warners also turned out a series of biographical films—*Disraeli* (1929 but reissued in the late 1930s), *The Life of Emile Zola* (1937), *A Dispatch from Reuters* (1940), and *Dr. Ehrlich's Magic Bullet* (1940)—that heralded the achievements of famous Jews. For Warners' antifascist film, see Kaplan and Blakley, *Warners' War*; Birdwell, *Celluloid Soldiers*; Colgan, "Warner Brothers Crusade."

35. Edward G. Robinson to Hal Wallis, October 20, 1938, box 36, folder 20, EGR Coll.; Kullen, "Little Caesar Joins the G-Men"; *Film Weekly*, June 15, 1939. For the problems involved in making *Confessions*, see Steven J. Ross, "Confessions of a Nazi Spy: Warner Bros., Anti-Fascism and the Politicization of Hollywood," in Kaplan and Blakley, *Warners' War*, 48–59.

36. Edward G. Robinson to D. R. Taft, December 22, 1938, box 29, folder 9, EGR Coll.; Robinson, *All My Yesterdays*, 218; Robinson to Taft, December 22, 1938, EGR Coll.

The *Motion Picture Herald* voted Robinson the "most effective film personality on radio." Alvin H. Marill, *The Complete Films of Edward G. Robinson* (New York, 1990), 35.

37. *LAT*, August 7, 1940. For reaction to the Hitler-Stalin pact and subsequent hearings in Washington and California, see M. J. Heale, "Red Scare Politics: California's Campaign against Un-American Activities, 1940–1970," *Journal of American Studies* 20 (April 1986): 5–32; Dunne, *Take Two*, 127–131; Stewart, *By a Stroke of Luck*, 249; Friedrich, *City of Nets*, 24, 47.

38. American Legion award quoted in Lasky, unpublished mss., 14, box 30, folder 17, EGR Coll. For Robinson's decision to end his radio show, see Gansberg, *Little Caesar*, 106.

39. Robert Sherwood to Edward G. Robinson, October 13, 1942, box 29, folder 15, EGR Coll.; for Robinson's military service, see correspondence in box 29, folders 15–16, 24–33, EGR Coll. For Robinson's work with the Hollywood Democratic Committee, see script and report on "The Common Man" Rally, February 4, 1944, box 8, folder 15, Hollywood Democratic Committee Papers (hereafter, HDC Coll.), Wisconsin Historical Society; HDC report, August 21, November 3, 1944, box 2, folder 7, Stephen Vaughn Papers, Wisconsin Historical Society.

40. Gansberg, *Little Caesar*, 111; Edward G. Robinson to Edwin Smith, February 13, 1943, box 29, folder 7, EGR Coll.

41. Robinson, *All My Yesterdays*, 121. Robinson's family problems are discussed in ibid.; Gansberg, *Little Caesar*; Robinson Jr., *My Father—My Son*.

42. *Los Angeles Herald Express*, February 5, 1944; Special Report, Los Angeles Office, "Communist Infiltration of the Motion Pictures Industries," August 25, 1943; also see "Letters from the Bureau Re: Communist Infiltration," August 14, November 9, 1942, Los Angeles File 100-15732, FBI Records, cited in Federal Bureau of Investigation, Confidential Files, *Communist Activity in the Entertainment Industry: FBI Surveillance Files on Hollywood, 1942–1958*, ed. Daniel J. Leab (University Publications of America, Microfilms, 14 rolls: hereafter, FBI Records). For the MPA's formation and early anti-Communist activities, see *Los Angeles Herald Express*, February 5, 1944; *Variety*, February 7, 1944; *Hollywood Citizen-News*, February 8, 1944; *PM*, February 15, 1944; *NYT*, April 23, 1944; *Los Angeles Examiner*, April 29, 1944; *LAT*, April 29, May 6, 1944; *Los Angeles Daily News*, June 6, 1944.

43. Robinson, *All My Yesterdays*, 270. For broadcasts and petitions supporting the United Nations and the Wagner-Murray-Dingell bill calling for creation of a "National Health and Welfare Program," see "Postcard Invitation, June 1945: Film Promoting UN," box 7, folder 1; and "Minutes of Emergency Meeting of Members of Hollywood Arts and Sciences Committee, May 22, 1945," box 8, folder 12, HDC Coll.; Edward G. Robinson to Medical Advisory Council, Hotel Astor, N.Y.C., April 19, 1946, box 29, folder 13, EGR Coll.

44. Edward G. Robinson to Harry S. Truman, March 13, 1946, box 37, folder 3, EGR Coll.

45. John H. Sengstacke (president, *Chicago Defender*) to Edward G. Robinson, October 19, 1944, box 29, folder 19, EGR Coll. During the war, he worked with the Civil Rights Congress and the Committee of 100—Dedicated to Justice for Negroes. He also narrated a radio documentary about domestic racism and wrote an article, "If I

Were a Negro," for the *Negro Digest*. For radio and other race-related activities, see Dore Schary to Robinson, March 13, 1945, and other letters in ibid.; Maril, *Films of Robinson*, 35; *NYT*, August 31, 1947.

46. Robinson to George Marshall, May 21, 1945, box 29, folder 27, EGR Coll.; telegram, Edward G. Robinson to Harry S. Truman, April 18, 1946, box 37, folder 3, EGR Coll. For activities on behalf of Jews, see correspondence in box 29, folder 20; box 37, folder 2, EGR Coll.

47. Robinson, *All My Yesterdays*, 248–249. For his involvement in labor struggles and in HICCASP, see Gansberg, *Little Caesar*, 119–128; the battle between the CSU and IATSE is discussed in the next chapter.

48. Gene Kelly, Oral History, December 20, 1958, 20, CUOHP; Myrna Loy, Oral History, June 1959, 36, series 2, vol. 5, Popular Arts Project, CUOHP. For liberal and left splits over anti-Communism, see Richard H. Pells, *The Liberal Mind in a Conservative Age: American Intellectuals in the 1940s and 1950s* (New York, 1985); Arthur Schlesinger Jr., *A Life in the Twentieth Century* (Boston, 2000). For Hollywood and the ADA, see Dunne, *Take Two*; Douglas, *See You at the Movies*.

49. Quoted in Gans, *Little Caesar*, 130; F. B. Putnam to Edward G. Robinson, March 24, 1946; Dick Mooney to Robinson, November 25, 1946; Robinson to Mooney, December 4, 1946, box 37, folder 4, EGR Coll.

50. Special Agent in Charge (hereafter, SAC), Los Angeles, to Director [J. Edgar Hoover], September 20, 1947, FBI Records. Los Angeles agents frequently complained to Hoover about the hasty and unprofessional manner in which HUAC investigators put together their files on alleged Hollywood Communists. See correspondence between local agents and Hoover beginning in August 22, 1947, contained in FBI Records.

51. L. B. Nichols to Clyde Tolson, September 10, 1947, FBI Records; Rankin quoted in Gerald Horne, *The Final Victim of the Blacklist: John Howard Lawson, Dean of the Hollywood Ten* (Berkeley, 2006), xi; Mildred Strunk, ed., "The Quarter's Polls," *Public Opinion Quarterly* 12 (Spring 1948): 150. Thomas was later jailed for accepting kickbacks.

52. Menjou quoted in Billingsley, *Hollywood Party*, 184; Cole, *Hollywood Red*, 272. For a similar encounter between Mayer and Melvyn Douglas, see Douglas, *See You at the Movies*, 113.

53. Marsha Hunt, Oral History, August 12, 1983, 56, Ronald L. Davis Oral History Collection, DeGolyer Library, Southern Methodist University (also available at the Herrick Library, AMPAS); CFA statement quoted in Gansberg, *Little Caesar*, 139. The Hollywood Ten included Alvah Bessie, Herbert Biberman, Lester Cole, Edward Dmytryk, Ring Lardner Jr., John Howard Lawson, Albert Maltz, Samuel Ornitz, Adrian Scott, and Dalton Trumbo. For the activities of the CFA, see Gansberg, *Little Caesar*, 139–140, 145–152; Alvin Yudkoff, *Gene Kelly: A Life of Dance and Dreams* (New York, 1999), 170–175; Lauren Bacall, *By Myself and Then Some* (New York, 2005), 177–184; Ceplair and Englund, *Inquisition in Hollywood*, 275–290.

54. Johnston quoted in Kahn, *Hollywood on Trial*, 26; also see *Washington Post*, October 27, 28, 1947; *NYT*, October 27, 1947.

55. Copy of Bogart's prepared statement, December 3, 1947, box 3f, Hedda Hopper Papers, AMPAS (hereafter, Hopper Papers). For studio pressures on Bogart, see

Bacall, *By Myself*, 183. For Warner's fear of box-office reprisals, see SAC to F.B.I. Director [J. Edgar Hoover], December 19, 1947, FBI Records.

56. R. B. Hood, SAC, L.A. to Director [J. Edgar Hoover], November 3, 1947; Hopper comments in Report from L.A. Office, November 17, 1947; R. B. Hood, SAC, L.A. to Director, November 20, 1947, FBI Records. One 1948 anti-Red tract blasted Katharine Hepburn for her opposition to the HUAC hearings and claimed that her "love for Joe Stalin is no secret." Myron C. Fagan, *Red Stars in Hollywood* (St. Louis, Mo., 1948), 3.

57. L.A. SAC to Director, December 19, 1947, 1, 36, FBI Records. For an analysis of declining boxoffice during this period, see John Sedgwick, "Product Differentiation at the Movies: Hollywood, 1946 to 1965," *Journal of Economic History* 62 (September 2002): 676–705.

58. Waldorf Statement quoted in Steven J. Ross, *Movies and American Society* (Oxford, U.K., and Malden, Mass., 2002), 217–228; L.A. SAC to Director, December 19, 1947, 1, 36, FBI Records. For studio leaders using the blacklist to reassert control over the industry, see Jon Lewis, "'We Do Not Ask You to Condone This': How the Blacklist Saved Hollywood," *Cinema Journal* 39 (Winter 2000): 3–30.

59. Lasky, unpublished article, 24, box 30, folder 17, EGR Coll.; espionage accusation quoted in Gansberg, *Little Caesar*, 153; E. H. Winterrowd to Colonel Harry Hawkins Vaughn, The White House, May 4, 1945; Report from L.A. Office, August 4, 1947, 2, FBI Records. For surveillance of his home, see Report to Director, October 7, 1947. HUAC asked the FBI for Robinson's file in September 1947. J. P. Coyne to D. M. Ladd, September 17, 1947, FBI Records.

60. Robinson letter in *Hollywood Reporter*, October 3, 1946; also see Edward G. Robinson to *International Photo Engravers Union Journal*, St. Louis, Missouri, October 2, 1946; Edward G. Robinson to William Wilkerson, October 2, 1946, box 30, folder 14-B, EGR Coll.

61. Joseph A. Caterina to Edward G. Robinson, October 17, 1947; Alexander Burke to Edward G. Robinson, October 23, 1947, box 30, folder 14-B, EGR Coll.; *Los Angeles Express*, April 13, 1947.

62. Anonymous letter to Emmanuel Goldenburg [*sic*] alias Edward G. Robinson, June, 16, 1949, box 30, folder 14-B; Edward G. Robinson to Alexander Burke, December 8, 1947, box 30, folder 14-B, EGR Coll.; press release, "News from 20th Century Fox: Dateline Hollywood," ca. 1949, 2, in Edward G. Robinson Biography file (microfiche), AMPAS.

63. *Philadelphia Inquirer*, June 9, 1949; W. R. Wilkerson, "Trade Views," *Hollywood Reporter*, June 13, 1949; Smith quoted in Gansberg, *Little Caesar*, 156.

64. R. B. Hood, SAC, L.A. to Director, November 3, 1947, 4–5, FBI Records. The conservative chill that fell over postwar Hollywood is discussed in Larry May, *The Big Tomorrow: Hollywood and the Politics of the American Way* (Chicago, 2000), 175–213; Brownstein, *Power and the Glitter*.

65. Report of Los Angeles SAC, December 14, 1950, FBI Records. The California Committee on Un-American Activities linked him to eleven Communist front groups. Robinson, *All My Yesterdays*, 242–245; also see *Red Channels* (New York, 1950) and Fagan, *Red Stars in Hollywood*; Myron C. Fagan, *Red Treason in Hollywood* (Hollywood, 1949); Myron C. Fagan, *Documentation of the Red Stars in Hollywood* (Hollywood, 1950).

66. Testimony of Robinson, HUAC, . . . October, December 1950, 3300, 3331, 3321.

67. J. Edgar Hoover to Edward G. Robinson, January 8, 1938, box 37, folder 2; Edward G. Robinson to J. Edgar Hoover, November 3, 1950 and Hoover to Robinson, November 8, 1950, box 30, folder 14-C, EGR Coll. His request to the MPA was considered at a February 15, 1951, meeting of the board. The FBI informant claimed that the board "would not believe Robinson anyway." Report of SAC, L.A., March 14, 1951, FBI Records.

68. Testimony of Robinson, HUAC, . . . October, December 1950, 3341, 3342, 3343.

69. Ibid., 3343.

70. Parsons column in *Los Angeles Examiner*, December 26, 1950; *Hollywood Reporter*, January 11, 1951; Darryl Zanuck to Edward G. Robinson, January 29, 1951, box 30, folder 14-D, EGR Coll. For coverage of Robinson's testimony, see *NYT*, December 22, 1950; [NY] *Journal American*, December 21, 1950; *New York Post*, December 21, 1950.

71. William P. Laffin (Commander Post #3, American Legion) to John Wood, January 11, 1951, Report of SAC, L.A., March 14, 1951, FBI Records; *Variety*, February 12, March 14, 1951. Like HUAC chair Thomas, Jackson was anxious to receive as much personal publicity as possible. By 1953, he was leaking confidential information to Hedda Hopper. Donald Jackson to Hedda Hopper, January 30, 1953, box 11, Hopper Papers.

72. Victor Lasky, unpublished profile of Robinson, ca. 1950, box 30, folder 17, EGR Coll.; *People*, December 31, 1952, 20. The conflict between Robinson and Reagan is discussed in Gansberg, *Little Caesar*, 119–129, 157, 159; Roy Brewer to Edward G. Robinson, February 4, 1947, Robinson to Brewer, February 11, 1947, box 29, folder 19, EGR Coll.

73. When Eddie and Gladys finally divorced in 1956, the actor was forced to sell most of his art collection. For family difficulties during this time, see *Los Angeles Herald Express*, February 15, 1952; *Los Angeles Express*, March 4, 1952; *LAT*, April 12, 1952; Gansberg, *Little Caesar*, 138, 161, 179, 202, 206.

74. Telegram to Edward G. Robinson from Bert [Allenberg], March 31, 1952; Bert Allenberg to Edward G. Robinson, April 9, 1952, box 30, folder 14-E, EGR Coll. For Yorty's efforts, see Sam Yorty to Ruth Shipley, Director, Passport Division, Department of State, April 29, 1952, box 30, folder 14-E, EGR Coll.

75. Robinson, *All My Yesterdays*, 268, 256. The play was based on Arthur Koestler's novel. The literature on the political impact of Senator Joe McCarthy and McCarthyism on HUAC and the Cold War is voluminous. For overviews of the era, see David Caute, *The Great Fear: The Anti-Communist Purge under Truman and Eisenhower* (New York, 1978); Stanley I. Kutler, *The American Inquisition: Justice and Injustice in the Cold War* (New York, 1982); Stephen J. Whitfield, *The Culture of the Cold War* (Baltimore, Md., 1996); Richard M. Fried, *Nightmare in Red: The McCarthy Era in Perspective* (New York, 1990).

76. *Communist Infiltration of Hollywood Motion-Picture Industry—Part 7. Hearings before the Committee on Un-American Activities House of Representatives. Eighty-Second Congress. Second Session. January 24, 28, February 5, March 20, and April 10, 30, 1952* (Washington, D.C., 1952), 2417, 2416, 2417, 2416.

77. Ibid., 2427, 2430, 2434.

78. *LAT*, May 1, 1952; *Los Angeles Examiner*, May 1, 1952; Robinson, "How the Reds Made a Sucker Out of Me," 68, 70.
79. Robinson, *All My Yesterdays*, 265, 271, 271.
80. Louis J. Russell to Edward G. Robinson, July 11, 1953; Robinson to Russell, July 13, 1953, box 30, folder 14-F, EGR Coll. For Robinson's testimony, see typescript copy of United States House of Representatives Committee on Un-American Activities, "Report of Proceedings. Executive Hearing: Edward G. Robinson, Monday, January 25, 1954," Dolores Anderson, Reporter; a copy can be found in the EGR Coll. On HUAC clearing Robinson of wrongdoing, see *Variety*, January 26, 1954.
81. Robinson, *All My Yesterdays*, 272.
82. Ibid., 276.
83. Edward G. Robinson to Ralph Dills, March 16, 1969; Ronald Reagan to Edward G. Robinson, ca. March 1969; Edward G. Robinson to George Murphy, March 16, 1969, box 37, folder 10, EGR Coll.; *Hollywood Reporter*, November 18, 1969.
84. Robinson, *All My Yesterdays*, 307; also see *Variety*, January 12, 1973. For Robinson's postage stamp honor, see *LAT*, October 24, 2000.
85. Testimony of Robinson, HUAC, . . . October, December 1950, 3342; Edward G. Robinson to Progressive Citizens of America, November 1950, box 47, folder 8, EGR Coll.
86. Robinson, *All My Yesterdays*, 263, 270n.
87. Author interviews with Betty Sheinbaum, November 12, 1999, May 9, 2006, Los Angeles, California.
88. Ronald Reagan with Richard G. Hubler, *Where's the Rest of Me?* (New York, 1965), 183; Bacall, *By Myself*, 184; *Hollywood Reporter*, September 13, 1961. For Tamm's decision, *LAT*, July 25, 1961.
89. George Pepper to David K. Niles, July 12, 1945, box 7, folder 15, HDC Coll.
90. *Los Angeles Examiner*, October 27, 1947.
91. *LAT*, July 16, 1979.
92. Author interview with Lee Grant, July 8, 2002, New York City. The FBI did accuse actors who were too vocal in the civil rights movement, such as Harry Belafonte, of being Reds.
93. Marill, *Films of Robinson*, 23.

CHAPTER 4

1. Theodore Kuperfman quoted in *Variety Weekly*, October 9, 1968; for Vegas odds, see George Murphy with Victor Lasky, *Say . . . Didn't You Used to Be George Murphy* (n.p., 1970), 381.
2. "The Way We Live," *NYT Sunday Magazine*, July 11, 2010.
3. Murphy, *Say*, 259. There has been surprisingly little written about George Murphy. Biographical information about his life has been culled from ibid.; "George Murphy—Biography," Universal Studies, mimeographed publicity sheet, October 1936, George Murphy microfiche file number 1, Margaret Herrick Library, Academy of Motion Picture Arts and Sciences (hereafter, AMPAS), Beverly Hills; *Los Angeles Express*, June 9, July 30, 1934; Hedda Hopper profile in *Chicago Tribune*, October 7, 1939; Richard English, "Hollywood's Yankee-Doodle Dandy,"

Saturday Evening Post, July 2, 1955, 28–29, 71–74; "George (Lloyd) Murphy," *Current Biography* (December 1965): 25–27.

4. Ronald Reagan with Richard G. Hubler, *Where's the Rest of Me?* (New York, 1965), 3, 40. Biographical information on Reagan is substantial. The most useful sources for understanding his early years are ibid.; Stephen Vaughn, *Ronald Reagan in Hollywood: Movies and Politics* (New York, 1994); Garry Wills, *Reagan's America: Innocents at Home* (New York, 1985); Anne Edwards, *Early Reagan* (New York, 1987); Michael Paul Rogin, *Ronald Reagan, the Movie and Other Episodes in Political Demonology* (Berkeley, 1987); Bill Boyarsky, *The Rise of Ronald Reagan* (New York, 1968); Robert Dallek, *Ronald Reagan: The Politics of Symbolism* (Cambridge, Mass., 1999); Edmund Morris, *Dutch: A Memoir of Ronald Reagan* (New York, 1999); John Patrick Diggins, *Ronald Reagan: Fate, Freedom, and the Making of History* (New York, 2007); Marc Eliot, *Reagan: The Hollywood Years* (New York, 2008); Neil Reagan, "Private Dimensions and Public Images: The Early Political Campaigns of Ronald Reagan," June 1981, Oral History Program, Special Collections, UCLA. The newspaper clipping files at AMPAS and the New York Public Library for the Performing Arts are helpful sources.

5. Reagan, *Where's*, 26.

6. *Los Angeles Express*, November 1, 1939. Dollar equivalencies are taken from www.measuringworth.com/ppowerus/, accessed May 8, 2010.

7. For his poor eyesight and service record, see *Los Angeles Express*, January 12, 1943; Vaughn, *Reagan*, 104–118.

8. *NYT*, June 28, 1982.

9. Leo Rosten, Oral History, June 1959, 51, series 3, vol. 7, part 1, Popular Arts Project, Columbia University Oral History Program, Special Collections Department, Columbia University (hereafter, CUOHP); Edward G. Robinson with Leonard Spigelgass, *All My Yesterdays: An Autobiography* (New York, 1973), 143. For Mayer, Koverman, and Murphy, see *Hollywood Reporter*, November 5, 1964. For Murphy's early political experiences at MGM, see *LAT*, May 24, 1964; Herbert Gold, "Nobody's Mad at Murphy," *NYT Magazine*, December 13, 1964.

10. Murphy, *Say*, 259; *Hollywood Reporter*, November 5, 1964; Murphy, *Say*, 262.

11. "American Institute of Public Opinion—Surveys, 1938–1939," *Public Opinion Quarterly* 3 (October 1939): 586.

12. For Murphy's battle against IATSE and its Chicago mob allies, see David Prindle, *The Politics of Glamour: Ideology and Democracy in the Screen Actors Guild* (Madison, Wis., 1988), 31–36; *LAT*, September 2, 1939; Murphy, *Say*, 219–224. For a fuller account of the mob takeover of IATSE Local 33, see Mike Nielsen and Gene Mailes, *Hollywood's Other Blacklist: Union Struggles in the Studio System* (London, 1995).

13. Murphy, *Say*, 264. For his activities in the 1940 campaign, see *LAT*, September 7, 18, 20, October 21, 22, 28, 30, 1940; Telegram: George Murphy to Hedda Hopper, October 22, 1940, Box 16f, Hedda Hopper Papers, AMPAS (hereafter, Hopper Papers); English, "Hollywood's Yankee Doodle-Dandy," 71. Once Murphy switched to the Republican Party, Ida's good friend Hedda Hopper began writing favorable articles trying to advance his career. *LAT*, October 1, 1939, *Chicago Tribune*, October 7, 1939.

14. Murphy, *Say*, 253, 264.
15. Ibid., 266; Eugene Lyons, *The Red Decade: The Stalinist Penetration of America* (Indianapolis and New York, 1941), 11; Murphy, *Say*, 281. For Murphy's initial suspicion of Communist penetration of Hollywood unions, see Murphy, *Say*, 280–282. For the deal struck between IATSE and producers, see George H. Dunne, *The King's Pawn: The Memoirs of George H. Dunne, S. J.* (Chicago, 1990), 147–149; testimony of Victor Clarke in House of Representatives, 80th Congress, *Jurisdictional Disputes in the Motion-Picture Industry Hearings before a Special Subcommittee of the Committee on Education and Labor First Session, Hearings Held at LA, Ca. August 11–September 3, 1947, 3 vols.* (Washington, D.C., 1948).
16. MPA, "Statement of Principles," reprinted in *Variety*, February 7, 1944; and "Statement of Policy," ca. 1944, mimeograph copy in box 16, Hopper Papers. For reports on the MPA's formation and early anti-Communist activities, see "Statement of Policy," box 16, Hopper Papers; Ronald Brownstein, *The Power and the Glitter: The Hollywood-Washington Connection* (New York, 1992), 87–92; *Variety*, February 7, 1944; *Hollywood Citizen-News*, February 8, 1944; *PM*, February 15, 1944; *NYT*, April 23, 1944; *Los Angeles Examiner*, April 29, 1944; *LAT*, April 29, May 6, 1944; *New Leader*, July 15, 1944. On the MPA inviting the HUAC back, see Garry Wills, *John Wayne's America* (New York, 1997), 195.
17. *Washington Post*, August 18, 1976.
18. Interview with Bernard Vorhaus in Patrick McGilligan and Paul Buhle, *Tender Comrades: A Backstory of the Hollywood Backlist* (New York, 1997), 674.
19. Vorhaus quoted in ibid., 674; Special Agent [name blacked out], Washington D.C., Memorandum for Mr. Clegg, September 17, 1941, box 1, folder 2, Stephen Vaughn Collection, Wisconsin Historical Society. For Reagan and the FBI, see FBI report, December 27, 1943, FBI Report August 4, 1947, L.A., cited in Federal Bureau of Investigation, Confidential Files, *Communist Activity in the Entertainment Industry: FBI Surveillance Files on Hollywood, 1942–1958*, ed. Daniel J. Leab (University Publications of America, Microfilms, 14 rolls: hereafter, FBI Records); also see Betty Glad, "Reagan's Midlife Crisis and the Turn to the Right," *Political Psychology* 10 (December 1989): 614; Wills, *Reagan's America*, 295–296.
20. Reagan, *Where's*, 139; John Cogley, *Report on Blacklisting*, vol. 1, *Movies* (n.p., 1956), 69. FBI records list Reagan as belonging to the Committee for a Democratic Far Eastern Policy, the United World Federalists, the International Rescue and Relief Committee, and the American Veterans Committee.
21. Reagan, *Where's*, 166; Vaughn, *Reagan*, 125; also see Neil Reagan, Oral History, 30–31. HICCASP was an amalgam of the Hollywood Democratic Committee and the New York–based Independent Citizens Committee of the Arts, Sciences and Professions. For an overview of the organization, see Reagan, *Where's*, 166–170; Larry Ceplair and Steven Englund, *The Inquisition in Hollywood: Politics in the Film Community, 1930–1960* (Berkeley, 1979), 218, 224–231, 237–239; Ronald Radosh and Allis Radosh, *Red Star over Hollywood: The Film Colony's Long Romance with the Left* (San Francisco, 2005); Gerald Horne, *The Final Victim of the Blacklist: John Howard Lawson, Dean of the Hollywood Ten* (Berkeley, 2006).
22. For the changing relationship between Moscow and the CPUSA, see Irving Howe and Lewis Coser, *The American Communist Party: A Critical History, 1919–1957*

(Boston 1957), 444–453; Ceplair and Englund, *Inquisition in Hollywood*; Radosh and Radosh, *Red Star*.

23. *Life*, July 29, 1946; Reagan, *Where's*, 167. Schlesinger's book was published in 1949. Arthur Schlesinger Jr., *The Vital Center: The Politics of Freedom* (New York, 1949).

24. Reagan, *Where's*, 167–168; resolution quoted in Vaughn, *Reagan*, 131. For de Havilland's background and involvement with HICCASP, see *Los Angeles Examiner*, September 7, 14, 1958; Vaughn, *Reagan*, 127–128.

25. *Los Angeles Examiner*, September 14, 1958; Reagan Testimony in Jeffers Case, July 1, 1955, 3, 411, box 3, folder 8, Vaughn Coll. For the decline of HICCASP and Lawson's role, see Horne, *The Final Victim*; Vaughn, *Reagan*, 130–132; Ceplair and Englund, *Inquisition in Hollywood*.

26. Reagan, *Where's*, 142.

27. Ibid., 133. Reagan mistakenly says he was elected to the Board in 1938; it was 1941. Lou Cannon, *Governor Reagan: His Rise to Power* (New York, 2003), 85. For Reagan's contracts and correspondence, see Ronald Reagan to Warner Bros., September 27, 1940, file 2838, folder 1, Jack Warner Papers, Warner Bros. Archives, USC; also see folders 2–3.

28. Bob Colacello, *Ronnie and Nancy: Their Path to the White House—1911 to 1980* (New York, 2004), 179.

29. A great deal has been written about the CSU-IA strikes. The best sources are George H. Dunne, *Hollywood Labor Dispute: A Study in Immorality* (Los Angeles, 1950); House of Representatives, *Jurisdictional Disputes in the Motion-Picture Industry*; Prindle, *Politics of Glamour*; Ceplair and Englund, *Inquisition in Hollywood*; Vaughn, *Reagan*; Nielsen and Mailes, *Hollywood's Other Blacklist*. For Murphy's recollection of the strike, Murphy, *Say*, 283–286.

30. FBI report, July 11, 1946, FBI Records. For Brewer's early work in Hollywood, see ibid.; Roy Brewer, "Oral History," 1980, UCLA Oral History Project, Special Collections, UCLA; Vaughn, *Reagan*; John Meroney, "Hollywood's Brewer and America's," *National Review Online*, September 19, 2006, accessed November 5, 2008. For Brewer and the FBI (which forgot to black out his name in one report), see SAC, L.A. to Director, November 14, 1947, FBI Records.

31. Brewer, "Oral History," 117.

32. Reagan, "Private Dimensions," 22. For reports of violence, see *LAT*, October 3, 6, 1946; *Los Angeles Express*, January 14, 1953.

33. Reagan, *Where's*, 170, 174. For more on the threats of acid, see Reagan's testimony, July 1, 1955, *Jeffers v. Screen Actors Guild*, quoted in Vaughn, *Reagan*, 140; *Los Angeles Express*, January 14, 1954; Brewer, "Oral History," 118.

34. George H. Dunne, S.J., "Christian Advocacy and Labor Strife in Hollywood," Oral History Collection, UCLA, 25–26, 148, 154, 28. Dunne insisted that Reagan's autobiographical account of the meeting was "a mélange of truth, half or partial truth, and untruth." Dunne, *King's Pawn*, 155. For Murphy's warnings, see Murphy, *Say*, 280.

35. Brewer quoted in Vaughn, *Reagan*, 143–144; Jack L. to Jack M. Warner, October 15, 1946, quoted in Vaughn, *Reagan*, 141.

36. Reagan drew upon Hayek's work in his 1964 "Time for Choosing" speech. Hayek's book was published in England in March 1944 and in the United States in April

1945. For Hayek's writings and influence, see John Patrick Diggins, *Ronald Reagan: Fate, Freedom, and the Making of History* (New York, 2007). For Reagan and the ADA, see Melvyn Douglas to Philip Dunne, June 21, 1947, box 13, folder 4, Melvyn Douglas Papers, Wisconsin Historical Society.

37. *Chicago Tribune*, May 18, 1947; *LAT*, May 18, 1947. Hopper prepared two columns on Reagan that ran the same day. The lengthier one ran in the *Chicago Tribune* and a shorter one in the *LAT*.

38. Reagan testimony quoted in Eric Bentley, ed., *Thirty Years of Treason: Excerpts from Hearings before the House Committee on Un-American Activities, 1938–1968* (New York, 1971), 144, 146.

39. Cooper quoted in *Chicago Tribune*, October 24, 1947; Reagan quoted in Bentley, *Thirty Years*, 147.

40. The Moscow–U.S. connection is explored in Radosh and Radosh, *Red Star*, 219–222. For Reagan and Brewer's involvement in clearing actors, see Jack Dales, "Pragmatic Leadership: Ronald Reagan as President of the Screen Actors Guild," Oral History, Special Collections, UCLA, 20–23; Brewer, "Oral History," 2–3, 5, 11.

41. Edward Dmytryk, Oral History, June 1959, 68–69, CUOHP.

42. House of Representatives, *Jurisdictional Disputes in the Motion-Picture Industry*. For a rank-and-file perspective on the CSU and their hatred of IATSE corruption, see Nielsen and Mailes, *Hollywood's Other Blacklist*.

43. Brewer, "Oral History," 118.

44. *Los Angeles Express*, June 19, 1948. For the final divorce, see *LAT* and *NYT*, July 19, 1949.

45. Reagan and Brewer were cochairs of the Labor League. *Hollywood Reporter*, November 18, 1948.

46. For Murphy and Dewey, see *LAT*, June 24, 1948.

47. Murphy, *Say*, 313. For his appointment to the RNC, see *NYT*, October 3, 1948. For Murphy's involvement in the campaign, see *Say*, 297–315; *Variety*, June 22, 1948; *LAT*, June 18, September 1, 22, 24, October 14, 25, 28, 1948. Murphy was also elected to the convention's permanent organization committee. For Dewey's use of television, see Sig Mickelson, *From Whistle Stop to Sound Bite: Four Decades of Politics and Television* (New York, 1989), 14.

48. Adolphe Menjou and M. M. Musselman, *It Took Nine Tailors* (New York, 1948), 162; *NYT*, June 22, 1952. For television statistics, see *Historical Stations of the United States*, 2:796. For television coverage of the 1948 conventions, see Erik Barnouw, *Tube of Plenty: The Evolution of American Television* (New York, 1975), 110–111; Robert J. Donovan and Ray Scherer, "Politics Transformed," *Wilson Quarterly* 16 (Spring 1992): 19; *Time*, July 14, 1952; Craig Allen, "Our First 'Television' Candidate: Eisenhower over Stevenson in 1956," *Journalism Quarterly* 65 (1988): 352–359. For television coverage of the 1952 and 1956 conventions and the impact of TV, see Kathleen Hall Jamieson, *Packaging the Presidency: A History and Criticism of Presidential Campaign Advertising* (New York, 1996), 39–121; Steve M. Barkin, "Eisenhower's Secret Strategy: Television Planning in the 1952 Campaign," *Journal of Advertising History* 9, no. 1 (1986): 18–28; David Culbert, "Television's Nixon: The Politician and His Image," in John O'Connor, ed., *American*

History/American Television: Interpreting the Video Past (New York, 1983), 184–207; Allen, "Our First 'Television' Candidate," 352–359.

49. *Time*, July 21, July 14, 1952. The three networks spent $10 million to cover the Republican Chicago convention and transmitted it to 108 stations. Ibid.

50. English, "Hollywood's Yankee Doodle," 72. This was the last presidential election in which more money was spent on radio ($3.1 million) than television ($2.95 million). In 1956, Republicans outspent Democrats on TV time by a 2:1 margin. Jamieson, *Packaging the Presidency*, 44, 95. For Murphy's work during the convention and his fundraising efforts in Hollywood, see Murphy, *Say*, 326–328, 332; Minutes of the Meeting of the Entertainment Industries for Eisenhower, August 18, 1952, and Goldie Arthur to Jack Warner et al., September 19, 1952, folder 2844, "Mimeo, Entertainment Industry . . . Full Financial Statement," November 29, 1952, folder 2949, Jack Warner Papers, USC; *Los Angeles Daily News*, October 8, 1952; *Beverly Hills Press*, June 10, 1954.

51. *Time*, November 3, 1952; Murphy quoted in Brownstein, *Power and the Glitter*, 134; survey comment quoted in Jamieson, *Packaging the Presidency*, 46. For BBDO and Murphy's media work, see English, "Hollywood's Yankee Doodle"; John E. Hollitz, "Eisenhower and the Admen: The Television 'Spot' Campaign of 1952," *Wisconsin Magazine of History* 66 (Autumn 1982): 25–39; Robert J. Donovan and Ray Scherer, "Politics Transformed," *Wilson Quarterly* 16 (Spring 1992): 19–33.

52. Dwight D. Eisenhower to Edward John Bermingham, January 26, 1954, document 689, *The Papers of Dwight David Eisenhower*, ed. Louis Galambos and Daun van Ee (Baltimore, Md., 1996), World Wide Web facsimile by The Dwight D. Eisenhower Memorial Commission of the print edition, http://www.eisenhowermemorial. org/presidential-papers/first-term/documents/689.cfm, accessed November 15, 2006; also see Eisenhower to George Murphy, August 4, 1954, document 1007; Eisenhower to Bermingham, November 24, 1954, document 561, in ibid. Ike considered appointing Murphy to an ambassadorship. *Los Angeles Examiner*, September 4, 1954. On January 18, 1956, Murphy and Montgomery visited the White House for an "off the record" meeting with Ike to prepare for the 1956 campaign. See Presidential Schedule, www.eisenhowermemorial.org/presidential%2Dpapers/ first%2Dterm/chronology/1956-01.htm, accessed November 15, 2006; also see Hedda Hopper Interview with Robert Montgomery, July 22, 1959, box 16, Robert Montgomery, Hopper Papers.

53. Murphy, *Say*, 338; *Los Angeles Examiner*, October 12, 1953; *Hollywood Reporter*, October 14, 1953. For reports on the selection process, see *Los Angeles Examiner*, October 8, 9, 1953; *Hollywood Citizen News*, October 9, 1953.

54. For reports of his speeches, see *Los Angeles Examiner*, November 13, 1950.

55. *Los Angeles Examiner*, August 6, 1951; Jocelyn Marteleur, "Meet Hollywood's Number 1 Citizen," *Screen Fan*, ca. 1952, AMPAS clipping files.

56. For Murphy's new position, see *Hollywood Reporter*, December 13, 1954; *Hollywood Citizen-News*, January 18, 1955.

57. For his political kinship with Desi, see *Los Angeles Mirror*, February 7, 1958.

58. Mary Pickford was an especially active and astute participant in the campaign. See her critique of Kennedy. Mary Pickford to George Murphy, November 4, 1960, Republican Activities: Nixon-Lodge folder, Mary Pickford Papers, AMPAS.

59. Ronald Reagan, "How Do You Fight Communism?" *Fortnight,* January 22, 1951; *LAT,* February 2, 1952; *Los Angeles Examiner,* July 19, 1952.

60. Reagan, *Where's,* 235, 234. The famed neurosurgeon let it be known that no Jew would ever be given tenure at Northwestern University's medical school while he was on the faculty. Author interview with Dr. Kurt Kent, December 16, 2000. Dr. Kent, now deceased, was the author's father-in-law. For Davis's politics and Nancy's influence, see Kitty Kelley, *Nancy Reagan: The Unauthorized Biography* (New York, 1991), 39–42, 118–119; Glad, "Reagan's Midlife Crisis," 613–615.

61. Allyson quoted in Bob Colacello, *Ronnie and Nancy: Their Path to the White House—1911 to 1980* (New York, 2004), 279; also see 200–202; 277–279; 313–314.

62. Quoted in Glad, "Reagan's Midlife Crisis," 598.

63. Reagan, *Where's,* 245. For an analysis of how changing income tax policies affected Hollywood, and the politics of its stars, see Eric Hoyt, "Hollywood and the Income Tax, 1929–1955," *Film History* 22, no. 1 (2010): 5–21.

64. *Los Angeles Examiner,* March 11, 1959. For Reagan's work on the mayoral campaign, see ibid., May 2, 1953; *Los Angeles Daily News,* May 1, 16, 1953.

65. *Chicago Tribune,* July 13, 1980; Morris, *Dutch,* 304–305. Reagan also received 25% ownership in the show. Dan E. Moldea, *Dark Victory: Ronald Reagan, MCA, and the Mob* (New York, 1986), 143. For Reagan's involvement with GE, see Thomas W. Evans, *The Education of Ronald Reagan: The General Electric Years and the Untold Story of His Conversion to Conservatism* (New York, 2008); Tim Raphael, "The Body Electric: GE, TV, and the Reagan Brand," *The Drama Review: TDR* 53 (Summer 2009): 117; Matthew Dallek, *The Right Moment: Ronald Reagan's First Victory and the Decisive Turning Point in American Politics* (New York, 2000), 36–37; Reagan, *Where's,* 251–267.

66. Ronald Reagan to William Clothworthy, June 16, 1980, in Kiron K. Skinner, Annelise Anderson, and Martin Anderson, eds., *Reagan: A Life in Letters* (New York, 2003), 146; Reagan, *Where's,* 263, 264, 258, 267.

67. *Chicago Tribune,* July 13, 1980.

68. For the evolution of conservative thought, see Russell Kirk, *The Conservative Mind, from Burke to Santayana* (Chicago, 1953); Michael Kazin, "The Grass-Roots Right: New Histories of U.S. Conservatism in the 20th Century," *American Historical Review* 97 (February 1992): 136–155; Alan Brinkley, "The Problem of American Conservatism," *American Historical Review* 99 (April 1994): 409–452; Leonard Moore, "Good Old-Fashioned New Social History and the 20th Century American Right," *Reviews in American History* 24 (1996): 555–573; Jonathan M. Schoenwald, *A Time for Choosing: The Rise of Modern American Conservatism* (New York, 2001); Gregory L. Schneider, ed., *Conservatism in America since 1930* (New York, 2003).

69. Cannon, *Governor Reagan,* 112.

70. Reagan, *Where's,* 267.

71. Quoted in Cannon, *Governor Reagan,* 112–113.

72. "Mr. Norm" quoted in Raphael, "The Body Electric," 120; *Hollywood Reporter,* November 14, 1955; Ronald Reagan to Richard Nixon, July 15, 1960, in Skinner, Anderson, and Anderson, *Reagan: A Life in Letters,* 704.

73. *Los Angeles Mirror*, February 1, 1961. There is disagreement over whether Reagan registered as a Republican in 1961 or 1962. According to the *Mirror*, it was 1961.

74. James N. Druckman, "The Power of Television Images: The First Kennedy-Nixon Debate Revisited," *Journal of Politics* 65 (May 2003): 563; Baker quoted in Mary Ann Watson, *Defining Visions: Television and the American Experience since 1945* (Fort Worth, Tex., 1998), 248.

75. Daniel J. Boorstin, *The Image: A Guide to Pseudo-Events in America* (New York, 1961), 183, 204; Raphael, "The Body Electric," 117.

76. U.S. House of Representatives, *Political Broadcasts—Equal Time: Hearings before a Subcommittee of the Committee on Interstate and Foreign Commerce: House of Representatives Eighty-Sixth Congress, June 29, 30 and July 1, 1959* (Washington, D.C., 1959), 242, 229.

77. *LAT*, August 28, 1961; *Los Angeles Examiner*, August 31, 1961; *LAT*, October 16, 17, 1961. Schwarz's school also served as a breeding ground for right-wing Republican activists; see Lisa McGirr, *Suburban Warriors: The Origins of the New Right* (Princeton, N.J., 2001); Sheilah R. Koeppen, "The Republican Radical Right," *Annals of the American Academy of Political and Social Sciences* 382 (March 1969): 78–81.

78. *Los Angeles Mirror*, January 3, 1962; for his denunciation of Medicare, see Ibid., June 17, 1961.

79. For an overview of these efforts and subsequent campaign, see Totton J. Anderson and Eugene C. Lee, "The 1964 Election in California," *Western Political Quarterly* 18 (June 1965): 451–474; Cannon, *Governor Reagan*; Dallek, *Right Moment*. For an analysis of the Republican ideological divide during this era, see Diggins, *Reagan*; Perlstein, *Before the Storm*.

80. The two best overviews of postwar conservatism are Rick Perlstein, *Before the Storm* (New York, 2001), and McGirr, *Suburban Warriors*. For the movement's ideological evolution, see sources in n. 68.

81. McGirr, *Suburban Warriors*, 30; also see Cannon, *Governor Reagan*, 122. The most prominent groups included Fred Schwarz's School for Anti-communism, the Orange County Freedom Forum, the California Free Enterprise Association, California's Committee to Combat Communism, Citizens for Fundamental Education, and the Young Americans for Freedom. Stephen Whitfield, *The Culture of the Cold War* (Baltimore, Md., 1996), 75.

82. For the UROC, see Anderson and Lee, "1964 Election," 458; *LAT*, March 8, 16, May 3, 1964.

83. In addition to supporting a variety of right-wing causes, Frawley helped finance Fred Schwarz's Christian Anti-Communist Crusade; see his obituary in *NYT*, November 9, 1998; John Gizzi, "Patrick Frawley, R.I.P.," *Human Events* 55 (January 1, 1999): 12.

84. Goldwater quoted in Dallek, *Right Moment*, 63; primary results are in Anderson and Lee, "1964 Election," 462. Murphy received 1,121,591 votes to Kaiser's 689,323, and Hall's 261,036.

85. *LAT*, May 18, 1964. For poll results, see ibid., April 10, September 16, 1964. Salinger defeated Cranston 1,177,517 to 1,037,748.

86. For Murphy's inner circle of supporters and advisers, see Murphy, *Say*, 382, 393; *LAT*, April 10, September 8, 1964.

87. *LAT*, September 29, 16, 2, 14, 1964; William Trombley, "New Role for Legendary George," *Saturday Evening Post*, May 30, 1964, 23; Gold, "Nobody's Mad at Murphy," 59.

88. *LAT*, October 14, 7, 1964; Murphy, *Say*, 388. For a discussion of the Rumford Act and Proposition 14, see Thomas W. Casstevens, *Politics, Housing, and Race Relations: California's Rumford Act and Proposition 14* (Berkeley, 1967); Anderson and Lee, "1964 Election," 466–470.

89. *Washington Post*, October 30, 1964; *NYT*, September 26, 1964; *Washington Post*, May 31, 1964; Murphy, *Say*, 373.

90. *New York Sunday News*, May 9, 1965; *LAT*, August 9, 1964; Marya Saunders, "Washington's Brash, New Star," *Family Weekly*, September 12, 1965; *LAT*, October 26, 1964.

91. Ibid., October 4, 1964; Murphy, *Say*, 383.

92. Murphy, *Say*, 394.

93. *Washington Post*, October 21, 1964; for poll, see *LAT*, October 15, 1964.

94. *Washington Post*, October 31, 1964; for polls, see *LAT*, November 2, 1964.

95. *LAT*, December 1, November 5, 1964; voter totals and party preferences are taken from Anderson and Lee, "1964 Election," 452, 465–467.

96. Neil Reagan, Oral History, viii. For earlier efforts to persuade Reagan to run, see *LAT*, December 12, 1961; *Los Angeles Mirror*, January 3, 1962.

97. The October 27, 1964, address can be seen and heard at www.youtube.com/watch?v=qXBswFfh6AY, accessed April 3, 2009.

98. David Broder and Stephen Hess, *The Republican Establishment: The Present and Future of the G.O.P.* (New York, 1967), 253–254; Thomas C. Reed, "Snapshots from an Early Reagan Era 1958–1970," unpublished manuscript, May 2006, 40. I wish to thank Mr. Reed for sharing his work with me.

99. *Hollywood Citizen-News*, November 8, 1964.

100. *LAT*, November 20, 1964; Dallek, *Right Moment*, 71.

101. *Washington Post*, June 1, 1965. For poll results, see *LAT*, April 21, 1965. For an overview of the events leading to Reagan's decision to run, see Reed, "Snapshots," 57–58; Dallek, *Right Moment*; Neil Reagan, Oral History, 23–25; Cannon, *Governor Reagan*.

102. Reed, "Snapshots," 40.

103. Stevenson quoted in Dallek, *Right Moment*, 109.

104. *LAT*, January 5, 1966; also see *Washington Post* and *NYT*, January 5, 1966.

105. *Washington Post*, June 1, 1965; Manning quoted in Dallek, *Right Moment*, 204.

106. *NYT*, June 6, 1966; *LAT*, April 8, 1965; *NYT*, June 1, 1966.

107. *LAT*, June 6, 1966; *NYT*, June 1, 1966; *LAT*, April 20, 1966.

108. Ronald Reagan to George Murphy, August 19, 1966, quoted in Dallek, *Right Moment*, 216. For primary results, see Totton J. Anderson and Eugene C. Lee, "The 1966 Election in California," *Western Political Quarterly* 20 (June 1967): 540. Reagan's courting of Republicans is described in Reed, "Snapshots," 65; McGirr, *Suburban Warriors*, 199–210.

109. Neil Reagan, Oral History, 28. Neil insisted his brother had a "photographic mind" and could memorize a script without ever having to study the lines.

110. Anderson and Lee, "1966 Election," 550.

111. *LAT*, June 10, 1965.
112. McGirr, *Suburban Warriors*, 210, 199–200.
113. *NYT*, September 12, October 2, 1966; *LAT*, October 4, 1966.
114. Ryan quoted in *Pageant*, July 1966, 23; California poll and quotes are in *NYT Sunday Magazine*, October 25, 1970.
115. *NYT*, November 5, 1966.
116. For campaign results, see Anderson and Lee, "1966 Election," 353–354; Johannes Pedersen, "Age and Change in Public Opinion: The Case of California, 1960–1970," *Public Opinion Quarterly* 40 (Summer 1976): 143–153.
117. Reed, "Snapshots," 69.
118. *LAT*, February 6, 1965; George Murphy to Hedda Hopper, September 16, 1965, Box 16f, Hopper Papers; Murphy, *Say*, 422. For Murphy's fundraising trips, see *NYT*, June 4, 1966.
119. *Times* quoted in Totton J. Anderson and Charles G. Bell, "The 1970 Election in California," *Western Political Quarterly* 24 (June 1971): 259. For totals and a thorough analysis of the election and the scandal, see ibid., 252–273; *Hollywood Citizen-News*, March 12, 27, 1970; *LAT*, November 15, 1970, May 5, 1992.
120. *LAT*, May 5, 1992.
121. Reed, "Snapshots," 101–102, 107, 124. For Reagan's rise and the subsequent conservative revolution, see Lou Cannon, *President Reagan: The Role of a Lifetime* (New York, 1991); Michael Schaller, *Reckoning with Reagan: America and Its President in the 1980s* (New York, 1992); Lee Edwards, *The Conservative Revolution. The Movement That Remade America* (New York, 1999); Boyarksy, *Rise of Reagan*; Schoenwald, *Time for Choosing*; Morris, *Dutch*.
122. Robert W. Kaufman, "Ronald Reagan: A Republican Messiah?" *North American Review* 253 (May–June 1968): 10.

CHAPTER 5

1. *Ebony* (September 1996). Belafonte got the date of the meeting wrong in the interview; it was 1956 and not 1953. For a more accurate account, see Taylor Branch, *Parting the Waters: America in the King Years 1954–64* (New York, 1988), 185.
2. Author interview with Harry Belafonte, July 11, 2002, New York City; John Lovell Jr., "The Belafonte Image," *Journal of Negro Education* 30 (Winter 1961): 44.
3. Belafonte quoted in "Control and Conscience," *Films and Filming* 18 (September 1972): 26.
4. Kirtley Baskette, "Harry Belafonte," *Modern Screen*, June 1957, 37.
5. For the formation of Belafonte's company, HarBel, see *Hollywood Reporter*, August 16, 1957; *Chicago Tribune*, September 26, 1957; "Belafonte Becomes 'Big Business,'" *Ebony* 13 (June 1958): 17–24.
6. Coretta Scott King, *My Life with Martin Luther King, Jr.* (New York, 1969), 334.
7. Johnson quoted in Harold Cruse, "Harlem Background—The Rise of Economic Nationalism and the Origins of Cultural Revolution," in Robert C. Twombly, *Blacks in America since 1865* (New York, 1971), 243; *LAT*, August 7, 1994. For the Harlem Renaissance and Marcus Garvey, see Nathan Irvin Huggins, ed., *Voices from the Harlem Renaissance* (New York, 1995); Winston James, *Holding Aloft the Banner of*

Ethiopia: Caribbean Radicalism in Early Twentieth-Century America (London and New York, 1998); Colin Grant, *Negro with a Hat: The Rise and Fall of Marcus Garvey* (New York, 2010).

8. Statistics are from *NYT*, March 24, 1939; *Washington Post*, March 23, 1935. For the riots, see Dominic J. Capeci Jr., *The Harlem Riot of 1943* (Philadelphia, 1977); Cheryl Lynn Greenberg, *"Or Does It Explode?" Black Harlem in the Great Depression* (New York, 1991). Few stars are more in need of a modern biography than Harry Belafonte. Information about his early years is taken from Hy Steirman, ed., *Harry Belafonte: His Complete Life Story* (New York, 1957); Arnold Shaw, *Harry Belafonte: An Unauthorized Biography* (New York, 1960); Genia Fogelson, *Harry Belafonte: Singer and Actor* (Los Angeles, 1980); interview of Harry Belafonte by Cornel West, in *Restoring Hope: Conversations on the Future of Black America*, ed. Kelvin Shawn Sealey (Boston, 1997); Mark Hayward, "Harry Belafonte, Race, and the Politics of Success," M.A. thesis, McGill University, 2000; Lisa Diane McGill, "Constructing Black Selves: Caribbean-American Narratives and the Second Generation," Ph.D. diss., Yale University, 2001; Larissa Jeanne Faulkner, "'Integration in Action': Belafonte, Black Authorship, and the Limits of Media Subversion (1955–1969)," Ph.D. diss., University of Iowa, 2004; Karen Beavers, "Lead Man Holler: Harry Belafonte and the Culture Industry," Ph.D. diss., University of Southern California, 2008. For useful periodicals, see Maurice Zolotow, "Belafonte," *American Weekly*, May 10, 1959; *LAT*, August 7, 1994; Sharon Fitzgerald, "Belafonte the Lionhearted" [Washington, D.C.], *American Visions* 11 (August–September 1996); *Ebony* 5 (September 1996); [Manchester, U.K.] *The Guardian*, November 16, 1996, December 22–December 28, 2005, and December 29–January 4, 2005.

9. Errol G. Hill, "Calypso and War," *Black American Literature Forum* 23 (Spring 1989): 72, 78.

10. Author interview with Belafonte; [Detroit] *Michigan Chronicle*, April 4, 2001.

11. Menjou quoted in Stephen J. Whitfield, *The Culture of the Cold War* (Baltimore, Md., 1996), 193. Robeson made 11 films and more than 300 recordings as a concert singer. For biographies, see Paul Robeson, *Here I Stand* (Boston, 1972, originally published 1958); Martin Duberman, *Paul Robeson: A Biography* (New York, 1989); and Jeffrey C. Stewart, ed., *Paul Robeson: Artist and Citizen* (New Brunswick, N.J., 1998).

12. Ossie Davis and Ruby Dee, *With Ossie and Ruby: In This Life Together* (New York, 1998), 178; author interview with Belafonte. In 1951, the Communist Party moved its national headquarters to Harlem. For Robeson's friendship with Belafonte and Poitier, see Aram Goudsouzian, *Sidney Poitier: Man, Actor, Icon* (Chapel Hill, N.C., 2004); Davis and Dee, *With Ossie and Ruby*.

13. Davis and Dee, *With Ossie and Ruby*, 177, 178.

14. *Chicago Daily Defender*, September 11, 1962.

15. "Lead Man Holler," *Time*, March 2, 1959; Zolotow, "Belafonte," 9.

16. *Time*, March 2, 1959; Steirman, *Belafonte*, 45–46, 50; *Time*, March 2, 1959.

17. For Belafonte's political activities during this period, see *Counterattack*, January 8, February 12, 1954; Branch, *Parting the Waters*, 88.

18. Zolotow, "Belafonte," 3; Belafonte quoted in Goudsouzian, *Poitier*, 133.

19. Sidney Poitier, *This Life* (New York, 1980), 262; *Time*, March 2, 1959; *Chicago Defender*, October 29, 1962.

20. For his early performances, see *Chicago Daily Defender*, September 23, 1950, April 7, 1951; *NYT*, February 6, 20, 1951, December 11, 1953.

21. Author interview with Belafonte.

22. Ibid.; Davis and Dee, *With Ossie and Ruby*, 195. For African Americans and the film industry, see Thomas Cripps, *Slow Fade to Black: The Negro in American Film, 1900–1942* (New York, 1977); Thomas Cripps, *Making Movies Black: The Hollywood Message Movie from World War II to the Civil Rights Era* (New York, 1993); Donald Bogle, *Bright Boulevards, Bold Dreams: The Story of Black Hollywood* (New York, 2005). For an early perspective on the problem, see Leon H. Hardwick, "Negro Stereotypes on the Screen," *Hollywood Quarterly* 1 (January 1946): 234–236.

23. Fitzgerald, "Belafonte the Lionhearted."

24. *LAT*, April 3, 1954. Schary minimized MGM's financial risk by producing the film with its less costly "B" unit. Paul Buhle and Dave Wagner, *Hide in Plain Sight: The Hollywood Blacklistees in Film and Television, 1950–2002* (New York, 2003), 148.

25. Shaw, *Belafonte*, 130–131; Hopper quoted in Jeff Smith, "Black Faces, White Voices: The Politics of Dubbing in Carmen Jones," *Velvet Light Trap* 51 (Spring 2003): 32. For reviews and box-office returns, see *Chicago Daily Defender*, September 4, 1954; *LAT*, March 7, 1958. For the controversy over making an all-black film, see *Los Angeles Tribune*, November 12, 1954.

26. *Counterattack* 8 (January 8, 1954): 4.

27. Robeson quoted in Goudsouzian, *Poitier*, 8; *Counterattack* 8 (February 12, 1954): 3; also see John Cogley, *Report on Blacklisting*, 2 vols. (New York, 1956), 2:8–9. For Robeson's declining income, see Carl T. Rowan, "Has Paul Robeson Betrayed the Negro?" *Ebony* 12 (October 1957): 32.

28. For Sullivan's intervention, see Sally Vincent, "Harry Belafonte Challenges Hollywood," *Manchester Guardian*, November 16, 1996; *Philadelphia Tribune*, February 5, 1999. For Belafonte's television appearances, including five on *The Ed Sullivan Show*, see the Internet Movie Database, IMDb.com; *Chicago Daily Defender*, April 9, July 5, 1952. Sidney Poitier encountered the same problem in 1953, when MGM demanded he sign a loyalty oath before they would approve his role in *Blackboard Jungle*. Sidney Poitier, *This Life* (New York, 1980), 172. For other African American actors attacked by Red-hunters, see *Counterattack* 7 (September 25, 1953); Ossie Davis, "Typescript of CBS Defense," n.d., folder 2, Ossie Davis and Ruby Dee Collection, Manuscripts, Archives and Rare Books Division, Schomburg Center for Research in Black Culture, New York Public Library (hereafter, Davis-Dee Coll.); Davis and Dee, *With Ossie and Ruby*, 232–234; Bogle, *Bright Boulevards*, 315–318.

29. According to New York Communist Party member Helen Meltzer, Robeson and Belafonte occasionally "showed up at [CP] meetings" in the late 1940s. Author interview with Helen Meltzer, July 24, 2002, Beverly Hills, California.

30. Harry Belafonte, "Giant Strides of U.S. Negroes," *New York Journal*, May 31, 1955.

31. For Belafonte integrating nightclubs, see *Chicago Daily Defender*, November 19, 1955; Kirtley Baskette, "Harry Belafonte," *Modern Screen*, June 1957, 37; Shaw, *Belafonte*, 156; Fogelson, *Belafonte*, 49.

32. For his TV appearances, see *Chicago Daily Defender*, October 8, 1955, April 9, July 5, 1962; *New York Journal*, November 5, 1955; *Look*, February 21, 1956; Fogelson,

Belafonte, 78–79. For the *Steve Allen Show*, see *Chicago Daily Defender*, November 29, 1958.

33. Fitzgerald, "Belafonte the Lionhearted." Between 1953 and 1962, Belafonte released sixteen record albums. For his recording career and the Calypso craze he unleashed, see "The Belafonte Boom," *Look,* August 21, 1956, 38; McGill, "Constructing Black Selves," 19–47.

34. *Chicago Daily Defender*, May 28, 1956. For his encounters with Stevenson, see *NYT*, October 18, 1955; *Chicago Daily Defender*, October 8, 15, 1956.

35. *Chicago Daily Defender*, February 9, 1957.

36. *Look,* June 25, 1957; Joan Fontaine, *No Bed of Roses* (New York, 1978), 245. For a copy of the cut scene, see the cover photo of Cripps, *Making Movies Black.* For the debate over interracial romance, see "'To Kiss or Not to Kiss' Is the Question Which Upset the Cast," *Ebony* 12 (March 1957): 33–34; "Island in the Sun," *Ebony* 12 (July 1957): 33–34, 36.

37. Alec Waugh, *Island in the Sun: A Story of the 1950s Set in the West Indies* (New York, 1955).

38. *Variety*, July 8, 1957; *Chicago Daily Defender*, August 24, 1957; *Variety*, June 14, 1957 (last two quotes). For the South Carolina threat, see *Look*, June 25, 1957. For the film's reception, see Albert Johnson, "Beige, Brown or Black," *Film Quarterly* 13 (Autumn 1959): 39–41; Whitney Strub, "Black and White and Banned All Over: Race, Censorship and Obscenity in Postwar Memphis," *Journal of Social History* 40 (Spring 2007): 685–715; Richard Iton, *In Search of the Black Fantastic: Politics and Popular Culture in the Post–Civil Rights Era* (New York, 2008), 223–226.

39. *Look,* June 25, 1957; *New York Journal*, October 24, July 12, 1957. For box-office returns, see *Variety*, June 19, 1957; *Hollywood Reporter*, July 18, 1957.

40. *New York Morning Telegraph*, July 24, 1957.

41. Author interview with Belafonte; *Pittsburgh Courier*, June 22, 1957; also see Bogle, *Bright Boulevards*, 356. That same year, he declined to star in the remake of Paul Robeson's *Emperor Jones* when the studio refused a script by black writer John Killens that changed Brutus Jones from a crap-shooting train porter into a slave who killed a white whipping boss and went on to lead the Haitian revolution. See *Chicago Daily Defender*, March 3, 1956; *Los Angeles Examiner*, February 13, 1957; John O. Killens, "Hollywood in Black and White," in *Cinema Nation: The Best Writing on Film from* The Nation, *1913–2000,* ed. Carl Bromley (New York, 2000), 154.

42. Author interview with Belafonte; Poitier quoted in Dennis John Hall, "Pride without Prejudice: Sidney Poitier's Career Surveyed," *Films and Filming* 18 (December 1971): 42.

43. Harry Belafonte, "Why I Married Julie," *Ebony* 12 (July 1957): 90. For Robinson's background, see Zolotow, "Belafonte," 14; Fogelson, *Belafonte*, 63–65.

44. Letters to the Editor, *Ebony* (September 1957): 10; "'I Wonder Why Nobody Don't Like Me': Harry Belafonte Is the Country's Most Popular Calypso Singer," *Life*, May 27, 1957.

45. *New York Herald Tribune*, April 14, 1958. Oscar Micheaux made "race films" for black audiences from 1919 to 1948. Pearl Bowser and Louise Spence, *Oscar Micheaux and His Circle: African-American Filmmaking and Race Cinema of the Silent*

Era (New Brunswick, N.J., 2000); Patrick McGilligan, *Oscar Micheaux: The Great and Only: The Life of America's First Black Filmmaker* (New York, 2008).

46. Statistics from Tino Balio, *Hollywood in the Age of Television* (Cambridge, Mass., 1990), 10.

47. Belafonte quoted in "Workers' Cultural Renaissance," AFL-CIO Web site, www .aflcio.org/aboutus/history/review/index.cfm, accessed November 6, 2006; *New York Morning Telegram*, July 6, 1959; *New York World Telegram and Sun*, September 1, 1959. For the formation of HarBel, see sources in n. 5.

48. *NYT*, March 15, 1959. For Pushkin, see *Chicago Tribune*, July 19, 1957; *NYT*, June 22, 1958; *Variety*, March 11, October 21, 1959; "HarBel Plans to Produce Western, Life of Pushkin," *Ebony* 14 (July 1959): 96–100; for King and Little Rock, see *Jet*, September 5, 1957; *The Papers of Martin Luther King Jr.*, ed. Clayborne Carson, 6 vols. (Berkeley, 1992), 4:373n1; *Chicago Daily Defender*, July 9, 1958. For Hannibal, *Los Angeles Examiner*, May 12, 1958, Steirman, *Belafonte*, 53; for Exodusters, *Variety*, October 21, 1959; *New York Morning Telegram*, July 6, 1959.

49. *NYT*, March 15, 1959; Belafonte quoted in Paul Buhle and Dave Wagner, *A Very Dangerous Citizen: Abraham Lincoln Polonsky and the Hollywood Left* (Berkeley and Los Angeles, 2001), 185–186.

50. Fogelson, *Belafonte*, 159; "Movie Maker Belafonte," *Ebony* 14 (July 1959): 95; *NYT*, November 15, 1957. For a history of SANE and the involvement of movie stars, see Milton S. Katz, *Ban the Bomb: A History of SANE, the Committee for a Sane Nuclear Policy, 1957–1985* (Westport, Conn., 1986). For HarBel's deal with MGM, see Fogelson, *Belafonte*, 159; "Movie Maker Belafonte," *Ebony* 14 (July 1959): 95.

51. Belafonte quoted in Abraham Polonsky, *Odds against Tomorrow: The Critical Edition*, ed. John Schultheiss (Northridge, Calif., 1999), 236; Shaw, *Belafonte*, 257; author interview with Belafonte. Belafonte explained that *Odds* was originally "written with greater honesty for two white guys, and the metaphor was laborer versus capitalist." Polonsky, *Odds*, 236. For Belafonte walking off the set, see *Washington Post*, November 20, 1978.

52. *Boxoffice*, April 13, 1959; *New York Herald Tribune*, May 21, 1959; *LAT*, May 30, 1959; *Saturday Review*, May 2, 1959.

53. *Hollywood Citizen-News*, May 14, 1952; "Movie Maker Belafonte," *Ebony* 14 (July 1959): 100. For UA production deal and production costs, see *NYT*, July 26, 1959; *Variety*, September 2, 1959; "Movie Maker Belafonte," 95.

54. Polonsky, *Odds*, 235, 252; *NYT*, March 15, 1959. For Polonsky's diary entries while writing the film, see "Diaries," November 1957–February 1958, March–November 1958, box 12, folder 3, Abraham Polonsky Papers, Wisconsin Historical Society (hereafter, Polonsky Papers).

55. *NYT*, March 15, 1959. The film eventually made a profit; see Cripps, *Making Movies Black*, 267.

56. Diary, March 18, 1958, box 12, folder 3, Polonsky Papers. For his participation in various demonstrations, see Michael S. Mayer, "Prayer Pilgrimage to Washington (1957)," *Encyclopedia of African-American Civil Rights*, ed. Charles D. Lowery and John F. Marszalek (Westport, Conn., 1992), 436.

57. Ossie Davis to Harry Belafonte, ca. summer 1958, box 1, folder 2, Davis-Dee Coll.

58. Ibid. Davis gave one of the eulogies for Malcolm X in February 1965.

59. *NYT*, September 30, 1958; *New York Post*, October 12, 1958; also see *Time*, March 2, 1959.

60. *Chicago Daily Defender*, November 1, 1958; also see Daniel Levine, *Bayard Rustin and the Civil Rights Movement* (New Brunswick, N.J., 2000), 110–111.

61. Belafonte, "Why I Married Julie," 95. For his earnings, see ibid., 95; "Belafonte Becomes Big Business," *Ebony* 13 (June 1958): 17–19, 22 24; *NYT*, December 13, 1959.

62. Poitier, *This Life*, 323; King, *My Life with Martin*, 144–145; Poitier, *This Life*, 278.

63. For Belafonte's role as the SCLC's largest donor, see Jim Bishop, *The Days of Martin Luther King, Jr.* (New York, 1971), 424. Belafonte also told me this was the case: King asked and he responded.

64. Stanley D. Levison to Martin Luther King Jr., March 1960, Carson, *Papers of King*, 5:381. For SCLC budget figures, see David Levering Lewis, *King: A Biography* (Urbana, Ill., 1978), 156. For the committee's activities, see *King Papers*, 5:5, 25–26, 381n5, 476; Branch, *Parting the Waters*, 274, 288; Goudsouzian, *Poitier*, 195; Adam Fairclough, *To Redeem the Soul of America: The Southern Christian Leadership Conference and Martin Luther King Jr.* (Athens, Ga., 1987), 66; *NYT*, March 29, 1960; *LAT*, May 1, 1960. SANE was the common abbreviation for the Committee for a SANE Nuclear Policy.

65. Author interview with Belafonte; Martin Luther King Jr., *Why We Can't Wait* (New York, 1963), 57, 58.

66. For the Emmy award and nominations, see *LAT*, June 21, 1960.

67. Branch, *Parting the Waters*, 307; C. David Heymann, *RFK: A Candid Biography of Robert F. Kennedy* (New York, 1998), 178.

68. William L. Benoit, "The Emergence of Discursive Conventions in Presidential Advertising, 1952–2000," *Advertising and Society Review* 4 (2003): n.p.; also see Goudsouzian, *Poitier*, 194. For a copy of the campaign spot, see www.livingroomcandidate .org/commercials/1960/harry-belafonte, accessed July 13, 2007. For King and Kennedy's meeting in New York, see Branch, *Parting*, 307, 314.

69. Author interview with Belafonte. For Belafonte's appointment to the Peace Corps, see *Los Angeles Examiner*, March 31, 1961.

70. Stokely Carmichael with Ekwueme Michael Thelwell, *Ready for Revolution: The Life and Struggles of Stokely Carmichael (Kwame Ture)* (New York, 2003), 222.

71. Branch, *Parting*, 558. For Belafonte's mediation, see Branch, *Parting*, 558, 578–579. For his work on behalf of SNCC, see *Chicago Daily Defender*, September 13, 1961; Branch, *Pillar*, 51. For donations to the music and art foundation, see *Time*, March 2, 1959.

72. King, *My Life with Martin*, 75, 225; King, *Why We Can't Wait*, 58. For Belafonte's role in the Birmingham struggles, see Glenn T. Eskew, *But for Birmingham: The Local and National Movements in the Civil Rights Struggle* (Chapel Hill, N.C., 1997), 215–290; Ralph David Abernathy, *And the Walls Came Tumbling Down: An Autobiography* (New York, 1989), 261; Branch, *Parting the Waters*, 705, 734–735, 784–804.

73. Author interview with Belafonte for both quotes. The most complete history of the march can be found in Thomas Gentile, *March on Washington: August 28, 1963* (Washington, D.C., 1983); also see *Los Angeles Herald Examiner*, August 28, 1963;

Variety, August 29, 1963; *NYT*, August 29, 1963. Heston's involvement is discussed in chapter 7.

74. Poitier, *This Life*, 280.

75. Goudsouzian, *Poitier*, 225; Poitier, *This Life*, 282; also see Branch, *Pillar*, 450–451; Poitier, *This Life*, 278–282.

76. Carmichael, *Ready for Revolution*, 412; Clayborne Carson, *In Struggle: SNCC and the Black Awakening of the 1960s* (Cambridge, Mass., 1981), 134. Belafonte served as artistic adviser to the Guinea government. Elizabeth Gritter, "Interview with Julian Bond," *Southern Cultures* 12 (Spring 2006): 76–79. For Project Airlift Africa, see *New Pittsburgh Courier*, January 23, 1960.

77. Henry Hampton and Steve Fayer, *Voices of Freedom: An Oral History of the Civil Rights Movement from the 1950s through the 1980s* (New York, 1991), 204. For King, SNCC, and Belafonte, see *NYT*, May 1, 1965; Donald T. Critchlow and Emilie Raymond, *Hollywood and Politics: A Sourcebook* (New York and London, 2009), 207–208; David Garrow, *Bearing the Cross: Martin Luther King, Jr., and the Southern Christian Leadership Conference* (New York, 2004), 390, 424; Fairclough, *To Redeem the Soul*, 249; Stewart Burns, *To the Mountaintop: Martin Luther King Jr.'s Sacred Mission to Save America* (New York, 2003), 287–288. For the Selma march, at which Belafonte performed, see *Reporting Civil Rights: Part Two: American Journalism 1963–1973* (New York, 2003), 364–391.

78. *The Worker*, July 18, 1965. Belafonte exaggerated his wartime experience; he never left the country during his military service.

79. Student Nonviolent Coordinating Committee, "Position Paper: On Vietnam," www2.iath.virginia.edu/sixties/HTML_docs/Resources/Primary/Manifestos/SNCC_VN.html, accessed May 12, 2007.

80. *The Nation* quoted in Maurice Isserman and Michael Kazin, *America Divided: The Civil War of the 1960s* (New York, 2008), 178; Young and Wilkins are quoted in Hampton and Fayer, *Voices of Freedom*, 339.

81. Author interview with Belafonte; *NYT*, March 28, 1966. For the European trip, see *Hartford Courant*, March 5, 12, 1966; *NYT*, March 25, 1966; Lewis, *King*, 318.

82. Goudsouzian, *Poitier*, 250; Hampton and Fayer, *Voices of Freedom*, 371. For debates within the black community over Vietnam, see David Halberstam, "The Second Coming of Martin Luther King," *Harper's Magazine*, August 1967, 39–51.

83. FBI Report, April 19, 1967, New York, quoted in Michael Friedly with David Gallen, *Martin Luther King, Jr.: The FBI File* (New York, 1993), 510.

84. Hampton and Fayer, *Voices of Freedom*, 345. For FBI surveillance, see FBI Records, October 15, 1966, April 11, 12, 1967 in Friedly, *King FBI File*, 509–510; Fairclough, *To Redeem the Soul*, 340.

85. *LAT*, September 1, 1967. For the antiwar rallies, see ibid., September 20, December 5, 22, 1967; Fairclough, *To Redeem the Soul*, 361. For "Broadway for Peace," see *Variety*, January 17, 1968; *NYT*, January 22, 1968.

86. *LAT*, March 7, 1968.

87. *NYT*, February 7, 1968; *Chicago Daily Defender*, March 2, 1968.

88. King, *My Life*, 333; Hampton and Fayer, *Voices of Freedom*, 470; author interview with Belafonte.

89. *LAT*, August 7, 1968.

90. *Washington Post*, December 3, 1993; *Chicago Daily Defender*, April 1, 1972. Belafonte originally cast Edward G. Robinson as his costar in *The Angel Levine*. Chiz Schultz to Mike Merrick, September 23, 1968, box 1, folder 1, Charles H. "Chiz" Schultz Collection, 1968–1990, Schomburg Center, New York Public Library.

91. *Washington Post*, June 17, 1984; WABC press release, January 26, 1979, two-part interview with Harry Belafonte on Sunday, February 4 and February 11, on WABC-TV. In subsequent years, he appeared in *White Man's Burden* (1995), *Kansas City* (1996), and *Bobby* (2006).

92. "The Storm over Belafonte," *Look*, June 25, 1957; *LAT*, August 7, 1994.

93. Author interview with Belafonte.

94. *LAT*, September 1, 1967; *Los Angeles Sentinel*, February 7, 1985. Belafonte worked closely with Michael Jackson and Quincy Jones in organizing the recording session.

95. *NYT*, March 21, 2006, October 10, 2002, March 21, 2006.

96. Ibid., December 4, 1989; "50 Who Changed America," *Ebony* 51 (November 1995): 108. During the 1980s and 1990s, Belafonte was given the Paul Robeson Award, the Dag Hammarskjold Peace Medal, the Martin Luther King Jr. Peace Prize, the Nelson Mandela Courage Award, the NAACP's first Thurgood Marshall Lifetime Achievement Award, and a National Medal of Arts from President Clinton. During the next decade, he received a lifetime Grammy Award, the Bishop Walker Distinguished Humanitarian Service Award for his work in Africa, and the inaugural Marian Anderson Award.

97. Newsobserver.com, April 17, 2010, www.newsobserver.com/2010/04/17/441069/keep-fighting-injustice-belafonte.html, accessed May 6, 2010; *Democracy Now* transcript of Belafonte speech, January 21, 2009, www.democracynow.org/2009/1/21/obama_presidency_an_opportunity_for_us, accessed May 1, 2010.

CHAPTER 6

1. *Los Angeles Herald Express*, August 20, 1979.

2. *Newsweek* and *Penthouse* quotes cited in Susan Elaine McLeland, "Fallen Stars: Femininity, Celebrity and Scandal in Post-Studio Hollywood," Ph.D. diss., University of Texas at Austin, 1996, 173–185; William Buckley, "Secretary Fonda," *National Review*, August 18, 1972; author telephone interview with George McGovern, June 16, 2006, Mitchell, South Dakota.

3. John Frook, "Jane Fonda Non Stop Activist: Nag, Nag, Nag," *Life*, April 23, 1971, 51.

4. Carol Burke, "Why They Love to Hate Her," *The Nation*, March 22, 2004, 14. *Motion Picture Almanac* annual survey quoted in David A. Cook, *Lost Illusions: American Cinema in the Shadow of Watergate and Vietnam 1970–1979* (Berkeley and Los Angeles, 2000), 339. Katharine Graham, Rosalynn Carter, Ann Landers, and Barbara Walters preceded her.

5. Jane Fonda, *My Life So Far* (New York, 2005), 37, 565.

6. *Chicago Tribune*, January 25, 1970. There are many works dealing with Fonda's life and politics. The better biographies include Fonda, *My Life*; Thomas Kiernan, *Jane Fonda: Heroine for Our Time* (New York, 1982); Fred Lawrence Guiles, *Jane Fonda: The Actress in Her Time* (Garden City, N.Y., 1982); James Spada, *Fonda: Her Life in*

Pictures (Garden City, N.Y., 1985); Michael Freedland, *Jane Fonda: A Biography* (New York, 1988); Christopher Andersen, *Citizen Jane: The Turbulent Life of Jane Fonda* (New York, 1990); Bill Davidson, *Jane Fonda: An Intimate Biography* (New York, 1990); Tom Collins, *Jane Fonda: An American Original* (New York, 1990); Peter Collier, *The Fondas: A Hollywood Dynasty* (New York, 1991); Russell Shorto, *Jane Fonda: Political Activism* (Brookfield, Conn., 1991); Mary Hershberger, *Jane Fonda's War: Political Biography of an Antiwar Icon* (New York and London, 2005); Andrew Irwin Schroeder, "Strategies of Cinema: Cultural Politics in the New Hollywood, 1967–1981," Ph.D. diss., New York University, 2002; Mary Hershberger, ed., *Jane Fonda's Words of Politics and Passion* (New York, 2006); McLeland, "Fallen Stars." For a hostile examination of her life and politics, see Henry Mark Holzer and Erika Holzer, *"Aid and Comfort": Jane Fonda in North Vietnam* (Jefferson, N.C., 2002).

7. Quoted in Suzanne Finstad, *Warren Beatty: A Private Man* (New York, 2005), 183.

8. Movie critic Stanley Kauffmann quoted in Andersen, *Citizen Jane*, 91.

9. Roger Vadim, *Bardot, Deneuve, Fonda*, trans. Melinda Camber Porter (New York, 1966), 230. For Vadim's view of Fonda's gradual politicization, see ibid., 224–230, 246, 255–256, 279–284.

10. Both quotes are from author telephone interview with Jane Fonda, May 16, 2007, Rowe, New Mexico. The book was Jonathan Schell's *The Village of Ben Suc* (New York, 1967). Fonda describes this period of politicization in Fonda, *My Life*, 139–140, 191–199.

11. Author interview with Fonda; Camus quoted in Spada, *Fonda*, 109; author interview with Fonda.

12. For her conversations about the Panthers, see Fonda, *My Life*, 213, 171–172; Schroeder, "Strategies of Cinema," 172.

13. For reports of her contact with the Black Panthers, see *LAT*, June 21, September 20, 1970; *NYT*, August 22, 1970; Andersen, *Citizen Jane*, 211–214. Gardner wrote the screenplay for *Zabriskie Point* (1970), Michelangelo Antonioni's film about American student radicalism, while Lane's *Rush to Judgment* (1966) offered a scathing critique of the Warren Commission report about the assassination of John F. Kennedy. For her involvement with the Native American rights movement, see *LAT*, March 6, June 6, 1970; *Chicago Tribune*, March 9, 1970; Andersen, *Citizen Jane*, 193–211.

14. Author interview with James Lafferty, August 28, 2010, Los Angeles, California. For the rise and growth of the antiwar movement, see Tom Wells, *The War Within: America's Battle over Vietnam* (New York, 1994); Maurice Isserman and Michael Kazin, *America Divided: The Civil War of the 1960s* (New York, 2008); Rick Perlstein, *Nixonland: The Rise of a President and the Fracturing of America* (New York, 2008).

15. By January 1971, 72% of the population favored withdrawal. Hazel Erskine, "The Polls: Is War a Mistake?" *Public Opinion Quarterly* 34 (Spring 1970): 141–142; Benjamin I. Page and Richard A. Brody, "Policy Voting and the Electoral Process: The Vietnam War Issue," *American Political Science Review* 66 (September 1972): 979–995.

16. *Chicago Sun-Times*, May 9, 1971. For Fonda's initial antiwar activism, see *Washington Post*, May 8, 10, 1970; *Chicago Tribune*, May 10, 1970; *NYT*, May 12, 30, 1970; *LAT*, May 17, 1970; *Hartford Courant*, May 23, 1970.

17. Author interview with Lafferty. For Hollywood films about Vietnam, see Robin Wood, *Hollywood from Vietnam to Reagan . . . and Beyond* (New York, 2003); Susan Jeffords, *The Remasculinization of America: Gender and the Vietnam War* (Bloomington, Ind., 1989); Linda Dittmar and Gene Michaud, eds., *From Hanoi to Hollywood: The Vietnam War in American Film* (New Brunswick, N.J., 1990).

18. *NYT*, October 24, 1970; *Hartford Courant*, May 25, 1970. For an account of similar events, see Tom Wolfe, *Radical Chic & Mau-Mauing the Flak Catchers* (New York, 1970).

19. *Washington Post*, July 29, 1972; Fonda quoted in David Talbot and Barbara Zheutlin, *Creative Differences: Profiles of Hollywood Dissidents* (Boston, 1978), 140–141.

20. Hershberger, *Fonda's War*, 24; Bo Burlingham, "Politics under the Palms," *Esquire*, February 1977, 52.

21. Ronald Brownstein, *The Power and the Glitter: The Hollywood-Washington Connection* (New York, 1992), 255; [George Washington University] *The Hatchet*, February 14, 1974, box 7, folder 2, Indochina Peace Campaign Records, 1940–1976, Wisconsin Historical Society (hereafter, IPC Records); Fonda, *My Life*, 263. For an analysis of Barbarella and Fonda's early cinematic persona, see McLeland, "Fallen Stars."

22. FBI quoted in Hershberger, *Fonda's War*, 29. For Fonda and the FBI, see Talbot and Zheutlin, *Creative Differences*, 135–136; Fonda, *My Life*, 255–263; Hershberger, *Fonda's War*, 51–72; Guiles, *Fonda*, 165–169.

23. Author interview with Lafferty. For the Winter Soldier investigations, see Andrew E. Hunt, *The Turning: A History of Vietnam Veterans against the War* (New York, 1999); Richard Stacewicz, *Winter Soldiers: An Oral History of the Vietnam Veterans against the War* (New York, 1997); Fonda, *My Life*, 259–268; Hershberger, *Fonda's War*, 27–36.

24. Kiernan, *Fonda*, 267; author interview with Fonda. Cockrel's son, Ken Jr., was elected mayor of Detroit in September 2008.

25. Spada, *Fonda*, 125; *LAT*, June 24, 1971.

26. Fonda, *My Life*, 272; Hershberger, *Fonda's War*, 44. The troupe also released a film, *FTA*, which played a limited run in the middle of 1972. For more on the FTA, see Hershberger, *Fonda's War*, 41–49; Fonda, *My Life*, 272–276; *Time*, March 1, 1971; *NYT*, March 21, 1971, September 4, 1972; *Hollywood Reporter*, August 16, October 31, 1971, January 24, July 26, 1972.

27. Burlingham, "Politics under the Palms," 118; for her other critics during this period, see Guiles, *Fonda*, 191–192.

28. For Hayden's background, see Tom Hayden, *Reunion: A Memoir* (New York, 1988).

29. Fonda, *My Life*, 285.

30. Quoted in Hershberger, *Fonda's Words*, 24.

31. Hershberger, *Fonda's War*, 88, 93.

32. Ibid., 28.

33. Fonda, *My Life*, 316, 318.

34. Bush quoted in Perlstein, *Nixonland*, 707; *NYT*, August 5, 1972.

35. *Variety*, September 27, 1972. Internal memos revealed the White House wanted to "use available federal machinery to screw our political enemies." Alan Schroeder, *Celebrity-in-Chief: How Show Business Took Over the White House* (Boulder, Colo., 2004), 104.

36. Jaskjy quoted in Hershberger, *Fonda's War*, 123; *LAT*, August 11, 1972. For a conservative critique of Fonda's trip and radio broadcasts, see Holzer and Holzer, *"Aid and Comfort."* For various state resolutions, see Hershberger, *Fonda's War*, 123–124; Fonda, *My Life*, 321; *NYT*, April 6, 1973.
37. FBI report quoted in Fonda, *My Life*, 323.
38. Author interview with Tom Hayden, March 21, 2008, Culver City, California.
39. Kiernan, *Fonda*, 335.
40. No Title, n.d., Mimeo of Indochina Peace Campaign Vision and Strategy for Organizing and Coalition Building: Marked "Read and Save" at top, box 1, folder 1, IPC Records. For Hayden's views of IPC goals and strategies, see Hayden, *Reunion*, 448–460; Tom Hayden, "Cutting Off Funding for the War: The 1973 Indochina Case," Huffington Post, March 20, 2007, www.huffingtonpost.com/tom-hayden/cutting-off-funding-for-w_b_43917.html, accessed March 21, 2007.
41. For examples of speeches by Fonda and Hayden, see "Vietnam Is One: Speeches by Jane Fonda and Tom Hayden, Indochina Peace Campaign, Tuesday, September 12, 1972," mimeographed document produced by the Alliance and the Motor City Labor League, box 7, folder 8, IPC Records.
42. Unidentified Philadelphia newspaper, March 5, 1974, box 7, folder 2, IPC Records. For an overview of the tour, see "The Tour and the Resources," ca. 1972, box 7, folder 1, IPC Records.
43. Fonda quoted in Spada, *Fonda*, 146.
44. Author interview with Lee Grant, July 8, 2002, New York City. Three documents are especially useful for laying out Fonda's responsibilities and contributions: see "Los Angeles Resource Center," ca. 1973, box 1, folder 9; Fonda's long letter to IPC chapters, instructing them on the most effective ways to lobby congressional representatives, "Dear Friends" letter signed by Jane Fonda, ca. 1974, box 7, folder 5; and a nine-page strategy memo marked "Read and Save" in box 1, folder 1, IPC Records. For the tour, see Hayden, *Reunion*, 459–460.
45. Conference, Santa Barbara, August 1973, box 1, folder 9, IPC Records; author interview with Stanley Sheinbaum, May 9, 2006, Brentwood, California. Gallup poll cited in *Washington Post*, January 1, 1973.
46. *LA Herald-Examiner*, May 22, 1973; for her USC visit, see ibid., April 13, 1973.
47. For the lawsuit and findings, see Fonda, *My Life*, 353–333; *Hollywood Reporter*, June 29, 1973; *LAT*, February 15, 1975. For the Church Committee, see Gary Hart, *The Good Fight: The Education of an American Reformer* (New York, 1993), 139.
48. Author interview with Fonda; *NYT*, December 6, 1981; Spada, *Fonda*, 142. For reports on Fonda's graylisting, see *NYT*, February 19, 1978; *Chicago Tribune*, March 4, 1979, February 3, 1980; *LAT*, December 6, 1981.
49. Spada, *Fonda*, 139.
50. Tom Hayden, "Tom Hayden for Senate," box 2, folder 1, IPC Records; author interview with Andy Spahn, July 16, 2002, Universal City, California; also see Hayden, *Reunion*, 466. For left critiques of Hayden's campaign, see *Village Voice*, August 11, 1972.
51. Author interview with Spahn; Columbia Studios quoted in Davidson, *Fonda*, 195.
52. Fonda, *My Life*, 368. For the campaign, see Andersen, *Citizen Jane*, 275–277.
53. *LAT*, September 25, 1982.

54. Author interview with Fonda. For an overview of CED, see *Time*, February 9, 1977; *LAT*, March 3, 1978, September 7, 1979; Jon Wiener, "Tom Hayden's New Workout (Campaign California)," *The Nation*, November 29, 1986, 603–606; Hayden, *Reunion*, 471–472.

55. *Chicago Tribune*, March 4, 1979.

56. Fonda quoted in Talbot and Zheutlin, *Creative Differences*, 138. For CED's political success, see *LAT*, April 20, August 12, 25, 1977, November 26, 1978, September 7, 1979, April 5, 1981; *Washington Post*, July 5, 1979.

57. Author interview with Spahn; *LAT*, September 25, 1982. For membership and political success, see *LAT*, September 7, 1979.

58. Fonda, *My Life*, 389–396.

59. Ibid., 402.

60. Fonda quoted in Talbot and Zheutlin, *Creative Differences*, 133.

61. Fonda, *My Life*, 359; *NYT*, February 3, 1974.

62. Gilbert quoted in Dan Georgakas and Lenny Rubenstein, eds., *The Cineaste Interviews: On the Art and Politics of the Cinema* (Chicago, 1983), 258; *Variety* figures quoted in Cook, *Lost Illusions*, 339. The film was made for $3 million.

63. Fonda, *My Life*, 407.

64. *Wall Street Journal*, March 30, 1979, January 21, 1984; for GE, see *NYT*, February 28, 1979.

65. Andersen, *Fonda*, 297–298.

66. Author interview with Fonda. For the women's movement during this era, see Ruth Rosen, *The World Split Open: How the Modern Women's Movement Changed America* (New York, 2006); Gail Collins, *When Everything Changed: The Amazing Journey of American Women from 1960 to the Present* (New York, 2009).

67. Freedland, *Fonda*, 223.

68. For her involvement with 9 to 5, see Fonda, *My Life*, 410–414; Andersen, *Fonda*, 299–300; *Chicago Tribune*, August 5, 1979; *NYT*, September 25, 26, 1979; *Washington Post*, September 27, 1979.

69. Nussbaum quoted in Fonda, *My Life*, 414. For Nussbaum's success, see *Washington Post*, December 22, 1980; *LAT*, December 26, 1980, March 6, 1981; *Chicago Tribune*, November 19, 1985.

70. For box-office figures, see www.imdb.com/title/tt0082846/business, accessed October 19, 2007.

71. Author interview with Fonda. The film would eventually earn $10 million. For box-office figures, see Spada, *Fonda*, 208; www.imdb.com/title/tt0083006/business, accessed October 19, 2007.

72. Fonda, *My Life*, 394. Box-office figures are quoted in Cook, *Lost Illusions*, 339.

73. *Variety*, October 29, 1979. Katharine Graham, Rosalynn Carter, Ann Landers, and Barbara Walters preceded Fonda. *LAT*, November 21, 1980.

74. *LAT*, May 3, 1982; for CED success in electing other California candidates, see ibid., September 25, 1982.

75. *LAT*, April 28, 1984, February 19, 1984. For boycotts and vilification campaigns against the star, see *Washington Post*, September 27, 1979; *LAT*, April 8, May 16, 1982, July 11, 1984; *Chicago Tribune*, May 18, 22, 1982.

76. Author interview with Hayden; author interview with Fonda.

77. Author interview with Marge Tabankin, June 24, 2002, Santa Monica, California; author interview with Hayden. Tabankin is the director of the Streisand Foundation and Steven Spielberg's Righteous Persons Foundation.
78. Author interview with Hayden. For a discussion of Network, see Brownstein, *Power and the Glitter*, 294–302; *LAT*, January 30, 1986; *Christian Science Monitor*, June 7, 1988.
79. *Washington Post*, May 5, 1985. Fonda won an Emmy for her role as a Kentucky farmwoman in the TV film *The Dollmaker* (1984); Lange starred in *Country* (1984) and Spacek in *The River* (1984).
80. For poll results, see *Chicago Tribune*, September 8, 1985; Fonda, *My Life*, 328. For an analysis of the backlash, see Susan Faludi, *Backlash: The Undeclared War against American Women* (New York, 1991).
81. *LAT*, April 28, 1984.
82. Ibid., July 11, 1984; *Chicago Tribune*, May 22, 1982; Woods quoted in Brownstein, *Power and the Glitter*, 313; Larry McCarthy quoted in ibid., 314.
83. For a discussion of the manipulated photo, see *LAT*, February 12, 2004.
84. For an interesting analysis of gender and the politics of the Vietnam War, see Jeffords, *Remasculinization of America*.
85. *NYT*, February 28, 1988.
86. Ibid., August 4, 1988.
87. Davidson, *Fonda*, 264, 265; Andersen, *Fonda*, 332.
88. Hayden quoted in Andersen, *Fonda*, 326; Fonda, *My Life*, 461.
89. Andersen, *Fonda*, 340. For Campaign California, see Wiener, "Tom Hayden's New Workout," 603–604.
90. Author interview with Hayden; Fonda, *My Life*, 470, 472.
91. Author interview with Lafferty; author interview with McGovern.
92. Author interview with Fonda.
93. Weinstein quoted in Rachel Abramowitz, *Is That a Gun in Your Pocket? The Truth about Female Power in Hollywood* (New York, 2002), 96; author interview with Lara Bergthold, July 22, 2002, Beverly Hills, California; HWPC manifesto quoted in Abramowitz, *Is That a Gun in Your Pocket?* 342.
94. Hollywood Women's Political Committee, *A Decade of Voices: In Celebration of the 10th Anniversary of the Hollywood Women's Political Committee, 1984–1994* (Los Angeles, 1994), n.p.; author interview with Spahn.
95. For the Creative Coalition, see Marc Cooper, "Postcards from the Left: Under the Cloud of Clintonism," *The Nation*, April 5–12, 1999, 21.
96. *Washington Post* and *LAT*, both September 28, 2007.
97. Author interview with Fonda.
98. Author interview with Hayden.

CHAPTER 7

1. Charlton Heston, *The Actor's Life: Journals 1956–1976* (New York, 1978), 177. For an account of Heston's picketing in Oklahoma City, see *Los Angeles Examiner*, May 28, 1961; Heston, *Actor's Life*, 120.
2. Vic Gold, "Hollywood Comes to Washington," *Washingtonian*, July 1982, 74.

3. *LAT*, April 29, 1979. Not strictly a conservative, Eastwood was widely admired by conservatives largely because of his cinematic image as a tough enforcer of law and order. Richard Schickel, *Clint Eastwood: A Biography* (New York, 1997).

4. Interview with Leslie Knowles: cover letter dated May 12, 1976, box 39, folder: Interview Transcripts, Charlton Heston Collection, Margaret Herrick Library, Academy of Motion Picture Arts and Sciences, Beverly Hills, California (hereafter, Heston Coll.); Charlton Heston and Jean-Pierre Isbouts, *Charlton Heston's Hollywood: Fifty Years in American Film* (New York, 1998), 49; *LAT*, December 2, 1972.

5. "Nader, Limbaugh Are Best Spokespeople," *O'Dwyer's PR Services Report,* July 1996, 20. The poll conducted by Porter/Novelli included Oprah Winfrey, Michael Jordan, Billy Graham, Robert Redford, Rush Limbaugh, and Ralph Nader.

6. Norman Kolpas, "The Quintessential Actor Charlton Heston," *Valley Magazine,* June 1986, 30; *Washingtonian,* July 1982, 74.

7. Charlton Heston, *In the Arena: An Autobiography* (New York, 1997). There is a disagreement over whether Heston was born in 1923 or 1924. I am going with the date Heston gave in his own work, 1924. Biographical information on Heston is drawn from ibid.; Charlton Heston, *The Courage to Be Free* (Kansas City, Kans., 2000); Michael B. Druxman, *Charlton Heston* (New York, 1976); Jeff Rovin, *The Films of Charlton Heston* (Secaucus, N.J., 1977); Michael Munn, *Charlton Heston* (New York, 1986); Bruce Crowther, *Charlton Heston: The Epic Presence* (London, 1986); Emilie Raymond, *From My Cold, Dead Hands: Charlton Heston and American Politics* (Lexington, Ky., 2006); Heston and Isbouts, *Heston's Hollywood*; Heston, *Actor's Life*; *Chicago Tribune,* February 22, 1951, December 11, 1960, February 19, 1989; Charlton Heston interviewed by Ronald L. Davis, July 18, 21, 1989, July 20, 1990, Ronald L. Davis Oral History Collection, DeGolyer Library, Southern Methodist University (copy at Margaret Herrick Library, AMPAS).

8. *LAT*, May 7, 1980.

9 *Los Angeles Examiner,* January 14, 1950.

10. *The Ten Commandments* (Paramount Pictures, 1956), Special Collectors Edition (2004). For a transcript of the prologue and analysis of the film's Cold War emphasis, see Alan Nadel, "God's Law and the Wide Screen: The Ten Commandments as Cold War 'Epic,'" *PMLA* 108 (May 1993): 416–417; Tony Shaw, *Hollywood's Cold War* (Amherst, Mass., 2007), 103–134; George C. Pratt and Herbert Reynolds, "Forty-Five Years of Picture Making: An Interview with Cecil B. DeMille," *Film History* 3 (1989): 141; Peter Lev, *The Fifties: Transforming the Screen 1950–1959* (New York, 2003), 162–168. For DeMille's politics, see Cecil B. DeMille, *The Autobiography of Cecil B. DeMille,* ed. Donald Hayne (Englewood Cliffs, N.J., 1959); Scott Eyman, *Empire of Dreams: The Epic Life of Cecil B. DeMille* (New York, 2010).

11. For other portrayals of Moses, see Richard H. Campbell and Michael R. Pitts, *The Bible on Film: A Checklist, 1897–1980* (Metuchen, N.J., 1981).

12. For changing images of masculinity during this period, see Tom Pendergast, *Creating the Modern Man: American Magazines and Consumer Culture, 1900–1950* (Columbia, Mo., 2000); James Burkhart Gilbert, *Men in the Middle: Searching for Masculinity in the 1950s* (Chicago, 2005); Michael S. Kimmel, *Manhood in*

America: A Cultural History (New York, 2006); Richard Meyer, "Rock Hudson's Body," Inside/Out: Lesbian Theories, Gay Theories, ed. Diana Fuss (New York, 1991), 258-288.

13. Chicago Tribune, March 25, 1956; DeMille, Autobiography, 415.
14. LAT, October 28, 1956; DeMille, Autobiography, 415. DeMille also used Heston's newborn son Fraser to play the infant Moses. For an analysis of the research that went into the film, see Henry S. Noerdlinger, ed., Moses and Egypt: The Documentation of the Motion Picture The Ten Commandments (Los Angeles, 1956).
15. Time, November 12, 1956; LAT, December 23, 1956.
16. For box-office figures and attendance, see NYT, November 10, 1957; Heston and Isbouts, Heston's Hollywood, 70. Daily Variety estimated that over 51 million people in the United States had seen it by the late 1960s. Daily Variety, December 28, 1960. For a complete run of newsletters from 1956 to 1971, see "Charlton Heston Newsletter," box 38, Heston Coll.
17. For production and box-office figures, see Heston and Isbouts, Heston's Hollywood, 97-117; Daily Variety, December 26, 1961, August 26, 1968.
18. LAT, September 22, 1959.
19. Charlton Heston interview with Jean Belmont, ca. 1960-61, tape 3, 12, box 39, folder: Interview Transcripts, Heston Coll. For his Moses-related commercial ventures, see Heston, Actor's Life, 72; "The Charlton Heston Newsletter," October 15, 1959, August 30, 1960, box 38, Heston Coll.; Christian Science Monitor, November 5, 1959; NYT, November 20, 1959; Chicago Tribune, December 31, 1959; Washington Post, May 3, 1960.
20. Ed Leibowitz, "Charlton Heston's Last Stand," Los Angeles, February 2001, 64. The introduction, photographs, and captions of Heston's Beijing Diary (New York, 1990) were all done by Lydia.
21. Heston, In the Arena, 396; author interview with theater director who wished to remain anonymous, April 3, 2009.
22. Transcript of Hedda Hopper interview with Heston, February 1952, 7, Hopper Coll.; Variety, November 2, 1960. For Heston's activities during the 1950s, see NYT, January 27, 1952; Chicago Tribune, November 29, 1953.
23. Heston interview with Belmont, 10-11, box 39, Heston Coll.
24. "Charlton Heston Newsletter," July 18, 1963, 1-2, box 38, Heston Coll.; Chicago Tribune, July 7, 1968; LAT, December 5, 1965.
25. NYT, September 25, 1960.
26. For Heston's involvement, see NYT, July 11, 1960; Heston, Actor's Life, 97; Heston, In the Arena, 260; Raymond, From My Cold, Dead Hands, 66.
27. For a discussion of slaves' preference for Moses over Jesus, see Eugene Genovese, Roll Jordan Roll: The World the Slaves Made (New York, 1974).
28. Heston, Actor's Life, 119.
29. Luper quoted in Raymond, From My Cold, Dead Hands, 70-71. For accounts and photographs of events, see Heston, In the Arena, 260-261; Heston, Actor's Life, 119-120; Los Angeles Examiner, May 28, 1961; LAT, May 28, 1961; Chicago Daily Defender, May 29, 1961; Christian Science Monitor, May 31, 1961. For West's reminiscence of the day, see NYT, March 15, 1990.
30. Heston, In the Arena, 261; Los Angeles Express, May 28, 1961.

31. *Variety*, July 17, 1963. For accounts of the various meetings, see Heston, *Actor's Life*, 177–178; Heston and Isbouts, *Heston's Hollywood*, 123; Thomas Gentile, *March on Washington: August 28, 1963* (Washington, D.C., 1983), 209.

32. Heston, *Actor's Life*, 177; author interview with Harry Belafonte, July 11, 2002, New York City. Belafonte's account was confirmed by Ed Asner; author interview with Ed Asner, October 4, 1999, Studio City, California.

33. Heston misremembered several other facts. In his autobiography and coauthored book, he noted that he served as SAG president at the time. Although he was on the organization's executive board, he did not become its president until 1965. Heston, *In the Arena*, 314–315; Heston and Isbouts, *Heston's Hollywood*, 123.

34. Heston, *Actor's Life*, 178; Heston, *In the Arena*, 315.

35. "Some rough notes—humbly set down," typed notes on committee goals with Heston's pencil markings at top of page, box 39, folder: Hollywood March on Washington, 1963, Heston Coll.; *Daily News* quoted in Gentile, *March on Washington*, 76; "Some rough notes," box 39, Heston Coll. Poll results are quoted in Raymond, *From My Cold, Dead Hands*, 74.

36. Heston, *In the Arena*, 316; for FBI warnings, see Gentile, *March on Washington*, 212. For a photomontage of the day's events, see *Life*, September 9, 1963.

37. *New York Amsterdam News*, September 7, 1963; Heston, *In the Arena*, 316; Heston, *Actor's Life*, 179.

38. Heston, *Actor's Life*, 179.

39. *Washington Post*, March 1, 1966.

40. Heston, *In the Arena*, 354. The misleading idea that Heston converted to conservatism in 1964 is repeated by several authors; see Alan Schroeder, *Celebrity-in-Chief: How Show Business Took Over the White House* (Boulder, Colo., 2004), 54–55.

41. Heston, *Actor's Life*, 210. For a discussion of Prop 14 and the 1964 campaign, see chapter 4. For Heston's involvement with the King fundraisers and documentary, see *Los Angeles Sentinel*, November 6, 20, December 4, 11, 1969; *LAT*, December 4, 1969.

42. *LAT*, December 5, 1965.

43. Charlton Heston and Martin Anderson, "My President, Way Back," *National Review*, June 28, 2004, 32. For the 1960 strike, see ibid.; David F. Prindle, *The Politics of Glamour: Ideology and Democracy in the Screen Actors Guild* (Madison, Wis., 1988), 82–91.

44. For Heston's work on behalf of SAG and the government, see Raymond, *From My Cold, Dead Hands*, 89–161.

45. *LAT*, February 27, 1966. For Heston's immediate impressions of Vietnam, see "The Charlton Heston Newsletter," March 30, August 18, 1966, box 38, Heston Coll.; Heston and Isbouts, *Heston's Hollywood*, 157–159. The *Army Times* poll is reported in *Washington Post*, June 29, 1965. The other stars included Gina Lollobrigida, Paul Newman, Kim Novak, Jayne Mansfield, and Vic Morrow.

46. Author interview with Fraser Heston, November 1, 2010, Los Angeles, California; *Variety*, May 10, 1967; *LAT*, April 2, 1967; Heston, *Actor's Life*, 282.

47. "Heston Newsletter," April 17, 1967, Heston Coll.; Heston, *Actor's Life*, 327. Ziffren was also Heston's lawyer. For Vaughn and Heston, see *Washington Post*, February 11, 1967; *Christian Science Monitor*, September 20, 1967.

48. Heston, *Actor's Life*, 296. For an overview of the gun control debates, see Raymond, *From My Cold, Dead Hands*, 176–181.
49. For changes in the Democratic Party, see Maurice Isserman and Michael Kazin, *America Divided: The Civil War of the 1960s* (New York, 2008), 291–294.
50. Michael Harrington, "The Welfare State and Its Neoconservative Critics," *Dissent* (Fall 1973): 20. For the rise of the neoconservative movement, see Peter Steinfels, *The Neo-Conservatives: The Men Who Were Changing American Politics* (New York, 1979); Irving Kristol, *Neoconservatism: The Autobiography of an Idea* (Chicago, 1999); Jonathan M. Schoenwald, *A Time for Choosing: The Rise of Modern American Conservatism* (New York, 2001); Donald T. Critchlow, *The Conservative Ascendancy: How the GOP Right Made Political History* (Cambridge, Mass., 2007); Thomas L. Jeffers, *Norman Podhoretz: A Biography* (New York, 2010); Raymond, *From My Cold, Dead Hands*, 2–5, 204–209.
51. *LAT*, December 3, 1972; author interview with Fraser Heston.
52. Heston, *Actor's Life*, 393.
53. *Washington Post*, October 31, 1972. For Clark, see Heston, *Actor's Life*, 394; for radio, see *Washington Post*, October 3, 1972.
54. *Washington Post*, January 20, 1973. For Heston's campaign activities, see Raymond, *From My Cold, Dead Hands*, 187–190.
55. Heston, *Actor's Life*, 396; *Washington Post*, December 5, 1973. Nixon crushed McGovern 47,168,710 to 29,173,222 in the popular vote and 520 to 17 in the electoral vote.
56. Dialogue from *Planet of the Apes* (20th Century Fox, 1968).
57. For a sampling of Hollywood SANE activists and their pronouncements, see *Los Angeles Express*, April 26, 1960; *Hollywood Reporter*, November 17, 1961, May 4, 1962; Dave Sendler, "Movie Star Robert Ryan Charges: 'Actors Are Unfit for Political Office!'" *Pageant*, July 1966, 21–25.
58. *Boston Globe*, August 17, 2007. For more mixed contemporaneous reviews, see *Chicago Tribune*, October 10, 1972; *Washington Post*, April 21, 1973; *Chicago Defender*, April 20, 1974.
59. Heston, *Actor's Life*, 480; typescript of Heston interview with Leslie Knowles, 15, May 12, 1976, box 39: folder: Interview Transcripts, Heston Coll.
60. Ford's supporters included Cary Grant, Rosalind Russell, Fred Astaire, Groucho Marx, Zsa Zsa Gabor, Ben Vereen, and Sonny Bono. Reagan's crew included John Wayne, Pat Boone, James Cagney, Merle Oberon, Efrem Zimbalist Jr., and Hal Wallis. *NYT*, July 11, 1976. For the Senate race, see *LAT*, April 16, May 29, 1976. For Heston's defense of environmental issues, see *Wall Street Journal*, October 25, 1978; Raymond, *From My Cold, Dead Hands*, 222–223. For his work on behalf of the NEA and NEH, see Heston, *In the Arena*, 526–530; Raymond, *From My Cold, Dead Hands*, 125–161, 215–216, 290–293.
61. William Keens, "Living and Thriving Forever: An Interview with Charlton Heston," *American Arts* (July 1981); box 38: Clippings, 1953–1988, Heston Coll.; *LAT*, January 21, 1981.
62. Kirk quoted in Alan Brinkley, "The Problem of American Conservatism," *American Historical Review* 99 (April 1994): 420. For a discussion of the divisions within the conservative movement, see ibid.; Michael Kazin, "The Grass-Roots Right: New

Histories of U.S. Conservatism in the 20th Century," *American Historical Review* 97 (February 1992): 136–155; Alonzo L. Hamby, *Liberalism and Its Challengers: From F.D.R. to Bush* (New York, 1992); Bruce J. Schulman, *The Seventies: The Great Shift in American Culture, Society, and Politics* (New York, 2001); John Patrick Diggins, *Ronald Reagan: Fate, Freedom, and the Making of History* (New York, 2007); and sources in n. 50.

63. Irving Kristol, quoted in Max Boot, "What the Heck Is a Neocon?" *Wall Street Journal*, December 30, 2002; Heston quoted in Rovin, *Films of Heston*, 121.

64. Roberta Plutzik, "Last of the Epic Heroes," *Horizon*, March 1980, 33; box 38: Clippings, 1953–1988, Heston Coll. For Reagan's ability to reshape television reportage, see Mark Crispin Miller, "Prime Time: Deride and Conquer," in Todd Gitlin, ed., *Watching Television* (New York, 1986), 183–228. For the changing relationship between television and politics, see Kathleen Hall Jamieson, *Packaging the Presidency: A History and Criticism of Presidential Campaign Advertising* (New York, 1996); James L. Baughman, *The Republic of Mass Culture: Journalism, Filmmaking, and Broadcasting in America since 1941* (Baltimore, Md., 1992).

65. For Hollywood and Central America, see Ronald Brownstein, *The Power and the Glitter: The Hollywood-Washington Connection* (New York, 1990), 282–292.

66. Heston quoted in Laura Anne Ingragam, "A Conservative in Hollywood," *Policy Review* 36 (Spring 1986): 19; *LAT*, May 18, 1982; Ronald Reagan to Charlton Heston, May 10, 1983, in Kiron K. Skinner, Annelise Anderson, and Martin Anderson, eds., *Reagan: A Life in Letters* (New York, 2003), 112. For Asner's firing, *Los Angeles Herald Examiner*, February 17, 1982; Raymond, *From My Cold, Dead Hands*, 230–231; *NYT*, February 23, 26, 1982; *Christian Science Monitor*, May 21, 1982.

67. Quoted in Raymond, *From My Cold, Dead Hands*, 221. Two of Heston's television ads, "Freeze #1 and #2," made for "Californians for a Strong America," can be found in the UCLA Film and Television Archive. For the debates, see Munn, *Heston*, 201–202; *LAT*, October 15, 1982; Chicago *Tribune*, October 22, November 29, 1982; *Los Angeles Herald Examiner*, October 30, 31, 1982. For Newman's point of view, see Shawn Levy, *Paul Newman: A Life* (New York, 2009), 330–332.

68. *LAT*, November 2, 10, 1982.

69. For Sorokin's comments and the final vote, see *LAT*, November 4, 1982; for Heston's Q clearance and films, see Stephen I. Schwartz, ed., *Atomic Audit: The Costs and Consequences of U.S. Nuclear Weapons since 1940* (Washington, D.C., 1998), 447; *San Francisco Chronicle*, November 9, 1989.

70. *NYT*, November 25, 1985; Heston quoted in Raymond, *From My Cold, Dead Hands*, 218; "An Interview with Charlton Heston," *Reason*, April 1987, 25.

71. For the impact of campaign finance reform and growing importance of Hollywood money and celebrities, see David Adamany, "The Sources of Money: An Overview," *Annals of the American Academy of Political and Social Science* 425 (1976): 17–32; Elmer B. Staats, "Impact of the Federal Election Campaign Act of 1971," in ibid., 98–113; "The 1971 Federal Election Campaign Act," www.campaignfinanceguide.org/guide-34.html, accessed June 12, 2008; Brownstein, *Power and the Glitter*, 206–211; Linda Marsa, "Who's That Hollywood's Getting Out," *Boxoffice*, October 1980, 52.

72. *LAT*, December 23, 1984; *NYT*, July 16, 1985. For poll results, see *LAT*, May 12, 1985, November 13, December 23, 1984, May 6, 16, 25, August 8, 1985; for a possible presidential bid, see *NYT*, January 3, 1986.

73. Maynard Good Stoddard and Cory SerVaas, "Charlton Heston: He'd Rather Pretend Than Be President," *Saturday Evening Post*, September 1984, 42; author interview with Fraser Heston.

74. Ed Leibowitz, "Charlton Heston's Last Stand," *Los Angeles*, February 2001, 62; for Heston's early morning habit, see ibid., 63. The Arts & Entertainment Network ran a series, "Charlton Heston Presents the Bible," in December 1992. *LAT*, December 19, 1992.

75. Ingraham, "A Conservative in Hollywood," 22; *San Francisco Chronicle*, August 18, 1988; *Christian Science Monitor*, November 23, 1992; also see Michael Levine, *A Branded World: Adventures in Public Relations and the Creation of Superbrands* (Hoboken, N.J., 2003), 104.

76. Leibowitz, "Heston's Last Stand," 65; author interview with Fraser Heston.

77. *Washington Post*, October 29, 1982; for election results, see *LAT*, November 3, 4, 1982. The best overview of Heston's involvement with the NRA is Raymond, *From My Cold, Dead Hands*, 243–282. For a history of the NRA, see Robert Spitzer, *The Politics of Gun Control* (Chatham, N.J., 1998).

78. LaPierre quoted in Raymond, *From My Cold, Dead Hands*, 262; Margot Hornblower, "Have Gun, Will Travel but Can Heston's Celebrity and Rhetoric Revive the N.R.A?" *Time*, July 6, 1998, 44. For declining membership, see *LAT*, September 12, 1997.

79. For a video of Heston's closing remarks, see www.youtube.com/watch?v=5ju4Gla 2odw&;;feature=related, accessed June 22, 2008.

80. Andrew Ferguson, "Moses in '96?" *Washingtonian*, September 1993, 25; *NYT*, May 6, 1997.

81. Heston, *Courage*, 191, 173, 192.

82. *NYT*, May 6, 1998; Heston, *Courage*, 184; for a copy of his December 7, 1997, speech to the Free Congress Foundation, see www.vpc.org/nrainfo/speech.html, accessed June 22, 2008.

83. Leibowitz, "Heston's Last Stand," 148; Levine, *A Branded World*, 104–105.

84. *LAT*, January 30, 1983. For his inclusion on Duke's Web site, see ibid.; Leibowitz, "Heston's Last Stand," 149.

85. Heston, *Courage*, 5–6.

86. Ibid., 210, 183; Heston, *In the Arena*, 570, 574.

87. John H. Richardson, "Heston," *Esquire*, July 2001, 66; Heston, *In the Arena*, 574. For his speech to the Harvard Law School Forum in February 1999, "Winning the Culture War," see Heston, *Courage*, 214–220. For the culture wars, see James Davison Hunter, *Culture Wars: The Struggle to Define America* (New York, 1992).

88. *National Enquirer* quoted in *USA Today*, July 31, 2000; also see *NYT*, August 1, 2000.

89. Heston, *In the Arena*, 575, 573; *NYT* April 4, 1998; Robert Dreyfuss, "Bush's Concealed Weapon," *Rolling Stone*, March 29, 2001, 35–37.

90. David Corn, "Looking for Mr. Right: Who's Running the Conservative Club in Town," *The Nation*, April 5/12, 1999, 52–54; *NYT*, May 21, 2000. For membership statistics, see Dreyfuss, "Bush's Concealed Weapon," 35–37.

91. *NYT*, August 10, 2000. For NRA election activities, see Neil Munro et al., *National Journal* 32 (November 11, 2000): 3626; Robert Dreyfuss, "The NRA Wants You," *The Nation*, May 29, 2000, 11–18; Raymond, *From My Cold, Dead Hands*, 276–277; Peter Stone, "In the NRA's Sights," *National Journal* 32 (July 22, 2000): 2366; Brian Anse Patrick, *The National Rifle Association and the Media: The Motivating Force of Negative Coverage* (New York, 2003).

92. Leibowitz, "Heston's Last Stand," 62; *U.S. News and World Report*, December 11, 2000. For examples of his columns, see "The President's Column," *American Hunter*, August 2000, 12; "The President's Column," *American Hunter*, September 2000, 14.

93. *NYT*, November 3, 2000; Jack W. Germond and Jules Witcover, "Who'd Ya Rather Have a Beer With?" *National Journal* 32 (October 28, 2000): 3440. For attendance at Heston rallies, see Cameron Hopkins, "A New NRA," *American Handgunner*, July 2001.

94. Leibowitz, "Heston's Last Stand," 149; Clinton quoted in Raymond, *From My Cold, Dead Hands*, 278; also see John B. Judis, "Two More Years," *American Prospect*, December 4, 2000, 10; Pamela Brogan, "Voter Distrust of Gore on Environment, Gun Control Blamed for Loss," November 9, 2000, Gannett News Service.

95. For statistics, see Cameron Hopkins, "A New NRA," *American Handgunner*, July 2001; [San Diego] *North County Times*, April 7, 2008; James Jay Baler, "Voting Freedom First," *American Rifleman*, January 2001, 78–80.

96. Hopkins, "A New NRA," July 2001; *NYT*, April 7, 2008; also see John Elvin, "Heston Headlines Annual CPAC," *Insight on the News*, February 5, 2001.

97. *Washington Post*, April 6, 2008. For more on Columbine, Heston, and the NRA, see Raymond, *From My Cold, Dead Hands*, 274, 280–281.

98. *LAT*, August 10, 2002.

99. *NYT*, October 23, 2002.

100. *LAT*, April 26, 2003; *Hollywood Reporter*, April 7, 2008. In March 2003, as I prepared to interview Heston, Carol Lanning, his assistant for thirty-two years, called to say his mental condition would no longer permit interviews.

101. For the *Fortune* rankings, see *Business Wire*, May 14, 2001; for Kerry and Edwards, see *NYT*, April 7, 2008.

102. *Atlanta Journal-Constitution*, April 6, 2008; *LAT*, April 8, 2008; *Atlanta Journal-Constitution*, April 6, 2008.

CHAPTER 8

1. Author observations, ADA dinner, September 29, 1999. For coverage of the event, see *NYT*, October 19, 1999; *LAT*, September 30, 1999.

2. Lynn Hirschberg, "Warren Beatty Is Trying to Say Something," *NYT Sunday Magazine*, May 10, 1998, 23.

3. *LAT*, September 30, 1999.

4. Author interview with Warren Beatty, March 17, 2004, Beverly Hills, California; for Beatty's childhood political aspirations, see *LAT*, September 3, 1960. Biographical information about Beatty is drawn from the following sources: Suzanne Munshower, *Warren Beatty: His Life, His Loves, His Work* (New York, 1983); John Kercher, *Warren*

Beatty (London and New York, 1984); James Spada, *Shirley and Warren* (New York, 1985); David Thomson, *Warren Beatty and Desert Eyes: A Life and a Story* (New York, 1987); John Parker, *Warren Beatty: The Last Great Lover of Hollywood* (New York, 1993); Ellis Amburn, *The Sexiest Man Alive: A Biography of Warren Beatty* (New York, 2002); Suzanne Finstad, *Warren Beatty: A Private Man* (New York, 2005); Peter Biskind, *Star: How Warren Beatty Seduced America* (New York, 2010).

5. Author interview with Beatty.

6. Ibid.

7. Ibid.

8. Kazan's political films included *Gentleman's Agreement* (1947), *Pinky* (1949), *On the Waterfront* (1954), and *A Face in the Crowd* (1957). For an excellent biography of Kazan, see Richard Schickel, *Elia Kazan: A Biography* (New York, 2005).

9. Author interview with Beatty.

10. *Life*, November 3, 1961; [London] *Daily Mirror*, October 19, 1961. For an overview of Beatty's films, see Lawrence J. Quirk, *The Films of Warren Beatty* (Secaucus, N.J., 1979).

11. Allen quoted in *American Movie Classics Magazine*, March 1999.

12. Jon Whitcomb, "The Healthy Ego of Warren Beatty," *Cosmopolitan*, February 1962, 13; transcript of interview with Jane Fonda, May 17, 1961, box 7f, Jane Fonda Folder (1959–65), Hedda Hopper Papers, Margaret Herrick Library, Academy of Motion Picture Arts and Sciences, Beverly Hills, California (hereafter, Hopper Papers). For his interaction with Hopper, see "Transcript of Hopper Interview with Beatty," ca. 1964–65, box 2f, Warren Beatty Folder (1961–64), Hopper Papers.

13. Salinger quoted in Muriel Davidson, "Warren Beatty: Public Images vs. Private Man," *Good Housekeeping*, ca. 1970, 166 (AMPAS clipping file); *NYT*, May 3, 1951. For a fuller version of the story, see J. Hoberman, *The Dream Life: Movies, Media and the Mythology of the Sixties* (New York, 2003), 56–57; John Kennedy, "Politics and Other Dirty Words," *George*, December 1995/January 1996, 182; Finstad, *Beatty*, 281–282.

14. Box-office figures are taken from U.S. Department of Commerce, *Historical Statistics of the United States: Colonial Times to 1970*, 2 vols. (Washington, D.C., 1975), 1:400; Paul Monaco, *The Sixties, 1960–1969* (Berkeley and Los Angeles, 2003), 271. For the making and impact of *Bonnie and Clyde*, see Peter Biskind, *Easy Riders, Raging Bulls: How the Sex-Drugs-and-Rock 'n' Roll Generation Saved Hollywood* (New York, 1998); Mark Harris, *Pictures at a Revolution: Five Movies and the Birth of the New Hollywood* (New York, 2008).

15. *New Left Notes* quoted in Rick Perlstein, *Nixonland: The Rise of a President and the Fracturing of America* (New York, 2009), 210.

16. First two quotes in *Chicago Tribune*, September 8, 1968; Penn in Biskind, *Easy Riders, Raging Bulls*, 23.

17. *LAT*, July 25, 1971; *Chicago Tribune*, August 17, 1971. Dollar equivalencies taken from www.measuringworth.com/ppowerus/, accessed May 8, 2010.

18. Ronald Brownstein, *The Power and the Glitter: The Hollywood-Washington Connection* (New York, 1990), 242; *Washington Post*, March 17, 1968; Davidson, "Warren Beatty," 3, 166.

19. Peter Biskind, "He Stars, She Stars," *Vanity Fair*, February 2000, 173. Humphrey finally announced his opposition to the war on September 30, 1968.

20. Author interview with Beatty. Peter Biskind estimated that from the mid-1950s until he met Annette Bening, Beatty bedded 12,775 women. Biskind, *Star*, 160.

21. For an overview of the 1972 presidential campaign, see Norman Mailer, *St. George and the Godfather* (New York, 1972); Gary Warren Hart, *Right from the Start: A Chronicle of the McGovern Campaign* (New York, 1973); George McGovern, *Grassroots: The Autobiography of George McGovern* (New York, 1977); Kathleen Hall Jamieson, *Packaging the Presidency: A History and Criticism of Presidential Campaign Advertising* (New York, 1996), 276–328.

22. Brownstein, *Power and the Glitter*, 234.

23. John Kennedy, "Politics and Other Dirty Words," *George*, December 1995/January 1996, 183; Thomas Thompson, "Will He Run?" *Los Angeles*, March 1975, 100; author interview with Beatty.

24. Author interview with Beatty.

25. Mailer, *St. George and the Godfather*, 25; *Washington Post*, June 5, 1972; Finstad, *Beatty*, 403.

26. Author telephone interview with George McGovern, June 16, 2006, Mitchell, South Dakota.

27. Ibid.

28. Ibid.

29. *Newsweek*, May 1, 1972; on turning down roles, see Munshower, *Beatty*, 51; for Christie, see Leo Janos, "Warren Beatty: King of Hearts," *Cosmopolitan*, June 1983, 221.

30. Biskind, *Star*, 169; Brownstein, *Power and the Glitter*, 247.

31. Author interview with Beatty; author interview with McGovern; author telephone interview with Gary Hart, February 24, 2009, Kitbridge, Colorado.

32. Author interview with McGovern. For more on Beatty's role in the campaign, see Brownstein, *Power and the Glitter*, 236–249; Biskind, *Star*, 161–175; Finstad, *Beatty*, 405–408.

33. Author interview with McGovern.

34. Ibid.

35. *LAT*, April 11, 1972.

36. Gary Hart, *The Good Fight: The Education of An American Reformer* (New York, 1993), 96.

37. Author interview with Beatty.

38. McGovern told me that Beatty urged him to add Humphrey to the ticket, but was unaware that the actor had gone to his hotel. Author interview with McGovern. On Beatty's meeting with Humphrey, see Parker, *Beatty*, 192–193.

39. For an interesting perspective on the 1972 campaign, see Ted Van Dyk, "How the Election of 1968 Reshaped the Democratic Party," *Wall Street Journal*, August 23, 2008.

40. Joan Dew, "Warren Beatty: More Than Just a Lover," *Redbook*, May 1974, 101; for the poll, see *NYT*, October 19, 1973.

41. Quoted in Finstad, *Beatty*, 403.

42. Beatty quoted in Quirk, *Films of Beatty*, 53.
43. Interview with Alan J. Pakula, May 14, 1983, 12, **P. box 59, no. 1, American Jewish Committee Oral History Collection, New York Public Library [Humanities-Jewish Division]. Other prominent conspiracy films included *Executive Action* (1973), *The Conversation* (1974), *Three Days of the Condor* (1975), and *All the President's Men* (1976). For the era's conspiracy features, see Michael Ryan and Douglas Kellner, *Camera Politica: The Politics and Ideology of Contemporary Hollywood Film* (Bloomington, Ind., 1990), 95–105; Gary Crowdus, ed., *The Political Companion to American Film* (Chicago, 1994), 310–318.
44. Quoted in Quirk, *Films of Beatty*, 187.
45. "Interview with Warren Beatty: Would He Run for Office? He Hinted He Might Last Year," *Viva*, July 1975, 100.
46. Beatty quoted in Quirk, *Films of Beatty*, 53; Parker, *Beatty*, 205. Beatty cowrote the script with Robert Towne, who won an Oscar for *Chinatown* and did an uncredited rewrite on *Parallax View*.
47. Finstad, *Beatty*, 414.
48. For box-office receipts and Beatty's earnings, see David A. Cook, *Lost Illusions: American Cinema in the Shadow of Watergate and Vietnam, 1970–1979* (Berkeley and Los Angeles, 2000), 113; Amburn, *Sexiest Man Alive*, 219–220.
49. Letter from Mrs. J. B. Williams, San Antonio, Texas, *People*, May 5, 1975. For Beatty's name being floated as a possible candidate, see *LAT*, November 12, 1974; Brownstein, *Power and the Glitter*, 248; Munshower, *Beatty*, 153–154.
50. Munshower, *Beatty*, 152; Thompson, "Will He Run?" 101; "Interview with Beatty," *Viva*, 100.
51. *Chicago Tribune*, February 23, 1975.
52. *New York Times*, January 28, 1975. For examples of Beatty's activism, see *Wall Street Journal*, May 31, 1974, August 20, 1980; *Variety*, August 14, 1974; *NYT*, March 10, 1975; *Washington Post*, May 3, 1975; *Oakland Post*, May 23, 1976; *LAT*, June 27, October 11, 1976
53. Quirk, *Films of Beatty*, 20; Beatty quoted in Andrew Schroeder, "Strategies of Cinema: Cultural Politics in the New Hollywood, 1967–1981," Ph.D. diss., New York University, January 2002, 285. For rumors of his possible Senate campaign, see *Los Angeles Herald-Examiner*, July 12, 1977; for *Time*'s profile, see Frank Rich, "Warren Beatty Strikes Again," *Time*, July 3, 1978.
54. Beatty quoted in Munshower, *Beatty*, 112.
55. Diller quoted in Biskind, *Easy Riders, Raging Bulls*, 364. For box-office returns, see Quirk, *Films of Beatty*, 211. For production histories of *Reds*, see Biskind, *Easy Riders, Raging Bulls*, 364–367; Peter Biskind, "Thunder on the Left: The Making of *Reds*," *Vanity Fair*, March 2006, 344–359; Finstad, *Beatty*, 426, 439–449; Kercher, *Beatty*, 117–125; Spada, *Shirley and Warren*, 194–200. For the biography of Reed used by Beatty, see Robert Rosenstone, *Romantic Revolutionary: A Biography of John Reed* (New York, 1975).
56. Author interview with Lawrence Bachmann, October 3, 2002, Beverly Hills, California. Beatty was not the first filmmaker to realize this. During the silent era, a wide range of radical and labor organizations made feature films aimed at swaying public opinion about their struggles. For an account of this intriguing time in film

history, see Steven J. Ross, *Working-Class Hollywood: Silent Film and the Shaping of Class in America* (Princeton, N.J., 1998).

57. Kurt Vonnegut, "The Passions of Warren Beatty," *Vogue*, April 1982, 315; William Buckley, "Really, Fellow Conservatives, It's Okay to See 'Reds,'" *Washington Post*, January 21, 1982. For reports of the White House screening, see *NYT*, December 9, 1981; Janos, "Warren Beatty," 272.

58. *LAT*, December 8, 1981; Richard Corliss, "7 Top Political Movies from Seven Decades," *Time International*, November 20, 2006. For marketing and reception, see Biskind, *Star*, 311–321. The film cost $33 to $35 million and grossed $40.4 million by the end of 1982. For production costs and box-office returns, see *Hollywood Reporter*, December 8, 1981; Aaron Latham, "Warren Beatty Seriously," *Rolling Stone*, April 1, 1982, 19.

59. For his earlier statement on open marriage, see E. J. Dionne Jr., "Gary Hart: The Elusive Front-Runner," *NYT*, May 3, 1987.

60. For Beatty's role in the 1984 and 1988 campaigns, see Biskind, *Star*, 322–325, 336–340; Brownstein, *Power and the Glitter*, 316–343.

61. Brownstein, *Power and the Glitter*, 325; author interview with Beatty; *NYT*, July 22, 1983.

62. Hart quoted in Amburn, *Sexiest Man Alive*, 300; author interview with Hart. For a more thorough account of Hart's ideas, see Hart, *Good Fight*.

63. Author interview with Hart.

64. Author interview with Jon Boorstin, August 10, 2009, Los Angeles, California. Boorstin worked with Beatty on *The Parallax View*.

65. Author interview with Hart.

66. Ibid.

67. For Gallup poll results, see Biskind, *Star*, 337.

68. Green and Hart quoted in Brownstein, *Power and the Glitter*, 322.

69. For reports of the New York speech and Beatty's role, see *NYT*, April 1, 1984; *Washington Post*, April 16, 1984.

70. Mondale captured 38.3% of the total primary vote to Hart's 35.9%.

71. *Entertainment Today*, September 7, 1984. For Bird and Green, see *LAT*, July 4, 1985, February 12, 1986; *NYT*, October 13, 1986.

72. pro.imdb.com/title/tt0093278/business, accessed November 27, 2009.

73. Author interview with Hart. For the candidate's platform, see Hart, *Good Fight*, 218.

74. Dionne, "Hart," *NYT*, May 3, 1987. Poll results in Biskind, *Star*, 372; also see 371–378, 395–397 for the 1988 campaign.

75. Both quotes from Dionne, "Hart," *NYT*, May 3, 1987. For the scandal, see John Steele Gordon, "Gary Hart's Monkey Business: How and Why a Candidate Got Caught," *American Heritage.com*, May 8, 1997, www.americanheritage.com/people/articles/web/20070508-gary-hart-donna-rice-george-mcgovern-democratic-presidential-primary-political-scandal.shtml, accessed November 27, 2009; Brownstein, *Power and the Glitter*, 334–336.

76. Beatty quoted in Brownstein, *Power and the Glitter*, 339; sexual McCarthyism quote in "On Movies, Money, and Politics," *The Nation*, April 5, 1999, 13.

77. For two quotes in "The Hart-Beatty Connection," *Newsweek*, January 25, 1988; Parker, *Beatty*, 293.
78. Redford quoted in Brownstein, *Power and the Glitter*, 332.
79. Author interview with Michael Dukakis, February 23, 2010, Los Angeles, California; author interview with Andy Spahn, July 16, 2002, Universal City, California.
80. Finstad, *Beatty*, 476. For Bening's background, see Parker, *Beatty*, 319–324; Finstad, *Beatty*, 476–479.
81. *Washington Post*, July 17, 1991.
82. Norman Mailer, "The Warren Report," *Vanity Fair*, November 1991, 232.
83. *LAT*, May 3, 1998.
84. *Newsweek*, May 11, 1998. For the story behind the making of *Bulworth*, see Hirschberg, "Beatty Is Trying to Say Something," 24–25, 53, 62; Peter Swirski, "*Bulworth* and the New American Left," *Journal of American Culture* 28 (September 2005): 293–230; Henry Louis Gates Jr., "The White Negro," *New Yorker*, May 11, 1998, 62–65; Finstad, *Beatty*, 495–500.
85. Finstad, *Beatty*, 496.
86. All quotes are taken from *Bulworth* (Fox, 1998).
87. Both quotes are from "On Movies, Money, and Politics," 13. For box-office figures, see Swirski, "*Bulworth*," 297.
88. *Hollywood Reporter*, March 30, 1999; "On Movies, Money, and Politics," 13.
89. *People*, July 19, 1999; *LAT*, August 10, 1999.
90. Author interview with Beatty. For Beatty's brainstorming sessions, see Peter H. Stone, "Behind the Beatty Boomlet," *National Journal* 31 (September 11, 1999): 2576–2577; *Wall Street Journal*, August 30, 1999; Jake Tapper, "My Dinner with Bulworth," *Salon.com*, September 2, 1999; Biskind, *Star*, 528–538.
91. *LAT*, September 30, 1999.
92. For a copy of Beatty's speech, see www.a9e.org/Beatty4President/beatty-adaspeech.html, accessed March 17, 2009.
93. *Variety*, October 4, 1999; *Los Angeles Sentinel*, October 14, 1999.
94. Author interview with Beatty; George Gallup Jr., *The Gallup Poll: Public Opinion 1999* (Wilmington, Del., 2000), 89–90; also see Jacob Weisberg, "Beatty vs. Buchanan?" *Slate*, August 19, 1999, www.slate.com/id/1003448/, accessed May 12, 2009.
95. David Plotz, "Warren Beatty: He Doesn't Really Want to Be President. He Wants to Be Campaign Manager," *Slate.com*, August 20, 1999, www.slate.com/id/33472/, accessed May 12, 2009; author interview with Beatty.
96. Author interview with Boorstin.
97. Author interview with Beatty.
98. *LAT*, November 4, 1999.
99. Author interview with Marge Tabankin, June 24, 2002, Santa Monica, California.
100. Quotes are taken from *36th Annual AFI Life Achievement Awards*, June 25, 2008, USA Network; also see *Variety*, June 13, 2008; *USA Today*, June 16, 2008.
101. *LAT*, May 25, 2005.
102. Author interview with Hart.
103. "Will Bulworth Run," *The Nation*, September 6/13, 1999.

CHAPTER 9

1. *NYT*, August 10, 2003. Despite repeated requests, Arnold Schwarzenegger declined to be interviewed for this book.

2. The line, delivered during his candidacy announcement on *The Tonight Show*, is from *Terminator 2. LAT*, August 3, 2003.

3. Joe Mathews, *The People's Machine: Arnold Schwarzenegger and the Rise of Blockbuster Democracy* (New York, 2006), 80–82.

4. Quoted in Nigel Andrews, *True Myths: The Life and Times of Arnold Schwarzenegger* (Secaucus, N.J., 1996), 186.

5. Author interview with Bonnie Reiss, November 20, 2009, Malibu, California. For Schwarzenegger's Master Plan, see George Butler's comments in the segment "Arnold Schwarzenegger's Photo Show and Politics," broadcast on the Weekend Edition of *All Things Considered*, December 8, 1990.

6. Biographical information on Schwarzenegger is drawn from Arnold Schwarzenegger with Douglas Kent Hall, *Arnold: The Education of a Bodybuilder* (New York, 1977); Wendy Leigh, *Arnold: An Unauthorized Biography* (Chicago, 1990); George Butler, *Arnold Schwarzenegger: A Portrait* (New York, 1990); Laurence Leamer, *Fantastic: The Life of Arnold Schwarzenegger* (New York, 2005); Louise Krasniewicz and Michael Blitz, *Arnold Schwarzenegger: A Biography* (Westport, Conn., 2006); Andrews, *True Myths*; Mathews, *People's Machine*; also see *NYT*, May 8, 1976; *Chicago Tribune*, June 6, 1976; *U.S. News & World Report*, November 26, 1990.

7. *Chicago Tribune*, June 6, 1976.

8. Quoted in Mathews, *People's Machine*, 34.

9. For a profile of Alfred Gerstl, see Leamer, *Fantastic*, 24–26.

10. *The Road to Serfdom* was first published in Great Britain in March 1944. It became a bestseller in the United States after *Reader's Digest* published an abridged version in April 1945. Hayek later taught at the University of Chicago, where he influenced future Nobel laureate Milton Friedman. Ronald Reagan insisted that Hayek was among the two or three people who most influenced his economic philosophy. Glenn Beck's endorsement of the book in June 2010 led to its becoming a bestseller on amazon.com. For Hayek's influence on Reagan, see Martin Anderson, *Revolution* (New York, 1988). For continued conservative and Tea Party attraction to Hayek, see *NYT*, October 2, 2010.

11. Mathews, *People's Machine*, 45. Schwarzenegger kept in close touch with Gerstl throughout his life and served as his best man when the Austrian widower remarried in 1999. *Christian Science Monitor*, September 24, 2003.

12. Author interview with Reiss; Leamer, *Fantastic*, 51–52.

13. *LAT*, July 2, 1974.

14. He formed Oak Productions with actor Burt Reynolds with the idea of staging Mr. Olympia contests for television; see *Chicago Tribune*, January 31, 1977. Schwarzenegger's books included Schwarzenegger and Hall, *Arnold*; Arnold Schwarzenegger, *Arnold's Bodyshaping for Women* (New York, 1979); Arnold Schwarzenegger, *Arnold's Bodybuilding for Men* (New York, 1981); and Arnold Schwarzenegger, *Encyclopedia of Modern Bodybuilding* (New York, 1985). For his various business

ventures, see "Sexy, Fun-Loving Schwarzenegger!" *Cosmopolitan*, July 1988, 139; Robert Kurson, "The Amazing Arnold!" part 2, *Esquire*, July 2003, 64; Leamer, *Fantastic*, 79, 91; *LAT*, July 2, 1974; *NYT*, May 8, 1976; *Chicago Tribune*, January 31, 1977; *Washington Post*, June 8, 1981; *People Weekly*, October 14, 1985.

15. Quoted in Leamer, *Fantastic*, 114. For Arnold being feted at Elaine's Restaurant, see *NYT*, January 13, 1977.

16. *LAT*, July 2, 1974; *NYT*, May 8, 1976; *Chicago Tribune*, June 6, 1976. For photographs of Schwarzenegger, see *LAT*, July 2, 1974, November 16, 1975, July 25, 1976; *Washington Post*, December 28, 1975, February 19, 1977; *NYT*, May 8, 1976, January 19, March 18, 1977; *Chicago Tribune*, January 31, March 18, 1977.

17. Quoted in Kurson, "Amazing Arnold!" 64.

18. *Vanity Fair* interview and Eunice Shriver quoted in Mathews, *People's Machine*, 40; also see "Commando in Love," *People Weekly*, October 14, 1985, 126.

19. Schwarzenegger quoted in Mathews, *People's Machine*, 40–41.

20. Parker quoted in ibid., 25. For his activities, see *Washington Post*, December 9, 1978; *NYT*, December 12, 1978, June 5, 1981; *Washington Informer*, July 13, 1983; *LAT*, June 2, 1987.

21. *NYT*, February 23, 1977, May 14, 1982.

22. Mathews, *People's Machine*, 47. For Schwarzenegger's involvement in party fundraising, see *LAT*, September 8, 1986; *USA Today*, August 17, 1988; *NYT*, September 15, 1988.

23. His movie grosses are reported in Alan Richman, "Arnold Meets the Girly Man," *Gentleman's Quarterly*, May 1990, 204.

24. For an overview of his movies and box-office success, see John T. Flynn, *The Films of Arnold Schwarzenegger* (Secaucus, N.J., 1996).

25. Author telephone interview with Joan Barnett, December 8, 2009, Boston, Massachusetts.

26. *LAT*, April 11, 1982. For the ways in which Schwarzenegger, Stallone, and other "hard-body" action heroes rewrote the legacy of Vietnam during the Reagan era, see Susan Jeffords, *The Remasculinization of America: Gender and the Vietnam War* (Bloomington, Ind., 1989); Michael A. Messner, "The Masculinity of the Governator: Muscle and Compassion in American Politics," *Gender and Society* 21 (August 2007): 464. For Reagan's speech, see www.americanrhetoric.com/ speeches/ronaldreaganatimeforchoosing.htm, accessed January 5, 2007.

27. For a perceptive analysis of Schwarzenegger's films, see Susan Jeffords, *Hardbodies: Hollywood Masculinity in the Reagan Era* (New Brunswick, N.J., 1994).

28. For box-office figures, see Dana Wechsler Linden and Dyan Machan, "Corporate America's Most Powerful People: Put Them at Risk!" *Forbes*, May 25, 1992, 158; www.imdb.com; www.boxofficemojo.com. For dollar equivalencies, see www .measuringworth.com/ppowerus/, accessed May 8, 2010.

29. Kurson, "Amazing Arnold!" 64.

30. *The Terminator* cost $6.4 million and grossed $78.4 million worldwide.

31. *LAT*, October 4, 1985. For Reagan's reaction, see Ryan P. Murphy, "Arnold Schwarzenegger: No Sweat," *Saturday Evening Post*, March 1989, 49.

32. Mathews, *People's Machine*, 41; Lynn Darling, "How Much Bigger Can Arnold Schwarzenegger Get?" *Esquire*, March 1985, 132. Net-worth figure is quoted in

Murphy, "Schwarzenegger: No Sweat," 47. Friends estimated his total assets in 1990 at $40 million. Andrews, *True Myths*, 193. In 1990, *Forbes* reported that he earned more money from real estate and investments than films. "Arnold Schwarzenegger's Photo Show and Politics," segment on Weekend Edition of *All Things Considered*, December 8, 1990.

33. Domestic grosses were $35.1 million for *Commando* and $56.5 million for *Predator*.

34. *NYT*, November 4, 1988.

35. Author interview with Reiss. For Schwarzenegger's involvement with the Reason Foundation, see Mathews, *People's Machine*, 47–48.

36. *Wall Street Journal*, February 7, 1991; Mathews, *People's Machine*, 46. For Friedman's comments, see Richman, "Arnold Meets the Girly Man," 204.

37. Arnold Schwarzenegger's introduction, "The Power of the Market," in *Free to Choose: The Updated and Revised Television Series* (PBS, 1990). For a transcript of his remarks, see www.freetochoosemedia.org/freetochoose/media_ftc1990.php, accessed February 16, 2010.

38. Margaret Warner, "Bush Battles the 'Wimp Factor,'" *Newsweek*, October 19, 1987. For Bush's masculinity, see Stephen J. Ducat, *The Wimp Factor: Gender Gaps, Holy Wars, and the Politics of Anxious Masculinity* (Boston, 2004); Alan Schroeder, *Celebrity-in-Chief: How Show Business Took over the White House* (Boulder, Colo., 2004), 26–27.

39. Ronald Brownstein, *The Power and the Glitter: The Hollywood-Washington Connection* (New York, 1990), 377.

40. For the initial meeting between the two men, see Andrews, *True Myths*, 194.

41. Quoted in Mathews, *People's Machine*, 49.

42. Author interview with Marty Kaplan, June 3, 2002, Beverly Hills, California; *NYT*, November 4, 1988. Bush received 48.9 million popular votes to Dukakis's 41.8 million, and 426 electoral votes to the Democrat's 111. For an overview of the campaign, see Kathleen Hall Jamieson, *Packaging the Presidency: A History and Criticism of Presidential Campaign Advertising* (New York, 1996), 459–484.

43. Quotes are from Bush speech, Republican National Convention, August 18, 1988; George Bush inaugural address, January 20, 1989. bartelby.org/124/pres63.html, accessed February 1, 2010. President Bush invited the Schwarzenegger family to join him at Camp David on two occasions. The only other celebrities invited for White House stays were Johnny Carson and comedian Dana Carvey, who played Bush on the TV show *Saturday Night Live. NYT*, January 14, 1991; Schroeder, *Celebrity-in-Chief*, 215–216; Mathews, *People's Machine*, 54.

44. Author correspondence with Richard Schickel, June 16, 2010; author correspondence with Bonnie Reiss, September 17, 2010.

45. *NYT*, March 4, 1993.

46. Author interview with Reiss.

47. Richman, "Arnold Meets the Girly Man," 202; "Pumping the Public Persona," *U.S. News & World Report*, November 26, 1990; 1993 statistics are taken from "Arnold: The Pied Piper of Fitness," *Saturday Evening Post*, November 1990, 107. For his work as chairman of the council, see "Arnold: The Pied Piper of Fitness"; Maynard Good Stoddard and Cory SerVaas, M.D., "Marketing Fitness with the President &

Arnold Schwarzenegger," *Saturday Evening Post*, July/August 1990, 44, 47; Lynn Hirschberg, "Making It Big," *Vanity Fair*, June 1990, 114; "The American Dream in Physical Form: Marketing Schwarzenegger," *The Economist*, September 15, 1990, 170. Mathews, *People's Machine*, 49–57.

48. "American Dream in Physical Form," 170; for box office, see Flynn, *Films of Schwarzenegger*, 180.

49. *NYT*, November 11, 1991; Aaron Latham, "Schwarzenegger as Governor of California?" *M Inc.*, October 1991, 112. For his activities and speculation about a potential political career, see *Boston Globe*, February 26, 1990; *NYT*, December 27, 1990, January 8, 1991; *Newsweek*, July 22, 1991; Bill Zehme, "Mr. Big Shot," *Rolling Stone*, August 22, 1991.

50. *LAT*, July 14, 1991. For box-office figures for this and his other films of the 1980s and early 1990s, see Flynn, *Films of Schwarzenegger*.

51. *Washington Post*, February 18, 1992, August 10, 1992; *NYT*, February 16, 1992, August 20, 1992; Sidney Blumenthal, "Springtime for Buchanan: Arnold for Bush," *New Republic*, March 9, 1992, 22–25.

52. *Washington Post*, February 18, 1992.

53. *NYT*, June 30, 1992; Mathews, *People's Machine*, 56.

54. For the 1992 campaign, see Jamieson, *Packaging the Presidency*, 485–516.

55. For the accusations and controversy, see Andrews, *True Myths*, 200–202; Leamer, *Fantastic*, 193–196, 211–212.

56. "Top 10 Celebrity Candidates," *George*, May 2000, 46. For a look at Eastwood's politics, see Richard Schickel, *Clint Eastwood: A Biography* (New York, 1996). Ventura worked with Schwarzenegger on *Predator* (1987), *The Running Man* (1987), and *Batman and Robin* (1997).

57. "Our leader" quote, *LAT*, February 1, 1995; author interview with Dan Schnur, February 15, 2010, Los Angeles, California; *NYT*, June 1, 1995; *U.S. News & World Report*, June 12, 1995. Schwarzenegger filmed a campaign spot in which he donned a leather jacket and sunglasses and delivered the line, "Governor Wilson will be back!" *LAT*, October 11, 1994.

58. *NYT*, November 24, 1999.

59. White's meeting with Schwarzenegger is discussed in Mathews, *People's Machine*, 62; for his medical problems, see *LAT*, April 18, 1997.

60. Interview quoted in *LAT*, October 1, 1999.

61. Ibid.

62. Both quotes in Tom Dunkel, "Millennium Man," *George*, November 1999, 135.

63. *LAT*, October 10, 2000.

64. For poll results, see Mathews, *People's Machine*, 67. Jack Mathews has written the most insightful examination of the inner workings of Schwarzenegger's gubernatorial campaign.

65. John Connolly, "Arnold the Barbarian," *Premiere*, March 2001, 88. For coverage of the scandal, see *National Journal*, February 24, 2001; *USA Today*, February 27, 2001; *LAT*, March 2, 7, 9, 19, 2001; *US Weekly*, March 12, 2001; *NYT*, March 13, 2001; [London] *Financial Times*, March 14, 2001; *Variety*, March 19, 2001; *Human Events*, March 26, 2001.

66. Author interview with Reiss. For his work with the Governor's Council and the evolution of the Inner City Games, see Daniel Weintraub, *Party of One: Arnold Schwarzenegger and the Rise of the Independent Voter* (Sausalito, Calif., 2007), 14–15; *NYT*, February 25, 1993; Mathews, *People's Machine*, 57–60; Dunkel, "Millennium Man," 118–120.

67. Prop 49 increased funding for before- and after-school programs; made all public schools eligible for after-school grants ranging from $50,000 to $75,000; and mandated that beginning in fall 2004, new funding for school programs could not be taken from the main education budget. For Schwarzenegger's Prop 49 campaign, see Mathews, *People's Machine*, 95–104.

68. Weintraub, *Party of One*, 14.

69. For an analysis of the problems that led to Davis's recall, see Larry N. Gerston and Terry Christensen, *Recall! California's Political Earthquake* (Armonk, N.Y., and London, 2004), 16–48; Leamer, *Fantastic*, 260–272; Mathews, *People's Machine*, 107–129.

70. Author interview with Schnur; author interview with Reiss. Schwarzenegger and Reiss, who headed the Inner City Games Foundation, met with Thomas, Bill Young, and Ted Stevens in a successful effort to reverse federal budget cuts for after-school programs. For a history of recall elections, see Donald Musch, *The Rise of Arnold Schwarzenegger, The Fall of Gray Davis: Recall Elections in the United States* (Livermore, Calif., 2004).

71. *LAT*, August 8, 2003.

72. Poll results cited in Mathews, *People's Machine*, 131.

73. Author interview with Reiss; *LAT*, August 7, 2003.

74. *LAT*, August 7, 8, 2003.

75. For the uses of TV by candidates, see Christine F. Ridout, "News Coverage and Talk Shows in the 1992 Presidential Campaign," *PS: Political Science and Politics* 26 (December 1993): 712–716; David Niven, S. Robert Lichter, and Daniel Amundson, "The Political Content of Late Night Comedy," *Harvard International Journal of Press/Politics* 8 (2003): 118–132; William Babcock and Virginia Whitehouse, "Celebrity as a Postmodern Phenomenon, Ethical Crisis for Democracy, and Media Nightmare," *Journal of Mass Media Ethics* 20 (2005): 176–191; Matthew A. Baum, "Talking the Vote: Why Presidential Candidates Hit the Talk Show Circuit," *American Journal of Political Science* 49 (April 2005): 213–234.

76. Statistics are taken from Matthew A. Baum and Samuel Kernel, "Has Cable Ended the Golden Age of Presidential Television?" *American Political Science Review* 93 (March 1999): 101, 99. Figures for the combined 2002 totals are taken from the FCC's "Ninth Annual Report on Competition in Video Markets," December 31, 2002; for a copy of the news release, see www.satellite-tv.info, accessed May 5, 2010; also see P. J. Bednarski, "More Than I Can Watch: The Number of TV Channels Is Growing Faster Than Our Interest," *Broadcasting and Cable*, July 17, 2001, 18.

77. Pew Research Center report quoted in Baum, "Talking the Vote," 215.

78. According to the Pew Research Center, 47% of eighteen- to twenty-nine-year olds got their news about presidential campaigns from late-night television. *LAT*, September 29, 2000.

79. For a perceptive study of Clinton's use of entertainment programs, see Ridout, "News Coverage and Talk Shows," 712–716.

80. Both quotes from author interview with Reiss.

81. Walsh quoted in Gerston and Christensen, *Recall!* 142.
82. Author interview with Schnur. For Schwarzenegger's entertainment appearances, see Babcock and Whitehouse, "Celebrity as a Postmodern Phenomenon," 185.
83. Author interview with Reiss. For his press conference and relationship with the media, see Cecilia Alvear and George Lewis, "Lights, Camera, Recall," *Nieman Reports* 57 (Winter 2003): 59; Mark Simon, "The Campaigning of Political Reporters," *Nieman Reports* 57 (Winter 2003): 48.
84. For the most detailed studies of Schwarzenegger's campaign, see Gary Indiana, *The Schwarzenegger Syndrome: Politics and Celebrity in the Age of Contempt* (New York, 2005); Gerston and Christensen, *Recall!*; Weintraub, *Party of One*; Mathews, *People's Machine*; Leamer, *Fantastic*.
85. Baum, "Talking the Vote," 217; Robert Feder, "Gore to Help Kick Off New Season on Oprah," *Chicago Sun-Times*, September 1, 2000.
86. Alvear and Lewis, "Lights, Camera, Recall," 60.
87. For his July media appearances, see Jeffrey Broxmeyer, "From Silver Screen to the Recall Ballot: Schwarzenegger as Terminator and Politician," *New Political Science* 32 (March 2010): 3n11.
88. Leamer, *Fantastic*, 308–309.
89. All quotes taken from ibid., 306–307.
90. *LAT*, August 8, October 3, 2003. Schwarzenegger polled 40%, Bustamante 32%, and McClintock 15%; Huffington dropped out on September 30. *NYT*, October 2, 2003. On October 4, four more women came forward with similar accusations of inappropriate sexual behavior. *LAT*, October 5, 2003; *Wall Street Journal*, October 6, 2003; Katha Pollitt, "Governor Groper? (Subject to Debate) (Arnold Schwarzenegger on the Oprah Winfrey Show)," *The Nation*, October 6, 2003, 9.
91. *NYT*, October 4, 2003; *LAT*, October 4, 2003; also see *NYT*, October 6, 2003.
92. For public reaction and loss of subscriptions, see *Wall Street Journal*, October 6, 2003; Babcock and Whitehouse, "Celebrity as a Postmodern Phenomenon," 184.
93. *NYT*, October 2, 2003. For a description of "Schwarzenegger University," see Mathews, *People's Machine*, xvii–xviii, 151–155, 173–174.
94. Mathews, *People's Machine*, 190; *LAT*, September 26, October 4, 2003.
95. Unfortunately, the link for the most complete polling data by Mitofsky International ("Exit Poll Analysis: The California Recall Election," October 7, 2003, www.mitofsky-international.com/ca-recall.htm, accessed on May 5, 2010) no longer works. However, much of the Mitofsky data can be found at www.cnn.com/ELECTION/2003/recall/pages/epolls/special.election.html and www.cnn.com/ELECTION/2003/recall/pages/epolls/governor.html, accessed March 1, 2011. For other exit polls, see William Schneider, "The Triumph of Change," *National Journal*, October 11, 2003; *Newsweek*, October 20, 2003; CNN exit poll, October 8, 2003, edition.cnn.com/2003/ALLPOLITICS/10/08/recall.results/, accessed May 5, 2010. For an analysis of the 2003 elections and exit polls, see Brian K. Arbour and Danny Hayes, "Voter Turnout in the California Recall: Where Did the Increase Come From?" *American Politics Research* 33 (March 2005): 187–215.
96. Figures are from the California Secretary of State, www.sos.ca.gov/elections/sov/2000_general/reg.pdf and www.sos.ca.gov/elections/sov/2002_general/sum.pdf, both accessed May 5, 2010.

97. *LAT*, October 7, 9, 2003. For exit poll statistics, see Mathews, *People's Machine*, 192.

98. For the fullest view of speech, Leamer, *Fantastic*, 320; also see *NYT*, November 18, 2003; *LAT*, November 18, 2003.

99. Approval figures are quoted in Mathews, *People's Machine*, 219. Schwarzenegger's successes and failures are analyzed in ibid.; Weintraub, *Party of One*; Leamer, *Fantastic*; Gerston and Christensen, *Recall!*

100. Mathews, *People's Machine*, 257; *LAT*, July 18, 2004.

101. Weintraub, *Party of One*, 83; for his accepting money from special interests, see Dan Morain, "Tracking Money in the California Recall Election," *[Cambridge] Nieman Reports* 57 (Winter 2003): 61; Weintraub, *Party of One*, 63. His declining approval ratings are cited in Weintraub, *Party of One*, 81.

102. Ibid., 209.

103. Quoted in Mathews, *People's Machine*, 384; for polling results, see field.com/field-pollonline/subscribers/Rls2346.pdf, accessed July 20, 2010.

EPILOGUE

1. *Washington Post*, September 6, 2007. For the June polling results, see *LAT*, June 12, 2007.

2. *Newsweek*, June 11, 2007. For the report on Thompson's brief campaign days, see *LAT*, December 9, 2007.

3. Winfrey appeared in three feature films and three made-for-TV movies. She finished second on the Gallup poll's most admired woman list every year since 1997 with the exception of 2001, when she was third (to Laura Bush and Hillary Clinton). No movie or television star finished higher than her. *Forbes* named her the world's most powerful celebrity in 2005, 2007, and 2008. For polls measuring the impact of Oprah's endorsement, see *LAT*, July 22, 2007; CBS Poll, September 8, 2007, www.cbsnews.com/stories/2007/09/08/opinion/polls/printable3244412.shtml, accessed October 10, 2008; Pew Center, "The Oprah Factor and Campaign 2008: Do Political Endorsements Matter," September 27, 2007. People-press.org/report/357/the-oprah-factor-and-campaign-2008, accessed October 10, 2008; graphics8.nytimes.com/packages/pdf/politics/20071211_POLL.pdf, accessed September 10, 2010.

4. For voting patterns and poll results, see Matthew A. Baum, "Talking the Vote: Why Presidential Candidates Hit the Talk Show Circuit," *American Journal of Political Science* 49 (April 2005): 215; National Annenberg Election Survey, "Oprah: Gender Gap in Political Knowledge Persists in 2004," September 17, 2004, www.annenbergpublicpolicycenter.org//NewsDetails.aspx?myId=91, accessed October 5, 2010; League of Women Voters, "Election 2004 Voter Turnout: Let's Turn It Up! A 2004 Election Guidebook for Local Broadcasters," www.lwv.org/AM/Template.cfm?Section=Home&;;section=Voter_Information1&template=/CM/ContentDisplay.cfm&ContentFileID=1024, accessed October 5, 2010; *LAT*, July 22, 2007; CBS Poll, September 8, 2007, www.cbsnews.com/stories/2007/09/08/opinion/polls/printable3244412.shtml, accessed September 18, 2010; Pew Center, "Oprah Factor and Campaign 2008."

5. An article about the findings of University of Maryland economists Craig Garth-
   waite and Tim Moore appeared in *NYT*, August 11, 2008. For a copy of their paper,
   see econweb.umd.edu/~garthwaite/celebrityendorsements_garthwaitemoore
   .pdf, accessed October 1, 2010. For various poll results, see Annenberg Election
   Survey, "Oprah: Gender Gap," and League of Women Voters, "Election 2004 Voter
   Turnout," Web sites cited in n. 4; *LAT*, July 22, 2007; CBS Poll, September 8, 2007,
   www.cbsnews.com/stories/2007/09/08/opinion/polls/printable3244412.shtml,
   accessed September 18, 2010.
6. *LAT*, January 9, June 4, 2008.
7. Author interview with Ed Asner, October 20, 1999, Studio City, California.
8. For the status quo nature of the Constitution and the Founding Fathers' fears concerning the excess of democracy, see Gordon S. Wood, *The Creation of the American
   Republic, 1776–1787* (Chapel Hill, N.C., 1969).
9. Reagan quoted in Betty Glad, "Reagan's Midlife Crisis and the Turn to the Right,"
   Political Psychology 10 (December 1989): 598.
10. Author interview with Tom Hayden, March 21, 2008, Culver City, California.
11. Jim Bettinger, "The Anger Journalists Never Fully Understood," *Nieman Reports* 57
    (Winter 2003): 50.
12. According to a 2002 *Hollywood Reporter* poll, 44% of respondents said they would
    not pay to see a film that "starred an outspoken actor they disagreed with." *Wall
    Street Journal*, May 8, 2006.
13. Reagan quoted by Warren Beatty in *Variety*, October 17, 2005; Hunter Walker, "Fox
    News Is the Preferred Network of GOP Presidential Candidates," September 27,
    2010, www.thewrap.com/television/column-post/fox-news-preferred-network-
    republican-presidential-candidates-21210, accessed October 10, 2010.
14. Figures quoted in *LAT*, November 7, 2010. For Beck's Web site, see www.glenn-
    beck.com. For an analysis of *The Daily Show*'s political impact, see Jonathan S.
    Morris, "*The Daily Show with Jon Stewart* and Audience Attitude Change during the
    2004 Party Conventions," *Political Behavior* 31 (2009): 79–102.
15. Author interview with Fraser Heston, November 1, 2010, Los Angeles, California;
    Reeve quoted on www.thecreativecoalition.org, accessed October 10, 2010.

INDEX

486 • INDEX